00110111 11000001 00010100 11101011 00001100 11001111 00010001 00001001
10011010 01011000 01010011 10000110 00101101 10011010 00011100 10010111
01110100 11000100 11001011 00011000 01101011 00110010 01110100 10101110
11100001 00101100 00011011 00010000 10001111 10101101 10111011 11111100
10001001 00111011 01000111 00111001 01111011 00001001 00011001 01111110
10100100 01110011 11001011 10111000 01001011 10110110 10100000 00000011
11111001 10110000 01011111 00111111 01111000 00001011 11111001 11000011
10100011 10111111 10111101 10000000 00001001 11101111 00100000 00110111
11000110 01110000 10000000 00001110 01000000 11101101 00010101 11111011
11010000 00100100 00110101 11111010 01110100 10001011 00111111 10101001

A History of Silicon Valley:
The Greatest Creation of Wealth in the History of the Planet,
2nd Edition

00011100 11001100 01001000 00011000 00011000 11010111 01101011 11011010
10110111 11101001 01100011 11010100 00101011 10111101 00111100 01010100
01101010 01010000 00000100 10001101 11110001 00110101 10110011 01110110
10101100 10111010 01010100 10010011 00100100 00010000 0   1011001
01111010 11011000 11101010 11000001 01011111 10001111 0  1110001
11101001 01110001 01111000 00101100 01110001 11110110 1   0000111
00000101 00111001 11011000 11101100 00000011 01100101 0   1010000
11001111 01011000 11011000 01001000 11101111 01000110 10111001 10010010
01111111 00111101 00001101 11101010 00011011 00010010 00000110 00001111
00100111 01001001 11011001 01010001 10010000 00110100 01010011 11010010

A History of Silicon Valley:

The Greatest Creation of Wealth in the History of the Planet,

2nd Edition

1900-2013

Arun Rao
with the collaboration of
Piero Scaruffi

O

**Omniware
Group**

Palo Alto, California

Business history - entrepreneurship - innovation - Silicon Valley

Rao, Arun with the collaboration of Piero Scaruffi
A History of Silicon Valley: The Greatest Creation of Wealth
in the History of the Planet, 2nd Edition
All Rights Reserved © 2013 by Arun Rao & Piero Scaruffi

Published by Omniware Group

Printed and published in the United States

ISBN-13: 978-1490330402
ISBN-10: 1490330402

Photo credits: Piero Scaruffi
Due to Bruce Damer for pictures of machines in his Digibarn.
Some pictures were also taken at the Intel Museum and at the Computer History
Museum.

"This 'telephone' has too many shortcomings to be seriously considered as a means of communication. The device is inherently of no value to us."
Western Union internal memo, 1876.

"I think there is a world market for maybe five computers."
Thomas Watson, chairman of IBM, 1943.

"There is no reason anyone would want a computer in their home."
Ken Olson, president, founder & CEO of Digital Equipment Corp., 1977.

Table of Contents

1. Introduction to Silicon Valley 9
2. Dream Makers: The Factors behind Silicon Valley's Success
      (1945-2013) 16
3. Pioneers: Stanford University, Radio Engineering, the Melting
      Pot, and an Artistic Genesis (1900-25) 28
4. Scouts: Electrical Engineering, Nuclear Engineering, the Navy,
      and a Culture of Innovation (1925-40) 37
5. Partners: A Case Study on Bill Hewlett, Dave Packard, and Fred
      Terman at HP and Stanford (1930-1970) 44
6. Moles: The Military Boom, Artistic Boom, and Economic Boom
      (1941-48) 58
7. Early Funders: The Early History of Venture Capital (1900-59) 64
8. Engineers: Stanford Industrial Park, Inventions, Discoveries, and
      Rebellion at the Dawn of the Computer Age (1949-61) ... 75
9. Graybeard Funders: Venture Capital in its Clubby Days
      (1955-78) 95
10. Hippies: Fairchild, the Spin-offs, the Minicomputer, Artistic
      Creativity, and Social Revolution (1961-68) 104
11. Chipmakers: A Case Study on Intel's Creation and Re-Creation
      (1965-98) 120
12. Geniuses: SRI, Arpanet, Software, Labor Fluidity, and Utopia
      (1968-71) 132
13. Lab Inventors: A Case Study on Xerox PARC and its
      Innovation Machine (1969-83) 143
14. Helpers: Lawyers and Investment Bankers in Silicon Valley
      (1970-2000) 158
15. Hobbyists: The Microprocessor, Computer Kits, Ethernet,
      Internet, the Alto, and Genetic Engineering (1971-75) ... 170
16. Entrepreneurs: Software, Storage, Unix, Biotech, Alternative
      Music, and Spirituality (1976-80) 184
17. Database Lords: A Case Study on Larry Ellison's Oracle Corp.
      (1977-2013) 196
18. Warriors: Personal Computers, Killer Applications, and SUN
      Microsystems (1980-83) 208
19. Early Failures: A Case Study on Good Ideas which Arrived
      Too Early (1980-94) 221
20. Magicians: A Case Study on Steve Jobs' Reality Distortion
      Field and Apple Computer (1976-2013) 227
21. Artists: New Paradigms of User-Computer Interaction, Open
      Architectures, Cisco, Synthetic Biology, and
      Cyberculture (1984-87) 251
22. Startups: Fab-less Firms, Networking, Mobility, and Nanotech
      (1987-90) 306
23. Surfers: The World-Wide Web, Netscape, Yahoo, Multimedia,
      and Bioinformatics (1990-95) 318
24. Funder Builders: The Heyday of Venture Capital (1978-2000) ... 335
25. Dot Com Failures: Startups that Went Bust in the Tech Boom
      (1991-2000) 344

26. *iBoomers: Google, Hotmail, Java, the Dotcoms, High-speed Internet, and Greentech (1995-98)* *351*
27. *Other Boomers: The Y2K Bug, Wi-Fi, Personal Digital Assistants, and DNA Mapping (1995-98)* *367*
28. *Googlers: A Case Study on Google from Search Startup to Big Brother (1995-2013)* *376*
29. *Monopolists: A Case Study on eBay, Google, Facebook, and Companies with Network Effects (1998-2013)* *390*
30. *Survivors: Paypal, Wikipedia, and Genomics (1999-2002)* *406*
31. *Lost Funders: Venture Capital Struggling in the Aughties (2001-12)* *421*
32. *Aughties Failures: A Case Study on Startups that Died of Indigestion (2001-10)* *426*
33. *Downsizers: Facebook, YouTube, Web 2.0, and Tesla Motors (2003-06)* *431*
34. *Sharks: The iPhone, Cloud Computing, Location-based Services, Social Games, and Personal Genomics (2007-2013)* *446*
35. *Conclusions about Silicon Valley and its Future* *488*
36. *A Timeline of Silicon Valley* *499*
37. *Bibliography* *521*

Arun Rao's Biography

Arun Rao is a Californian investor. He has previously contributed articles to the Economist magazine on business issues and the financial markets. Arun has worked at three investment firms, two of which are in Silicon Valley. He is a graduate of the Wharton School of Business at the University of Pennsylvania and the UCLA Anderson School of Management.

Piero Scaruffi's Biography

Piero Scaruffi received a degree in mathematics (summa cum laude) in 1982 from the University of Turin, Italy, where he did work in the general theory of relativity. In 1983 he relocated to Silicon Valley to work at Olivetti's Advanced Technology Center, where he was employed first to port the Unix e-mail program to Olivetti's version of Unix and then to implement the first object-oriented system (Smalltalk) for a Wintel personal computer. In 1985 he started and managed Olivetti's Artificial Intelligence Center, leading a number of joint projects with universities in the US and Europe. After a visiting scholarship at Stanford University to conduct research on cognitive science, in 1999 he joined Intellicorp. There he continued to work on artificial intelligence-based business solutions.

Since 2003 he has been a free-lance consultant for Silicon Valley and European companies. He has lectured in three continents on "Theories of Mind" and "History of Knowledge," most recently at UC Berkeley. He has published a number of books on artificial intelligence and cognitive science, the latest one being "The Nature of Consciousness" (2006). Meanwhile, he pioneered internet-based journalism with thousands of articles on music, science, cinema, literature, and history. In 1985 he started his first e-zine, distributed by e-mail over the Internet. Between 1986 and 1990 he created an online database, downloadable via FTP. That database mutated into his own website Scaruffi.com in 1995. In 2006 the New York Times ran an interview with him titled "The Greatest Website of All Time."

Meanwhile, Piero has continued writing poetry both in Italian, for which he was awarded several prizes in the 1980s, and in English. His book "Synthesis" (2009) collected poems and meditations. In parallel, Piero has become a controversial music critic. His latest books on music are: "A History of Jazz Music" (2007), and "A History of Rock and Dance Music" (2009). He has organized several interdisciplinary cultural events in the Bay Area, notably the monthly "Leonardo Art Science Evenings" (LASERs) held at Stanford and USF. He has also been on the board of the art magazine "Leonardo" (MIT Press). An avid traveler who spends months on the road, he has visited more than 130 countries in the world as of 2012.

Contact Us:

Questions, comments, complaints, corrections, bulk order requests, distribution requests, or other feedback?

Please contact us at: **p@scaruffi.com**

[page left blank]

1. Introduction to Silicon Valley

One Industry Leads to the Next

This book is a history of the high-tech industry in the San Francisco Bay Area. It is difficult to write a history of Silicon Valley without mentioning what else was going on in computers around the world. Therefore this book is also a minor history of computing and biotechnology in disguise.

A meta-theme of this book concerns how one industry led to the next one in an apparently endless cascade of continuous reinvention: gold led to railways that led to shipping operations that led to ports that had two side effects. First, ports created coastal cities that needed electrical power that required high-voltage power transmission that established the region as a leader in electrical engineering. Second, ports needed radio communications that needed electronics that created the semiconductor industry that led to the microprocessor that led to the personal computer that created the software industry that benefited from the Internet that created huge fortunes that were invested in biotech and greentech. That is, in a nutshell, the history of the Bay Area during the 20th century. The question is how.

Silicon Valley. Or just "the Valley." Officially, its name is the Santa Clara Valley. It stretches between the Santa Cruz Mountains and the San Francisco Bay, from Redwood City through Palo Alto, Mountain View, Sunnyvale, and Santa Clara, down to San Jose. Then it continues on south toward the farming community of Gilroy. The real technological locus is between San Jose to Redwood City or San Carlos, with a far edge of San Mateo. The Valley historically did not include the city of San Francisco. Yet with many startups and venture capital firms based there, by 2013 the city of San Francisco and parts of the East Bay (Berkeley and Emeryville) belong to the Valley too, a metaphysical space within the Bay Area.

The journalist Don Hoefler is credited with coining the phrase: "Silicon Valley," though Bostonians visiting in the 1960s had previously used that term. With his first publication on January 11, 1971, Hoefler wrote a series of articles titled "Silicon Valley US" for a weekly tabloid called "Electronic News." In it, he described groups of electronics firms, especially semiconductor companies, thriving and multiplying in Santa Clara County. Some sources suggest Ralph Vaerst, then President of Ion Equipment, suggested the name "Silicon Valley" to Hoefler, who had worked as a publicist in one of the most important early firms in the Valley, Fairchild Semiconductor Corp. in Mountain View.

The legend came with the great companies built there with small amounts of initial capital. Companies that changed the world. A portly man named Arthur Rock helped raise money to fund a team of rebels,

Gordon Moore and Robert Noyce, with $2.5 million to create Intel Corp. It was the first massive semiconductor company and still the industry innovator in 2013. Apple Corp., the world's greatest consumer electronics company of 1980-2011, was initially funded with a small bank loan by a twenty-two year old kid (Steve Jobs), his older buddy (Steve Wozniak), and a technology executive who guaranteed the loan (Mike Markkula). Genentech, the first company to synthesize human insulin for diabetics, started with $250,000 and gave its early investors a 3500% return. Yahoo and Google, which made the web understandable and searchable, each began with two Stanford grad students. The Yahoo founders had a fast growing directory. The Google founders had an algorithm that would eventually be the heart of a $260 billion company (in early 2013). Great things happened over a few decades. It was magical.

Tech Depends on Context and a DIY Culture

Silicon Valley did not exist in a vacuum. Its history cannot be divorced from the history of the Bay Area's economy and society at large. Even more importantly, its ascent cannot be dissociated from the artistic and cultural renaissance that took place in the region. All the great centers of technological progress boasted artistic creativity at the same time: Athens, Italy during the Renaissance, Belle-Epoque Paris, and Berlin at the turn of the century. Silicon Valley was part of a region in which creativity was treasured, along with a provocative, subversive and irreverent attitude. Alternative lifestyles and a utopian counterculture seem to have always been in the genes of the Bay Area, starting with the early poets and visual artists and then continuing with the hippie generation. Scholarly books tend to discuss too many abstract models and ignore the most important of all factors: creativity. Silicon Valley has consistently boasted a very high degree of creativity. One could argue that everything else is a detail.

Somewhat related is a mindset of independence and individualism that predates Silicon Valley and that led to the "do it yourself" (DIY) philosophy of the hobbyists who started Silicon Valley. Traditionally, the emphasis on Silicon Valley's development has been on technology transfer from universities, in particular commercialization via startup company creation. While that certainly played an important role, the hobbyist (whether a university alumnus or not) played an equally important role. The hobbyists represent the passion to toy and tinker with novel technology. It was part of the US psyche, but in the Far West it had the additional advantage of being far enough from all the industrial colossi.

That attitude might explain Silicon Valley better than any economic theory. We tend to take for granted that Silicon Valley is an economy of high-tech companies and we think it is natural that they were started by engineers, not businessmen. But maybe we should instead look at Silicon Valley businesses from the opposite direction: because this was a place where engineers rather than businessmen started companies, then it was inevitable that their companies would be high-tech companies.

There now seems to be agreement among scholars that Silicon Valley started in the early years of the 20th century, meaning that behaviors normally associated with Silicon Valley were pioneered back then. I feel that one should go even further back. As one analyzes how the various waves of business got started, one realizes that the one thing they have in common is a spirit of the Wild West. The Wild West's eccentric and independent character is the predecessor to all the inventors and gurus of Silicon Valley.

The prominent attitude towards risk-taking may also derive from the pioneers of the Wild West.

Each and every mass-consumed product has changed society, from Coca Cola's soda to McDonald's burgers, from Levi's blue jeans to Hollywood's movies. However, Silicon Valley has specialized in products that cause much bigger social change of a more endemic kind. There are, in fact, places in the world where much more sophisticated technology is created, from nuclear power plants to airplanes. But personal computers, web services and smart phones have changed our lives in a more invasive and pervasive manner. Somehow these are the technologies in which Silicon Valley excels. It is not about the complexity and sophistication of the technology, but about the impact it will have on human society. In a sense, Silicon Valley "loves" socially destabilizing technologies. Could it be that this happens because Silicon Valley arose from what used to be a very unstable quasi-anarchic society?

Much has been written about the "knowledge economy" of Silicon Valley. The average engineer's knowledge is usually limited to his field. In fact, it is hyper-specialized. The anecdotal histories of Silicon Valley are full of self-made multimillionaires but they rarely talk about the thousands of engineers who retired early because their hyper-specialized skills became useless and it was just too difficult for them to retrain. Those specialists actually had very limited knowledge which was often worthless outside their cubicle. By definition, labs that are full of specialists are designed to produce incremental improvements on existing technology, not groundbreaking innovation. Most of the innovation came from elsewhere.

At the same time, though, the great innovators of Silicon Valley (Fairchild, HP Labs, Intel, Xerox PARC, Apple, and Google) built companies not so much around a technology as around their people. They hired the best and nurtured highly creative environments. The way companies cared for creating superior "firepower" inside their labs, rather than for a "return on investment," may have more to do with innovation than any other myth of Silicon Valley. And, again, a big chunk of innovation came from the independent eccentric hobbyist (whether inside or outside academia), who did have a lot of "knowledge" about the technology and the industry, but not because of the famed networks of venture capitalists and entrepreneurs. Hobbyists invest all their spare time into their hobby, absorbing knowledge from magazines, blogs and party chats.

Many have written about the importance of venture capitalists in the development of Silicon Valley. However, we need to give credit to the biggest venture capitalist of all: the government. The history of high-tech in the Bay Area constitutes a prime example of the benefits of technologies that move from military to civilian use, and of government intervention in general. The initial impulse to radio engineering and electronics came from the two world wars, and was largely funded by the armed forces. It was governments (American and British) that funded the development of the computer, and NASA (a government agency) was the main customer of the first integrated circuits. The US government's Advanced Research Projects Agency (ARPA) created the Internet. The World-Wide Web was created at CERN, a center funded by multiple European governments (the worst possible nightmare for those who hate government bureaucracies).

Much has been made of the way Silicon Valley attracts and spawns businesses, trying to explain it in terms of academic and financial factors. However, this model would not work in Siberia or the Congo, and not even in most of Western Europe and Japan. In fact, there were very few places where it could have worked, and there are still very few places where it can work in 2012. The Bay Area managed to attract brains from all over the world due to its image as a sunny, "cool," advanced and cosmopolitan region, a dreamland for the highly educated youth of the East Coast, Europe and Asia. Because the Bay Area was underpopulated, those national and international immigrants came to represent not an isolated minority but almost a majority, a fact that encouraged them to behave like first-class citizens and not just as hired mercenaries. The wave of college-level immigration got started in the 1960s, before the boom of Silicon Valley, and for reasons that are more related to the "summer of love" and surfing than microprocessors.

Nothing Invented in Silicon Valley

Residents of Silicon Valley invented very little. Computers were not invented in Silicon Valley. Silicon Valley never had the largest hardware company or the largest software company in the world. Silicon Valley did not invent the transistor, the integrated circuit, the personal computer, the Internet, the World-Wide Web, the browser, the search engine, social networking, or the smart phone. Neither biotech nor greentech are from Silicon Valley. Instead, Silicon Valley was instrumental in making all these go "viral." Silicon Valley has a unique, almost evil, knack for understanding the socially destabilizing potential of inventions and then making money out of them; Schumpeter's "creative destruction" turned into destructive creativity. That is, ultimately, what people mean when they talk about Silicon Valley as a factory of innovation.

The eccentric independent is truly the protagonist of this story. Foreigners, especially Europeans, wonder why Silicon Valley happened where it happened. One simple answer is that the US in general is friendlier than Europe towards the eccentric independent, and California in particular is the friendliest. The suit and tie is a nice metaphor. In Europe, you can't possibly be a successful employee if you don't wear a suit and tie. Therefore the employees who rise in the hierarchy tend to be the ones who are better at dressing up, and not necessarily the ones who are more knowledgeable, competent, and creative. In California, even billionaires wear blue jeans and t-shirts.

Another reason why it could not happen in Europe is the risk-averse mindset that can be summarize in an autobiographical anecdote. An engineer worked for a decade at a European multinational. Every time one of the engineering team had an idea for a new product line, the management would ask a trick question: "Has anybody else done it yet?" If they answered "yes," the management would conclude: "Then we are too late." If they answered "no," the management would conclude: "Then there is no need for it." A case in which engineers could work on something new just did not exist. Silicon Valley, instead, amplified the passion of the US for risk-taking. Silicon Valley cultivated a philosophy of risk-taking and turned it into a science.

Another key difference between Silicon Valley and most of the world, particularly Europe, is the mindset of faculty at universities. European universities are static, feudal bureaucracies in which a professor is the equivalent of a baron granting favors to assistants. He is, in turn, the vassal of a department head for life. On the contrary, the Bay Area's universities and colleges encourage their faculty to take leaves of absence and start their own companies.

Why did it happen on the West Coast and not on the East Coast, which was more educated, wealthy, and cosmopolitan? It's why the hippies were born in San Francisco, or why the Free Speech Movement was born in Berkeley: a unique strand of anti-establishment sentiment and a firm belief in changing the world. Too little is written about the "failures" of Silicon Valley, the many industries that had a strong base here, including massive research programs at the local universities, but never made it big: artificial intelligence, lasers, virtual reality, etc.

There were a number of financial stimuli to the development of Silicon Valley. Once fortunes were created, though, Silicon Valley benefited from the generosity of its own millionaires. Philanthropy and "angel" investing provided a secondary boost to the creation of creativity. "Be creative when you are not yet rich, and support tech creativity when you get rich:" that could be the motto of Silicon Valley's entrepreneurs. The lifestyle of the Bay Area creates social pressure to "be different" and social pressure to "be good." Rich, self-made people who meet at a party don't just boast of how they made their money: they also boast of how they are spending it to help worthy causes or to help fledging startups. In a sense, here self-made multimillionaires feel a sense of gratitude towards the system that allowed them to become self-made multimillionaires. It's a phenomenon that has been part of the fabric of US society, and here you find its most sublime expression.

Therefore a major theme is that Silicon Valley was a sociological and economic experiment before it was a technological and entrepreneurial experiment. Silicon Valley fostered a marriage of advanced technology and unbridled capitalism via a triangular relationship with utopian collectivism: Silicon Valley wed utopian collectivism and advanced technology (the sociological experiment), and, at the same time, Silicon Valley wed utopian collectivism and unbridled capitalism (the economic experiment). Silicon Valley was an alternate universe.

The Greatest Legal Creation of Wealth in the History of the Planet

In numerous investor presentations in the 1990s, during what in hindsight we know was the Tech Bubble, the venture capitalist John Doerr often said: "The Internet is the greatest legal creation of wealth in the history of the planet." Presumably Doerr didn't count "illegal" periods of "wealth creation" or transfer like when the Romans sacked Carthage or when Britain sucked resources out of its 18th century colonies. Yet Doerr wasn't far off. Internet companies went from zero to $400 billion from 1995 to 2000, a mere five years (and then crashed to a fraction of that). From 1975 to 2000, more billion dollar companies were created in Silicon Valley than in any other part of the world or in human history, though measurement difficulties make it hard to compare this phenomenon to previous decades or centuries.

Doerr apologized after the bust in 2001 that his oft-repeated quote helped fuel the dot-com bubble that focused investors more on a "mercenary" drive to make quick (and illusory) stock market profits off Internet start-ups rather than on incubating businesses with revolutionary technology. He then cheekily described the Internet as "the largest legal creation (and evaporation) of wealth in the history of the planet." Yet even disregarding the stock bubble, Doerr's firm, Kleiner Perkins, had invested $1.3 billion in 250 technology ventures by 2000, of which successful firms created 192,000 jobs, achieved $73 billion in sales. After the bust, the great Internet firms of Cisco, Google, and Oracle (whose databases power the Internet) would survive and thrive, while joined by upstarts such as Facebook and Salesforce.com.

The Difference between Wealth and Money

One thing that people in Silicon Valley intuitively understand is something very different from the mentality of Wall Street, large corporations, or politicians.

Simply put: <u>wealth is not money</u>.

Money is a paper marker used for transactions; it is a useful social device which acts a measure of value, a bartering tool to aid transactions (a medium of exchange), and sometimes a holder of value (note that gold holds its value better than any paper currency). Money is zero-sum, unless a central bank prints more or banks generate more through the lending process. Money is a marker. It is a way of moving wealth.

Wealth consists of goods and services that improve people's lives. It includes tangible goods (food, clothes, houses, cars, appliances, gadgets) and intangible activities (vacations, airplane services, haircuts, manicures, health and education services, etc.).

As Paul Graham, an entrepreneur and angel investor, states in his excellent essay, "How to Make Wealth (May 2004)," what most businesses really do is make wealth. They do something people want. Profit is only a measurement tool and one shouldn't confuse the marker with the core activity. Graham goes on to discuss:

- The fixed-pie fallacy that many people believe, in contrast to the Valley view that the rich can get richer along with everyone else getting richer – it pays to cooperate and make a bigger pie;
- What a job is – a very slow way of creating wealth;
- The importance of craftsman culture, which is evident when someone can create wealth with their own mind and hands;
- What sort of incentive structure makes a startup culture possible – mostly measurement of individual contributions (which a small company can do) and leverage of a team's abilities (which is most valuable in a technology startup, where a small innovation can scale easily to make millions of people's lives better and easier).

Graham's essay is worth reading many times over. It should be taught in every business school, entrepreneurship program, and government policy course.

This is a book about the people who built Silicon Valley, their dreams, and the institutions they left us that still stand today. It is an analytical history describing key people, events, and trends, weighing their relative importance and impact economically and socially. By describing Silicon Valley's mentality and its institutions, we aim to disseminate its productive elements across the world, spreading wealth and sparking dreams.

2. Dream Makers: The Factors behind Silicon Valley's Success (1945-2013)

The Uniqueness of Silicon Valley

Silicon Valley is different. If you drive up and down its two arterial highways, the I-101 and I-280, talking to entrepreneurs, venture capitalists, corporate executives and others, you can sense something uncommon and special. Many think it is unique. The closest competitor, Boston's Route 128 area, struggles to compete.

This chapter examines some of the themes behind Silicon Valley, including: the big corporations that act as Silicon Valley's engines; the universities which are feeders of intellectual capital (smart people); the venture capital, angel, and legal infrastructure; the sunny and warm weather; the influx of driven and entrepreneurial immigrants; the culture of starting companies and failing; and the inspiration of people following dreams to change the world.

The venture capitalist Don Valentine of Sequoia Capital thought it would be difficult to duplicate the Valley. In an interview, he cited the universities and warm weather but then said it would be "very hard to narrow down to six or seven simple declarative sentences." He believed that venture capitalists were important because the good ones didn't just invest, that is, buy and sell things, but rather helped build companies and industries. Valentine stated that the Valley was "a state of mind" where "you don't have the stigma of failure." Hence a young entrepreneur could start a company, fail, and then try again more intelligently and maturely. Valentine also acknowledged the value of immigrants, especially Chinese and Indians, over the last 30 years. [1] Many of the themes Valentine hinted at are developed below, starting with the corporate engines.

The Corporate Engines of Silicon Valley

Outsiders forget that Silicon Valley is not powered by startups, but its big engines: multi-national technology companies with tens of billions of dollars in revenue. The local paper of record, the San Jose Mercury Daily News, keeps track of the "Silicon Valley 150." In 2012, some of the biggest engines in the Valley were:

---

[1] Valentine, Donald T. "Interview with Don Valentine," Silicon Genesis: An Oral History of Semiconductor Technology. April 21, 2004, Menlo Park, California.
http://silicongenesis.stanford.edu/transcripts/valentine.htm.

SV150 Companies with Biggest Profits in 2012

Name	City	Date Founded	2012 Profits ($billion)
Apple	Cupertino	1976	41.7
Hewlett-Packard	Palo Alto	1939	14.4
Intel	Santa Clara	1968	11.9
Google	Mountain View	1998	10.6
Oracle	Redwood City	1977	10.2
Cisco Systems	San Jose	1984	8.4
eBay	San Jose	1995	3.8
Gilead Sciences	Foster City	1987	2.5
Franklin Resources	San Mateo	1947	1.9
Applied Materials	Santa Clara	1967	1.4

Source: SEC Edgar 10-Q filings and analyst estimates on Bloomberg; HPQ AMAT numbers are EBITDA to adjust for accounting writedowns

Besides the companies in the table, some other large engines that most outsiders wouldn't recognize include Symantec, VMWare, Juniper Networks, McAfee, Netapp, Nvidia, Electronic Arts, Sandisk, Synopsys, Varian, Xilink, and of course, Facebook. Billion dollar companies, all in high tech, dominate the Valley (Franklin Resources is the exception, being a financial services company). They are the machines undergirding the technology ecosystem.

New technologies arose from a range of the big engines due to a "spill-over" effect. This happened when research by large companies produced excess technology that they did not develop efficiently. IBM created hard disc and magnetic disc technologies used by Valley startups (Shugart, Seagate, Quantum, Maxtor). IBM also created relational database technology that helped others (Oracle, Sybase, Informix). Similarly, Xerox PARC did the same for the personal computer (PC), graphical user interface (GUI), and local networks (Apple, Microsoft, 3Com).

The Valley owes its genesis to two important companies creating settled industries there. There was a bit of path dependency in the local industrial history, where one initial industry led to skills creation that was vital to future developments. First Federal Telegraph Corp. (FTC) the radio company arose and its eco-system followers like Litton Industries and AMPex in the 1920s. Second came Shockley and then Fairchild Semiconductor. They both led to the establishment of the integrated circuit, memory, and semiconductor industries in the Valley in the 1950s. A whole industry sprang from Fairchild Semiconductor and National Semiconductor, its strongest competitor.

Some important undercurrents about the Valley are apparent from its engines in 2012:

- The biggest industries are computer software and hardware, then biotech, then business services.
- The core of these companies is formed by engineers making technical products. Hence there is always a high demand for highly-skilled engineering labor (and the San Jose Metropolitan Statistical Area has the US's highest per capita average income as of 2012, so these engineers are paid well).
- All of the nine listed in the table above received venture capital funding, as did almost every billion dollar company in Silicon Valley (HP, Salesforce, and Siebel were perhaps the exceptions). These were young startups in the not-too-distant history (the oldest was HP, incorporated in 1947, though it dated to a partnership formed in 1939) that grew into massive engines. The funding infrastructure mattered.
- Most new startups in the Valley are sold to the big engines and are not kept independent and private or taken into an IPO. So most entrepreneurs are thinking carefully about what the engines want to acquire and process.

As the engines consume engineers and startups as their fuel, we turn next to the providers of those.

The Feeders of Intellectual Capital

Silicon Valley is built around the best matrix of technical talent generators in the world. Four schools in particular stand out: Stanford University, the University of California, Berkeley (UC Berkeley), the University of California, San Francisco (UCSF), and San Jose State University (SJSU). Together, they put out such a mass of engineering and scientific talent (both in quality and quantity), that they act as feeders of smart, creative people, or human capital, which is essential to the large engines and startups of the Valley. This group of talent attracts others from not just the US, but around the world. Whether it was Arthur Rock who came to the Valley because of the scientific talent around Stanford, Vinod Khosla who came to study at Stanford, or Bill Joy who left Berkeley to form SUN Microsystems, they all came for the engineering/science programs.

Stanford is perhaps the most important. As the venture capitalist Bill Draper once said: "Silicon Valley is so lucky, starting with Stanford. I don't think there'd be a Silicon Valley without Stanford." Stanford started out with one of the best radio engineering departments in the country in the 1930s.

What made Stanford special was the Professor (and later Dean) Fred Terman. He consciously set out to build a great engineering school and to build strong businesses around the university. He pioneered academic-industrial relations during a time when most engineering departments (esp. elite ones like MIT) would fire professors or kick out graduate students for having extracurricular interests in industry. This was a systematic vision to create an ecosystem of complementary institutions. Terman also attracted millions in federal funding at key times, along with professors and students with an entrepreneurial bent. Today, Sand Hill Road, which hems one side of the Stanford campus, houses more than two dozen venture capital firms investing billions of dollars. Many technology startups tend to launch nearby in Palo Alto, Mountain View, or Redwood City. Google, Yahoo, Youtube, Silicon Graphics, SUN Microsystems, and other major companies started on the Stanford campus, in dorm rooms and offices. Some consider Stanford to be the epicenter of Silicon Valley (Sunnyvale is the only other contender).

The University of California, Berkeley comes next. It has the greatest number of science and engineering programs that rank in the top 5 programs for the US. Many consider UC Berkeley the best public university in the world, with brilliant professors and students across a range of disciplines. Famous startups from UC Berkeley include Apple Computer (Steve Wozniak was a UC Berkeley undergrad when he left to form Apple), Inktomi Corp., and Cadence Design, all multi-billion dollar companies. Other prominent UC Berkeley alumni include Gordon Moore and Andy Grove (who started and ran Intel Corp.), Sanjay Mehrotra of San Disk Corp., and Edward Wang of VMware Corp. Less known is the fact that the venture capitalist Tom Perkins made his first fortune collaborating with Dick Jaenecke and Henry Rhodes at UC Berkeley to make early laser devices at their startup University Laboratories Inc. (ULI); they sold the company in a few years and each cashed out for millions. Jaenecke was 25 and joked around that the only problem with an early retirement was that all his golf and tennis friends were in their sixties.

Stanford and UC Berkeley are powerful magnets for talent. Every year the Shanghai Jiao Tong University (of China) puts out its Academic Ranking of World Universities comparing 1,200 higher education institutions worldwide. Their quantitative formula takes into account alumni winning Nobel Prizes and Fields Medals (10%), staff winning Nobel Prizes and Fields Medals (20%), highly-cited researchers in 21 broad subject categories (20%), articles published in Nature and Science (20%), and the Science Citation Index and Social Sciences Citation Index (20%). In 2011 Stanford and Berkeley ranked 2nd and 4th respectively, *in the entire world.*

The University of California, San Francisco (UCSF) is one of the best medical research complexes in the world. It has excellent programs in research and treatment for kidney and liver transplantation, neurosurgery, neurology, oncology, ophthalmology, gene therapy, women's health, fetal surgery, pediatrics, HIV/AIDS, and internal medicine. It is the third largest recipient of US government (NIH) medical funding in the US, to the tune of about $440 million in 2007. Its scientists pioneered techniques in recombinant DNA and human synthetic insulin production. If someone wants to develop novel techniques or commercialize them in the field of medicine, there probably are only one or two other places in the world that have both the scientific talent and the nearby startup infrastructure. As one example, Genentech was a product of UCSF research.

Finally, last and often overlooked is San Jose State University (SJSU). SJSU provides a low-cost, quality education in a range of engineering fields, especially computer science and computer engineering. Its engineering school has nearly 4,700 students, and it is by far the largest feeder of engineering talent (by volume) into Silicon Valley. Famous alums include Gordon Moore of Intel (who spent 2 years there), Ray Dolby of Dolby Labs, and Omid Kordestani of Google (an early, key employee and vice-president at the search firm).

Finally, here is a stunning fact. The tiny town of Berkeley alone had 31 Nobel Prize winners, more than any country in the world except the US, Britain, Germany, and France. Add Stanford's 16 and UCSF's 3 for a grand total of 50 in a region of about 19,000 square kilometers, smaller than Belize or Slovenia. The Bay Area has more Nobel Prize winners than any other country in the world other than the US as a whole.

What did all these schools produce? Rich people and nerds. Paul Graham wrote an essay called "How to Be Silicon Valley" where he jokes that these were all you needed to have an environment conducive to startups. Beyond that, Graham believes that a personality to a place (an open, tolerant attitude) along with hordes of youth, usually well-educated university students with science and engineering backgrounds, contributes. In Graham's mind, the Bay Area was a magnet for young and optimistic people for decades before the technology became mainstream. For Graham, "it was a place people went in search of something new. . . synonymous with California nuttiness." And that culture of granola, skiing, surfing, hiking, yoga, and tech optimism, hasn't died.[2]

While the four schools provide the raw human brainpower and energy, a broader infrastructure of venture capital firms, angel investors, and law firms also support the incubation of startup companies.

The Venture Capital, Angel, and Legal Infrastructure

Two further institutional elements are crucial to Silicon Valley: first and well-acknowledged is the venture capital and angel infrastructure; second and much less known is the legal infrastructure, ranging from law firms to actual laws and regulations unique to California.

The venture capital firms and angel networks are deep in the Valley; they are deeper and richer in the Valley than anywhere else in the world. To give an example, according to Entrepreneur magazine, of all the private

---

[2] "Paul Graham Essays." Paul Graham Website. n.d. Web. 3 Nov. 2010. http://www.paulgraham.com/articles.html.

venture firms to do 10 or more early stage deals in 2007, 6 out of the 10 have offices in the Valley. According to the National Venture Capital Association (NVCA), a majority of the largest venture investments in 2011 were in Silicon Valley, and the Valley took the largest share of total funding, as the table below shows.

Total US Venture Capital Investment in 2011

Regions Defined	Total $ Invested	Average $ Per Deal	Deals
All	$28,425mn	$7.74mn	3,673

	Amount	Total %	Deals
Silicon Valley	$11,630mn	40%	1,158
New England	$3,204mn	11%	441
NY Metro	$2,727mn	10%	379
LA/Orange County	$1,976mn	7%	208
Texas	$1,460mn	5%	153
Midwest	$1,432mn	5%	269
Southeast	$1,091mn	4%	185

Source: PWC/ NVCA/ Money Tree Report, Thomson Reuters data, Jan. 2012

The Valley accounted for 33% of the nation's total venture funding in that quarter, equaling the total funding of the next three largest regions. The Valley's angels (rich people funding seed and early stage companies) are often the first to source deals, as recent examples of Google, Facebook, and Linkedin show.

More importantly, serial entrepreneurs and venture capitalists operate within unspoken networks of trust. When trust is broken, the aggrieved party will often choose not to sue the transgressor, but rather make their experience known and hurt the transgressor's reputation. For example, when Sabeer Bhatia of Hotmail (sold to Microsoft for $400 million) was displeased with what he believed was predatory behavior by his venture firm, Draper Fisher Jurvetson (DFJ), he let it be known in an interview. It seems Bhatia's statements were either hasty or false, and DFJ strongly contested his statements. Nevertheless, they were hurt in the venture community, with entrepreneurs investigating them more deeply. Reputation matters, as a good reputation lowers transaction and due diligence costs. One interesting way that entrepreneurs have gotten around the problem of reputation is to rate venture capitalists and term sheets (documents offering money with certain terms) at a website: thefunded.com.

Beyond capital, the legal infrastructure in the Valley is impressive. Today firms like Wilson Sonsini Goodrich & Rosati P.C., Cooley Godward Kronish LLP, DLA Piper LLP, Gunderson Dettmer LLP offer a range of free services like incorporation, term sheet generators, and legal forms for startups. It's quite easy for a startup team with a modicum of credibility (whether seasoned entrepreneurs or students from Stanford, Berkeley, or SJSU) to access these free services. The law firms hope to cheaply acquire clients who will become the next Google or Facebook.

There has also been a strong push for standardized terms for an early/seed stage startup, including these elements identified by the angel Chris Dixon (warning – this is complicated stuff):

- Investors get either common stock or 1x non-participating preferred stock.
- Pro rata rights for investors (no super pro rata rights)
- Founder vesting with acceleration on change of control.
- A board consisting of one investor, one management member, and one mutually agreed upon independent director. (Or two venture capitalists, two management members, and one independent member).
- Founder salaries at a "subsistence" level and no more (no salaries for wealthy founders).
- If small angels are investing alongside big venture capitalists, they should get the same economic rights as the venture capitalists but no control rights.
- Option pool – normally 10-20%, coming out of the pre-money valuation.
- Other terms (registration rights, dividends etc) should be standard NVCA terms.

Dixon suggested that entrepreneurs and venture capitalists reduce their negotiations to only two elements: the pre-money valuation of the startup (what it is worth before outside investments) and the amount invested/raised. Having a set of standardized terms and simplifying negotiations would be important. First, it would help entrepreneurs raise money faster using less energy (lower transaction costs). Second, it would promote healthier relationships between entrepreneurs and venture capitalists, helping a business grow smoothly.

Beyond deal terms and specific law firms, some elements of California state law have been very helpful. First of all, California does not allow non-compete clauses in employment contracts, so someone can leave a large company or startup and work for a competitor right away. This facilitates the movement of technology and ideas. Second, Silicon Valley and California don't actively enforce the law of trade secrets and proprietary information. Professional work in Silicon Valley involves employees changing jobs frequently. The law of trade secrets conceptualizes all information about how to do jobs or narrow technical tasks that are not generally known; this is the property of the employer, who normally can sue departing employees who disclose or might disclose such trade secrets. California courts, however, do not vigorously enforce trade secrets law and local judges and juries dislike such suits, rarely awarding relief. Plaintiff companies pay for such suits in diminished internal morale and recruiting ability (who would want to work at a firm suing former employees?). So while California's laws "on the books" do not materially differ from other jurisdictions' laws, and while nearly all technical and scientific employees sign standard agreements on trade secrets, invention assignment, and proprietary information, such agreements are not easily enforceable by courts.

Finally, some general cultural and legal features facilitate the formation of startups, including: rapid job mobility; short job tenures; heavy use of temporary labor, independent contracting and other contingent labor; weak internal labor markets; weak loyalty to individual firms; career paths that often involve starting a business or joining a startup; hiring for specific skills; labor market intermediaries that facilitate short-term hiring, such as temporary help agencies and Internet job boards; flexible compensation involving bonuses and stock options; and strong inequality in earnings and labor market participation. As incentives go, the stock option culture is critical. It incentivizes employee-owners to toil for long hours and so potentially get a long payout (hence condensing 10 years of "normal" productivity into an intense 3 year period).

While members of young startups don't have much free time due to their long hours, they certainly appreciate what free time they have, and good weather on those rare moments of leisure is an attractive part of their life.

Sunny and Warm Weather

One oft-cited but underappreciated fact of Silicon Valley's development is its sunny, Mediterranean weather. Many entrepreneurs were attracted by the weather, including William Shockley, whose company, Fairchild Semiconductors, is considered to be a seminal technology startup. Offshoot companies from Fairchild gave birth to the semiconductor and later the entire computer and software industries in the Valley. Shockley was a Palo Alto native and one big reason he came back was the pleasant weather. As any California native will attest, year-round sunny weather is hard to resist.

A Mediterranean climate has a mild, rainy winter and a hot dry summer, which is perfect for grape cultivation (and hence winemaking). Only about 2% of the earth's land surface has a Mediterranean climate. All these regions are costal:

- The actual Mediterranean Basin, including the coastal parts of countries such as Spain, Italy, Greece, Morocco, Algeria, and Tunisia;
- Parts of Southwest and Southern Australia;
- Parts of central Chile;
- Parts of Western South Africa, notably the Cape Town region;
- A sliver of North America, from the Bay Area down to Baja California.

A more striking description compares the seasonal weather patterns of Palo Alto (the heart of Silicon Valley) and Cambridge (the heart of the Boston/Route 128 region). Note that Palo Alto is warmer in the winter with averages in the low 50s Farenhiet (10 Celcius) compared to the low 30s (-5 Celcius) in Cambridge, and Palo Alto is generally cooler in the summer, with average Farenheit temperatures in the high 70s (low 20s Celcius) compared to the low 80s (high 20s Celcius) in Cambridge. Programmers and engineers who come to the Valley notice this – they are data-driven, after all.

Silicon Valley's weather is so temperate that it tends to attract one essential group: immigrants with science and engineering backgrounds from countries such as India, China, Russia, and Eastern Europe. They all are averse to a Bostonian winter. Both authors of this book at one point lived in Redwood City, California, near Woodside and Palo Alto, whose temperate, sunny weather led to an official motto of "Climate best by government test." Numerous other people, such as Don Valentine, Ram Shriram, Larry Ellison, and others have referred to the sunny weather as an important reason as to why they stayed in California.

The Immigrant Influx

Silicon Valley is a talent magnet. It doesn't just attract talent from a Californian pool of 37 million people or an American pool of 310 million people. It attracts talent from a global pool of 6,800 million people (especially the 2 billion plus pool of China and India). Most importantly, the Valley gets talent from the science, technology, engineering, and mathematics (STEM) fields and is purely meritocratic. No one cares where you're from, where you went to school, or what religion you're a part of. While immigrants make up only 12% of the US population, they constitute over 24% of the US science and technology workforce and over 47% of US science and technology PhDs in 2009. This has powerful implications.

For example, one study in 1999 by Anna Lee Saxenian of the University of California, Berkeley, showed that foreign-born workers account for about a third of the skilled scientific and engineering workforce in Silicon Valley. Indians and Chinese dominated, with nearly 75% of the total. Saxenian found that in 1998, Chinese and Indian immigrants were running a quarter of the high-tech businesses in Silicon

Valley, collectively accounting for more than $16.8 billion in sales and over 58,000 jobs. More specifically, Chinese and Indian CEOs were running 13% of Silicon Valley technology companies started between 1980 and 1984 and 29% of those started between 1995 and 1998. In a 2008 extension to her study, Saxenian and her partners estimated that of all companies founded from 1995 to 2005 in the Valley, 25% had at least one immigrant co-founder, and the companies produced $52 billion in sales and employed 450,000 workers in 2005 (but only a third of the founders were from India and China). Interestingly, for US-born founders in the Valley, most came disproportionately from five other US states besides California: New Jersey, Michigan, Georgia, Virginia, and Massachusetts.

Allowing more skilled immigrants has a direct impact on innovation. According to one study, a 10% increase in the number of foreign graduate students would raise patent applications by 4.5%, university-patent grants by 6.8%, and non-university patent grants by 5.0%. Note that it was government intervention that allowed immigration, specifically the Hart-Celler Act of 1965, and the Immigration and Nationality Act of 1990, both of which created and expanded special visas for highly skilled immigrants and their families. The latter nearly tripled the number of skilled visas from 54,000 annually to 140,000 annually.

Chinese and Indian immigrants were also prolific networkers, starting more than two dozen business and trade associations. Satish Gupta, an Indian immigrant, founder of SenSen Networks, and an early member of TiE (The Indus Entrepreneurs), a Valley networking group, felt that, for new immigrants doing startups, "contacts are everything." For him, informal immigrant networks work primarily with trust. "Trust has to do with the believability of the person, body language, mannerisms, behavior, cultural background" and other factors. Even social caste or financial status could be involved.[3]

The ethnic networks are important. As Vinod Khosla, a cofounder of SUN Microsystems and a major venture capital investor said: "the ethnic networks clearly play a role here: people talk to each other, they test their ideas, they suggest other people they know, who are likely to be of the same ethnicity. There is more trust because the language and cultural approach are so similar." Also, once a successful Indian entrepreneur invests in a company, he provides the legitimacy that allows the entrepreneur to get a hearing from the region's more established venture capital funds.

The Culture of Starting and Failing

Silicon Valley works because it encourages smart failure. One oft-repeated piece of advice is "fail often but fail quickly." As the co-founders

---

[3] Saxenian, AnnaLee. "Silicon Valley's New Immigrant Entrepreneurs." University of California, Santa Cruz, Working Paper 15, May 2000.

of MIT Entrepreneurship Review discovered after visiting the Valley, there still exists a trial-and-error or evolutionary process where failures could create opportunities and better innovations. Also failure is "encouraged and rarely punished," reflecting a still existing pioneer spirit of the American West.[4]

But failing isn't the entire rub. As Doug Leone, a Sequoia Capital partner stated: "Successes and failures should be balanced. If you haven't failed, you haven't tried; but if you've only failed, you don't know how to do things right."

A more perceptive view regarding failure comes from Bill Coleman. He was a serial entrepreneur and co-founder of BEA Systems (sold to Oracle for $8.5 billion in 2009). Coleman believed Silicon Valley's secret was "failure, tolerance of massive amounts of failure. One in 20 companies makes it here, but if you fail you try again." In contrast, other business cultures punish failure harshly and a businessperson doesn't get a second chance. Coleman himself had many failed startups (Visicorp and Dest Systems). So when he built BEA Systems, he recruited a senior staff consisting of people who were in at least one company that had failed. Coleman believed that "you learn not just about failure and how to make things work, you learn the psychology of failure and how you react to it." One example Coleman gave was SUN Microsystems, which did everything that was possibly wrong in creating products, but corrected course quickly. In Coleman's view, "a startup is not a technology company - it is a learning machine."[5]

There are few business cultures in the world that are as tolerant of failure as the Valley. People who fail and learn from it become better entrepreneurs and managers. They become intelligent risk-takers, knowing how to work the odds and create wealth. Or as one successful entrepreneur stated at the 2010 TiE Conference: "A startup is just a machine to turn one-dollar bills into twenty dollar bills – that's it." This book will have three chapters on failures, as the failed ventures in the Valley have much to show about what makes the Valley and its people successful.

The Inspiration to Follow Dreams to Change the World

Creating wealth is a powerful motivator. If enough people focus on it, it's conceivable that poverty could be a historical oddity. Yet most entrepreneurs and venture capitalists in the Valley point to something greater than wealth (or money). The most motivated ones have a vision for

[4] Lemos, Rob & Erdin Beshimov. "East Meets West - 5 Observations on Silicon Valley from an MIT Sloan Perspective." Silicon Valley Watcher, Jan. 12, 2010.
http://www.siliconvalleywatcher.com/mt/archives/2010/01/east_meets_west.php.
[5] Foremski, Tom. "Thought Leader: Valley Veteran Bill Coleman On Failure And The Guild Of Entrepreneurs . . ." Silicon Valley Watcher, March 5, 2009.
http://www.siliconvalleywatcher.com/mt/archives/2009/03/thought_leader_7.php.

what they want the world to be. They already have more money tha
need and have created more wealth than they can give away in
lifetimes. They work because they have a dream to change the world.

Some visions include:

- Steve Jobs of Apple Computer didn't just want to sell hardware
  devices and well-packaged microchips and mobile I/O devices. He
  wanted to change the way people imagine about and interact with
  each other and the world using technology. He wanted to promote
  design so beautiful that his company's inventions would make it to
  museum cases (as an example, Olivetti typewriters from the 1960s
  and 1970s, paragons of design, were in a SFMOMA exhibition in
  2010).

- Google's founders, Larry Page and Sergey Brin, didn't just want
  to be ad peddlers; rather, they wanted to collect and organize all
  the world's information so it could be easily searchable. They
  wanted to recreate the mythical Library of Alexandria by
  digitizing every book. Or as Susan Wojcicki, Brin's sister-in-law
  stated about their plans in 2000 (before Google even had a revenue
  model): "They actually would do some of the math behind it, and
  calculate, like, how many [scanning] machines it would take, how
  many hours it would take. So they knew with certain assumptions
  that it was a doable project."

- Facebook's founder Mark Zuckerberg didn't want to just make a
  social network selling ads and digital goods. He wanted to
  understand the connections between every person in the world due
  to properties of their social graphs, and then help them
  communicate in a more effective way. Every person could and
  should become a storyteller; every person could be a Homer,
  Walter Cronkite, or Glenn Beck.

- Vinod Khosla didn't just want to get a standard 30%+ IRR for
  investors in his funds. He wanted to solve the problem of non-
  renewable energy sources, helping the world find a perpetual,
  clean, and sustainable renewable energy mix. This wasn't just a
  pipe dream: Khosla convinced former British Prime Minister Tony
  Blair to join him.

Ultimately, Silicon Valley was built of both dreams and institutions.
Dreams are idiosyncratic; they start in an individual's mind and spread like
fire as an entrepreneur motivates a team to build a company. Institutions
provide all the necessary resources: the talented people, the productive
work environment, the supportive infrastructure, the right cultural mindset,
and so on. As many residents of the Valley have said: "Silicon Valley is a
state of mind." Yet it is also a place where the right institutions have been
built, where every newcomer can, to paraphrase Isaac Newton, stand on
the shoulders of giants, or at least build apps cheaply on the cloud
infrastructure laid before them.

3. Pioneers: Stanford University, Radio Engineering, the Melting Pot, and an Artistic Genesis (1900-25)

After the Gold Rush

Just over twenty thousand people lived in San Jose around 1900. When James Lick died in 1876, he was the wealthiest man in California. His "high-tech" occupation had been piano manufacturing. Lick had accumulated a little fortune by building and selling pianos in South America. In Peru he had met Domingo Ghirardelli, a maker of chocolate. When Lick moved to California, he invited Ghirardelli to set up shop in San Francisco, an advice that turned out to be golden: one year later gold was discovered near Sacramento, and both immigrants benefited by the economic boom. Lick was smart enough to buy land all around the Bay Area, while living in the village of San Jose.

Lick was planning to use his fortune to build himself the largest pyramid on Earth. Yet somehow the California Academy of Sciences convinced him to fund the Lick Observatory, the world's first permanently occupied mountain-top observatory, to be equipped with the most powerful telescope on Earth. That observatory, erected in 1887 on nearby Mount Hamilton, was the only notable event in the early history of San Jose. If you feel that Lick was a bit out of his mind to think of building a pyramid to himself, don't forget that his contemporary, Joshua Norton of San Francisco, had proclaimed himself "Emperor of the United States" in 1859 and subsequently the "Protector of Mexico." Those were strange days.

Stanford University

Until 1919, the only road connecting San Jose to San Francisco was the old "El Camino Real," a dusty country road at the time known as US 101. It snaked its way through orchards and barren hills. The only way to travel quickly was the Southern Pacific Railroad. It had been acquired by the railway empire of Leland Stanford, the president of the company charged with the western section of the first transcontinental railroad. Stanford was a former California governor and a US senator. The Stanfords donated land and money to start a university near their farm after their only son, Leland Junior, died. They had a station built on the Southern Pacific route called University Park, later renamed Palo Alto.

Stanford University opened in 1891. It was not the first university of the Bay Area. The Berkeley campus of the University of California had opened in 1873 at the other end of the bay. However, Leland was a man with a plan: his express goal was to create the Harvard of the West, something like New York State's Cornell University. At the time, despite the huge sums of money offered to them by Leland, neither the President of the Massachusetts Institute of Technology (MIT) in Boston, nor the President of Cornell were willing to move to such a primitive place as the Bay Area from their comfortable East Coast cities. Leland had to content himself with a humbler choice, a relatively young Cornell graduate named David Starr Jordan. In 1892 Leland hired Albert Pruden Carmen from the College of New Jersey (later renamed Princeton University) to teach electricity, a new discipline within the Physics Department. The following year, another Princeton graduate, Fred Perrine, became the first professor of electrical engineering within a department furnished with equipment donated by local electrical firms.

Santa Clara Valley

The Santa Clara Valley, located between Palo Alto and San Jose, was known as the "Valley of Heart's Delight" because it was an endless expanse of orchards. Its agriculture output was growing rapidly and, due to the invention of the refrigerated railroad car, it soon became the largest fruit production and packing region in the world. At one point there were 39 canneries in the valley, notably the San Jose Fruit Packing Company. At the peak, Chinese workers represented 48% of agricultural labor in the Santa Clara Valley. The agricultural boom increased the demand for firewood and lumber, which made the fortune of the Santa Clara Valley Mill & Lumber Company of Felton. But mostly the boom made the fortune of the "railroad barons" who provided the main form of transportation for goods and people. In fact, Santa Clara county confronted the arrogant railroad empires in a case that became famous in and had consequences for the whole nation. In 1886 the US Supreme Court decreed that corporations should have the same rights as persons, and therefore the Southern Pacific Railroad Company was entitled to deduct mortgage from its taxable income just like any household. Finally, ports dotted the bay, notably Redwood City's port that shipped lumber to San Francisco. Redwood City was located in the "Peninsula," the stretch of land between San Francisco and Palo Alto.

Most of the Peninsula belonged to San Mateo County and was underpopulated. The county road from San Francisco to Belmont (north of Redwood City) served the wealthy San Franciscan who had bought a mansion in the countryside, typically for the summer, when San Francisco was blanketed by fog. These mansions usually controlled a large tract of land and constituted self-sufficient agricultural units. World War I helped populate one town, Menlo Park, just north of Palo Alto, where the Army established Camp Fremont to train tens of thousands of soldiers. Not much else was going on in the sleepy bay accidentally discovered in 1769 by Spanish explorer Gaspar de Portola.

Much was happening in the rest of the US. The nation was booming with innovative ideas revolutionizing agriculture, industry, mining, and transportation. Since there were more and more numbers to crunch, it is not surprising that inventors started devising several computing machines. The most influential were William Burroughs' adding machine of 1885 and Hermann Hollerith's tabulator of 1890 (chosen for the national census). However, the new sensation at the turn of the century was electricity. It enabled a whole new spectrum of appliances, from the light bulb to the phonograph.

Electrical Engineering

The railway brought people to the Bay Area, and created the first fortunes. But then, the Bay Area needed electricity. California had plenty of water coming down from its mighty Sierra Nevada mountain range. Entrepreneurs understood that dams (hydroelectric plants) could provide the electrical power needed by the coastal cities, and engineers were working on solving the problem of how to distribute that power. The East Coast had not faced the problem of carrying high-tension voltage over long-distances, but that was precisely the problem to be solved on the West Coast. Stanford professors and students, under the leadership of the new head of the Electrical Engineering Department, Harris Ryan, another Cornell alumnus who had arrived in 1905, helped solve the problem. They inaugurated a cooperative model between university and industry. The Bay Area's electrical power companies used the Stanford High Voltage Laboratory (as well as the one at UC Berkeley) for the development of long-distance electric power transmission. That cooperation, in addition, raised a generation of electrical engineers that could match the know-how of the East Coast.

Radio Engineering and Federal Telegraph

Around 1900, San Francisco's inhabitants showed a voracious interest in the radio technology invented in Europe. The Italian inventor Guglielmo Marconi, then in Britain, had galvanized the sector with his long-distance radio transmissions. Marconi started in 1897 and culminated with the radio message from the US President Theodore Roosevelt to the British king Edward VII of 1903. Marconi's company set up radio stations on both sides of the Atlantic to communicate with ships at sea. However, it was still difficult to create a wireless communication system.

In 1906 an independent engineer named Lee DeForest had invented the vacuum tube in Chicago without quite understanding its potential as a signal amplifier. His invention, the "audion," was useful to amplify electrical signals, and therefore relevant to wireless transmissions. Prior do DeForest in 1904, the British chemist John Ambrose had invented the two-element amplifier, or "diode," and a few months before DeForest the

Austrian physicist Robert von Lieben had already built a three-element amplifier, or "triode." But DeForest was in the right place. In 1910 DeForest moved to San Francisco and got into radio broadcasting. He had pioneered technology when he had broadcast from New York a live performance by legendary Italian tenor Enrico Caruso. DeForest started using the term "radio" to refer to wireless transmission when he formed his DeForest Radio Telephone Company in 1907. However, his early broadcasts did not use the audion yet. Interest in radio broadcasting was high in the Bay Area, even if there were no mass-produced radios yet. Charles Herrold in San Jose had started the first radio station in the US with regularly scheduled programming, including songs, using an arc transmitter of his own design. Herrold had been one of Stanford's earliest students and founded his own College of Wireless and Engineering in San Jose.

The Bay Area stumbled into electronics almost by accident. In 1909 another Stanford alumnus, Cyril Elwell, had founded the Poulsen Wireless Telephone and Telegraph Company in Palo Alto. It was later renamed the Federal Telegraph Corporation (FTC) and commercialized a new European invention. The Danish engineer Valdemar Poulsen had previously invented an arc transmitter for radio transmission, but no European company was doing anything with it. Elwell understood its potential was not only technological but also legal: it allowed him to create radio products without violating Marconi's patents. Elwell acquired the US rights for the Poulsen arc. His radio technology, adequately funded by a group of San Francisco investors led by Beach Thompson, blew away the competition of the East Coast. In 1912, he won a contract with the US Navy, the biggest consumer of radio communications. Thus commercial radio-telegraphy, that is, long distance signal transmission, developed first in the US. The "startup" was initially funded by Stanford's own President, David Starr Jordan, and employed Stanford students, notably Edwin Pridham. Jordan had just inaugurated venture-capital investment in the region.

In need of better receiver amplifiers for the arc transmissions, FTC hired Lee DeForest, who had finally realized that his audion could be used as an amplifier. The problem with long-distance telephone and radio transmissions was that the signal was lost en route as it became too faint. DeForest's vacuum tube enabled the construction of repeaters that restored the signal at intermediate points. Hence the audion could dramatically reduce the cost of long-distance wireless communications, making mass radio viable. FTC began applying the audion to develop a geographically distributed radio-telegraphy system. The first tower they had built, in July 1910, was on a San Francisco beach and it was 90 meters tall. Yet the most impressive of all was inaugurated later at Point San Bruno, just south of San Francisco. It was a large complex boasting the tallest antenna in the world at 130 meters.

By the end of 1912 FTC had grown. Besides California, it had stations in Texas, Hawaii, Arizona, Missouri, and Washington. However, the Poulsen arc remained the main technology for radio-telephony, long distance voice transmission. Ironically, FTC was no longer in that business. Improvements to the design by recent Cornell-graduate Leonard Fuller allowed the audion to amplify a signal a million times eventually led FTC to create the first global wireless communication system. The audion was still used only for receivers, while most transmitters were arc-based. It was only in 1915 that DeForest realized that a feedback loop of audions could be used to build transmitters as well. DeForest had already sold the patent for his audion to Graham Bell's AT&T Corp. in New York. AT&T had used it to set up the first coast-to-coast telephone line by early 1915, just in time for the Panama-Pacific International Exposition. Meanwhile, DeForest had moved to New York. There, in 1916, he shocked the nation by broadcasting the results of the presidential elections with music and commentary from New York to stations within a range of 300 kilometers. He used an audion transmitter. Radio-telephony would switch from the Poulsen arc to his audion during the 1920s. In due time, Leo Fuller took Elwell's place as chief engineer of FTC. By 1920 the former Marconi engineer Haraden Pratt was hired to launch commercial wireless telegraph service and sugar magnate Rudolph Spreckels bought control of FTC.

The wireless industry was booming throughout the US, aided by sensational articles in the mainstream press. Earle Ennis had opened a company (Western Wireless Equipment Company) to sell wireless equipment for ships. He also ran a radio broadcast to deliver news to ships at sea. In 1910 he organized the first air-to-ground radio message, thus showing that the same technology could be used by the nascent airline industry.

Because of its maritime business, the Bay Area became one of the largest centers for amateur radio. The Bay Counties Wireless Telegraph Association was founded in 1907 by amateurs such as Haraden Pratt, Ellery Stone, and Lewis Clement. Among the amateurs of the second decade were Charlie Litton, an eleven-year old prodigy who operated an amateur station in Redwood City in 1915, and Frederick Terman, a teenager who operated an amateur station in Palo Alto in 1917. Some of those amateurs went on to create small companies. Magnavox Corp. was founded in 1910 in Napa, north of the Bay Area. It was the brainchild of Peter Jensen, one of the Danish engineers imported by FTC to commercialize the Poulsen arc, and Edwin Pridham, a Stanford graduate who also worked at FTC. In 1917 they introduced a new type of electrical loudspeaker.

Little did the hobbyists and small companies know that their devices would in times of war constitute a strategic industry for the Air Force, Navy, and Army. During World War I, Elwell's technology would be a pillar of naval communications for the US. The Navy had set up radio stations all over the world. In January 1918, US President Woodrow Wilson proudly spoke live to Europe, the Far East, and Latin America.

After World War I, it became clear that radio technology was strategic defense technology and it couldn't be left in the hands of West Coast independents. The US government compelled a large East Coast company, General Electric, to buy the US business of Marconi. The US government also helped the new company to acquire the most important radio patents. Thus a new giant, RCA, was born and soon became the dominant player in consumer electronics as the number of radios grew from 5,000 in 1920 to 25 million in 1924. Hence FTC was doomed and other Bay Area-based radio companies had to live with only military applications.

Radio engineering created two worlds in the Bay Area that would greatly influence its future: a high-tech industry and a community of high-tech amateurs.

Culture and Society

Cultural and social changes in San Francisco provided a crucial backdrop to the high-tech industry, even from early times. San Francisco was still living with the legacy of the "Gold Rush" of 1849. The "Barbary Coast," as the red-light district was known, was a haven for brothels and nightclubs, making the city something like a cross of modern Las Vegas and Thai Pattaya. The thousands of Chinese immigrants who had been lured to California to build railways, mine gold, and grow food had fathered a new generation that settled in "Chinatown," the largest Chinese community outside Asia. The port served steamers bound for the coast or Asia as well as ferry traffic to the bay and the Sacramento River. It supported a large community of teamsters and longshoremen that also made it the most unionized city in the US.

Dubious characters still roamed the landscape. The career of despised media tycoon William Randolph Hearst got its start in 1887 when his mining-entrepreneur father handed him the San Francisco Examiner. But there were also honest, enterprising men, such as Amadeo Giannini, who founded the Bank of Italy in 1904 to serve the agricultural economy of the Santa Clara Valley. This bank was later renamed Bank of America. At the turn of the century one could already sense San Francisco's predisposition towards rebellion. John Muir's Sierra Club, formed in 1892, led the first environmental protest when the state planned a dam in Yosemite. The American Anti-Imperialist League organized the first anti-war movement when the US went to war against Spain. This was largely architected by Hearst to sell more copies of his newspapers. The Union Labor Party became the first pseudo-socialist party to win a mayoral election in a US city. Yet most of this was irrelevant to the rest of the nation. San Francisco only made the national news in 1906 because of the earthquake and resulting fire that leveled most of the city (strategic locations like whiskey warehouses were saved by eager citizens).

California was also blessed with some of the most reformist governors in the country, notably Hiram Johnson (1911-1917), who democratized California and reduced the power of the political barons. William Stephens (1917-1923) did something similar to curb the political power of unions. Their policies focused on raising the living standards of the middle class, and therefore of the suburbs.

Immigration made San Francisco a cosmopolitan city. There had already been Italians when California was still under Mexican rule. They were fishermen and farmers. By the turn of the century, old and new Italians had created an Italian quarter in North Beach. Then came the Japanese, who replaced the Chinese in agriculture. At the beginning of the century San Francisco boasted two Japanese-language newspapers: "The New World" and the "Japanese American." Mexicans immigrated from 1910 to 1930, following the Mexican revolution and the construction of a railway.

San Francisco was also becoming friendly toward the arts. In 1902, the California Society of Artists was founded by a cosmopolitan group that included the Mexican-born painter Xavier Martinez and the Swiss-born painter and muralist Gottardo Piazzoni. At the California School of Design, many students were influenced by muralist and painter Arthur Mathews. As one of the founders of the American Arts and Crafts Movement, he tried to reconcile craftsmanship with industrial consumerism. A symbolic event took place after the 1906 earthquake when Mathews opened his own shop as a craftsman and a painter to publish one of the earliest art magazines in town, the Philopolis. Another by-product of the American Arts and Crafts Movement was Oakland's California College of the Arts and Crafts, founded in 1907 by Frederick Meyer.

More and more artists were moving to San Francisco. They created the equivalent of Paris' Montmartre artistic quarter at the four-story building called "Montgomery Block," also nicknamed "Monkey Block," the epicenter of San Francisco's bohemian life. Maynard Dixon was influenced by the Panama-Pacific International Exposition during the 1920s and he created an original Western style of painting. In 1921 Ansel Adams began to publish his photographs of Yosemite. It was another small contribution to changing the reputation of that part of California and the birth of one of the most vibrant schools of photography in the world. Literature, on the other hand, lagged behind, represented by Frank Pixley's literary magazine the "Argonaut," located at Montgomery Block. Another art colony was born in the coastal city of Carmel, about two hours south of San Francisco. Armin Hansen opened his studio there in 1913 and was followed by Percy Gray and impressionist master William Merritt Chase.

Architects were in high demand both because of the fortunes created by the railway and because of the reconstruction of San Francisco after the earthquake (for example, Willis Polk). Mary Colter studied in San Francisco before venturing into her vernacular architecture for the Southwest's desert landscape. The Panama-Pacific International Exposition of 1915, held in San Francisco, for which Bernard Maybeck built the exquisite Palace of Fine Arts, symbolized the transformation that had taken place in the area: from emperors and gold diggers to inventors and investors (and soon, defense contractors).

Classical music was represented by its own school of iconoclasts. Charles Seeger taught unorthodox techniques such as dissonant counterpoint at UC Berkeley. Starting with "The Tides of Manaunaun" (1912), pianist Henry Cowell, a pupil of Seeger, began exploring the tone-cluster technique. That piece was based on poems by John Osborne Varian, the father of Russell and Sigurd Varian, who had moved to Halcyon, a utopian community founded halfway between San Francisco and Los Angeles by theosophists. Varian's sons Russell and Sigurd later became friends with Ansel Adams through their mutual affiliation with the Sierra Club.

The Prehistory of Office Automation

Elsewhere, mainly in the commercial centers of New York and Detroit, the sector of computing machines was taking birth. It was fueled by the frantic growth in statistical and bookkeeping activities, with the initial boost coming from the US Census Bureau. In 1911, Hollerith's Tabulating Machine Company was acquired by a new company based in New York. In 1924, it changed its name to International Business Machines (IBM) under President Thomas Watson. These "tabulating machines" processed punched cards that stored information. The idea of using holes to program machines was not new: the same principle had been used to "program" silk looms and player pianos. IBM's main rival, Powers Accounting Machine, also based in New York, would later be merged by James Rand with Remington, the main manufacturer of typewriters since 1873. Remington had introduced the first mass-produced model and the QWERTY keyboard. Besides government agencies, the main customers of tabulating machines were insurance companies and railroad companies.

Other inventors created useful business machines too. In 1894 Charles Kettering at John Patterson's National Cash Register (NCR) of Ohio had invented the electrical cash register. In 1922 NCR sold more than two million electrical cash registers, about 90% of the market. This revolutionized retail commerce, since store owners no longer had to hover around cash boxes and could focus on growing multi-location chains. In 1925 Burroughs of Detroit introduced a portable adding machine, still weighing quite a bit but "portable" by a strong man. It became a runaway success for bookkeeping calculations in large firms and was the first step towards automating an office.

By the 1920s most businesses were fully equipped with labor-saving machines such as typewriters, dominated by Remington Rand, adding machines, dominated by Burroughs, tabulating machines, dominated by IBM, and cash registers, dominated by NCR. Clearly first-movers had a huge advantage in the tech industry and it didn't look like Silicon Valley would become dominant.

4. Scouts: Electrical Engineering, Nuclear Engineering, the Navy, and a Culture of Innovation (1925-40)

Stanford and Electrical Engineering

A pivotal event in the history of the Bay Area's high-tech industry took place in 1925. Frederick Terman, a ham radio fan who had also studied at MIT in Boston with Vannevar Bush, joined Stanford University. He worked at Harris Ryan's pioneering radio-communications laboratory. Terman was the son of a Stanford professor. He represented a highly educated generation that had been raised in the Bay Area, a step forward from the unlettered immigrants of previous decades. Within two years, the young apprentice became a visionary on his own, fostering a new science on the border between wireless communications and vacuum-tube electronics. Terman didn't just perfect the art of radio engineering. He encouraged his students to start businesses and not just join big companies. Many of those students were coming from the East Coast. He encouraged them to stay in the Bay Area. Terman viewed the university as an incubator of business plans. It was a step up from Harris Ryan's philosophy of encouraging cooperation between academia and industry.

A vibrant industry was taking hold around Stanford University by the time Ryan retired in 1931. While Cyril Elwell's Federal Telegraph Corporation (FTC) moved east, several Bay Area startups were FTC spin-offs or radio company affiliates.

Stanford's student Ralph Heintz, a former radio amateur and employee of Earle Ennis, had started a business to install short-wave radios on ships and airplanes. In 1926 he founded Heintz & Kaufmann in San Francisco. Soon Henitz had to start manufacturing their own vacuum tubes to compete with RCA, for which they hired radio hobbyists Bill Eitel and Jack McCullough.

Litton Engineering Laboratories had been founded in 1932 by ham-radio hobbyist, Stanford student, and FTC manager Charlie Litton. He started it in his parents' Redwood City home to manufacture tools for vacuum tube manufacturers (the same job he had at FTC).

Eitel-McCullough, later Eimac, was formed in 1934 in San Bruno by Heintz's employees Bill Eitel and Jack McCullough to develop better vacuum tubes for the amateur or ham radio market. These would become the Armed Forces' favorite tubes during the war. Another FTC employee, German-born Gerhard Fisher invented the metal detector in 1928, and founded Fisher Research Laboratories in 1931 in his home's garage in Palo Alto. Many of these independents who scouted the market for radio communications and electronics had started out as ham radio amateurs, some of them at a very early age.

Berkeley and Nuclear Engineering

Meanwhile, another industry came to the Bay Area because of one creative scientist and his groundbreaking invention. UC Berkeley had opened LeConte Hall in 1924 to enlarge its Department of Physics. It had gone on a hiring spree to fill it with young talent. In January 1931, one of these young physicists, Ernest Lawrence designed the first successful cyclotron, a particle accelerator.

It was theoretically known that nuclear particles undergo transformations as they travel faster, but no lab had devised a machine yet that could accelerate particles to the point that this phenomenon would be observable. It was called a "cyclotron" because its principle was to send particles in a loop through the same accelerating field, thus increasing their speed with each cycle.

A former FTC executive, Leonard Fuller, had become the head of the Electrical Engineering Department at the UC Berkeley and had managed to obtain from FTC a 1000-kilowatt generator that Lawrence used to build his device, actually quite small at just 66 centimeters in diameter. The Radiation Laboratory that Lawrence opened that year in August right halfway between LeConte Hall and the campus' bell tower became one of the most celebrated research centers for atomic energy. It later moved up the hill and was renamed Lawrence Berkeley Lab, attracting several of the world's most promising scientists to Berkeley. Another nuclear physicist, Robert Oppenheimer, had joined UC Berkeley in 1929, one year after Lawrence. He was important in shaping the intellectual mood of the campus with his passion for Eastern philosophy and his donations to socialist causes. During the 1930s, several of his friends, relatives (including the woman he married in 1940), and students were affiliated with the Communist Party.

Atomic Energy and Big Science

The relevance of atomic energy became more and more self-evident as the 1930s progressed, and not only for particle physics. John Lawrence, brother of the Lawrence Berkeley Labs' founder, realized that it could be useful in another field too. In 1936 he founded the Donner Laboratory to conduct research in nuclear medicine. In 1939 Ernest Lawrence was awarded the Nobel Prize in Physics, the first time the prize came to the Bay Area. As important as Lawrence's engineering/scientific achievements was his concept of "big science." He created a large interdisciplinary team of engineers and scientists to focus on a practical project. It didn't come just out of good will, but also out of necessity. The construction of his increasingly bigger cyclotrons required an increasingly large number of specialists in different disciplines. Lawrence's team would include four future Nobel Prize winners (Edwin McMillan, Luis Alvarez, Glenn Seaborg and Emilio Segre) plus mechanical engineers such as William Brobeck. Last but not least, Lawrence was skilled at obtaining donations from philanthropists, a difficult task in the middle of the Great Depression.

The Stanford counterpart to Lawrence was Swiss physicist Felix Bloch, who fled the Nazis in 1934. He and Oppenheimer organized a joint Berkeley-Stanford seminar on theoretical physics that brought European science to the West Coast. Bloch would become Stanford's first Nobel Laureate. Meanwhile, young graduate Bill Hansen imported know-how about Lawrence's accelerator and set out to find a way to use high-frequency waves to accelerate electrons to high energy.

New Inputs

The military was creating cities from empty land. The vast activity in radio engineering led the Navy in 1933 to open a base between Palo Alto and San Jose. It was called the Naval Air Station Sunnyvale and later renamed Moffett Field. The contacts that had existed between the Bay Area's engineering companies and the military bureaucracy found a major outlet. In 1939 the US government would up the ante by establishing the Ames Aeronautical Laboratory, later renamed the NASA Ames Research Center, at Moffett Field. The area to the north would develop into the town of Mountain View. The area to the south would develop into Sunnyvale Originally the two were part of just one huge Mexican ranch.

The local tradition of radio engineering led an immigrant to settle in San Francisco to conduct his experiments. In 1927, Philo Farnsworth, a stereotypical amateur who had been discovered in Utah by San Francisco venture capitalists Leslie Gorrell and George Everson, carried out the first all-electronic television broadcast. It was based on a theory that he had conceived as a teenager. Farnsworth's team included the young Russ Varian and Ralph Heintz. In 1931 the investors decided to cash in. They sold the company to the Philadelphia Storage Battery Company, later renamed Philco. At the time, Philco was the main maker of home radios in the US and therefore in a much better position to mass-manufacture television sets. The power of RCA, however, was such that the Russian-born scientist Vladimir Zworkyn of their New Jersey laboratories was credited by the media with inventing television. Farnsworth's reputation was saved by his good San Francisco friend, Donald Lippincott, formerly an engineer turned attorney, who in 1930 defended the young inventor's intellectual property against RCA. Lippincott exemplified a tradition of heavy intellectual-property litigation in the Bay Area that would be crucial to the development of the high-tech industry run by young inventors.

Culture and Society

Meanwhile, San Francisco was changing. Initially starting as Sodom on the West Coast, it had become one of the financial capitals of the US. In 1930, its Ferry Building was the second busiest transportation terminal in the world after Manhattan. The Bayshore Highway opened in 1932 to Palo Alto and in 1937 reached San Jose. In 1964 it would be renamed US I-101, previously the designation for El Camino Real. The rapidly spreading urban area required the building of the Oakland Bay Bridge and of the Golden Gate Bridge, completed respectively in 1936 and 1937. The latter was the longest bridge yet built in the world. Rich patrons allowed the city to open its own Museum of Art (1935) and to found the first professional ballet company in the US (1933).

Capitalizing on the pioneers of the previous generation, the arts flourished. Among the new talents were: the surrealist sculptor Adaline Kent, one of Ralph Stackpole's students at the California School of Fine Arts; the Japanese-born painter Chiura Obata, famous for his 1927 paintings of the Sierra Nevada, who founded the East-West Art Society; and the bizarrely reclusive Achilles Rizzoli, who between 1935 to 1944 created intricate visionary architectural drawings in the "Art Nouveau" style. German-born Abstract Expressionist painter Hans Hofmann moved to UC Berkeley in 1930 and became the most influential teacher of the Bay Area, pushing for curricula that were heavy on modern art. It turned the Bay Area into one of the US's friendliest regions for experimental artists.

The Bay Area was probably the only place in the world where the dominant fine art was photography, perhaps as a reaction to the Los Angeles movie industry. Besides Ansel Adams, the Bay Area produced: Dorothea Lange, famous for her work on the homeless of the Great Depression; Imogen Cunningham, famous for her industrial landscapes of the late 1920s; and James Weston, based in Carmel, famous for his still lifes and nudes of the late 1920s. Seven Bay Area-based photographers (including Adams, Cunningham, Weston and Weston's apprentices Willard Van Dyke and Sonya Noskowiak) founded Group f/64. This was in opposition to Alfred Stieglitz's pictorialism that had dominated photography in the first decades of the century. The group held their first, highly-publicized exhibition in 1932.

Another art that was relatively unique to San Francisco was wall painting, heavily influenced by Diego Rivera's work in Mexico. In 1936 muralist Edith Hamlin painted the Western-themed murals for the Mission High School. Whereas the dominant art form of movies in Los Angeles generated high revenues and the arts on the East Coast created world-famous movements, San Francisco's artists were mostly independents and eccentrics, just like the hobbyists of radio engineering.

High culture came in 1935 when art historian Grace Morley founded the San Francisco Museum of Art, the second museum in the US devoted exclusively to modern art. Again, San Francisco had its own idea of what "modern art" was. In 1946 Morley hired filmmaker Frank Stauffacher to start the "Art in Cinema" series. This inspired the California School of the Arts to assign a film course to Sidney Peterson. Peterson, who had been a painter and sculptor in France at the time of Dada, directed the manifesto of the San Francisco avant garde with poet James Broughton: "The Potted Psalm" (1946).

San Francisco celebrated its status as a vibrant center of innovation with the 1939 World's Fair. The "Golden Gate International Exposition" was held on an artificial island in the middle of the bay named Treasure Island. Its highlight was Ralph Stackpole's 24-meter tall colossus "Pacifica," dynamited in 1942 to make room for a naval base. In the years that it lasted, 16 million visitors came to visit.

Another oasis for artists came about in a strange way. In 1911, James Phelan had a villa built in the south bay, precisely in the hills of Saratoga overlooking Santa Clara Valley. He had made his fortune during the Gold Rush as a trader and a banker and had then become the mayor of San Francisco. He later became a US Senator from California. Phelan had bequeathed this villa, named "Montalvo" in honor of the 16th century Spanish writer who coined the name "California," to the state so that it could be turned into a cultural center to support promising artists, writers, musicians and architects. It took a while, but in 1939, Villa Montalvo opened the doors to an artist residency program, the first one in the Western United States.

The great musical innovator of the Bay Area was Henry Cowell, a bisexual who spent four years in prison for that "crime." In 1930 he commissioned the Russian instrument builder Leon Theremin to create the first electronic rhythm machine, the "Rhythmicon." Cowell later taught the influential course "Music of the Peoples of the World" at UCSF. He promoted atonality, non-Western modes, percussion ensembles, and even chance composition. He also was probably the first classical composer to live a parallel life as a successful pop songwriter. In San Francisco his pupil Lou Harrison took advantage of the Bay Area's ethnic Babel and incorporated Chinese opera, Native-American folk, jazz, and later the gamelan music of Indonesia into Western classical music. In New York, his other pupil John Cage became famous by expanding on several of his master's intuitions.

Rich patrons also funded San Francisco's legendary nightlife, a legacy of "Barbary Coast" that religious groups tried in vain to suppress. In 1936 Joe Finocchio opened the gay bar "Finocchio's" on Broadway. Those were the years of the Great Depression, which had started with the financial collapse of 1929. However, not a single bank failed in San Francisco. The Bay Area was certainly affected by the crisis, but it fared a lot better than the rest of California and of the US. In fact, it was during the Great Depression that San Francisco leapfrogged to the higher ranks of metropolitan areas, despite remaining a relatively small city in itself. After growing rapidly since the earthquake (416,000 people in 1910), the population stabilized at 634,000 during the 1930s. Residential growth was now spreading to the north, east and south.

At the time San Francisco was famous around the country for its ethnic diversity, but little else. At the end of the 1930s San Francisco was still a relatively lawless place. A popular joke was that the organized crime of Chicago and New York had no chance to infiltrate San Francisco because the entire city was just one big racket.

Stanford and US Industry

Stanford University was becoming a major center of innovation, and its doctrine of encouraging entrepreneurship was beginning to pay off. In 1937 Fred Terman's students William Hewlett and David Packard started working on an audio-oscillator. In January 1939 they founded a company called Hewlett-Packard in a Palo Alto garage. Their first customer was Walt Disney. The Hollywood animation company purchased their oscillator in 1939 for the animated film "Fantasia." Stanford University's Professor William Hansen teamed up with two hobbyists who had a brilliant idea. They were the brothers Sigurd Varian, an airplane pilot, and Russ Varian, a Stanford dropout who had roomed with Hansen and been a former engineer in Philo Farnsworth's television laboratory. They were refining an electronic device that worked as an amplifier for generating electromagnetic waves at higher frequencies than radio frequency (microwaves). Working with Hansen at Stanford they developed the klystron tube, the first generator of microwaves. This invention revolutionized and greatly improved radar technology. It enabled airborne radars, Sigurd Varian's original motivation on the eve of World War II. The radar dish broadcasts pulses of microwaves, which bounce back whenever they hit an object in a time interval that reveals the distance of the object.

These pioneers knew each other well via Stanford. In 1938 Terman organized a research team around Russ Varian, with Charles Litton reporting to him and Dave Packard reporting to Litton.

In 1940 the cash-rich Sperry Corporation of New York, which specialized in aircraft navigation equipment, basically "bought" Hansen and the klystron from Stanford. It rewarded Stanford with a huge investment in its electrical engineering lab, allowing the lab to grow even more rapidly. Stanford already had a national reputation in high-voltage power transmission. It had now found the money to expand in electronics too. The Varian story was a further refinement of the FTC story: interaction between industry and a university led to an advanced technology whose first customer was the government and whose first application was warfare.

Progress in Electronic Computation

Mostly unbeknownst to the Bay Area scientists who were working on radio engineering and atomic energy, significant theoretical progress was being made elsewhere in the theory of computation. In 1937, the British mathematician Alan Turing described a machine capable of performing logical reasoning by manipulating symbols like a mathematician, the "Turing machine." He then described a "universal Turing Machine," capable of simulating any Turing machine by reading a symbolic description of the machine to be simulated. It was a purely abstract concept, but it proved the feasibility of a machine capable of solving all problems. In technical terms it was a "programmable" machine. A few years later the Hungarian-born mathematician John Von Neumann at Princeton University showed how it would be more efficient to build a computing machine that holds both its data and its instructions, the "stored-program architecture." The idea spread quickly due to Princeton's policy of making its research publicly available.

A major research center had been created in 1925 by AT&T in New York and named after AT&T's founder Alexander Graham Bell. From the beginning, Bell Labs had featured a department for applied mathematics, led by Thornton Fry. Here George Stibitz had the idea of using relay circuits, the same kind of circuits that AT&T was deploying for telephone systems, to perform binary arithmetic computations. In 1937 he built a relay-based binary calculator, the "Model K."

The computer had many more fathers. In 1938 John Atanasoff at Iowa State College had conceived a rudimentary electronic digital computer. It was not programmable though. Konrad Zuse built the first program-controlled computer in 1941 in Germany, the "Z3," the first hardware implementation of the universal Turing machine. It still employed electro-mechanical relays. For practical purposes, though, the "differential analyzer" was still the most advanced computing device. It was a mechanical analog computer, capable of performing sophisticated computations as fast as a professional mathematician. Vannevar Bush, the Professor of Electrical Engineering at MIT in Boston who had graduated Terman in 1924, constructed a computer in 1931. It was installed in 1935 at the Moore School of Electrical Engineering of the University of Pennsylvania to help the Ballistics Research Laboratory of the Army calculate the trajectory of bombs. The "soldiers" assigned to perform computations for the artillery were usually women. They were called "computers."

5. Partners: A Case Study on Bill Hewlett, Dave Packard, and Fred Terman at HP and Stanford (1930-1970)

The Team that Built Silicon Valley

Fred Terman was the founder of Silicon Valley, if any single person can be given credit for it. He was one of the most successful American administrators of science, engineering, and higher education in the 20th century. He made the Stanford engineering department one of the best in the country and laid the foundations that would make Stanford one of the world's pre-eminent research universities. He single-handedly created the university-government-industry partnership model that still characterizes Silicon Valley in the twenty-first century. Bill Hewlett and Dave Packard were two of Terman's favorite engineering students and certainly his most successful protégés. They left behind a Global Fortune 50 company that in 2012 sold products around the world (it is Silicon Valley's largest corporation by revenues). The pair also founded multiple multi-billion dollar charitable foundations.

The history of the three men is best combined, as is the partnership of Stanford University with the federal government and private industry like the Hewlett Packard Corporation (HP). Their friendship and admiration for each other was genuine. David Packard showed it at Terman's Memorial Service in January 1983, in Stanford California, when he mentioned knowing Terman for more than 50 years. Packard said he enjoyed Terman's "friendship and benefited in many ways and on many occasions from his council, his advice, and his wisdom. . . Fred Terman was an engineer's engineer." Terman was unique in that he loved technical theory but also loved to build useful products and companies, to see practical things get done.[6]

Bill Hewlett showed the depth of his affection after hearing of his best friend Packard's death in a March morning in 1996. Another friend came by to pay his condolences. The friend went into the kitchen and saw Hewlett sitting on his wheelchair by a table in the breakfast nook. Hewlett was staring into the distance; his staff watched him sitting there from the

---

[6] Sharpe, Ed. "The Life of Fred Terman." Southwest Museum of Engineering, Communications and Computation, Vol. 3, Iss. 1. http://www.smecc.org/frederick_terman_-_by_ed_sharpe.htm

early morning into the afternoon hours, with a deep and sad look on his face.[7]

The HP history is an admirable one of two close friends building a multinational company which during their lives was one of the world's most admired companies for both its profit growth and its employee-oriented culture.

Terman in California

In 1905 the Terman family moved to Southern California from the Midwest. Fred Terman's father needed the warm climate to get over tuberculosis so he took a Stanford Education School professorship in 1910. The family moved to the place where Fred Terman would both grow up and die. Terman went to Palo Alto High School just as Federal Telegraph Corp. (FTC), funded by Stanford President David Starr Jordan, became a major radio company in Palo Alto.

FTC is important for both the Valley and Terman. Cy Elwell's company convinced the inventor Lee DeForest to leave the East Coast and come to Palo Alto to be his Chief Scientist. DeForest created the electronic amplifier, found in so many electronics devices today. Yet he was still being persecuted and had even been sent to jail for stock fraud charges relating to a previously failed New York startup. Elwell had to post bail. California was a much more amenable place to work for a risky electronics venture. FTC went on to have the first intercontinental radio broadcast in 1919 (Annapolis Maryland to Bordeaux France). It was one of the major radio manufacturing companies in the US. Alas, the glamour of Federal Telegraph didn't last, as it slowly faded around a handful of products till Marconi acquired it in 1931. Two entrepreneurial employees left to found Magnavox.

Federal Telegraph was doubly important because all the neighborhood techie kids became amateur radio enthusiasts, hanging around Federal Telegraph's labs. In fact, ham radio may have been the first Silicon Valley boom, with its low cost of entry and simple technology, and hence accessibility to a large group of technical-minded people. The inspiration of radio never left Terman – environment was destiny in his case.

Terman studied Chemical Engineering at Stanford, then took a double graduate course load in Electrical Engineering to get a PhD in the subject. With his studies in Palo Alto maxed out, he went to Boston Tech, later renamed as MIT. Terman studied under Arthur Kennelly, electronics whiz and discoverer of the earth's ionosphere, Norbert Weiner, nonlinear mathematician and cybernetics theorist, and most importantly, Vannevar Bush, his faculty research advisor. This relationship was very important to

---

[7] Malone, Michael S. Bill & Dave: How Hewlett and Packard Built the World's Greatest Company. New York: Penguin Portfolio, 2007, p. 362.

the future development of Silicon Valley and Stanford. Bush was a sociable, politically well-connected engineer. He would become President of the Carnegie Institution, help found the National Science Foundation, and most importantly, he was director of President Roosevelt's Office of Scientific Research and Development. This organization gave massive amounts of US federal funding to engineering schools to develop military technology, and it favored a small group of schools, of which MIT and Stanford sat at the top.

Terman wasn't the sole star graduate of Stanford. Charlie Litton was a mechanical genius and a few years behind Terman, graduating in 1924, just as Terman returned to Stanford. Litton was a self-taught expert at creating glass or metal vacuum tubes, used in all radios and eventually early computer. After working for Bell Labs and then Federal Telegraph, Litton formed Litton Engineering Labs in Redwood City in April 1932.

Litton Engineering Laboratories designed and manufactured glass-working machinery and equipment for power vacuum tubes used in radios. Twenty years later it was a billion dollar company. Litton became one of the US's wealthiest people and an early model of a technology millionaire. Yet Litton would say when he was asked about his success: "I was just a lucky kid." Litton himself lived as an eccentric technology entrepreneur: he breakfasted in the late afternoon, went to the office in evening, and worked till morning so he could have a productive day during the night's quiet hours. Once he built a new building for the company by showing up with a bulldozer to do foundation excavation. Litton lived a simple life and liked to hike in the Sierras. The vacuum tube side of the company became Litton Industries (of California) in 1946. It sold products only to the Department of Defense. In 1953, Litton sold the stock of Litton Industries (of California) to Electro-Dynamics and it became Litton Industries, Inc. He could stop worrying about operating a company or taking care of his estate, and so could focus on research. Litton later moved to Carson City, Nevada, where he died in 1973.

Upon returning to Stanford, Terman contracted tuberculosis and became immobilized. He lay in bed with sandbags on his chest for nine months and then suffered a burst appendix with the resulting vision problems lasting for years. However Terman used the time to write a book on electrical transmission and found that he could join circuit theory with amplifiers and vacuum tubes. He became more interested in radio engineering. While in bed, he received offers from both Stanford and MIT to teach, and he chose Stanford due to loyalty and the good weather. It was a good decision as MIT turned its back on radio, even though retail US sales went from $2 million to $325 million between 1920 and 1925. Stanford, on the other hand, had a well-stocked radio lab because of a partnership with private companies like AT&T, Western Electric, and Pacific Telephone.

In 1932 Terman published his textbook on radio engineering. After numerous editions, it was the seminal text on radio technology. Terman was a hard worker; he never took vacations and he wrote daily. He married Sibyl Walcutt around that time, in what would be a 47 year marriage till she died in 1975.

Terman's Precocious Protégés

Terman's two most famous students also grew up on the West Coast. Bill Hewlett grew up in San Francisco on Union Street. His father was a physician and promising professor at Stanford. Yet he died young in 1925, leaving a wife and a teenage son. Dave Packard grew up in Pueblo, Colorado. Packard's father was a lawyer, his mother a teacher. Packard was a star scholar-athlete growing up, and would outshine Hewlett in terms of publicity for their lives.

In the fall of 1930, Hewlett and Packard met as freshmen at tryouts for the Stanford football team. Stanford had at that point a football team for 40 years. It had played in four Rose Bowl tournaments and won a national championship a few years before. Glenn S. "Pop" Warner was the coach at Stanford. Packard had lettered in three sports: football, basketball, and track. He was a star athlete, unlike Hewlett who had heart but very little athletic talent. In his studies, Packard was also a star electronics student whereas Hewlett was a mediocre student who had a knack for mechanical things. Packard made the football team and not Hewlett. Yet the two met on the playing fields and saw each other over the years on campus. They became close friends in their senior year. They would take trips in Hewlett's car, a rarity in the Depression, to go hiking in the mountains or go fishing. After graduation in 1934, they went on a two-week backpacking trip to the San Juan Mountains in Colorado. So began a 60-year friendship and business partnership.

Terman and his radio lab were the biggest influence on both of them. Terman would take his students on tours to local entrepreneurs' labs: Charlie Litton's lab; Kaar Engineering in Palo Alto; Eitel-McCullough in Burlingame; and Philo Farnsworth's lab in San Francisco, where the first TV emission was sent. Packard was inspired to see "young entrepreneurs working on new devices in firms which they themselves had established." Terman confided to Packard that most of the firms they had visited were founded by men with little formal education. Terman believed formally-trained engineers with a little business sense might be even more successful.[8]

It was liberating to graduate in the Depression. There were so few jobs that graduates had to start something. Packard knew Terman by hanging

---

[8] Malone, Michael S. Bill & Dave: How Hewlett and Packard Built the World's Greatest Company. New York: Penguin Portfolio, 2007, pp. 29-69.

around the radio lab. He took Terman's graduate course in radio engineering as a senior in 1933 and said of it: "That was the beginning of a series of events that resulted in the establishment of the Hewlett-Packard Company." The smartest engineering student was Barney Oliver, later HP's Chief of Research.

Packard graduated and went to GE in February 1935. He hated it but learned "management by walking around" when he worked on the shop production floor to lower defects in mercury vapor rectifiers. Terman guided Hewlett to get a graduate degree and pursue studies in resistance capacity oscillators. This would be HP's first product. Hewlett spent some time in MIT to get his degree, then returned home to a job Terman found him building oscillators. Packard visited to see his girlfriend Lucille "Lu" Salter, and he held a "business meeting" with his buddy Hewlett to discuss businesses they could start. They were a team looking for an idea and took minutes. The meeting was dated August 23, 1937 and the topic under discussion was "tentative organization plans and tentative work program for a proposed business venture." They discussed products like high-frequency receivers and medical equipment, or something for TV. Ultimately they started their business and partnership without a product. They were a team of two who liked and trusted each other and wanted to build a company. They were friends before they became partners: they had the same values, interests, and ambitions.

Packard took a one-year leave of absence with an offer to work in Terman's lab, a low risk departure from GE, and a 50% pay cut. He worked with Russell Varian, an interesting entrepreneur himself. Varian graduated high school at 21 and was a dirt poor student at Stanford. He knew where all the fruit and nut trees on campus were for snacking and helped invent the klystron tube. This was as important as integrated circuits and the digital computer, crucial to radar detection and eventually air travel, cellular telephony, and microwave ovens. Millions in royalties over time came to Stanford professors and the university itself from the invention. Packard worked at a new klystron lab at Litton Labs, which Litton loaned to Varian. The early entrepreneurs cooperated and helped each other out often.

The Modest Start and Immodest Growth of Hewlett Packard Corp.

In 1938, Hewlett and Packard rented a house at 367 Addison Avenue in Palo Alto. Packard and his new wife Lucille lived inside while Hewlett moved into the shack of a garage, took a cot, and put up shelves and workbenches. Many consider the garage to be the metaphysical birthplace of Silicon Valley. They flipped a coin to name the company, and Hewlett won, so it became the Hewlett-Packard Company. With no products, they took contract work. They designed lane signaling equipment for a bowling alley, a synchronous motor drive for the telescope at Lick Observatory, a self-flushing toilet, audio oscillators to tune harmonicas, and an exerciser with electric impulses to let people get workouts while sitting. Basically, they lived on Lu's income as a secretary.

The two men wanted to make something. Hewlett knew circuit technology and Packard was good at manufacturing. They signed a partnership agreement in January 1939. Hewlett's audio oscillator seemed to have market demand, so they built a professional case and called it the 200A, priced at $54.40. The price was picked randomly to seem thoughtful, but was dumb because it was priced below cost. Yet the competition's product was about ten times the price, so they raised their price quickly and still sold it. The first major sale was to Disney for its Fantasia movie. They quickly decided to dump contract work and become manufacturers. An early contract salesman sold the product in Southern California to Hollywood movie makers and aerospace buyers. By the end of 1939 they had $5,369 in sales, pre-tax profit of $1,653, $500 cash, no debt, and many orders. The pair even went to Litton's lab to do design work. Litton magnanimously saw HP not as a competitor but as "compatriots." Later when a fire destroyed the Litton Labs factory, Packard allowed them to use HP facilities at night. Bill married Flora Lamson, a UC Berkeley biochemistry grad. It was very rare in those days for a woman to go to college, let alone study the hard sciences.

As the business grew, Hewlett and Packard built audio oscillators in a new shop on the corner of Camino Real and Page Mill, the first true HP facility. Hewlett and Packard had to be versatile to: invent, build, and price products; package and ship them; deal with customers and sales reps; keep accounting books; write ads and market the product; sweep up the shop and clean the toilets. They even burnt the entire shop once and broke the windows multiple times. They barely made payroll in 1940 at one point, by building a fixed-frequency oscillator for ITT, since they had done an all-cash business. The experience forced them to get a line of credit from Palo Alto National after being refused by Bank of Italy, now Bank of America. An initial $500 loan led to millions of dollars of profits for the banks for developing the relationship.

Growth signs were healthy. Their first products after oscillators were basically lab testing tools (a distortion analyzer, a harmonic wave analyzer, a square wave generator) to help engineers in other manufacturing labs test devices they were making. In June 1940 HP gave $5 to 5 local charities, 18 months after the partnership was founded, with 5 employees. For the year, all employees got a production bonus. Revenues grew to $34,396 in 1940, $106,548 in 1941, and nearly $1 million by 1943. Much of the business was from the US Naval Research Lab, with key contracts referred their way by Terman.

While things were going well, a strange thing happened. Hewlett was called to war duty by the Army Signal Corps in late 1941 and he left for 4 years. Packard ran the company in his absence but did not re-negotiate their partnership percentages or contract. They both worked on trust as Packard waited patiently for Hewlett to return. Packard moved into a factory cot and worked through many nights; he took the same salary that Hewlett earned at the US government. Noel Eldred came in as an operations executive to help.

After the war ended, Hewlett returned as if nothing had happened, to a much larger company. Yet there was a post war slump, with revenues falling from $1.6 million in 1945 to less than $800,000 in 1946. The founders had to fire employees, reducing the workforce from 200 to 80. The experience was so painful that they never again had a mass layoff, even during the harsh 1973-74 recession. In the mid-1960s, when an HP executive John Minck asked Hewlett why they gave buyouts to independent sales representatives instead of just firing them like their competitors did, Hewlett responded: "Goddamnit, Minck, you just don't understand the situation. These reps are all personal friends. For a decade we did business with them, on a handshake. We owe them most of our success." The humanity learned from hard times stuck.

Terman Guides the Development of Stanford's Engineering and Science Programs

In 1941, Vannevar Bush at MIT hired Terman to run a radio research lab at MIT. Terman ran the lab with its staff of 850 to develop electronic countermeasures and jammers for the Navy and Air Force. HP later recruited many talented lab members. Terman made numerous federal government contacts that he would later pass on to startups. He also connected entrepreneurs with the influx of contracts from the Office of Naval Research (ONR).

By 1946 Terman returned to Stanford as Dean of the Engineering School. Terman had come with a plan for putting Stanford's engineering school on the map as one of the premier programs in the nation. At the Harvard radio lab, he learned a formula for success. It involved using government funding, mainly ONR contracts, for two ends: to build a premier faculty in areas of electronics, which Terman was confident would be the major engineering growth area in the post-war environment; to create a large PhD program, transforming Stanford's curriculum from one offering just practical engineering training to one rooted in the hard subjects of physics, chemistry, and mathematics. Terman created the Stanford Honors Cooperative Program in 1954 for engineers to work after undergraduate studies and do part-time studies for masters. The program soared from 16 students to 243 in first three years, and drew in a third of the graduate students in the department. By 1950, Stanford, with a much smaller faculty, awarded as many electrical engineering PhD degrees as MIT.

Terman's biggest focus was on attracting people. He called his plan "steeples of excellence," and he said: "It's better to have one seven foot jumper on your team than any number of six foot jumpers." Terman would rather have one star professor than a group of merely good ones. The steeples were small groups of experts who were leaders in their professions. Terman wanted these professors to be self-financing. So instead of using government grants to increase salaries of faculty already on staff, Terman pursued what he termed "salary splitting." He would pay for half of the salary of a new faculty member from grants and contracts, as opposed to the operating budget. Research associates and other personnel working on sponsored projects would be entirely covered from contract funds. Both groups would have to be entrepreneurial in getting funds to make their positions stick. These faculty members would over the years attract millions in grant money and the finest students from around the world, starting a virtuous cycle of talent attracting talent. Terman's other goal was for the program to be strong in areas of mainstream interest and importance rather than in "niche" areas.

In sum, Terman had many components in the 1950s for his "recipe for distinction," such as: using government grants and contracts to finance "steeples of excellence;" splitting faculty salaries to grow the faculty; concentrating on graduate student research and production of MS and PhD degrees; establishing the Stanford Research Park as a means to create profitable exchange relations between industry and Stanford research labs, particularly in areas of electronics; creating a Honors Cooperative Program as incentive for companies to locate near Stanford; encouraging the licensing of Stanford inventions and establishing faculty consulting relations as means for getting Stanford ideas into the core of industry.

Terman became Stanford's provost, the highest academic officer in the university, in 1955. He stayed there till retirement in 1966, when he went on the HP board. Under Terman, the total government grants and contracts to Stanford went from $3 million in 1951 to over $50 million in 1964.

HP Develops the Valley's Big Hi-Tech Company Model

On August 18, 1947, the HP partnership was changed into a corporation. Packard was President and the outside man (public relations, marketing, and finance) while Hewlett was the Vice President and the operations and research man. Yet they could also do each other's work, as Packard designed a series of highly profitable voltometers and Hewlett kept them light on debt. The company had 36 products in its catalog. That year's revenues of $851K grew to 1948's revenues of $2.2 million, and employment went up to 128 people.

The most extraordinary thing was their policies. "Management by Walking Around" (MBWA) was an extension of their open factory floor. Basically, instead of waiting for subordinates to report to their own hermetic offices, as much of corporate America was then organized, the founder-executives would walk around the offices and factory and pro-actively engage everyone else. Another breath of fresh air was the "Open Door" policy, again very different from corporate America at that point. Any employee could take a problem to his supervisor, or next level up. If the employee still felt dissatisfied, he could take it straight to Hewlett or Packard, who would then mediate and teach lower supervisors better management skills. The two founders trusted their employees, and had all equipment parts rooms left open. Once when Hewlett came late at night to do a project and came across a locked parts room, he cut off the lock and left a note for the manager to never lock the room again.

Hewlett and Packard had unique views about business. One key view was that while profit was important, it was not the sole objective of a company. Packard gave a speech in 1948 to a gathering of corporate CEOs where he stated that beyond profit, a company had responsibilities to employees, customers, suppliers, and society. The other CEOs and executives laughed and dismissed him as naïve. The debate still hasn't ended in 2012, as the "profits and shareholder value maximization as sole objective" view is still a short-sighted modern school of thought, propagated by University of Chicago types following the lead of the brilliant economist Milton Friedman. Or as Packard said in a 1960 training speech, he felt that many people wrongly assumed a company exists to make money. While money was an important result of a company's existence, Packard felt the measure of success should be how well a company makes its product (with costs and profits being constraints).[9]

One nice fact was that the founders were always in harmony. Or as the technology pioneer John Granger stated: "You could ask either of them a question on any matter, any important matter, and you'd be sure the answer you got reflected the feeling of the other one as well... they understood one another perfectly."

HP did very well in the 1950s. From 1950 to 1960, revenues grew from $2 million to over $60 million, and employees went from 146 to over 3,000. The core management team in 1942 was Noel Porter in production, Barney Oliver in R&D, Frank Cavier in finance, and Noel Eldred in sales. Three out four were Stanford grads who trained under Terman. The team stayed stable for almost the next 20 years, till their death or retirement.

---

[9] Yuen, Albert. Bill & Dave's Memos. A Collection of Bill Hewlett and David Packard's Writings. Palo Alto: 2DaysofSummer Books, 2006, pp. 39.

This was very unusual as Silicon Valley became a disloyal and promiscuous place, with managers coming and going like flies on fly-light. Lucille added a homey touch by buying a wedding gift for every married employee and a blanket for every child. During company picnics, Bill, Dave, and senior executives served food and answered questions.

The two founders developed some other unique views and traditions. They bought a parcel of land in the Santa Cruz Mountains, an hour away from Palo Alto, in a redwood forest for retreats and camping called Little Basin. They also bought a ranch at San Felipe for personal family time and off-site management meetings. These properties became a way of developing their friendship and business partnership. For example, they learned lessons on leading people from corralling cattle, as Packard noted: "Press them too hard, and they'd panic, scattering in all directions. Slack off entirely, and they'd just head back to their old grazing spots." They also encouraged company traditions like: the two coffee breaks, at 10AM and 3PM daily, where the company provided coffee, donuts, and Danish rolls and everyone mingled; the Friday afternoon beer bust, where employees left early to have beer at a local bar and talk shop; and casual dress Fridays, which eventually became casual dress everyday across Silicon Valley.

While times were good the founders still made mistakes, including some dumb ones. In the 1950s they made the mistake of developing an electronic lettuce thinner for farmers in the Salinas Valley. It was foolish and their lesson was not to stray too far from their core competency of electronic testing and measurement equipment. Also in 1954 they produced the 150A low frequency oscilloscope, which was much worse than the competition (Tektronix), who had a much more reliable device with better repairmen and service. Their lesson was to wait to launch a better product, and to improve their support services.

Meanwhile, in 1949 Terman was developing the Stanford Industrial Park, consisting of 9,000 unused acres of land near campus. He wanted to attract companies to hire faculty and graduates as consultants and workers, and simultaneously the university could provide real-time training to workers for graduate degrees in the Honors Co-op Program. Terman teamed with the university's business manager, Alf Brandin, to create modern facilities with landscaped setbacks, parking hidden behind shrubs and trees, and flowing lawns from one property to another. Stanford signed long-term leases with the tenants. Varian Associates was the first occupant. Terman convinced several other electronics firms to move research facilities to the 450 acre sector of land designated for commercial development by the Board of Trustees in 1950. The plan also called for the development of the Stanford Shopping Center, and later the Medical Center that would move from San Francisco to the Stanford Campus in 1958. In the early 1950s, Terman even encouraged William Shockley to locate his company in Mountain View, near Stanford; the company and its progeny would have a lasting influence on the Valley.

Near the park was the new HP corporate headquarters at 1501 Page Mill Road. It was a modernist building with a sawtooth roof and lots of glass and natural light. Inside the space was split with dividers, or proto-cubicles, for the workers, which created a new level of white-collar worker. Only Hewlett and Packard had formal offices, and this was more for visiting dignitaries than for daily use. HP went public on November 6, 1957 at $16 per share, the same month as the Walt Disney Company. The company opened a European headquarters in Geneva, Switzerland, in 1959 and started selling aggressively into that market.

One turning point amidst all the growth was to institutionalize the principles of the founders. A 1957 retreat at the Sonoma Mission Inn, north of San Francisco, was on how to deal with growth and organizational structure. One decision was to decentralize the firm around divisions like GM. The thought was that at about 1200 people, the company was at the right size to divide into two or more units. Packard also articulated his "Management by Objective" program: "If managers know what kinds of decisions are wanted, they are best able to make those decisions from their level rather than from above." He believed managers just need guidelines from above, and then the autonomy to execute.

With their senior managers, Hewlett and Packard then created corporate objectives, a philosophy or set of values to guide the company. These were: Profit, "the best single measure of our contribution to society;" Customers, to create quality, useful products that have value; Field of Interest, to focus but seek growth; Growth, as a corollary of success – useful products should be scaled; and Employees, to give job security and personal satisfaction from work. Later objectives were: Organization, an environment that fosters individual motivation, initiative, and creativity; and Citizenship, to be good citizens of a community and contribute to local institutions. The Sonoma retreat formalized annual off-sites for executives, often with a skit lampooning the founders.

Hewlett and Packard were also comfortable with profit sharing and stock option plans, but the danger was complacency and the risk of becoming too inward or hermetic. They instituted a plan where employees could buy shares at a 2% to 5% discount to market prices. This reduced salary overhead and re-invested funds in the company, creating long-term owners. However, they were disappointed that many short-sighted employees sold the stock right away. A few held on for more than a decade and became millionaires. The founders later added a vesting period.

The late 1950s and the decade of the 1960s were good times. In October 1958, HP acquired the F.L. Moseley Company, which sold "Autograf X-Y plotters," early printers. This would later become the base of the firm's profitable printer family. John Young, the future CEO and chosen successor, joined in 1957 from Stanford's MBA program. He held marketing to sales roles, becoming a division manager for the Microwave division at a young age. In the 1960s, Hewlett encouraged communications luncheons, where a senior executive had lunch with people one to two levels lower and asked: "Tell me what you've been doing, tell me what we should be doing." Lunches would begin formally and strained till an icebreaker question showed the executive was serious; then a stream of questions would come forth. HP hired a major polling company, International Survey Research Corp., to regularly poll employees on opinions about their workplace and compare it to other companies. Over 90% of employees were consistently satisfied in the 1960s. In 1967, the company introduced flex-time at a HP plant in Boeblingen, Germany. Workers could arrive between 6:30am to 9:30am and work an 8 hour day. This gave them the ability to balance work and family lives, while keeping a core six hours from 9:30am to 3:30pm for meetings. The founders gave employees the freedom to make choices.

The Business Philosophy of Bill and Dave

A few key business principles made Hewlett and Packard unique, in addition to the ones mentioned above. Both men were products of the Great Depression, and so they didn't want to run a "hire-and-fire operation," but wanted to share the company's prosperity with workers. Moreover, they wanted to run the company on a "pay-as-you-go" basis and finance growth with earnings, not debt.

Fostering innovation was also important. Hewlett met all new ideas with enthusiasm, excitement, and support. A few days later, he would come in an inquisition mode to ask tougher questions and probe the idea more, but with no decision. Later, he would meet with the inventor-proposer and come up with a judicious decision – hence not stifling the desire to innovate. Hewlett felt that "the creative process works best when it is not too structured, but it must, in the long run, be tamed, harnessed and hitched to the wagon of man's needs." As an employer, Hewlett believed it was very difficult to spot a creative individual using a resume or a quick analytical interview. Instead, engaging in the creative process to solve problems was long and arduous, where problems were "organized and dissected, then key issues isolated and defined." Next came a period of gestation where an engineer could mull over issues, consciously or unconsciously working at them at odd hours of the day or night. Hewlett's analogy for this problem-solving was "trying to place a name on the face of someone you've met before," where the final solution came the same way you eventually recall the name.[10]

---

[10] Ibid 230-232.

Hewlett emphasized that being on the cutting edge was very important for motivating talented engineers. If they didn't feel they were pushing boundaries, they could always leave HP for academia or other companies that were, and this brain drain would be lethal for a company's innovation.

Meanwhile, both founders understood the importance of people, the core of any organization. Hewlett thought that the "efficient utilization of people," getting them to think, innovate, and bring imagination and inner motivation, was the most important skill of a leader. Packard presented in the 1958 Sonoma retreat his rules to deal with people, whether managing up or down:

- Think about the other person first.
- Build up the other person's sense of importance and don't forget to respect the other person's "personality rights" (the right to be different). Try to understand and empathize with the other person (consider how you would react in similar circumstances in their shoes).
- Give sincere appreciation. Don't openly try to reform people.
- Eliminate the negative. Focus on the solution and what works and not on what can't be done.
- Examine your first impressions on people, products, and companies (especially dislikes based on differences).
- Take care with the little details (watch your smile, tone of voice, your greeting, your appearance, your use of names and dates, etc.).
- Develop a genuine interest in other people. [11]

Hence soft skills, people skills that most engineers or tech company heads lack, were high up in the thoughts of these institution builders.

Between 1970 and 1981, 30% of Fortune 500 companies fell off the list after two financial crises, rampant inflation, oil and commodity shocks, and so on. HP grew sales from $365 million to $3.6 billion, and employees from 16,000 to above 66,000. Profits grew at a rate of 27% annually, with 26 manufacturing plants around the world, and sales in 65 countries.

Packard left the company in January 1969 to become Deputy Secretary of Defense under Mel Laird. It was a very unsatisfying two years for him in Washington while Hewlett ran the company effectively with Ralph Lee and Ed Porter. So 37 years after Hewlett left to join the US Army and relied on Packard, Packard did the same and knew he could rely on Hewlett. The measure of Hewlett's character was shown in the brutal 1972 to 1974 recession. As revenues and profits dove, he instituted a policy of no layoffs, but a 10% across the board pay cut, along with a nine day workweek. Only sales kept going full-time, to maximize revenue. The order applied from the CEO to janitors – it was a pragmatic solution for tough times, and it saved the skin of many people creating gratitude and

[11] Ibid. 249-51.

love for the company. As Hewlett disapproved of arbitrary firing, he put down a solid policy to avoid it, stating: "It is not humane. It is not HP-like. It is not justified." The broader policy was to give notification and training to employees, move them around, and finally, if that didn't work, part with respect (and solid documentation).

Eventually both founders would retire and a competent John Young would take over one of the most admired companies in the US and around the world.

6. Moles: The Military Boom, Artistic Boom, and Economic Boom (1941-48)

The Bay Area as a Strategic Weapon

The Japanese attack on Pearl Harbor dragged the US into World War II in December 1941. WWII had an enormous impact on Bay Area scientists since they had the most advanced radio technology in the nation. Fred Terman was assigned by the US government to lead the top-secret Harvard Radio Research Laboratory. Terman had graduated from MIT in 1924 with a thesis supervised by Vannevar Bush. In June 1941, the US government established a new agency (the Office of Scientific Research and Development) to coordinate nation-wide scientific research for the US military, and put Bush in charge of it. Traditionally the US government (like every other government) had relied on top-secret military labs (or their private contractors) to develop military technology. Bush, instead, directed funding to and influenced the direction of research programs at universities. He chose Terman, who could tap into the know-how of Stanford. Bush's approach created a new template for interaction between science and government, as well as between science and war. Terman was basically in charge of electronic warfare, a new kind of warfare that was fought in labs instead of tanks, ships or planes.

UC Berkeley was also strategic because of its know-how in nuclear physics. In 1942, the US government launched the "Manhattan Project" to build a nuclear bomb, and appointed UC Berkeley Professor Robert Oppenheimer in charge of it. Oppenheimer applied Lawrence's concept of "big science" and assembled a large team of physicists to design the weapon. The project soon exceeded the capacity of the Berkeley campus and was moved to Los Alamos in New Mexico. It was Lawrence himself who designed an electromagnetic process to separate the explosive U-235 isotope from the U-238 isotope of uranium that led to the building of the facility at Oak Ridge in Tennessee. In parallel Edwin McMillan and Glenn Seaborg at the Radiation Lab in Berkeley used the cyclotron to discover a new element, plutonium, and immediately realized that it was even better than U-235 at sustaining an explosive chain reaction. The government rushed to build another plant, this time to produce plutonium, at Hanford in the state of Washington. The "Trinity" bomb that was detonated in July 1945 in the desert of New Mexico used plutonium. The bomb dropped on Hiroshima one month later used U-235, the one dropped on Nagasaki used plutonium.

Business was mainly affected by World War II in terms of providing high-tech components to the booming defense industry. This was a lucrative business that turned several small companies into giants.

Companies also benefited from the war by cultivating new technologies. The Dalmo Manufacturing Company, based in San Carlos since 1944, had evolved from the shop that Tim Moseley had opened in 1921 in San Francisco to manufacture simple electrical appliances. During World War II it developed the first airborne radar antenna, which was crucial for the air force to win the war. The invention was largely the work of the Russian-born engineer Alexander Poniatoff, who had joined the company in 1934. Moseley's company (now a joint venture with Westinghouse renamed Dalmo-Victor and based in nearby Belmont) was becoming a major defense contractor. Meanwhile, in 1944 Moseley himself invested in Alexander Poniatoff's new company Ampex, located in San Carlos, to manufacture electrical parts for radar that were hard to find. Poniatoff, however, moved into a new field, the tape recorder, a novelty that a US soldier, Jack Mullin, had brought back from occupied Germany. It was one of Germany's fields of excellence: the magnetic tape had been invented by Fritz Pfleumer in 1927. The first tape recorder (later dubbed Magnetophon) had been introduced by AEG in 1935 and perfected into a high-fidelity system in 1941. AEG used tape made by IG Farben, a manufacturer of the lethal gas used in Nazi extermination camps. In 1947, Ampex delivered its own tape recorder, which had been requested by pop-star Bing Crosby and soon became a favorite among pop and movie stars.

The First Computers

One of the major technological outcomes of World War II was the computer, another "imported" technology. The British had built a series of machines, all of them dubbed "Colossus," to help decipher encrypted German messages. In 1943, British engineers led by Tommy Flowers, working for the Post Office Research Station in north London, built the Colossus Mark 1. It was the world's first programmable digital electronic computer, and the first electronic computer to be used extensively. It was "electronic" because it used vacuum tubes. The closest thing in the US was the result of a joint project between IBM and Harvard University: a prototype code-named Automatic Sequence Controlled Calculator (ASCC) that Harvard preferred to call "Harvard Mark I," designed by Howard Aiken of the Harvard Computation Lab and completed in February 1944. It was the first computer programmed by punched paper tape, but it still employed electro-mechanical relays, just like Zuse's Z3 (and it wasn't as programmable as the Z3). One of its "programmers" was Grace Murray-Hopper, a female Navy officer dispatched to the Harvard Computation Lab. The paper tape was a significant innovation: all the previous computers required human intervention during the calculation, while the paper tape contained all the instructions needed to run without any human help.

Whatever the merits of these early machines, they provided momentum to fulfill Turing's dream. In 1946 the ENIAC, or "Electronic

Numerical Integrator and Computer," was unveiled by Professor John Mauchly and his student Presper Eckert at the University of Pennsylvania's Moore School. It contained 18,000 vacuum tubes and occupied about 160 square meters of space. That too had been funded by the US military. "Project PX," started in 1943 by the Army's Ballistics Research Laboratory (BRL) to replace the old Bush differential analyzer. The ENIAC was not able to store a program internally: a group of programmers (mostly women) had to organize switches and wires to "enter" the program into the computer. Also, the ENIAC was a decimal computer, not binary. Luminaries such as Vannevar Bush and Howard Aiken were very critical of the project.

An improved version of the Harvard Mark I, the SSEC (Selective Sequence Electronic Calculator), built by astronomer Wallace Eckert at Columbia University, was unveiled by IBM in 1948: it contained 12,500 vacuum tubes and 21,400 relays.

In December 1947, the brand new discipline of computer science was given a boost by the invention of the transistor: AT&T Bell Labs' engineers John Bardeen, William Shockley and Walter Brattain demonstrated the principle of amplifying an electrical current using a solid semiconducting material. As the name implies, a semiconducting material lies in between electrical conductors and insulators. Germanium and silicon are two of the most common semiconducting materials. Unlike conductors, which always conduct, and unlike insulators, which never conduct, the behavior of a semiconducting material can be customized by "doping" it, i.e. by disturbing it with an electromagnetic field or by heating it. In other words, pure germanium and silicon conduct poorly, and "dopants" are added to increase conductivity: either extra electrons (negative-type dopant) or extra holes (positive-type dopant). The trick in the fabrication consisted of joining "positive-type" semiconductors with "negative-type" semiconductors, where positive or negative refers to the majority electrical charge. That "p-n junction" is the elementary unit of a semiconducting device. A transistor is simply made of two "p-n junctions" (usually n-p-n). Shockley immediately realized the potential of the transistor: it was a better amplifier than the vacuum tube and it was easier to mass manufacture.

Other revolutionary ideas revolved around the concept of information. In 1945 Vannevar Bush at MIT envisioned the Memex, an electromechanical device capable of accessing archives of microfilms (which at the time were the most widely used format of storage after paper), of creating paths of navigation by linking pages, and of combining microfilms with annotations. In 1947 MIT Professor Norbert Wiener founded cybernetics, having realized that machines and animals shared two fundamental concepts: control and communication. That very year John Von Neumann at Princeton University advanced the notion of self-reproducing automata. In 1948 Claude Shannon at AT&T's Bell Labs was researching how much information could be sent on a noisy phone line. In the process, he came up with a mathematical definition of "information," founded information theory, and coined the term "bit" to describe the fundamental unit of information. Shannon's definition implied that an unexpected occasional event contains more information than a regular behavior. In 1950 Turing (still in Britain) proposed a test to determine whether a machine could be considered intelligent or not. Human imagination was jumping way ahead of human technology.

Interest in electronic computers was skyrocketing, although only a handful of people had actually seen one and even fewer were capable of using them. The main centers for research on electronic computing were Boston (Harvard and MIT), Philadelphia (UPenn's Moore School of Electrical Engineering, BRL) and New Jersey (Bell Labs, Princeton, RCA Labs).

The Bay Area and the Cold War

The Bay Area finally got involved in computers via a newly created offshoot of Stanford University. In 1946 Stanford spun off the Stanford Research Institute (SRI). Its purpose was to create an industrial research center that would leverage Stanford's high-tech know-how for commercial products. After six months, SRI moved off campus (to Menlo Park, which had swollen after the government had run a large military hospital there between 1943 and 1946) and began to relax its ties with the university. One of its very first projects was to improve the ENIAC: SRI replaced some key components with the latest electronic novelties and obtained a smaller machine. The original ENIAC was a 30-ton monster that covered 167 square meters of floor space and contained 17,468 vacuum tubes, 70,000 resistors, 10,000 capacitors and 1,500 relays.

At the same time Fred Terman returned to Stanford University as the dean of the engineering school, and used his connections with the US military (notably the recently instituted Office of Naval Research) to found and fund a new Electronics Research Lab (ERL). The Korean War began in 1950 and brought another huge infusion of money from the Office of Naval Research to carry out research in electronics, which Terman used to open an Applied Electronics Laboratory (AEL). After the Soviet launch of the first artificial satellite, Sputnik, the US government rapidly increased funding for research, and the beneficiaries were mainly MIT on the East Coast and Stanford University on the West Coast.

After the invention of the klystron, Bill Hansen continued his research into accelerating electrons and in 1947 inaugurated his first linear accelerator.

Meanwhile, his former assistants, the Varian brothers, opened their own business in San Carlos in April 1948 to work on radio, radar and television. The ties with Stanford were still strong: Ed Ginzton, an alumnus of the klystron project, was both a director at Varian Associates and a Stanford professor. The Varian brothers chose San Carlos because that city north of Palo Alto was becoming an electronic industrial center. San Carlos was a mini-urban experiment: it had been built *ex-novo* between 1917 and 1925 just north of Redwood City by the Mercantile Trust Company following the arrival of the Southern Pacific railway. San Carlos was still a very tiny village in 1930, but then Charles Litton (1930s), Dalmo (1944) and Eitel-McCullough (1945) opened offices there. Around them other companies were created to serve the electronics industry.

The San Francisco Renaissance and the Economic Boom

It was during World War II that the foundations for the "San Francisco Renaissance" were laid down. San Francisco had previously lacked a literary scene that could match its visual arts. The poets Kenneth Rexroth and Madeline Gleason started it. In 1954, Gleason founded the Poetry Center at San Francisco State University and, in April 1947 organized the first "Festival of Modern Poetry." Rexroth and Gleason helped Berkeley poet Robert Duncan, one of the first openly gay intellectuals who wrote "The Homosexual in Society" in 1944. Rexroth also befriended poets William Everson, a former Catholic monk, Muriel Rukeyser, a Jewish feminist, and Philip Lamantia. In the 1940s San Francisco also witnessed a dramatic increase in black immigrants. Most of them settled around Fillmore Street, the "Harlem of the West." That street became the epicenter of nightlife and of live music.

The end of the war was unleashing the industrial potential of the US. Industrial production rose by almost 50% in the ten years after the war. The civilian economy, busy engineering the lifestyle of the winners, was an avid consumer of new appliances. The defense economy, busy countering the moves of the Soviet Union in the "Cold War," was an avid consumer of new weapons. In 1946 a new entity joined the US government in funding technological innovation: the venture capital firms. Three big firms debuted in 1946. First was Boston's American Research and Development Corporation (ARD), led by the French-born former Harvard Business School's Professor Georges Doriot with assistance from MIT's President Karl Compton and Federal Reserve Bank of Boston's President Ralph Flanders, which was the first publicly owned venture-capital firm (that would fund spin-offs of MIT and Harvard). Second was New York's J.H. Whitney & Company, led by Jock Whitney (his partner Benno Schmidt coined the term "venture capital"). Third came New York's Rockefeller Brothers, led by Laurance Rockefeller (later renamed Venrock). They were often attracted by the potential of commercializing technologies invented during the war. The exuberance of private investors spread to California, where at least two such ventures were incorporated in

1946: Industrial Capital, founded by San Francisco's stock broker and "angel" investor Edward Heller, and Pacific Coast Enterprise.

The US was beginning one of the longest and fastest periods of economic expansion in history. The population of California had been less that 100,000 people in 1850 and 1.5 million people in 1900. During World War II, it rose from seven million to over nine million in just four years.

7. Early Funders: The Early History of Venture Capital (1900-59)

Background on the Venture Capital Industry

Venture capital is private money to fund early-stage, high-potential and high-risk, growth companies. The provider of the money generally wants an equity stake and a return of capital within five to ten years through:

i)   An initial public offering (IPO) of the company, or
ii)   A sale of the company to a strategic investor, usually a large and well-established technology company.

Long-term harvesting through dividends and share buybacks are generally not used by venture capital firms, for reasons discussed below.

Most venture capital is invested in high technology industries such as software, computer hardware, biotechnology, clean energy, etc.. Yet some venture capital firms invest in scalable low-tech business ideas like consumer products and retail. Venture capital is directed toward new companies with a limited operating history, which are too small to raise capital in the public markets, secure a bank loan, or complete a debt offering. In exchange for the high risk that venture capital firms assume by investing in smaller and less mature companies, they get significant control over a company's decisions through board seats, plus a large portion of the company's equity (so large that founders sometimes call them "vulture capitalists").

The startup game goes like this: An aspiring entrepreneur starts with a team, an idea, and some artificial currency (stock). Her goal is simple: to increase the value of the business and so the stock, so she and her team can cash out. The trick is to swap portions of the stock for resources that make the business more valuable: people and labor hours, more and better ideas, and money. The initial people want stock and they bring sweat labor and their ideas, or intellectual property (designs, patents, contacts, trade secrets, etc.). The venture capital firms give cash in stages for the team to hit milestones to prove the business. Yet at any point, the team can pull the plug, or the business can die if the milestones aren't met and the venture capitalists don't give more capital. Game over. Alternatively, the company can make a promising product and so sell itself to a corporate acquirer or to the public markets in an IPO. The entrepreneur and her team can cash in and leave. Or they can double down, sell the product to customers over time, and try to be corporate managers and build a real company. Success.

Venture capital firms are typically comprised of small teams with technology backgrounds (scientists, researchers, tech execs) or with business training from investment banks, consulting firms, or corporate

M&A divisions. Venture capitalists bring managerial, governance, and technical expertise, as well as capital, to their investments. Confusingly, both a venture capital firm and a partner/associate of a venture firm, a "venture capitalist," are both referred to as a "VC." Venture capitalists pool together funds for their investments from institutional investors (pension funds, foundations, endowments) and high net worth individuals, through creating a partnership (most commonly a limited partnership, where the venture firm is the general partner, or "GP," and the outside investor is the limited partner, or "LP").

Venture capital and startup generation are often associated with job creation, the knowledge economy, and business or technological innovation. One stunning fact comes from Robert Litan, who directs research at the Kauffman Foundation, which specializes in promoting entrepreneurship and innovation in America: "Between 1980 and 2005, virtually all net new jobs created in the U.S. were created by firms that were 5 years old or less . . . That is about 40 million jobs. That means the established firms created no new net jobs during that period."[12] The National Venture Capital Association estimates there were 12.1 million jobs at venture-backed companies in the US as of 2009, and those companies accounted for 21% of US GDP.

Some of the themes from the history of venture capital include:
- Origins within family offices of very wealthy families such as the Phipps, Rockefellers, and Whitneys;
- The influence of one man, George Doriot, in single-handedly creating much of the modern venture capital industry;
- Early informal partnerships in Silicon Valley due to a confluence of factors, most importantly the high-tech semiconductor industry and offshoots of Fairchild Semiconductor;
- Great venture firms like KPCB, Sequoia, and NEA refining the partnership-based model of investing with institutional capital;
- The loosening of ERISA rules and the boom and busts of the 1980s and 1990s, in which success mixed with excess;
- An industry somewhat lost in the 2000s and searching for a viable model again.

One of the most insightful sayings about the Valley has been repeated by Don Valentine and John Doerr, two of the most successful venture capitalists: "Silicon Valley is a state of mind."

---

[12] Stangler, Dane & Robert E. Litan. "Where Will The Jobs Come From?" Kauffman Foundation Research Series: Firm Formation and Economic Growth, November 2009. http://www.kauffman.org/uploadedFiles/where_will_the_jobs_come_from.pdf

Origins of Modern Venture Capital, 1900-1945
Benno Schmidt of J.H. Whitney claimed he and his partners put together "risk capital" and "our business is the adventure" to first describe the industry as "private venture capital" in 1946. Schmidt claimed they shortened "adventure capital" to "venture capital." However, the first documented use of the words "venture capital" can be traced to 1920, when the Industrial Securities Committee submitted a report on it: "The enlistment of venture capital is necessary for the development and growth of the country, as well as for the safety of all investment securities."[13] These investors saw venture capital as part of a traditional portfolio for large investors, as an investment in "business in the experimental stages."

Prior to 1920, a few wealthy families, such as the Phipps, the Rockefellers, and Whitneys, informally invested in new ventures. They were amateurs. Yet as the stock market took off in the 1920s, these individuals switched their investment allocations to the public markets, and venture funds declined. When the markets crashed from 1929-1931, wealthy individuals shunned all risky investments and delegated more to institutions.

A number of other factors led to a paucity of venture investing from 1931 to 1946. First, as tax rates rose through the 1930s and 1940s, especially due to higher tax brackets for the rich and interpretations of rules by the IRS, wealthy families shunned venture investing. Second, as power shifted from individuals to institutions, the new "institutional investors" found that state fiduciary rules limited their investing to only securities on approved lists, usually the safest bonds and preferred stock. This combined with the natural risk aversion of institutional investors, leading to the decline of venture funding. Third, the public's distrust of investment bankers, the difficulty of getting transitional funding for a growing venture due to the new securities laws of 1933 and 1934, and bankers' reluctance to take risk impeded the growth of venture capital. Fourth, the excess profits tax that Congress raised in 1933 penalized young companies more than established ones, since their rates of return were highly variable and the tax would hit them in their peak years. Fifth, inventors and entrepreneurs had little bargaining power with holders of capital after the depression, and so many chose to bootstrap their own companies or join larger corporations.

During those lean years, most venture funding was being done by large corporations and the US government. Corporations could expense their venture creation as "R&D costs," and could raise the large amounts of capital that some new ventures needed. Generally, the US government avoided venture funding, and New Deal programs funneled capital to large projects like the TVA. Government banking agencies like the

---

[13] Fenton, Frederic R. (Secretary) "Proceedings of the Ninth annual Convention of the Investment Bankers Association of America." Chicago: Lakeside Press of RR Donnely, 1920, p. 157.

Reconstruction Finance Corporation (RFC) could not finance risky ventures (though the RFC made loans to some small businesses). Rather, most government venture capital came during World War II, as government, industry, and universities formed a research network, and subcontracting programs for federal procurement encouraged technology transfer to small firms. One example is the development of synthetic rubber production from scratch, where $700 million was invested in 51 plants over two years. Most importantly, many state governments started giving institutional investors more leeway to finance risky investments, often dropping approved investment lists for a "prudent man rule," a discretionary standard. Also, a tax code change in 1942 gave capital gains a more favorable treatment. Finally, the GI Bill after WWII put millions of Americans in college, educating a generation of technologists and entrepreneurs, while increasing funding for research in pure science many times over.

The Venture Pioneers of 1946

Five important venture organizations were started after World War II, around 1946, as businessmen and government officials realized the importance of venture funding. The organizations were J.H. Whitney and Company, Rockefeller Brothers and Company (later Venrock), the American Research and Development Corporation (ARD), and two in Silicon Valley: Industrial Capital Corp. and Pacific Coast Enterprises. These were daring experiments, as conventional wisdom was that the US would fall back into a depression after WWII ended. This is why US government bond yields were so low around 1945, and most investors clung to government bonds yielding a little above 2%. Venture capital investors, however, were bolder and willing to take more risk for a potential higher return.

J.H. Whitney & Company was founded by John Hay "Jock" Whitney and his partner Benno Schmidt in February 1946, after Whitney wrote a $5 million check to capitalize the firm. Whitney had been investing since the 1930s, founding Pioneer Pictures in 1933 and acquiring a 15% interest in Technicolor Corporation with his cousin Cornelius Vanderbilt Whitney. Benno Schmidt was working at the State Department in 1946 when one day he got a call from Whitney, one of the wealthiest men in the country. Whitney wanted to stake a new firm with $5 million to finance young companies in new industries. Schmidt told Whitney that he had no business experience whatsoever. Whitney replied: "I'm not looking for somebody who has a lot of business experience. I'm looking for someone who has had a lot of experience with life." Schmidt signed on and became a partner for 52 years.

Schmidt and Whitney did good deals. An early deal of the new firm was buying Spencer Chemicals after World War II and converting its munitions plant into a fertilizer facility (the $250,000 of initial equity was eventually worth over $10 million). Whitney's most famous investment was in Florida Foods Corporation. The company developed an innovative method for delivering nutrition to American soldiers, which later came to be known as Minute Maid orange juice and was sold to The Coca-Cola Company in 1960. Eventually, J.H. Whitney & Company left the venture capital space to become a buyout firm.

Rockefeller Brothers Co. had its roots in the 1930s, when Laurence S. Rockefeller (1910-2004) pioneered early-stage financing by investing in the entrepreneurs of Eastern Airlines and McDonnell Aircraft. Over the years, the family's investment interests included the fields of aviation, aerospace, electronics, high temperature physics, composite materials, optics, lasers, data processing, thermionics and nuclear power. Beginning in August 1969, the VC firm Venrock was founded to continue the family's heritage of investment and building entrepreneur-backed companies, beginning with its investment in Intel, based on the advice of Arthur Rock. Venrock still existed in 2012, having invested $2.5 billion in over 440 companies resulting in 125 IPOs and 128 M&A exits over its 40+ year life.

These early family venture funds share a few goals: achieving high returns on an initial investment to get favorable capital gains tax treatment (versus the higher-tax burden from dividends and interest from established companies); creating a more effective way to finance new ventures from their entrepreneurial friends and associates; and pushing an ideological view of free market capitalism over state-sponsored socialism. All three goals came together with a sense of noblesse oblige, as the rich felt they needed to lead the way back for a prosperous economy and free enterprise system. The most important firm founded in 1946, however, was not a family venture capital firm.

The Father of Venture Capital: Georges Doriot of ARD

Non-family venture models essentially began with the American Research and Development Corp. (ARD), founded by Georges Doriot, who many believe was the "Father of Venture Capital." Before WWII, Doriot was a banker at Kuhn, Loeb & Company, the premier investment bank of its time (along with JP Morgan & Co.). Doriot then became a Harvard Business School professor, where he formed close bonds with many students and taught an eccentric business philosophy (rather than mutable facts or fancy theories) in his Manufacturing Class. Note that Doriot was also an uber-capitalist and elitist, as shown by a speech he gave in 1934 where he denounced FDR's popular and socialist New Deal programs as "one thing that has done more harm to the morals of the nation" and that "those who pay the taxes have more right to govern than those who don't."

During WWII, Doriot partnered with Ralph Flanders, Merrill Griswold, and Karl Compton (a former President of MIT) to encourage private sector investments in new products for the war effort. He even joined a private company, Enterprise Associates, which raised $300,000 from twenty stockholders to finance the final stages of promising research projects and look for entrepreneurs and ideas to finance. Doriot was pulled even further into the war when he became the head of the Military Planning Division in the Office of the Quartermaster General of the US Army, where his role was putting together teams to develop technologies and transform ideas into products and weapons for the battlefield (one example is the food ration bars for soldiers on the line, packages containing meat, biscuits, a powder-made drink, a sweet, gum, and cigarettes).

After WWII, members of previous committees that Doriot sat on formed the American Research and Development Corporation (ARD) on June 6, 1946, as a Massachusetts corporation. ARD raised $3.5 million through a public equity offering (a mistake, as we shall see), of which $1.8 million came from nine institutional investors like MIT, Penn, and the Rice Institute. ARD's significance lay in that it was the first institutional venture capital firm that raised capital from sources other than wealthy families although it had several notable investment successes as well. One of the incorporators, Ralph Flanders, gave a speech in 1945 to the National Association of Security Commissioners explaining the need for "new methods of applying development capital" and that the nation could not "depend safely for an indefinite time on the expansion of our big industries alone." Hence ARD sought to bring together cash-poor entrepreneurs with great ideas and an institutional investor community that had become too risk averse.

ARD's investment record was typical of the economics of many venture firms. A few failed (Island Packers, tuna fish packing), a few made modest amounts of money (Tracer Labs), and one investment made the fund (Digital Equipment, a chip manufacturer). ARD's criteria was "taking calculated risks in select [growth] companies", with guidelines such as projects having passed the test tube stage, with patent or IP protection, and an "attractive opportunity for eventual profits." Doriot also thought entrepreneurs were more important than ideas and joked in the 1949 annual report that "An average idea in the hands of an able man is worth much more than an outstanding idea in the possession of a person with only average ability." ARD raised $4 million more in 1949, and Doriot found that selecting companies was the easy part and that the "hardest task [was] to help a company through its growth pains."

Doriot had an interesting business philosophy. He felt the study of a company was not the study of a dead body, but rather of things and relationships which were alive and constantly changing. For him, business was "the study of men and men's work, of their hopes and aspirations... a study of determination of successive goals and of victorious competitive drive towards them." Doriot also fostered an entrepreneur's paranoia that "someone somewhere is making a product that will make your product obsolete." He pushed managers to delegate down, grow slowly, and examine small decisions which could lead to vital errors. In the end, he felt work was a part of living, that work was not just an activity necessary for existence but also a worthwhile part of existence.[14]

ARD and Doriot went through hard times, as by 1953 venture investing was out of fashion again. By 1954 the number of proposals fell and the company made no investments. Also, the SEC created problems by examining and questioning the valuation of the underlying portfolio companies (a speculative endeavor). The stock price slumped below the net asset value at which the accountants had valued the company's assets per share.

ARD's greatest investment was Digital Equipment (DEC) in 1958, its sole investment of that year, where it put in $70,000 in equity and $30,000 as a loan. 70% of the equity went to ARD, 20% to founders Ken Olsen and Harlan Anderson, and 10% was set aside for a more seasoned management team (a spot which went unfilled, so everyone's share increased pro rata). ARD invested $30,000 more in 1958. Olsen and Anderson went on to build a powerhouse, based on their new technology (their first product was a module to test computer memory devices), and their natural frugality and penchant for hiring MIT engineers. In 1959, the PDP-1 was an interactive computer that DEC sold at a fraction of the cost of an IBM mainframe. While DEC prospered, Doriot invested $190,000 in a Texas oil rig manufacturer named the Zapata Off-Shore company, run by a young war hero named George H. W. Bush (later President of the US).

ARD was prospering by the spring of 1961, when Doriot gave a talk he titled "Creative Capital." Of the $11 million invested in 66 ventures, ARD's portfolio was now worth $30.3 million. Doriot's thoughts on venture investing were that:

- The best returns were from the riskiest companies, which were started from scratch.
- The best companies were built over time with steady progress and solid management, and were not overnight successes.
- Specialized technical areas were the best places to invest, as patents and know-how gave small companies the ability to compete with larger ones.
- The hardest thing to do was to convince entrepreneurs to seek and accept outside help, whether it was for generating sales, getting a bank credit line, or hiring the right team.

---

[14] Doriot, Georges F. "Manufacturing class notes: Harvard Business School, 1927-1966", Board of Trustees, The French Library in Boston, 1993.

Doriot was busy on the side of ARD too. He helped start the pre-eminent French business school, INSEAD, along with international venture capital companies, Technical Development Capital Ltd. (a British VC firm started in 1962 with $2 million in capital) and the European Enterprise Development Company (a French-Euro venture capital firm started in 1963 with $2.5 million in capital).

The first real trouble ARD and Doriot got into with the government was in 1963, when the SEC contacted Doriot. The SEC objected to ARD's officers, Doriot's young men who screened ideas and sat on portfolio companies, holding stock options in ARD affiliates. Doriot complained that this was the best way to motivate people, but the SEC saw a conflict of interest in a public company doing this. This problem was one strong factor pushing the entire industry into private partnerships, where contracting was not inhibited and parties could do anything they wanted without government interference.

A second, more important problem was losing key people. Doriot relied on his associates to find and screen deals, and Bill Elfers was his right hand man who made many decisions. When Doriot refused to retire or set a retirement date in 1965 (after leading ARD for nearly 20 years), Elfers left. Elfers and Arthur Rocks separately used the limited partnership (LP) entity form seen in the oil wildcatting business (used by Texas millionaires since 1900). The advantages were numerous, with the key one being attracting good venture capitalist partners and compensating them properly with the right incentives. This was something Doriot couldn't do at ARD, a public corporation. Elfers started Greylock Capital in 1965, raising $5 million from J.H. Whitney & Company along with 5 other wealthy families (the Watsons of IBM, Warren Corning of Corning Glass, Sherman Fairchild of Fairchild Semiconductor, etc.). Another Doriot associate, Charles P. Waite griped that when one portfolio company, Optical Scanning, went public, the CEO made $10 million but Waite just got a $2,000 raise. He left for Greylock. Later associates of Doriot founded Morgan, Holland Ventures, the predecessor of Flagship Ventures (founded in 1982 by James Morgan), Fidelity Ventures (started by Henry Hoagland in 1969), and other firms.

But 1963 also brought good news. DEC went public, selling $8 million of stock at $22 per share, and ARD's 65% stake was valued at $38.5 million. When ARD eventually liquidated the stake, it was worth $400 million, a 70,000% return. This made tensions worse in the ARD office, as only four ARD employees had DEC options, making them millionaires, while the rest, who also worked on the deal, got peanuts.

By 1968, Doriot realized ARD was not competitive anymore. The SEC was still hounding the firm. Talent was leaving for other venture partnerships or corporate venture arms. Doriot wanted to merge ARD with an industrial firm, and eventually he merged it with Bill Miller's Textron Corp in 1972. Doriot reached out to three executives to succeed him, and all rejected the offer. The most important of the three was Thomas J. Perkins, a student of Doriot, who would go on to work with Bill and Dave at HP and start the most famous venture firm in the West Coast, if not the US. More on Perkins later, but one main reason he didn't join ARD was the compensation structure and the limited upside. Many say ARD failed for a reason other than compensation: Doriot just couldn't leave and empower a successor, and the ARD board stood behind him, the intellectual and moneymaker, instead of pushing him out for younger talent (Elfers worked magic at Greylock). Textron didn't solve any of the compensation issues, and ARD faded away within it.

Doriot lived by his principle that "you will get nowhere if you do not inspire people." He was fond of telling a story about three men breaking stones on a medieval road. They were asked what they were doing: One said, "I earn a living." One said, "I break stones." One said, "I help build cathedrals." Doriot wished his students and associates to build cathedrals together.

Economics and Legal Structure of Venture Capital Firms

The paradox of venture capital investing is that most investments will fail, but on the whole, a venture capitalist should make a 2x to 4x multiple on the invested capital. Because no one can know *ex ante* (before an investment) what will succeed and what will fail, venture firms must invest in large groups of companies (at least ten, and as many as a few dozen). For a sample of any ten investments, three to five will be written off to zero (complete failures), three to four will break even or eke out a small return (moderate failures at 1.5x to 2x multiples), and the remaining one to two will generate an outsized return (5-10x or more). The winning investments are tail events or positive "black swans," that is, improbable events that are hard to predict *ex ante* but which carry out-sized benefits or returns (and which seem obvious in hindsight, *ex post*). Hence, while some diversification is prudent for most asset classes, it is central to the venture capital model. To some extent, this is a calculated shotgun approach, especially for the earlier stages (such as the "seed" stage), and the composition and balance in a pool of investments matters more than any single investment. This economic logic leads to the ideal incentive and legal structure.

Venture capital funds are typically structured as limited partnerships, with the limited partners (LPs) being institutional investors and the general partner (GP) being the venture firm, which serves as an investment advisor and has complete control over the fund. As noted above, when institutions started displacing wealthy individuals, they became the biggest LPs in venture funds (though even today, technology company CEOs and select centi-millionaires form an old-boys network that can invest directly in venture funds). Most venture capital funds have a fixed life of 10 years, with one year extensions allowed for sales and IPOs in dry exit markets.

Venture capitalists are compensated through a combination of management fees and carried interest (often referred to as a "two and twenty" arrangement):

- Management fee: An annual payment made by LPs to the fund's GP to pay for the GP's expenses. In a typical venture capital fund, the general partners receive an annual management fee equal to up to 2% of the committed capital during the investment period, and a smaller amount (as low as 0.5%) for the harvest period.
- Carried interest or performance fee: A share of the profits of the fund (typically 20%), paid to the GP as a performance incentive. The remaining 80% of the profits are paid to the LPs.

Why partnerships and not a corporate structure? As Doriot's experience at ARD showed, the following reasons were important:

- Partnerships could fund daily operations (salaries, offices, etc.) with the management fee and so didn't need to raise money through more equity offerings or company sales, giving them flexibility;
- Partnerships could compensate the general partners with carried interest, but corporations had a hard time creating similar incentives (Doriot and the equity investors got the lion's share of returns from ARD's investments, while his junior team was salaried and received almost no upside);
- Partnerships could take a long view by marking asset values sensibly, unlike corporations such as ARD, which was harassed by the SEC on its reporting of asset values for many years;
- A limited fund life, per the partnership structure, forces the GP to return investors money in a timely way, which fits most LPs expectations of a return of capital in 7-12 years.
- Partnerships avoided the problem of raising additional funds and compensating junior members that corporations had. Doriot had to constantly haggle with companies to pay interest/dividends or with equity investors to put in new capital (and about the valuation level of the current portfolio), where GPs only have to launch a new limited partnership and so can start from scratch. Multiple funds also allow younger partners to take higher carry stakes and also simplify performance measurement for LPs.
- Partnerships could avoid the problem of a dominant founder who doesn't age well and understand new technology trends. Or as Dick Kramlich stated it: "One of the purposes of a partner is to save another partner from himself."

It can take anywhere from six months to several years for venture capitalists to raise money from institutional investors. At the time when all of a fund's money has been raised, the fund is said to be "closed" and the

10 year lifetime begins. A fund's "vintage year" generally refers to the year in which the fund was closed; this helps institutional investors stratify venture funds and compare their performance.

The investing cycle, or "commitment period," for most funds is generally three to five years, after which the venture capitalist focuses on managing and making follow-on investments in an existing portfolio. This means LPs have a fixed commitment to the fund that is initially unfunded and subsequently "called down" by the venture capital fund over time as the fund makes its investments. The remaining years are a "harvest period" where companies are expanded and then sold. This limited life structure can occasionally create a conflict between venture capitalists and entrepreneurs, as investors prefer to cash out early whereas entrepreneurs want to hold on.

One example of founder versus venture capitalist strife was the sale of Zappos to Amazon in 2009. Some reports suggested the venture capitalist, Mike Moritz, pressured the founder, Tony Hsieh, to sell early despite Hsieh's wish to wait for an IPO and maintain control of the company to nurture its unique customer-oriented culture. Hsieh was emotional and wanted to stay independent. Moritz was cold and rational, as Zappos relied on a revolving line of credit of $100 million to buy inventory; it had to hit projected revenue and profitability targets each month, or the banks could walk away from the loans during the 2009 credit crunch and create a possible cash-flow crisis that could bankrupt Zappos. Other problems with asset-backed inventory also existed. Moritz concluded Amazon would be a safe place for Zappos to borrow money, and Moritz's investment would be safe from these non-trivial risks.

Because a fund may run out of capital prior to the end of its life, larger venture capital firms usually have several overlapping funds at the same time; this lets the larger firm keep specialists in all stages of the development of firms almost constantly engaged. Smaller firms tend to thrive or fail with their initial industry contacts; by the time the fund cashes out, an entirely-new generation of technologies and people is ascending, whom the general partners may not know well, and so it is prudent to reassess and shift industries or personnel rather than attempt to simply invest more in the industry or people the partners already know.

Finally, most venture investments are structured as convertible preferred stock. If a startup fails, the venture fund, as a preferred stock owner, gets priority in a sale or liquidation to earn its money back (generally to break even or minimize losses). If a startup succeeds, the venture fund can convert the preferred stock into common stock and share in the startup's upside. This type of financing was seen early in the industry's history, with ARD using convertible debt (with interest at twice the government rate) or convertible preferred stock.

8. Engineers: Stanford Industrial Park, Inventions, Discoveries, and Rebellion at the Dawn of the Computer Age (1949-61)

Commercial Computers

Key early computer components were created in the US and Britain in the 1940s. In October 1944, the Army funded a project for Mauchly and Eckert to develop a binary (not decimal) computer capable of storing a program internally. They hired John von Neumann as a consultant, who in June 1945 delivered the design for the Electronic Discrete Variable Automatic Computer (EDVAC). It was eventually deployed at the University of Pennsylvania three years after the two inventors had already left the university to start their own company (EMCC). Meanwhile, Alan Turing in Britain in February 1946 had been commissioned by Britain's National Physical Laboratory to create an electronic computer. He delivered the design for the Automatic Computing Engine (ACE). The Pilot ACE, deployed in May 1950, had 1,450 thermionic valves (vacuum tubes). Turing's ideas moved quickly to the US.

Still in Britain, Frederick Williams at the University of Manchester developed a tube that was a variation on the cathode-ray tube. These Williams tubes could be used to implement Random Access Memory (RAM), a type of computer memory that was convenient for storing a program (in previous computers the program had to be entered manually each time, either through switches or paper tapes). Williams' team set out to build a computer. Williams' assistant Tom Kilburn ran the first computer program in June 1948. The computer was ready in 1949, and British defense contractor Ferranti built the commercial version, the Manchester Mark 1, in 1951.

The first stored-program electronic computer to be deployed in the US for general use was the SEAC in May 1950 at the National Bureau of Standards (NBS) in Washington, basically a scale-down version of the EDVAC (originally intended as an "interim" computer when it was conceived in 1948). It was also the first computer to use semiconductor devices (10,500 germanium diodes) instead of vacuum tubes for its logic. It had a memory of 512 words of 45 bits each (the equivalent of about 2.5 kilobytes). A program was entered via teletype or paper tape as a string of hexadecimal characters. The console to control the computer had no keyboard but just switches and dials. The NBS trained a relatively large staff of programmers. The "interim computer" was designed by a huge team of 33 people, organized in two groups: the engineers, headed by Sam Alexander and featuring Bob Elbourn, Ruth Haueter (the sole female engineer) and Sidney Greenwald; and the mathematicians, headed by Ed Cannon and featuring Ida Rhodes, Ethel Marden and Joe Levin.

The age of differential analyzers was coming to an end. The last one was the Magnetic Drum Digital Differential Analyzer (MADDIDA), built in 1951 in Los Angeles by Northrop Aircraft.

Corporate interests in the US were also plowing ahead. In 1950, the Remington Rand Corporation of New York purchased Mauchly's and Eckert's computer business (EMCC). Rand turned it into their Univac division with the aim of creating the "UNIVersal Automatic Computer" (a computer useful for business as well as scientific purposes). Mauchly and Eckert dutifully delivered this the following year to the US Census Bureau, their first and only customer before they were rescued by Remington Rand. In 1951 Grace Murray-Hopper, a pupil of Aiken at Harvard who had joined the Eckert-Mauchly Computer Corporation in 1949, developed the first compiler for a computer programming language, the A compiler for the Univac, a language that eventually evolved into B-0 or Flow-matic (1955).

IBM was involved in computers too. The main customer for IBM's early computers was the Naval Surface Weapons Center at Dahlgren, Virginia. The Center bought the electromechanical Mark II in 1948 and then the semi-electronic Mark III in 1951, both designed again by Howard Aiken like the Harvard Mark I. In 1952 IBM introduced its first electronic computer, dubbed IBM 701, designed at a facility north of New York (the Poughkeepsie Engineering Laboratory) by the team assembled by Ralph Palmer, a former electronic engineer of the Navy who had no experience with the Harvard project but had just introduced IBM's line of electronic calculators.

All the first computer customers were part of the military establishment. Remington Rand responded in 1953 with the Univac 1103. In 1946 the Navy had set up a company in Minneapolis, Engineering Research Associates (ERA), to build its top-secret computer, first the Atlas (operational in December 1950 and only available to the Navy) and then the Atlas II (of which 20 were built and sold to the general market). In 1952 Remington Rand bought Engineering Research Associates (including a young Seymour Cray) and commercialized the Atlas II as the Univac 1103 (in 1954). Then Gene Amdahl architected the IBM 704 of 1954, which used vacuum tubes, had RAM and also came with a rudimentary "operating system." The RAM of both the Univac 1103 and the IBM 704 replaced the cathode-ray tube storage with a new kind of storage, "magnetic core." However, IBM's first mass-produced computer, designed at yet another laboratory in upstate New York, was the low-cost 650, also introduced in 1954, but it was still decimal, not binary, and had a rotating drum memory instead of the magnetic-core RAM.

The era of commercial computers had begun with a race between Univac and IBM. Univac had acquired the technology from outside and needed to integrate the Remington Rand research center of Connecticut with the EMCC facility of Pennsylvania and with the ERA facility of Minnesota. IBM had created the technology internally, notably at Aiken's and Palmer's laboratories.

IBM probably won out (in the long term) because of its involvement in a groundbreaking and important military project, the Semi-Automatic Ground Environment (SAGE). With funding from the Navy, that was interested in a flight simulator, between 1948 and 1951 a team led by Jay Forrester had built the Whirlwind computer at MIT, the first real-time system and the first computer to use a video display for output. Norman Taylor had worked on the Whirlwind from its inception in 1948 and Jack Gilmore had written the assembler program.

SAGE was created because the Air Force needed a system to rapidly process the data coming from a radar network in case of a Soviet attack against the US. SAGE was assigned to MIT's Whirlwind team in 1954 with the goal to create a system for monitoring and intercepting enemy rockets. IBM was in charge of adapting the Whirlwind computer to the task, and the result was the AN/FSQ-7 computer, which (first delivered in 1958) still remains the largest computer ever built: it weighed 275 tons and covered 2,000 square meters of floor space, and contained 55,000 vacuum tubes. Another innovation was a radar device that would send data to the computer in digital format by modem over telephone lines (a feature developed by AT&T that jumpstarted its digital telecommunications business). Half of IBM's computer-related revenues of the 1950s came from two military contracts: the guidance computer for the B-52 bomber, and SAGE. SAGE alone accounted for sales of $500 million in the 1950s.

Early IBM computers that later became industry standards were the 704 and 709. The 704 used ideas originally developed for yet another military contract. In 1950 a government agency, the Navy Bureau of Ordnance, commissioned a superfast computer for the Naval Surface Weapons Center at Dahlgren (Virginia), which IBM named Naval Ordnance Research Computer (NORC). Built between 1950 and December 1954 in collaboration with Columbia University under the direction of astronomy professor Wallace Eckert, this vacuum-tube computer that used RAM with Williams tubes was indeed the fastest computer of its time. It also introduced an architectural innovation: an input-output subsystem that executed while the computation continued, to minimize in-between time (a feature that was transferred to the commercial computer IBM 709 in 1960 and then became a standard for all computers).

The transition from the early task-oriented computers to the general-purpose IBM and Univac computers had largely been enabled by the development of Random Access Memory (RAM). Its first successful and affordable implementation was in terms of magnetic-core memory, a technique that emerged out of research conducted in the 1950s mainly around Boston. Two groups contributed to its refinement: Chinese-born physicist An Wang at Harvard's Computation Laboratory under Aiken since 1949 (and at his own Wang Laboratories since 1951) and Jay Forrester's Whirlwind project at MIT. Wang can also be credited for introducing the idea of outsourcing hardware manufacturing to the Far East, as magnetic-core memories were probably the first computer component whose price declined rapidly due to cheap labor in the Far East. Magnetic-core memories replaced the old assemblies of relays and/or vacuum tubes that were not effective in retrieving and returning data.

Within ten years the computer industry had undergone a dramatic transformation. Initially computers were wartime government projects. Then small companies such as EMCC and ERA (mainly working for government agencies) tested the new technology and the private market for it. Finally, the large office automation players (Remington Rand, IBM, NCR, Burroughs) entered the field. Burroughs' Philadelphia research center built the Unitized Digital Electronic Computer (UDEC) in 1951 and the company sold the first unit in 1953. NCR purchased the California-based CRC in 1953. The electronics mega-corporations (General Electric, RCA, AT&T, and Western Electric) were followers, not leaders; their first computers were respectively the ERMA (1956) and the BIZMAC (1956). In 1955, General Electric's revenues were $3 billion, whereas IBM didn't even reach half a billion: General Electric had the know-how, the engineers and the capital to dwarf IBM and Univac in the computer field; but it didn't. On the contrary, in 1955 IBM passed Remington Rand for number of installed computers and became the world leader in computers.

The computer had been invented by scientists interested in solving complex mathematical problems such as nonlinear differential equations and had found its first practical application in military-related tasks. The first companies to realize the non-military potential of the computer were the ones making typewriters, cash registers, adding machines and tabulating machines, not the ones making electronic components.

Jay Forrester's Whirlwind project and the subsequent SAGE project gave Boston a huge lead in computer science over the rest of the country. In 1951, the Air Force chose MIT to create a state-of-the-art laboratory for computer science, the Lincoln Laboratory, which probably became the main center for training computer scientists in the entire world.

Another major center for computer innovation was the University of Illinois at Urbana-Champaign (UIUC). In 1951, a team there developed the ORDVAC, based on Von Neumann's EDVAC. It became the second computer entirely built within a university, although on behalf of the Army. It was followed in 1952 by its more famous twin, the ILLIAC I (Illinois Automatic Computer), which remained to be used by the university. They boasted 5 kilobytes of memory (1024 40-bit words). Incidentally, a member of that team, Saburo Muroga, returned to Japan to build that nation's second computer, the Musashino-1, following Okazaki Bunji's FUJIC at Fuji. In 1960, Donald Bitzer at UIUC used this very ILLIAC computer to create PLATO, the first computerized system for learning that inaugurated the field of computer-based education. Despite the limitations of input/output devices, Bitzer realized that graphics were crucial for using computers to teach.

The Birth of the Semiconductor Industry

An important decision was made by AT&T, the owner of Bell Labs, to share the technology of the transistor with anyone who could improve it. Jack Morton organized a symposium to disseminate know-how about semiconductors among scientists and engineers from all over the world.

The first symposium, held in September 1951, specifically targeted defense contractors. Yet the second one was open to everybody who had purchased the license for the transistor technology. Several electrical companies understood the long-term potential of transistors: Sylvania, a vacuum-tube company based in Massachusetts that had expanded during World War II and that introduced one of the earliest transistors in 1949; Motorola, which opened its Semiconductor Division in Arizona in 1949; Texas Instruments, one of the companies that bought the license in 1952; and, of course, Western Electric itself, AT&T's manufacturing arm, that opened a factory in Pennsylvania (at Laureldale) to make transistors and diodes exclusively for the government. A "startup" that understood the importance of the invention was Transitron Electronics. Leo and David Bakalar (the latter a graduate from MIT who had worked at Bell Labs on transistors) founded in 1952 near Boston, to take advantage of Western Electric's transistor license.

The first applications of transistors had nothing to do with computers. Raytheon became the largest manufacturer of transistors by selling transistors used in hearing aids. What made a "transistor" a household name were the first portable radios: the Regency TR-1 (October 1954), which used Texas Instruments' transistors and the TR-52 (March 1955) by the Tokyo Telecommunications Company (later renamed Sony). By then the cost of a transistor had been reduced to $2.50 and the Regency (that contained four transistors) was sold for $50. The portable radio marked the birth of consumer electronics, a trend towards miniaturization and lower prices that would eventually bring ever more powerful appliances in every house and even every pocket.

The first fully transistorized computer, the TRADIC (TRAnsistor Digital Computer), was built by AT&T's Bell Labs for the Air Force in 1954, but AT&T was barred from commercial computer business. It was followed in 1955 by the TX-0, built at MIT and basically a transistorized version of the Whirlwind. IBM did not introduce a transistorized stored-program computer until 1960, the 7070 (meant as a replacement for the 650).

The Computer Industry on the West Coast

The West Coast computer industry was located far from the research centers of the large office automation companies (IBM, NCR, Burroughs, Remington). It was peripheral to the strategies of the electronic giants (General Electric, RCA, Honeywell, AT&T) and left out of the loop of the large government-funded computing projects (Boston's Lincoln Lab and UPenn's Moore School). On the West Coast the computer industry was limited to serve the needs of the booming aviation industry of Los Angeles, namely Northrop Aircraft, Raytheon, Rand and Hughes.

These projects too were mostly funded by government agencies. The staff of the National Bureau of Standards (NBS) was valuable to the computer industry of the West Coast because many of those programmers accepted to move west and joined the aviation industry. To start with, in July 1950 UCLA completed a computer for the government's National Bureau of Standards, code-named Standards Western Automatic Computer (SWAC) and designed by Harry Huskey, who in 1947 had been a member of Turing's ACE team. The SWAC contained 2,300 vacuum tubes.

Northrop, however, did not believe in electronic computers. In 1950 some of its engineers, who had worked on the Magnetic Drum Differential Analyzer, quit to form Computer Research Corporation (CRC) and work on computer contracts for the Department of Defense, but was acquired by NCR in 1953.

The rest of Northrop's computer lab was sold to Bendix, a maker of appliances and radios based in Indiana. In March 1956 Bendix introduced their first digital computer, the Bendix G-15, designed by Harry Huskey and inspired by Turing's ACE. It took input from paper tape or punched cards and sent its output to a typewriter (about ten characters per second) or a pen plotter. It was much smaller than the monsters created by IBM and Univac, a premonition of the minicomputers to come.

New computers were sprouting up. In 1957, some of the former Northrop engineers led by Max Palevsky quit Bendix and joined Packard Bell (a Los Angeles-based maker of consumer radios) to open their computer labs. Raytheon developed the code-named Hurricane (later

Raydac) in 1953 for a Naval Air Missile Test Center, which supposed to replace the SWAC at the NBS.

The RAND Corporation had been chosen as one of the five sites for development of a computer designed by Von Neumann in 1946 at the Institute for Advanced Studies in New Jersey (IAS). It was completed in 1953, a few months after the IAS machine became operational. The IAS machine was the one that popularized the term "Von Neumann architecture" to refer to stored-program computers (in which computation is due to the interaction between a processor and a memory, with the memory storing both instructions and data).

Finally, there were at least two spin-offs from the California Institute of Technology (CalTech): the Librascope division of General Precision (that built another "small" computer); and the ElectroData division of Consolidated Electrodynamics Corporation (CEC), spun off in 1954 to market its first computer, sold to Burroughs. The dynamics in Los Angeles were significantly different from the East Coast: engineers moved from one company to another, and several of them started new companies. All of them were funded, directly or indirectly, by military projects.

The Stanford Industrial Park

In the Bay Area, the Terman doctrine of close interaction between academia and industry was further implemented in 1951 when Stanford University, prodded by the rapidly growing Varian that needed more space, created the Stanford Industrial Park. Located along Page Mill Road, the southern border of the campus, the park was meant to be an area for companies interested in high-tech innovation. Stanford had meant to lease the unused land to companies, and Terman simply proposed that land be leased "only" to high-tech companies. There had been industrial parks before, but none so oriented towards technological innovation. Its first tenant (in 1953) was going to be Varian, then Hewlett-Packard, General Electric (1954), Eastman Kodak, Zenith (1956), Lockheed (1956), and many others.

Incidentally, it wasn't the only scheme devised to increase Stanford's revenues. In September 1955 the Stanford Shopping Center opened its doors to the first tenant: this part of Stanford was reserved for retailers and would become a celebrated open-air shopping mall.

The founders of Hewlett-Packard created a unique corporate culture. Their management style had little to do with the cold, opportunistic style of the East Coast. Instead of focusing only on profits, HP focused on its human resources. Employees were treated like family members. Hewlett-Packard probably introduced the custom of addressing even the owners of a large company by their first names. Hewlett-Packard pioneered the idea that the workers of a company are co-owners of it, giving them stock options. While most companies hired specialists whose value depended on how long their specialization was valuable, HP pioneered the practice of retraining employees for different functions in the company, thus avoiding the career pitfall of hyper specialization. Lay-offs were anathema, no matter how well or badly the company was doing. HP was also one of the first companies to promote women to higher management positions. Hewlett-Packard invested first not on technology or customers but on its own workforce. Before it created products, it created a sense of community. The company had done well during the war, providing high-quality electronic equipment, and it was rapidly expanding. Revenues grew from $5.5 million in 1951 (215 employees) to $88 million in 1961 (5,040 employees).

Varian (whose revenues had increased more than tenfold during the Korean War) went public in 1956, Hewlett-Packard in 1957, and Ampex in 1958. The IPO (Initial Public Offering) meant that the region was becoming less dependent on the big conglomerates of the East Coast. These three companies had raised the money they needed without having to sell bits to the incompetent East Coast electronics companies. These IPOs also marked the beginning of a partnership between Silicon Valley and Wall Street.

The Valley was finding other places to apply computer technology. In 1950 the Stanford Research Institute was hired by Bank of America to design a computer for the automation of check processing. In September 1955, the prototype of the ERMA (Electronic Recording Machine Accounting) was ready and the following year the machine was manufactured by General Electric and NRC. It was the first successful use of a computer for a banking application, and even pioneered optical character recognition.

The Culture of Invention

The Bay Area was becoming an ever more attractive location for business. The inventions continued to flow. Notably, in 1956 Charles Ginsburg at Ampex Corporation, heading a team that included a young Ray Dolby, built the first practical videotape recorder, a device that changed the way television programming worked (previously, all programs had been broadcast live, and, obviously, at the same time in all time zones). In 1961 Laurence Spitters, a Wall Street investment banker who had moved to San Francisco and joined Ampex in 1958, founded Memorex in Santa Clara taking three Ampex engineers with him to work on computer magnetic tape .

UC Berkeley had its own stored-program computer project, CALDIC (California Digital Computer), completed in 1954 by Professor Paul Morton who employed former ENIAC staff from Pennsylvania and local students (including a young Doug Engelbart).

The number of engineers produced by Stanford and UC Berkeley was beginning to draw the attention of East-Coast companies. In 1952

IBM opened its first West-Coast laboratory in San Jose. In September 1956 this lab unveiled the Random Access Method of Accounting and Control (RAMAC) 305, another vacuum-tube computer and the first to use magnetic-disk storage, invented at this lab in 1954. Its RAMAC 350 hard-disk drive had a capacity of five megabytes. This computer shipped with a processing unit, a card-punch machine, a console (card feed, typewriter, keyboard), a printer and the 350 hard-disk drive.

The Defense Industry

The defense industry was still the main employer of the Bay Area. In 1956 sales in the US of electronic equipment exceeded $3 billion, and half of that went to the military. During the Korean War (1950-53), California finally overtook New York as the state receiving the largest share of military contracts (26% of all contracts). The majority of the money went to the aircraft industry based near Los Angeles, but next was the Bay Area. Afraid that the Soviet Union was leapfrogging their missile technology, in 1953 the Army, due to Terman, commissioned Sylvania to create a missile detection system. Sylvania set up an Electronic Defense Lab (EDL) in Mountain View, near Moffett Field, not the first defense contractor to get involved in military projects at this location. This project, directed by Stanford alumnus Bill Perry, lasted several years and eventually led to Sylvania's Ballistic Missile Early Warning System (BMEWS). In 1958 IBM shipped its first transistorized 709 (originally built with vacuum tubes) specifically for this project, before that machine was renamed IBM 7090. In 1959 Sylvania was bought by General Telephone to form General Telephone and Electronics, or GT&E. By then Sylvania's EDL had become one of Santa Clara Valley's largest companies, with over 1,000 employees.

In 1954, Charlie Litton sold his San Carlos-based vacuum-tube operations to Litton Industries. Despite its name, Litton was based in Los Angeles and owned by Tex Thornton, a former vice-president at Hughes Aircraft with strong ties to the Defense Department (he had started Electro Dynamics Corporation in 1953). Litton's original business in San Carlos became the Electron Devices Division of Thornton's Litton Industries. Thornton was one of the businessmen who understood that the Cold War would require increasingly sophisticated weapons. By 1959, he could count on sales of $120 million, of which about 50% came from the government. By 1963 sales would top half a billion dollars. Meanwhile, in 1954 General Electric opened its Electric Microwave Lab at the Stanford Industrial Park to manufacture electronic devices for radars and missile defense systems. In 1957 Paul Cook opened Raychem in Redwood City to manufacture wires and cables for the military and aerospace industries.

When the Department of Defense awarded Lockheed a contract to work on the project for a submarine-launched ballistic missile (the

Polaris), Lockheed relocated its electronics research group to the Stanford Industrial Park and built a factory for its Lockheed Missiles Division near Moffett Field in Sunnyvale. That same year the US decided to invest in satellites to spy on the Soviet Union (a project code-named "Corona") and that division of Lockheed got the contract and opened another factory, the Advanced Projects division. Within ten years it would become the main employer of the region.

The Valley's companies were still small by the standards of the East-Coast conglomerates. In 1956 both General Electric and RCA had revenues of over $700 million. In comparison, Varian was the largest of the native Bay Area companies and barely reached revenues of $25 million. HP had more employees but less in revenues ($20.3 million).

The Culture of Discovery

In those years the scientific reputation of Stanford and UC Berkeley grew rapidly. In 1952, Felix Bloch of Stanford University was awarded the Nobel Prize in Physics, the first for Stanford. Berkeley had already accumulated more Nobel Prizes than any other university in the five years since the end of the war: John Northrop and Wendell Stanley (1946), William Giauque (1949), Glenn Seaborg and Edwin McMillan (1951) all won the prize.

At the end of the war Robert Oppenheimer realized that the future would need a new kind of weapons laboratory, one that wouln't just build them but also improve them. He helped conceive Sandia National Laboratories, established near Los Alamos and assigned to the University of California. Later, President Truman decided to transfer its management to AT&T.

When the US decided to develop a "hydrogen" bomb to stay ahead of the Soviet Union (that had detonation its first atomic bomb in August 1949), in 1952 the Atomic Energy Commission established a branch of the Lawrence's Radiation Laboratory (later renamed Lawrence Berkeley Lab) in the town of Livermore (on the underdeveloped east side of the bay), soon to become known as the Lawrence Livermore Laboratory. The lab in Livermore was charged with military projects, while the lab in Berkeley was free to conduct theoretical research. In 1954 the lab in Berkeley, which had relocated up the hill from the UC Berkeley campus, installed a 10,000-ton synchrotron (nicknamed "Bevatron") that could accelerate protons to 6.2 BeV (one billion electronvolts), enough to create antimatter on Earth: the first antiproton was detected in October 1955.

The lab in Livermore, instead, became one of the sites for the top-secret Project Sherwood with Princeton and Oak Ridge to produce a "controlled" nuclear fusion reaction. Fusion is the kind of nuclear reaction that takes place in the sun and generates enormous amounts of energy out of hydrogen. The goal of Project Sherwood was to turn hydrogen (the most available element on Earth) into energy for industrial and domestic purposes. Unfortunately, fusion seems to happen only at very high temperatures. The project was started in 1951 under British physicist James Tuck of Los Alamos, who had worked on fusion for nuclear weapons within the Manhattan Project, but in 1953 Berkeley alumnus Amasa Bishop was appointed the new director.

In August 1955 Homi Bhabha chaired the United Nations' Conference on the Peaceful Uses of Atomic Energy and said: "I venture to predict that a method will be found for liberating fusion energy in a controlled manner within the next two decades. When that happens the energy problem of the world will truly have been solved forever for the fuel will be as plentiful as the heavy hydrogen in the oceans."

Culture and Society

The Californian governors of the post-war era helped modernize the state. Earl Warren (1943-1953), a charismatic politician, unified the state behind him and launched an ambitious program of public works, basically continuing the New Deal. He built state universities and community colleges as well as a vast network of freeways. Goodwin Knight (1953-1959) and Pat Brown (1959-1967), a San Francisco lawyer, continued these policies. The political climate was so united that at one point Warren was nominated by all three main parties and Pat Brown switched from one party to another. These governors invested heavily in the infrastructure of the state while wisely managing its finances. Due to the prosperity created by their policies, immigrants flocked to the "Golden State" from all over the country.

Meanwhile, San Jose experienced a population boom in the 1950s due to the soldiers who relocated there after World War II. They could find affordable suburban housing and well-paid jobs. In 1955 a new fast road connected San Jose to San Francisco, the I-280 freeway. Up until the 1950s, the Bay Area was mainly known as a haven for unorthodox artists and writers. Very few engineers dreamed of moving from imperial Europe, whos cities and universities still dominated the world, to provincial California. Fewer engineers dreamed of moving from the political and industrial hubs of the East Coast and the Midwest to the picturesque but isolated Bay Area. It was mainly the artists who found that distant western outpost fascinating.

The cultural life of San Francisco was beginning to take off, although in a rather bizarre manner. In 1951 Zen apostle Alan Watts moved from Britain to San Francisco, where he became a major influence on the assimilation of Eastern philosophy into Western lifestyle. He started a radio program in 1953 at Berkeley's KPFA station. Meanwhile, Peter Martin can be credited as the man who imported the spirit of New York's intelligentsia into San Francisco. In 1952 he began publishing a literary magazine titled "City Lights." The following year,

Lawrence Ferlinghetti was convinced by Ken Rexroth to move to San Francisco. He opened a bookstore, "City Lights," which was an experiment in itself: the first all-paperback bookstore in the nation. The bookstore soon became the headquarters of alternative writers.

In October 1955, Allen Ginsberg's recitation of his poem "Howl," organized by Rexroth at the Six Gallery, transplanted the "Beat" aesthetic to San Francisco. Other writers came to inspire the local "Beat Generation." Jack Kerouac moved to San Francisco in 1956 and Robert Creeley moved to San Francisco in 1957. Among the local talents who embraced the new style were Michael McClure and Jack Spicer (part of Robert Duncan's Berkeley circle). The most lasting influence was perhaps that of two poets who had studied in Oregon at Reed College. Gary Snyder and Philip Whalen, because they adopted Zen Buddhism, started a trend that would make California an international center of Zen and would make Zen a staple of the counterculture. Snyder, in particular, delved into Chinese and Japanese poetry, bringing to California the passion for exotic cultures (instead of contempt for their poor emigrants).

At the same time, San Francisco still maintained its old sexually permissive atmosphere. In 1955 the police staged a coordinated campaign of persecution against homosexuals, but its outcome was to cement solidarity within that community, and, for example, in the same year the "Daughters of Bilitis" was founded in San Francisco, the first exclusively lesbian organization in the US. In 1959 Stanford University hired Austrian-born chemist Carl Djerassi, who four years earlier at Syntex of Mexico City had invented synthetic progesterone, which accidentally turned out to be "the birth-control pill." Syntex was run by Uruguayan-born Alejandro Zaffaroni and manufactured synthetic steroid hormones.

A notable event in the artistic life of the Bay Area was the 1945 establishment of the Photography Department at the California School of Fine Arts (later renamed the San Francisco Art Institute), due to Ansel Adams. It recognized photography as a fine art in a way that no other academic institution had yet done. In 1946, Adams convinced other distinguished photographers to accept positions at the school: Minor White, a former student of Alfred Stieglitz in New York, Berkeley's Dorothea Lange, and San Francisco's Imogen Cunningham.

Another notable event was the birth of the art movement later dubbed "Bay Area Figurative Painting." The founder was David Park, who moved to San Francisco in 1943 to teach at the California School of Fine Arts and later exhibited the first abstract paintings with figurative elements. He influenced Elmer Bischoff, who started teaching at the School of Fine Arts in 1946, and Richard Diebenkorn, who began teaching at Oakland's California College of Arts and Crafts in 1955. In 1947 and 1949 New York's abstract expressionist Mark Rothko taught at the same school. The Contemporary Bay Area Figurative Painting

Exhibition at the Oakland Art Museum of September 1957 featured Park's, Bischoff's and Diebenkorn's student Henry Villierme, the leader of the second generation.

Junk and found object art started to develop too. Starting in 1952, Wally Hedrick began constructing collages of metal objects that he scavenged in junkyards (cans, lamps, radios, appliances). Jess Collins in 1952 founded the King Ubu Gallery, which in 1954 Hedrick renamed Six Gallery and turned into an artist-run cooperative. Around it revolved artists such as Manuel Neri and Mary-Joan "Jay" DeFeo, a UC Berkeley alumna who had absorbed influences from Native-American, African and prehistoric art. Most of them were also grouped in Bruce Conner's Rat Bastard Protective Association (an non-existent association, just a term coined in 1959). They represented the counterpart to the Beat movement in the visual arts. Bruce Conner, who had arrived in 1957 in the city, upped the ante of the movement with his chaotic sculptures of junk wrapped in sexy nylon stockings.

San Francisco's avantgarde cinema scene came to life due to Frank Stauffacher's "Art in Cinema," held in the San Francisco Museum of Modern Art since 1946. It marked the first time in the US that an art museum presented a series of experimental films. Despite the focus on avantgarde films, the events often drew a sold-out crowd. The San Francisco International Film Festival debuted in 1957. It eventually became the longest-running film festival in the Americas. Little of this fervor reached the Peninsula. In 1955, peace activist Roy Kepler opened a bookstore in Menlo Park to sell paperbacks, which at the time were shunned by most high-brow bookstores. His Kepler's bookstore remained an outpost of alternative culture in the Peninsula.

A bizarre contribution to the cultural life of the Bay Area came from the Central Intelligence Agency (CIA). In 1953 the CIA launched a secret project, "MK-Ultra," to develop a truth drug that would control the mind of its victims. This was in response to reports that the Communists in North Korea had brainwashed US prisoners of war. The CIA administered Lysergic Acid Diethylamide (LSD) to the volunteers of the program. One of these volunteers was a Stanford student named Ken Kesey.

Electronic Brains

The computer industry was still largely absent from the Bay Area. In the rest of the nation it was however progressing rapidly. In 1956 there were 800 computes in operation in the US. By 1959 there were about 6,000. The press, which had barely followed the original efforts, was now fascinated by these machines that journalists dubbed "electronic brains."

The brains helped automate manual tasks. In 1949 John Parson in Michigan invented "numerical control," the computer-based automation of machine tools. In 1951 David Shepard at AFSA, the government agency that would later be renamed National Security Agency (NSA), devised a computer program capable of recognizing printed text and went on to build a "reading machine" called "Gismo." The first commercial system was installed at Reader's Digest in 1955. When IBM introduced a similar product in 1959, it named it Optical Character Recognition (OCR). In 1951 Princeton University's student Marvin Minsky built SNARC (Stochastic Neural Analog Reinforcement Calculator), a machine that simulated the way the neural network of the brain learns.

In 1952, a "Conference on Mechanical Translation" was organized at MIT by Yehoshua Bar-Hillel, attended in particular by Leon Dostert, who in 1949 had built (on machines donated by IBM) a computer-based system for language interpretation at the Nuremberg trial of Nazi officers and subsequently had established the Institute of Languages and Linguistics at Georgetown University in Washington. In 1954, George Devol, a former radar specialist who had joined Remington Rand, designed the first industrial robot, Unimate, which was finally used by General Motors.

Researchers wanted to optimize computers. John McCarthy of MIT organized the first conference on artificial intelligence at Dartmouth College, the goal being to study how computers could be made as intelligent as humans (not just number crunchers). Allen Newell at RAND Corporation in Los Angeles and Carnegie Mellon University's Herbert Simon in Pittsburgh unveiled the "Logic Theorists" in 1956 and in 1957 the "General Problem Solver," a computer program that represented another step in abstracting a Turing machine. It not only separated data and instructions, but even knowledge (about the domain of the problem) and inference (the logical methods that lead to solutions). Also in 1957 Frank Rosenblatt conceived the "Perceptron," a machine that simulated the neural structure of the brain and that could learn by trial and error (one of the few scientists who followed Von Neumann's advice). Also in 1957 Morton Heilig invented the "Sensorama Machine," a pioneering virtual-reality environment. In 1959 McCarthy and Minsky, who had joined MIT in 1958, founded the Artificial Intelligence Lab. In 1959 Norbert Wiener's pupil at MIT, Oliver Selfridge, described "Pandemonium," a computer modeled after the neural networks of the brain and capable of machine learning that could be used for problems of pattern recognition that eluded existing computers.

Not everyone thought computers were electronic brains. In 1955, on his death-bed, John Von Neumann warned the computer community that the brain (the original computing device) worked according to wildly different principles than the ones employed in computers: not a sequence of instructions but a network that self-reorganizes dynamically.

The Art of Programming

Software was considered such a negligible part of computing that it didn't even have a name (the term "software" was introduced in 1959). During the 1950s most programs came bundled with the computer. The computer manufacturer was in charge of providing the applications, which typically targeted the big sectors (banking, manufacturing, retailing) to which the manufacturer was marketing the machines. In other words, the application program was just one of the many accessories that helped sell the machine.

There were also user-written programs, but they were not really "sold." They were made available to the community of users of the same machine. "Share" was the name of the IBM user group (originally formed in 1955 by aerospace companies of the Los Angeles area that used the 701) and "Use" was the name of the Univac user group. It was the manufacturer itself (IBM or Univac) that facilitated the flow of know-how. The largest organizations could also afford to maintain in-house teams of programmers for developing ad-hoc applications; but, again, these were not for sale.

Software became a real industry after John Backus at IBM in New York unveiled the FORTRAN programming language in 1957. It was the first practical machine-independent language. This language basically created the job of the software engineer. The following year another seminal programming language was introduced: COBOL (Common Business Oriented Language), which was defined by a Conference on Data System Languages (CODASYL) called by the Department of Defense, and largely based on Grace Murray-Hopper's Flow-matic.

Both manufacturers and customers were beginning to realize that computers were powerful hardware but their usefulness depended on their software applications. However, given the limitations of the hardware, it was not possible to create large, sophisticated applications even if one wanted to. SAGE was the notable exception, a task originally estimated at one million instructions. And SAGE, in fact, did spawn the first software company: RAND Corporation, selected in 1955 to write the code for SAGE, created a new System Development Division that in 1957 was spun off as System Development Corporation (SDC). SDC created from scratch a whole new profession by training about two thousand programmers at a time when most countries had zero programmers and only a few countries had more than 100. Software was not taught in college at the time (the first masters program would come only in 1979). For the record SAGE was only completed in 1962, the largest computer project in the world.

Software consulting slowly gained in importance. John Sheldon and Elmer Kubie of IBM's scientific software division had already started the Computer Usage Company in March 1955 in New York specifically to provide software consulting. The biggest software consulting company in the late 1950s was CEIR (Corporation for Economic and Industrial Research), originally a financial consulting firm. Founded in 1957 by Herbert Robinson in Washington after fulfilling a contract with the Air Force, it had a software division headed by Orchard Hayes whose custom software applications rapidly became the main source of revenues. Fletcher Jones, one of the founders of Share, started Computer Sciences in Los Angeles in 1959. Their "labs" were valuable training grounds for self-taught programmers.

The Minicomputer

Most computers at this point were still the size of entire rooms. While few minicomputers had any commercial impact, they contributed to create the myth of the machine that could take over the world. Size did matter: the bigger ones had greater processing power and so more intelligence. There was, however, one event that would have a great commercial impact. In 1957 Georges Doriot's ARD Corp. (the American Research and Development Corporation) made a modest investment in a computer company started near Boston by a former MIT scientist and SAGE engineer, Ken Olsen. It was the Digital Equipment Corporation (DEC). Its "mini-computer" PDP-1 (Program Data Processor), basically a streamlined version of the TX-0 (the first transistorized computer built at MIT), was introduced in 1960 at a price of $125,000. The PDP-1 came with a keyboard and a monitor in a much smaller (and cheaper) package than the IBM and Univac computers. It could process 100,000 instructions per second and had a memory of 4,000 words (each word being made of 18 bits). The PDP-1's first customer was MIT's Project MAC.

Factory Automation

Two important steps toward automating factories were taking place.

First, in 1958 Patrick Hanratty at General Electric unveiled Pronto, a numerical-control programming language that allowed computers to control machine tools, while the Automatically Programmed Tool (APT) was still being developed by Douglas Ross at MIT (APT would become the industry's standard). This was an important step towards automating a factory.

What numerical control did was to introduce the concept of "real time" in commercial computing. It placed the computer inside a "living" system, the factory. The computer was no longer an isolated machine that could compute an exotic scientific problem in isolation and leisurely, but a cog in a complex clockwork that had to interact with other machines on the fly. For these applications the sensor was as important as the processor.

Second, the development of Computer-Aided Design (CAD) helped automation and it is entangled with the story of spy satellites. In 1957, Kodak executive Richard Leghorn was in the unique position of knowing the top-secret plans for flying spy satellites over the Soviet Union. He had originally proposed them when he was in the Air Force he know of the state-of-the-art in photography. He obtained money from Laurance Rockefeller and founded Itek in Boston to build reconnaissance cameras just in time to sell them to the CIA for its Corona project, beating the competition of camera leader Fairchild Camera and Instrument. With that money in 1960 Itek funded the Electronic Drafting Machine (EDM), a machine to automate the design process of engineering departments. This required the ability to display graphics and not only text on monitors, something that had been experimented by the Whirlwind/SAGE project at MIT. In fact, the brains behind the project were two MIT whizzes who had worked on the Whirlwind/SAGE project: Norman Taylor, who had been hired by Itek, and Jack Gilmore, who had started one of the earliest software companies. They decided to use a PDP-1 just released by another SAGE alumnus, Ken Olsen. In 1962 they delivered the first Digigraphics system, the forerunner of graphics workstations.

Semiconductors in the Bay Area

A series of events in the second half of the 1950s led the Bay Area into the nascent computer industry. The defense industry was still driving a big chunk of the Valley's economy. It was so prevalent that in 1955 Stanford University merged the Applied Electronics Laboratory and the Electronics Research Laboratory into the Systems Engineering Laboratory under the direction of Fred Terman to focus on electronic warfare. The Cold War was proving to be a gold mine for electronics. NASA too opened a research center at Moffett Field in Mountain View (1958). New ideas for defense-related business were floating around. It was not easy, though, to start a new company. In 1955 private investors or "angels," including John Bryan, Bill Edwards, and Reid Dennis (an employee of the Fireman's Fund in San Francisco), established "The Group" to invest together in promising electronics companies of the Bay Area. They invested their own money.

The timing could not have been more auspicious for semiconductors. William Shockley, inventor of the transistor, had joined Beckman Instruments, a company based in Los Angeles that was willing to open an entire research center for transistors. In 1956, Beckman opened its Shockley Semiconductor Laboratory division in Mountain View to work on semiconductor-based transistors that would replace vacuum tubes. Shockley's transistors had used germanium but he was aware that in 1954 Texas Instruments had introduced silicon transistors, and knew it was the right direction. He tried in vain to convince former coworkers at Bell Labs to follow him west. Eventually he settled on hiring young local engineers, all of them still in their 20s. Among them were Philco's physicist Robert Noyce and Caltech's chemist Gordon Moore.

Just one year later, in October 1957, eight of these engineers, including Robert Noyce, Gordon Moore, Jean Hoerni and Eugene Kleiner, quit the Shockley Transistor Laboratories to form Fairchild Semiconductor in Mountain View. They obtained funding from Sherman Fairchild's New York-based Fairchild Camera and Instrument due to the help of a young investment banker, Arthur Rock. It was the first venture-funded "startup" company in the Bay Area. Fairchild's main selling point was that transistors could be made with a cheap and ubiquitous material like silicon instead of the germanium that the industry had been using. Shockley called them traitors and maybe they were. Yet they legitimized the practice of quitting a company and starting a competing company, thus betraying their employer but also advancing the state of technology.

The rupture was made possible by the realization that the semiconductor industry did not require a huge capital investment: silicon can be found everywhere and it is cheap. Unlike the old economy of big, complex, and expensive products, in the semiconductor industry starting a competitor in competition against one's own employer was relatively easy. The problem was other competitors: Texas Instruments in Dallas, Motorola in Phoenix, and Transitron and Raytheon in Boston.

The Beginnings of Venture Capital

There were still few groundbreaking ideas coming out from the Bay Area electronics sector, but somehow there was an interest in funding ideas. In 1957 Dean Watkins of Stanford's ERL (where he had supervised the project for traveling-wave tubes or TWTs, tubes that allowed the amplification of radio signals to very high power) started Watkins-Johnson to manufacture components for electronic intelligence systems. It was one of the first venture-capital funded companies in the Santa Clara Valley, and one of the most successful of its generation, with sales doubling in four years. Its main investor was Tommy Davis, a realtor in southern California.

At the same time, spurred by the Cold War and by the need to boost the post-war economy, the US enacted a law to help start new companies: the Small Business Investment Company Act of 1958. The government pledged to invest three dollars for every dollar that a financial institution would invest in a startup (up to a limit). In the next ten years, this program would provide the vast majority of all venture funding in the US. The Bay Area was a major beneficiary.

Numerous venture firms sprung up. In 1958 Draper, Gaither and Anderson was founded in Palo Alto by Rowan Gaither (founder of the RAND Corporation), William Draper, and Fred Anderson. It was the first limited-partnership venture-capital firm in California, although short-lived. A limited partnership made it easier to compensate partners with carried interest and reduced investors' risk. One year later, Frank Chambers established the venture-capital company Continental Capital in San Francisco. In 1961 Tommy Davis and Arthur Rock (an investment banker who had been a student of Georges Doriot at Harvard and who had just relocated from New York after facilitating the Fairchild deal) founded the limited-partnership company Davis & Rock in San Francisco. They mainly raised money on the East Coast for investment in the Bay Area. In 1962 Bill Draper and Franklin Johnson formed Draper & Johnson. In 1961 the Venture Capital Journal started being published in San Francisco.

The Integrated Circuit

The major jump for computers came with the invention of the integrated circuit. It was Jack Kilby at Texas Instruments who (in 1958) invented the integrated circuit, a tiny silicon device containing a large number of electronic switches. With Kilby's technique, multiple transistors could be integrated on a single layer of semiconductor material. Previously, transistors had to be individually carved out of silicon or germanium and then wired together with the other components of the circuit. This was a difficult, time-consuming and error-prone task that was mostly done manually. Putting all the electrical components of a circuit on a silicon or germanium "wafer" the size of a fingernail greatly simplified the process. It heralded the era of mass production. The first customers of integrated circuits were the Air Force and NASA.

The golden team at Fairchild Semiconductor merely improved the idea. In 1959, Jean Hoerni invented the planar process that enabled great precision in silicon components, and Robert Noyce designed a planar integrated circuit. Fairchild introduced the 2N1613 planar transistor commercially in April 1960, and the first commercial single-chip integrated circuit in 1961 (the Fairchild 900), a few months after the Texas Instruments' SN502.

Meanwhile, Fairchild continued to harness talent, such as Don Farina, James Nall, Bob Norman (from Sperry Gyroscope), Don Valentine (their Los Angeles sales manager), and Charles Sporck (production manager), all hired in 1959. Later hires were Jerry Sanders (1961, sales, from Motorola), Jack Gifford (1963, Los Angeles sales and in 1966 product marketing in Mountain View), Mike Markkula (sales). However, Fairchild Semiconductor made a big mistake when it did not focus on integrated circuits. A number of engineers who disagreed (led by David Allison) left Fairchild to start Signetics in 1961. Signetics benefited from the decision in 1963 taken by the Department of Defense to push for architectures based on integrated circuits. Throughout 1964, Signetics dwarfed Fairchild and everybody else in the manufacturing of integrated circuits.

Fairchild is important in the history of Silicon Valley's semiconductor industry not only for the technology it patented but also for the people it hired and trained. In fact, its contribution might be bigger as a creator of talent than as an innovator. Fairchild represented a corporate culture that treasured human resources: it hired the best of the best, and then it trained them to become even better. To use a physics metaphor, the potential energy at Fairchild was probably bigger than all the kinetic energy it ever produced.

An early supporter of the Bay Area's semiconductor industry was Seymour Cray, a former Univac engineer who had founded the Minneapolis-based Control Data Corporation (CDC) in 1957. He built the first large transistorized computer in 1960 (the CDC 1604). Cray sponsored research at Fairchild that resulted in a transistor made of silicon that was faster than any transistor ever made of germanium. Cray's new "super-computer," the CDC 6600 was first delivered in 1964 to the Lawrence Livermore Lab and would employ 600,000 transistors made by Fairchild. General Electric, RCA and Texas Instruments made germanium-based products. Fairchild became the first silicon-only company. The Bay Area was beginning to get into computer hardware, but it was still largely software illiterate.

The Advent of DNA

Meanwhile, the great scientific news of the decade came from England. In April 1953, Francis Crick and US-born James Watson, two molecular biologists working in Britain at the Cavendish Laboratory (the Department of Physics of Cambridge University), discovered the double helical structure of DNA. The code of life looked amazingly similar to a computer program. The always alert Fred Terman, who was then Stanford's provost, foresaw the potential of biotechnology. He decided to invest in Stanford's chemistry department.

9. Graybeard Funders: Venture Capital in its Clubby Days (1955-78)

Early Venture Capital in Silicon Valley

Venture capital sprung from government action. One of the first steps toward a professionally-managed venture capital industry was the passage of the Small Business Investment Act of 1958. The launch of the Soviet Sputnik satellite scared the US Congress enough to pass the law. It officially allowed the US Small Business Administration (SBA) to license private "Small Business Investment Companies" (SBICs) to help the financing and management of the small entrepreneurial businesses in the United States. SBICs had problems. They could borrow four dollars for every one to invest, and many did. But this was unsuitable for risky venture investing. Government guarantees for the debt usually meant taxpayers subsidized dumb deals and bankers made off with the best.

Due to these problems, many venture capital pioneers are conflicted about whether the SBIC program did much to advance the art and practice of venture investing. The booming IPO market proved the model of investing in new companies, as some SBICs cash out at attractive levels. SBICs did give a boost to early venture firms, and some like Franklin "Pitch" Johnson thought the new law made the US "see that there was a problem and that [venture investing] was a way to do something... it formed the seed of the idea and a cadre of people like us." Bill Draper, the first West Coast venture capitalist, has been more blunt: "[Without it] I never would have gotten into venture capital. . . it made the difference between not being able to do it, not having the money." Many believe SBICs filled a void from 1958 to the early 1970s, by which point the partnership-based venture firms took off. The US government, however, lost most of the $2 billion it put into SBIC firms.

So why did Silicon Valley lead the way with its venture capital industry? Geography and history were part of the answer. Before WWII, the northeast dominated because the technical skill was in Boston (MIT) and the capital was there too (Boston and New York City). The West Coast took over because of the sunny weather and the federal funds that boosted the engineering departments at Stanford and Berkeley (along with shrewd institution building by Fred Terman, described in another chapter in this book). Additionally, the West Coast was much more a meritocracy, where young engineers could lead companies and young bankers could fund them. Fairchild itself was the nucleus of many semiconductor startups in the 1960s. So due to the Valley's world-class engineering departments, strong commercial track record (HP, Fairchird, Varian, etc.), and a seasoned group of entrepreneurs, smart venture capitalists started moving West.

Four Venture Capital Firms Set the Tone

Four venture capital firms formed in the 1960s are worth noting. Most of these greybeards had financial backgrounds and not strong technical backgrounds.

The first notable firm of the 1960s was Davis and Rock, founded by Arthur Rock and Tommy Davis in 1961 with $5 million. Rock initially began more as an agent than as a principal in an investment company, doing deals on the side. He was a banker at Hayden, Stone & Co. in New York and had been flying to California to do technology deals. One early deal in 1957 was getting some scientists who left Shockley Labs a new home at Fairchild Semiconductor, after Sherman Fairchild (an inventor and the largest owner of IBM stock) decided to back them for $1.5 million. After four years on red-eye flights, Rock moved to California because of the scientific energy around Stanford, created by Terman. He founded his own firm and played a key role in launching Teledyne, Intel, Apple, and many other high-tech companies.

An early big deal for Rock was Scientific Data Systems, funded for $280,000 in 1962 and sold for $990 million in 1969. Rock's biggest deal was funding Intel in 1968, after Noyce called him to say "Gee, I think maybe Gordon [Moore] and I do want to leave Fairchild Semiconductor and go into business for ourselves." This was because Fairchild had died, and the bureaucratic new CEO in New Jersey didn't want to pay the scientists options or give them management control of the division, a big mistake. Rock raised $2.5 million for Gordon and Noyce's team, as no venture firm was large enough to fund that amount as a single commitment. Rock even wrote their business plan. He always attributed Intel's success to the scientific talent and the great manager-engineer CEOs (Noyce first, then Moore, then Grove).

Rock's firm was financially thriving. Between 1961 and 1968, Davis & Rock invested $3 million (after raising $5 million) and returned $100 million to their investors. Yet Davis and Rock dissolved in 1968, despite a stellar run because Rock was a difficult man to work with (junior partners didn't want to stay with him).

A second notable early West Coast venture capital company was Draper, Gaither & Anderson (officially the first venture firm in the West Coast in 1959). It was later re-formed as the Draper and Johnson Investment Company in 1962, by William Henry Draper III (a student of Doriot's) and Franklin P. ("Pitch") Johnson, Jr. Bill Draper's father was responsible for the economic reconstruction of Germany and Japan under the Marshall Plan, and put Bill in touch with an associate, Fred Anderson, to start a venture firm in 1959. In 1962, Draper and Johnson started their firm with $150,000 of their family money and $300,000 of SBIC money. In 1965, they merged their ship with Sutter Hill Ventures and brought Paul Wythes on board. Sutter Hill set the early tone of the Valley, partnering with other venture firms to syndicate investments (i.e. split them into pieces to co-invest in). While in the venture capital business, Bill Draper invested in Apollo Computer Dionex, Integrated Genetics, Quantum, Activision, Measurex, Hybritech, and LSI Logic.

Draper's earthy philosophy was about people. He believed that if you back the right person, "he'll get you out of a bum business, a bum product idea, a bum service idea, and move you into a better one." But the wrong person with a great idea would never get anywhere and instead just bumble and fumble.[15]

Bill's son, Tim Draper, left Alex Brown & Sons in 1985 to become the third generation of venture capitalists in his family with the formation of Draper Fisher Jurvetson. Tim restructured a family-owned Small Business Investment Company (SBIC) that had been set up by his father in 1979. Tim then created an early-stage venture capital fund, which invested in successes like Hotmail, Skype (where a $2.5 million investment turned into $2.5 billion), Baidu, and so on. Pitch Johnson went on to form Asset Management Company, in 1965, and over his career he made over 250 venture investments, including legendary ones like Amgen, IDEC Pharmaceuticals, Octel, Sierra Semiconductor, Tandem Computer, Teradyne, and Verity.

The third notable firm was Sutter Hill Ventures, founded by Bill Draper and Paul Wythes in 1964. Wythes had held technical marketing and sales positions at Beckman Instruments and Honeywell. He went on to be a Founding Director of the National Venture Capital Association, the main industry association, and served on over 27 boards and led Sutter Hill investments in Tellabs, Xidex, Linear Technology and AmeriGroup. Sutter Hill pioneered a few techniques: the warehousing of people, today called having entrepreneurs-in-residence where talented entrepreneurs simmer for a while to come up with a venture; the offering of simple terms of straight preferred stock and a handshake (no complicated term sheets); the backing people from a diversity of backgrounds, including immigrants and women (e.g. Andy Gabor of Diablo Corp. or Donna Dubinsky of Palm Corp.). Wythes philosophy on his work is pithy: "Venture capitalists don't create successful companies, entrepreneurs do... we are in the business of building businesses. We're not trying to do financial transactions."

In 1969, the entire venture capital community could meet at the Mark Hopkins Hotel in San Francisco for lunch. There were about 20 people. Many had intimate connections with Arthur Rock, who partnered with and mentored others. These venture firms were the beginning of the institutionalized venture capital business where funds were dedicated specifically to starting companies. They had small amounts of money and

---

[15] Draper, William H. III. "Early Bay Area Venture Capitalists: Shaping the Economic and Business Landscape," oral history conducted by Sally Smith Hughes in 2009, Regional Oral History Office, The Bancroft Library, University of California, Berkeley, 2008.

a limited number of practitioners. But they set the stage for the great venture firms of the 1970s, of which three have set the standard.

Fred Terman and the Venture Capital Industry

The fourth notable firm was the Mayfield Fund, started by Tommy Davis, who moved to California from the East Coast to join a land development company, Kern County Land and Development Company (KCLD), so he could ride horses in his spare time. Davis worked in the Central Valley farm country but started making investments in Silicon Valley and eventually linked with Stanford dean Fred Terman.

Terman's involvement with venture capital started when Stanford President Wally Sterling met George Montgomery of KCLD in February 1957. KCLD was a Southern California-based financial company primarily involved in the agriculture, land, and oil businesses. Montgomery told Sterling that he and his associate, Tommy Davis, wanted to invest in the electronics industry. Sterling had Terman contact Montgomery.

Montgomery and Davis were developing ideas about how to invest in the electronics business. Initially, Terman brushed them off and suggested KCLD contract with professors Joe Pettit and Edward Ginzton to advise them on small companies to purchase. Montgomery and Davis, though, decided they were not interested in owning shares of stock in a bigger company like HP or Lockheed. They were more interested in growth and wanted to be directly involved in the creative construction of a young technology and to interact directly with management.

Davis wrote Terman a letter in 1957 explaining that he wanted to combine KCLD's capital with the technical skills and creative ability of engineers to build up young companies. Engineers would benefit financially through their equity stake in the company and emotionally through having control over their own venture and surroundings. They could also rely on KCLD to build up the operations element with legal, accounting, personnel, and other functions done for them. Davis wanted to "offer a vehicle for young creative talents that few companies could or would be willing to provide, especially the large electrical, electronic and aircraft companies." Both the engineers and KCLD would keep a large portion of ownership and hence be responsible for the venture's success.[16]

The letters between Tommy Davis and Fred Terman showed their ideas about what a venture capital firm should be. When KCLD wanted Davis to focus on buildings and oil wells, he joined Rock in 1963. After one partnership cycle, he left to start the Mayfield Fund in 1969 with Wally Davis, with about $3 million raised. Davis wanted a connection to Stanford through an advisory board to his new venture capital firm. He wanted Stanford engineering school faculty who were close to new ideas

---

[16] Davis to Terman, 9 August 1957, Terman Papers SC 160, Series III, Box 34, Fol. 6.

that could potentially form the basis of a startup company. Davis recruited Stanford engineering professors such as Bill Miller, John Linvill, Bob, and Michel Boudart as advisors for the first Mayfield Fund. These advisors were special limited partners in the fund. They received a part of the carried interest of the fund and were touted as a "Brain Trust" to raise money. Davis formed a close relationship with Stanford University and its technical professors, something all the venture firms do today. Mayfield focused on early-stage hi-tech companies, and its impressive roster of investments included 3Com, Amgen, Atari, Compaq, Genentech, Sandisk, and more.

Terman viewed consulting and startup companies as recruitment and retention issues. Terman's own goal was to get premier faculty to join Stanford. The prospect of being able to launch a company growing out of their research was an attraction in Terman's view and frequently was an incentive to come to Stanford, but not the reason for recruiting faculty in the first place. Similarly, in order to retain high quality faculty it was important that the University not create obstacles to entrepreneurial activity. Terman's policy was not to push people into entrepreneurial activity, but not to stand in their way if they wanted to pursue it.

Later Stanford did have a formal plan for venture capital investment. Rod Adams wrote a memo in 1978 called "Venture Capital: A Policy Paper for Stanford University." He argued that Stanford should benefit not just from the licenses on intellectual property at Stanford's Office of Technology and Licensing, but also from a flow of ideas, tacit knowledge, and techniques that would not necessarily get patented or lead to the formation successful companies in the area. Stanford could, however, benefit by investing in venture capital funds whose purpose was to shape these sorts of resources into viable high-tech firms. Adams's idea was for a staff of trained specialists within the Stanford Management Company (SMC) to use their local contacts within the financial industry to invest as limited partners in the best funds. These investments started in 1981 at 1% of the endowment and later increased to approximately 6% of the endowment by 2002.

Kleiner Perkins, Sequoia Capital, and NEA Multiply Money

The growth of the venture capital industry was fueled by a number of venture firms on Sand Hill Road, running along the northern boundary of Stanford's campus. The three most important firms historically were Kleiner, Perkins, Caufield & Byers (Kleiner Perkins or KPCB) and Sequoia Capital, both founded in 1972, plus New Enterprise Associates (NEA), founded in 1978.

First, KPCB was in 1972 the world's largest venture capital partnership when it raised $8 million; about 50% of the fund came from the secretive Pittsburgh billionaire Henry Hillman. Gene Kleiner was an alumnus of Fairchild Semiconductor and Tom Perkins was a protégé of David Packard at HP plus a favored student of Doriot's at Harvard. Both were deeply plugged into the Silicon Valley network, and neither wanted to meet the other when the investment banker Sandy Robertson put them in touch. KPCB's model would be different because they practiced hands-on management, organized portfolio companies in an informal keiretsu (a group of companies with interlocking business relationships), and formalized the business by distributing audited quarterly and annual reports to investors. They also had investor friendly terms like: an 8-year fund life limit; a clause saying all capital must be returned in full to limited partners before the GP received any compensation; a restriction that no profits could be re-invested; a term that the GPs could not invest in deals outside the partnership for their personal benefit.

After a few early failures such as a semiconductor deal, a tennis shoe resoling company, and a snowmobile-to-motorcycle conversion kit company, Kleiner and Perkins decided to focus on their strengths: computers.Their deal flow plus connections to engineering professors and entrepreneurs were critical. Still, the phones didn't ring at all in those early years. As Kleiner stated: "We just didn't wait around for deals to come to us. You had to create the deals to be really successful." For example, Perkins teamed up with an old colleague at HP, Jimmy Treybig, to create a company making fault tolerant computers that could operate on a reduced level when one part failed. Banks were an ideal customer as they needed computers that didn't fail. In 1974 Treybig and Perkins founded Tandem Computers. The company went public in 1977 and had $2.3 billion in sales by 1996.

One of Perkin's great innovations was his keiretsu method of investing. It comes from the Japanese word "keiretsu," which describes a set of interlocking relationships among Japanese suppliers and manufacturers (which in turn came from the zaibatsu of pre-WW II). Basically KPCB encouraged its companies to help each other by forming buy-sell, licensing, or endorsement arrangements. It provided companies with regular updates on the strategies and plans of their peer group, along with organizing half a dozen formal gatherings of portfolio company CEOs and other key executives each year. Perkins' protégé, John Doerr, stated it thus: "Keiretsu are rooted in the principle that it is really hard to get an important company going and that the fastest and surest way to build an important new company is to work with partners."

One example was Destineer, which KPCB incubated with Mobile Telecommunications Technologies in 1990 to develop a one-way and two-way nationwide messaging service. Since Wireless Access, another Kleiner Perkins company, was developing advanced pager technology, a Kleiner Perkins partner suggested that the two companies work together. The two companies, along with Motorola and Destineer, co-developed protocol, networking, and chip technologies, all of which have been fused into SkyTel, Mobile's paging network.

After the dot.com bust, when the word keiretsu become disfavored, Brook Byers stated "It's not keiretsu, it's relationship capital." It could more broadly be seen as a network, a Rolodex, or just outside business help with domain knowledge or potential sales leads.

Tom Perkins further elaborated on his investment philosophy in his memoir, where he wrote that "money is the least differentiated of all commodities. With water, you've got Calistoga, Perrier, and San Pellegrino, all noticeably different. With sugar there's the cane and beet variety; some can tell the difference. But with money it's all the same." Perkins felt a venture capitalist was in the business of selling money to entrepreneurs and so needed to add value to differentiate oneself. He attributed his success to not just waiting for "fully fleshed-out business plans, and full teams" coming in through the mail or the front door. Instead, he incubated ventures that he brainstormed with entrepreneurs, and he actively built high-tech teams.[17]

Kleiner himself had some interesting apothegms. Two of them were: "When the money is available – take it" and "The more difficult the decision, the less it matters what you choose."

Another big 1970s win for Kleiner and Perkins was born from failure. KPCB had hired Bob Swanson to handle deals, but nothing worked out, so they politely asked him to leave. Swanson started learning about the emerging field of biotechnology and started trading ideas with Herb Boyer, a biochemistry professor at UCSF. Boyer had developed a technique to make drugs by splicing DNA from one organism directly into the genes of another, and thought it would take 10 years to commercialize. Tom Perkins used KPCB's funds to do a proof-of-concept trial, then bought a 25% stake for $100,000 in 1976. The company would become Genentech and it was the first commercial venture to synthesize insulin in 1978, helping millions of diabetics worldwide. Genentech's 1980 IPO raised $35 million. KPCB did quite well.

Second, Sequoia Capital was started by Don Valentine in 1972. He had come to California due to the military, and then worked at a string of technology companies, ending as a salesman at Fairchild Semiconductor. He left for National Semiconductor. At both companies he evaluated technology and markets while running sales and marketing, and he found the same problem. Engineers could do amazing things but capital for projects was scarce. So Valentine had a system for how to invest corporate capital.

Valentine focus at Fairchild and National was in investing in companies that addressed very large markets and solved a specific kind of

---

[17] Perkins, Tom. Valley Boy: The Education of Tom Perkins. New York: Gotham Reprint, 2008, p. 131.

problem. At National, with its limited engineering resources to make custom circuits, he had to help the company to decide what business to accept and what to decline. Over a period of four or five years Valentine created "a more intuitive investment selection process based on huge markets and solutions that made a significant short-term commercial sense."[18] The market came first, technology second.

Due to his success, Valentine was approached by The Capital Group, a large Los Angeles-based mutual fund company. It was launching a business in the creation of a trust company, and their clients wanted some exposure to the venture capital business. Valentine was invited to join that start-up and create a venture capital company which would be part of The Capital Group. That's how Sequoia was started, though Valentine took it independent from Capital Group in 1975. One early big success was Nolan Bushnell's Atari, which was three years old in 1976 with a $3 million profit on $40 million in sales. Atari needed money to grow. Valentine put in Sequoia money and raised funds from the Mayfield Fund, Time Inc., and Fidelity Ventures. Within that same year, Bushnell realized Atari needed more money and the entire company was sold to Warner Communications for $28 million, netting the venture capital investors a quick profit.

Valentine's greatest deal was funding Apple Computer. Bushnell had suggested that Steve Jobs and Steve Wozniak visit Valentine. Valentine got them to focus on marketing and "think big." He teamed the young kids with Mike Markkula, a thirty year old marketing manager, so they could launch Apple in 1977. The company raised $517,500 in January 1978 from Venrock ($288,000), Sequoia ($150,000), and Arthur Rock, with a promise to keep the shares for 5 years. Valentine, in a dumb move, sold his stock in the summer of 1979 for tax reasons and to make distributions to investors. It was a big mistake, as Rock's $57,000 stake was worth nearly $22 million by 1980 (it would be worth over ten billion dollars by 2012 if he had kept it). Other notable successes were funding Cisco in 1987 and Yahoo in 1997.

Valentine developed an "aircraft carrier" method of investing, where a "carrier" company would sail with a fleet of other companies for servicing and defense purposes. So a strong portfolio company would be supported by smaller ones. Apple was a carrier and 13 other companies were the smaller ships to serve it (e.g. Tandon Corp. to make disk drives for Apple's computers). This is a center-periphery model compared to Kleiner's distributed network model of portfolio investments. Valentine was also uncomfortable just relying on the quality of people. He wanted to know the potential market size, momentum toward there, and the exact product and application.

---

[18] Valentine, Donald T. "Interview with Don Valentine," Silicon Genesis: An Oral History of Semiconductor Technology. April 21, 2004, Menlo Park, California. http://silicongenesis.stanford.edu/transcripts/valentine.htm.

One interesting point Valentine mentioned about VC: semiconductors were the core. Valentine estimated in 2004 that Sequoia has financed probably 600 different companies, with about 40 of those companies being semiconductor companies. Semiconductors were a fundamental business to the digital revolution. By the early 1970s, there were many semiconductor companies based in the Santa Clara Valley as well as early computer firms using their devices and programming.

In 1973, with the number of new venture capital firms increasing, leading venture capitalists formed the National Venture Capital Association (NVCA). The NVCA would serve as the industry trade group. Venture capital firms suffered a temporary downturn in 1974, when the stock market crashed and investors were naturally wary of this new kind of investment fund.

Third, Dick Kramlich, Chuck Newhall, and Frank Bonsal started NEA in 1978 with $17 million. Kramlich had previously joined Arthur Rock in 1969 to do some investments. That partnership had turned $6 million into $40 million. NEA changed the venture model in two ways: it raised the first billion dollar fund, and it tried to go national, having offices in both Silicon Valley, the Boston Route-128 corridor, and in other key cities. Chuck and Frank stayed on the East Coast and Dick operated from the Valley. They communicated daily by telephone, making early investments in Apple and 3Com. By NEA-3 in 1984, the third partnership fund, they had raised $125 million. Yet so much money was chasing deals that prices were high and NEA made bad deals too. By 2000, NEA had about 130 IPOs, nearly 130 companies acquired, and $4.3 billion distributed, including Immunex, Juniper (a $3 million investment for NEA that turned into $1.5 billion), Silicon Graphics, 3Com, PowerPoint, and Healtheon.

Other investors were active in the venture world, at least in the growth stage and on the East Coast. The famous investment banker Andre Meyer at Lazard Freres involved his partners' capital in various growth venture investments such as Avis (car rentals) and Allied Concord (specialty finance). One of his younger partners, John Vogelstein, was tasked to a failing deal and eventually left. He joined Warburg Pincus, which traces its roots to E.M. Warburg & Co., an investment banking and private investment counseling firm founded in 1939 by the German-Jewish banker Eric Warburg. In 1966, Warburg's firm joined with Lionel I. Pincus & Co., a venture capital and financial consulting firm. Lionel Pincus and John Vogelstein, who joined in January 1967, brought a "professionalized approach" to venture capital. Warburg Pincus and the National Venture Capital Association, which Pincus helped found, played a central role in negotiating with the Labor Department to revise ERISA regulations which had restricted investments in those asset classes. Finally, Charles Waite at Greylock and Richard Burnes at Charles River Associates were doing interesting work in Boston.

10. Hippies: Fairchild, the Spin-offs, the Minicomputer, Artistic Creativity, and Social Revolution (1961-68)

The Era of Large Computer Projects

IBM was the 800-pound gorilla of computers in the decade of love and protest. After its successful introduction in 1960 of the 7000 series that was transistorized, IBM owned more than 81% of the computer market. However, the market wasn't too big. Computers were cumbersome and expensive. In 1960, the price of an IBM 7030 was $13.5 million. They were even more expensive to run. Only the government and a few large corporations could operate one.

However, IBM had struck some lucrative contracts. One of them was for automating American Airlines' reservation system. Someone at IBM had noticed that an airline's reservation system was very similar to the monitoring problem solved by SAGE. IBM basically adapted SAGE to the airline business, and the result was a system called SABRE, the first online transaction processing. It debuted in 1960 and took over all reservations by 1964.

In the next three years, several foundational elements of computing were established by researchers throughout the country in a remarkable series. In 1961, Fernando Corbato at MIT created the first working time-sharing system, Compatible Time Sharing System (CTSS). This allowed many users to share the same computer and to remotely access a computer, an IBM 7090/94. The idea of time sharing spread both to academic and industrial centers to minimize the cost per user of using a computer. Next, Charles Bachman at General Electric in New York developed the first database management system, Integrated Data Store or IDS. AT&T introduced the first commercial modem. Steve Russell and others at MIT implemented the computer game "Spacewar" on a PDP-1, a sign that enthusiastic computer engineers were beginning to see the computer as a vehicle for entertainment.

Standards, graphics, and new programming languages followed. In 1963, a standards committee worked out the "American Standard Code for Information Interchange" (ASCII) to encode character symbols in the digital format of the computer. That year, MIT-student Ivan Sutherland demonstrated "Sketchpad," a man-machine graphical communication system. It was the first computer program ever with a Graphical User Interface (GUI) and the first computer program to display three-dimensional objects on a two-dimensional screen. Gyorgy Kemeny and

Thomas Kurtz invented the BASIC programming language for the Dartmouth College time-sharing system.

Something monumental happened in 1964. IBM introduced the System/360, a computer that was controlled by a full-fledged "operating system," the OS/360. IBM's chief architect, Gene Amdahl, had designed a family of computers that were software-compatible and, to some extent, modular. Customers could migrate and upgrade their software applications at will. The processor and the memory of the machines of this generation were enclosed in a metal cabinet called a "mainframe," and somehow the term came to identify that generation of computers. This eventually led to the mass production of software applications.

This computer was the result of a government contract, although not a military one. In January 1956, two government agencies had sponsored a project code-named "Project Stretch." One was the National Security Agency (NSA), which needed to process character strings and the other one was the Atomic Energy Agency, which needed to carry out numerical calculations. In April 1961, Gene Amdahl had completed the new transistorized computer, now renamed the IBM 7030, which was good at encoding both characters and numbers. On this project, Werner Buchholz coined the term "byte" for eight bits. Only nine 7030s were built. They were sold to government agencies and large research centers. Yet the 7030's architecture laid the foundations for the 360, a mainframe for both the scientific and the business communities.

IBM was still the industry leader. By 1965 IBM had a 65% market share of the electronic computer industry. Its main competitors were called "the seven dwarfs" and were: Burroughs in Detroit, mostly targeting banks; Sperry Rand in New York (formerly Remington Rand, which included Univac and ERA), which still relied on military contracts; Control Data in Minneapolis, an offshoot of ERA that consistently beat the competition in terms of processing speed; Honeywell in New Jersey, whose computer business was purchased from Datamatic and started in 1955 near Boston; NCR, which in 1953 had purchased Los Angeles-based Computer Research Corporation and began to specialize in computers for banking; and finally the New York-based conglomerates General Electric and RCA.

It was difficult to compete with these mainframe companies. A group of computer engineers including Max Palevsky from Packard formed Scientific Data Systems (SDS) in September 1961 in Los Angeles. They raised $1 million from Arthur Rock and the Rosenwald family, heirs to the Sears Roebuck fortune. They introduced their first model, the 24-bit silicon computer SDS910. It was basically a mini-computer, meant to challenge IBM and the other mainframe manufacturers. Their first customer was NASA. The SDS 940 was built in April 1966 for the time-sharing system at UC Berkeley, funded by DARPA's Project Genie.

The Era of Large Computer Networks

Seeds were also being planted for connecting computers through a network. In 1962 Paul Baran worked at the RAND Corporation, a Los Angeles-area "think tank" that mainly consulted for the armed forces. He proposed that a distributed network of computers was the form of communication least vulnerable to a nuclear strike, a highly sensitive topic during the Cold War. At the same time Joseph Licklider, an MIT professor of psychology and a SAGE alumnus who had become a consultant, was preaching about the power of computer networks. In 1965, Ted Nelson coined the word "hypertext" to refer to nonsequential navigation of a document.

The most influential ideas of those years were tied to government agencies. The Department of Defense established the Advanced Research Projects Agency (ARPA) in February 1958. Within a few years, this agency provided the highest proportion of funding for computer engineering research in the US. In October 1962, ARPA created a specific office devoted to computers, the Information Processing Techniques Office (IPTO). IPTO hired the visionary Licklider from MIT and BBN to be its first director. In his new capacity, Licklider sponsored the pioneering time-sharing system Project Machine Aided Cognition (MAC) at MIT. This "project" was a laboratory that opened in July 1963 and was devoted to artificial intelligence and time sharing. It featured Marvin Minsky as the director and John McCarthy as the resident visionary. Corbato envisioned a successor to CTSS, eventually named Multiplexed Information and Computing Service (MULTICS), a collaboration between MIT, General Electric, and Bell Labs.

Licklider also dispatched money to the budding research centers in the Bay Area: Stanford University and UC Berkeley (neither of which had a graduate program in computer science yet) plus Douglas Engelbart's team at SRI. Licklider's funds established a West-coast counterpart to Project MAC, called Project Genie. It started in 1964 at UC Berkeley and its main achievement was a public-domain time-sharing system. Several team members started a company, Berkeley Computer Corporation (BBC), to market it.

Another benefactor of Engelbart was NASA's Office of Advanced Research and Technology in the person of Bob Taylor. He had joined NASA in 1961 after working for Maryland-based defense contractor Martin Marietta. NASA was interested in using computers for flight control and flight simulation, not purely "number crunching." Licklider was succeeded at IPTO in 1963 by Ivan Sutherland, who in 1965 hired Bob Taylor away from NASA. Taylor used ARPA to promote his views. He wanted computers to be more useful than for just rapid large-scale arithmetic, and one way was to connect them in a network.

Taylor was a crucial person in the US government, funding key projects in computer science research. In February 1966, Taylor launched an ARPA project to create a computer network, later named ARPAnet, the predecessor to the Internet. Wes Clark was a UC Berkeley graduate who joined the Whirlwind project at MIT and designed MIT's minicomputer LINC (Laboratory INstrument Computer) in 1962. Then at Washington University of St Louis, Clark suggested not having each node write its own software on its own mainframe in order to connect to a network. Instead, the network should hand each node a small "gateway" computer, later named "router," in charge of networking functions, the same one at each node, letting the local mainframe do what it normally did. Bolt Beranek and Newman (BBN) won the contract to develop the Interface Message Processor (IMP), a customized version of the Honeywell DDP-516. It was the first router.

Software and Services

Two major software ventures were created in Texas. Ross Perot founded Electronic Data Systems (EDS) in 1962 and invented the business of outsourcing. EDS would gladly implement custom software for any mainframe customer that did not have the in-house resources to do it. University Computing Company (later renamed Uccel) was founded in 1963 on the campus of Southern Methodist University by Sam and Charles Wyly with funding from Swiss billionaire Walter Haefner. Their product was the Tape Management System (TMS). Within a decade, EDS and Uccel would become two of the largest software companies in the world.

As the costs of owning and operating a mainframe were prohibitive for most companies, time-sharing became a lucrative business. In 1964 Tymshare started one of the most popular time-sharing services in Cupertino. It was the company that brought the software business to Silicon Valley in earnest. Tymshare later created a circuit-switched network that predated the Internet.

The impact of computers on existing jobs varied greatly between "white-collar" industries like professional services and "blue-collar" industries like manufacturing. The ones that became disposable were the white-collar workers, notably the accountants. From the very beginning of commercial computing, a computer was used to crunch numbers faster than an army of accountants, 24 hours a day, 7 days a week. Luckily for accountants, only the very large firms could afford a computer.

The history of manufacturing applications is tied to the Midwest, where many of the US's manufacturing giants resided. Their major problem was to guarantee the smooth flow of materials through the several stages of a production process. The structure that was used to list all the components of a product was called a "bill of material" (BOM). It was in the Midwest that IBM first tried to automate the management of the BOM. These firms were aware of Japan's "lean manufacturing," designed by Taichi Ohno at Toyota, which made factories much more efficient. In 1961 Joe Orlicky at J.I. Case, a manufacturer of tractors, implemented such an automated system on an IBM RAMAC 305. IBM engineers expanded that idea into more general systems named BOMP ("Bill Of Materials Planning") in 1963, LAMP ("Labor & Material Planning") in 1964, and PICS ("Production Information and Control System ") in 1966. Eventually the field got the name MRP (first "Material Requirements Planning" but later "Manufacturing Resource Planning"). Each generation integrated more functions to further optimize the plant. In 1966, IBM was asked to cooperate with Rockwell and Caterpillar in designing a BOM system for the Apollo mission to the moon. The result was the Information Management System (IMS), a hierarchical database destined to become IBM's main software product.

The computer industry had started from government contracts. Fundamentally, computer manufacturers designed computers in collaboration with research laboratories for their use. Then the computer manufacturer would give the computer a business name, publicize it as a general-purpose machine, and educate large customers on what that machine could do for them. That changed in the 1960s. Increasingly the specifications were driven by private customers. The successful computer manufacturers learned to listen to their customers. The importance of software became more obvious. Software represented the application, i.e. the very reason that a customer purchased or rented a computer. Software caused a trend away from the general-purpose computer towards specialized vertical-market machines. In turn, vertical markets increased the demand for specialized software.

Computers in the Bay Area

Project MAC and the Arpanet, plus government-funded research on computer graphics and artificial intelligence at MIT, further increased Boston's lead over the rest of the nation. However, the Bay Area received Project Genie at UC Berkeley, leaving the San Jose area and the Santa Clara Valley in particular with no significant computing investment. Meanwhile, the computer industry was still mostly concerned with the big financial institutions of the East Coast and the manufacturing base of the Midwest. No major business or industrial user of computers existed in the Bay Area other than Bank of America. Silicon Valley was still insignificant from a tech perspective.

Science in the Bay Area

Stanford University was hyperactive at this time. Ed Ginzton continued Hansen's work on a particle accelerator propelled by ever more powerful klystron tubes (i.e. microwaves). Ginzton was the co-founder with Russell and Siguard Varian of Varian Associates. He still kept one foot in Stanford and had built by 1952 a one-billion electron-volt (1GeV) particle accelerator, the Mark III. It was the most powerful in the world and led to Stanford's Microwave Laboratory. In 1951, Pief Panofsky had been hired away from the Berkeley's Radiation Lab, where he had designed the latest proton accelerator. The two joined forces to launch "Project M" to build a more powerful machine. The result was the Stanford Linear Accelerator Center (SLAC), the longest linear accelerator in the world, which started operating in 1962.

Other East-Coast transplants thrived at Stanford. In 1963, John McCarthy, the founding father of artificial intelligence, moved to Stanford from MIT. He opened the Stanford Artificial Intelligence Laboratory (SAIL) on the hills a few kilometers away from the campus. It became a West-Coast alternative to Project MAC. Another transplant from the East Coast, Herbert Simon's pupil Ed Feigenbaum, designed the first knowledge-based or "expert" system, Dendral. It was an application of Artificial Intelligence to organic chemistry. It differed from Simon's Logic Theorist because it aimed at the specific domain of organic chemistry. Just as humans tend to be experts only in some areas, the project emphasized the importance of domain heuristics, the "rules of thumb" that experts use to find solutions to problems. Following his former scientist Carl Djerassi, Al Zaffaroni relocated biotech pioneer Syntex from Mexico City to the Stanford Industrial Park in 1963, and the following year the birth-control pill was introduced commercially.

Stanford's inventions even reached into music. In 1967, John Chowning, a graduate in music composition and a pioneer of computer music, was using the computer at the Stanford Artificial Intelligence Lab. He invented "frequency modulation synthesis," a technology that allowed an electronic instrument to simulate the sound of orchestral instruments. Yamaha refined this invention in the 1970s to manufacture electronic keyboards.

At SRI, Douglas Engelbart toyed with the first prototype of a computer mouse, part of a much bigger project funded by NASA to reinvent human-computer interaction. Indirectly, McCarthy and Engelbart started two different ways of looking at the power of computers. McCarthy represented the ideology of replacing humans with intelligent machines, whereas Engelbart represented the view of augmenting humans with machines that can make them smarter.

Stanford had become an ebullient scientific environment and it was rapidly expanding beyond the original quadrangle. In 1968, Niels Reimers established an office at Stanford University, later renamed Office of

Technology Licensing (OTL), to literally market Stanford's inventions to industry. By 2001 Stanford's OTL income would pass the $1 billion mark.

Fairchild's Golden Years

Progress at Fairchild had been rapid, and mainly due to two new employees from the Midwest: Dave Talbert and Bob Widlar. In 1963 Widlar produced the first single-chip "op-amp." In 1964 Talbert and Widlar created the first practical analog integrated circuit that created a new world of applications. Their work set the standards for the design of semiconductor devices.

Another isolated genius at Fairchild was Frank Wanlass, a Utah engineer who worked for Fairchild for less than two years. He completely changed the face of the semiconductor industry. In 1963 he invented a new technique to build integrated circuits called Complementary Metal-Oxide Semiconductor (CMOS). A Metal-Oxide Semiconductor (MOS) element consists of three layers: a conducting electrode (metal), an insulating substance (typically, glass), and the semiconducting layer (typically, silicon). Depending on whether the semiconductor has been doped with electrons (n-type) or holes (p-type), the MOS circuit can be nMOS or pMOS. CMOS, by combining both types in appropriate complementary symmetry configurations, greatly reduced current flows. Due to CMOS, MOS circuits had low power consumption, low heat, and high density, making it possible to squeeze hundreds of transistors on a chip and eventually to drop semiconductors into digital watches and pocket calculators. Wanlass quit Fairchild in December 1963 to join General Microelectronics (GMe), where the first MOS product was completed in 1964, months ahead of Fairchild. Yet Wanlass quit again after just one year and moved to the East Coast, and then back to his native Utah. The CMOS technology spread due to Wanlass' bee-like job changes and to his willingness to pollinate.

Initially the main customers for MOS circuits were government agencies like NSA and NASA. Lee Boysel, a young Michigan physicist working at Douglas Aircraft in Santa Monica, met Wanlass in 1964 and learned about MOS technology. In 1965 Lee Boysel moved to IBM's Alabama laboratories to apply his MOS skills. In 1966 Fairchild hired Boysel from IBM to start a MOS group. Boysel perfected a four-phase clocking technique to create very dense MOS circuits. In 1967, at a time when computer memory made of transistors were still a rarity, Boysel proved that he could build an entire computer with MOS technology.

Finally, there was another independent genius, Federico Faggin from Italy. He relocated to Fairchild's Palo Alto labs in 1968. Faggin invented silicon-gated MOS transistors. Silicon control gates are faster, smaller, and more energy-efficient than the aluminum control gates that had been commonplace. When both contacts and gates were made of silicon, the manufacturing process was simpler. It was this invention that allowed for the exponential growth in chip density, that is, the number of transistors that could be packed into a chip. Fairchild introduced the first silicon-gate integrated circuit in October 1968.

On the business side, Fairchild wasn't doing well. Under the casual management of Noyce, it was basically run by the marketing people. The competitors were catching up and the company posted its first loss in 1967.

The Semiconductor Community

Several semiconductor companies dotted the landscape between Stanford and San Jose, and almost all of them could trace their roots back to Fairchild. They were:

- Amelco (a division of Teledyne), co-founded in 1961 by three Fairchild founders including Jean Hoerni. It developed one of the first analog integrated circuits;
- Molectro, founded in 1962 by James Nall of Fairchild. In 1965 it hired the two Fairchild geniuses, Bob Widlar and Dave Talbert, and was acquired in 1967 by East-Coast based National Semiconductor. National eventually relocated to Santa Clara in 1968 after "stealing" many more brains from Fairchild (notably Charlie Sporck, Pierre Lamond, Don Valentine, Floyd Kwamie and Regis McKenna);
- General Microelectronics (GMe), founded in 1963 by Fairchild engineers (including Don Farina and Phil Ferguson), that developed the first commercial MOS (Metal-Oxide Semiconductor) integrated circuits in 1965 (for the Victor 3900 calculator), and was eventually (1966) bought by Philadelphia-based Philco (that in turn had been acquired by Ford Motor);
- Applied Materials Technology (AMT), founded in 1967 by Mike McNeilly;
- Electronic Arrays, founded in 1967 by Jim McMullen;
- Intersil, started in 1967 by Jean Hoerni to produce low-power CMOS circuits for electronic watches (funded by a Swiss watchmaker); and
- Monolithic Memories, founded in 1968 by Fairchild engineer Zeev Drori.

Fairchild was generating the same phenomenon of "spin-offs" similar to Federal Telegraph two generations earlier. Virtually the only semiconductor companies that were not based in the Santa Clara Valley were Texas Instruments, Motorola, and RCA. They did not have a genealogical tree like Fairchild's spin-offs. The Bay Area was unique in encouraging engineers to expand their ideas outside their employer and to continuously innovate over already successful businesses.

The vast incestuous network of local spin-offs was creating a self-sustaining manufacturing community. It mixed Darwinian competition and selection with symbiotic inter-dependent cooperation. It was this odd coupling of competition and cooperation that made the rapid pace of technological progress in semiconductors possible. The startups were very jealous of their industrial secrets but at the same time aware of who was working on what, and not shy to band together when advantageous.

As a whole, the system of companies which were easily born and easily "killed" was highly flexible and therefore capable of adapting quickly to changing circumstances. The system "metabolized" a complex technology by way of inter-related specialized technologies. The system exhibited a form of collective learning from the responses to its actions. The network as a whole, in fact, constituted an efficient organism that, just like biological organisms, was capable of adaptation, evolution, reproduction, metabolism and learning. It is not true that Silicon Valley companies shared knowledge. They were actually were jealous of their industrial secrets, but the network as a whole shared trade secrets through employee mobility and short-lived alliances.

In 1965, Gordon Moore predicted that the processing power of computers would double every 12 months (later revised to 18 months). This came to be known as "Moore's law." The semiconductor industry experienced a rapid acceleration towards increased power, smaller sizes and lower prices.

The Military Sponsors

The military played a fundamental role in fostering this process. The new technologies were too expensive and unstable to be viable for the general market. The military was the only entity that was willing to experiment with novel technologies, and it did not bargain on price. The "Cold War" was even more powerful than World War II in motivating the US government to invest in research. Global intelligence and communications were becoming more important than the weapons themselves, which were really used only in Vietnam. And these systems were built out of microwave devices that were the Bay Area's specialty. The US government served as both a munificent venture capitalist that did not expect a return (not even co-ownership) yet acted as an inexpensive testbed. In 1965 Hewlett-Packard employed about 9,000 people, Fairchild had 10,000, and Lockheed's Missile Division had 28,000 employees. The defense industry was still dominant.

For communications, the field of digital signal processing was born due to the military. In 1964 the head of Sylvania's Electronic Defense Lab (EDL), Stanford alumnus Bill Perry, took most of his staff and formed Electromagnetic Systems Laboratory (ESL) in Palo Alto. He worked on electronic intelligence systems and communications in collaboration with Stanford and in direct competition with his previous employer. His idea was to embed computers in these systems. By turning signals into digital streams of zeros and ones, ESL pioneered the field of digital signal processing. It was initially for the new satellite reconnaissance systems designed by Bud Wheelon, a former Stanford classmate who in 1962 had been appointed director of the Office of Scientific Intelligence at the CIA.

ESL's innovation was not only technological, but in employee compensation too. Perry's intention was to replicate Hewlett-Packard's corporate culture, and in fact to better it. HP handed out stock only to management, but ESL was the first company to extend the program to every employee. Perry went on to become defense secretary under President Bill Clinton.

An important boost to integrated circuits came from NASA's Apollo mission to send a man to the moon. NASA had been using analog computers, but for this mission in August 1961 it commissioned MIT's Instrumentation Lab to build a digital computer. The Apollo Guidance Computer (AGC) was the first computer to use integrated circuits. Each unit used more than 4,000 integrated circuits from Fairchild. That number represented a significant share of the worldwide market for integrated circuits. In 1964 NASA switched to Philco's integrated circuits, thus turning Philco into a semiconductor giant and enabling it to buy General Microelectronics.

The semiconductor boom also created a fertile ground for hobbyists. Halted Specialties Company would become the first electronics superstore of Silicon Valley. It opened its doors in 1963 in Santa Clara to sell electronic components and instruments.

Few of the companies that had thrived in the age of microwave electronics made a successful transition to the age of the integrated circuit. The protagonists had changed. What had remained was the template of collaboration among university, industry, and the military.

Tech Companies beyond Semiconductors

Other tech companies besides semiconductors started to thrive also. In 1961 Laurence Spitters, a Wall Street investment banker who had moved to San Francisco and joined Ampex in 1958, founded Memorex in Santa Clara. He took three Ampex engineers with him to manufacture high-precision magnetic tapes that could also be used as data storage. At the other end of the bay, Berkeley wasn't just the site of student riots and psychoactive drug tests. In 1965, UC Berkeley's Lotfi Zadeh invented Fuzzy Logic. Ray Dolby, a former Ampex employee, founded Dolby Labs in Britain in 1965 and relocated to San Francisco in 1976. Also new investment companies sprouted, notably Sutter Hill Ventures, formed in 1964 by Bill Draper and Paul Wythes.

Towards a More Humane Electronic Brain

One big trend was that computers were becoming more affordable. In 1965, the Digital Equipment Corporation (DEC) of Boston unveiled the mini-computer PDP-8, which used integrated circuits. Designed by Gordon Bell and Edson de Castro, it was much smaller and cheaper than an IBM mainframe, selling for only $16,000. The success of this model launched Massachusetts Route 128 as a rival to Silicon Valley for innovation in computing. DEC spawned several companies, notably Data General, founded in 1969 by Edson de Castro, the brain behind the PDP-8. Its Nova introduced an elegant architecture that fit a 16-bit machine on a single board and that only had one instruction format, each bit of which had meaning. Also, unbeknownst to most in the US, in 1965 Italian computer manufacturer Olivetti introduced an affordable programmable electronic desktop computer, the P101.

Crowning this race to miniaturization, in 1967 Jack Kilby at Texas Instruments developed the first hand-held digital calculator. Computers were getting smaller and cheaper. However, very few people had personally seen one, and even fewer knew how to operate them. Computers were still an exotic topic. In 1966 there were 2,623 computers in the US, and 1,967 of them were owned by the Defense Department. Integrated circuits had been manufactured since 1958, but very few computer models employed them in 1965.

Hewlett-Packard was still concentrated on instrumentation. It got into computers (the HP 2116A in November 1966 using integrated circuits), desk calculators (the 9100A in 1968), and hand-held calculators (the HP-35 in 1972) only because they were the natural evolution of instrumentation. The 2116A was marketed as an "instrumentation computer" and boasted interfaces for more than 20 scientific instruments. It had been designed by engineers from Data Systems, a Detroit company that HP had acquired in 1964. Data Systems already marketed a computer, the DSI 1000. However casual and half-hearted, it was the beginning of the computer industry in Silicon Valley.

Computers were becoming more affordable, but they were still impossible to operate. In 1967, Nicholas Negroponte, originally an architect with a vision for computer-aided design, founded MIT's Architecture Machine Group to improve human-computer interaction. He had the same goal as Douglas Engelbart's team at SRI. Also in 1967 the artist Gyorgy Kepes, who had joined MIT's School of Architecture and Planning in 1946, founded MIT's Center for Advanced Visual Studies, a place for artists to become familiar with computer technology.

The chimera of having computers speak in human language had been rapidly abandoned, but there was still hope that computers could help translate from one human language to another. After all, computers had been invented to decode encrypted messages. The Hungarian-born Peter Toma, hired in 1958 by the Georgetown University machine-translation team, spent a decade refining his Russian-to-English machine-translation software until he could demonstrate his SYSTRAN on an IBM/360 in 1964. The ALPAC (Automatic Language Processing Advisory

Committee) report of 1966 discouraged the US from continuing to invest. Toma was forced to complete his program in Germany and he returned in 1968 to California to found Language Automated Translation System and Electronic Communications (LATSEC). It sold SYSTRAN to the military at the peak of the Cold War.

Unbeknownst to the masses and to the media, an important experiment in e-learning was conducted at Stanford for the first time in the world. Two psychology professors, Patrick Suppes and Richard Atkinson, created a computer-based program to teach children from lower-income families. Later, Suppes became the Terman of e-learning, encouraging local startups in this field.

Lasers

Laser technology was one of the other high-tech industries flowering in Silicon Valley. A Stanford graduate, Ted Maiman, working at Hughes Research Laboratories in Los Angeles, had demonstrated the first laser in May 1960. He beat the more famous teams of Charles Townes at Columbia University and Arthur Schawlow at Bell Labs, not to mention the very inventor of the laser, Gordon Gould, who had moved to the firm TRG (Technical Research Group) from Columbia. In 1959 Gould had coined the term, which stands for "Light Amplification by Stimulated Emission of Radiation." Schawlow joined Stanford's Microwave Lab in 1961.

Meanwhile, Eugene Watson and Earl Bell had worked at Varian in the 1950s, where Herb Dwight had led the project to build the first practical helium-neon laser. To capitalize on that invention, in 1961 Dwight and Bell founded Spectra-Physics in Mountain View, the world's first laser startup. In 1962 they hired Watson as a sales manager. Revenues soared mostly because labs all over the world wanted a taste of the new technology. Watson and Spectra-Physics' young scientist James Hobart then opened Coherent Radiation Laboratories at the Stanford Industrial Park. They staffed it with Spectra-Physics engineers and commercialized the more powerful lasers invented at Bell Labs (the carbon-dioxide laser) and at Spectra-Physics (the ion laser). Another spin-off of Spectra-Physics would be Chromatix in Sunnyvale. Spectra-Physics went on to build in 1974 the first bar-code scanner ever used in a store.

The laser was a formidable invention. No other invention would be integrated so quickly in society and become so pervasive in such a short time. Its uses were in bar-code scanners, compact discs, cutting and welding, holography, precision surgery, etc.

Culture and Society

The culture-makers of San Francisco could care less about computers. The arts were moving in the opposite direction, towards primitive, grotesque, and provocative forms of expression. The assault on the senses was global. In 1959, dancer and mime Ron Davis founded the R.G. Davis Mime Studio and Troupe, better known as the San Francisco Mime Troupe. It specialized in silent anti-establishment mimed comedies inspired by the Italian "commedia dell'arte." In 1961, Bruce Baillie and Mildred "Chick" Strands founded the San Francisco Cinematheque to show experimental films and videos. At the same time, Bruce Baillie started the artist-run cooperative Canyon Cinema that also distributed the films (one year before Jonas Mekas started the more famous Film-Makers Cooperative in New York). Composers Morton Subotnick and Ramon Sender established the San Francisco Tape Music Center to foster avant-garde music. Pauline Oliveros' dadaistic chamber music and Terry Riley's repetitive patterns had little to do with classical music. Subotnick indulged in chaotic live electronic music, due to Berkeley-based hobbyist Don Buchla, who built his first electronic synthesizer in 1963.

The experimental music of the Bay Area was, again, representative of an alternative lifestyle and an anti-conformist approach to innovation. Unlike Europe and the East Coast, where the audience was mainly elites and music specialists, in San Francisco experimental music reached a broad and diverse audience. It was, yet again, the spirit of the eccentric independent, indifferent to the rules and traditions of the genre. In 1962, Michael Murphy, a former Stanford student who had spent two years in India to practice meditation, opened the "Esalen Institute" at Big Sur to promote the integration of Eastern and Western philosophy and "spiritual healing." Esalen became the epicenter of the "human-potential movement," named after Aldous Huxley's lectures. The idea was that humans are not fully realizing their potential, but if they did, they could lead much better lives.

The visual arts found a new haven in the East Bay. Peter Voulkos, who had started the "Funk" movement by applying the aesthetics of abstract expressionism to ceramic sculptures, had moved to UC Berkeley in 1959. UC Davis, located between Berkeley and Sacramento, became a major artistic center. Pop art was pioneered by Wayne Thiebaud even before Warhol made it famous in New York. Ceramic artist Robert Arneson became the local leader of the funk aesthetics pioneered by Voulkos. William Wiley, who joined Davis in 1963, expanded funk to painting. Roy De Forest joined the faculty in 1965. The most influential of the Davis group was perhaps Wayne Thiebaud's assistant Bruce Nauman, who went on to dabble in a variety of media (photography, neon, video, printmaking, sculpture, performance). He established a praxis of interdisciplinary art. Meanwhile, the first public showing of computer art was held at San Jose State University in May 1963, organized by Joan Shogren, who had programmed a computer with "artistic" principles.

Something even more monumental was happening in the Bay Area. In 1964, Mario Savio at UC Berkeley started the "Free Speech Movement," the first major case of student upheaval, peaking with the "Sproul Hall Sit-In" of December in which 768 protesters were arrested. This movement eventually would lead to massive student marches and riots around the nation and Western Europe. Meanwhile, in the South Bay Ken Kesey organized the "Merry Pranksters," a group of young freaks who traveled around the country in a "Magic Bus." They lived in a commune in La Honda and experimented with acid.

LSD began to be manufactured in large quantities by Owsley "Bear" Stanley at the UC Berkeley campus. It soon became widely available and relatively cheap. UC Berkeley had hosted an Institute for Personality Assessment and Research since 1949. The CIA was involved from its inception and probably contributed to the diffusion of psychoactive drugs on campus. Incidentally, the most famous of LSD gurus, Timothy Leary, was at the time the director of the Kaiser Foundation Psychological Research in Oakland and taught at UC Berkeley. Yet he did not try LSD until 1960, when he returned to Harvard. Whatever the original source of hallucinogenic drugs, they became the common denominator of the Bay Area's cultural life, and the symbol of an attack on the "American way of life."

In 1965 the cultural world became even more effervescent. Ron Davis of the San Francisco Mime Troupe published the essay "Guerrilla Theatre." Ben Jacopetti inaugurated the Open Theater as a vehicle devoted to multimedia performances for the Berkeley Experimental Arts Foundation. Family Dog Productions organized the first hippie festival. The authorities had lost control of the situation and a youth culture was taking over the area, mainly in the Haight-Ashbury district. Word of mouth was spreading throughout the US and young people were attracted to San Francisco's extravagant and tolerant society. By 1966 the media could not ignore the phenomenon anymore. Stewart Brand organized the "Trips Festival," collating Ken Kesey's "Acid Test," Jacopetti's Open Theater, Sender's Tape Music Center, and rock bands. The Jefferson Airplane and the Grateful Dead popularized a new genre of music inspired by psychedelic drugs, acid-rock. Willie Brown formed the Artists Liberation Front at the Mime Troupe's Howard Street loft. The first issue of the San Francisco Oracle, an underground cooperative pamphlet, was published. Emmett Grogan and members of the Mime Troupe founded the "Diggers," a group of improvising actors and activists whose stage was the streets and parks of the Haight-Ashbury district and whose utopia was the creation of a Free City. The first "Summer of Love" of the hippies was going on, including a three-day "Acid Test" with the Grateful Dead performing. Huey Newton, Bobby Seale, Angela Davis, and other African-American, Oakland-based activists founded the socialist-inspired and black-nationalist "Black Panther Party." This was the violent counterpart to the pacifist "flower power" ideology of the hippies. The revolution was widespread and octopus-like.

The gay community, which on New Year's Day of 1965 had staged a widely publicized "Mardi Gras Ball," was indirectly a beneficiary of the hippie phenomenon. Eureka Valley, the area south of the Haight-Ashbury, was a conservative middle-class neighborhood that did not quite appreciate the crazy circus going on a few blocks away. Many families decided to leave for the suburbs and Eureka Valley became a ghost town. Gay couples, unwelcome elsewhere, were able to snatch up cheap Victorian homes and renovate them. The district soon became known for its main street, Castro Street.

Drugs, free speech, experimental music, non-marital sex, and gay love were main elements of the Bay Area's counterculture and defiance of social and political norms. This would be the same environment that scientists and hobbyists would later thrive in.

By the late 1960s, San Francisco's arts scene was still moving away from technology and towards nature and humanity. In January 1967, a "Human Be-In" was held at the Golden Gate Park. The beach town of Monterey hosted the first major rock festival and John Lion started the Magic Theatre. In 1968, Stewart Brand published the first "Whole Earth Catalog," a sort of alternative yellow pages that listed products targeting the hippie lifestyle and featured articles on all sorts of counterculture topics. Chip Lord founded the Ant Farm to promote avantgarde architecture and design.

The national media went berserk reporting from San Francisco about the bizarre youth counterculture. Millions of young people around the world started imitating it. The whole hippie phenomenon paralleled the Bay Area's flare in interest for computer science and the growth of its semiconductor industry. Indian musician Ali Akbar Khan founded the Ali Akbar College of Music in 1967 in Berkeley to teach and spread Indian classical music, which was becoming increasingly popular among rebellious youth like everything else from India and the Far East.

At the same time, many new residential areas were being created between San Francisco and San Jose. The underpopulated Bay Area fostered a different urban model than the one popularized by Manhattan's skyscrapers. There was plenty of free space south of San Francisco, and therefore no need for high-rise buildings. Earthquakes also helped shape the urban environment as an endless flow of flat buildings with no particular center. The community lay horizontally, reached by walking instead of elevators. The main square had disappeared. Even Main Street and Broadway (the two staples of urban topography in most US towns) were missing. San Francisco was called "the city" because the cities of Silicon Valley were not cities.

One of the most important events of 1965 for Silicon Valley had nothing to do with technology per se. The Immigration Act of 1965 greatly increased the quotas of immigrants allowed from various countries. It allowed immigration based on rare skills, such as software or hardware engineering. For example, only 47 scientists migrated to the US from Taiwan in 1965, but in 1967 the number was 1,321. That immigration law started a brain drain of engineers and scientists from Europe and especially the Far East towards Silicon Valley. This would have far-reaching consequences.

11. Chipmakers: A Case Study on Intel's Creation and Re-Creation (1965-98)

Three Men Start a Memory Chip Company

In 1965 Gordon Moore predicted that the power and complexity of integrated circuits would double every 18 months. Hence computers would be about twice as fast every two years and the range of applications would grow geometrically with this speed. This prediction would later be known as "Moore's law." Its implications were that the collective intelligence of humans would start growing faster, as Doug Engelbart wrote in his papers.

One of the most important companies pushing this advance was Intel Corp, founded by Gordon Moore and Robert Noyce. They chose Andy Grove as Director of Operations and their first employee. Moore and Noyce were plain-spoken American engineers.

Gordon Moore had grown up as a straight-talker in San Francisco and Pescadero, California. He was a lazy student who attended San Jose State and UC Berkeley. He eventually became serious and got a PhD from Caltech in chemistry and physics in 1954.

Bob Noyce was from the small Iowa town of Grinnell. Noyce barely managed to graduate from Grinnell College, where he studied under Grant Gale (who had one of the first few transistors invented at Bell Labs), after Noyce stole a farmer's pig as a prank. Luckily, Noyce went on to get a PhD in physics from MIT in 1953. He would go on to invent the integrated circuit in 1959, while Jack Kilby independently did so at Texas Instruments.

Grove came from a very different background. Grove had grown up in a Budapest occupied by Germans and then Russians; he had experienced the horrors of murder, pillage, and rape as a Jewish kid in genocidal times (he later named one of his books "Only the Paranoid Survive"). In 1963 Grove fled Hungary and eventually worked his way to New York City, where he got a degree in chemical engineering in City College, and then a PhD at UC Berkeley in 1963.

Noyce and Moore had met at Shockley Semiconductor in 1956, which was founded by William Shockley the year before. Shockley had co-invented the transistor and wanted to cash in on it by producing them. He recruited a dream team of scientists and engineers, most not even 30 years old yet, as he presented himself as a lone-wolf genius like Thomas Edison. Other stars were Jean Hoerni, Jay Last, Sheldon Roberts, Julius Blank, Victor Grinich, and Eugene Kleiner. Unfortunately Shockley was a horrible manager and a bit of a crank in business, so this group of eight, later called the "traitorous eight" left in a year.

In October 1957 the "traitorous eight" created a startup within Sherman Fairchild's company, called Sherman Semiconductor. It would be one of the few early successes of the semiconductor age. Hoerni invented an efficient way to manufacture semiconductors, called the planar process. Noyce invented the integrated circuit to jam many transistors into a small space. Both were practical problems of production, and both processes became industry standards that were crucial to the development of the semiconductor industry. Each of the traitorous eight invested $500 in 1957, and two years later that would be worth $250,000. Moore hired Andy Grove in 1963, and Grove had two remarkable gifts: first, he was a talented, problem-solving engineer for technical issues; second, he was good at dealing with people, and quite good at "managing up." Grove would eventually see Moore as an avuncular figure, while becoming friends with Noyce.

Fairchild was a great place to work and for entrepreneurial engineers and many left to start their own semiconductor companies. It was an important hub. In a 1969 conference for the industry, 400 participants attended and over 90% were formerly Fairchild employees. The Valley was a mobile place. Employees were loyal to each other, their network, rather than any company. For example, in spring 1967, Charlie Sporck, the manufacturing manager of Fairchild, left; by the fall, 35 other Fairchild employees joined him at National Semiconductor, which would be one of the early stars in the industry.

After a good ten year run, in 1968 Noyce and Moore decided to form Intel after Noyce was passed over for the Sherman Semiconductor CEO role. He became frustrated with feckless bureaucrats running Fairchild from the East Coast. They were soon joined by Grove, the third employee, who would become and remain President and CEO of Intel into the 1990s. Noyce and Moore were rich men and confident their company would succeed. Grove was scared to death and had nightmares about the move. Les Vadasz, a Hungarian engineer at Fairchild, was employee number four. Moore thought Fairchild failed because it failed on the direction of technology, investing in bipolar circuits instead of MOS transistors. Grove thought that Fairchild just had such bad management; it was hard to get anything done.

To obtain start-up capital, Noyce and Moore approached Arthur Rock, a venture capitalist, with a one-page business plan stating their intention of developing large-scale integrated circuits. Rock had helped start Fairchild Semiconductor, Teledyne, and Scientific Data Systems. He had confidence in Noyce and Moore and raised $2.5 million in capital. The company was incorporated on July 18, 1968, as N.M. Electronics (the letters stood for Noyce Moore). It quickly changed its name to Intel, formed from the first syllables of "integrated electronics." Noyce and

Moore issued partner stock to themselves for $1, and sold the rest for $10 to outsiders. Rock prevented Grove from being a partner and buying the cheap stock. Intel raised another $2 million in capital before going public in 1971. In 1968 Intel had half a million dollars in losses. Still, its star-packed board was positive on its future, so they didn't complain. They let Moore, Noyce, and Grove continue on.

DRAM

The price of magnetic core memories had been declining steadily for years. The founders of Intel, however, believed that semiconductor computer memory could fit a lot more information (bits) and therefore become a cheaper method to hold large amounts of data. Intel's first product in 1969 was the 3101, a 64-bit Schottky bipolar memory chip for high-speed random access memory (RAM). It was a niche product. The 3101 was popular enough to sustain the company until the 1101, a metal oxide semiconductor (MOS) chip, was perfected and introduced in 1969. The following year, Intel introduced the 1103, a one kilobyte (K) dynamic RAM, or DRAM, which was the first commercially-available chip large enough to store a significant amount of information. With the 1103, Intel finally had a chip to replace magnetic core chip technology. DRAMs eventually became indispensable to the personal computer.

Intel was not alone in believing in new memory technology. An IBM researcher, Robert Dennard, achieved the first breakthrough in 1966, when he built the first DRAM. His DRAM, or dynamic random access memory, needed only one transistor and one capacitor to hold a bit of information, thus enabling very high densities. It was called "dynamic" because it needed to be refreshed continuously. Lee Boysel at Fairchild Semiconductor achieved a 256-bit dynamic RAM in 1968. Then he founded Four Phase Systems in 1969 to build 1024-bit and 2048-bit DRAMs (kilobits of memory on a single chip). Advanced Memory Systems, founded in 1968 not far from Intel by engineers from IBM, Motorola, and Fairchild Semiconductor, introduced one of the first 1K DRAMs in 1969. Intel introduced its own in 1970, the 1103.

Before DRAMs, the semiconductor firms mainly made money by building custom-designed integrated circuits. Like all customized solutions, they did not have a huge market (often just one customer) but were lucrative and safe. DRAMs, instead, were general-purpose and rapidly became a commodity. Their advantage was that they could be sold by the thousands. Their disadvantage was that the semiconductor firms had to learn to live with competition, i.e. with a constant downward pressure on prices. By 1972 Intel had more than 1,000 employees and posted revenues of $23 million.

Despite major production problems, Intel got the DRAM out and it put the company on the map. Moore thought the difficulty of using the chip paradoxically helped it, as engineers knew their jobs were safe in utilizing the chip in their projects (it required much engineering support). While the chip had many flaws, it was "good enough" for many customers, and two years later it was the biggest selling semiconductor in the world. Intel was a thriving memory chip company.

Reversed and Advanced Engineering

The new business model meant that the entry point was lower. Many other firms opened up. In 1969 Advanced Micro Devices (AMD) was founded by Jerry Sanders, the marketing guru of Fairchild Semiconductor. AMD invented a sort of parasitic business plan: let others invent and then improve over their original design. While it was less "creative," this approach required sophisticated engineering skills to reverse engineer the products of other companies (typically, Intel) and then tweak it to obtain a better product.

By then IBM had shot far ahead of the competition. The competition relied on the anti-trust laws to manufacture "clones" of IBM mainframes. They were called the "bunch" from the initials of their names: Burroughs, Univac (that in 1971 bought RCA's computer business), NCR, Control Data Corporation (that had acquired Bendix), and Honeywell (that in 1970 bought General Electric's computing business).

Honeywell had jumped late into computers but had made some bold acquisitions and hired bright engineers. Bill Regitz was one of them, a specialist in core memory systems from the Bell Labs. He became a specialist in MOS (Metal Oxide Semiconductor) technology and came up with an idea for a better DRAM (using only three transistors per bit instead of the four or more used by the previous mass-market DRAM chips). He shared that idea with Intel (and eventually joined Intel) and the result was the Intel i1103, a 1,024-bit DRAM chip, introduced in the fall of 1970. It wasn't the first one, but it was the first one that could be easily used to build computer memories. Hewlett-Packard selected it for its 9800 series, and IBM chose it for its System 370/158. It became the first bestseller in the semiconductor business.

Within two years Intel was dominating the market for DRAMs. By the end of the year not only Intel but the whole Santa Clara Valley had become the place to go and buy semiconductor technology: five of the seven largest US semiconductor manufacturers were based here. However, core memory was still the memory of choice among large computer manufacturers, still accounting for more than 95% of all computers in the mid 1970s.

Building a Microprocessor and Managing a Company

Intel had two major events in 1971. First, it went public on October 13 at a price of $23.50 per share, after having its first profitable year. An investor who bought 100 shares for $2,350 would have a stake worth $2 million in 1996. Second, Intel introduced its first microprocessor, the Intel 4004, the world's first commercial microprocessor. Like many of Intel's innovations, the microprocessor was a byproduct of efforts to develop another technology. When a Japanese calculator manufacturer, Busicom, asked Intel to design cost-effective chips for a series of calculators, Intel engineer Ted Hoff was assigned to the project. Hoff and Federico Faggin conceived a plan for a central processing unit (CPU) on one chip. The 4004, which crammed 2,300 transistors onto a one-eighth-inch by one-sixth-inch chip, had the power of the old room-sized ENIAC computer, which depended on 38,000 vacuum tubes. Hoff and Faggin had invented a general purpose processor circuit that could be programmed for a wide range of jobs. However, no industry observer knew that microprocessors would be a big business and most felt it was a niche product, just like personal computers (PCs). As Grove said, when someone came to him with the idea of a personal computer, he thought it could only be used to store recipes and said: "I personally didn't see anything useful in it, so we never gave it another thought." *No one knew how microprocessors would be used!*

Intel had a strong financial year in 1971. Revenues of $9.4 million were double the amount of the previous year, with a profit of $1.1 million from a licensing deal with Microsystems International. Licensing at that point was standard process, as customers demanded a "second source" for a guaranteed supply of product, and more likely, for price competition. However, the practice of second sourcing hurt memory manufacturers and impeded innovation, as companies taking a risk to develop a new product earned lower profits for their risk-taking. In Intel's favor, the 1103 was a profitable product that no one could reverse engineer, and it helped Intel's sales reach $855 million by 1980, a 66% sales growth figure. Intel's policy at that point was to beat competition by constantly innovating and staying ahead. This meant a high R&D budget and also high margins on its products.

In 1972 Intel bought Microma, a digital watch company making solid state quartz watches with liquid crystal displays. Intel thought it could make the watch's chip and the display as complementary items, but it had production issues. More importantly, Intel failed at the consumer marketing game and lost big by paying for ads (one ad by itself cost $600,000). Intel shut down Microma by 1978 and transferred its employees to other divisions. It was easier to close a division when no one was fired, as fewer people fought to keep a dud alive.

Grove was a focused and determined manager with a unique management style. He worried about the Peter Principle, which states that everyone is promoted out of jobs at which they excel and stalled in jobs at which they are mediocre or bad. Grove wrote that "management is the art of absorbing a task in one lump from above, cutting it into smaller lumps and pushing them down one level in such a way that if the members of the lower level each take one of their own lumps, the mother lump automatically gets done." In his mind, bad managers didn't transmit tasks down rapidly, didn't partition lumps well, or didn't follow up to make sure sub-lumps got done. For effectiveness, each layer should transmit its lump downward very rapidly.[19]

Grove ran meetings in a disciplined way, with clear agendas and a focus on at tackling issues sequentially, while not getting distracted. He created a "late list," active from 1971 to 1988. If you came to work after 8:05, you had to sign in; this included everyone, including VPs and the CEO. It angered many employees but Grove stuck to it. He wanted everything measured quantitatively. He used ranking and rating systems on all managers, linking them to objectives. It was a tough culture of "constructive confrontation." The downside was that Grove found it hard to compliment people and had to make an effort to do so. He had a style based on fear and was passionately focused on winning in the marketplace. Fear led to excellence, and Grove wrote that "fear plays a major role in creating and maintaining such passion. Fear of competition, fear of bankruptcy, fear of being wrong, and fear of losing can all be powerful motivators."[20]

Intel had initially focused on the microprocessor as a computer enhancement to allow users to add more memory to their units. But soon it was clear that the microprocessor's great potential was for everything from calculators to cash registers and traffic lights. These broad applications were made possible by Intel's introduction of the 8008, an 8-bit microprocessor developed along with the 4004 but oriented toward data and character (rather than arithmetical) manipulation. Intel introduced the 8008 in 1974. It was a watershed as the first truly general purpose microprocessor. For $360, Intel sold a whole computer on one chip, while conventional computers sold for thousands of dollars. Customers went mad. The 8080 soon became the industry standard and Intel the industry leader in the 8-bit market.

As Intel grew, it had some important recruits in 1974. A recession-year class included Craig Barrett, a Stanford PhD joining as a technology development manager, and Paul Otellini, a Berkeley MBA. Both would later become Intel CEOs. Early Intel company characteristics were its secrecy, its ability to hire and keep great talent by offering great stock option packages, and its practice of filling executive positions "two in a box," so the strengths of two people would complement each other.

In 1974 Intel had sales of $140 million with about 3,100 employees. In 1976, Intel would share its design for microprocessors with Advanced Micro Devices (AMD), which would become a big competitor.

---

[19] Tedlow, Richard. Andy Grove: The Life and Times of an American. New York: Portfolio, 2006, p. 150.
[20] Ibid p.225.

In response to ensuing competition in the manufacture of 8-bit microprocessors, Intel introduced the 8085, a faster chip with more functions. The company was also developing two more advanced projects, the 32-bit 432 and the 16-bit 8086. The 8086 was introduced in 1978 but took two years to achieve wider use. During this time, Motorola produced a competing chip (the 68000) that sold more. Intel responded with a massive sales effort to establish its architecture as the standard. In 1979 Grove became President and Chief Operations Officer of Intel.

When Intel released the 8086 microprocessor, it was a big and expensive bet. Intel had lots of competitors, especially Zilog and Motorola whose 68000 was technically superior. Intel decided to compete against Motorola on customer service and support, knowing its technical specs were worse. Intel also pitched the chip to IBM and won, helping the 8086 become the industry standard for the 16-bit microprocessor market. This was a huge strategic inflection point as it would create a network effect position for Intel in the microprocessor wars. It also helped Microsoft, which won the battle to outsource the operating system for software. Intel, by having IBM adopt its chip, could now sell to IBM clone companies as the industry standard. Never before had IBM gone to an outside standard for a key technology, and it was a big mistake.

Intel's rapid growth, from the 12 employees it had when it began in 1968 to 15,000 in 1980, necessitated a careful approach to corporate culture. Noyce, Moore, and Grove remembered their frustration with Fairchild's bureaucratic bottlenecks. In Intel they carefully defined a flat, meritocratic management style. They had informal weekly lunches with employees and kept communication lines open while the company was small. The founders installed a carefully outlined program emphasizing openness, decision-making on the lowest levels, discipline, and problem solving rather than paper shuffling. Moreover, the company's top executives eschewed such luxuries as limousines, expense account lunches, special dining and wash rooms, and private parking spaces to establish a sense of teamwork with their subordinates. No one flew first class. When Fortune magazine made an index in 1993 of return to shareholders per square foot of CEO office space, Grove was at the top of the list by far.

In 1981, IBM began to use the 8086 in its first PCs. IBM could make a PC every 45 seconds but that wasn't fast enough for demand. IBM's sales would reach $5 billion for just its PC division in 1984, making the division as #75 on the Fortune 500 list. While the PC took off, Intel faced tough times.

A big recession hit in 1982. At a low point of the economy and Intel's sales, Moore was depressed that nobody had tried to acquire Intel. He was ready to sell out at $25 per share, a cheap price. During the 1974 recession, Intel had been forced to lay off 30% of its employees and morale crashed. During the 1981-1982 recession, instead of laying off more employees,

Intel accelerated new product development and asked employees to share the pain. Managers asked exempt employees to work two extra hours per day, without pay, for six months. A brief surge in sales the following year did not last, and, again, instead of more layoffs, Intel imposed pay cuts of up to 10%. Most workers hated such measures, but by June 1983, Intel undid all the cuts and awarded retroactive raises. Moreover, in December 1982, IBM paid $250 million for a 12% stake in Intel. This gave Intel a needed boost and cemented its relationship with IBM, which would raise its stake to 20% before selling it in 1987.

The recession in 1982 masked Intel's introduction that year of its 80286 microprocessor. This chip quickly came to dominate the upper-end PC market after IBM came out with the 286-powered PC/AT. Intel's sales boomed by 1984, rising 45% to $1.6 billion, putting Intel at #226 on the Fortune 500 list. Intel's compounded annual growth rate in sales and profits for the three years were 27% and 94%.

In 1985 Intel released the 80386 microprocessor, popularized in 1987 by the Compaq Deskpro 386. Despite its initial bugs, the 386 became one of the most popular chips on the market. While the 286 had enough speed and power to challenge larger computers, the 386 offered even more speed and power along with the ability to run more than one program at a time. The 386 featured 32-bit architecture and 275,000 transistors, more than twice the number of the 286.

Good times were quickly replaced by bad ones. The PC boom ended in 1984 as many businesses bought one, but Intel had built up too much plant capacity and an overhead structure twice as high. Also foreign competition was tough. By the dark year of 1986, Intel was hurting again with sales of $1.3 billion and a loss of $170 million. IBM executives worried about Intel going bust. IBM was also annoyed that Intel was selling chips to PC-clone manufacturers, and IBM's share of Intel sales fell from 20% in 1985 to 6% in 1986. IBM was feeling pressure from PC clone companies like Compaq, Zenith, Tandy, Epson, and Acer. Compaq was founded in 1982 by three former Texas Instrument engineers and by 1985 had $625 million in revenue. Intel again had to institute layoffs, plant closings, and salary cuts. The good news was that Intel kept R&D high to come up with the next big chip.

In 1989 Intel introduced the 80486; it was basically a mainframe-on-a-chip. The 486 included 1.2 million transistors and the first built-in math co-processor; it was 50 times faster than the 4004, the first microprocessor. It took Intel 130 person years to design it at a cost of $200 million (nearly twice as much as the 386). Intel also ran an ad campaign with a big red X and circle around the 386 as it tried to promote the 486, a gutsy ad campaign to kill one product for another. It was also targeted directly at consumers, not manufactures. Intel's stock price doubled that year.

Destroying Intel's Main Business to Start Over

During the early 1980s, Intel began to slip in its memory markets. Fierce competition in DRAMs, static RAMs, and EPROMs forced Intel to concentrate on microprocessors. While competitors claimed that Intel simply gave away its DRAM market, Moore said the company deliberately focused on microprocessors as the least cyclical field in which to operate.

Intel had to leave the semiconductor memory business. The founders were forced into that decision because Japanese competitors came in with a 10% rule: quote a price 10% below the prices of Intel's and AMD's chips. The Japanese firms' market share went from under 30% in 1976 to above 50% in 1988; US companies lost the most. For Intel, memory sales fell from 90% of revenues in 1972 to about 20% in 1988. Intel's managers were dealing with industry change, a strategic inflection point.

Strategic inflection points come when the balance of power shifts but few notice because it's less perceptible. For IBM, it was when Intel and Microsoft owned key technologies and became more powerful from 1982-1986. Most strategic inflection points don't come with a bang but rather on "little cat feet," and so are often not evident till much later. The question managers would have to ask were: Is your key competitor about to change? If you had a silver bullet to kill one competitor, who would it be?

Intel had to make a traumatic decision on how to compete, as DRAM memory chips were the center of Intel's product line. The executives had lots of meetings and bickered about the strategy. Two dogmas made the decision hard: 1) Intel was on the technological edge for memory and the company defined itself for pushing the boundaries (though they were increasingly not lucrative), and 2) the sales force wanted to sell a full line of products to customers, not to tell them to go elsewhere (though margins on memory were disappearing). There was a crucial difference between memory business and microprocessors: in memory, much of the value came from low-cost manufacturing, whereas for microprocessors, much more value came from product definition (choosing features), product design (creating schematics for circuits and doing logic simulation), and process design (figuring out a process to efficiently make the product).

In the end, Grove posed a thought experiment in mid-1985 to Moore: "If we got kicked out and the board brought in a new CEO, what do you think he would do?" Moore replied: "He would get out of memories." Grove responded: "Why shouldn't you and I walk out the door, come back, and do it ourselves?" Grove was listening to middle management who were closer to the issues. However, it was easier to start something than to kill something. The founders ended up deciding to kill the DRAM business and move its highly talented people to other business lines. One lesson was that Intel had to protect its intellectual property and so manufacture its own products; anything else would be an invitation to make a product a commodity. Intel's corporate culture changed dramatically after the crisis that almost sank it. Power shifted from Noyce to Andy Grove, who replaced Noyce's idealistic philosophy and casual management with a brutal philosophy of Darwinian competition and iron discipline.

In 1987, Andy Grove became CEO of Intel; he would replace Moore as board chairman in 1997. Grove focused the company more. Intel's new strategy would have three parts: manufacture its own chips; market itself as the "vendor of choice" as customers narrow down the group; and extend its architectural leadership by getting more programmers to write for its chips, getting a high installed base and so a network effect on its platform. Licensing meant turning your business into a commodity, so Intel stopped doing licensing. It meant walking away from military business because of a demand to second source. Also, for each new generation of chips, the price to build a fabrication lab went up ($50 million for the 286 and $100 million for the 386 lab). Intel became the sole source for the 80386 in October 1985. It was a big move, as IBM could have chosen to leave Intel. Intel convinced IBM to stay by building multiple source across the US that only it owned - also Barrett developed and executed on a "copy exactly" manufacturing process worked well to increase reliability.

At the end of 1988, Intel had about 21,000 employees with double the productivity per employee from 4 years before. That year Intel started its legal battle with Advanced Micro Devices (AMD) concerning their 1976 information sharing agreement. In 1990 Bob Noyce died and Craig Barrett was promoted to Executive Vice President, where he was 2nd in command at Intel.

Pentium and Branding a Chip Inside a Box

Intel had started creating a branding strategy even for the 486 and before the Pentium processor. In 1991 the "Intel Inside" campaign had started. Sales and profits in 1991 were up 22% to $4.8 billion and $819 million. The next year, Intel's annual net income topped $1 billion for the first time, following a very successful, brand-building marketing campaign. Intel's ads aggressively increased consumer interest in and demand for computers that featured "Intel Inside."

Intel's foray into branding was one-half finance and one-half romance. It was expensive to build a brand. It was even tougher to brand a component inside a box, a chip no one sees. A brand can be seen as the capitalized value of trust between a company and its customers; this makes it valuable. Intel spent about $500 million from 1990 to 1993 to build the "Intel Inside" brand. By late 1993, the company's brand equity totaled $17.8 billion, more than three times its 1992 sales.

In 1993 Intel released its fifth-generation Pentium processor. This trademarked chip could execute over 100 million instructions per second (MIPS) and support real-time video communication. The Pentium processor, with its 3.1 million transistors, was up to five times more powerful than the 33-megahertz Intel 486 DX microprocessor (and 1,500 times the speed of the 4004). Craig Barrett was promoted to Chief Operations Officer. Intel had a 50% revenue increase in 1993, reaching $8.8 billion.

In 1994 a mathematical bug was discovered in the Pentium microprocessor by a researcher. Intel initially denied the error and claimed it was so small that it would affect few users. While this was correct from an engineering perspective, it was a marketing disaster, as every mom-and-pop Intel chip purchaser wanted a new chip and not a defective one. Intel stingily offered a partial replacement for companies it decided were using the Pentium chip for those limited high-end uses it felt were compromised. After consumer rage reached a high level, Intel finally backtracked and offered a replacement for anyone who bought a defective chip.

In 1995 the Pentium Pro microprocessor was introduced. It was a great year, as sales of $16.2 billion were 41% higher, with net income of $3.6 billion. The next year Intel and AMD settled their spat after 8 years of litigation.

A short note about the "Wintel" (Windows-Intel) relationship: Intel had a complementor relationship between itself and Microsoft, where they both sold goods (microchips and operating systems) to PC manufacturers that complemented each other. Generally, firms want their complementor price to be low. Intel would want Microsoft's products to be cheap so people would pay more for an Intel chip. However, Intel had the weaker position, as it sold one chip for each PC, whereas Microsoft would sell multiple operating systems (versions of Windows) and application suites (versions of MS Office). In 1996, Intel tried to launch an NSP initiative, a special software program to help software developers make apps for advanced video/graphics without a special chip. The point was for developers to bypass Windows and create instructions directly for the microprocessor. It was a clear encroachment on Microsoft's territory, and Bill Gates quickly killed it.

One thing Intel did differently than Microsoft was settle its antitrust lawsuit. In early 1999 Intel reached a settlement with the Federal Trade Commission on an antitrust suit. It avoided the protracted litigation and negative publicity that hurt its Wintel partner, Microsoft, in the late 1990s.

In 1997 Intel released the Pentium II. Previously, Intel had focused on designing new, more powerful chips for the top end of the market. It allowed previous-generation microprocessors to migrate down to the lower segments of the market. However, with the introduction of the Pentium II in May 1997, Intel adopted a new strategy of developing a range of microprocessors for every segment of the computing market. The Pentium II, with 7.5 million transistors, was a top-end model that clocked at 300 MHz. While the Pentium II was originally designed for high-end desktop PCs, it was soon adapted for use in notebook and laptop computers. Within a year Intel launch of the Celeron processor, which was designed specifically for the low-price, value PC market, a rapidly growing segment since Compaq started selling a sub-$1000 PC in early 1997. Demand for Intel's new chips was high and it caused revenues to hit $20.9 billion by 1996, while net income soared to $5.2 billion. In 1998 Intel for the first time designed a microprocessor, the Pentium II Xeon, for midrange and higher-end servers and workstations.

In 1998 Andy Grove stepped down as CEO and Craig Barrett took his place. Many CEOs and management scholars consider Grove one of the best US corporate managers from 1970 on. Grove had some advice for businesspeople, starting with: "Enjoy your work. Be totally dedicated to the substance of your work, to the end result, the output." Grove also suggested people respect the work of all those who respect their own work. Finally, it was important to be straight with everyone and to stop and think your way through to your own answers.

In general Grove defined managing as "getting things done through other people" and that people issues were one of the biggest part of it (hiring, settling conflicts, helping people plan careers, coaching strengths, being around as a shoulder to cry on, etc.). Grove wrote in his book *High Output Management*: "The job of a manager is to elicit peak performance from subordinates." In managing and building Intel, Moore, Noyce, and Grove had done a stellar job of it.

12.   Geniuses: SRI,   Arpanet, Software, Labor Fluidity, and Utopia (1968-71)

Bay Area High-Tech Creativity

The hippie's anti-military ideology indirectly affected SRI. Student protests against SRI's reliance on military projects caused Stanford to spin off SRI as an independent non-profit entity, which later renamed itself SRI International. In 1969, SRI's Artificial Intelligence group, led by Charlie Rosen, demonstrated "Shakey the Robot," a mobile robot that employed artificial intelligence techniques. The next year, Stanford University's Ed Feigenbaum launched the Heuristic Programming Project to create "expert systems" that could match the behavior of human experts in specific domains.

Computer Manufacturing

Meanwhile, Hewlett-Packard was ready to enter the minicomputer market with the 3000 in 1972. HP used a new strategy to design this machine: it employed both hardware and software engineers to write the specifications. The result was that the 3000 was one of the first computers to be completely programmed in a high-level language instead of the prevailing assembly languages. It soon came with a database management system (IMAGE), something that in the past only mainframes had been able to offer. The PDP of DEC had introduced a "do-it-yourself" mindset in data centers. By enabling staff with little computing skills to manage strategic data, the HP/3000 pushed that mindset one floor up to the business offices. The success of this machine would transform HP's culture. To start with, HP would use this product to expand from its traditional industrial base into the business world. In a few years revenues from the 3000 would account for almost half of total revenues, propelling HP to the forefront of the minicomputer industry.

Besides HP, IBM had to face a new competitor that was based in the Bay Area. The chief architect of IBM's mainframes, Gene Amdahl, started his own business in 1970 in Sunnyvale to build IBM-compatible mainframes, less expensive and faster than IBM's models. Amdahl's first machine would come out in 1975.

The Floppy Disk

IBM's San Jose laboratories were assigned the task of developing a cheap storage medium to load the 370 mainframe's microcode and replace the cumbersome tape units. Previous IBM mainframes had used non-volatile read-only memory to store the microcode. The 370 instead used a read and write semiconductor memory that had become affordable and reliable, besides solving many engineering problems. Semiconductor memory was volatile; it was erased whenever the power was switched off. Therefore IBM had to provide a medium to reload the microcode. In 1971 David Noble came up with a cheap read-only 80-kilobyte diskette: the "floppy disk." It made it easy to load the control program and to change it whenever needed. It was originally designed to be written once and read many times, but just one year later a team at Memorex led by Alan Shugart built the first read-write floppy-disk drive, the Memorex 650. It obviously could serve more purposes than just loading control programs into a mainframe.

The Videogame

People also began to realize that advanced computer technology could be used for purposes totally unrelated to computing. Inspired by Steve Russell's ten-year old but still popular "Spacewar," in 1971 Ampex employees Nolan Bushnell and Ted Dabney quit their jobs and created the first arcade videogame, "Computer Space." It was a free-standing terminal powered by a computer and devoted to an electronic game that anyone could use. When, Magnavox introduced the first videogame console, Ralph Baer's transistor-based "Odyssey," Bushnell was inspired again, this time by an electronic ping-pong game. He founded Atari in Santa Clara and asked his engineer Allan Alcorn to create a similar game. "Pong" launched in 1972 as a runaway success.

The Financial and Legal Infrastructure

The high-tech industry of the South Bay began attracting serious capital in 1968 when ARD's investment in Digital Equipment Corporation (DEC) was valued at $355 million. It was the first well-publicized case of an investment in a computer company that paid off handsomely. The same model could be replicated on the West Coast. New investment companies were founded: Asset Management by Franklin Johnson (1965); Hambrecht & Quist by William Hambrecht and George Quist in San Francisco (1968); Bryan & Edwards by John Bryan and Bill Edwards (1968); Crosspoint Ventures by John Mumford (1970); and so on. As their returns beat national stock index averages, New York firms such as Bessemer Securities opened branches in the Bay Area.

At the same time, a law firm located in the Stanford Industrial Park, evolved from a firm that a Redwood City attorney John Wilson had started in 1961. Its customers were Tymshare, ESL, and Coherent Laser. Wilson's firm just added two Berkeley graduates: Larry Sonsini in 1966 and Mario Rosati in 1971. This laid the foundations for the typical Silicon Valley law firm, which specialized in setting up startups, writing contracts between founders and venture capitalists, taking startups public through IPOs, and, controversially, accepting equity in its clients as a form of payment.

Biotech's First Steps

In 1959 the medical department of the University of the Pacific had moved to Stanford University's campus in a joint venture between the City of Palo Alto and Stanford University. In 1968 this medical center was purchased by Stanford University and renamed as Stanford University Hospital. Coupled with the success of Syntex, this event symbolized the coming of age of the area in pharmaceutical research.

A few early biotech companies were created. Alza was founded in 1968 by former Syntex's President Alejandro Zaffaroni in Palo Alto and rapidly became a successful pharma company, leading the way for the next big thing. Cetus was the first biotech company of the Bay Area. It was founded in 1971 by Donald Glaser, a Nobel-winning nuclear physicist at UC Berkeley. He had switched to molecular biology and wanted to develop methods to process DNA. In those days, the composition of DNA was still largely a mystery and biotech's main business was to devise automated methods to research DNA.

Arpanet

By the end of 1960s the Bay Area didn't yet boast a major computer manufacturer. Hewlett-Packard was still mostly manufacturing electronic equipment. Even worse was the software situation: Silicon Valley had no major software company. It was no surprise, therefore, that all the important decisions still took place on the East Coast. In 1968, the hypertext project run by Dutch-born Andries van Dam at Brown University, originally called Hypertext Editing System, yielded the graphics-based hypertext system FRESS for the IBM 360. Influenced by Douglas Engelbart's NLS project at the SRI, FRESS featured a graphical user interface running on a PDP-8 connected to the mainframe. This system also introduced the "undo" feature, one of the simplest but also most revolutionary ideas introduced by computer science.

Paul Baran's old idea that a distributed network was needed to survive a nuclear war had led the US government's Advanced Research Projects Agency (ARPA) in 1966 to launch a project for one such network under the direction of MIT scientist Lawrence Roberts. He had implemented one of the earliest computer-to-computer communication systems. In October 1969 Arpanet was inaugurated with four nodes, three of which were in California: UCLA, in the laboratory of Leonard Kleinrock (who had developed the mathematical theory of packet switching for communication between computers); Stanford Research Institute in Doug Engelbart's

Augmentation Research Center; UC Santa Barbara; and the University of Utah. Bolt Beranek and Newman delivered one Interface Message Processor (IMP) to each node. The IMPs communicated via software that sent messages over ordinary telephone lines. As a historical note, the Arpanet had been preceded by the Octopus network, implemented in 1968 at the Lawrence Livermore Laboratories by connecting four Control Data 6600 mainframes.

Unix

In November 1971 Bell Labs unveiled its Unix operating system. It was the successor to MULTICS (Multiplexed Information and Computing Service), a time-sharing operating system for General Electric's mainframe GE-645 that had been jointly developed by MIT's Fernando Corbato and Bell Labs. Two Bell Labs scientists, Kenneth Thompson and Dennis Ritchie had worked on a smaller version of Multics, which became Unix, written in the assembly language of the PDP. In 1973 they also rewrote it in a programming language called C, developed by Ritchie the year before. That marked the first time that an operating system was written in a high-level language, and therefore easy to port across computers (although de facto until 1976 Unix only ran on DEC PDPs).

In 1958 AT&T, the owner of Bell Labs, was served with an antitrust court order that forbade it to ever enter the computer business and that forced it to license any non-telephone inventions to the whole world. This odd ruling turned Unix into a worldwide phenomenon, as it spread from one corner of the computer world to the other.

Remote Computing

Meanwhile, the time-sharing industry had popularized the concept of remote computing. For example, Ohio-based CompuServe, founded in 1969 as a spin-off of the University of Arizona's time-sharing system, made money by renting time on its PDP-10 midrange computers (what later would be called "dial-up" service). Computers were especially valuable for "real-time" transactions, when they had to process multiple critical transactions in milliseconds, a problem typical of financial applications. In July 1969 IBM introduced the transactional system CICS (Customer Information Control System).

The Unbundling of IBM

In June 1969 IBM preempted an antitrust lawsuit by opening up its software business to competition. Its decision might also have been driven by the increasing costs of developing software. IBM was "bundling" the software with the computer. In theory the software was free, yet its cost was factored into the price of the computer. As the cost of developing software increased, IBM was forced to charge higher prices for computers that could have been much cheaper, and the customer was forced to pay for all the software that came with the computer regardless of what was really used.

This historical "unbundling" created a golden opportunity for independent software companies, as the market for mainframe applications was huge. Until then, only Max Palevsky's Scientific Data System (SDS) had charged customers for software. Initially IBM's customers were not amused when told that they had to pay for software that used to be free, but soon the advantages of having a free market for software applications became obvious. Multiple companies introduced competing packages addressing big industries. Suddenly software companies were no longer "consultants" working on custom applications but third-party vendors selling off-the-shelf packages.

The first packaged product from an independent software company was probably Autoflow, an automatic flowcharting system unveiled in 1965 by consulting firm Applied Data Research (ADR). It was originally founded in 1959 by a group of Univac programmers, notably Martin Goetz, formerly of Sperry Rand. Before Autoflow the business of software was a pure custom service. Nobody had tried to sell the same applications to multiple customers. Standard applications were bundled for free with the computer by the manufacturer. Goetz also went down in history as the first person to be awarded a patent for a software "invention" in 1968; it was for a sort program that he had developed in 1964.

Informatics was founded in 1962 by Walter Bauer, the former manager of information systems at Ramo-Wooldridge in Los Angeles, and Frank Wagner, a former president of Share. It introduced the term "informatics" into popular jargon. In 1964 Informatics acquired Advanced Information Systems from aviation giant Hughes and turned its file management system into a product, Mark IV, that went on to become the first best-seller of the software industry. Bauer modeled the business after IBM's business model, assuming that selling software wasn't different than selling hardware

In 1968 John Cullinane started the first software company funded by Wall Street investors, Cullinane Corp., in Boston. The first startup. Cullinane's vision was that it made more sense to sell applications to the department that used them than to the data processing department. His idea was to purchase successful custom applications and generalize them so that they could be resold to other customers.

Software, whether developed by computer manufacturers, software companies, or in-house facilities of large users, was growing chaotically. For too long software had been conceived as a mere appendage to hardware. Millions of lines of code had been written with no standards and often no methodology. Now the computer manufacturers were plagued with "bugs" in their operating systems that were impossible to fix, and customers were plagued with mission-critical applications that contained "spaghetti code" which was difficult to update and difficult to port to other machines. In 1968 the Dutch mathematician Edsger Dijkstra wrote an article titled "GO TO Statement Considered Harmful." It was a simple, somewhat illiterate statement about how "not" to write software. Computer programmers had conceived programs as sequences of instructions. It was time to conceive them as the complex architectures that they were. In October 1968, NATO organized a conference in Germany focusing on methodologies for software development titled "Software Engineering." In 1969 Joseph Piscopo founded Pansophic Systems in Chicago; it was a pioneer of Computer Aided Software Engineering (CASE).

The importance of software was also recognized when Los Angeles-based Computer Science Corp (CSC), the largest software company in the country, became the first software business to be listed on the New York Stock Exchange. The world of computing was beginning to be called "Information Technology" (IT).

The Software Industry in Perspective

The first software companies were consulting operations that helped data centers program their computers to provide applications to their organization. The term "user" tended to apply to the data processing center, not to the department that actually used the results of the application program. The typical customer in the 1950s was a government agency or a research laboratory. As prices decreased and "standard" software became more useful for practical office chores, computers spread to financial and industrial corporations. Initially they too thought that the "user" of a computer was the data processing center. The standard software that came bundled with a computer solved simple problems of accounting and recording. Organizations that had spent millions to buy computers wanted to do more with those computers. There were few "programmers" around and organizations were reluctant to hire "programmers" (still an uncharted profession). So it made sense that some of those programmers decided to start companies specializing in writing programs for data processing centers. On the one hand, these organizations did not want to hire programmers who were needed only for the duration of a project but were useless for the main business of the organization. On the other hand, the programmers themselves were not excited to work for an organization because there was no career path for them. Their status and salary was certainly higher than it had been for the early (female) programmers, but they had no prospects for promotions within the organization. Thus the software business was born as a form of outsourcing.

The main problem that the early software companies encountered was in estimating the costs of a software project. There was no science behind it. It was based on intuition and negotiation: you charged what the customer was willing to pay. Since the costs were so difficult to estimate, it was natural that software companies started to pay attention to which code was being rewritten for different applications. Code could be recycled from one project to the next, thus reducing the unpredictability of development costs.

The other problem that the early software companies had to face had to do with the perception that software was not a product. Customers were reluctant to pay for software, since they saw it as an integral part of the computer. They naturally expected the computer to solve their problem, not to become an additional problem. The data processing centers quickly realized the reality: the computer was indeed an additional problem that needed a whole new class of solutions. It took longer for the other departments of an organization to accept that the computer was not a solution but a problem, albeit one that potentially could lead to higher productivity and competitiveness.

The next step for software companies was to resell an entire application to multiple customers, and the category of software products was finally born. Suddenly, organizations were willing to pay good money for software applications, while software companies were able to control the costs. Software was becoming a lucrative business.

At the beginning, many software companies seemed unconvinced that software products were useful. These companies had very few sales people. Their official reason was that only few people understood their software products, but in reality those sales people did not understand the product as much as they understood the customer, i.e. how to convince the customer to buy the product. The product was something that most customers were not asking for and sometimes did not even understand. The sales person had to create a market that did not exist. The sales person was someone in between the organizational consultant, the explorer, and the itinerant medicine peddler.

All of this happened far away from the Bay Area. Most software companies were based on the East Coast or in the Midwest, because most computer users were based on the East Coast or in the Midwest. The only major exception was Los Angeles, where the aviation industry was based. The Bay Area had only two major users of computers: Bank of America in San Francisco (that had already installed the ERMA in 1955) and the Lawrence Livermore Laboratories in the East Bay (an early adopter of the PDP-1 in 1961 and of the CDC 6600 in 1964). Not much, however, existed in the Santa Clara Valley. In 1975, just months before the introduction of the first Apple computer, the whole market for software products in the US was still worth less than $1 billion.

Case Study: Bell Labs

AT&T founded Bell Laboratories ("Bell Labs") in 1925 and funded it heavily because AT&T had a monopoly on telephone communications in the US. Bell Labs was, in fact, an odd case of a private research laboratory funded by its customers with approval from the government. The government allowed AT&T to charge the cost of the research on the customers' phone bills. In the late 1960s, Bell Labs in New Jersey had about 50,000 people. From the 1930s it had been a magnet for engineers throughout the country.

Bell Labs mostly worked on long-term projects because the organization and its products had a life expectancy measured in decades. Bell Labs themselves were not making products that would be sold in stores, i.e. that marketing campaigns could turn into front-page news. Its employees were similar to tenured faculty, but without the obligation to teach and with greater accountability. Throughout their history they had virtually no connection with nearby aristocratic Princeton University, where people like Einstein were working. In 1936, Mervin Kelly had become the director of Bell Labs. His fame was due to the vacuum tube that his group had perfected, but he was keenly aware of the limitations of the device: it was unreliable and it sucked a lot of power. In 1945, at the end of the war, he established the solid-state team, an interdisciplinary group, under the supervision of the relatively young William Shockley, a Palo Alto-raised physicist. Kelly had created an environment that valued collaboration over cooperation: it was anathema to compete with fellow scientists. Shockley did just that with John Bardeen and Walter Brattain, the "first inventors" of the transistor. Then Shockley would migrate to the San Francisco Bay Area and transfer his know-how to what would become Silicon Valley.

In a sense, Silicon Valley was born out of Shockley's betrayal of Bell Labs' ethics. Shockley's ego was the original sin that begat Silicon Valley. Meanwhile, AT&T shared its technology with the rest of the country out of two considerations, one purely political (they had to avoid being accused of being the monopoly that they were) but the other one moral. As internal correspondence shows, they realized the importance of the discovery and felt a moral duty to share it with the scientific world. After the transistor, other notable inventions to come out of the Bell Labs would be: the solar cell in 1954 by Daryl Chapin, Calvin Souther Fuller, and Gerald Pearson; the laser in 1958 by Arthur Schawlow, and Charles Townes; the communications satellite Telstar in 1962; the touch-tone telephone in 1963 by Leo Schenker and others; the Unix operating system in 1971 by Kenneth Thompson and Dennis Ritchie; and the cellular phone system, first tested in Chicago in 1978. Bell Labs' researchers won several Nobel Prizes in those decades: Clinton Davisson (1937), the three inventors of the transistor (1956), Phillip Anderson (1977), and Arno Penzias and Robert Wilson (1978), who discovered the cosmic background radiation. Bell Labs's researchers would win two more in the 1990s.

However, Bell Labs remained mainly focused on refining a giant communication platform. It was not disrupting innovation, but sustaining evolution. Its researchers ended up missing on packet switching and fiber optics, two of the most important innovations in their field. The labs also had a history of racial discrimination, particularly against Jews, which did not help diversity. Clearly Bell Labs was not as good at importing foreign immigrants as California would be. Its scientists were mostly on the reserved and austere side, with the notable exception of Claude Shannon, the inventor of communication theory, who was wildly eccentric and known for riding his unicycle at work and juggling with one arm.

Labor Fluidity

Silicon Valley already exhibited unique job dynamics that would accelerate in the age of software. First of all, California was blessed with a strong economy that often outperformed the rest of the US. Therefore there were plenty of jobs available. It was an employee's market and not an employer's market. The job of the "head hunter," an employment broker, was more important than elsewhere since recruiting talented people was not easy. Second, California law forbade any labor contract that limited what an employee could do after quitting. Section 16600 of the California Business and Professions Code, a clause that dated back to the 19th century, was enforced by courts. In the rest of the US, trade secrets were guarded jealously and employees were forbidden to join competitors.

The job market in the Bay Area exhibited high turnover. Silicon Valley's engineers exhibited a preference for horizontal instead of vertical mobility, that is, for hopping sideways from job to job instead of following a career of promotion after promotion. Europe and the East Coast had an entrenched concept of vertical mobility of moving up in a career in a company. Sometimes, even at the expense of skills, an engineer might be promoted to a role that had nothing to do with engineering simply because it was the only available higher-level position. However Silicon Valley was about horizontal mobility, changing jobs in order to maximize one's skills based on available opportunities across the industry. In fact, many engineers believed that staying with the same company for more than a few years did not look "good" on a resume. This created a system that was an odd and involuntary model of cooperation.

High job turnover and no legal protection for trade secrets were clearly not beneficial to the individual company, but they boosted the entire ecosystem because they fostered an endless flow of knowledge throughout the community. No educational institution could spread knowledge as fast and efficiently as this job mobility did. This resulted in rapid dissemination of knowledge within an industry and across companies, as well as in cross-fertilization of ideas across research groups.

Somewhat related to the high-speed job market was the status symbol of being an engineer. Probably no other region in the world held its engineers is such high esteem. The skilled engineers represented a higher social class in Silicon Valley than marketing executives, lawyers, or politicians. The status symbol of being an engineer was only second to the status symbol of being an entrepreneur.

Culture and Society

The effervescent cultural scene of San Francisco attracted artists whose eccentric visions were tamed in their native East Coast. In particular, George Kuchar, the prophet of lo-fi cinema, moved from New York to the San Francisco Art Institute in 1971.

The leading art in San Francisco, however, mixed fiction and painting: the comics. A number of eccentric cartoonists, most of whom had moved west during the "Summer of Love," lived in the Haight-Ashbury neighborhood. They repudiated Walt Disney's poor-heart ethics and adopted mocking tones and a vulgar language: the "underground comix" movement was born. The pioneer was Joel Beck, one of the original contributors to the Berkeley Barb, with the full-length comic book "Lenny of Laredo" in 1965. Yet the movement coalesced in 1968 when publisher Don Donahue opened "Apex Novelties" and Robert Crumb penned the comic book "Zap Comix." Gary Arlington opened the first comics-only store in the US in the Mission District. Then came other original strips: Bill Griffith's strip "Young Lust," which mocked sexual attitudes; Roger Brand's comic magazine "Real Pulp Comics," which promoted the burgeoning counterculture scene; Trina Robbins' "It Ain't Me Babe Comix," the first all-female comic book; Dan O'Neill's collective "Air Pirates"; Gilbert Shelton's "The Fabulous Furry Freak Brothers"; and Justin Considine's "Binky Brown Meets the Holy Virgin Mary."

The contradictions of the "hippie" era peaked with the election of a conservative governor who seemed to stand for everything that California was not. Ronald Reagan, a former Hollywood actor who was governor from 1967 till 1975, ended an enlightened age in which the state of California was focused on building its infrastructure. Reagan inaugurated an age in which citizens revolted against government and cared more about improving their economic conditions (for example, by lowering taxes) than investing in the future. The dream land of idealistic immigrants was on its way to become a pragmatic state of greedy bourgeois.

The post-hippie era in California also witnessed the rapid political growth of the grass-roots environmental movement. It started with the article "Tragedy of the Commons," published in *Science* in 1968 by Garrett Hardin of UC Santa Barbara. The first victory of the movement came in 1969 when the Sierra Club managed to stop Walt Disney from building a tourist resort in the mountains of a national park. Anti-nuclear sentiment also increased, leading David Brower to split from the Sierra Club and start Friends of the Earth in Berkeley. In the fall the United Nations organized a conference titled "Man and his Environment" in San Francisco. One of the speakers, California-based peace activist John McConnell, the editor of the utopian *Mountain View* magazine, proposed an international holiday. In March 1970, San Francisco allowed him to hold the first "Earth Day." Soon after, the United Nations held its first "Conference on the Environment" in Sweden. One of the people who traveled from the US to attend it was Peter Berg, who founded Planet Drum in Berkeley. The influence of the environmentalists would be felt for decades.

At the same time that the Reaganite establishment was curbing public spending on ideological grounds, a rising environmentalist movement pressed to curb the infrastructure boom of the previous decades on almost opposite ideological grounds. The effect of this "double whammy" was to be felt decades later.

Britain and Japan's Computer Failures

In the 1940s Britain had pioneered computers. In the 1960s Japan was experiencing the most spectacular economic boom in the world. These two countries were the only countries that could potentially compete with the US. Their stories were different. The British computer industry had all the know-how to match developments in the US. The Japanese computer industry had to start from scratch in the 1950s. In both cases the government sponsored long-term plans and brokered strategic alliances among manufacturers. In Britain leadership came from the National Research Development Corporation (NRDC). In Japan, it came from the Ministry of International Trade and Industry (MITI).

In both countries, initial research came from a government-funded laboratory. In Britain the National Physical Lab (NPL) and in Japan the Electrotechnical Lab (ETL). However, the outcomes were completely different. Japan created a vibrant computer industry within the existing conglomerates (notably Fujitsu, Hitachi and NEC), whereas Britain's computer industry imploded within two decades. In 1972 Fujitsu and Hitachi partnered with Amdahl to reverse engineer IBM's mainframes. By 1979 Fujitsu would pass IBM to become Japan's main computer manufacturer. By then International Computers Limited (ICL), created by merging all the main British manufacturers, went broke. Eventually, Fujitsu would acquire it.

13. Lab Inventors: A Case Study on Xerox PARC and its Innovation Machine (1969-83)

The Creation of a Corporate Research Lab

Xerox's Palo Alto Research Center (PARC) was the US's most successful corporate research lab in the 1970s. Researchers invented the personal computer, the graphical user interface (GUI), the laser printer, and Ethernet networking technology. Many agree that the wellspring that made PARC so successful was its highly talented employees. Six factors brought these people together in a creative environment. First was Xerox's seeming endless pool of cash devoted to research. Second was a buyer's market for talent. PARC was started in a weak economy when after the Vietnam War the federal government was cutting back on research staff. Third was the state of computer technology, which was at an inflection point due to Moore's Law. Fourth was its quality management, which knew how to hire the best researchers, give them a broad mandate, and then let them play without directives, instructions, or deadlines. Freedom to experiment was invaluable. Fifth were the premium salaries that Xerox paid its researchers, about $30,000-35,000 in 1970, a nice amount for a new PhD. Sixth was a paucity of startup opportunities; when PARC was started, computer science researchers couldn't easily find funding for a startup, though that would change.

While Xerox never commercialized all the wonderful technologies at PARC, the company did earn billions from these innovations, and so made its money back many times over. A handful of people deserve credit for starting PARC. Jack Goldman, Xerox's Chief Scientist, submitted in May 1969 his proposal for an "Advanced Scientific & Systems Laboratory" to pursue research in computing and solid-state physics. Goldman told Xerox executives: "If you hire me, you will get nothing of business value in five years. But if you don't have something of value in ten years, you'll know you've hired the wrong guy." Xerox's CEO, Peter McCullough, had the vision and long-term good sense to approve and champion it. In 1969 McCullough had Xerox purchase Max Palevksy's Scientific Data Systems (SDS) for $920 million in stock. It was a computer company with a second rate minicomputer product that Xerox would divest years later. Yet McCullough wanted the company to explore in that direction and he had Jack Goldman take the lead for PARC to create "the office of the future."

Goldman first recruited some star managers. The most important was Bob Taylor, a former Department of Defense Advanced Research Projects Agency (ARPA) director. Next, coming in early 1970, George Pake accepted the job of director PARC and persuaded Goldman to locate it in Palo Alto, California, near Stanford University. Taylor had a gift for finding and cultivating talented researchers in the computer science field. After the GI Bill paid for Taylor's study of psychology at the University of Texas, he eventually joined JCR Licklider at ARPA. By December 1970, ARPAnet, the precursor to the Internet, became formally operational, with four nodes up and running.

ARPA was a beast with a $14 million budget for computer science research, more than the top 5 other grant-givers combined. Taylor eventually became Ivan Sutherland's deputy at ARPA, and then soon began running the Information Processing Techniques Office (IPTO). Taylor would approach the best computer science programs in the country and work with PhD students and junior faculty to find cutting edge projects to promote, many in the field of human computer interaction. Taylor was important because at ARPA he funded the country's first computer science grad programs at Stanford, CMU, and MIT. He knew all the young researchers in the field and had their trust. He knew enough to ask good questions and direct them, but was candidly not a specialist and would not micromanage research. So Taylor built one of the best professional networks in the field, and met people like Alan Kay, who said in 1972 that "90% of all good things that I can think of that have been done in computer science have been done funded" by ARPA. The ARPA model was to find good people, give them a lot of money, and then step back. If the researchers didn't deliver in three years, they were dropped.

Alan Kay was one of the moving forces behind PARC. In July 1969, Kay's doctoral dissertation, "The Reactive Engine," was accepted at the University of Utah (he only got into the PhD program because Don Evans, the director, never looked at grades). Within Kay's paper were early descriptions of his "Dynabook" personal computer, basically an early laptop. Kay was a non-stop idea machine; half of his ideas were brilliant and unworkable, the other half could be tested and be revolutionary. He had been a frenetic child prodigy who could never sit still. Kay hated the time-sharing computer terminals that everyone had to use at that point. Whether it was a mainframe or a minicomputer, you had to share them. They had blinking green text and were only accessible to a nerdy few. Kay wanted an interface children could use, more like finger paints and color television.

Kay had a completely different view of what a computer was and what it should do; his vision came from his passion for education. In a sense, he envisioned children as the ultimate users of computers, and therefore computers as tools for children. Once framed this way, the problem became one not of faster processing but of better interaction. It was not humans who had to learn the language of computers but computers who had to learn the "language" of humans.

Kay had the vision of a mobile computer that he named Dynabook; he also promoted "object-oriented" educational software. Kay designed a completely new software environment to develop software applications: Smalltalk. It was inspired by Simula 67, a programming language for simulations that had been defined in Norway by Ole-Johan Dahl and Kristen Nygaard. They all had created a GUI with children in mind, with overlapping windows and a "desktop" metaphor. Alan Kay's team included Adele Goldberg and Dan Ingalls, who developed most of the programming language. PARC also hired most of the gurus behind the Berkeley Computer Corporation (BCC) that had tried to commercialize Berkeley's Project Genie, notably Charles Thacker.

Perhaps as important as the technology was the work ethic at Xerox PARC, an ethic that basically consisted in not having a work ethic at all. Xerox funded the center and left the scientists free to do what they wanted with the money. Unlikely as it may sound for someone coming from government agencies, Taylor fostered an environment that was casual, informal, and egalitarian, with no dress code and no work hours. Xerox PARC came to symbolize for research centers the equivalent of the alternative lifestyle preached by the hippies, if not a premonition of the punk ethos.

As PARC took off, the 1970s was a tough decade for Xerox. In 1970 IBM brought out its first office copier, ending Xerox's historic monopoly and introducing a period of painful retrenchment at Xerox. Also as some executives tried to later kill PARC, Xerox board member and Nobel laureate John Bardeen (co-inventor of the transistor) fought to save PARC in board meetings, believing the $1.7 million budget was worth it.

Douglas Engelbart and SRI's Augmentation Research Center

Before delving more into PARC, it's important to understand its neighboring institution, the Augmentation Research Center (ARC), and Douglas Engelbart. Near the end of World War II, Engelbart was midway through his college studies at Oregon State University when the Navy drafted him. He served two years as a radar technician in the Philippines, where, on a small island in a tiny hut up on stilts, he read Vannevar Bush's 1945 article "As We May Think." Bush wrote about computing and a future when a "memex" device would augment human intelligence. A human could use it to store "all his books, records, and communications, and which is mechanized so that it may be consulted with exceeding speed and flexibility." Engelbart's experience as a radar technician convinced him that information could be analyzed and displayed on a screen. He dreamt of knowledge workers sitting at display "working stations," probing through information space and harnessing their collective intellectual capacity to solve problems. Engelbart returned to complete his

Bachelor's degree in Electrical Engineering in 1948 and he got a PhD from UC Berkeley in 1955. After a year of teaching at Berkeley as an Assistant Professor, he took a position at the Stanford Research Institute (SRI) in Menlo Park. In October 1962, Engelbart published a key document about computing and his beliefs on the modern workplace: "Augmenting Human Intellect: A Conceptual Framework."

At SRI, Engelbart had a dozen patents to his name and he proposed research to augment the human intellect using computers. ARPA, a US government research agency, funded him and he launched the Augmentation Research Center (ARC) within SRI. ARPA gave the team funds to explore Man-Computer Symbiosis, plus technology for "time sharing" of a computer's processing power between a number of concurrently active on-line users. Engelbart and his team developed computer-interface elements such as bit-mapped screens, the mouse, hypertext, collaborative tools, and precursors to the graphical user interface in the mid-1960s, long before the personal computer industry did. At that time, most individuals were ignorant of computers; experts could only use mainframes with proprietary systems and difficult-to-master text interfaces. After two years of unproductive work for ARPA, Bob Taylor at ARPA funded a project to experiment and evaluate various available screen selection devices, or pointers, for use in on-line human-computer interaction.

Taylor's ARPA grant led to the modern computer mouse. Engelbart conceived of the device and Bill English actually built the first wooden prototype. In 1967, Engelbart applied for a patent (with Bill English) for a wooden shell with two metal wheels: a computer mouse (US Patent 3,541,541). They described the device as an "X-Y position indicator for a display system." No one at the lab remembered who gave it the name "mouse," but someone did because the tail came out the end. Sadly, Engelbart and English never received any royalties for the mouse. SRI held the patent but had no idea of its value; it later licensed the mouse to Apple Computer for about $40,000.

A year later, Engelbart gave the "Mother of All Demos." On December 9, 1968, Engelbart and his group of 17 researchers gave a 90-minute, live public demonstration of their work, the "oN-Line System" (NLS). It was at a session of the Fall Joint Computer Conference held at the Convention Center in San Francisco, attended by about 1,000 computer professionals. A number of experimental technologies that have since become commonplace were first presented here. It was the public debut of the computer mouse, hypertext (interactive text), object addressing, dynamic file linking, video conferencing, teleconferencing, email, and a collaborative real-time editor (where two persons at different sites communicated over a network with audio and video interface).

A year later, Engelbart's lab became the second node on the Arpanet (the predecessor network that evolved into the Internet). On October 29,

1969, a link was established between nodes at Leonard Kleinrock's lab at UCLA and Engelbart's lab at SRI. Both sites would serve as the backbone of the first Internet. In addition to SRI and UCLA, UCSB and the University of Utah were part of the original four network nodes. By December 5, 1969, the entire 4-node network was connected. Engelbart's ARC lab soon became the first Network Information Center; it managed the directory for connections among all Arpanet nodes. One could say that Engelbart's lab in Palo Alto was the physical home of the most important Arpanet/Internet node for its first few years.

During his time at SRI, Engelbart developed a complex philosophy about man improving through technology, a sort of co-evolution through human-computer interactions. Engelbart was strongly influenced by Benjamin Lee Whorf's hypothesis of linguistic relativity. Whorf argued that the sophistication of a language controls the sophistication of the thoughts expressed by a speaker of that language. In parallel, Engelbart believed that the state of current technology controls people's ability to manipulate information. Better manipulation led to more innovation and new, improved technologies. People could even work in groups, where the collective IQ would be larger than the sum of the parts (witness the modern laptop, created by teams of specialists using other computers to design and prototype a laptop's different components). Engelbart pithily stated to Reader's Digest: "The rate at which a person can mature is directly proportional to the embarrassment he can tolerate. I have tolerated a lot." He was paid more by Reader's Digest for this quote than for his many inventions.

By 1976, Engelbart slipped into relative obscurity. Some of his ARC researchers became alienated from him and left to join Xerox PARC. Engelbart saw the future in collaborative, networked, timeshare (client-server) computers, while younger programmers preferred working on personal computers (individual machines that would not be shared and controlled by a centralized authority). Eventually funding from ARPA stopped by 1977 and SRI transferred the lab to Tymshare, which tried to commercialize some of Engelbart's software. However Engelbart was marginalized and relegated to obscurity. Management, first at Tymshare, and later at McDonnell Douglas (which took over Tymshare in 1984), liked his ideas but never committed the funds or the people to further develop them. Engelbart retired from McDonnell Douglas in 1986 and in 1988 founded the Bootstrap Institute with modest funding to promulgate his ideas.

Hiring the Best Computer Scientists Around

On July 1, 1970, Xerox's Palo Alto Research Center (PARC) officially opened its doors at 3180 Porter Drive, near Stanford University. For the location, Yale's New Haven was the first choice, but Goldman was put off by the snobbery of the university and its hostility to enterprise next door to it. Berkeley had no dedicated real estate near the campus, and Santa Barbara had no large airport. The physical and cultural climate in Palo Alto helped. Pake had hired Bob Taylor to help him staff the Computer Science Lab. Taylor forced the researchers to build things they could use daily and avoid prototypes and playthings that just sat on a shelf. He described his position at Xerox like this: "It's not very sharply defined. You could call me a research planner."

Taylor made two key hires for PARC. First, in November he hired the engineers of the failing Berkeley Computer Company, including Butler Lampson, Chuck Thacker, and Peter Deutsch. Second, Taylor raided Doug Englebart's lab at SRI's Augmentation Research Center, where there was no desire to make a product or prototype, but just to search for knowledge. Bill English, a brilliant hardware engineer, left for PARC and other Englebart protégés followed.

PARC's first big project came from a corporate squabble. The researches decided to build a clone of the DEC PDP-10, which was the standard minicomputer machines of the time that all the researchers wanted. Xerox had tried to force them to take an inferior SDS machine because Xerox owned SDS. Instead, the PARC researchers lost the battle to buy a PDP-10 but won the war by just ordering parts and putting together a PDP-10 clone. It was a great bonding exercise and a waste of one year. They called it the MAXC as a comeuppance to Xerox management and the poor products that Max Pavelksy's SDS made.

The PARC researches were tinkerers and hackers. They liked to make things. Generally the office had a feeling of collegiality and a grad school environment. It had lots of informal collaboration or "Tom Sawyering," with someone proactively setting forth an idea or project and then convincing others to join to attack it. If the problem or project got momentum, the ad hoc team could spend 3-6 months on it; if not everyone dispersed and looked for something else. One project was to make replicas of the expensive Bose 901 speaker systems, where a set cost $1,100. They reverse-engineered the speakers and made 40 pairs for the team at a cost of $125 per set. Alan Kay once said "a true hacker is not a group person. He's a person who loves to stay up all night, he and the machine in a love-hate relationship." Hackers were nerdy kids who were smart but un-interested in conventional goals. Computing was ideal because no credential or PhD was required and coders could be independent artisans, selling directly to customers based on the quantity and quality of output and not pedigree or something else.

One PARC institution was "Dealer," a weekly meeting in a lounge with sofas and bean bag chairs at lunch time, usually Tuesdays. Attendance was mandatory for the computer science researchers. It began with housekeeping, and then one person would be the "dealer" and take over, to set a topic for discussion and rules of debate. Topics were unconstrained, like how to take apart and re-assemble a bike, how programming algorithms are similar to kitchen recipes, or a presentation on the sociolinguistics of the Nepalese language and culture. Discussion and blunt talk were common, with people calling each other out with ejaculations like "bullshit" and "nonsense," not to mention denunciations like "That's the stupidest thing I've heard" or "It'll never work." It was a feral seminar, a match of intellects.

By the summer of 1972, Kay and a hand-picked team completed the first version of their revolutionary object-oriented programming language, Smalltalk, which would heavily influence such modern programming systems as C++ and Java. Kay had the idea in a shower in Building 34 on the Xerox campus for an entirely new syntax of computer programming based not on data and procedures, but on "objects" that would be discrete modules of programming. Object-oriented languages are easier to code in because as a program becomes more complex, much complexity is kept within an object. So a programmer can manipulate the program more easily and stick to the big picture rather than getting lost in the granular code. Because anything could be an object, like a list, word, or picture, Smalltalk did well for a graphical display. It was the language that enabled the Alto to be really useful.

Around that time, Stewart Brand wrote an article about PARC titled "Spacewar." It was about a game called Spacewar which joined computers and graphic displays. It was play, part of no one's scheme or theory, and just done for competitive fun. Yet it encompassed many of the things the researchers were trying to do for computing. As Brand noted, it was interactive in real-time, used live graphics, served as a human communication device, was on stand-alone computers, and was quite fun in a way that only games could be.

The PARC researchers would go on to make numerous devices that lived up to these principles.

The Miraculous Inventions of PARC

In early 1971 Gary Starkweather transferred from Xerox's other research lab in Rochester to PARC, bringing with him the concept of the laser printer. Starkweather was a scientist outcast at the other lab in Webster, where he created a laser technology to "paint" an image onto a xerographic drum with greater speed and precision than ordinary white light. In November 1971 Starkweather completed work on the world's first laser computer printer. He had modulated a laser to create a bit-mapped electronic image on a xerographic copier drum. The commercial project was approved and killed three times, saved only by Jack Lewis, a Xerox executive who ran the printing division and ignored orders. In 1972, the Lawrence Livermore Lab in Berkeley put in an order for the printers, which Xerox declined to fulfill (too low production run-unwilling to create an early adopter market). A corporate committee decided to delay for three years until a conventional high-speed printer, the 9000 series, was made and sold. The Xerox 9700 laser printer only came out in 1978, and that was after Burroughs showed it in a demo at the Hanover Messe. The laser printer and its successors would generate billions in sales.

In September 1972, after MAXC was completed, Thacker and Lampson invited Kay to join their project to build a small personal computer. The machine would be known as the Alto, and have a keyboard, screen, and processor in portable, suitcase-sized package (it would later have a mouse and GUI interface). The idea was that processors would be cheap enough in 5-10 years for every person to have their own "personal computer" instead of sharing time on an office computer.

In November 1972, Thacker began design work on the Alto. The original plan was to make 30 units for the PARC computer science lab. The screen would be 8.5x11" to mimic paper and the projected cost was $10,500 per machine. In the end, Xerox made 2,000 Altos at a cost of about $18,000 per machine, which fell to $12,000 after a high-volume program was put in place. There were some technical innovations like micro-parallel processing (to shift the memory access problem to the microprocessor) and a new high-performance display that used less memory (and so allowed the user to actually run apps).

Meanwhile, in June 1972, Bob Metcalfe encountered a technical paper by Norman Abramson describing Hawaii's ALOHAnet, a radio network. Metcalfe would use several principles in that paper while designing the first Ethernet, a computer networking technology for local area networks (it's how most office Internet networks are connected even in 2012). A month later, Bob Metcalfe wrote a patent memo describing his networking system, using the term "Ethernet" for the first time. Metcalfe had come from Harvard after they rejected his doctoral thesis on how networks transmit data in digital packets because it was "insufficently theoretical." He would later use the concepts in that thesis to build a multi-billion dollar company and transform the networking industry (he also resubmitted his thesis with more math, and it was accepted). Metcalfe had a huge advantage over many researchers because he was the Arpanet liaison or "facilitator" at MIT in 1971, and so saw the early networking technical issues and he had valuable personal connections with people on Arpanet. Instead of getting a university position after graduation, Metcalfe chose Xerox for the high pay, beautiful weather, and pure research freedom with no teaching responsibilities or worry about tenure. Metcalfe hooked up MAXC to Arpanet, but other local network proprietary systems were too expensive. Taylor had set specs for a local area network linking the Altos whose cost was no more than 5% of the computers it connected and was simple, with no complex hardware, and that was reliable and easily expandable (didn't want to splice cable all the time). Metcalfe used Abramson's paper, adapting it for Altos and building in redundancy (a string of verification bits known as "checksum") and an algorithm to deal with interference. It would also require a physical line and Metcalfe called it the Ethernet.

Initially none of the Alto users wanted to use Ethernet at a $500 cost, and it competed with "sneakernet," that is, people using hard disks and walking between labs with sneakers to transfer data. But when an early version of Starkweather's laser printer was connected to the Ethernet, the "EARS" system was too valuable. Ethernet for the network, the Alto for the personal computer, a Research character generator for early word processing, and a Slot machine (the name for the laser printer) to make professional paper documents. On March 31, 1974 Metcalfe filed a patent for Xerox (awarded two years later). He then quit for a job at Citibank, where he got higher pay and a chance to work on its electronic fund transfer system. He was the first top researcher to leave PARC.

The Alto is the First Personal Computer (PC)

In April 1973, the first Alto became operational, displaying an animated image of Sesame Street's Cookie Monster. The Alto was described in a memo in 1972 by Butler Lampson (himself inspired by the "Mother of All Demos" of Doug Engelbart); Chuck Thacker was the main designer of the Alto. Lampson's memo had proposed a system of interacting workstations, files, printers, and devices linked via one co-axial cable within a local area network, whose members could join or leave the network without disrupting the traffic.

The Alto was revolutionary because it was a personal workstation for one, not a room-sized, time-sharing computer for many, meant to sit on a single desktop. It is credited as being the first "personal computer" (PC) in a world of mainframes (note that some would argue for other PCs being first, like the Olivetti P101). The Alto had a bit-mapped display, a graphical user interface (GUI) with windows and icons, and a "what you see is what you get" (WYSIWYG or "wizzy-wig") editor. It also had file storage, a mouse, and software to create documents, send e-mails, and edit basic bitmap pictures. Also in April 1973, Dick Shoup's "Superpaint" frame buffer recorded and stored its first video image, showing Shoup holding a sign reading, "It works, sort of." It was the first workable paint program.

The Alto got better as PARC's programmers built apps for it. In fall 1974, Dan Ingalls invented "BitBlt," a display algorithm that later made possible the development of key features of the modern computer interface (overlapping screen windows, icons, and pop-up menus which could be manipulated with a click of the mouse). This was the desktop metaphor used by 99% of personal computers around the world even in 2013. At the same time, Charles Simonyi, Tim Mott, and Larry Tesler began work on two programs which would become the world's first user-friendly computer word processing system.

The Alto, BitBlt, and Bravo basically created the modern industry of desktop publishing, used by office workers around the world. Ordinary people at home or work could turn out professional quality newsletters, magazines, books, quarterly letters, and so on, faster and more easily.

Bravo, the word processor, has a fascinating story. Charles Simonyi, a Hungarian computer science student who defected to the US, was a key actor. His defection, as a side note, caused the Hungarian government to fire his father from a teaching job at a Budapest engineering institute, showing how the vaunted "Soviet science" system devoured its best talent for idiotic political reasons. Simonyi built on Burt Lampson's ideas for holding an entire document in memory using "piece tables" to create an app called Bravo. It was the first "what you see is what you get" WYSIWYG word processor on a computer at a reasonable speed – a useful application. People started coming to PARC to use it for personal stuff like PTA reports, letters to professional bodies, resumes, and so on. Their friends writing PhD theses wanted to use it. Larry Tesler and Tim Mott improved the Bravo user interface to create something similar to the menu-based interface people use in MS Word in 2005. It had features like "cut," "paste," and so on, after watching how non-engineers actually interacted with the interface.

In early 1975, Xerox established the System Development Division, as a stronger attempt to commercialize PARC technology. More than five years later, SDD would launch the Xerox Star. Meanwhile, a Sante Fe startup called MITS was selling the Altair 8800, a hobbyist's personal computer sold as a mail-order kit. It made the cover of Popular Electronics and caught the attention of a generation of youthful technology buffs—among them, Bill Gates and Paul Allen.

In February 1975, PARC engineers demonstrated for their colleagues a graphical user interface for a personal computer, including icons and the first use of pop-up menus. This concept would later be stolen by Steve Jobs and Bill Gates and be developed into the Windows and Macintosh interfaces of today. A month later, PARC's permanent headquarters at 3333 Coyote Hill Road formally opened.

Others Commercialize on PARC Technology

Due to one bad corporate decision, a billion dollar product was lost. In August 1977, Xerox shelved a plan to market the Alto as a commercial project. It closed the door to any possibility that the company would be in the vanguard of personal computing. If Xerox had followed through with its plan, it would have released a PC in mid-1978, beating the IBM PC by three years with a much better machine. The project was killed because Xerox President, Archie McCardell, was an accountant who didn't get technology. Also, because of Xerox's poor organizational structure, the Altos would have to be made by a Dallas manufacturing facility that made typewriters. The managers in Dallas just wanted to keep making the same product and get their highest short-term bonuses. Xerox's top execs just didn't get the Alto or PCs. They were used to a leasing business model where customers leased a copy machine and paid annual fees for the copies used based on the meter. Their fear was that if there was no print copy, "how would Xerox get paid" over and over again?

However, Xerox did sell some early Altos running Bravo to the Carter White House in 1978, and eventually to Congress for their offices. John Ellenby tried to more aggressively push the sales of Altos. But after senior management interfered too much (over the course of 3 years), Ellenby quit Xerox in 1980. He started his own company, Grid Systems, making some of the world's first laptop computers.

At the same time, during a "Futures Day" at the Xerox World Conference, Boca Raton, Florida, personal computers, graphic user interfaces, and other PARC technologies were introduced to a dazzled sales force. Other than the laser printer, however, few reached market under the Xerox name.

In June 1978, PARC scientists completed the Dorado, a high-performance PC, and Notetaker, a suitcase-sized machine that became the forerunner of a generation of laptops. The next month, PARC made a mistake by starting a program in silicon-based integrated circuits and building an expensive fabrication lab. Building a fab lab briefly put Xerox in competition with Intel, a hardware component company which Xerox had no business competing against (and Xerox never made money in that business). Xerox was attempting to do something internally that it could do much better and more cheaply by sourcing externally.

In December 1979, two key events occurred. First, Stanford University Professor James Clark designed the "Geometry Engine," the first 3-D computer graphics chip and later the foundation of his billion-dollar company, Silicon Graphics, Inc. He had used design principles formulated at PARC. The company's chips allowed the computer-aided design of cars, aircraft, roller-coasters, and movie graphics like "Jurrasic Park." Clark's first test chip was built by Lynn Conway at PARC, who came from IBM in 1972. She had written a book with Carver Mead on VLSI chip design (how to pack more circuits into a microprocessor). PARC then offered professors at a dozen schools the use of PARC's lab to create their own specialty microprocessors. Clark moved to PARC's offices and focused for 4 months in the summer of 1979 to create his chip.

At the same time Carver Mead went to Xerox headquarters to suggest they do a better job of commercializing PARC technology. He suggested Xerox set up an internal venture capital arm to fund startups with technology made by their scientists. Xerox would take an equity role and have a strategic position, while incentivizing entrepreneurial scientists to run companies. Xerox declined, one of the greatest corporate mistakes ever.

The second big event in December 1979 was when Steve Jobs and a team of Apple Computer engineers visited PARC twice and took copious notes. They came because one of Jobs' key designers, Jef Raskin, had many relationships with PARC researchers and he was impressed with their work. Jobs had signed a deal with Xerox letting Abe Zarem's Xerox Development Corporation, a subsidiary, invest in Apple pre-IPO in exchange for "marketing help." It turned out that the technology demos were much more important, and they gave Jobs a demo that no other outsider had received at that point. After observing its hardware and software in action, Jobs and his team took steps to incorporate Alto's design principles and the GUI into the Apple Lisa and Macintosh. Jobs even poached some PARC talent, like Larry Tesler, who would eventually become Apple's Chief Scientist.

In September 1980, PARC finally released its first invention to the world for commercialization. Along with Intel and Digital Equipment, Xerox issued a formal specification for the Ethernet and made it publicly available for a nominal licensing fee. Ethernet quickly became the networking technology of choice. PARC scientists also worked on an Internet Protocol standard, called PARC Universal Packet, or "Pup," which eventually became a crucial part of the Arpanet standard known as TCP/IP. It became the standard for much of the data passing through the Internet. At the same time, John Shoch invented an early computer virus, a "worm," which temporarily shut down the entire network and all the Altos at PARC one day in 1978.

Xerox did have a new computer product; it just wasn't a good one for the market. In April 1981, Xerox unveiled at a Chicago trade show to wide acclaim the Star workstation as the Xerox 8010 Information System, with a beautiful GUI and desktop metaphor. It was the commercial offspring of the Alto and other PARC technology. However, the Star was slow and cost $16,600. Moreover, customers needed to buy 2 to 10 at a time, and had to install Ethernet and a laser printer. The costs were daunting. By August IBM unveiled its Personal Computer, forever altering the commercial landscape of office computing and making the Star obsolete. IBM's machine only cost $5,000 and didn't have the pretty GUI. It didn't have icons, windows, a desktop metaphor, e-mail, or Internet; it crashed randomly. Yet it was good enough for basic business tasks and apps and it sold very well. Only 30,000 Stars were sold, compared to millions of IBM PCs.

PARC's talent was frustrated and wanted to leave. Earlier that year, Charles Simonyi was thinking about next steps. Bob Metcalfe suggested he talk to a 22-year old kid named Bill Gates who ran a startup called Microsoft. Gates and Simonyi hit it off right away with high-bandwidth conversations on the nature of computing, the role of technology, and future product ideas. Simonyi felt the Xerox corporate brass didn't know much about technology and didn't care – they were bean-counters, ex-Ford finance people that McCardell had hired to run the company. Gates on the other hand was a visionary and a first-rate, cut-throat businessman. As Simonyi put it, "you could see that Microsoft do things one hundred times faster, literally." So Simonyi left PARC for Microsoft, where he became a "messenger RNA of the PARC virus." Within six years, the market capitalization of Microsoft was higher than Xerox's, and Simonyi plotted a strategy to exploit a range of markets that Xerox fumbled on: word processors, spreadsheets, e-mail, and voice recognition. Simonyi especially helped on the project to create Windows, a first-rate GUI operating system that competed with Apple.

Another dispirited engineer who left PARC in 1981 was Chuck Geschke, who was frustrated that Xerox wasn't commercializing their work. He went on to found Adobe Corp., a billion-dollar company that used postscript, a typesetting language, to help computer users make crisp, printable, presentable, and professional documents with text and graphics. The company's technology became the de facto standard of computer typesetting and held that position in 2013.

By May 1983, Apple introduced the Lisa, a personal computer with a graphical interface based on principles developed at PARC. Jobs joked that Xerox couldn't compete with his scrappy startup because Xerox's cost structure was too high. The company was fat and bloated. As one Xerox engineer joked, "If we built a paper clip it would cost three thousand bucks."

In September 1983, Bob Taylor resigned from PARC under pressure. Within a few months many of the center's top computer engineers and scientists resigned in sympathy. Many went to Taylor's new employer, the DEC Systems Research Center. In January 1984, Apple introduced the Macintosh, the popular successor to the Lisa and the most influential embodiment of the PARC personal computer, with a striking "1984"-style television commercial during the Super Bowl.

Xerox's Inventions Spread to Others

Xerox PARC's inventions continued to spread through Silicon Valley, but mostly at other companies. In January 1990, Adobe released Photoshop for the Macintosh, thus completing the desktop-publishing revolution. Photoshop, actually developed by Thomas Knoll, a student at the University of Michigan, allowed ordinary computer users to do things that were difficult even for a professional printer. IBM itself introduced the Interleaf desktop-publishing software for its personal computers.

Operating systems made some headway. In 1988 a Los Angeles-based company called Elixir ported the Xerox Star windowing GUI to the IBM PC and to MS-DOS. Yet it was too little too late to compete with the Macintosh. Smalltalk, the first object-oriented environment, had never been marketed by Xerox. Los Angeles-based Digitalk had already developed in 1983 a version of Smalltalk for the IBM PC, the first commercial release of Smalltalk. In 1989 Adele Goldberg, who had taken over management of Smalltalk at Xerox PARC from Alan Kay, founded ParcPlace in Mountain View to market a version of Smalltalk for Unix, Windows, and Macintosh platforms. Both companies were trying to capitalize on the appeal of Smalltalk's elegant software development environment and graphical user interface, but Smalltalk was an interpreted language and therefore very slow. Last but not least, it was not endorsed by any major company.

Document management and Visual BASIC also had roots in Xerox PARC. Documentum, based in Pleasanton and founded in January 1990 by Howard Shao of Xerox PARC and John Newton of Ingres, was incubated by Xerox's own venture-capital arm, Xerox Technology Ventures, to consolidate PARC's efforts in document management software. In 1988 Alan Cooper of Digital Research sold Microsoft a visual form generator ("Ruby") that, combined with Microsoft's BASIC programming language, would become Visual Basic. The spirit was pure PARC: a friendly environment to develop business applications on personal computers. It also introduced a new way for people to augment a system by seamlessly integrating third-party software code "widgets" into the system.

Finally, PARC's other great invention, ethernet, had spawned an industry of its own and the demand for "broadband" was increasing dramatically. Sensing an opportunity, Indian-born inventor Vinod Bhardwaj founded Sunnyvale-based Kalpana in 1987; in 1990, it introduced the first Ethernet switch. A "switch" is a device that connects the computers of a Local Area network (LAN). The switch optimizes the traffic of data packets, thereby reducing bandwidth usage and increasing the overall bandwidth of the network. Another early player in that market was Crescendo Communications, founded in 1990 by Italian-born former Olivetti executives Luca Cafiero and Mario Mazzola.

Did Xerox PARC Blow It?

Why did PARC invent so many great technologies and then fail to commercialize them? The first part of this chapter listed factors leading to success. Now we turn to why Xerox failed at commercialization. As Steve Jobs said in a speech in 1996: "Xerox could have owned the entire computer industry... could have been the IBM of the nineties... could have been the Microsoft of the nineties."[21]

One reason is that the company's decision-making on dozens of occasions was not about new technologies and opportunities, but about personalities, politics, and short-term incentives. High tech companies

---

[21] Cringely, Robert X. "Triumph of the Nerds: The Television Program Transcripts: Part III." PBS Special, 1996, http://www.pbs.org/nerds/part3.html.

require brutal hours and superhuman effort, so employees want to share in the upside with equity, not salaries and bonuses.

The second was that the company's managers saw it as a copier company, not as a computer or a publishing company, let alone an enabler of the "office of the future." The managers were fixated on the leased copier business model, and the sales force was trained on copiers and typewriters, not new office technology. Also the purchasing managers for computers were professional IT people, not the managers who ordered copiers.

A third reason was that Xerox wouldn't allow entrepreneurial scientists to do spinouts and avoid the corporate bureaucracy. New ventures had to be led by people running established divisions, people who hated risk-taking. So Xerox lost talent like Clark, Simonyi, Geschke, Metcalfe, and others who did startups that became billion-dollar companies much bigger than Xerox.

Finally, the fault lay with PARC itself, which often acted as a pure research center. The scientists were generally far away from customer development, sales, or intrapreneurial development. The few Xerox execs (not PARC researchers) who tried to commercialize products were crushed by the corporate bureaucracy. So while PARC was a success at innovation, it was mostly a failure at commercialization.

14. Helpers: Lawyers and Investment Bankers in Silicon Valley (1970-2000)

The Most Maligned Group

One underappreciated aspect of Silicon Valley was the infrastructure of professional "helpers" that supported startups. Between the large corporate engines, the nimble entrepreneurs, and the legions of venture capitalists, stood the workhorse professionals who supported the smooth functioning of the Valley. These were the corporate lawyers and investment bankers, plus the accountants and journalists (who will not be covered in this chapter). The professionals were sometimes maligned, and as the venture capitalist Tom Perkins once unfairly referred to investment bankers: "[T]hey are a necessary evil." The lawyer Larry Sonsini called it a "synergistic grouping of entrepreneurs, venture capitalists, lawyers, accountants coming together to really build enterprises."

For the lawyers, a handful of specialized law firms dominated the Valley. First and pre-eminent was Wilson Sonsini Goodrich & Rosati, as it was the largest high-tech law firm in the Valley. Next came a handful of firms such as Cooley, Fenwick and West, and Gunderson Detmer. Some notable failures were Brobeck Phleger & Harrison and the Venture Law Group.

The investment bankers have had a tougher time, as most of the boutique Silicon Valley bankers have gone bust or folded into larger enterprises. This includes firms like Montgomery Securities, Robertson Stephens, and Hambrecht and Quist. In 2012, the initial public offering (IPO) and mergers and acquisition (M&A) business in Silicon Valley is dominated by the large broker-dealer banks such as Goldman Sachs, Credit Suisse, Morgan Stanley, Deutsche Bank, and so on.

Wilson Sonsini Goodrich & Rosati

In 2012, Wilson Sonsini Goodrich & Rosati (WSGR) was legal counsel to more than 300 public and 3,000 private companies, representing firms such as Apple Computer, Hewlett-Packard, VA Linux Systems, Novell, Netscape Communications, and Micron Technology. The firm also served investment banks and venture capital firms that financially support both technology and other companies. WSGR is based in the heart of Silicon Valley with a satellite office in San Francisco and small offices in other hi-tech centers such as Austin, Texas, McClean, Virginia, and Kirkland, Washington. The firm's gleaming glass-walled offices at 650

Page Mill Road are affectionately referred to as the "Death Star" by its competitors and Stanford neighbors.

If every institution is the lengthened shadow of one person, then Wilson Sonsini the law firm could point to the name partner Larry Sonsini. He was perhaps Silicon Valley's most feared and sought-after lawyer and acted as corporate consigliere to many CEOs. Sonsini was a soft-spoken and disciplined man, often dressed nattily in dark Italian suits. He worked in the Valley's environment of frenetic shouters wearing chinos or blue jeans, t-shirts or polo-shirts, and often flip-flops. In contrast, Sonsini's papers would be arranged neatly in evenly-spaced stacks across his office desk. During his 40 plus years as a lawyer, Sonsini helped to publicize many of the leaders of the technology boom, including Netscape Communications, Pixar, Google, Apple, and SUN Microsystems.

Sonsini graduated from the UC Berkeley undergraduate and law school programs and he joined McCloskey Wilson & Mosher as its first associate in 1966. His mentor was John Wilson, then 50, who after a distinguished legal career in the East had moved to the Valley in 1956. The firm's location near Stanford University helped it represent companies formed from research conducted there. By 1966 the firm had established ties with some key players in the new venture capital field, including Laurance Rockefeller, Davis and Rock, and Draper, Gaither and Anderson. Wilson was even involved in the formation of the Mayfield Fund and was a part-time partner there for a while.

Wilson Sonsini's legal business model was to represent entrepreneurs and startups first, venture firms and banks second. Both Wilson and Sonsini wanted to continue to represent their clients as they grew, rather than handing them off to larger firms when they went public, which was common practice. Or as Sonsini said, "we started to develop the recipe for how to build companies… I was becoming a piece of the recipe."[22]

One key ingredient was co-investing. In 1969 the partners created WM Investment Company to take advantage of stock options that some of its startup clients offered instead of cash for payment of services. It was a way of dealing with a very practical problem of poor clients. Many other Valley law firms eventually adopted this practice as a way to participate in their clients' long-range success. This practice created a potential for conflicts of interest. For example, if a lawyer holds stock in a client company and then has to decide whether the client needs by law to disclose information that may cause its stock price to fall, the lawyer's judgment could be clouded. Also, some partners had access to deals that others didn't, causing a partnership conflict. So in 1978 Wilson Sonsini set up WS Investments, a fund designed to manage both problems. Each partner's pay would automatically be docked to create the fund. Deductions were mandatory and so each partner would have pro rata equal

[22] Parloff, Roger. "Scandals rock Silicon Valley's top legal ace." Fortune, November 17, 2006.
http://money.cnn.com/magazines/fortune/fortune_archive/2006/11/27/8394382/index.htm.

stakes in every company. Typical investments were in the $25,000 to $50,000 range, and payouts could be large (the Google investment was worth nearly $20 million after the company's IPO in 2004).

In the 1970s, WSGR gained new partners and a new name. John B. Goodrich, a tax expert, joined to start the tax department in 1970 and Mario M. Rosati was recruited to build the trust and estates practice. After McCloskey left to enter politics in 1973, the firm changed its name to Wilson, Mosher & Sonsini. Eventually in 1978 the firm assumed its current name: Wilson Sonsini Goodrich & Rosati. Note that the tax and trust and estates departments were strategic additions to serve startups and their founders. WSGR was also one of the first firms to build a technology department of PhDs and others with advanced degrees. These teams understood the technology and would focus upon technology problems in licensing, distribution of product, intellectual property protection, intellectual property litigation, and so on.

The event that marked Wilson Sonsini's arrival on the national business stage was its representation of Apple Computer in its IPO in 1980. It was the largest IPO since Ford Motor Company's in 1956, and the notion that two local Palo Alto firms (Wilson Sonsini and Fenwick) would handle it was a big deal. While the 1970s were the time of semiconductor companies, the 1980s brought Apple and a range of computer companies (hardware, peripherals, software).

In 1984 the firm entered the mergers and acquisition advice business of providing mature technology firms with counsel. The firm had helped ROLM Corp. get started in 1969 and had handled its IPO in 1975. Then Larry Sonsini represented ROLM when IBM acquired it for $1.8 billion. The ROLM transaction implied the firm needed more manpower if it were to provide a full range of legal services. By 1986 it expanded to 97 lawyers, sometimes by lateral hiring of mature attorneys from rival law firms. Driven and hard-headed entrepreneurs appreciated Sonsini. TJ Rodgers, the founder and CEO of Cypress Semiconductor, noted that he didn't take orders well but he liked Sonsini for being professorial and nonjudgmental. Sonsini's attitude was "you can choose to do this, you can choose to do that, and these will be the consequences." An entrepreneur was not being forced or pushed into anything. Instead Sonsini explained why a frustrating, arcane, and inefficient system of laws made sense and should be followed.[23]

The 1980s were a good time, as a mini-bull market kept the firm busy with a string of technology IPOs. By 1988, Wilson Sonsini's average profits per partner reached $430,000. It was much more than any San Francisco firm and outpaced the nearest competitor by $100,000, according to The Recorder, a San Francisco legal newspaper. Sonsini personally found the Valley to be unique because of lateral movement for

---

[23] Ibid.

startup employees (going to one company while looking to work for another), plus the equity compensation culture (due to US tax policy in that granting of stock options isn't a taxable event). Sonsini also opined on the failure culture: "Failure is not a stigma. The fact that you started an enterprise and failed at it probably makes you more valuable as an entrepreneur."

Silicon Valley's lawyering style is less adversarial and more cooperative than normal. While many East Coast lawyers are in the business of protecting wealth and fighting hard for their clients, most Valley lawyers understand the importance of cooperation as all transactions are repeat transactions (the Valley is a small environment). A scorched earth strategy is a poor one, as the prevailing Valley sentiment is to make the pie larger, rather than the traditional view of dividing a fixed pie. For many businesses, lawyers are combatants. However in the Valley the focus of business is to create wealth. Neither lawyers nor clients want to spend weeks arguing with theatrics or threats.

Internally, WSGR also set different norms. It is a consensus driven culture and group heads wield much power. There is no automatic "lockstep" increase in pay and no tenure; associates and partners must earn their keep every year. Finally the firm pushes diversity very hard, including ethnicity, gender, color, and creed. Still, there are few female partners in this rough environment.

The 1990s technology boom brought even more clients, deals, and conflicts. For example, in 1995 Wilson Sonsini represented its client Seagate when it acquired Conner Peripherals, another client. The CEOs had to sign a conflict-of-interest waiver. With the healthcare and biotechnology industries expanding, Wilson Sonsini represented several life science firms in the 1990s, including Abgenix, Cardiac Pathways Corporation, Cell Genesys, and Vivus. Non-tech clients included Home Depot and Monaco Coach Corporation. The decade ended with Wilson Sonsini doing 118 initial public offerings in 1999, representing both companies and underwriters; this was the most for any law firm in the nation. The firm bulked up to handle the workload, peaking in size at close to 800 lawyers in 2000. Other national law firms popped up, opening 40 satellite offices. It was a bad time, as Wilson Sonsini partner Boris Feldman admitted "it was a period of raw greed." Restrained greed was always an important component in the Valley, where the sense was if you built a good company, you'd be rewarded for it. But during the Tech Bubble, people forgot the element of building value and went mad. Feldman felt the "values in the Valley were, if not corrupted, then certainly strained."[24]

In 1999 and 2000, Sonsini later admitted it was "somewhat of a practice" for Valley lawyers to insist on getting investment opportunities

---

[24] Ibid.

in their startup clients as a pre-condition of representing them. Even some Wilson Sonsini lawyers did this. Yet after the peak, the Tech Bust was sobering, and Wilson Sonsini had to lay off dozens of lawyers, along with the rest of the Valley. Still, times were exciting, as Sonsini recalls: "I remember when I met with Larry Page and Sergey Brin, two Stanford students, one Saturday in my office, who said they wanted to start a company, and they wanted to call it Google. I thought, you can't name a company Google. Well, now it's a verb."

The aughties proved tough as Larry Sonsini got caught up in the HP boardroom scandal in 2005 and the corporate options backdating scandal in 2006. While he was found to have clean hands in both situations, they rocked the Valley. Also, while Sonsini sat on nine public boards in February 2002, by 2010 he was down to just one (Echelon Corporation). He had come to believe that the presumption should be against sitting on public boards, to keep boards more independent and lawyers with fewer conflicts.

Other Big Silicon Valley Law Firms

The other important Silicon Valley law firms are Cooley, Fenwick and West, and Gunderson Dettmer.

Cooley was founded in the 1930s when Arthur Cooley and Louis Crowley started a law partnership in the Humboldt Bank building in San Francisco. Later important partners were lawyers such as Fred Supple, Bill Godward, Rowan Gaither, Ed Huddleson, Gus Castro, and Sandy Tatum. The firm's name has changed many times, and today the firm simply goes by Cooley LLP. In 1958, Cooley formed Draper, Gaither and Anderson, the first venture capital partnership to be organized on the West coast. The Firm also formed Raychem in 1957 and National Semiconductor in 1959, two early technology stars. Later Cooley took Genentech public in 1980 and Amgen in 1983; they were the largest biotech companies by market capitalization. As Cooley was a San Francisco-based firm, in 1980 it opened a second office in Palo Alto. In 1992, Cooley took Qualcomm public and soon opened an office in San Diego. Cooley eventually opened offices in other technology centers like Boulder (Colorado), Reston (Virginia), Boston (Massachusetts), and Seattle (Washington). It eventually merged in the fall of 2006 with Kronish Lieb Weiner & Hellman LLP, a New York firm with bankruptcy, tax, and complex commercial and white-collar litigation practices. In 2012, Cooley had some important clients such as Google, eBay, Facebook, NVIDIA, Tivo, Brocade, Bluetooth, Adobe Systems, and so on.

Fenwick and West was founded by four attorneys who moved to Palo Alto in 1972. The firm incorporated Apple Computer in 1976 and took Oracle Corporation public in 1986. It was involved in major M&A transactions including the largest Internet merger in history (VeriSign's $21 billion acquisition of Network Solutions) and the largest software

merger in history (Symantec's $13 billion acquisition of Veritas Software).
By 2012, Fenwick and West was the 2nd-largest law firm headquartered in
Silicon Valley.

Gunderson Dettmer was a smaller, boutique firm, but many angels in
the Valley, such as Chris Dixon, preferred it to the large firms due to its
flexibility and lean structure. That contrasted with two notable law firm
failures: Brobeck Phleger & Harrison and the Venture Law Group.

Brobeck was formed in 1926 and had traditional clients, such as Wells
Fargo, for many years. Yet during the Tech Boom, its lawyers chose to
focus on serving technology clients (neglecting anti-cyclical business like
bankruptcy and litigation), taking equity instead of cash, spending lavishly
on marketing (advertising on TV), and building a fancy headquarters. The
firm's revenues jumped from $214 million in 1998 to $314 million in
2000, when the firm became top-heavy with 754 attorneys (with a profits-
per-partner figure of more than $1 million a year). As the firm started to
lay off staff in 2002, key lawyers jumped to other firms and took their
clients with them. What was left was a large building with few partners
and lots of debt, which ended in a dissolved partnership.

The Venture Law Group was formed in 1993 to serve only startups.
The firm prospered during the Tech Boom as it took equity stakes and
cashed out big. In 1999, the firm's equity investments generated more than
$30 million, and in 2000 investments generated more than $100 million.
The firm's business model was hence rooted in equity compensation and
not cash. From 2000 to 2001, revenues fell from $64 million to $54
million, and even more in 2002. Eventually, the Venture Law Group was
absorbed by a larger, more traditional San Francisco law firm, Heller
Ehrman (which incidentally also went bust during the 2008 financial
crisis).

Defunct Investment Banks of Yore

Sadly the history of investment banks in Silicon Valley was one of
failure. Investment bankers were essential to the Valley infrastructure as
they helped companies scale up from smallish, private venture capital
money to massive public equity capital. The investment bankers were
essential since under US securities laws and SEC regulations, before an
IPO was completed and money raised, a company needed to follow a set of
procedures and do a road show, where management met with different
groups of investors in cities around the US, to raise capital from the public.
The investment bankers (stock underwriters) used the tour to build a book
of orders for the company (stock issuer). In good times, the stock was
oversold by two or three times. Very rarely did investment bankers have to
take on the risk of purchasing the leftover shares of an undersold issue to
hold on their own books. Some would argue the most important function
of an investment bank was its list of contacts: institutional investors such
as pension funds and mutual fund managers on the one hand, and the

companies ready for IPOs on the other. Essentially, investment bankers were SEC-licensed gatekeepers and middlemen.

Not everyone was a fan of investment bankers. Tom Perkins believed the term investment banker was misleading. The Wall Street banks didn't invest or provide basic banking services; rather they just marketed the stock of an IPO like glib salesmen. Perkins wrote that "the term fee-charging middlemen is clearly less attractive, but it's much closer to an accurate description of their actual function." Even at his career's end, Perkins found investment bankers exceptionally short-term oriented on any given transaction and focused only on their resulting fee. For Perkins, investment bankers were a "necessary evil."[25]

Perkins' partner, Frank Caufield, had an even more caustic comment about bankers: "They have all the self-restraint of lobotomized sharks." One must, however, keep in mind the social value of an investment bank. Any growing enterprise needs large amounts of capital that only the public markets can provide. The public equity, corporate structure offers a company and its investors many advantages: i) two layers of limited liability (protecting investors from the liabilities of the company and the liabilities of other investors, while protecting the company from the liabilities of investors); ii) tradable and fungible, hence liquid, stock ownership; iii) a fast way to raise further money through shelf registration and access to debt and commercial paper markets. And investment bankers are the sole gatekeepers for the public equity markets, making sure that both buyers and sellers of stock get a fair deal.

Silicon Valley was historically served by four independent, San Francisco-based boutique investment banks from the 1960s to the late 1990s. Their Wall Street competitors called them the HARM group, though they preferred the moniker of the Four Horsemen: Hambrecht & Quist, Alex Brown & Sons, Robertson, Stephens, and Montgomery Securities. By 2000, each of those firms had been gobbled up by a large, Wall Street bank. This was followed by defections of large numbers of investment bankers and other key employees. There were several reasons the banks couldn't stay independent:

- The big Wall Street investment banks started to compete strongly during the Tech Boom, and they had greater resources to do so. For example, the bigger investment banks offered companies a full array of products for raising money, including loans, bonds and specialized forms of stock. The Four Horsemen focused mainly on traditional stock offerings;
- Depression-era regulations like Glass-Steagall were removed, allowing commercial banks with large balance sheets to enter the business and outcompete the boutique investment banks;

---

[25] Perkins, Tom. Valley Boy: The Education of Tom Perkins. New York: Gotham Reprint, 2008, p. 113.

- Most of the Four Horsemen sold out before the top of the bubble so their senior partners could cash in, perhaps sensing there was a bubble and that their long-term competitive position was weak.

In 2012, a handful of Wall Street banks, such as Goldman Sachs, Morgan Stanley, Credit Suisse, Deutsche Bank, and so on dominated the Valley IPO and M&A scene. Jeffries Group survived as the only independent bank, but its headquarters were in Los Angeles.

The Four Horseman Boutique Investment Banks

The oldest investment bank in Silicon Valley, Alex Brown & Sons, was actually a Baltimore bank started by Alexander Brown and which did an early US IPO, the Baltimore Water Company, in 1808. Eventually the firm moved to New York by the late 19th century to do railroad financings, and it opened up a San Francisco office after World War II. The company had the good fortune to do the IPO of some growth companies of the times, including Microsoft, Oracle Systems, Starbucks, and United Healthcare. Alex Brown & Sons was bought by Bankers Trust in 1997 to form BT Alex Brown. Two years later, in 1999, BT Alex Brown was acquired by Deutsche Bank.

The genesis of investment banking in San Francisco was with Sanford "Sandy" Robertson. Robertson came to California in 1965 as an investment banker for Smith Barney and did early deals with Applied Technology and Spectra-Physics, during which he met Tom Perkins when Spectra-Physics acquired Perkins' laser company University Labs. However, as Robertson tells it, his co-workers in New York City made fun of his "ray gun company" and he decided to leave and start his own firm, realizing he had no future doing West Coast technology deals for an East Coast bank. So he started Robertson, Colman & Siebel in 1969, raising $100,000 from 8 limited partners, including Eugene Kleiner, and another $100,000 each from the three principals ($1.1 million total). The limited partners brought deals, advice, credibility, and technology knowledge

Robertson's early deals included the Wangco IPO, a tape drive manufacturer, and in the fall of 1972, the IPO of Applied Materials, which would become a multi-billion dollar semiconductor company. One of Robertson's proudest moments was introducing Eugene Kleiner and Tom Perkins, by asking them to breakfast at Ricky's Hyatt House. The two men instantly hit it off, and Robertson said this was "the best merger I ever did in my life ... introducing those two guys to each other and raising their first fund [$8.4 million in 1972]." In 1971, Thomas Weisel, an Olympic-caliber athlete, joined the firm, which was renamed Robertson, Colman, Siebel & Weisel. Weisel was a quick study and in October 1978, Weisel, the junior partner, pulled off what was described later as a mutiny. Weisel became chief executive of the firm and prompted the departure of

Robertson and Colman. Weisel changed the name of the firm to Montgomery Securities.

Montgomery Securities ended up being a dominant boutique investment bank that specialized in the high-tech and health care sectors. Montgomery was the lead banker for high-tech companies like TriQuint, Cyrix, and Quarterdeck. It also reached deeply into the broader market, handling offerings by Avis Rent-A-Car and Guitar Center. The 1990s were good years for the firm, as it more than doubled to 1,400 employees. Eventually Weisel sold the firm in 1997 for a rich $1.2 billion payout to Nationsbank, despite the firm's meager capital of only about $200 million. A year after the sale, Weisel left to start a new, competing firm named Thomas Weisel & Partners. He recruited several of his highest-ranking colleagues to join and used his Montgomery payout to fund the initial operations.

Sandy Robertson was not finished, however, after his ouster in 1978. He went on that year to found Robertson, Colman, Stephens & Woodman along with partners Robert Colman and Dean Woodman (the firm's name was shortened to Robertson Stephens & Company in 1989). Robertson Stephens and Montgomery Securities would remain fierce rivals for two decades. Just during the 1990s, Montgomery and Robertson Stephens generated more than $11 billion in offerings in which they served as lead managers, easily putting the combined investment banks into Wall Street's Top 10.

Robertson believed investment banking was a great business, as bankers made strategic, high-level decisions and got to "play God" along with a company's board. He also pointed out that because there was very little financing in the 1970s, a $1 million deal was the largest. If a startup needed a second financing, it was a washout round at 10 cents to the dollar, and at the third round the entrepreneurs got completely washed out. This forced entrepreneurs to be lean and focus on expenses. All this changed in the fat, 1980s markets.

Robertson Stephens helped bring forward companies like SUN Microsystems, Excite and, in the biotech arena, Chiron. It became a leading underwriter of growth companies in the technology, Internet and e-commerce, health care, retailing, consumer products, and real estate sectors. The firm handled more than 500 initial public offerings over a 30-year period, often using Wilson Sonsini as the corporate counsel. Before being sold, the firm led or co-managed 10 of the top 25 IPO performers in 1997 and 8 of the top 25 IPO performers in 1998. Tech Boom deals included advising Excite on its merger with @Home, E-Trade on its purchase of Telebanc, and WebMD in its transactions with Microsoft and Healtheon.

In June 1997, a long tale of sales began as the partners sold Robertson Stephens to BankAmerica for $540 million. The combined firm would operate as BancAmerica Robertson Stephens for approximately 11 months. In 1998, BankAmerica agreed to a merger with NationsBank, which had recently become the parent company of arch-rival Montgomery Securities. The significant internal tensions between Montgomery and Robertson Stephens led to the sale of Robertson Stephens to BankBoston in 1998 for $800 million, a nice profit for BancAmerica. Shortly after the sale of the firm to BankBoston, Sandy Robertson left the firm and was succeeded by COO Bob Emery. Robertson Stephens changed hands again the following year when Fleet Financial merged with BankBoston in 1999 to form FleetBoston Financial. As the technology banking business became more competitive due to the major Wall Street banks, Robertson Stephens held its own and completed the underwriting of 74 IPOs with a total value of $5.5 billion between 1999 and 2000.

By 2001, Robertson Stephens was suffering from the bust after the dot-com bubble due to a lack of interest in new technology IPOs and a lack of companies well suited for IPO. Robertson Stephens had a net loss of $61 million in 2001, compared with a net profit of $216 in 2000 (revenue had dropped from $1.56 billion to $543 million). Fleet put Robertson Stephens up for sale in April 2002 and struggled to come to terms with a buyer, as many analysts thought the firm was worth $100 million at most. Senior executives of Robertson Stephens pushed hard for a potential management buyout. However, the deal talks ended in acrimony as Robertson Stephens' executives didn't want to give up their guaranteed revenue-sharing pay from previous years. In July 2002, the Fleet team in disgust decided to shut the bank down, firing nearly 950 people in a fast liquidation.

The final horseman in San Francisco was Hambrecht & Quist (H&Q), founded by Bill Hambrecht and George Quist in 1968. H&Q underwrote IPOs for Apple Computer, Genentech, and Adobe Systems in the 1980s. Most of its early people were engineers, as both Hambrecht and Quist were financial types. They looked for tech-savvy partners who made judgments based on science and people as "the numbers were the last thing you looked at." Genentech raised capital with no revenues, promising some insulin sales in 18 months; it took four years. H&Q also developed a model of not just raising capital, but investing in its companies. Hambrecht explained: "small companies were not very attractive financings from an economical point of view. But if we were a shareholder, and we could benefit as a shareholder, we thought, okay, that would be a good business model. And as it turned out, if you go back for the thirty years H&Q was in the business, about 40% of the profits came from the venture and 60% frominvestment banking."

In the 1990s, H&Q also backed the IPOs of Netscape, MP3.com, and Amazon.com. Competition in the investment banking industry in the late 1990s limited H&Q's growth potential, so in 1999, Chase Manhattan Bank acquired H&Q for $1.35 billion. The firm was renamed Chase Securities West and is currently part of JPMorgan Chase. After leaving H&Q, Bill

Hambrecht popularized a Dutch auction model allowing anyone, not just investing insiders, to buy stock in an IPO. Among the companies that adopted this model were Overstock.com, Ravenswood Winery, and Salon Media Group. Most famously, Hambrecht's new firm nabbed a role co-managing Google's large IPO, by persuading the founders to try a Dutch auction method.

A final story on how Hambrecht changed tech banking was with Farinon Electric, when Hambrecht went to see Bill Farinon one day and had an epiphany. Farinon's company had $2 to $3 million in revenue and was profitable, but small; his father-in-law, who had put up the money, needed some liquidity.

Farinon asked Hambrecht: "Can I go public?"

Hambrecht said: "Look, to go public you have to have five years of earnings; you have to have $1 million of after-tax earnings; you've got to have this, you've got to have that." Hambrecht gave him the four or five guidelines that they used on Wall Street.

Farinon asked confusedly: "Who set up those rules?"

Hambrecht said, "I don't know. They're just the rules. I don't know."

Farninon jumped at the banker and shouted, "Look, those goddamn rules. They were set up for you guys! So you could make a lot of money. They have nothing to do with me. How about looking at this from my point of view? I want my company to stay independent. I need some money."

Then as Hambrecht walked out the door, Farinon fumed and finally looked up and said, "Do you think I have a good company here?"

Hambrecht replied, "Oh yes. I think you really do."

Farinon said, "Would you put in some of your own money?"

Hambrecht replied, "Absolutely, I would love to buy stock."

Farinon pleaded, "If you're willing to buy stock for yourself, why aren't you willing to sell it to the public?"

Hambrecht relented and later made that his firm's credo. If he was willing to put up his own personal money, then he was willing to sell it to the public.[26]

Surviving Investment Banks

The Silicon Valley investment banking scene was dominated by the big Wall Street investment banks in 2012, with Deutsche Bank, Morgan Stanley, JP Morgan, Goldman Sachs, Credit Suisse, and Barclays doing the most tech IPOs. Thomas Weisel stayed independent till early 2010, when Stifel Financial Corp. acquired it for $318 million. Stifel participated in nine tech, media, and telecom deals from 2005 to 2009, compared with

---

[26] Hambrecht, William R. "Early Bay Area Venture Capitalists: Shaping the Economic and Business Landscape ," conducted by Sally Smith Hughes in 2010, Regional Oral History Office, The Bancroft Library, University of California, Berkeley, 2011, p. 15.

Weisel's 96. While the combined company, with estimated revenue of $1.6 billion, had research coverage on more US public companies than any Wall Street firm (1,143), its main office was not in the Valley.

Perhaps the last remaining independent bank was Jeffries Group, founded in 1962 in a telephone booth outside the Pacific Stock Exchange in San Francisco, by Boyd Jeffries. Jeffries was more of a niche broker than an investment bank for a long time, was acquired by IDS and then became independent again going on to become a public company in 1983. It specialized in junk bonds and the oil and gas sector for a while. The firm only became a true investment bank for startups and small companies in the 1990s, under the new CEO Frank Baxter. The number of equity analysts grew from 0 to 38 in 1993, and revenue from investment banking jumped 127%. Sandy Robertson said in the late aughties: "There is a hole in the marketplace where the Four Horsemen have gone. Jefferies has a chance to fill it. They always had great trading and great distribution. Now they got the whole puzzle."

15. Hobbyists: The Microprocessor, Computer Kits, Ethernet, Internet, the Alto, and Genetic Engineering (1971-75)

The Microprocessor

A microprocessor is a programmable set of integrated circuits; basically, a city of logic gates compressed into a chip. It had been theoretically possible for years to integrate the Central Processing Unit (CPU) of a computer on a chip. It was just a matter of perfecting the technology. In 1970 Lee Boysel at Four Phase Systems had already designed the AL1, an 8-bit CPU. It was the first commercial microprocessor.

Yet the microprocessor that changed the history of computing was being developed elsewhere. Ted Hoff at Intel bet on silicon-gated MOS technology to hold a 4-bit CPU onto a chip. In 1970 he hired Federico Faggin, the inventor of silicon-gated transistors. Faggin implemented Hoff's design in silicon, and in November 1971 Intel unveiled the 4004, a small thumbnail-size electronic device containing 2,300 transistors and capable of processing 92,000 instructions per second. Intel's tiny 4004 chip was as powerful as the ENIAC, but millions of times smaller and ten thousand times cheaper. By August 1972 Intel had ready an 8-bit version of the 4004, the 8008, whose eight-bit word allowed it to represent 256 ASCII characters, including all ten digits, both uppercase and lowercase letters and punctuation marks.

Intel was not convinced that a microprocessor could be used to build a computer. It was up to Bill Pentz at California State University in Sacramento to prove the concept. In 1972 his team built the Sac State 8008, the first microcomputer, and helped Intel fine-tune the microprocessor for the task of building computers.

Intel's initial motivation to make microprocessors was that microprocessors helped sell more memory chips. A few months earlier Intel had introduced another important invention, the EPROM, developed by the Israeli-born engineer Dov Frohman. An EPROM (Erasable Programmable Read Only Memory) is a non-volatile memory made of transistors that can be erased. By making it possible to reprogram the microprocessor at will, it also made it more versatile. The 4004 and the 8008 had been produced in small quantities, the latter mainly as the basis for DEC's own processors. In April 1974 Intel unveiled the 8080, designed at the transistor level by Japanese-born Masatoshi Shima. It lowered both the price and the complexity of building a computer while further increasing the power (290,000 instructions per second). It was bound to happen.

Meanwhile, at least 60 semiconductor companies had been founded in the Santa Clara Valley between 1961 and 1972, many by former Fairchild engineers and managers. It was a highly competitive environment, driven by highly-educated engineers.

The center of mass for venture capital had steadily shifted from San Francisco towards Menlo Park. In 1972, the venture capital firm Kleiner Perkins, founded by Austrian-born Eugene Kleiner of Fairchild Semiconductor and former Hewlett-Packard executive Tom Perkins, opened offices on Sand Hill Road. It was followed by Don Valentine of Fairchild Semiconductor who founded Capital Management Services, later renamed Sequoia Capital. That year the electronics writer Don Hoeffler coined the term "Silicon Valley," the new nickname of the area between Pale Alto and San Jose, which fell in the Santa Clara Valley. In 1974 Reid Dennis and Burton McMurtry founded the investment company Institutional Venture Associates. In 1976 it split into two partnerships, McMurtry's Technology Venture Associates and Dennis' Institutional Venture Partners, while Tommy Davis launched the Mayfield Fund. In 1968, Harvey Wagner and several UC Berkeley professors founded Teknekron, one of the world's first startup incubators focused on IT.

The Impact of Microprocessors

Very few people knew what "silicon" was, but many began to understand that it was important to build smaller and cheaper computers that could be embedded into just about any device. For example, in 1973 Automatic Electronic Systems (AES) of Canada introduced the "AES-90." It was a "word processor" that combined a screen (a cathode ray tube or CRT monitor), a floppy disk, and a microprocessor. The term "word processing" had first been used in 1964 by IBM for its MT/ST system, but it was just a typewriter connected to a magnetic tape.

The most direct impact was on calculators. MITS (Micro Instrumentation and Telemetry Systems) of New Mexico built the first calculator to use the Intel 8008, MITS 816, in 1971. A year later, Hewlett-Packard, Texas Instruments, Casio (a Japanese manufacturer of mechanical calculators), and Commodore all debuted small calculators. Texas Instruments soon produced its own microprocessors, notably the 4-bit TMS 1000 series that integrated the CPU, the ROM, and the RAM on a single chip. In 1973 Japan's Sharp developed the LCD (Liquid Crystal Display) technology for the booming market of calculators.

Mail-order Computer Kits

The Intel 8008 was used by companies targeting the electronic hobbyist market, which was huge. These companies were mostly selling kits by mail-order that hobbyists could buy to build exotic machines at home. The first two companies were Scelbi, first advertised in March 1974 by a Connecticut-based company, and Mark-8, developed by Virginia Tech's student Jon Titus and announced in July 1974. However, they were all beaten at the finish line by Vietnamese-born engineer Andre Truong Trong Thi, who used the 8008 to build the Micral in February 1973 for a governmental research center in France. It was an assembled computer, not just a kit.

Magazines such as "Radio Electronics," "QST" and "Popular Electronics" were responsible for creating excitement about the microprocessor. Basically, the microprocessor reached a wider audience than its inventors had intended because of hobbyist magazines. Otherwise it would have been known only to the few large corporations that were willing to buy microprocessors in bulk. The most creative and visionary users were not working in those corporations.

Networking Computers

At the same time that microprocessors were revolutionizing the concept of a computer, progress continued in the field of networking, although its impact would be felt only decades later. In 1972 Ray Tomlinson at Boston's consulting firm Bolt, Beranek and Newman (BBN) invented e-mail for sending messages between computer users. The visible hand of government was at work again, and one of its decisions was influential in the development of computer networks, although not as popular as the creation of the Internet. In 1971, the government banned AT&T from entering the data-processing business, in particular the online services that obviously AT&T would have dominated with its existing long-distance network. By doing so the government basically treated "data processing" as a special, strategic field in which competition was deemed essential to innovation. The history of computers and networks would have been very different if a monopoly had been able to control the development of data telecommunications. In 1973 Efrem Lipkin, Mark Szpakowski, and Lee Felsenstein at UC Berkeley started the "Community Memory," the first public computerized bulletin board system, using a Scientific Data Systems' time-sharing machine. It was based at Leopold's Records.

In 1973 Bob Metcalfe at Xerox PARC coined the term "Ethernet" for a local-area network that they were building. PARC wanted all of its computers to be able to print on their one laser printer. Unlike the Internet, which connected remote computers using phone lines, the Ethernet was to connect local computers using special cables and adapters. Unlike the

Internet, which was very slow, the Ethernet had to be very fast to match the speed of the laser printer. The first Ethernet was finally operational in 1976. Metcalfe also enunciated "Metcalfe's Law:" the value of a network of devices increases exponentially with the number of connected devices. This was popularly translated in terms of users: the value of a network increases exponentially with the number of the people that it connects.

Groups of computer users were already working together, sharing "notes" on files that were accessible by the whole network. The most popular of these early note-sharing systems (later "groupware") was perhaps PLATO Notes, written in August 1973 by University of Illinois student. David Woolley wanted to keep track of software "bug" reports on their mainframe-based time-sharing system PLATO, used to host the educational software of the Computer-based Education Research Laboratory (CERL). As the PLATO time-sharing system spread to more and more organizations, PLATO Notes, renamed Group Notes in January 1976, rapidly evolved into an online community discussing a broad range of topics. Plato was commercialized in 1975 by Control Data Corporation in Minneapolis and it spread around the world.

Another early piece of "groupware" was the Emergency Management Information System And Reference Index (EMISARI). Murray Turoff at the New Jersey Institute of Technology created it in 1971 on a Univac mainframe. It was a computer conferencing system to let geographically-distributed government agencies discuss opinion surveys.

Meanwhile the Arpanet had 2,000 users in 1973 and Vinton Cerf of Stanford University had nicknamed it the "Internet." A study showed that about 75% of its traffic was e-mail messages: the Internet had become a replacement for telephone and mail communications (not the intended purpose). The following year Cerf and others published the Transmission Control Protocol (TCP), which became the backbone of Internet transmission: it enabled Arpanet/Internet computers to communicate with any computer, regardless of its operating system and of its network.

A transformation was taking place in the nature of the Arpanet that was not visible from outside. The Arpanet, a military tool, had been handed out of necessity, not by design, to Unix hackers. These hackers were imbued with a counterculture that was almost the exact opposite of the military culture. So the Arpanet was increasingly being "hijacked" by a bunch of hackers to become a social tool, although originally only used to chat and play games.

The Arpanet had not been designed with any particular application in mind. In fact, its "application neutrality" would remain one of the main drivers of innovation. It actually appeared to be ill suited for any application. The Arpanet worked pretty much like a post office: it made a "best effort" to deliver "packets" of data in a reasonable timeframe, but packets might be delayed and even lost. Email could live with a delay of minutes and even hours, but not with a loss of text. A phone call, on the other hand, could live with the loss of a few milliseconds of voice but not with a delay. Being application-agnostic, the Internet solved no problem well.

Electronic commerce between companies already existed, but had never been standardized. In 1968 the railways had pioneered a standard for their paper documents. That consortium, the Transportation Data Coordinating Committee (TDDC), came up in 1975 with a set of rules for exchanging electronic documents. Its name was later changed to Electronic Data Interchange Association (EDIA) and Electronic Data Interchange (EDI) became the place for electronic commerce. Electronic commerce was, instead, forbidden within the Arpanet, which in theory was reserved for ARPA-funded research projects. These wide-area networks worked over traditional telephone lines. In April 1973 Martin Cooper at Motorola demonstrated the first portable, wireless or "cellular" telephone.

The Hobbyist Market

The hobbyist market was growing. A large number of young people were children of engineers. They were raised in technology-savvy environments. Many of them picked up electronic kits as teenagers and eventually continued the local tradition of the high-tech hobbyists. In fact, that tradition merged with the mythology of the juvenile delinquent and with the the hippie ideology in legendary characters like John Draper (better known as Captain Crunch), the most famous "phone phreak" of this age who in 1971 built the "blue boxes" capable of fooling the phone system. One of his fans was Steve Wozniak, back then an engineer at the Cupertino public radio station KKUP.

The year 1974 ended with an advertisement in hobbyist magazines of Ed Roberts' kit to build a personal computer, the Altair 8800, based on Intel's 8080 microprocessor and sold by mail order for $395. It was the first product marketed as a "personal computer." Roberts' company MITS, which used to make calculators, was based in Albuquerque, New Mexico. Two students, Bill Gates and Paul Allen, wrote a BASIC interpreter for it, and then founded a company named Micro-soft, initially also based in Albuquerque. MITS sold 2,000 Altair 8800 systems in one year and started the whole personal-computer frenzy, despite offering only 256 Kbytes of memory (static RAM). Additional static RAM and cards could be used to connect to input/output units (e.g., a teletype) but were not included in the price. Basically, the Altair was meant for hobbyists. Roberts assumed that his customers were technically savvy enough to buy the missing pieces, connect them together and program the box.

One of the most daring architectures built on top of the Intel 8080 came from Information Management Science Associates (IMSAI), a consulting company for mainframe users founded by William Millard in 1972 in San Leandro, in the East Bay. Its engineers realized that a number of microprocessors tightly coupled together could match the processing power of a mainframe at a fraction of the price. In October 1975 they introduced the Hypercube II, which cost $80,000; the comparable IBM 370 mainframe cost about $4 million. Ironically, they were more successful with IMSAI 8080, a clone of the Atari 8800 that they sold to the hobbyist market starting in December 1975, while only one Hypercube was ever sold, to the US Navy.

The Hobbyist Revolution

In 1973 Gary Kildall, who was an instructor at the Naval Postgraduate School in Monterey, developed the first high-level programming language for Intel microprocessors, PL/M (Programming Language /Microprocessor). It was "burned" into the Read Only Memory (ROM) of the microprocessor. Intel marketed it as an add-on that could help sell its microprocessors. However, when Kildall developed an operating system for Intel's 8080 processor, CP/M (Control Program/Microcomputer), which managed a floppy drive, Intel balked. Intel was not interested in software that allowed users to read and write files to and from the disk; but makers of small computers were.

The 8080 had inspired several companies to create 8080-based kits, notably MITS and IMSAI. Both needed software for the ever more popular floppy disk. MITS offered its own operating system. IMSAI bought Kildall's CP/M. Kildall's CP/M was largely based on concepts of the PDP-10 operating system (VMS). Kildall then rewrote CP/M isolating the interaction with the hardware in a module called BIOS (Basic Input/Output System). This way CP/M became hardware-independent, and he could sell it to any company in need of a disk operating system for a microprocessor. In 1974 Kildall started his own company, Digital Research, to sell his product on hobbyist magazines. CP/M soon became a standard.

Kildall's operating system was a crucial development in the history of personal computers. It transformed a chip invented for process control (the microprocessor) into a general-purpose computer that could do what minicomputers and mainframes did.

Several hobbyists rushed to mimic Altair's concept. A group of Bay Area-based hobbyists formed the Homebrew Computer Club in March 1975. They met at Gordon French's garage in Menlo Park and later at SLAC's auditorium. These were young people who had been mesmerized by the do-it-yourself kits to build computers. Some of them would go on to build much more than amateur computers. For example, Hewlett-Packard engineer Steve Wozniak demonstrated the first prototype of his Apple at the Homebrew Computer Club meeting of December 1976. Bob Marsh and Lee Felsenstein, formerly an activist of Berkeley's Free Speech Movement in 1964, used the Intel 8080 to design the Sol-20 for Processor Technology in Berkeley. It was released in June 1976 and became the first microcomputer to include a built-in video driver, and the archetype for mass-produced personal computers to come.

The Hobbyist Community

The role played by hobbyists should not be underestimated. The computer market was split along the mainframe-minicomputer divide. IBM and the "BUNCH" sold mainframes. DEC, HP, and others sold minicomputers. These large corporations had the know-how, the brains, and the factories to produce desktop computers for the home market. They did not do it.

The market for home computers was largely created by a group of hobbyists. They were highly individualistic home-based entrepreneurs who worked outside the big bureaucracies of corporations, academia, and government. Many of them had no higher education and no business training. Many of them had no connections whatsoever with universities or government agencies. However, it was a grass roots movement of hobbyists that created what the corporate world had been unable to do. They created their own community using magazines, stores, and clubs to obviate the lack of financial, technological, and marketing infrastructure.

One could argue the personal computer was not invented by an individual, by a laboratory, or by a company; it was invented by a community. In fact, its dynamics was not too different from the dynamics of a community that had taken hold a decade earlier in the Bay Area: the community of the counterculture (agit-prop groups, hippie communes, artistic societies). Until then progress in computer technology had been funded by governments, universities and corporations. The next step would be funded by humble hobbyists spread all over the nation.

To serve the growing community of computer hobbyists, in 1975 a Los Angeles hobbyist, Dick Heiser, had the idea to start a computer store, Arrowhead Computers. It became the first computer retail store in the world. In December 1975 a member of the Homebrew Club, Paul Terrell, opened a store in Silicon Valley, the Byte Shop, which became a reference point for the local hobbyists, and sold the first units of Wozniak's Apple hobbyist computer. In 1976 William Millard of IMSAI 8080 fame opened the "Computer Shack," a store located in Hayward (again in the East Bay) that offered everything a personal computer user needed. That store would soon become a nation-wide chain, Computerland. It sold computers to the public, a proposition that only a few years earlier (when computers were astronomically expensive and impossible to use) that would have been inconceivable. The retail sale of a computer represented a monumental paradigm shift not only for the industry but also for society as a whole.

Journalists and hobbyists were the true visionaries, not corporate executives with their gargantuan staffs of planners and strategists. The journalists relayed news across the country. The hobbyists organized the newsletters, clubs, and conferences that cemented the community. It was the editor of one such magazine (Dr. Dobb's editor Jim Warren) who in April 1977 organized the first personal computer conference in San

Francisco, the "West Coast Computer Fair." It was attended by 13,000 people, the largest computer conference ever. Newsletters, clubs such as the Southern California Computer Society, and user conferences proliferated in the following years.

This hobbyist network had another role. It compensated for the fact that most of those early microcomputers came with no customer support, very little quality control, and only the most elementary software. The network provided the education and the support that large computer manufacturers provided to their customers. The network even did the marketing and proselytizing. At the same time, the network influenced the manufacturers. The community of users probably helped shape the personal computer market more than any technological roadmap.

Microprocessor Wars

Meanwhile, a business decision in Texas involuntarily launched another wave of personal computers. Texas Instruments owned the market for CPUs used in calculators. When in 1975 it decided to increase the price of the CPU to favor its own calculators, the other manufacturers were left scrambling for alternatives. Texas Instruments had realized it was getting difficult to compete with Intel. Intel boasted a full line of state-of-the-art semiconductor products: RAMs, EPROMs and CPUs. Microprocessors (CPUs) drove memory sales which then funded improvements in microprocessors.

The market for calculators collapsed. Out of the ruins, Commodore decided to change its business. Tom Bennett at Motorola in Arizona had created the 8-bit 6800 in 1974, a more advanced microprocessor than anything that Intel had introduced yet. Chuck Peddle, a former employee of Tom Bennett's at Motorola, developed the 8-bit 6502 at MOS Technology (1976); it was much cheaper ($25) than the 6800 ($180) or Intel's 8080 ($360). He was hired by Commodore to build an entire computer, the Commodore PET (Personal Electronic Transactor), demonstrated in January 1977.

Competition to Intel eventually came from Silicon Valley itself. In 1975 Jerry Sanders' Advanced Micro Devices (AMD) introduced the AMD 8080, a reverse-engineered clone of the Intel 8080 microprocessor, putting further pressure on prices. AMD then developed the 4-bit 2901 chip that used the faster Schottky bipolar transistors instead of the unipolar MOS transistors used by Intel. Federico Faggin left Intel with coworker Ralph Ungermann right after finishing the 8080, taking Shima with them, and, having convinced Exxon to make a generous investment, started his own company, Zilog. It became a formidable competitor to Intel when in July 1976 it unveiled the 8-bit Z80 microprocessor, which was faster and cheaper than the 8080 (designed at transistor level by the same Shima). National Semiconductor had already introduced PACE in December 1974, the first 16-bit microprocessor.

The new startups invested heavily on microprocessors, forcing competition at the technological level. The established companies used microprocessors as a weapon, forcing competition at the price level.

Relational Databases

On the software front, a new field of databases was born at IBM's San Jose laboratories, later renamed Almaden Research Center). In 1970 Edgar Codd had written an influential paper, "A Relational Model of Data for Large Shared Data Banks," in which he explained how one could describe a database in the language of first-order predicate logic. A Relational Database group was set up in San Jose. In 1974 Donald Chamberlin defined an algebraic language to retrieve and update data in relational database systems, SEQUEL, later renamed SQL (Structured Query Language). It was part of the development of the first relational database management system, code-named System R, begun in 1973 and finally unveiled in 1977 (running on a System 38). However, IBM's flagship database system remained the IMS, originally developed in 1968 for NASA's Apollo program on IBM's mainframe 360. That was the most used database system in the world. Since IBM was not eager to adopt a new technology, it did not keep it secret and the idea spread throughout the Bay Area.

In particular, IBM's work on relational databases triggered interest in a group of UC Berkeley scientists led by Michael Stonebraker, who started the Ingres project in 1973, a project that would transplant the leadership in the field of databases to the Bay Area and create large fortunes.

Software for Manufacturing

Some significant progress was being made in software applications for manufacturing applications. Evans & Sutherland was formed in 1968 by David Evans, who had worked on the Bendix G15 and on UC Berkeley's time-sharing system, and Ivan Sutherland, an MIT pioneer of graphical user interfaces (GUIs). Both were now employed at the University of Utah, creating a pioneering Line Drawing System (LDS) in 1969 that in 1973 evolved into their Picture System, a graphics system for Computer Aided Design (CAD). They employed bright young engineers such as Jim Clark, Ed Catmull, and John Warnock, who went on to establish the field of computer graphics in the Silicon Valley.

In the 1970s, Manufacturing Resource Planning (MRP) was one of the success stories of the mainframe software industry. In 1972 some IBM engineers in Mannheim, Germany, founded Systemanalyse und Programmentwicklung (SAP, later read as "Systeme, Anwendungen und Produkte") taking with them some software that IBM had inherited from Xerox and that IBM didn't want anymore. SAP set out to create integrated business and manufacturing applications for large firms, and eventually introduced a mainframe-based product that integrated manufacturing, logistics, distribution, inventory, shipping, invoicing, and accounting. That became the reference for Enterprise Resource Planning (ERP) applications, a term coined in the 1990s. Another pioneer was based in Mountain View. Sandra Kurtzig became one of the first multimillionaire women of the computer industry by starting ASK. In 1974, it introduced ManMan, a "universal manufacturing program" running initially on the Tymshare's time-sharing service, and later on the HP3000 mini-computer. It enabled mid-sized manufacturing companies to control the operation of an entire factory. Unlike SAP, ASK aimed for a broader market.

User Interfaces

Experiments with new kinds of hardware and software platforms were changing the vision of what a computer was supposed to do. Engelbart's group at SRI had lost funding from ARPA (and was eventually disbanded in 1977). Several of its engineers started moving to PARC, which was a pioneer in graphical user interfaces, optical character recognition, and WYSIWYG applications.

In 1973 Xerox PARC unveiled the Alto, the first workstation with a mouse and a Graphical User Interface (GUI). Inspired by Douglas Engelbart's old On-Line System and developed by Charles Thacker's team, it was a synthesis of all the software research done at PARC and it was far ahead of contemporary computers. More importantly, it wasn't just a number cruncher. The Alto was meant for a broad variety of applications, from office automation to education. It wasn't based on a microprocessor yet, but on a Texas Instruments 74181 chip. In 1974, Hungarian-born Charles Simonyi developed Bravo, the word processor that introduced the "what you see is what you get" (WYSIWYG) paradigm in document preparation.

In 1974 a strong believer in artificial intelligence, former MIT student Ray Kurzweil, introduced Optical Character Recognition (OCR) software that could read text written in any font. Coupled with a scanner and a text-to-speech synthesizer, it yielded the first reading machine for the blind. Xerox would eventually acquire the software in 1980.

Meanwhile, scientists at IBM were still innovating. In 1972 IBM introduced the 3270 terminal to connect to mainframes. Previous terminals (generally known as "ASCII terminals") interacted with the mainframe at every keystroke, basically sending characters back and forth. The 3270 instead presented the user with a form to fill, and sent the form to the mainframe only when completed. Because it greatly reduced the input/output interactions with the mainframe, it allowed many more terminals to connect to the mainframe at the same time.

In 1974 IBM also introduced the Interactive System Productivity Facility (ISPF), one of the earliest integrated development environments, which allowed programmers to design menu-driven applications. It basically marked the end of the punched cards. Previously, a program was entered by punching the cards and then feeding them in the card reader of the mainframe. With the 3270 and the ISPF the programmer could enter ("edit") the program directly on the terminal.

Two major innovations came from a Route 128 company. In May 1972 Boston-based Wang Labs introduced the 1200, a word-processing machine. Harold Koplow, a designer of Wang calculators, had simply wired together a calculator, a typewriter and a cassette so that the user could type a document, store it, retrieve it, edit it, and print it. He had rewritten the microcode of the calculator so that it would perform word-processing functions instead of mathematical functions. In 1975 Wang added a CRT monitor so that the typist could check the text before printing it. This was one of the inventions that changed every office in the world. For centuries people had to retype a page in order to correct trivial mistakes or to make simple changes. For decades people had to use a photocopier to make copies of a document. That era ended in 1975. When in 1977 Wang's Office Information System also added an Intel 8080 microprocessor, AES's pioneering vision finally went mainstream.

Unbeknownst to most people, one of the most influential technologies of the future was being developed in Europe. In 1972 Bent Stumpe, a Danish-born engineer at the CERN in Geneva (the joint European laboratory for particle physics), invented the concept of a touch screen that reacts to being touched with a finger. In 1977, CERN inaugurated its use for industrial control and the Danish industrial-control manufacturer NESELCO commercialized the technology in the world's first touch-screen computer. Simultaneously, in 1972 Donald Bitzer's PLATO project at the University of Illinois' Education Research Laboratory (CERL) introduced a new terminal based on plasma display for the PLATO IV release.

The State of Computing Jumps Ahead

During the 1950s and 1960s computers had evolved rapidly from the ENIAC. Most of the credit goes to a few companies that devised how to sell computers to corporations and to the government agencies that de facto subsidized those companies with large projects. However, there had only been an evolution and not a revolution. Computers had evolved into faster and cheaper machines that were also easier to program and maintain. They were now employed to perform mission-critical industrial and business applications, not only scientific ones. They had not changed significantly, though. The Arpanet, the Unix operating system and the minicomputer, instead, represented a different kind of progress, one that could be more appropriately termed as a revolution. Each of them changed the way computers were used, what they did, and who used them. In fact, they changed the very meaning of a "computer." The term itself became misleading, as computers were beginning to be used less to "compute" than to perform many other functions.

Again, this revolution had taken place mostly far away from the Bay Area, although centers like the SRI and the Xerox PARC were beginning to put the Peninsula on the map. PARC's experiments with graphical user interfaces, desktop computers, and local area networks expanded the computer culture of the Bay Area. PARC also played the role of a venture capitalist investing in new technologies. By hiring Robert Taylor, Xerox transplanted the futuristic vision of ARPA's IPTO into the Bay Area. The IPTO's mission, in turn, represented two decades of computer research in the Boston area. Xerox was transferring Boston's lead in computing to the Bay Area, which also happened to be the world's capital of semiconductor engineering. This was similar to what Shockley had done when he had transferred the East Coast's lead in semiconductors to the world's capital of radio engineering. And, again, the recipient of the transplant was a community imbued with a different spirit than the one of the scientists of the East Coast.

Biotech, Energy, and Lasers

While the semiconductor industry was booming, another Bay Area industry was in its infancy. A local biomedical drug industry had been created by the success of Alza. Silicon Valley soon developed as a center for biomedical technology, the industry of medical devices that draws from both engineering and medicine.

Meanwhile, several groups of biologists were trying to synthesize artificial DNA in a lab, trying to extract a gene from any living or dead organism and insert it into another organism ("recombinant DNA"). In 1972 Paul Berg's team at Stanford University synthesized the first recombinant DNA molecule. In 1973 Stanford University's medical Professor Stanley Cohen and UCSF's biochemist Herbert Boyer invented a practical technique to produce recombinant DNA. They transferred DNA from one organism to another, creating the first recombinant DNA organism. That experiment virtually launched the discipline of "biotechnology," the industrial creation of DNA that does not exist in nature but can be useful for human purposes. Boyer had just discovered that an enzyme named EcoRI allowed him to slice DNA molecules to produce single strands that could be easily manipulated. Cohen had just devised a way to introduce foreign DNA into a bacterium. They put the two processes together and obtained a way to combine DNA from different sources into a DNA molecule. Cohen decided to continue research in the academia, while Boyer decided to go into business.

The Asilomar Conference on Recombinant DNA, organized by Paul Berg in 1975 near Monterey, set ethical rules for biotechnology. Meanwhile, the Polish geneticist Waclaw Szybalski coined the term "synthetic biology," opening an even more ambitious frontier: the creation of new genomes, and therefore of biological forms, that don't exist in nature.

That attention to biology was not coincidental. In 1970, Stanford had set up an interdepartmental Human Biology Program focused on undergraduate students. The founders were all distinguished scholars: Joshua Lederberg, a Nobel laureate who was the head of Genetics at the Medical School; David Hamburg, chair of Psychiatry at the Medical School; Norman Kretchmer, chair of Pediatrics, Donald Kennedy, chair of Biology; Paul Ehrlich, who had jump-started environmental science with his book "The Population Bomb" (1968); Sanford Dornbusch, former chair of Sociology; and Albert Hastorf, former chair of Psychology. This was an impressive cast, and Lederberg and Hamburg were already teaching a pioneering course titled "Man as Organism" since 1968. However, there was little support for this idea from the establishment. The reason that Stanford went ahead was money. The Ford Foundation believed in multidisciplinary approaches and its generous funding made the program possible. The class on "Human Sexuality," started in 1971 by Herant Katchadourian, attracted a record 1,035 students in its first year. The Human Biology Program would continue to 2012 and still remain the single most successful program at Stanford.

A major oil crisis hit the world in 1973. It was a wake-up call that the US did not control the main material required by its economy: oil. It became the first drive to seriously explore alternative sources of energy, although it would take many more crises and wars before the government would launch a serious plan to get rid of fossil fuels. In 1973 the Lawrence Berkeley Lab founded the Energy and Environment Division, which came to specialize in lithium-ion batteries. The federal government, instead, chose Colorado as the site for the main research center in alternative sources of energy. In 1974 it mandated the establishment of the Solar Energy Research Institute, later expanded to wind and biofuel and renamed National Renewable Energy Laboratory (NREL).

Research on lasers at Stanford University yielded a major discovery in 1976. John Madey invented the "free-electron laser," a laser that differed from previous varieties (ion, carbon-dioxide and semiconductor lasers) because it could work across a broader range of frequencies, from microwaves to X-rays.

Culture and Society

By the mid-1970s San Francisco's art scene was shifting towards video, performance art, participatory installations, mixed media, and time-based art, often accompanied with live electronic music. Alternative art spaces popped up in the Mission and South of Mission (SOMA) districts, notably notably Southern Exposure, New Langton Arts, and Gallery Paule Anglim. "Conceptual" artists Howard Fried and Terry Fox pioneered video art and performance art. Lynn Hershman's "The Dante Hotel" pioneered site-specific installations. The ultimate site-specific installation was David Ireland's own house at 500 Capp Street, which the artist began to remodel in 1975 with sculptures made of found objects. Chip Lord's Ant Farm created one of the most influential installations in 1974 in the desert of Texas, "Cadillac Ranch," using parts of old cars. The Ant Farm also organized multimedia performances such as "Media Burn" during which they burned in public a pyramid of television sets.

Alternative art spaces and projects were booming. In 1970 Tom Marioni founded the Museum of Conceptual Art (MOCA), one of the first alternative art spaces in the nation. There he debuted his "Sound Sculpture As" together with Paul Kos's "The Sound of Ice Melting," which recorded the sound of disintegrating ice; these two pioneered sound sculpture. In 1973 British painter Harold Cohen joined Stanford University's Artificial Intelligence Lab to build AARON, a program capable of making art, thus creating an artistic equivalent of the Turing test: can a machine be a good artist if experts appreciate its art? The project would continue for several decades. In 1975 John Chowning founded Stanford's laboratory for computer music, later renamed Center for Computer Research in Music and Acoustics (CCRMA).

The Bay Area stole a bit of Hollywood's limelight in 1971 when film producer George Lucas opened Lucasfilm in San Francisco, a production company that went on to create "American Graffiti" (1973), "Star Wars" (1977), and "Indiana Jones and the Raiders of the Lost Ark" (1981). The "underground comix" movement continued to prosper, but now the reference point was the magazine "Arcade" started by Bill Griffith of "Young Lust" fame and Swedish-born cartoonist Art Spiegelman, later more famous for the character "Maus."

The city's main sociocultural development was the rapid rise of the gay community. The first "Gay Pride Parade" was held in 1970. Around that time gays and lesbians started moving to the "Castro" district in large numbers. It was the first openly gay neighborhood in the US and it would elect Harvey Milk, the first gay politician in the US, later that decade. Arthur Evans formed the "Faery Circle" in San Francisco in 1975. It evolved into the "Radical Faeries" movement at a conference held in Arizona in 1979. It later became a worldwide network of groups that mixed gay issues and new-age spirituality, staging hippie-style outdoors "gatherings."

16.   Entrepreneurs: Software, Storage, Unix, Biotech, Alternative Music, and Spirituality (1976-80)

The Value of Software

Steve Jobs' vision at Apple Computer was to create a computer that was a home appliance. Still, the Apple II was just a hobbyist novelty like most small computers based on microprocessors. It never became a home appliance, but it got transformed into something as pervasive: an office tool. The transformation was not due to a hardware idea from Apple but to software. In 1979, Harvard Business School student Dan Bricklin and his friend Bob Frankston shipped VisiCalc, the first spreadsheet program for personal computers. That was the moment when sales of the Apple II truly started to take off.

A software application made the difference between selling thousands of units to hobbyists and selling millions of units to the general public. The Apple II only had 64 kilobytes of memory, and the application could only use a memory space of 48 Kbytes. VisiCalc fit in 32. Apple went public the following year. Its IPO (initial public offering) raised a record $1.3 billion, creating more instant millionaires than any other event in history at that point. Visicalc was ported to the Tandy TRS-80, Commodore PET and the Atari 800, becoming the first major application that was not tied to a computer company. The company that understood the value of software was Tandy, whose TRS-80 boasted an unprecedented library of applications (mostly games, but also word processors and spreadsheets).

Software companies tended not to understand the value of software. Bricklin and Frankston founded Software Arts in Boston to commercialize VisiCalc, which they had originally prototyped on MIT's Multics system and funded with their own money. But their company never sold its product. They gave it to a publisher, Daniel Fylstra's Personal Software (later renamed VisiCorp), that paid them royalties. Eventually this led to a legal dispute that indirectly allowed the competition to overtake VisiCalc. It never occurred to Bricklin and Frankston to look for venture capital to jumpstart their business.

Of course, not everybody shared Steve Jobs' vision. Just like in the old days, an IBM executive had predicted a very small market for computers, so in 1977 DEC's founder Kenneth Olsen proclaimed that "there is no reason anyone would want a computer in their home."

The Pace of Progress in Semiconductors

Meanwhile, the war of the microprocessors was still raging. In June 1979 Intel introduced the 16-bit 8088 (containing 29,000 transistors), and in September 1979 Motorola introduced the 16-bit 68000 microprocessor (containing 68,000 transistors). In between the two, Zilog introduced the 16-bit Z8000 (only 17,500 transistors). At the same time, sales of DRAM continued to skyrocket. Intel then assigned the task of designing the 8086 (eventually released in June 1978) to a software engineer, Stephen Morse: it was the first time that a microprocessor was designed from the perspective of software.

Chips got more powerful and foreign manufacturers entered the market. In 1974 the size of the chips had reached 4 kilobytes and in 1975 it was already 16 kilobytes. In 1977 the semiconductor industry of Silicon Valley employed 27,000 people. By 1979 there were 16 companies selling DRAMs of 16 kilobytes. Five of them were based in Japan.

Progress in semiconductor technology was no longer making the headlines, but continued faster than ever. By 1980 integrated circuits (the vast majority of which were manufactured in the US) incorporated 100,000 discrete components. In 1978 George Perlegos at Intel created the Intel 2816, an EEPROM (Electrically Erasable Programmable Read-Only Memory), basically an EPROM that did not need to be removed from the computer in order to be erased.

In 1977 the market for memory chips of all kinds was twice the size of the market for microprocessors. Combined, the two markets had grown from $25 million in 1974 to $550 million in 1979. However, it was not obvious yet that computers were going to be the main market for microprocessors. In 1978 the industry sold 14 million microprocessors, but only 200,000 personal computers were manufactured. The vast majority of microprocessors were going into all sorts of other appliances, calculators, and controllers, with Japanese conglomerates becoming increasingly aggressive.

An impressive phenomenon of the era was the number of hardware spinoffs launched by enterprising Chinese immigrants trained in some of Silicon Valley's most advanced labs: Compression Labs (CLI) by Wen Chen (1976) to make video conferencing and digital television components; Solectron by Roy Kusumoto and Winston Chen (Milpitas, 1977) to make printed circuit boards; Data Technology Corporation (DTC) by David Tsang (Milpitas, 1979) for floppy-disk and hard-disk drives; Lam Research by David Lam (Fremont, 1980) for equipment for chip manufacturing (or "etching"); Integrated Device Technology by Chun Chiu, Tsu-Wei Lee and Fu Huang (San Jose, 1980) for semiconductor components; Weitek by Edmund Sun, Chi-Shin Wang and Godfrey Fong (San Jose, 1981) for chips for high-end computers; fiber-optic pioneer E-Tek Dynamics by Ming Shih (San Jose, 1983); magnetic-disk manufacturer Komag by Tu Chen (Milpitas, 1983); etc.

The Business of Storing Data

Another front was being opened by companies studying how to store data. More computers around meant more data to store. It was intuitive that some day the industry for data storage would be a huge one. Audiocassettes were used for data storage by most microcomputers of the first generation, including the Apple II, the Radio Shack TRS-80 and the Commodore PET. Floppy disks had become increasingly popular, especially after Alan Shugart developed the smaller version (originally in 1976 for Wang). The first "diskettes" were manufactured by Dysan, a storage-media company formed in 1973 in Santa Clara by Norman Dion.

The growing number of applications running on personal computers required a growing number of floppy units. Finis Conner, working for Shugart of Memorex fame, had the idea of building a fixed, rigid disk of the same physical size as Dysan's flexible diskette that would provide both high performance and high capacity, equivalent to an entire bunch of floppy drives. Shugart and Conner formed Shugart Technology in December 1979 in Scotts Valley (south of San Jose), later renamed Seagate Technology, with funding from Dysan. In 1980, Seagate introduced the first hard-disk drive for personal computers (capable of 5 Megabytes), and soon hard disks would greatly improve the usability of small machines. That same year Sony introduced the double-sided, double-density 3.5" floppy disk that could hold 875 kilobyte.

Seagate also published the specifications of a computer interface that would allow users to connect different peripherals to the same personal computer, a device-independent "parallel" connection. They named it SASI (Shugart Associates Systems Interface), later renamed SCSI (Small Computer System Interface) when it was adopted as an industry standard. In 1981 the manager of the SASI project, Larry Boucher, quit Seagate to found Adaptec in Milpitas (north of San Jose), taking with him several Seagate engineers in a move that evoked the memory of Shugart's own exodus from IBM of 1969. Adaptec specialized in manufacturing computer cards (at factories in Singapore) to solve the growing problem of input/output bottlenecks in personal computers as the machines had to deal with a higher and higher traffic of data.

Storing data was not enough. It was also important to guarantee that the transactions of those data were reliable. Since computers and their software were prone to crashes, this was not a trivial problem, particularly in the arena of financial transactions. Former HP employee James Treybig convinced a few HP engineers to work at a fault-tolerant machine and started Tandem Computers in Cupertino. In 1976 they delivered the first product, the Tandem 16, based on a CPU derived from the HP3000 and running a proprietary operating system. Many of these CPUs were managed as a team so that if one failed the others could continue its job. Tandem servers were ideal for mission-critical business applications carried out by banks. Tandem's monopoly of fault-tolerant computers would last until at least 1982.

The exponential growth of digital communications led to the rapid expansion of the field of cryptography. The most pressing problem was to secure communications over distances between parties that had never met before and who could not exchange a secret key in private before beginning their digital communications. This problem was solved in 1976 by combining ideas from Stanford (Whitfield Diffie and Martin Hellman) and UC Berkeley (Ralph Merkle), opening the era of Public-Key Encryption (PKI). The following year the Israeli cryptographer Adi Shamir at MIT invented the RSA algorithm and added digital signatures to PKI.

The ever larger amount of data stored on disks created ever bigger databases, which, in turn, required ever more powerful database management systems. Larry Ellison, a college dropout from Chicago who had moved to California in 1966, had been employed at Ampex in Redwood City. He worked as a programmer on a database management system for the Central Intelligence Agency (CIA) codenamed "Oracle," under the management of his boss Bob Miner, the son of Middle-Eastern immigrants. In August 1977 Bob Miner and Ed Oates (also an Ampex alumnus, now at Memorex) founded the Software Development Laboratories to take advantage of a software consulting contract facilitated by Larry Ellison at his new employer, Precision Instruments (also a manufacturer of tape recorders, based in San Carlos, mainly serving NASA and the Navy). The startup used offices in PI's Santa Clara building. When Ellison joined them, he steered them towards developing an SQL relational database management system of the kind that IBM had just unveiled in San Jose but targeting the minicomputer market. Miner and their fourth employee Bruce Scott (another former member of Miner's team at Ampex) wrote most of it in the assembly language of the PDP-11. The company was soon renamed Relational Software and relocated to Menlo Park, and in 1978 the CIA purchased the first prototype. In 1979 Relational officially shipped the first commercial SQL relational database management system, Oracle. In 1982 the company would be renamed one more time and would become Oracle Corporation.

A rival project, Michael Stonebraker's relational database system Ingres at UC Berkeley, was demonstrated in 1979. For all practical purposes, Ingres looked like a variant of IBM's System R for DEC minicomputers running the Unix operating system. Being open-source software like UC Berkeley's Unix (BSD), within one year Ingres was deployed by many universities around the country as the first available relational database system (IBM's System R was not available outside IBM). In 1980 Stonebraker himself started a company, Relational Technology, later renamed Ingres, to market the system. That same year, Roger Sippl and Laura King, who had implemented an experimental relational database system, started Relational Database Systems in Menlo

Park, a company that was later renamed Informix. In 1984 some of Stonebraker's students (notably Mark Hoffman and Bob Epstein) formed Systemware, later renamed Sybase, in Berkeley.

All of these startups had something in common: they did not target the huge market of mainframe computers. They targeted the smaller market of minicomputers, in particular the ones running the Unix operating system. IBM's IMS dominated the database market for mainframe computers, but IBM had failed to capitalize on the experimental System R developed at its San Jose laboratories. IBM eventually released a relational database management system, the DB2, in 1983, but it was running only on its mainframe platform. IBM still showed little interest in smaller computers. This allowed Oracle, Sybase and Informix to seize the market for database systems on minicomputers.

Early Telecommunications and Networks

The other field still in its infancy was the field of telecommunications. The company that put Silicon Valley on the map of telecommunications was probably ROLM, founded by a group of Stanford students. In 1976 they introduced a digital switch, the CBX (Computerized Branch Exchange), a computer-based PBX (private branch exchange) that competed successfully with the products of Nortel and AT&T. Meanwhile, the Southern Pacific Railroad of Burlingame renamed a subsidiary selling private phone lines since 1972, from Southern Pacific Communications to "Sprint" (Switched PRIvate Network Telecommunications). Its Burlingame laboratory was another early source of know-how in telecommunications. Sprint would be later acquired by GTE and then by United Telecom of Kansas.

Networking was taking off. In 1979 Bob Metcalfe, the "inventor" of the Ethernet, left Xerox PARC to found 3Com (Computers, Communication and Compatibility) in Santa Clara. The idea was to provide personal computer manufacturers with Ethernet adaptor cards so that businesses could connect all the small computers in one local-area network. In 1979, Zilog's cofounder Ralph Ungermann and one of his engineers at Zilog, Charlie Bass, formed Ungermann-Bass in Santa Clara to specialize in local-area networks, particularly in the Ethernet technology.

Meanwhile, in Georgia in 1977 Dennis Hayes, a hobbyist who was employed at National Data Corporation on a project to provide bank customers with modems for electronic money transfers and credit card authorizations, started working on a modem for personal computers. He created a device that converted between analog and digital signals and therefore allowed personal computers to receive and transmit data via telephone lines. He soon founded his own company, Hayes Microcomputers Products, and announced the Micromodem 100 that could transmit at 110 to 300 bits per seconds (bauds). This modem was a lot simpler and cheaper than the ones used by mainframes, and, more importantly, it integrated all the functions that a modem needed to perform. Texas Instruments too introduced a 300-baud modem for its TI 99/4 in 1980.

The mother of all computer networks was still largely unknown, though. In 1980 the Arpanet had 430,000 users, who exchanged almost 100 million e-mail messages a year. That year the Usenet was born, an Arpanet-based discussion system divided in "newsgroups," originally devised by two Duke University students, Tom Truscott and Jim Ellis. It used a protocol called UUCP (Unix-to-Unix Copy), originally written in 1978 by Mike Lesk at AT&T Bell Laboratories for transferring files, exchanging e-mail and executing remote commands. Despite the fast growing number of users, at the time nobody perceived the Arpanet as a potential business.

In 1977 DARPA, working closely with SRI International, chose the San Francisco Bay Area to set up a "packet" radio network (Prnet) capable of exchanging data with Arpanet nodes. It was the beginning of wireless computer networking. After early experiments by Canadian ham radio amateurs, in December 1980 Hank Magnuski set up in San Francisco a ham radio to broadcast data (the birth certificate of the AmPrnet). The first wireless products for the general market would not appear for a decade, but, not coincidentally, would come from a company based in Canada, Telesystems, and a company based in the Bay Area, Proxim (founded in 1984 in Sunnyvale).

Video Games

Computers also started making an effect in the gaming/entertainment industry. The Atari 2600 home videogame console was a runaway success that yielded Atari more than 50% of the market. In 1980 Atari hired Alan Kay from the Xerox PARC to work on computer graphics for its products.

The business of gaming software came to the Bay Area via Broderbund, founded after hobbyist Doug Carlston had written the game "Galactic Empire" for the TRS-80 in 1979. This came one year after Toshihiro Nishikado, a veteran game designer who had developed Japan's first video arcade game in 1973, created the first blockbuster videogame, "Space Invaders." In 1980 it was ported to the Atari 2600, and broke all sales records, creating the demand for videogame consoles that made the video arcade obsolete. "Galactic Empire" thrived in its wake.

Hobbyists were also finding ever-newer uses for microprocessors. For example, in 1977 Dave Smith, a former UC Berkeley student who had started a company to make music synthesizers, built the "Prophet 5," the first microprocessor-based musical instrument, and also the first polyphonic and programmable synthesizer. Dave Smith also had the original idea that led (in 1983) to the MIDI (Musical Instrument Digital Interface), a standard to attach musical instruments to computers.

Fundamental for the development of the multimedia world was the introduction in 1978 of Texas Instrument's TMS5100, the first digital signal processor. Daniel Kottke, one of Apple's earliest employees who helped Wozniak assemble the very first Apple computers in Jobs' garage, also assembled a portable Apple to compose and play music for his own use (in 1980).

User Friendliness

Progress was also needed in developing user-friendly computers. The Xerox Alto had been the single major effort in that area. Xerox never sold it commercially but donated it to universities around the world. That helped trigger projects that later yielded results such as the Stanford University Network (SUN) workstation. In 1979 Steve Jobs of Apple had his first demonstration of an Alto at Xerox PARC, and realized that the mouse-driven GUI was the way to go. Xerox eventually introduced in April 1981 the 8010 Star Information System, which integrated a mouse, a GUI, a laser printer, an Ethernet card, an object-oriented environment (Smalltalk), and word-processing and publishing software. Programming this computer involved a whole new paradigm, the "Model-View-Controller" approach, first described in 1979 by Trygve Reenskaug. Xerox PARC was also experimenting with portable computers: the NoteTaker, unveiled in 1976 but never sold commercially, was basically a practical implementation of Alan Kay's Dynabook concept (by a team that included Adele Goldberg). In 1977 Xerox PARC gave a presentation to Xerox's management of all the achievements of the research center, titled "Futures Day." Despite the spectacular display of industrial prototypes, the management decided that Xerox should continue focusing on document processing. This started the exodus of brains from Xerox PARC towards the Silicon Valley startups.

Computer graphics began to be commercialized. In 1979 filmmaker George Lucas hired Ed Catmull to open a laboratory in San Rafael devoted to computer animation for his San Francisco firm Lucasfilm. Catmull had studied with Ivan Sutherland at the University of Utah, established the Computer Graphics Laboratory at the New York Institute of Technology in 1975, and helped create a computer animation in a scene of the film "Futureworld" (1976) that was the first ever to use 3D computer graphics. His firm morphed into Pixar.

The 1980s also witnessed the birth of the first computer graphics studios. Carl Rosendahl started Pacific Data Images (PDI) in 1980 in his Sunnyvale garage. Richard Chuang and Glenn Entis created a 3D software platform (initially running on a DEC PDP-11) that turned PDI into the first mass producer of computer animation, initially for television networks but later also for feature films.

The Bay Area was also the hub for a lively debate on artificial intelligence. In 1950 Alan Turing had asked, "When can the computer be said to have become intelligent?" In 1980 UC Berkeley philosopher John Searle replied, "Never." Searle led the charge of those who attacked the very premises of artificial intelligence. Nonetheless, in the same year Stanford's Ed Feigenbaum and others founded IntelliGenetics (later renamed Intellicorp), an early artificial intelligence and biotech startup, and the first of many to capitalize on the "expert systems" pioneered by Stanford University. French conglomerate Schlumberger acquired in 1979 the whole of Fairchild Camera and Instrument, including Fairchild Semiconductor and the following year hired Peter Hart from the SRI International to establish the Fairchild Laboratory for Artificial Intelligence Research (FLAIR), later renamed the Schlumberger Palo Alto Research (SPAR) Center, a clear reference to Xerox PARC.

The Unix Generation

Betting on the Unix operating system was a gamble. The dominant computer company, IBM, had no intention of adopting somebody else's operating system. AT&T (the owner of Bell Labs) had made Unix available to anyone that wanted to use it. No major computer manufacturer was interested in an operating system that all its competitors could use too.

The vast majority of the users of Unix were at Bell Labs and in universities around the world. Universities that received the source code of the operating system began to tinker with it, producing variants and extensions. UC Berkeley had received its copy in 1974. Within three years its version, assembled by former student Bill Joy as the "Berkeley Software Distribution" (BSD), became popular outside Berkeley. The second BSD of 1978 included two pieces of software developed by Joy himself that became even more popular: the "vi" text editor and the "C shell." Berkeley made it very easy for other universities and even companies to adopt BSD. Unix hence became by far the world's most portable operating system. Until then, however, the vast majority of Unix implementations used a PDP-11. Eventually, in 1980, a company, Onyx, started in Silicon Valley by former Harvard Professor Bill Raduchel, had the idea to build a microcomputer running UNIX. The Onyx C8002 was based on a Zilog Z8000, had 256-kilobyte RAM and included a 10-megabyte hard disk for the price of $11,000, a cheaper alternative to the PDP-11. It was followed by Apollo in the same year, then SUN Microsystems in 1981 and Silicon Graphics in 1982.

Consulting and software companies followed until a major Unix backer arose. In 1979 Larry Michels founded the first Unix consulting company, Santa Cruz Operation (SCO), another major act of faith in an operating system that had no major backer in the industry. In 1980 Microsoft announced the Xenix operating system, a version of Unix for the Intel 8086, Zilog Z8000 and Motorola M68000 microprocessors. What was missing was the killer application. Help arrived from the US government. In 1980, when the time came to implement the new protocol

TCP/IP for the Arpanet so that many more kinds of computers could be interconnected, DARPA (Defense Advanced Research Projects Agency) decided not to go with DEC (which would have been the obvious choice) but to pick the Unix operating system, specifically because it was a more open platform. Until that day there had been little interaction between the Internet world and the Unix world. After that day the two worlds began to converge. It is interesting that DARPA decided to unify the "nodes" of the network at the operating system level, not at the hardware level.

Membership in the Unix world mainly came through academia. Just about every Unix user had been trained in a university. All software refinements to the Bell Labs code had come from universities. However, the Unix community soon came to exhibit "counterculture" dynamics that mirrored the dynamics of the computer hobbyists who had invented the personal computer.

Unix was another case of a technology ignored by the big computer manufacturers and left in the hands of a community of eccentric independents. They could not avail themselves of the financial, technological and marketing infrastructure of the computer business. The big difference, of course, was that in this case the universities served as local attractors for the community more than magazines, clubs or stores. The Internet played the role that magazines had played in the 1970s, helping to disseminate alternative ideas throughout the nation. Another difference was that the average Unix innovator was a highly educated scientist, not just a garage engineer (hence the widely used expression "Unix guru" instead of the more prosaic "computer hobbyist"). However, just like hobbyists, Unix users came to constitute a counterculture that reenacted the rituals and myths of the counterculture of the 1960s. Both movements were founded on dissent, on an anti-establishment mood. Last but not least, both the personal computer and the Unix account had an appeal on this generation as a medium of individual expression in an age in which the media were castrating individual expression.

Both in the case of the personal computer and of the Internet, it was not a surprise that the invention happened: it was feasible and there was a market for it. The surprise was how long it took. The business "establishment" created a huge inertia that managed to postpone the inevitable. Viewed from the top, government funding from the 1910s till the 1960s had accelerated innovation whereas large computer corporations in the 1970s had connived to stifle innovation (outside their territory).

The Visible Hand of Capital

The amount of money available to venture capitalists greatly increased at the end of the decade because of two important government decisions. First, venture capital became a lot more appealing. In 1978 the US government enacted the "Revenue Act," which reduced the capital gains tax rate from 49.5% to 28%. Second and more importantly, in 1979 the government eased the rules on pension funds, allowing them to engage in high-risk investments.

The investment returns numbers were likely important too. Arthur Rock had invested less than $60,000 in Apple in January 1978 and reaped almost $22 million in December 1980 when Apple went public. For several years Kleiner-Perkins was able to pay a 40% return to the limited partners of its high-tech fund. The base of the Bay Area's venture capital industry started moving from San Francisco to 3000 Sand Hill Road, in Menlo Park, a complex of low-rise wooden buildings a few blocks from the Stanford Research Park. Within a few years several more venture-capital funds were founded and several of the East-Coast funds opened offices here.

The Invisible Hand of Government

Government spending also helped in less visible manners. In 1977, the Defense Department hired Bill Perry, the former ESL founder, to head their Research and Engineering Lab. The US had just lost the war in Vietnam, and one country after the other was signing friendship treaties with the Soviet Union. The US government decided that it was likely to lose a conventional war against the Soviet Union. The only hope to defeat the Soviet Union lay in launching a new generation of weapons that would be driven by computers, a field in which the Soviet Union lagged far behind. In the next four years the budget for the Defense Advanced Research Projects Agency (DARPA) was increased dramatically, leading to a number of high-tech military projects: the B-2 stealth bomber, the Jstars surveillance system, the Global Positioning System (GPS), the Trident submarine, and the Tomahawk cruise missile. Many of these projects depended on technology developed in Silicon Valley.

Biotech

The age of biotech started in earnest in the Bay Area with Genentech. It was formed in April 1976 by Herbert Boyer (the co-inventor of recombinant DNA technology or "gene splicing") and by 28-year-old venture capitalist Robert Swanson, who set up offices at Kleiner Perkins' offices in Menlo Park. They subcontracted experiments to the laboratories of UCSF, the City of Hope, and the California Institute of Technology in Pasadena (whose student Richard Scheller became one of their early employees) to genetically engineer new pharmaceutical drugs. Genentech's first success came in 1977 when they produced a human hormone (somatostatin) in bacteria, the first cloning of a protein using a synthetic recombinant gene. In 1978 Genentech and City of Hope produced human insulin; a year later Genentech cloned the human growth hormone.

The biotech business had begun with human proteins made in bacteria. The field got another boost in 1977 when Fred Sanger at Cambridge University in Britain developed a method for "sequencing" DNA molecules (genomes), i.e. for deciphering the sequence of the constituents of a DNA molecule, a process not all too different from deciphering the sequence of characters in a computer message. Another method was developed by Walter Gilbert's team at Harvard University. Gilbert joined forces with MIT Professor Phillip Sharp and founded Biogen in Geneva in 1978. In 1979 Walter Goad of the Theoretical Biology and Biophysics Group at Los Alamos National Laboratory established the Los Alamos Sequence Database to collect all known genetic sequences from a variety of organisms and their protein translations (basically, a catalog of genes and their functions), hiring the consulting firm BBN (Bolt Beranek and Newman), the same firm that had set up the Internet.

More biotech companies surfaced in those years on both coasts of the US. In 1979 Sam Eletr, who had been the manager of a medical instruments team at HP Labs, founded GeneCo in Foster City, near Oracle. It was later renamed Applied Biosystems to build biotech instrumentation: first a protein sequencer and later a DNA synthesizer. Also notable in the Bay Area was Calgene, formed in 1980 by UC Davis scientists. Scientists from UCSF and UC Berkeley formed Chiron in 1981 in Emeryville.

A decision by the Supreme Court opened the floodgates of biotech startups. In 1980 it ruled that biological materials (as in "life forms") could be patented. Due to these scientific and legal developments, the Bay Area's first biotech company, Cetus, went public in 1981, raising a record $108 million. In 1983 Kary Mullis at Cetus would invent the "polymerase chain reaction," a process capable of amplifying DNA, i.e. of generating many copies of a DNA sequence.

Outside the Bay Area the most successful company in recombinant DNA technology was perhaps Los Angeles-based Applied Molecular Genetics (later abbreviated to Amgen), founded in April 1980 by four venture capitalists who hired a stellar team of scientists from Caltech and UCLA. In 1983, Taiwanese-born physiologist Fu-Kuen Lin cloned the hormone erythropoietin (better known as EPO), later patented as Epogen, into the ovarian cells of hamsters; two years later Larry Souza cloned another hormone, granulocyte colony-stimulating factor (G-CSF), later patented as Neupogen. Revenues passed $1 billion in 1992.

Culture and Society

The Bay Area's cultural life was booming at the same time that the computer industry was beginning to boom; and it was still rather eccentric by the standards of mainstream culture. The Residents started the new wave of rock music with their bizarre shows and demented studio-processed litanies. In 1976 William Ackerman launched Windham Hill to promote a new genre of instrumental music, "new age" music. It was the soundtrack to a "new age movement" that simply updated Esalen's "human potential movement" and the spiritual element of the hippie generation for the new "yuppies" (young urban professionals), thereby creating an alternative spiritual subculture that promoted Zen-like meditation, astrological investigation, extra-sensorial powers, crystal healing, holistic medicine). At the same time punk-rock reached California where it mutated into a particularly abrasive and vicious form, hardcore, notably with the Dead Kennedys. Meanwhile the gay community patronized disco-music. Punk-rock was headquartered at the Mabuhay Gardens (on Broadway) and disco-music at the I-Beam (Haight-Ashbury).

Non-musicians were doing well too. In 1976 playwright Sam Shepard relocated to San Francisco to work at the Magic Theatre. The Herbst Theatre was established in 1977 on the site of the 1945 signing of the United Nations' charter. In 1977 George Coates founded his multimedia theater group, Performance Works. In 1978 Mark Pauline created the Survival Research Laboratories, which staged performances by custom-built machines. In 1980 Sonya Rapoport debuted the interactive audio/visual installation "Objects on my Dresser."

There were already many examples of philanthropy. For example, in 1979 Stanford University's professor and former Syntex scientist Carl Djerassi purchased land in the Santa Cruz Mountains west of Stanford and started the Djerassi Resident Artists Program. The program would attract dozens of world-class artists to create sculptures in the forest. In the mid-1980s John Rosekrans would establish the Runnymede Sculpture Farm on the family's vast estate in Woodside, acquiring over 160 outdoor monolithic sculptures.

The Bay Area was a tolerant but boring place. In 1977, San Francisco's city supervisor Harvey Milk became the first openly gay man to be elected to office in the US. Meanwhile, Silicon Valley was just a place to work. The only major entertainment was represented by the amusement park Great America, which opened in 1976 in Santa Clara. The rest of Silicon Valley was one large set of strip malls and dingy buildings.

17. Database Lords: A Case Study on Larry Ellison's Oracle Corp. (1977-2013)

Selling Databases to the CIA

In 1977, three errant software engineers, Larry Ellison, Bob Miner, and Ed Oates, founded Software Development Laboratories. They completed their first product, Oracle Version 1, in less than one year. Their customer was the Central Intelligence Agency (CIA). The engineers had significant experience designing customized database programs for government agencies. Miner and Ellison had persuaded the CIA to let them work on a lapsed $50,000 contract to build a relational database program, after they did some consulting work for a company called Omex.

A relational database allows business users to match data by using common characteristics (a set of relations). Relational databases, as implemented in relational database management systems (RDBMS), have become the main place to store digital information used for financial records, manufacturing and logistical information, personnel data, all Internet records, and much more. They have become the guts of the global technology infrastructure. For example, a data set containing all the real-estate transactions in a town can be grouped in many ways: by the year the transaction occurred; by the sale price of the transaction; by the buyer's last name; and so on. An RDBMS allows an organization to store massive amounts of data forever.

Oracle databases were the guts of the electronic world. To put these databases in context, 98% of the Fortune 100 companies depended on Oracle software to manage their information in 2001. Every time someone would use a credit card, buy a plane ticket, reserve a hotel room, order from any catalogue, surf the Internet, search Google or Yahoo, get cash from an ATM, settle phone bill, or so on, odds were that the person interacted with an Oracle database.

The idea for the product came from IBM research. Ellison and Miner had come up with the RDBMS idea after reading about it in the IBM Journal of Research and Development, realizing that no one had commercialized it. The key insight Ellison and Miner had was that IBM was interested in RDBMS, which many believed would allow computer users to retrieve corporate data from almost any form. This came from an IBM innovation called the Structured Query Language (SQL), a computer language that would tell a relational database what to retrieve and how to display it. Ellison and Miner had a hunch that IBM would incorporate the new relational database and SQL into future computers, mostly mainframes. So they set out to provide a similar program for digital minicomputers and other types of machines, when conventional wisdom was that it wouldn't work and would be too slow. It would be the first commercial, relational database. The founders renamed the company RSI.

To start the company, Ellison and Miner pooled $1,500 in savings to rent office space in Belmont, California. Ellison became President and CEO and took charge of sales and marketing for the new company, while Miner supervised software development. They convinced the venture capitalist Donald Lucas to become chairman of the board after he stumbled upon their company; employees were working late into the night in its early offices on 3000 Sand Hill Road. While the first version of the program was never officially released, Version 2 came out in 1979 and was the first commercial SQL RDBMS. It ran on a PDP-11, a popular computer at that point. The product attracted customers who used it for simple business functions and came out two years before the IBM version.

In the start-up days of Oracle, Bob Miner was the lead engineer, programming the majority of Oracle Version 3 by himself. As head of engineering, Miner's management style differed from Larry Ellison, who ran Oracle's hard-driving sales team. While Miner expected his engineers to produce, he did not agree with the demands laid upon them by Ellison. He thought it was wrong for people to work extremely late hours and he wanted them to see their families.

Ellison just wanted results. Bruce Scott, an early Oracle database engineer, felt Oracle was successful mainly because of Ellison's charisma, vision, and determination. One example Scott gave was when the engineers in the startup had space allocated to them and needed to get their terminals strung to the computer room next door. They didn't have anywhere to string the wiring. Larry walked in, picked up a hammer, and slammed a hole in the middle of the wall. He said, "There you go," and then walked away.[27]

In 1981 RSI began developing simple reporting tools after recognizing that customers wanted to write applications to enter and format data into usable reports. By 1982, RSI was profitable with 24 employees, 75 customers in the mainframe and minicomputer space, and reported annual revenues of nearly $2.5 million. Ellison was hiring salesman to aggressively increase revenues while Miner was more circumspect. Ellison hit the road and did demos of the product across the intelligence community to the CIA, NSA, Air Force Intelligence, and so on. Ellison was working 14 hours or more a day, and even had to cut his own salary at one point. His second wife left him as he focused on making products.

About a quarter of Oracle's 1982 revenues were poured back into research and development. This led to the 1983 Oracle innovation of the first commercially available portable RDBMS. The portable RDBMS

---

[27] Oracle Anniversary Timeline, Profit Magazine, May 2007, p. 26-30
http://www.oracle.com/oramag/profit/07-may/p27anniv_timeline.pdf.

enabled companies to run their DBMS on a range of hardware and operating systems, including mainframes, minicomputers, workstations, and personal computers. Oracle doubled its revenues to over $5 million in 1983. That same year, Miner and Oates rewrote the database code in the C programming language. After that, their RDBMS would no longer be bound by any single platform and could be easily modified for many types of computers. RSI became Oracle Corporation.

The next few years brought more product innovations and growing revenue. In 1985 Oracle released versions 5.0 and 5.1 to operate in client/server mode so multiple desktop business applications could access a single database on a server. Oracle also began to explore clustering, an early move toward flexible, scalable software. Revenues hit $23 million in 1985 and doubled to a record $55.4 million in 1986.

Two important events happened in 1986. First, the database industry decided to make SQL as the industry's standard language for relational database management systems. This in turn led to increased market acceptance of Oracle's SQL-compatible RDBMS. Second, on March 15, 1986, a decade after the founding of the company, Oracle had an initial public stock offering of 2.1 million shares on the NASDAQ exchange. The company had a market value of $270 million and Ellison owned 39% of the stock. At the time, the company had 450 employees and was the fastest-growing software company in the world. It had recorded 100% or better growth in revenues in eight of its first nine years. Much of this growth came from Oracle's targeted end users: multinational companies with a variety of previously incompatible computer systems. By 1986 Oracle's customer base had grown to include 2,000 mainframe and minicomputer users. These customer firms operated in such fields as the aerospace, automotive, pharmaceutical, and computer manufacturing industries, not to mention government organizations.

The IPO would reward investors well. Twenty years later, Oracle had a global workforce of 65,000 and annual revenue topping $15 billion. A $10,000 investment in the IPO of Oracle back in 1986 would by October 2006 be worth over $4 million. Revenues would go from $20 million in 1986 to $11 billion in 2001, when the companies would have operating margins of 35% and a cash pile of $6-8 billion dollars.

In 1986 Oracle expanded its RDBMS product line and released a distributed DBMS based on the company's SQL*Star software. Under the distributed system, computer users could access data stored on a network of computers in the same way and with the same ease as if all of a network's information were stored on one computer.

Getting into the Applications Market

By 1987 Oracle was fairly successful. It had topped $100 million in sales and had become the world's largest database management software company, with more than 4,500 end users in 55 countries. But Ellison was restless, and he wanted to branch out from databases into applications (computer programs) that used the information in databases for business purposes. Oracle created an applications division and began building its own business-management software, integrated closely with its database.

Ellison had decided by this point that he was a product guy and didn't like most of the CEO duties. So he concentrated on that and delegated all the rest, something Ellison called "closer to abdication than delegation." Ellison was also a brilliant recruiter of programming talent because he knew the product so well. While the sales and executive team could have a revolving door, there was a "kernel group" who created the core product and stayed, accumulating knowledge and experience to continuously make the software better.

Oracle a year later introduced a line of accounting programs for corporate bookkeeping, including a database for personal computers to work in conjunction with the Lotus Development Corporation's popular Lotus 1-2-3 spreadsheet program. The company also introduced its Oracle Transaction Process Subsystem (TPS), a software package designed to speed-up processing of financial transactions. Oracle's TPS opened a new market niche for the company, targeting customers such as banks needing to process large numbers of financial transactions in a short period of time. Meanwhile, hot backup allowed employees to continue working in the system while administrators duplicated and archived data (so it reduced overhead costs). The technology behind this, PL/SQL, generally allowed users to process data while it remained in the database.

In 1989 Oracle was booming. The company was added to the S&P 500 index of stocks. Oracle relocated from Belmont to a new, larger office complex in nearby Redwood Shores, California. Seeking to break into new markets, Oracle formed a wholly-owned subsidiary, Oracle Data Publishing, in December 1989 to develop and sell reference material and other information in electronic form. Oracle closed its books on the 1980s posting annual revenues of $584 million, netting $82 million in profit.

Times were good but the growth bought trouble. In March 1990 Oracle's revenues jumped 54% but net earnings rose only by 1%. Oracle's first flat earnings quarter, attributed to an accounting glitch, shook Wall Street out of its long love affair. Oracle had been booking revenues too aggressively by discounting product and shipping incomplete or buggy software. The day after the earnings announcement the company's stock plummeted $7.88 to $17.50 in record one-day volume with nearly 21 million of the company's 129 million shares changing hands.

In April 1990 a dozen shareholders brought suit against Oracle, charging the company had made false and misleading earnings forecasts.

On the heels of this lawsuit, Oracle announced it would conduct an internal audit and immediately restructure its management team with Ellison assuming the additional post of chairman, while Lucas remained a director. Oracle also formed a separate domestic operating subsidiary, Oracle US, aimed at addressing its domestic management and financial problems, which the company attributed to poor earnings.

Part of the problem was Ellison's management style. He was a sprinter who would work hard, rest, and then sprint again. Ellison could get bored of the company and then take weeks off to travel the world or spend time on his yachts. He could listen to his executives with intensity or completely ignore them. Ellison felt good when everyone said he was nuts because it was a sign that Oracle was trying to do something innovative. But Ellison also paradoxically cautioned, "when people say you're nuts, you might be nuts. You've got to constantly guard against that possibility. You don't want people saying you're nuts too often."[28]

For the fiscal year ending May 31, 1990, Oracle initially posted record sales of $970.8 million and profits of $117.4 million; but these results were below Oracle's own estimates. The company's stock price fell from a high of $28.38 to $19.88 then plunged to $11.62 in August after an internal audit forced the company to restate earnings for three of its four fiscal quarters. Jeff Walker, the CFO, had messed up in receivables and cash management, and Ellison had not been a good supervisor. At one point, Walker sought a cash infusion from the outside, but Ellison held back as he didn't want to dilute his personal equity stake. As a result, Oracle negotiated a $250 million revolving line of credit from a bank syndicate. A few weeks later the company reported its first-ever quarterly loss of nearly $36 million with expenses outpacing revenues by 20%. The corporate bank account had only $3 million at its low point. The stock tumbled once again, hitting a low of $4.88.

Ellison had to make major changes, which started with changing his management team. Oracle also moved to reduce its annual growth rate goals from 50% to 25%, laid off 10% of its domestic workforce of 4,000, consolidated financial and administrative operations, and folded various international units into a single division. A lot of top talent left at that point, including people like Tom Siebel. It was a low point for Ellison, as he had borrowed on his Oracle stock and so received margin calls. Meanwhile, Ellison's third wife Barbara left him and Miner, his co-founder, wanted out by selling. The company's board wanted to kick Ellison out, but Don Lucas stood on his side. Ellison had to start paying attention to accounting and legal, not to mention the sales teams. Ellison started fighting back and said: "I've always been more motivated by fear of failure than greed. And I hate losing."

---

[28] Symonds, Matthew & Larry Ellison. Softwar: An Intimate Portrait of Larry Ellison and Oracle. New York: Simon and Schuster, 2004, p. 37.

For 1991 Oracle topped the $1 billion sales mark for the first time in history and at the same time posted its first annual loss of $12.4 million. In October the company secured a new $100 million revolving line of credit from another bank syndicate. Oracle negotiated an agreement for $80 million in financing from Nippon Steel Corporation, which also agreed to sell Oracle products in Japan. In return, Nippon was given rights to purchase as much as 25% of Oracle's marketing subsidiary in Japan, duly named Oracle Japan.

The year 1992 brought much change. Ellison brought in Ray Lane, a senior partner from the consulting firm Booz Allen Hamilton, to help turn around the sales team, while his partner Robert Shaw came to build up Oracle's consulting arm. They would be two great hires and they helped turn Oracle around. They built their own executive teams and forced Ellison to listen and respond to criticism and unpleasant facts. In 1992, Oracle7 also came out after four years of research and development and two more years of customer testing. It supported a larger number of users than previous versions, handled more transactions, allowed data to be shared between multiple computers across a network, and improved application development features. It won industry praise and emboldened Ellison to talk up database technology for the Internet. Bob Miner also left in 1992 as he had trouble managing a large team of engineers and soon found out he had cancer.

By the end of its 1992 fiscal year, Oracle's balance sheet had improved as sales inched modestly upward and earnings rebounded, with the company reaching $1.18 billion in sales and $61.5 million in profits. Oracle entered 1993 with no bank debt, solid long-term financing in place, and in an improved financial position controlled by a revamped management team.

Ellison and Lane came up with a three-part strategy. First, they wanted to build Oracle 7's database market share at whatever cost. Second, they had to make sure their database was the best on the market by beating Sybase and Informix decisively. Third, Ellison wanted to branch out of databases into other applications. He was interested in video-on-demand (which would be a dead end).

By 1993, Lane was doing so well in US sales that he moved to global sales and was eventually heading to become the company's President. Ellison also made the mistake of firing the entrepreneurial Geoff Squire, who would go on to build Veritas into a strong software company.

By mid-1994 Oracle's sales had reached $2 billion and its consulting services accounted for 20% of sales. Consulting became an important part of Oracle's model. While its competitor, SAP, had a nice relationship with Anderson Consulting, the world's largest IT systems integrator, Oracle was pressing down hard.

The standard in the enterprise software business was for a large company to buy dozens of "best of breed" applications from a range of vendors. Then the company would hire an IT consulting company, like Accenture, to connect all these bits of software, with their multiple databases and systems. Data would become fragmented, duplicative, and conflicting across the databases behind the multiple programs. The analogy would be buying dozens of car parts from different places and then putting together your own car (without the different parts-makers having a common standard tying them together).

Since so many of Oracle's applications were so bad, its consultants pushed a "best of breed" strategy and then worked to integrate outside applications. Meanwhile, Ron Wohl would take over application development at Oracle and try to improve the internal products. The battles between Wohl and the Lane/Shaw duo would be rough, as the latter didn't like selling the buggy software coming out late from Wohl's team. Meanwhile Oracle also started buying and partnering with other, smaller software companies.

Fighting Microsoft over Internet Strategy

By 1995 Larry Ellison had "found Jesus" and had a specific vision and strategy for the Internet. During a keynote presentation at a conference in Paris, Ellison introduced his vision of the network computer, a small, inexpensive device that would run applications via the Internet. The keynote speech took the technology world by storm and would pit Ellison against Bill Gates of Microsoft, who still believed in the PC/server model of computing.

With Oracle's revenues topping $4 billion, in May 1996 Ellison took on the "Wintel" (Microsoft Windows software plus Intel's processing hardware) monolith by unveiling the "Network Computer" (NC). It was a kind of stripped-down PC with no hard drive and therefore no applications. Joining with such partners as SUN Microsystems and Netscape, Ellison offered to free corporations from the costly upgrades Intel and Microsoft forced on them with every new release of Windows and the x86 family of processors. Using Ellison's $500 NC, data and applications could be stored and accessed as needed via the World Wide Web or remote server computers, equipped, naturally, with Oracle's databases. Since corporations would no longer have to buy storage and applications for each computer, they could save millions with no loss in functionality, and Oracle would have a vast new market for its database products. By late 1996 this strategy had evolved into the "Network Computing Architecture," a complicated new three-tier world for corporate computing consisting of a client computer (the computer accessed by the user), an applications (such as word processing software) server, and a database server.

While Ellison battled Microsoft, he was still practical. In 1996 Oracle ported all of its development tools, object technology, and modeling and analysis tools to NT. Recognizing that Microsoft's Windows NT operating system was becoming increasingly popular with small businesses, Oracle delivered a multi-node scalable database for Windows NT clusters.

In 1997 Ellison unveiled Oracle8, based on his vision of the Internet and network computing. Meanwhile, the "best of breed" consulting strategy was falling apart, as it was difficult and expensive to link many different application programs. That same year, Ray Lane wanted to leave for the Novell CEO post, but Ellison bribed him to stay with $2.5 million in options. Many Oracle applications weren't good enough, so Ellison had to fire Ron Wohl and take over the applications development group himself. He would have to start making applications for things like order management, tables, and accounting; all were things Ellison had found boring before, but he now had to master them. Ellison also started to feel that Lane wanted him to fail.

Selling its Own E-Business Application Suite

Oracle prepared to release version 11i of its E-Business Suite in 2000. It would provide the most substantial integration of CRM and ERP applications to date. It was intended as an entire ecosystem of enterprise computing and the IT consulting industry, as Oracle claimed customers could get all they wanted from one place. There was no need to find a "best of breed" supplier and then pay expensive consultants for years to patch together systems. Ellison was changing the company's strategy to have a single, global database support a range of business applications, a suite from marketing, sales, supply chain, manufacturing, customer service, accounting, and so on

It was an attack against Microsoft's client/server model of computing again. The difficulty with that was anytime new software or hardware was updated, it had to be installed across hundreds of computers or more. That required costly IT labor hours.

Ellison also started in 1999 to get more involved in sales force compensation, an important issue. He took this responsibility away from Lane and created a better compensation plan. It was transparent, had stretch targets, and allowed the best salesmen to make more money and the worst to clear out. He also corrected dysfunctional incentives, such as this one: if a salesman sold a million dollars of Oracle product directly, he got $100,000; if he sold Oracle product through a partner and made the company $600,000, he got $120,000. So the sales force pushed the less profitable deals for large bonuses.

Another big event in 1999 was the arrival of Safra Catz, a former DLJ investment banker, who became Ellison's chief of staff. As a former lawyer and banker, she had a forensic approach to digging out facts and then analyzing them. Ellison appreciated her methodical approach, saying: "In an argument when nobody has any facts... the person with the strongest personality wins. But when one person has the facts and the other doesn't, the one with the facts always wins. When both people have facts, there's no argument." After Catz arrived, Ellison started stripping Lane of more responsibility.

Oracle also launched its rebuilt application server, Oracle9i Application Server. It included Web caching technology that dramatically increased Web site performance and scalability and cached dynamically generated as well as static pages.

Oracle shipped Oracle E-Business Suite Release 11i, the first Internet-enabled suite of business applications built on a single data model for seamless, real-time business intelligence. It was a big deal because Ellison was turning against the client/server model of computing for an Internet "cloud" model. The hardest part was convincing Oracle's own engineers that this was the right direction and to get them to support the new product strategy. Ray Lane fought Ellison's technology decision and was aghast at making the Internet the core of the company's platform.

Ellison had a brilliant strategy for selling 11i. He first implemented the entire software internally at Oracle, and showed that it saved Oracle $1 billion annually. Oracle then spent $300 million marketing this message: "By using our own E-Business Suite, Oracle saved $1 billion in one year." The message was mostly correct; the new suite required that companies adapt their business processes to it, but it was cheaper and more powerful, as an independent Economist Intelligence Unit study showed.

Oracle finished fiscal 2000 with revenues of $10.2 billion and earnings at an all-time high of $6.3 billion due to an extra $4 billion from selling shares in Oracle Japan. By the following year, Oracle prospered like its former self of the 1980s with soaring sales, new product releases, and a myriad of new ventures both in the United States and abroad. The company finished the year with sales close to $11 billion and $2.6 billion in earnings.

In June 2000, Ellison fired Ray Lane, the company's President and Ellison's heir apparent, saying: "It's like a marriage that went bad. I don't know [what went wrong]." Lane had cleaned up the US sales force and helped the consulting business grow, yet Ellison didn't see him as his replacement anymore. Lane never had a real social relationship with Ellison, who stated it this way: "Ray's a duck hunter. I raise mallards every spring. We couldn't be more different in personality and pastimes."

In 2001 Oracle released Oracle9i Database, with technology supporting software as a service. Oracle also redesigned its business applications to run on wireless and mobile devices. Oracle9i Database added Oracle Real Application Clusters, giving customers the option to run their IT on connected, low-cost servers—expanding performance, scalability, and availability of the database.

In 2002 Oracle Database 10g was introduced. An early database for grid computing, it allowed groups of low-cost servers to be connected by Oracle software and run applications faster than the fastest mainframe, in addition to offering self-management capabilities.

Meanwhile, Ellison started re-tooling the Oracle sales culture to get creativity out of the process and make it more "engineered." Ellison wanted a new process that involved first identifying a customer's decision maker and documenting it in their sales system. Then, the salesman could send a set of key customer references and case studies showing how other customers got better performance on a lower cost system, with case studies. Third, the salesman could send a proposal quantifying cost savings in hardware, software, and labor by implementing a specific Oracle product at that customer's company. Finally, the salesman could send a contract with standardized terms and a price quote.

By 2004 Oracle began to offer easy-to-implement, low-risk, affordable solutions for small and medium-sized businesses with Oracle E-Business Suite Special Edition and Oracle Database Standard Edition One. In 2005 Oracle OpenWorld was the biggest event in Oracle's history, opening its doors to more than 28,000 attendees, and offering more than 800 sessions and activities. Oracle was the king of American IT technology conferences; only Steve Jobs could do better.

Growth through Targeted Acquisitions

From 2003 onward, Oracle's growth strategy shifted towards acquiring other companies making business software. The motivations behind Oracle's largest acquisitions were to increase market share in large business software markets, to expand profitability by consolidating high-margin, customer support revenue while cutting labor costs, and to offer a complete technology "stack" of software applications and hardware.

All of Oracle's large deals over the next six years met these requirements. Peoplesoft, Siebel, and Hyperion all strengthened Oracle's market share position in the applications market while contributing captive customer bases that pay highly profitable support fees. BEA Systems was important for its stake in the middleware market, which helped Oracle integrate so many applications it sold. Finally, SUN Microsystems brought recurring support revenue. It was also interesting for two other reasons: first, it demonstrated Oracle's willingness to move into servers and storage (including hardware); second, Oracle took control of Java, a key programming language for Web and Internet development. In 2010, Ellison succinctly stated: "our strategy is in creating and acquiring intellectual property."

In mid-2003 Oracle initiated a hostile takeover of PeopleSoft Inc. for $5.1 billion. The Pleasanton, California-based PeopleSoft, was in the process of acquiring J.D. Edwards & Company and was not amused by Oracle's takeover bid, no matter how attractive the offer. For its part, Oracle raised its offer several times in the succeeding months, to as high as $9.4 billion, only to be met by a storm of controversy. Few people, save Ellison, were in favor of the takeover. Shareholders of both firms were unhappy. The US Department of Justice got involved over antitrust issues.

By the end of 2003, Ellison was determined to win the battle, whatever the cost. Oracle's year-end revenues fell for the second year in a row to $9.5 billion. By January 2005, Oracle had cleared the hurdles and closed the PeopleSoft acquisition, adding PeopleSoft Enterprise, JD Edwards EnterpriseOne, and JD Edwards World applications to its product lines. This was followed by the acquisitions of Siebel, Retek, Oblix, and other strategic companies.

In 2006 Oracle released Oracle Database 10g Express Edition, its first free database edition for developers and learning DBAs. Oracle acquired several companies including Sleepycat Software, the makers of the world's most popular open-source database, Berkeley DB, and released Oracle Secure Enterprise Search, a new standalone product that enabled secure, high-quality, easy-to-use search across all enterprise information assets.

In July 2007 Oracle bought Hyperion Solutions Corporation, a global provider of performance-management software solutions, through a cash tender offer for $52.00 per share, or approximately $3.3 billion. Earlier that year, Oracle filed a court case in the Californian courts against a major competitor, SAP AG, for malpractice and unfair competition. In October 2007 Oracle announced a bid to buy BEA Systems for a price of $17 per share, an offer rejected by the BEA board, which felt that it undervalued their company. In January 2008 Oracle bought BEA Systems for $19.375 per share in cash for a total of $7.2 billion net of cash. In 2008, Oracle started marketing servers and storage in a co-developed and co-branded data warehouse appliance named the HP Oracle Database Machine.

In April 2009 Oracle announced a bid to acquire SUN Microsystems for $7.4 billion ($9.50 per share). After a bidding battle with IBM, in January 2010 Oracle acquired SUN. SUN Chairman Scott McNealy had to leave the company he co-founded 28 years earlier. He wrote in a bittersweet memo, "My hat is off to one of the greatest capitalists I have ever met, Larry Ellison." McNealy preferred that SUN would be the great and surviving consolidator, but he was happy with the sale and his payout.

SUN's technology gave Oracle a place in the server, storage, and processor domains. Oracle became a direct competitor to more companies, even hardware customers to whom Oracle sold its database and other software for use on servers sold by those competitors. Now IBM, Hewlett-Packard, Cisco Systems, and EMC would be direct competitors. SUN made most of its revenue from selling computers but Oracle executives said they didn't regard SUN as a hardware company. As Oracle President Safra Catz stated, hardware would mean factory ownership and large capital investments. However, SUN outsourced nearly all the manufacturing, assembly, and servicing of its hardware. It was more of a hardware design company.

Oracle's sales pitch was one of integrated products: hardware and software built to work together so that customers didn't have to do the integration work themselves or pay an expensive third-party consulting firm, like Accenture, to do it. Also it would reduce software development costs and bugs, and improve security. Finally, SUN's computer designers could tailor hardware to the combined company's software, promising further gains in efficiency.

Beyond hardware, Ellison said that SUN's Java programming language and its Solaris operating system were the main attractions, calling the highly popular programming language Java "the single most important software asset we have ever acquired." Oracle could offer a more complete set of corporate software, ranging from SUN's hardware, operating system, and programming tools to Oracle's existing database and business applications. The end goal would be to help companies automate operations like finance and customer relations management.

Oracle was always a hard-charging company, as two incidents show. In July 2010 Oracle was indicted for fraud by the US Department of Justice, after an employee tip-off and investigation starting in 2007. The government accused Oracle of defrauding the US General Services Administration (USGA), which negotiated contracts for the government, on a software contract running from 1998 to 2006, involving more than $1 billion in sales. Oracle had agreed to give federal buyers discounts of up to 40%, which Oracle said was steeper than the discounts it gave similarly sized corporate customers. In reality, Oracle's sales force was authorized to give similar-sized customers discounts ranging from 40% to 70%, where 90% of other corporate deals contained discounts larger than what Oracle gave to the government. Oracle failed to inform the government of other customers' better deals and went out of its way to manipulate deals so that they wouldn't have to report them to the government. In 2011, Oracle stopped supporting its products for Intel and HP's Itanium chip servers, choosing to litigate instead of supporting a marginal product (that still generated $1bn of revenues for HP).

By 2013, Ellison's buying spree included over 80 companies bought for over $50bn, including cloud companies like Taleo and Eloquo and the networking gear company Acme Packet Inc. Instead of making much in-house, Oracle had decided to buy new products made by others and just plug them into its massive sales machine.

18. Warriors: Personal Computers, Killer Applications, and SUN Microsystems (1980-83)

The Coming of the Personal Computer

In 1980 IBM enjoyed a near-monopoly in the mainframe-computer market and decided to enter the personal computer (PC) market. IBM opened a small Entry Systems Division in Florida under the direction of Donald Estridge, who opted for building a computer from off-the-shelf, widely available components. One reason for this decision was that IBM was still wary of an antitrust lawsuit brought against it by the government in 1969. The best way to avoid accusations of monopolistic practices was to make the specifications available to its competitors. IBM put William Lowe in charge of the top-secret project, code-named "Acorn."

IBM had two key decisions to make about its PC, regarding the processor and the operating system. To start with, IBM chose the Intel 8088 microprocessor instead of a proprietary IBM microprocessor (IBM had already acquired the rights to manufacture Intel chips). IBM did not have an operating system for Intel's processors, so it was necessary to buy one from a third party. When in 1978, Intel had introduced the 8086, a young Seattle programmer, Tim Patterson, had been hired by Seattle Computer Products (SCP) to develop a CP/M-compatible operating system for it. In December 1980 he finished work on his 86-DOS. In 1981, Bill Gates talked his way into delivering an operating system for the 8086. His Microsoft bought the rights on 86-DOS from SCP and hired Patterson to port 86-DOS to the first prototype of the machine provided by IBM. It was renamed MS-DOS and Microsoft decided to retain the rights on the operating system.

IBM launched its machine as the IBM PC in August 1981. The basic version with 16 kilobytes of RAM and a cassette unit sold for $1,600. Another revolutionary move by IBM was to let outside distributors such as Sears & Roebucks and Computerland sell the PC. Previously, the best-selling computer in IBM's product line had sold only 25,000 units over five years. The PC would sell a million units in less than three years.

The IBM PC legitimized the personal computer. No other computer company before IBM had entered the personal-computer market. The PC companies such as Apple, Tandy, and Commodore were not considered real computer companies by the corporate world but rather more as toy makers for hobbyists.

The business models chosen by IBM and Microsoft would have far-reaching consequences. Because IBM had used off-the-shelf components for their PC, and because Microsoft had retained the rights on MS-DOS, it didn't take long for engineers all over the world to realize that one could build a "clone" of the IBM PC. The only difficult trick was to replicate the BIOS (Basic Input/Output System), the software written to "bootstrap" the computer. Rod Canion and other former Texas Instruments engineers founded Compaq to reverse engineer IBM's BIOS. In January 1983, after licensing MS-DOS from Microsoft, Compaq introduced the 8088-based Portable PC, fully compatible with the IBM PC but even smaller (a premonition of the laptop). It was equipped with 128 kilobytes of RAM and priced at $3,000 (the same configuration cost $3,800 on the IBM PC). Soon there would be an entire PC-clone industry worth more than the entire personal-computer industry of the previous years. Compaq was the most aggressive because it had hired marketing and sales executives from IBM. It was not a garage-style startup but a carefully planned large-scale operation. Compaq's strategy was to sell almost exclusively through retailers and resellers.

The personal-computer industry was already mature before the introduction of the PC-clone. About 1.4 million personal computers were sold in 1981, half of them in the US. However, less than 1% of all households in the US had one. That changed in 1982. Another winner in 1981, at the low end of the spectrum, was the Commodore VIC20. It sold 800,000 units in 1982. Its successor, the slightly more powerful Commodore 64 had a price tag of only $600 and would fare even better. It was the first affordable, color computer. It could be directly plugged into a television set and came with 64 kilobytes of RAM. The technology was only part of the reason for its success. Commodore decided to sell it in retail stores instead of electronics stores, thus addressing a much bigger audience. It went on to sell more than 20 million units (four times the units sold of Apple II).

Next to these giants there were the many makers of computers based on the Zilog Z80: Sinclair, Osborne, Sony, Sharp, NCR, Olivetti, Philips and, of course, most models of the popular Tandy Radio Shack TRS-80 series, which was still a best-seller. Notably, in April 1981, Osborne Computer delivered the Osborne 1. It was a portable computer running the CP/M operating system that weighed only 11 kgs and cost $1,800. Hardware engineer Lee Felsenstein, a fellow member of the Homebrew Computer Club, designed it and basically, it was a commercial version of the Xerox NoteTaker. The company had been founded in 1980 in Hayward by British-born hobbyist Adam Osborne, an old member of the Homebrew Computer Club. A few months later, in 1982, Japanese manufacturer Epson introduced an even smaller computer, the HC-20, designed around a Motorola microprocessor dressed up by Hitachi. In April 1982, GRiD Systems introduced a portable computer based on the Intel 8086 microprocessor, the 1101. The company had been founded by a former Xerox PARC scientist on the Alto team, John Ellenby; it had gone public before it even had a product. Manuel Fernandez, a refugee from Cuba who had become the CEO of Zilog during the Z80 era, founded Gavilan. In May 1983, Zilog introduced the first portable MS-DOS computer marketed as a "laptop" for $4,000.

Finally, there was Apple. In 1982, it became the first personal-computer company to pass the $1 billion mark in revenues. Unlike the IBM PC, which featured an operating system used by many other manufacturers, the Apple II relied on a proprietary Apple operating system that did not encourage independent software companies. Willingly or unwillingly, IBM had established an open software standard, whereas Apple still lived in the era of closed proprietary architectures. It wasn't clear which of the two strategies would be the winning one. That year almost three million personal computers were sold worldwide.

The Coming of Software

A major reason for the skyrocketing sales in personal computers was that they were becoming more useful. And that was due to the software, not the hardware. A number of word-processing and spreadsheet programs could run on the IBM PC. In the next few years, a lot of software applications turned the PC into a necessity for any office. They caused the rapid decline of application-specific machines, for example Wang's word-processing machine Office Information System, the wildly successful 1977 descendant of the Wang 1200.

Software application companies sprung from nothing and made useful office software. In 1981, Los Angeles-based Context Management Systems introduced Context MBA for Apple computers. It was a software package that integrated spreadsheet, database, charting, word-processing, and communication functions. In 1982 they ported it to the PC. In January 1983, the Massachusetts-based Lotus Development Corporation, founded the year before by Mitch Kapor of VisiCorp, introduced the spreadsheet program "Lotus 1-2-3" for MS-DOS and the IBM PC. It was developed by MIT alumnus and Lotus co-founder Jonathan Sachs, who had already developed a spreadsheet for Data General's minicomputer. Visicorp's VisiCalc had been ported to the IBM PC, but it was still limited to Apple II's 8-bit architecture and 48 kilobyte memory space. Lotus 1-2-3, on the other hand, was written specifically for the IBM PC in assembly language, taking advantage of its 16-bit Intel processor and of its 640 kilobyte memory space. It became a bestseller. Lotus instantly became the second largest software company for personal computers after Microsoft, with sales in 1983 of $53 million.

Software Plus, founded in 1980 by George Tate and Hal Lashlee, was a Los Angeles-based distributor and publisher of software for personal computers, a booming business. In 1981, they stumbled into the Vulcan database management system for the CP/M operating system developed at home by Wayne Ratliff, an employee of NASA's Jet Propulsion Labs, modeled after the database system of his lab's Univac mainframe. Software

Plus acquired the program, changed its own name to Ashton-Tate, turned Vulcan into a popular product, dBase ($700), and in 1982 ported it to MS-DOS. Finally, Ray Noorda's Novell in Utah in 1982 came up with the idea of a network operating system to allow several personal computers to share the same files and printers. Their NetWare for DOS was the first stepping-stone to enable personal-computer users to work as a team.

A complementary network effect was created between the PC-clones and the software manufacturers. The IBM PC could not run the many applications written for the CP/M operating system, but that rapidly became a non-issue. Due to IBM's size and to Microsoft's licensing skills, in 1982 fifty companies bought a MS-DOS license. As more computers used MS-DOS, the motivation to make software applications for MS-DOS increased. As more applications were written for MS-DOS, the motivation for hardware manufacturers to buy a MS-DOS license increased. Furthermore, Microsoft invested the money in greatly improving the operating system. In March 1983, MS-DOS 2.0 offered features derived from the Unix operating system, such as subdirectories and pipes, that made it much more competitive against CP/M on technical grounds.

Many software companies were started in 1982 in Silicon Valley, a fact that began to alter the relative proportion between hardware and software. Some notable ones included Autodesk, Symantec, Activision, Electronic Arts, and Adobe.

Autodesk was founded in 1981 in Sausalito to commercialize Mike Riddle's Interact, the first Computer-Aided Design (CAD) program for CP/M and MS-DOS personal computers, the first affordable tool for creating detailed technical drawings. Riddle, a user of ComputerVision's CAD system for graphical workstations, teamed up with John Walker's Marinchip Systems that had built a computer based on a Texas Instrument microprocessor.

Symantec was founded in March 1982 in Sunnyvale to pursue artificial intelligence-based research, notably in natural-language processing. Gary Hendrix, who had worked at the SRI International with Charlie Rosen, a pioneer of perceptron (neural-network) machines, founded and hired a group of specialists from Stanford University. Symantec went on to specialize in development tools for software engineers, i.e. software to help build other software.

Borland was founded in 1983 in Scotts Valley, between San Jose and Santa Cruz, by three Danish developers and a Frenchman who had cut his teeth on the Micral project. They targeted the growing needs not of the end user but of the software developer.

Activision was founded in October 1979 by music industry executive Jim Levy and a group of Atari game designers. It became the first company focused on game design. Until then, games for a console had been published exclusively by the console manufacturer. Activision introduced the praxis of giving credit and even publicizing the creators. Its first success, "Pitfall," drove many others to start similar companies.

Trip Hawkins, an Apple marketing manager, founded Electronic Arts in May 1982 in San Mateo. He aimed to market home computer games not as mere games but as a form of interactive digital media. Both EA's business plan and its ethics treated game publishing just like book publishing, plus it treated videogame production just like a movie studio treated movie production.

Adobe was founded in December 1982 in Mountain View to commercialize printer software made by John Warnock and Charles Geschke. They had worked at Xerox PARC on the page-description language InterPress, whose purpose was to enable all computers of a network to print on any printer of the network. By then they were both in their 40s. They left Xerox to develop a simpler language, PostScript. PostScript was the first building block for desktop publishing, which still needed a viable computer platform and a suitable software environment (both unsuccessfully pioneered by Xerox's Star). Unlike most startups, Adobe was profitable from its first year.

Generally speaking, an important transition was underway. Computers were formed by two interacting substances: hardware and software. At the beginning the cost of a computer was entirely the cost of its hardware parts and of assembling them. Until the 1970s, the hardware still represented most of the cost. However, in the 1980s, the falling prices of hardware components had enabled ever more sophisticated software applications and triggered a growing demand for them. This meant that the cost of software was escalating at the same time that the cost of hardware was plunging. This vicious loop also constituted a new powerful motivation for the hardware industry to continue producing more powerful chips in order to support ever-larger software applications. Semiconductor components had become commodities, while software now represented the luxury item. Software was also the place where profit margins could be very high.

One could see the same phenomenon in the world of mainframes, which still accounted for the majority of IT revenues. Computer Associates, was formed in 1976 by Charles Wang and Russell Artzt. It was a joint venture with a company owned by Swiss billionaire Walter Haefner. The firm was initially focused on system utilities for mainframe computers. But in the early 1980s, it inaugurated a cynical strategy of growth not through invention but through ruthless acquisitions that would eventually gobble up all the historical software companies of the mainframe world: Uccel in 1987 for a record $830 million; ADR in 1988; Pansophic in 1991; and Cullinet in 1989.

Losers

The growing complexity of computer applications also induced a growing concern for the user experience. User interfaces were still too technical for a machine that aimed at becoming a home appliance used by ordinary people. After Xerox invested in Apple in 1979, Steve Jobs was given a "demo" of the Alto. That demo set the course of Apple for the 1980s. In January 1983, Apple introduced the Lisa, the first personal computer with a GUI, the "WIMP" (Window, Icons, Mouse, Pull-down menus) paradigm pioneered by the Xerox Alto. The Lisa, based on a Motorola 68000 microprocessor and equipped with one megabyte of RAM and five megabytes of hard-disk storage, heralded the second building block of desktop publishing. Unfortunately, it was too expensive at $10,000 and too slow to truly capture the imagination and wallets of the masses. In October VisiCorp introduced the equivalent GUI for the IBM PC, VisiOn. Neither application lived up to the expectations of their creators.

The principal victim of the personal-computer boom was the videogame console. In the early 1980s there were many best-sellers: Atari 2600 and 5200, Bally Astrocade, Coleco Vision, Emerson Arcadia 2001, Fairchild Channel F, Magnavox Odyssey, Mattel Intellivision, Sears Tele-Games, etc. However, personal computers were getting cheaper and were beginning to offer graphics and sound. A personal computer could play videogames but also run many other useful applications. In 1983, the US market for videogame consoles crashed.

Winners

The semiconductor industry in Silicon Valley was booming, serving a market that ranged from watches to airplanes. The startups continued to multiply:

- Linear Technology, founded in 1981, and Xilinx, a Zilog spin-off formed in 1984, addressed programmable logic (chips that customers could program themselves);
- Maxim, founded in 1983 by former Fairchild's marketing executive and AMDs' co-founder Jack Gifford, perfected the analog integrated circuits that Fairchild pioneered;
- Cypress Semiconductor, an AMD spin-off formed in 1982 by a team of CMOS experts, and Altera, founded in 1983, focused on high-performance integrated circuits.;
- VLSI Technology, a Fairchild spin-off of 1979, and LSI Logic, formed in 1981 by Fairchild's engineer Wilfred Corrigan, specialized in ASICs (Application-Specific Integrated Circuits) for embedded systems.

Meanwhile, voice messaging became a household feature after Octel Communications, founded in 1982 by Robert Cohn and Peter Olson in Milpitas (near San Jose), introduced a voice-mail system. It was smaller and cheaper than the traditional ones because it used Intel and Zilog microprocessors.

SRI International's scientist Stan Honey founded Etak in Sunnyvale in 1983 with seed money from Atari's founder Nolan Bushnell. Etak became the first company to digitize maps. In 1985 it introduced the Navigator, a navigation system for cars. It was based on the Intel 8088 and the maps were stored on cassette tapes.

Few people heard of "Elk Cloner," a program that a 15-year-old high-school student, Rich Skrenta, unleashed on an Apple II in 1982. It was the first personal-computer virus. Elk Cloner was capable of spreading from floppy-disk to floppy-disk, and therefore from computer to computer. What this hacker had implicitly realized is that the widespread adoption of personal computers had connected millions of people, even though the "connection" still relied on copying files on floppy-disks.

Expert Systems

A mini-bubble within the bubble of software existed for startups that specialized in "expert systems." These were systems based on artificial intelligence (AI) techniques developed at Stanford and operating in a narrow domain, such as troubleshooting or configuring complex equipment. The novel approach to computing adopted by these systems consisted in emphasizing the knowledge required to solve a problem.

An expert system had two fundamental components: a knowledge base, constructed by eliciting knowledge from a human expert, and an "inference engine," which contained a set of algorithms to perform inference on the knowledge base. This was therefore a nonsequential kind of computing that differed from most software in which the solution is achieved via a sequence of instructions. Expert systems targeted complex problems for which a traditional program was not feasible. Just like a human expert, an expert system could only provide a "plausible" solution, not necessarily a perfect one. The favorite programming languages for these programs were Prolog and Lisp. In fact, there were also startups specializing in "Lisp machines."

A few startups tried to build expert systems. In 1981, Stanford Professor and expert-system pioneer Ed Feigenbaum founded Teknowledge, which for a while was the most hyped of the AI startups. In 1983, Intellicorp introduced its flagship object-oriented development environment, Knowledge Engineering Environment (KEE), also running on Lisp Machines. Brian McCune, an alumnus of the Stanford Artificial Intelligence Laboratory (SAIL), was one of the founders in 1980 of Advanced Information and Decision Systems (AIDS) in Mountain View, later renamed Advanced Decision Systems (ADS). It was a consulting firm specializing in AI research for the Department of Defense. He and Richard Tong, a Cambridge University graduate, designed a concept-based text-retrieval system, Rubric, a progenitor of search engines.

Workstations

One step up from the personal computer, the world was completely different. The early 1980s were the age of the workstation, similar to a personal computer because it was dedicated to a single user but more powerful, especially in graphics. It was also designed to be connected to a network. This kind of computer targeted the engineering market. They were usually based on the Motorola 68000 and they usually ran the Unix operating system. The market came to be dominated by Apollo, a firm founded in 1980 in Boston by former NASA scientist William Poduska. Other firms quickly followed: SUN (1981), Silicon Graphics (1982) and Hewlett-Packard (1983). They all stole market share from DEC's much more expensive minicomputers. Both SUN and Silicon Graphics originated at Stanford University.

SUN Microsystems was founded in February 1982 in Palo Alto by two foreign Stanford students, German-born Andrea Bechtolsheim of the computer science department and Indian-born Vinod Khosla of the business school. In 1981, Bechtolsheim, while working at the Stanford University Network, had modified a Xerox PARC's Alto into a workstation running Unix and networking software. His goal was simply to have machines for individual researchers that would make it as easy as possible to be connected and share data. Khosla realized that this could become a business. They joined forces with Scott McNealy, a former Stanford graduate and now at Unix startup Onyx, and hired Berkeley graduate Bill Joy of BSD fame. He developed a dialect of Unix, SunOS, based on BSD (Berkeley's version of Unix). Backed by venture capitalists such as Kleiner Perkins, SUN was started to market that concept. Unlike the Apollo workstation, which used custom hardware and a proprietary operating system, the SUN workstation used standard off-the-shelf hardware components and a standard operating system (Unix). Thus, in a sense, it replicated the business model of the IBM PC. Soon, the concept of the SUN workstation was competing with Microsoft. The SUN workstation was basically a more powerful personal computer that also happened to be hooked to a network. It ran Unix instead of Windows. It used a Motorola 68000 processor instead of the Intel x86 processors used by Windows-based computers. Also the SUN corporate culture was to the Microsoft culture what the counterculture was to the mainstream.

Silicon Graphics was started in November 1981 by Jim Clark and Abbey Silverstone of Xerox to manufacture graphic workstations. Previously, Evans & Sutherland's Picture System had pioneered hardware implementations of computer graphics. At Stanford University in 1980, former Evans & Sutherland's employee Jim Clark and his student Marc Hannah developed an improved version called the "Geometry Engine." The original idea was to have Motorola 68000-based workstations connected to a DEC VAX minicomputer that boasted high-performance graphics needed for engineering design. Later those workstations became stand-alone Unix computers. Silicon Graphics benefited from an exodus of HP engineers, including Jim Barton who went on to create a real-time version of Unix (essential for flight simulation) and the first video-on-demand system, Full Service Network, for Time Warner.

Workstation developers talked about the RISC (Reduced Instruction Set Computer) architecture, which promised faster CPUs. For three decades, there had been a trend towards implementing more and more complex functions directly in the hardware of a computer. The principle behind the research in RISC architectures was that, while it is helpful to be able to perform complex operations, applications mostly execute simple operations. Hence, it might be more efficient to perform those frequent simple operations faster than to implement infrequent complex operations.

So again, many startups were formed to exploit RISC:

- Ridge Computers was founded in 1980 in Santa Clara by a group of Hewlett-Packard engineers;
- David Patterson and Carlo Sequin launched the RISC project at UC Berkeley in 1980;
- The following year, John Hennessy started a RISC project at Stanford University. Hennessy eventually left Stanford, founded a company, MIPS, and in 1985 released the first major RISC processor, the R2000. Silicon Graphics would switch to MIPS processors in 1986. MIPS was also adopted by Nintendo in Japan and by Siemens and Bull in Europe;
- SUN introduced its SPARC architecture in 1986, based on Berkeley's RISC project; and so did Pyramid Technology, formed in 1981 by former HP employees;
- British computer manufacturer Acorn showed a RISC processor in 1985, the Acorn Risc Machine or ARM, designed by Sophie Wilson. It would become the company's most successful product, causing the birth in 1990 of a spin-off, Advanced RISC Machines (ARM), which in 1991 would introduce its first embeddable RISC chip.

The giant in the field of minicomputers was DEC. In October 1977, it introduced a 32-bit family of computers, the VAX, to progressively replace the various 16-bit PDP-11 models. DEC had designed a proprietary multi-user operating system for the VAXes, the VMS. However, in 1978 Bell Labs had already ported the PDP-11 Unix to the VAX platform. Unix had become the preferred operating system for universities and DEC hardware had always been a favorite of universities. Therefore DEC involuntarily had one of the most popular Unix platforms. DEC calculated that in 1985 about 25% of all VAXes was running Unix. The VAX with Unix was also the computer of choice for the Internet, since Unix had become the operating system for the Internet and the PDP-11s had become the preferred minicomputers for the Internet.

The Great Unix Wars

Unix was important to all software developers. In 1983, Oracle announced that its engineers (basically Bob Miner and Bruce Scott) had rewritten its database management system in the C programming language, the language preferred by all Unix systems. It was an achievement that made Oracle's product easily portable across computer platforms. It was therefore ported to the most popular minicomputers and even to mainframes that already had C compilers. It was also the first 32-bit relational database management system.

Something important happened in 1983 that had little to do with Unix technology but would have repercussions on Unix computers. The US government decided that AT&T, the company that owned Bell Labs and the Unix operating system, was a monopoly violating the anti-trust laws. The government ordered the dismemberment of this conglomerate, at the time the largest company in the world. AT&T had been forced since 1958 to make non-telephone technologies available to others. But now, broken up into separate companies, it was free to make money out of the Unix operating system. Before the end of the year, AT&T had a commercial version ready, which was renamed Unix System V. That was the beginning of the great Unix wars of the 1980s, pitting System V against BSD, i.e. AT&T's corporate profit-driven world, versus the idealistic Bay Area hobbyists (notably SUN, which was rapidly dwarfing the competition).

To further complicate the Unix landscape, in 1983 Richard Stallman at MIT started working on a free clone of Unix that would contain no Unix code, code-named GNU. In 1985, he issued a GNU manifesto and launched the Free Software Foundation that denounced proprietary software.

In theory, the Internet belonged to the US government through DARPA. In practice, most decisions were taken by the various scientists that cooperated casually in maintaining it. For example, SRI International had always maintained the "directory" of Internet nodes, a text file that returned a physical network address for each node. In 1983, Paul Mockapetris at SRI was assigned the task of developing the Domain Name System, so that each node would be identified by a "domain name" in a hierarchy of domain names. The concept was refined by the community via "Requests for Comments" (RFCs). The following year the first DNS was implemented in Unix by students at UC Berkeley. This process was eventually formalized (in January 1986) in an Internet Engineering Task Force (IETF), which was open to everybody.

The Counterculture and the Computer Culture

Just like the personal computer and the Unix, the Internet too was largely shaped by a community of eccentric independents. From the beginning, Arpanet was run by a powerful government agency. Yet its director, Lawrence Roberts, had relied not on top-down decisions but on a decentralized model that involved the very users of the Internet to submit proposals for future directions. He organized retreats for Arpanet users. It was a government-mandated collaborative effort and another case in which the consumer was the producer, a community of "prosumers." In a sense, the Arpanet was conceived from the beginning as a project in progress, not as a fully specified project, a concept that is more likely to surface in military projects than in commercial product development. One of the side effects of this approach was that the Arpanet changed mission over time, transforming from a military project to survive a nuclear attack into a system for interpersonal communication and knowledge sharing. It fostered collaboration among geographically remote research labs, which was already not one of the initial goals.

Even more unexpectedly, Arpanet became a popular tool for intranode communications and collaboration, as each node started connecting its multiple computers among themselves. E-mail itself was a user idea, never planned by the Arpanet's bureaucracy. Nobody commissioned it, approved it, or promoted it. A user deployed it and other users started using it. By 1973 it probably accounted for the majority of Arpanet traffic. Again, the pseudo-socialist and anarchic idealism of the counterculture had found another form. The ethos of the Internet, just like the ethos of the Unix world and the ethos of the early personal-computer hobbyists, was not the brutal, heartless ethos of the corporate world or Wall Street. It was the utopian ethos of the hippie communes transposed into a high-tech environment.

The nature of the revolution in personal computers, Unix, and the Internet mirrored more closely the continuous renovation of rock music than anything else. Rock magazines and radio stations were used to hail a "next big thing" every month and got music listeners to expect a new genre every month. Similarly, computer magazines and later Usenet groups started talking about a technological "next big thing" every month and thus created the expectation for it in computer users.

However, the parallel between counterculture and the high-tech industry had an obvious limit: the personal computer, Unix, and the Internet had nothing to do with San Francisco itself. The headquarters of personal-computer innovation was the Santa Clara Valley, the part of the Bay Area that had witnessed the fewest student riots, hippie be-ins, and rock concerts. Stanford, in particular, had been largely indifferent to the whole counterculture. Unix and the Internet had now strong roots in Berkeley, but it was only in part a phenomenon of the Bay Area. It looked as if the marriage between counterculture and high-tech culture had to take place in neutral territory, close enough to the epicenter but far enough not to be affected by its more extreme manifestations.

Lasers and Nanotechnology

The personal computer was much larger than all the other industries. Yet the early 1980s were also, for example, the era of semiconductor lasers. Startups specializing in these high-power lasers included: Stanford Research Systems (SRS), founded in 1980 in Sunnyvale; Spectra Diode Labs, a 1983 joint venture between Spectra-Physics and Xerox PARC; and Lightwave, founded in 1984 in Mountain View. Despite the immense and rapid success of laser technology in all sorts of applications, the laser industry never took off like the computer industry. There were many parallels with the computer industry. Stanford had one of the best research teams in the world. Ed Ginzton was for lasers what Terman had been for electronics. Ginzton's laboratory at Stanford spun off several startups and employees fluctuated among those companies and founded new ones. While lasers were similar to computers, this is a significant example of an industry based in Silicon Valley that did not achieve momentum.

Micro-Electro-Mechanical Systems (MEMS) represented the infancy of nanotechnology. These were miniaturized devices made of microsensors, microactuators and microelectronics. In 1982, Kurt Petersen wrote the influential paper "Silicon as a Mechanical Material" and founded Transensory Devices in Fremont (later IC Sensors in Milpitas), a pioneering company in commercializing MEMS devices. Petersen envisioned a broad range of inexpensive, batch-fabricated, high-performance sensors and transducers easily interfaced with the rapidly proliferating microprocessor.

In 1980 Stanford Electrical Engineering professor John Linvill had the idea for the Center for Integrated Systems, a lab that worked closely with industry to bring together material, hardware, and software engineers for the purpose of designing integrated circuits. For example, Gregory Kovacs would design sensor systems that combine detectors on silicon wafers the same way electrical circuits are integrated on computer chips.

Anarchy

The 1980s was the age of the spiritual revival that turned so many former hippies into new-age adepts. Arguing for a return to a more natural way of life, they were fiercely opposed to science and rationalism, and viewed technology as evil. The intellectual zeitgeist of the Bay Area was hardly in sync with its high-tech boom. The dichotomy between luddites and technophiles would remain a distinctive contradiction of the Bay Area, just like materialism and spirituality could coexist in the lifestyle of the same "yuppie" (young urban professional).

An important contribution to these booming industries came from people who were completely immune to the intellectual mood of the Bay Area: immigrants. The 1970s had witnessed the first wave of immigration of engineers from Europe and Asia. In the early 1980s they contributed significantly to the boom of Silicon Valley. For example, Chinese and Indian executives ran 13% of Silicon Valley's high-tech companies founded between 1980 and 1984. Additionally, the Bay Area had been attracting young people from the other states of the US since the 1960s. It was sunny, "cool," advanced, cosmopolitan, and laden with opportunities. It had the mythological appeal of the Far West and the quasi-mystic appeal of the Promised Land. At the same time it had become a pleasant and wealthy place to live, a dreamland for the highly educated youth of the East Coast and the Midwest. Silicon Valley was quite unique to have much ethnic diversity and deep technological saturation. It was also a place where the boring corporate world was non-existent and despised. In 1980, there were about 3,000 electronics firms in the Bay Area. The vast majority had less than 10 employees and only 15% of them had more than 100.

Silicon Valley exhibited a propensity towards spawning new firms even when the market was not ready for an avalanche of products. Viewed from above, the creation and destruction of companies was chaotic. The lifespan of startups was getting shorter, not longer. What mattered was not the life expectancy of an individual company but the success of the entire ecosystem. The price to pay for the latter was a short lifespan for most of the individual companies.

High labor mobility was crucial to the implementation of this model of continuous regeneration as well as to sustain the breathtaking growth of successful startups. The mobility of labor was also enabled by an anti-union spirit. This was not trivial. After all, San Francisco was the most unionized city in the country at the beginning of the 20th century and socialist agit-prop groups were ubiquitous in San Francisco and Berkeley during the 1960s. Perhaps it was precisely a desire not to be identified with the old-fashioned business style of San Francisco that led Silicon Valley to adopt the opposite stance towards unions.

The old computing world, mainly based on the East Coast, was controlled top-down at two levels. First, the users of a mainframe or mini had to be hired by a company or university, so access was controlled top-down by the owner of the expensive computer. Second, the technology of that mainframe or mini computer was proprietary, hence controlled top-down by the computer manufacturer. The personal-computer world, instead, was decentralized and anarchic at both levels.

It was ironic how an invention whose original purpose was purely military and reserved for a tightly-guarded and small number of laboratories was rapidly evolving into a ubiquitous data processing and communication device for ordinary offices and even households.

19. Early Failures: A Case Study on Good Ideas which Arrived Too Early (1980-94)

The startup and venture capital world went through a boom from 1981 to 1987. In hindsight, it was a precursor to the 1990s technology boom and bust, a much larger bubble. Three failed products exemplify the boom well: the Commodore Amiga, the Apple Newton, and the Go PenPoint OS. These promising failures show that the line between extreme success and bankruptcy can be a thin one. Being right with a product but launching into an unprepared market with the wrong timing means you are wrong. The market must be primed, yet variables such as product specs, marketing plans, and market readiness are important but difficult to gauge.

Commodore's Amiga Computer

The Commodore Amiga, a product that went from solid success to abject failure, actually began at Atari. The engineer Jay Miner wanted a console with a 16-bit processor and a floppy drive, but Atari executives didn't want to cannibalize their 8-bit console (or its developer systems and licensing fees from ROM media), so they discouraged him. Miner left in 1982 and, with the help of Larry Kaplan, raised $7 million to form the Hi-Toro Corp. The company made successful peripherals for the Atari 2600 while they developed their own competing console, which they called the Lorraine Project. Besides being a more powerful console, the attraction of a floppy drive was that it was cheaper for developers to make software, as they wouldn't need an expensive workstation or proprietary cartridges from Hi-Toro. Developers could use standardized 3.5" floppy drive disks. The company also changed its name to Amiga after lawyers found a Japanese lawn-mover company that had the name Hi-Toro.

In 1983, Atari was burning as customers defected to better products and its game launches failed (one example was a poorly designed but expensive game based on the movie "ET"). An early prototype of the Amiga was ready for the 1983 Comdex (CES) show in Chicago. Atari made a $500,000 loan to the near-bankrupt Amiga for the Lorraine motherboard design, expecting that it would not be paid back and they would keep the technology (getting it for a song). It was a classic case of a startup taking on too big a problem with too little funding; its technology was promising, but the early investors would not be able to capitalize on it. However, before Atari's loan came due, Commodore bought Amiga, repaid the loan, and put the Lorraine design (to be named the Amiga computer) on track for release in 1984. To make it ship on time, the new

Amiga computer (the Amiga 1000) had a TRIPOS operating system (OS), which at that point was more advanced than the recent Mac OS or Microsoft's MS-DOS 2.11 OS. The Amiga's OS's metaphor was for a "workbench" with "projects" stored in "drawers," and not a "desktop" with "files" stored in "folders." The computer was a big hit, as it combined solid graphics, video, and audio capability; it was the first multi-media, multi-tasking computer. The computer also had both a command-line interface and a graphical user interface (GUI).

The competition fought back. Atari released the Atari ST in July 1985 for half the Amiga's price and the Macintosh Plus competed strongly with a large collection of software. Amiga hit back with more cost-competitive devices such as the Amiga 2000 and the Amiga 500, which at one point was the leading home computer in much of Western Europe, selling over 6 million units. In 1987, the company posted a $28 million profit.

With success came failure. Commodore tried to move the Amiga into the living room with a bundled TV tuner, releasing the CD32 and CDTV models as 32-bit consoles. It tried to differentiate the product as not being a computer (it couldn't be sold in the computer section of a retail store). Unfortunately, the new devices failed to attract developers; most computer buyers wanted a separate and larger TV screen. Commodore started to lag further as Wintel PC-clones took off in the early 1990s. As Intel took a chip design lead and Microsoft won the OS war, the Amiga became an underequipped PC whose models cost more than much more advanced Wintel clones. Commodore went bankrupt in 1994 and the Amiga computer was bought by Escom, which itself went bust in 1997.

So while the Commodore Amiga introduced the modern, multi-tasking PC with a GUI interface, the company itself was not flexible to adapt to the Wintel onslaught of the 1990s; instead, competitors like Compaq, HP, Dell, and Gateway captured the market.

Apple's Newton Personal Digital Assistant

The Apple Newton was arguably the forerunner of all pad tablets, personal digital assistants (PDAs), and smartphones, but it was a grand failure itself. Apple's CEO John Sculley was trying to create a transformational product after the founder Steve Jobs was forced out of the company. Initially it was supposed to be a "Knowledge Navigator" about the size of an opened magazine (like tablets in 2012). So Sculley had Jean Louis Gassee and Steve Sakoman start a skunk works project within Apple in an abandoned warehouse on Bubb Road in Cupertino (like the Macintosh team did before). Sakoman's goal was a tablet computer priced the same as a desktop computer, about the size of a folded A4 sheet of paper, and that would recognize handwriting from a pen stylus and have a special GUI.

Initially the engineers made a classic mistake. They piled in too many features into the product, like a hard drive, an active matrix LCD screen, and infrared networking technology, to create a $6,000 product called Figaro (it was launched in 1992 and failed quickly). Also, for most of its design lifecycle, the Newton had a large screen, lots of internal memory, and an object-oriented graphics scheme. An early design use case was for a residential architect working quickly with a client to sketch, clean up, and modify a two-dimensional home plan. This was a poor choice of a target user.

Technically the project was bogged down, with the handwriting recognition being incredibly difficult. As Apple's sales slowed in 1989, Sculley was fighting to re-position the company and Gassee left with Sakoman to start Be Inc. to make computers. Sculley had put Larry Tesler, a former Xerox PARC researcher, in charge of the team with Michael Tchao in charge of marketing it. Another competing internal project at Apple, called Pocket Crystal, was spun out.

A smaller version of the Newton with Hyper-Card software was prepared for an April 1992 launch and a $1,500 price. Then an even more scaled down "Junior" product with a $500 price was planned. Apple also decided to partner with Sharp, the world's largest LCD manufacturer, and to build the Junior and share costs. Siemens and Motorola also licensed the technology. The Junior was released as the "MessagePad" in August 1993, after about 2 years of 16 to 20 hour days from the Newton team, and the suicide of one software engineer, Ko Isono, in December 1992. The price range was $700-900 and the device could send mobile faxes and connect to other devices with infrared ports; its key features were Notes (to take notes), Names (to organize contacts), and Dates (an early calendar). But at launch time, Tesler had left the team, the Apple board had kicked out John Sculley, and AT&T had a cheaper PenPoint tablet computer out.

The Apple Newton limped on for the next four years as the Palm Pilot trounced it in the PDA category. Palm offered a cheaper product aimed at specific user pain points. The $300 Palm Pilot was released in 1996 and sales took off. After 3Com bought Palm in 1998, its designers left to create a PDA joined with a phone (a smartphone), which eventually become the Handspring Treo (which in 2003 merged back into Palm). Eventually, in 1997 Steve Jobs returned to Apple and shut down the Newton in 1998. Jobs in 1998 tried to buy Palm and Handspring. One notable non-competitor was the Microsoft WinCE software for PDAs. As one raffle winner of a Compaq-made WinCE stated: "It was clunky, with a horrible user interface, too slow to use, had no battery life, and was still tied to Microsoft's own software. It made the Palm V [which] I already had look like a magical object dropped from the future by a superior alien race."

Observers offer many reasons why the Apple Newton failed:
- Apple pre-announced it too early, nearly two years before it launched, creating unrealistic expectations for a transformation product, which was then rushed out.

- The Newton was physically too large and operated too slowly; certain actions took too long, like scrolling through notes.
- The entire foray into handwriting was a mistake, especially the need to detect cursive, consuming much developer time with little end-user satisfaction.

In sum, the Newton was a great category opener but a failure in itself. Despite shipping over 100,000 units in the first year, Apple lost the market. A decade later, Steve Jobs came back with the iPhone, a revolutionary smartphone, but that is another story.

GO Corporation's PenPoint Operating System

Pen computing was first conceived in February 1987 when Mitch Kapor and Jerry Kaplan discussed the idea on a cross-country private jet from Boston to San Francisco. A bit later, Kleiner Perkins funded Kaplan and his idea, offering $1.5 million for 33% of the company. On August 14, 1987, GO Corp. was formally incorporated. The initial team was supposed to be Kapor, Kaplan, Peter Miller, and Steve Sakoman of Apple Corp. (who declined in a few weeks to compete with an Apple product). The entire project was documented beautifully in Kaplan's book "Startup," which is one of the best books written about Silicon Valley's startup culture.

GO faced hard competition from the start. In July 1988, the founders foolishly showed Bill Gates of Microsoft a deskbound prototype of GO's pen computer, hoping he would cooperate. Instead, he chose to send a stream of executives over to mine them for information and then build his own pen computer at Microsoft. Luckily, GO's connection with the venture capitalist John Doerr led to a March 1989 presentation to the Research Board, a group of the top information systems executives in the country. One of those execs at State Farm later decided to meet with GO and eventually back the concept over competitors like IBM, Hewlett Packard, and Wang.

At this point, GO had a key strategic decision to make. It needed to find an outside vendor to partner with to develop the hardware and to get financing. Unfortunately, GO chose to work with IBM instead of HP, and in March 1990 IBM agreed to license GO's Penpoint operating system. The conditions of the loan and later investments would be very punitive and help to destroy GO. In January 1991 GO's Penpoint "developer's release" was announced to broad computer industry acclaim. In October, IBM began promoting Pen OS/2 as an alternative to Penpoint. By April 1992, when Penpoint version 1.0 was released, IBM announced its Thinkpad pen computer. In dealing with his frustrations of an unpredictable environment typical of the startup world, Kaplan wrote that an entrepreneur is "faced with an endless stream of arbitrary challenges that bear down on you with the relentlessness of an automatic pitching machine. The trick is to know when to swing and when to duck."[29]

GO biggest major problems came from Microsoft. In March 1991 GO and Microsoft faced off publicly for the first time at the PC Forum in Tucson. Microsoft hindered GO at every turn. It licensed the API ostensibly to build apps, but then studied the API code and brought out its own mobile API, Pen Windows, shortly after. Microsoft pressured other programmers to not write apps for Penpoint, but instead work solely on Pen Windows. At one point, Microsoft found a way to levy a 100% tax on Penpoint, by forcing its hardware licensee companies to pay Microsoft for Pen Windows even though the licensee company used the Penpoint product. The competition was nasty but effective, clearly an antitrust violation. Officials at the Federal Trade Commission (FTC), one government antitrust agency, wanted to sue but decided against it. In April 1991, Kaplan briefed the FTC staffers about possible antitrust violations by Microsoft.

Eventually, GO partnered with AT&T and ending up getting acquired and dissolved by the phone behemoth. In July 1991, GO agreed to sell its hardware design group to AT&T and other investors. EO, an offshoot of GO, was formed to build pen computers based on Penpoint. But in May 1992, John Sculley finally discussed Newton, Apple's "personal digital assistant," at the Consumer Electronics Show in Chicago. In July 1992 GO announced a partnership with AT&T; later that year, EO and AT&T demonstrated the E0440 personal communicator at COMDEX. By June 1993, AT&T bought a majority position in EO, and in August, after AT&T considered dropping GO's Penpoint for Apple's Newton, it acquired GO and merged it into EO. Kaplan and the CEO at that point, Bill Campbell (formerly at Apple and later at Intuit), did the right thing for employees by selling the company and preserving jobs (they also basically destroyed any personal ownership stake they had left). By January 1994, the EO–GO merger was completed and AT&T shut down EO in July.

GO failed for many reasons which Kaplan doesn't directly address in his book. First, the product was likely too big a project for a startup. It was very difficult for even a big company like Apple to do it, and the time to market for a new technology in a new market was far too long. Second, Kaplan wasn't very sensitive to cost control, and so spent money freely, necessitating a lot of time spent fundraising and then joining up with some unattractive corporate bedfellows, like Intel (which backfired on GO later). Third, GO picked the wrong corporate partners. Perhaps local Silicon Valley companies like Apple or HP would have been better. Choosing IBM was a poor decision as IBM was a predatory partner and competitor; Intel was likely a bad decision too as it was close strategically to Microsoft

---

[29] Kaplan, Jerry. Startup: A Silicon Valley Adventure. New York: Penguin Books, 1996, p. 101.

and didn't have much invested to see GO succeed (it's bet on GO was a cheap option bet).

An interesting prologue was that Kaplan filed a lawsuit against Microsoft in June 2005, but federal courts rejected it as not timely (defendants would be prejudiced when "memories fade, documents are lost, witnesses become unavailable"). Kaplan argued that Microsoft only showed its misdeeds in 2002, which included pressuring Intel to keep its distance from GO, coercing other developers not to write software for GO, stealing trade secrets, and creating "PenWindows" after having access to proprietary GO materials. While GO's failure wasn't inevitable, it took another few years for the first genuinely successful pen computer or PDA, the Palm Pilot, to take off in 1996. GO's Penpoint operating system was basically three to five years too early.

20. Magicians: A Case Study on Steve Jobs' Reality Distortion Field and Apple Computer (1976-2013)

Prequels: Early Personal Computers

Before Steve Jobs and Apple Computer, there was Douglas Engelbart, Xerox PARC, and Jef Raskin. Doug Engelbart was a Berkeley professor who took a position at Stanford Research Institute (SRI) to study next generation computing. He was influenced by Vannevar Bush's article "As We May Think" on using next generation computing to enhance human ability. Engelbart got government funding to start an Augmentation Research Center at SRI. Engelbart invented the computer mouse and received a patent for it in 1967 with Bill English. His lab at SRI was one of first two points that connected the ARPAnet, the predecessor of the Internet. Engelbart was well-known in computing circles for his "Mother of All Demos" in the Fall Joint Computer Conference in San Francisco on December 6, 1968. During that conference, he publicly showed for the first time ever the computer mouse, as well as interactive text, video conferencing, teleconferencing, email, hypertext, and a collaborative real-time editor. Engelbart was a master of presentation but a hard person to work for. He was a spiritual precursor to Steve Jobs, though Jobs commercialized his innovations while Englebart never had working products.

In 1970, Xerox opened its Palo Alto Research Center (PARC), and employed a star team of computer scientists, including key members who left Engelbart's lab. Raskin started taking several trips to PARC as a visiting scholar for the Stanford Artificial Intelligence Laboratory. In 1973, PARC completed the Alto, the first true PC and computer with a graphical user interface (GUI). Both were major influences on Steve Jobs at Apple and Bill Gates at Microsoft, who openly stole PARC's ideas. PARC also had the first laser printer, which was connected to a group of Altos using the first Ethernet network.

In 1967, Jef Raskin (later co-creator of the Macintosh) wrote his PhD thesis on the Graphical User Interface at Penn State University. In his thesis he first coined the term "QuickDraw," which would eventually become the name of the Mac's graphics routine 17 years later. Raskin was later responsible for connecting Jobs to Xerox PARC and the innovations happening there.

Apple Computer's hometown, Cupertino, was a young city created only in October 1955. It was Santa Clara County's 13th city, originally known as the "Crossroads" because it developed around the crossroads of

Stevens Creek Boulevard and Saratoga-Mountain View Road (later Saratoga-Sunnyvale Road, and then De Anza Boulevard). The area had one large employer, who was also one of the state's richest men: Henry Kaiser. He owned the local rock quarry and cement plant, renamed Kaiser Permanente Cement Plant in 1939. After the war, Cupertino's Homestead High School started a class on electronics under John McCollum, one of the earliest computer classes in the world. One of McCollum's students and assistants was a kid named Steve Wozniak.

The relationship between Steve Jobs and Steve Wozniak ("Woz") began in 1968, when Bill Fernandez introduced his high school buddy Jobs to his neighbor Wozniak. Wozniak was a dropout and garage tinkerer who had an uncanny ability to focus and could spend days designing circuit boards and tinkering. Jobs was also a dreamer and a dropout, who had once toured India as a teenager, only to see extreme poverty and realize spiritual enlightenment was overrated. As Jobs said of India and its ever-present poverty: "It was one of the first times that I started to realize that maybe Thomas Edison did a lot more to improve the world than Karl Marx and Neem Kairolie Baba put together." At one point, Jobs and Wozniak worked as Alice in Wonderland characters at a shopping mall in San Jose. Jobs had experimented with LSD and Buddhism in the 1960s. He had grown up on Stewart Brand's "Whole Earth Catalog" and actually knew very little about semiconductors.

Their first major collaboration came when they discovered an obscure AT&T technical manual in the basement library of SLAC that allowed them to illegally hack into the international phone system for free. They made and sold a number of blue boxes to do this and Jobs found the experience illuminating because it taught him that a little bit of ingenuity would allow a young hacker to control billions of dollars worth of sophisticated infrastructure. Jobs later noted in a 1995 interview: "I don't think there would ever have been an Apple computer had there not been blue boxes." The highlight of this experience came when the pair called the Vatican asking for the Pope and posing as Henry Kissenger. They woke up a bunch of cardinals and then burst out laughing, giving their trick up.

In 1972, Jobs became one of the first 50 employees at Atari, a high-flying Valley startup founded and run by the entrepreneur Nolan K. Bushnell. Jobs later asked Wozniak for help in creating the sequel to the smash hit "Pong," called "Breakout." In 1975 Wozniak began attending meetings of the Homebrew Computer Club. Wozniak was intrigued by the Altair 8800, but could not afford one. He decided to build his own microcomputer and began work on what would become the Apple I. Meanwhile, Jobs was attending meditation retreats and studying Zen Buddhism with Kobin Chino, a major influence on Jobs' life, encouraging the spontaneous, the intuitive, and the simple.

Many years later, Jobs would reminisce about Zen Buddhism and the people in the Indian countryside who used their intellect less and their intuition more, developing it further than in the rest of the world. Jobs opined:

> Intuition is a very powerful thing, more powerful than intellect, in my opinion. That's had a big impact on my work. . . If you just sit and observe, you will see how restless your mind is. If you try to calm it, it only makes it worse, but over time it does calm, and when it does, there's room to hear more subtle things—that's when your intutition starts to blossom and you start to see things more clearly and be in the present more. Your mind just slows down, and you see a tremendous expanse in the moment. You see so much more than you could see before. It's a discipline; you have to practice it.[30]

Apple the Startup

In April 1976, Apple Computer was started in Cupertino by the hobbyist Wozniak the hippie Jobs. Wozniak had designed their first microcomputer in his Cupertino apartment and built it in Jobs' garage in nearby Los Altos. Wozniak used MOS Technology's 6502 microprocessor ($20) because he could not afford the more advanced Motorola 6800 or Intel 8080 (both about $170). The user had to provide his own monitor but an Apple I could be hooked up to an inexpensive television set.

Apple the startup happened quickly and in an un-organized way typical of startups. In March 1976, Wozniak had finished work on a microcomputer kit. Wozniak first asked his employer, Hewlett Packard, if they were interested in an $800 machine that ran BASIC; management was not interested. Wozniak then teamed up with Steve Jobs and Ron Wayne to form Apple Computer Company. Wozniak and Jobs funded their company with $1,000; Wozniak sold his prized HP 65 calculator for $500, and Jobs sold his VW bus for the same amount. In May, they introduced the Apple I at the Home Brew Computer Club meeting. Most members showed little interest, but Paul Terell, President of the Byte Shop chain, made an order for 50 units at $500 a unit to sell for $666.66. Since they didn't have cash, Jobs badgered a local supply house, Kierulff Electronics, to give them 30 day credit terms for $20,000 of goods.

Wozniak was a star engineer in that he designed both the hardware and the software of the Apple I. The key difference between the Apple I and its predecessors, such as the Altair, was in the amount of its memory. Wozniak felt that a computer without a programming language was an oxymoron and strived to build a computer powerful enough to run a real programming language. The main requirement was to install more memory than the first personal computers had. Unfortunately, static RAM was

---

[30] Isaacson, Walter. Steve Jobs. New York: Simon and Schuster, 201, p. 49. This is one of the best tech biographies ever written. It's worth buying and reading.

expensive. Therefore he had to turn to cheaper dynamic RAM. A 4K DRAM chip had just been introduced in 1974. It was the first time that RAM, a type of semiconductor memory, was cheaper than magnetic core memory. Being much cheaper than the static RAM used by the Altair, the DRAM allowed Wozniak to pack more of it in the Apple than the Altair. The key design issue was how to continuously refresh the dynamic RAM so that it would not lose its information (as a reference, the static RAM used by the Altair did not lose its information). Roberts, basically, had merely dressed up an Intel microprocessor in order to create his Altair. Wozniak, instead, dressed up a memory chip in order to create the Apple I. In June, Apple finished and delivered part of the Byte Shop order one day before deadline, with 12 units for $6,000. The two kids made a profit of $3,000.

The 4K computer Wozniak created was capable of running a real programming language. Since there was no language yet for that microprocessor, Wozniak also had to write, in assembly language, the BASIC interpreter for the Apple I. Note that Wozniak's motivation in creating the Apple I was not a business plan but simply the desire to own a computer; a desire constrained by a lack of money. The Apple I was the result of an optimization effort more than anything else: Wozniak had to minimize the parts and simplify the structure.

Wozniak, however, shared the same "business" vision that Roberts had with the Altair. His personal computer was meant for hobbyists, those technically savvy users who were going to program the computer themselves to solve their problems. Wozniak had simply made it much easier to write a program. He did not envision that the average user of a personal computer would be someone who "buys" the application programs already written and packaged.

It was, however, the Apple II, still based on a 6502 and released in April 1977, which really took off. The Apple II desktop computer was fully assembled, requiring almost no technical expertise. It boasted the look and feel of a home appliance. It had a monitor and a keyboard integrated with the motherboard shell, as well as a ROM hosting a BASIC interpreter and a RAM of 4 kilobytes, but no operating system. Part of its success was due to Apple's Disk II, the first affordable floppy-disk drive for personal computers, which replaced the cassette as the main data storage medium.

Later in the fall, Jobs and Wozniak showed an Apple II prototype to Commodore representatives and asked for $100,000, some Commodore stock, and salaries of $36,000. Commodore turned the ragged-looking pair down. The Apple II was a major innovation not for its color screen, but for its expansion slots that made upgrading easy and its operating system that was free and already loaded on, making the machine a plug-and-play. The machine was also quiet with no fan because Jobs found that a fan distracted him in his meditation practice. Finally, the pair convinced Rod

Holt, an Atari associate, to design a neat switching power supply that was lighter, cooler, and smaller than any other on the market. They went to the first "Personal Computer Festival" in Atlantic City on Labor Day that year to show their product, where the feedback they received was to make a completed product and not just a kit. The computer had to be a real product and not a hobbyist item.

The two founders needed more money for the company. In August, Jobs was pestering Frank Burge of the major national ad agency Regis McKenna to work with them. Burge met the team working in their garage but was unconvinced. Jobs then pestered Burge's boss with calls three or four times a day, and his secretary gave in and so Regis McKenna took the call and granted them an interview. When they met and McKenna wouldn't take the account, Steve refused to leave his office. McKenna finally took the account and decided to advertise for them in Playboy magazine, a publication for young men who were the target customers. As Apple didn't have any money, McKenna recommended that Steve contact Don Valentine, a venture capitalist. Jobs wore him down with calls. Valentine visited the garage and felt that Jobs was a "renegade from the human race." He pointed Jobs to Mike Markkula, a marketing expert. Markkula was a retired techie and marketing executive who was rich because of Intel stock options. Like Wozniak and Jobs, Markkula was a loner, but he was also a professional and looking for the next big thing. He took a look at Apple and soon decided the company could join the Fortune 500 in less than 5 years (he was right).

On January 3, 1977 Apple Computer, Inc. was officially incorporated. Mike Markkula invested $91,000 in Apple, with the intent to invest $250,000. The company also secured loans of $250,000 on Markkula's credit. Jobs, Markkula, and Wozniak took about 30% each and Holt got 10% for his work. Markkula would serve as Jobs' management mentor at Apple, teaching him how to run a business, and then eventually firing him. Markkula also recruited Mike Scott as President and managed Jobs. An early Apple marketing executive, Floyd Kvamme, recalled Markkula's attention to user experience. On Kvamme's first day at the company, Markkula told him to go out and buy an Apple Computer, then take it home and set it up, to better understand the customer's needs. Meanwhile, the friendship between Jobs and Wozniak started to erode, mostly because of Jobs' "holier-than-thou" attitude which came from his deep, intuitive connection with the end user. Jobs was both right and insufferable.

Markkula also became a father figure to Jobs and taught him subtle things about marketing. He emphasized that one should start a company to make something you believe in, to build a durable institution, and not to just get rich. Markkula taught Jobs his three principles: 1) empathy, an intimate connection for the feelings of customers; 2) focus, an elimination of unimportant opportunities to drill deeply on the few important products or details, and; 3) "impute," which means that people form opinions about products based on signals and appearances, so the presentation of products matters as much as the quality (both matter, not just the quality). For Jobs, this meant that the image and marketing of a company and its products were critical, so he spent much time on details like the thickness of packaging and the tactile nature of plastics used.

In April, the Apple II was publicly introduced for $1295. Within months Apple sold 300 computers. That year Jobs' girlfriend Chris-Ann gave birth to a baby girl of his and he mostly gave up drugs, but stayed vegetarian. Jobs started hiring "A-players" to join the company and in the summer of 1979 Apple sold $7.3 million worth of private stock to 16 buyers, including Xerox and some venture capital firms. Jobs was a millionaire on paper at 24. He bought a house in Los Gatos with no furniture other than cushions and a bedroom mattress, plus a Mercedes coupe. He also donated money to a Nepalese charity.

In January 1978, 34-year-old Jef Raskin joined Apple Computer as employee #31. He eventually became the Manager of Advanced Systems, where he created what became known as the Macintosh Project for a $500 portable computer. He worked on it from 1980 until his departure in 1982. Raskin focused on designing computers from the user interface out. Most other manufacturers tended to provide the latest and most powerful hardware, and let the users and third-party software vendors figure out how to make it usable. While Raskin worked on the Macintosh and its graphics-based system, Jobs worked on an alternate project, the Lisa Project, a character-generator-based machine.

Apple was just one of many companies that used the 6502. Commodore was another one (its PET was released in October 1977). The Atari 800, announced in late 1978 and designed by Jay Miner, was also based on the 6502. British computer manufacturer Acorn, founded in 1978 near Cambridge University by German-born Herman Hauser, also used the 6502 computer for the BBC Micro that was deployed throughout the British educational system. However, most companies used the 6502 for something else. In October 1977, Atari introduced a videogame console, the VCS (Video Computer System, later renamed 2600). Previous generations of videogame machines had used custom logic. The videogame console that pioneered the use of a microprocessor was Fairchild's Video Entertainment System, released in August 1976 and based on Fairchild's own F8 microprocessor.

The other popular low-cost microprocessor was the Zilog Z80, used for example in Tandy/Radio Shack's TRS-80 microcomputer, another bestseller of 1977. The companies that missed the market were, surprisingly, the ones that dominated the market for calculators. Texas Instruments' TI 99/4 was based on its own 16-bit TI 9940 processor that was simply too expensive; and the even more expensive Hewlett-Packard HP-85, based on an HP custom 8-bit processor, was something halfway between a mini and a micro.

The year 1977 was a turning point, as 48,000 personal computers were sold worldwide. The following year more than 150,000 were sold, of which 100,000 were Tandy/Radio Shack TRS-80s, 25,000 Commodore PETs, 20,000 Apple IIs, 5,000 IMSAIs, and 3,000 Altairs.

A New Hope: The Darling of Silicon Valley

In December 1979, Jobs took his first visit to PARC in exchange for allowing Xerox to invest $1 million in Apple. The same month, Jobs returned again to PARC with several vice presidents and management heads to see a demo of the wonderful PARC Alto personal computer and its features like windows, menus, and so on in a graphical user interface. By March 1980, the Lisa project was revamped to include all the features of the Alto, with several more. Later that summer, Jobs hired 15 Xerox employees to work on the Lisa Project.

One misconception was that Apple just copied Xerox's work at PARC, and that is untrue. The Apple team copied and significantly improved upon the Xerox GUI and mouse. For example, the Alto GUI was set up so you couldn't use the mouse to drag a window on a screen. With Apple, you drag windows and files and also drop them into folders. With the Alto GUI, you had to select a command to do anything. With Apple, you could just resize the window by pressing a button on it, and you had pull down menus from a bar atop the screen to select commands. Finally, the Xerox mouse had three buttons, didn't roll smoothly, and cost $300. Apple hired IDEO, the design firm, to create a cheap and simple mouse that cost $15. As Jobs fumed about Xerox's management: "They were copier-heads who had no clue about what a computer could do; they just grabbed defeat from the greatest victory in the computer industry."

The year ended with a bang. On December 12, 1980, Apple went public. Apple's share rose 32% that day, making 40 employees instant millionaires (the most for any IPO in history up to that point). Jobs, the largest shareholder, made $218 million dollars alone. Markkula made $203 million that day, a 220,700% return on investment. Jobs supposedly said: "When I was 23, I had a net worth of a million dollars. At 24, it was over $10 million dollars. At 25, it was over $100 million." However, neither Jeff Raskin, nor Daniel Kottke, both early Apple employees, were allowed to buy stock and so made no money during this time. Wozniak in 1980 started a plan to distribute his stock to other key employees and friends, but Jobs never did.

In January 1981, Jobs forced himself into the Macintosh Project, after earlier dismissing and often trying to cancel it. He saw greater potential there and pushed Raskin aside, hiring his old Apple II partners like Wozniak and Jerry Mannock. The team moved into a separate space and Jobs set a goal for a machine to get to market in a year, a ridiculous timetable. Jobs wanted the core computer to be the size of a telephone book, and rejecting the conventional wisdom, did not want it to be expandable. Eventually Jobs' plan was for the Macintosh to come out the same time as the Lisa at a price of $1,500, including software. He made up the estimated sales number of 500,000 units in year one.

Jobs was a micromanager who mixed catch phrases, sharp retorts, and some original insight. Jobs often took credit for others' ideas, and his group joked that he had a "reality distortion field" around him. As Bud Tribble of the Mac team said: "In [Jobs'] presence, reality is malleable. He can convince anyone of practically anything. It wears off when he's not around, but it makes it hard to have realistic schedules." Jobs could state a vision of an unlikely or illogical version of the future and then make it true. He did it by believing it himself, conning others into believing it, and then making it happen on a grueling schedule.

Jobs thought about design and usability problems non-stop and he often denigrated the ideas of those who worked for him. He would later come back claiming others' ideas as his own while proposing them anew. Jobs' team tended to be bright men, yet homogenous, and his interviewing questions were along the lines of "How many times have you taken acid?" and "When did you lose your virginity?" Jobs generally didn't like the wives or girlfriends of his all-male team and was difficult to interact with in the real world. He often sent dishes back in restaurants, only to not have cash at the meal's end and so have someone else pay. Jobs was basically an egotistical, insufferable wunderkind at that point in his life. He was also brilliant.

Two examples show the extent of Jobs' ability to motivate his team. First, he once approached Larry Kenyon to complain about the time it took a computer to start up. Jobs asked: "If it could save a person's life, would you find a way to shave ten seconds off the boot time?" Kenyon suggested he might be able to. Then Jobs showed Kenyon on a whiteboard that if there were 5 million people using the Mac and it took 10 seconds more each day, that would save three hundred millon hours per year, about one hundred lifetimes saved. Kenyon was impressed and a few weeks later he presented an OS that booted 28 seconds faster. Second, Jobs considered himself an artist and would take his team to places such as the Tiffany glass exhibit in the Metropolitan Art Museum in New York City. He wanted to show them that great art could be mass produced and that if they were making things, they should put effort in making them beautiful. Jobs emphasized a minimalist product design ethos, but also kept the products intuitive to users and fun, with a sense of play.

In 1981, Mike Markkula became President of Apple and approved the Macintosh from being an experimental project to a real product. Raskin left soon after and would go on to release the Canon Cat, a beautiful PC product that won several design awards but failed to become popular due to lack of production by Canon.

Competitors were not far behind. In June, Xerox introduced an improved variation of the Alto, the $16,595 Xerox Star. It included dragging and double clicking of icons. In August, IBM introduced the IBM PC for $1565. With 16K RAM and a 5.25" floppy drive, running the first version of MS-DOS, it was a poor computer, barely reaching the efficiency of the Apple II released 4 years earlier, but it sold well. Yet, 1981 was a big year for Apple in terms of name recognition; in the beginning, only 10% of Americans knew of it and by the end about 80% did.

Apple continued developing the Mac and Lisa in 1982. In January 1983, the Lisa was introduced for $9998, but it was a big flop compared to the much cheaper IBM PC. Apple's stock sank. The Apple IIe was introduced for $1395. It became the most successful and most popular Apple computer and would be produced for 10 more years.

Apple hit three major milestones in 1983. In the spring, its ad company, Chiat/Day, created a "1984" ad for use in Super Bowl XVIII in January 1984. The 30-second version of "1984" appeared in theater previews across the country. In the ad, an attractive female prisoner breaks into a drab prison where a Big Brother lecturer is on a large screen. She dashes to the screen and spins around with a huge sledgehammer, and then lets it go to smash the screen, which explodes in a blinding flash of light. A voiceover says: "On January 24th Apple Computer will introduce the Macintosh. And you'll understand why 1984 won't be like 1984." The ad was so admired that it was often replayed for free. It also temporarily boosted the company's sales, employee morale, and stock price.

Second, in April 1983 Jobs convinced John Sculley, then President of PepsiCo, to become President and CEO of Apple. The two lines he used to recruit Sculley were: "Do you want to spend the rest of your life selling sugared water or do you want a chance to change the world?" and "It's better to be a pirate than to join the Navy."

Third, in May 1983 Apple entered the Fortune 500 at #411 after only five years of existence. It had become the fastest growing startup company in US corporate history.

In January 1984, a $2495 Macintosh and $3495 Lisa 2 were introduced. The Macintosh did well initially after the 1984 ad, but failed to meet Jobs' target of 500,000 units. Internally the Macintosh team was angry about how underpaid they were and demanded raises. Meanwhile the Apple II team members, whose products sold the most, were angry that they were being displaced and that the Macintosh team was getting so many perks like massages, free food, and outings. Trouble was brewing. In April, the Apple IIc was introduced at the Apple Forever Conference in San Diego. Later that year, the Apple IIc won an Industrial Design Excellence Award. However sales for all the products were below targets and inventories were rising.

The Graphical User Interface (GUI)

A new era began in January 1984 when Apple introduced the Macintosh, because it was the first cheap computer with a GUI. Based on a 32-bit Motorola 68000 CPU, it still featured a proprietary Apple operating system with the Lisa GUI. It went on sale for $2,000. The Mac was the result of a project started in 1979 by Jef Raskin who had dreamed of a "computer appliance" and had hired his former student Bill Atkinson from UC San Diego.

The Macintosh created a new industry: desktop publishing. In 1985 Apple also introduced the LaserWriter, the first printer to ship with Adobe's PostScript. Aldus of Seattle, a company founded in 1984 by Paul Brainerd who coined the term "desktop publishing," introduced PageMaker, a software application that made it easy to create books on a Mac. In 1987 Adobe followed with Illustrator, a PostScript-based drawing application. All the pages were actually rendered in the printer, which meant that the laser printer contained a more powerful processor, with 1.5 megabytes of RAM, than the Macintosh itself. The "desktop publishing" buzzword was spread by marketing executive John Scull, who pulled together Apple, Adobe, and Aldus and virtually invented the whole industry.

The Macintosh emphasized the user interface over anything else. For example, before the Macintosh each application had its own set of keyboard commands. The Macintosh introduced a standard set of commands: Z for "Undo," X for "Cut," C for "Copy," V for "Paste," W to close a window, etc. Each and every Macintosh application had to comply with this standard.

The Macintosh also introduced a new marketing concept: "Buy me because I'm cool." It was the "look and feel" that mattered. Previously, personal computers had sold well because of their killer applications. All computer manufacturers still thought of software as a means to the end of selling hardware. Apple turned the concept upside down: the hardware was a means to power appealing software. In a sense, fashion had come to the computer industry. Apple became the master of style, the equivalent of Italian fashion designers for digital devices. The Macintosh was most used with its killer application in mind, and that was desktop publishing. However, that would not have been enough to justify that the company ignored legacy compatibility, as Apple II applications did not run on the Mac.

The Macintosh marked a dramatic change in philosophy for Apple. The Apple II was Wozniak's machine: an open platform for which anyone could write software and attach hardware extensions. Crucially, Apple refused to license the Mac's operating system, whereas Microsoft's operating system worked on any IBM clone. The Macintosh was Jobs' machine: a closed platform that can only run Apple-sanctioned software and attach to Apple-sanctioned hardware. In a sense Jobs had hijacked

Wozniak's vision of an open world of computing and turned it into a walled garden. By then Wozniak's health had been severely impacted by a 1981 airplane accident that he miraculously survived. Unlike IBM (that spawned an entire generation of clones), Apple did not tolerate any clones. Ironically, the combination of IBM's open platform and Apple's closed platform contributed to turn Microsoft into the world's largest software company and to make Bill Gates the richest person in the world. Apple had the better product, but Jobs' decision to opt for a closed world handed the victory to the lesser product, the Intel/Microsoft machines.

Competition pressed down against Apple. During 1984 Ashton-Tate announced its Framework for the IBM PC. It integrated word-processing, database management, and business graphics within a windowing environment. In November, Microsoft responded with Windows 1.0 for MS-DOS, a rather mediocre imitation of the Lisa GUI. Unlike Apple, which controlled its own hardware, Microsoft had to deal with the hardware delivered by PC manufacturers. But PC manufacturer were only interested in cutting prices to be more competitive, not in tweaking their hardware to run a better GUI. Therefore Microsoft couldn't match the Apple GUI until the hardware of PC clones became adequate. It was no surprise that these operating environments for the PC market stagnated.

Also in August 1984 IBM introduced a multitasking operating system named TopView for its new 80286-based PC AT. It never became popular and eventually lost to Windows. A Bay Area programmer, Nathan Myhrvold, had the idea of cloning TopView for MS-DOS and founded Dynamical Systems Research in Oakland. To be on the safe side, Microsoft bought the company in 1986 and hired Myhrvold. Five years later, he would establish Microsoft Research and eventually become the company's chief technology officer.

The Empire Strikes Back: Jobs Forced Out and Apple Loses its Direction

Jobs' first stint at Apple was perhaps destined to be short. The board was frustrated with the company's performance. Board member Arthur Rock told Sculley to take charge and correct the problems of rising inventories and unhappy employees. Meanwhile, board chairman Jobs was plotting to get rid of Sculley. On May 24, Jobs tried to force Sculley out of Apple by mounting a coup against him. On May 28th, the board, including Markkula, sided with Sculley and stripped Jobs of all his duties. "I felt betrayed by Mike," Jobs later said, "But I still have a very warm spot in my heart for him." Markkula expressed similar ambivalence: "I thought the way Steve left was at best ungentlemanly," he said, referring to Jobs' angry departure. Jobs' title became "global thinker" after the board vote and his remote office was to him a "Siberia," in a remote Apple building.

To process the events of his dismissal, Jobs went home to a dark house and listened to Bob Dylan in the dark. He then went on a trip to Paris and then the Tuscan hills outside Florence. He told a journalist: "You can't always get what you want; sometimes you get what you need." Seeing Jobs out, Bill Gates in July sent Scully a proposal suggesting he license the Mac OS to companies who might create Mac clones. After Jobs returned, Sculley and the management team ignored Jobs, who would go home depressed. Jobs stopped coming in to work. The stock price dropped and in for the quarter ending in June Apple announced its first loss ever of about $17 million, with sales dropping 11%. Sculley told the press: "There is no role for Steve Jobs in the operations of this company either now or in the future."

Jobs didn't know what to do. He thought about politics but then decided that creating new, innovative products was what he loved doing. By September, Jobs announced his intent to create a new computer company with other "lower-level" employees, creating a new computer for the university market. He distributed his resignation letter to Apple and several other news media figures, after initially (falsely) telling the board he wouldn't compete with Apple and that he would let Apple invest in the company.

On September 23, Apple filed suit against Jobs. Apple claimed Jobs knew sensitive technology secrets that he might use in his new company, and that he was poaching key Apple employees, which violated Jobs' duty of loyalty as an ex-Chairman. Apple later dropped the lawsuit when Jobs shamed the company by saying: "It's hard to think a $2 billion company with 4,300 plus people couldn't compete with six people in blue jeans." Jobs left in September 1985, after selling nearly all his stock, about $90 million worth, except one share, which he kept to get Apple's annual reports. He still professed a love for the company he founded.

Jobs reflected on these experiences with maturity in a Stanford University Commencement Speech in June 2005. He was fired by his hand-picked board and CEO at age 30 after his garage startup grew from two people into a $2 billion company with over 4,000 employees. Jobs felt "the focus of my entire adult life was gone, and it was devastating." He met with previous entrepreneurs David Packard of HP and Bob Noyce of Intel and "tried to apologize for screwing up so badly." Since Jobs was a public failure he even thought about running away from the Valley or becoming a professor. Yet he still loved what he did and felt he'd been rejected but was still in love. He decided to start over and later realized that "getting fired from Apple was the best thing that could have ever happened to me. The heaviness of being successful was replaced by the lightness of being a beginner again, less sure about everything." Jobs could enter another creative period, founding NeXT Computer and building up the animation company Pixar. Jobs also met his wife Laurene, started a family, and grew up a bit. He said "It was awful-tasting medicine but I guess the patient needed it. Sometimes life's going to hit you in the head with a brick."[31]

After Jobs left, Apple started on a path toward stagnation, losses, and a brush with bankruptcy. There was no room for hobbyists in an industry that was trying to turn the personal computer into a commodity. Apple had its first quarterly loss and laid off 20% of its workforce, an action that went against the old culture of the company.

Meanwhile Steve Jobs himself had launched a new company, NeXT, to build the next generation of computers with an even more advanced GUI than the Macs. Yet he opted for proprietary hardware and a proprietary operating system, and even a new programming language (the object-oriented Objective-C). Ross Perot invested $20 million in NeXT for 16% of the stock. However the NeXT Computer would be a year and a half late to market. In October 1988, the NeXT Computer was released for $6500. It included a 25 MHz processor, 8 MB RAM, 250 MB optical disk drive, math co-processor, digital processor for real time sound, faxmodem, and a 17" monitor. Apple's newest Mac was half as fast, with no peripherals for $1000 more. In September 1989, the NeXTstep OS was introduced, followed a year later by the NeXTstation which was released for $4995.

These design choices dramatically inflated the investment and discouraged third-party software developers. Unusual for the time, NeXT also invested in sophisticated audio features, mostly designed by Julius Smith of Stanford's CCRMA from 1986 on. Furthermore, the NeXT computer was the first to implement Adobe's brand new Display PostScript, which "printed" directly on the computer's screen, thus ensuring that the user saw on the screen exactly what he would get from the printer. NeXT was an ambitious project, ahead of its time.

Jobs did lose a big opportunity at NeXT. In 1987 he met with John Akers, the CEO of IBM, who wanted a new operating system for the IBM PC. Jobs fought over contract terms and negotiated hard. IBM became frustrated and its lead champion of the deal left. So IBM paid for Next's NeXTstep operating system but didn't use it. Instead IBM promoted Microsoft Windows and its own program, OS/2. Jobs had missed his chance to usurp Microsoft's key OS product, as it would have been likely that other PC manufacturers would follow IBM. NeXT, and not Microsoft, could have gotten a license fee for operating system software on every computer, a solid monopoly. NeXT had lost an important battle to be the next platform of the PC. By June 1991, Ross Perot resigned saying his investment was one of his biggest mistakes.

Apple had some superficial success, but it was rotting within. In 1987, Apple had six different Mac Pluses, though its product pipeline was dry.

---

[31] Jobs, Steve. "Stanford Commencement Speech 2005." Available online: http://www.stanford.edu/class/ee204/Apple2008.html.

The Macintosh personal computer had moved Apple into the business office market. Corporate buyers saw its ease of use as a distinct advantage. It was far cheaper than the Lisa and had the necessary software to link office computers. The first Apple computer with color graphics, the Macintosh II, debuted in March 1987, priced at $3,900. Its other improvement was a plug-and-play bus architecture that made it easier to add expansion cards. The "Mac" was a critical success. It helped cement the community of Apple fans, but the "open architecture" created by the IBM-Microsoft axis was winning in the broader market over Apple's closed, proprietary architecture. The competition was close behind. Compaq introduced the first Intel 386 PC, replacing IBM as the PC technology leader. In 1987, Apple renamed the Lisa 2/10 the Macintosh XL and discontinued all other Lisa configurations.

By 1988, over one million Macintosh computers had been sold, with 70% of the sales to corporations. Vendors created software connecting Macintoshes to IBM-based systems. Apple grew rapidly: its 1986 sales of $1.9 billion and income of $217 million grew in 1988 to sales of $4.1 billion and income of $400 million.

1988 to 1994 were slog years for Apple as it stagnated and Microsoft moved ahead. In January 1991 Microsoft released the second version of Windows, version 2.03. Compared to Windown 1.01, which was almost unusable, Microsoft made many improvements, many of which were taken from the Mac. These included Mac-like icons and overlapping instead of tiling windows. Even so, Windows was still not up to par to the first Alto OS, written 15 years before.

Sculley and his management team made a string of bad decisions over the next few years. First in 1988, the executives thought a worldwide shortage of memory chips would get worse, so they bought millions when prices were high. The shortage ended quickly and prices fell. Second, Sculley reorganized Apple again in August 1988 into four operating divisions: Apple US, Apple Europe, Apple Pacific, and Apple Products. Many longtime Apple executives were frustrated with the changes and left. Third, Apple fended off a lawsuit in December 1989, where Xerox Corp. claimed that Apple was unlawfully using Xerox technology for its Macintosh software. Apple won this lawsuit in1990, but had started its own lawsuit against Microsoft and Hewlett-Packard, charging copyright infringement over its graphical user interface (GUI). In the spring of 1992, Apple lost its case when a court decided copyright protection cannot be based on "look and feel" (appearance) alone. Instead, developers would have to come up specific features to protect. Finally, headcount became bloated. Apple had 5,500 employees in 1986 and over 14,600 by the early 1990s.

Apple had soared in the early 1980s due to large, expensive computers based off of many, but not all, of Wozniak and Jobs' innovative designs. The company had a committed, yet relatively small following. At a time when the industry was seeing slow unit sales, the numbers at Apple were rising because of smaller and cheaper desktop computers. In 1990, desktop Macs accounted for 11% of the PCs sold through American computer dealers. A year later, the figure was 19%. The notebook PowerBook series, released in 1991, found a 21% market share in less than six months. However, profit margins were lower and the company was not coming up with innovative products anymore. After another reorganization and massive set of layoffs in 1990, profits fell by 35% the next year. Apple's board of directors fired Sculley in 1993 after Apple's PC market share had shrunk from 20% to 8% under his watch.

The next two CEOs, Michael Spindler and Gil Amelio, didn't last long. Spindler broke tradition by licensing Apple technology to outside firms. A group of Apple clones hit the market, diluted the brand, and even hurt Apple's profits. Spindler did introduce the Power Macintosh line in 1994, but the company underestimated demand and produced too few. It previously overestimated demand for an earlier release of its PowerBook laptops.

Spindler, unfortunately, wanted to compete against Microsoft in the business and office machine market, not realizing that only price and performance mattered there. Apple's edge in style and design didn't matter there, and his strategy would fail. Later in 1994 Apple released the first PowerMacs using the PowerPC 601 and also System 7.5, with a bunch of new features everybody already had as shareware.

The next two years were bad ones. In 1995, Power Computing released the first Mac clones, including the very successful Power 100. In 1996, Apple licensed the Mac OS to Motorola, giving it authority to sub-license for the first time. Then Apple licensed the Mac OS to IBM. In early 1996, a deal to sell Apple to SUN Microsystems failed and Apple's revenue continued falling. As Spindler tried to cut costs, Jobs reportedly said: "The cure for Apple is not cost-cutting. The cure for Apple is to innovate its way out of its current predicament." By 1995, Apple had $1 billion worth of unfilled orders. Customers and investors were angry. The Apple board replaced Spindler with Gil Amelio in February 1996.

Amelio was a former Rockwell executive and Apple fan who had turned around National Semiconductor. He had no experience selling goods in the consumer marketplace. Amelio's tenure was short but forceful. He cut Apple's payroll by a third and slashed operating costs. However, he also couldn't oversee the creation of beautiful, desired products and he took a fat paycheck. The company's financial losses grew to $816 million in 1996 and $1 billion in 1997. The stock, which had traded at more than $70 per share in 1991, fell to $14 per share. Apple's market share in PCs was 16% in the late 1980s, but it had fallen to less than 4%.

Meanwhile not all was well at NeXT either. In January 1992, Steve Jobs announced NeXTstep 3.0, a version of NeXTstep that could run on an

Intel 486 simultaneously with MS-DOS. NeXT would eventually move its OS entirely to the Intel x86 platform. In February 1993, Jobs laid off 280 of his 530 NeXT employees on "Black Tuesday," sold his hardware line to Canon, and tried to become a Microsoft-like company by concentrating only on the NeXTstep OS for the Intel x86 platform.

Microsoft was doing well but Apple wasn't. In spring 1992 Microsoft introduced Windows 3.1, a big success. Microsoft did not make another major update for three years. Meanwhile that Spring Motorola shipped the first 50 MHz and 66 MHz PowerPC 601.

Amelio had a hard time at Apple. Bill Gates called often to offer Windows NT as a replacement for the Apple operating system. Then Steve Jobs started calling and offering the NeXTStep operating system, as did former Apple executive Jean-Louis Gassee offering his new Be operating system. Amelio had a team evaluate them all technically and Apple chose NeXTStep. Another positive of Amelio's leadership was inventory management, where Amelio converted lots of unsold products into cash. It was a lesson that Steve Jobs would later thank Amelio for.

Amelio was ousted from the company in July 1997, having spent less than three years there. Yet before his departure, he made a significant deal that brought Apple's savior to Cupertino. In December 1996, Apple paid $377 million for NeXT. It was a small, $50-million-in-sales company still run by Steve Jobs. Concurrent with the acquisition, Amelio hired Jobs as his special advisor, marking the return of Apple's visionary 12 years after he had left. In September 1997, two months after Amelio's exit, Apple's board of directors named Jobs interim chief executive officer. Apple's recovery occurred during the ensuing months.

The Return of Steve Jobs: Apple's Rise on the Back of the iMac

By August, Apple advisor Steve Jobs became de facto head and in September he became interim CEO at a salary of $1. Jobs was back home at the place he truly loved as a more mature designer-CEO. Jobs immediately discontinued the licensing agreement that spawned Apple clones. Jobs eliminated 15 of the company's 19 products, withdrawing Apple's involvement in printers, scanners, portable digital assistants, and other peripherals. From 1997 on, Apple would focus exclusively on desktop and portable Macintoshes for the professional and consumer markets. Jobs closed plants, laid off thousands of workers, and sold stock to rival Microsoft Corporation. Jobs replaced the board with his own picks and even worked on changing Apple's culture. He proclaimed no more pets at work and no business class travel; he also had a complete ban on talking to the press without a PR official watching.

In January 1997, Apple launched a new operating system strategy with Mac OS 7.6. Soon after, the Mac OS 8 was finally released and sold 1.25

million copies in less than 2 weeks. Jobs announced an alliance with Microsoft at the Macworld Expo in Boston. Among the agreements were: a cross-platform license where Microsoft could use Apple's design elements from its operating system; an agreement that Apple would use MS Office and Explorer as its default office and browser programs; Microsoft would invest $150 million in Apple. As the saying went, keep your friends close, but your enemies closer.

Jobs introduced new products and dabbled in retail. In January 1998, Jobs announced a projected $47 million profit for the first quarter at Macworld Expo. Apple had returned to profitability; it would be the first profitable year since 1995. That month, Mac-clone Power Computing went out of business for good. In February, after a little over five years, the Newton/eMate line was discontinued by Apple.

The next month, Apple unveiled a retail strategy. Jobs opened 149 Apple "stores within stores" in CompUSA locations across the country. This helped many Mac users who hated the small, incomplete, and out-of-stock Apple sections most retail computer stores provided.

In May, Apple announced the iMac and new PowerBook G3 models. By August, Apple had 150,000 preorders for the iMac. Apple's stock went over $40/share, the highest stock market price in three years. In August 1998, Apple finally introduced its new all-in-one computer reminiscent of the Macintosh 128K: the iMac (Amelio claimed most of the project had been completed under his watch). The iMac design team was led by Jonathan Ive, who would later design the iPod and the iPhone. The iMac featured modern technology and a unique design, with the monitor and computer in the same box. It had no floppy disk drive like other computers, and that was a risk that worked. The iMac sold close to 800,000 units in its first five months. Later that year Mac OS 8.5 was released to an ecstatic audience. Surveys showed that 43% of all iMac buyers were new to the Macintosh platform.

During the next few years, Apple purchased a few software companies to create a portfolio of professional and consumer-oriented digital production software. In 1998, Apple purchased Macromedia's Final Cut software for digital video editing. The following year, Apple released two video editing products: iMovie for consumers and Final Cut Pro for professionals. In 2002 Apple purchased Nothing Real for their advanced digital compositing application Shake, as well as Emagic for their music productivity application Logic, which led to the development of their consumer-level GarageBand application. iPhoto's release the same year completed the iLife suite. Jobs also tried to buy the hardware maker Palm, but its CEO Donna Dubinksy, a former Apple exec, refused on the grounds that she never wanted to work with or for Jobs again.

As the Internet boom went on in the late 1990s, thousands of would-be entrepreneurs flocked to Silicon Valley to start Internet companies they could flip quickly for millions. Jobs said "the rewarding thing isn't merely to start a company or to take it public." Instead, he felt it was like parenting, where after the miracle of a birth, the more rewarding thing is to help your child grow up. Many entrepreneurs wanted to start companies but not stick with them because of the many moments filled with despair and agony (firing people, cancelling products, etc.). But for Jobs, "that's when you find out who you are and what your values are."[32]

Meanwhile, in a big move Apple expanded its retail strategy further. On May 19, 2001, Apple opened the first official Apple retail stores in Virginia and California. Apple would go on to create memorable stores. For example, the entrance of the Apple Store on Fifth Avenue in New York City was a glass cube. It had a cylindrical elevator and a spiral staircase that went into the subterranean store.

In March 2001, Jobs released Apple's new operating system, Mac OS X, based on his work at NeXT. Mac OS X combined the stability, reliability and security of Unix with the ease of use afforded by an overhauled, beautiful user interface. As Jobs said: "We made the buttons on the screen look so good you'll want to lick them." To help users migrate from Mac OS 9, the new operating system allowed the use of OS 9 applications through Mac OS X's Classic environment.

That same year, Apple introduced the iPod portable digital audio player, its first game-changing device after the PC. The iPod was a masterpiece of design; simple and striking within its white box. Jobs was a master of framing. Instead of saying it had a 5-gigabyte hard drive, he said it was large enough to hold 1,000 songs. To minimize the iPod's $399 price tag, Jobs said, "There are sneakers that cost more than an iPod." The product was phenomenally successful; it sold over 100 million units within six years.

Once a year, Jobs took his most valuable employees to a retreat. He picked the "Top 100," who were the people he claimed he would bring if he could take only a hundred people on a lifeboat with him to another company. At the end of each retreat, Jobs would stand at a whiteboard, which gave him control and allowed him to focus the group, to ask: "What are the ten things we should be doing next?" After writing many ideas down and crossing off the things he thought were dumb, the group converged to the ten best. Jobs would then delete three more and push the group to narrow down the seven left to three. "We can only do three," he would say, and all of Apple's top ideas came from these retreats.

In 2003, Apple created its iTunes Store, offering online music downloads for 99 cents a song and integration with the iPod. Within a year it had 70% of the download market and had sold 85 million songs. The service quickly became the market leader in online music services, with over 5 billion downloads by June 19, 2008. The difficulty in creating the

---

[32] Young, Jeffrey S. & William L. Simon. iCon Steve Jobs: The Greatest Second Act in the History of Business. New York: John Wiley & Sons, 2005, p. 265.

store wasn't technical, but rather in getting the music companies to sign on and sell music on a medium they were hostile to. Jobs managed to convince them by sheer force of personality and by his celebrity.

Both the operating system and the iPod were launched from secrecy at Apple events where Steve Jobs, the master showman, spoke. Jobs would work with the technical crew for weeks on end before the launch and he would be intimately familiar with the product as its champion and visionary. Jobs would avoid rehearsals or scripts, but would work closely with the show's producer and lighting and visual people to get the right effects. By doing so, Apple launches would have hundreds of press people covering its magical act for free, giving the company tens of millions in effective and free advertising.

At the Worldwide Developers Conference keynote address on June 6, 2005, Steve Jobs announced that Apple would begin producing Intel-based Mac computers in 2006. On January 10, 2006, the new MacBook Pro and iMac became the first Apple computers to use Intel's Core Duo CPU. By August 7, 2006 Apple had transitioned the entire Mac product line to Intel chips, a year sooner than announced. The MacBook Pro with its 15.4" widescreen was Apple's first laptop with an Intel microprocessor. It was announced in January 2006 and is aimed at the professional market. The Power Mac, iBook, and PowerBook brands were retired during the transition; the Mac Pro, MacBook, and MacBook Pro became their respective successors.

Apple's success during this period was evident in its stock price. Between early 2003 and 2006, the price of Apple's stock increased more than tenfold, from around $6 per share (split-adjusted) to over $80. In January 2006, Apple's market cap surpassed that of Dell. This was sweet, as nine years before, Dell's CEO Michael Dell had said that if he ran Apple he would "shut it down and give the money back to the shareholders." Although Apple's market share in computers grew, it remained far behind competitors using Microsoft Windows, with only about 8% of desktops and laptops in the US.

Game Changers: Apple Moves beyond PCs to Phones, Pads, and Music/Movies/TV

Delivering his keynote at the Macworld Expo on January 9, 2007, Jobs announced that Apple Computer, Inc. would from that point on be known as Apple Inc. because computers were no longer the singular focus of the company. This change reflected the company's shift of emphasis to mobile electronic devices from personal computers. Jobs also announced the iPhone and the Apple TV. The following day, Apple shares hit $97.80, an all-time high at that point. In May, Apple's share price passed the $100 mark. iTunes was also evolving in response to buyer dislike of digital rights management (DRM) software that made sharing difficult. In

February 2007, Jobs defied the music industry and said he would sell music on the iTunes Store without DRM if record labels would agree. Two months later Apple and EMI, a large music label, jointly announced the removal of DRM technology from EMI's catalog in the iTunes Store. Other record labels followed later that year.

The Mac, iPod, iTunes, iPhone, and iPad became the five pillars of Apple's business. In July 2008 Apple launched the App Store within iTunes to sell third-party applications for the iPhone and iPod Touch. Within a month, the store sold 60 million applications and brought in $1 million daily on average. Jobs speculated that the App Store would become a billion-dollar business for Apple, with margins above 80%. The sixth pillar was raised.

These products were successful because of marketing and Jobs' genius at design. Unlike most marketers, Jobs hated focus groups, saying: "It's really hard to design products by focus groups. A lot of times, people don't know what they want until you show it to them." Instead, Jobs had a different philosophy, more suited for a designer-king leading his people. For Jobs, design was a funny word. Most people thought design meant how a product looked. But for Jobs, if you dug deeper, design was really how a product worked, so to design something well you had to take the time to study it and get it. You had to thoroughly understand a product and see how it affected and improved someone's life.[33]

As an example, Jobs talked about how he disliked most consumer devices, except for a new washing machine and dryer his family got. His family spent two weeks at the dinner table talking about options and arguing about design. They then chose a European washer, Miele, which was slow but used less water and treated clothes more gently. Jobs said of it: "They did such a great job designing these washers and dryers. I got more thrill out of them than I have out of any piece of high-tech in years."

On December 16, 2008, Apple announced that after over 20 years of attending Macworld, 2009 would be the last year Apple would be attending the Macworld Expo. Almost exactly one month later, on January 14, 2009, an internal Apple memo from Jobs announced that he would be taking a six-month leave of absence, until the end of June 2009, to allow him to better focus on treating cancer that he developed. Apple's COO, Tim Cook, took over until Jobs returned.

After years of speculation and multiple rumored "leaks" Apple announced a large screen, tablet-like media device known as the iPad on January 27, 2010. Jobs claimed the idea for the iPad came before the iPhone. The idea to ditch the keyboard for a "multi-touch display" came about in the early 2000s, although Jobs claimed the company was working on a telephone at the time. At that point a prototype came to him that used the device's now-famous scrolling mechanism. Jobs thought: "My God we

---

[33] Ibid 281.

can build a phone out of this." But the tablet product was put on the shelf and the iPhone went into development for several years before making its debut in 2007. Apple started selling the iPad tablet computer in April 2010.

The iPad ran the same touch based operating system that the iPhone used and so also ran many of the same iPhone apps. This gave the iPad a large app catalog on launch even with very little development time before the release. Later that year, the iPad was launched in the US and sold more than 300,000 units on that day and reaching 500,000 by the end of the first week. At one million iPads in 28 days, it took less than half of the 74 days it took to achieve this milestone with iPhone. Walt Mossberg of The Wall Street Journal, the premier gadget analyst in the US, called the iPad a "pretty close" laptop killer. In May 2010, Apple's market cap exceeded that of competitor Microsoft for the first time since 1989.

In June 2010, Apple released its fourth generation iPhone. It introduced video calling, multitasking, and a new stainless steel design, which acted as the phone's antenna. Yet it had weak signal strength problems at times.

Apple at this point was competing head-on with Microsoft and Google. Its operating system on computers was preferred over Microsoft Windows for ease-of-use, though not for the applications, which Microsoft had locked in. The Apple iPod easily defeated Microsoft's clunky Zune player, and its phone was much more successful than any phone with a Windows Mobile operating system.

More importantly, Apple competed against Google on two major fronts. First, the Google Android mobile operating system was the best competitor Apple had. Android was "open" and so gave application developers more freedom and creative control to make things. Apple was "closed" and so disliked by many app developers. Jobs had characterized Apple's system as "integrated," meaning the user experience was consistent and safe, like a gated community. In contrast, Android was "fragmented," meaning the users had more freedom, but also had to worry about security on the Internet, viruses, and malware. Second and more broadly, both were competing to be next generation content delivery systems. Apple had the iTunes store and Google had the Android store and Google TV.

With the iPad, a consumer had the anti-Internet in her hands, offering major media companies the ability to essentially re-create the old, closed business model. Big Media could push content to users on their terms rather than users going out and finding content, or using a search engine to find content, via the Google model.

The battle in 2011 between Apple and Google over the mobile operating system, and in general for all media devices, came down to an age old computer battle for the application programming interface (API), the platform on which applications (apps) are built. Every operating system had its APIs; these defined what the system does, how it looked to the user, and how programmers at other companies could build applications on the API.

As Jerry Kaplan of Go Corp. memorably explained, when a firm created an API, it was like trying to start a city on a tract of land. First the firm tried to persuade other programmers to build their businesses on it. This attracted customer/users, who wanted to live there because of all the "shops" the programmers had built on the land. This caused more programmers to want to come and build apps to rent space to be near customers. Eventually the process gathered momentum and the city grew faster than competitors. Once the city reached a high point, the owner of the API became a king making rules, collecting tolls, setting taxes on programmers and users, and holding back prime real estate (keeping confidential APIs for personal use). As Jobs said in 2004: "I've always wanted to own and control the primary technology in everything we do."

In 1999, Pixar was designing its new headquarters and Steve's hands were all over it. Jobs was a strong believer in face-to-face meetings and disdained email or calls to make decisions. "Creativity comes from spontaneious meetings, from random discussions," he said. "You run into someone, you ask what they're doing, you say "Wow,' and soon you're cooking up all sorts of ideas." So he designed the headquarters with a large central atrium that people were forced to enter into, with the mailboxes and café clustered together. There were only two sets of huge bathrooms in the entire building, on either side of the atrium, on both floors. In 2011, Jobs was also involved in the Norman Foster circular "spaceship" design of the new Apple headquarters, which incorporated many of the same ideas.

The Saga of Apple

In July 2011, Apple had more cash and securities, at $76 billion, than the cash reserves of the government of the US (which was facing a temporary liquidity crunch due to debt ceiling debates). Google was on a buying spree due to its inferior technology while Apple rarely bought anything from others, an impressive demonstration of technological superiority. Apple had always been a strange company, a distant second to Microsoft in operating systems for personal computers, but possibly better respected than Microsoft, as if Microsoft's rise was mere luck while Apple's survival was pure genius.

Meanwhile, Apple continued to refine its MacOS to the point that Microsoft's Windows look positively troglodytic to the Apple base. The iPod and the iPhone increased Apple's reputation in designing wildly appealing products, even though neither fully dominated its market. There were lots of digital music players, and Google's Android was growing a lot faster than Apple's iOS. The MacOS and iOS had, however, an incredible following worldwide, unmatched by any other desktop and mobile software platform. And, last but not least, Apple ruled the handheld tablet market with the iPad, almost 70% of the market in mid-2011, though that would come down to 44% in early 2013. Apple had never embraced social computing, just like it had been slow to embrace the Internet to start with, and it was late in cloud computing. The iCloud was only announced in June 2011.

Yet there was a general feeling that Apple did things only when it was capable of stunning the world. No other company could afford to be so late to the market and still be expected to make a splash.

The philosophical difference between Google and Apple was even wider than between Google and Microsoft. Apple still conceived the Web as a side-effect of computing, not as the world inside which computing happens, whereas Google, whose slogan was "nothing but the Web," was pushing the vision of the Web as *the* computing platform.

Google's business model was even more profound. It was mostly buying and distributing relatively trivial technology and letting people use it for free, with the advertisers footing the bill, turning the Web into a giant advertising billboard. Meanwhile, Apple was expecting people to pay a premium for its devices and services, just like any other traditional, quality-branded good.

In fact, one of Apple's great and unlikely success stories was its retail stores. The "Apple store" was popular worldwide, making Apple of the most valuable brands in the world. Revenues for Q1 went from $2bn, to $3.9bn, to $6.1bn from 2010 to 2012. Apple's retail stores made $6,050 in sales per square foot in 2012, the most of any American retailer, and twice that of the second best, Tiffany and Co., which earned $3,017 in sales per square foot. Most of the other top retailers made $1,000-2,000 in sales per square foot. Google was trying to make computing more or less free, while Apple was trying to make computing as fashionable as cosmetics and apparel. Apple had tried this before, when its closed platform Macintosh had competed with Microsoft's open platform Windows. Now it was the relatively closed iPod, iPhone and iPad versus Google's Android platform.

In many ways the iPod, the iPhone and the iPad marked a regress in computing. They were computers, but limited to a few functions that they did very well. For the sake of making those functions as mobile as the transistor radio, the first great mass-market portable electronic device, Apple reduced the power of the computer. In theory application developers could add their own applications to the iPhone, but in practice Apple had veto rights over which applications were allowed, curtailing freedom of choice and the free market. When Steve Jobs, the ultimate icon and mythological figure of Silicon Valley, died in October 2011, his legacy was the legacy of the whole of Silicon Valley. A new discipline that, borrowing other people's inventions, was not solely about the functionalities of a product and was not solely about the "look and feel" of a product, but was very much about the way that the human mind and the human body should interact with technology, the intersection of technology and the humanities. It was a discipline born at the confluence of the utopian counterculture of the Sixties, the tech hobbyist culture of the 1970s and the corporate culture of Wall Street; and it was about creating a new species, a machine-augmented Homo Sapiens. Just as Silicon Valley as a whole, Jobs had mostly copied other people's ideas, but turned them into existential issues. Jobs elevated to a sophisticated art the idea that producer and consumer should engage in one and the same game, exhibitionism, and then congratulate and even worship each other like fraternal deities.

21. Artists: New Paradigms of User-Computer Interaction, Open Architectures, Cisco, Synthetic Biology, and Cyberculture (1984-87)

Office Automation

Office tools such as the spreadsheet, word-processor, and presentation programs represented one of the fastest growing markets in the booming 1980s. In many cases, they were the real reason to own a PC. In 1987 Microsoft unveiled a spreadsheet program for Windows called Excel. These applications began to make Windows more appealing. The most popular word-processors for MS-DOS were WordStar and WordPerfect. Microsoft's own word-processor, MSWord was adapted from Xerox's Bravo by Charles Simonyi after he joined Microsoft. It was not successful until, ironically, Microsoft made it available on the Apple Macintosh in 1985. Only in 1989 would Microsoft release a version of Word for Windows. In 1984 Robert Gaskins and Dennis Austin had developed Presentation, later renamed PowerPoint. It was an application for the Macintosh to create slide presentations. In August 1987, Microsoft bought the whole company and ported the product to Windows. For a while the leader in this sector was Software Publishing, which had acquired Harvard Graphics' 1986 presentation program for Windows.

Desktop publishing was not new to the users of the expensive Unix workstations. Boston-based Interleaf, founded by David Boucher and Harry George, had introduced a document processor that integrated text and graphics editing for the Unix workstation market. Steve Kirsch saw an opportunity in that idea and founded FrameTechnology in 1986 in San Jose to commercialize FrameMaker, a publishing platform invented by British mathematician Nick Corfield. But those were products for the high end of the market.

Both on the software and on the hardware fronts there was a push towards making it easier to produce high-quality documents on a PC. In 1985 Hewlett-Packard introduced its own laser printer for the home market, the LaserJet. In January 1987 Aldus released PageMaker for Windows.

Graphics

The Macintosh was just one of many events of 1984 that displayed a phenomenal acceleration in using computers as graphic media. In 1984, Wavefront was founded near Los Angeles by Bill Kovacs, a creator of graphic applications with Evans & Sutherland's Picture System. Wavefront introduced the first commercial 3D-graphics software, Preview. It ran on a Silicon Graphics workstation.

Commodore and Atari meanwhile waged a corporate war. In 1985, Commodore launched the Amiga 1000, a 16-bit home computer with advanced graphics and audio, a multimedia device. It was designed by former Atari employee Jay Miner with a GUI by Carl Sassenrath and it ran a multitasking operating system. It was Commodore's response to the Macintosh. Atari's entry in this market was the ST. Both used the Motorola 68000 microprocessor. The two companies had a major feud because Commodore founder Jack Tramiel had been fired and had bought Atari, bringing key engineers with him to the rival company. Neither computer could attract the kind of third-party software that Apple and especially the MS-DOS camp could attract. Therefore both languished regardless of their technological merits.

Software was becoming the key to sell a computer. In 1986, Berkeley Softworks was a third-party vendor in the Bay Area. It was founded by videogame expert Brian Dougherty, who created GEOS (Graphic Environment Operating System), a GUI for the Commodore 64. It provided the look and feel of the Macintosh even on old 8-bit computers with very limited RAM. It rapidly became the third most popular operating system after MS-DOS and the Mac OS.

Nobody could yet offer photo-quality images on a computer, but at least in 1987 an international standard for image file format was introduced, the JPEG (Joint Photographic Experts Group). The timing was perfect because in 1986 camera manufacturer Kodak had built the first megapixel sensor, capable of representing a photograph with 1.4 million pixels (a pixel being the fundamental unit of a computer display). The world was getting ready for scanning, storing, manipulating, and transmitting images.

There were two obvious kinds of audience for graphics computers outside the computer industry: artists and film studios. In 1984 Joel Slayton at San Jose State University established the CADRE laboratory ("Computers in Art, Design, Research, and Education") that bridged the artistic and high-tech communities. In 1986, Steve Jobs bought Lucasfilm's Pixar division that had worked on computer animation and turned it into an independent film studio run by computer-graphics veteran Ed Catmull. Pixar introduced the Pixar Image Computer, the most advanced graphics computer yet, although it was a commercial flop.

Clearly, personal computers and workstations were mature enough that now the attention was focused on making them easier to use as well as capable of dealing with images and sound.

Virtual Reality

"Virtual reality" was basically an evolution of the old computer simulation systems, such as the ones pioneered by Evans & Sutherland. The software was interactive, meaning that it recreated the environment based on the user's movements so the user was able to interact with a computer via body movements. Virtual reality evolved with applications for the military, exploration, videogames, and online multi-user worlds.

The history of virtual reality dated back to the 1960s and was associated with military applications. Charles Comeau and James Bryan at Philco built a head-mounted display in 1961 called Headsight. Meanwhile, Bell Helicopter designed a head-mounted display for pilots that communicated with a moving camera. Ivan Sutherland at ARPA had speculated about the "Ultimate Display" in 1965. In 1966 he moved to Harvard University where he took Bell Helicopter's head-mounted display and connected it to a computer. Its images were generated by the computer rather than by a camera. When he moved to the University of Utah, he created a rudimentary virtual-reality system in 1969 on a PDP-1 attached to a Bell Helicopter's display with funding from the Central Intelligence Agency (CIA), ARPA, the Office of Naval Research and Bell Laboratories.

Thomas Furness at Wright-Patterson Air Force Base in Ohio started work in 1969 on a helmet for pilots that displayed three-dimensional computer graphics. His "Visually Coupled Airborne Systems Simulator" was first demonstrated in September 1981. He then used it to design a virtual cockpit, the "Super Cockpit," first announced in 1986. It allowed a pilot to fly a plane through a computer-simulated landscape by moving his head and his hand. Furness went on to establish in 1989 the University of Washington's Human Interface Technology Lab (HITL) in Seattle. Meanwhile, in 1979 Eric Howlett in Boston invented an extreme wide-angle stereoscopic photographic technology called Large Expanse Extra Perspective (LEEP).

Other researchers designed virtual reality devices for mapping and exploration. In 1979 Michael Naimark at MIT's Center for Advanced Visual Studies debuted the Aspen Movie Map, a project directed by Andy Lippman that allowed the user to navigate a representation of a city stored on laserdiscs. Aspen was the chosen city. The "movie map" had been created over two years by wide-angle cameras mounted on top of a car. In 1984 UC Berkeley alumnus Michael McGreevy joined NASA Ames Research Center and started the project for the Virtual Planetary Exploration Workstation, a virtual-reality system for which he built the first low-cost head-mounted display, the Virtual Visual Environment Display system (VIVED). The system was hosted on a DEC PDP-11 interfacing an Evans and Sutherland Picture System 2.

Videogame experts also become involved. In 1985 Scott Fisher, an MIT alumnus who had worked both at the Center for Advanced Visual

Studies in 1974-76 and at Negroponte's Architecture Machine Group in 1978-82, moved to the Bay Area. He joined Alan Kay's research group at Atari and the left for NASA Ames. There he built the VIrtual Environment Workstation (VIEW), incorporating the first "dataglove." By moving the dataglove the user moved in the virtual world projected into her head-mounted display. In 1984, a lab at NASA Ames in Mountain View created the first virtual-reality environment. In 1985, Jaron Lanier, another self-taught videogame expert, established VPL Research at his house in Palo Alto, the first company to sell Virtual Reality products, notably the "Data Glove" invented by Thomas Zimmerman.

The history of virtual reality also overlaps the history of computer games. A Multi-User Dungeon (MUD) is a computer game played by many users simultaneously on different computers, all of them connected to the same virtual world. There were predecessors but the game that created the term and started the trend on the Internet was MUD. It was created in 1978 in Britain by Essex University student Roy Trubshaw and launched online in 1980. In 1986 Lucasfilm launched "Habitat," a social virtual world created by Randy Farmer and Chip Morningstar. It ran on a Commodore 64 computer connected via dial-up lines. Each user in this virtual world was represented by an "avatar."

New Paradigms of User-Computer Interaction

With new technologies came new paradigms of computer-human interaction. In 1987 a Virginia-based company, Linus Technologies, introduced the first pen-based computer, WriteTop. It allowed the user to write directly on the screen. It was PC-compatible and cost $2,750. Also in 1987 Jerry Kaplan, formerly chief technologist at Lotus and co-founder of Teknowledge, started GO Corporation in Silicon Valley to manufacture similar portable computers with a pen-based user interface. GO never delivered anything of any consequence. Yet it went down in the history of the Valley for the impressive amount of venture capital that it managed to amass and burn through: $75 million.

In 1987 Apple demonstrated its HyperCard software, which allowed Macintosh users to create applications using interconnected "cards" that could mix text, images, sound, and video. The cards constituted a hypertext. Designed by Bill Atkinson, it was another idea derived from Xerox PARC, which had built a hypertext system called NoteCards in 1984. NoteCards in turn was based on the old experiments of Ted Nelson and Douglas Engelbart. HyperCard also pioneered the idea of "plug-ins," of external software that is allowed to access the application's internal data in order to extend its functionalities.

An early handheld mobile computer came out in 1984. It went largely unnoticed in the US, but the Psion Organiser was the archetype of a "personal digital assistant." The company was established in Britain in

1980 by David Potter as the software arm of local computer manufacturer Sinclair.

The Semiconductor Wars

Governments, at least in the US and Japan, quickly realized the strategic importance of semiconductors. The US owed its lead in the Cold War to its semiconductor advantage. Japan owed its lead in all sorts of gadgets to semiconductors. Eventually the ferocious competition between companies was escalated to a governmental level and the outcome indirectly helped Silicon Valley focus on the microprocessor.

Silicon Valley's technological lead was undisputed in the 1980s. In 1985, Intel introduced the 32-bit 80386 that contained 275,000 transistors and was capable of performing three million instructions per second. The first 32-bit microprocessor had been shipped already in 1983 by National Semiconductor (the NS32032) and the second had been Motorola in 1984 (the MC68020). Yet it was the Intel 80386 (abbreviated as 386) that shook the market. It boasted almost 100 times more transistors than the 4004 and could run both MS-DOS and Unix.

However, 1985 was the year of the first crisis of the semiconductor industry, brought about by cheaper Japanese products. The Japanese government, via the Ministry of International Trade and Industry (MITI), had sponsored a project headed by Yoshio Nishi at Toshiba for Very Large-Scale Integration (VLSI). Its primary goal was conquering the DRAM market. In 1984 Japanese firms introduced the 256K DRAM chips. Silicon Valley's companies could not compete with the low prices of those chips.

Silicon Valley had gotten its start by selling customized military systems, not by selling commodities. It relied on a network of local know-how and on intimate relationships with the customer. Commodities, instead, rely on economy of scale. So Japan started to win. In 1981, US manufacturers had enjoyed a 51.4% share of the world's semiconductor market, whereas Japanese companies had 35.5%. In 1986 the situation had been reversed, with Japan's share reaching 51% and US companies reduced to a 36.5% share. Specifically, by 1985 Japanese firms had gained 70% of the DRAM market. Intel, AMD, and Fairchild had to exit the DRAM market. It was mainly a Silicon Valley problem, because non-Silicon Valley firms such as Motorola, Texas Instruments, and Micron continued to manufacture competitive DRAMs. Thousands of hardware engineers were laid off in Silicon Valley, pushing the region towards software.

What saved Intel was the microprocessor. The "computer on a chip" was too complex and required too big a manufacturing investment to be handled like a commodity. Japanese microprocessor technology was simply licensed from the US. In 1984, the world market for microprocessors was worth $600 million: 63% of those sales went to US companies, 30% to Japanese companies, and 7% to European companies. But the situation was even better for the US: 99% of those microprocessors were designed under license from a US manufacturer.

Government intervention helped the chip manufacturers. In 1984, the US government passed the Semiconductor Chip Protection Act, which made it much more difficult to copy a chip. In 1987 the US government set up Sematech (SEmiconductor MAnufacturing TECHnology), a consortium of US-based semiconductor manufacturers funded by DARPA; it was an antidote to the MITI program. The semiconductor industry recovered and Silicon Valley-based companies such as VLSI Technology, Linear Technology, LSI Logic, Cypress Semiconductor, Maxim, Altera, and Xilinx went on to become international juggernauts.

The Bay Area was beginning to have the larger share of computer-related innovations. In the mid 1980s, only a handful of events compared with the boom of Silicon Valley. A few came from Japan, which was going through its own technological boom. In 1984 Sony and Philips introduced the CD-ROM for data and music storage. In 1984 Fujio Masuoka at Toshiba invented flash memory, a cheaper kind of EEPROM, soon to become a favorite for small appliances such as digital cameras. In 1983 Nintendo launched the Family Computer, a videogame console designed by Masayuki Uemura. They renamed it the Nintendo Entertainment System two years later in the US, where it single-handedly resurrected the videogame console.

Experimenting with Business Models

In 1985, IBM had shipped its four millionth PC, but the following year IBM made a historical mistake. Determined to stamp out the clones, IBM decided to introduce a new computer based on a proprietary architecture built on top of the old Intel 286 microprocessor. Compaq, which had been growing faster than any other company in the history of the US, did not miss the chance to introduce in September 1986 a faster machine based on the 386. When in April 1987 IBM at last delivered a 386-based machine, the Personal System/2 (PS/2), it ran a new operating system, OS/2, co-developed by IBM and Microsoft. This greatly confused the customers. Its lasting legacy would be a Video Graphics Array (VGA).

Unlike Apple, which was losing money due to its proprietary operating system, Redmond-based Microsoft was booming. Its operating system, MS-DOS, worked on most computers. Microsoft went from 40 employees and $7.5 million in revenues in 1980 to $140 million in revenues and 910 employees in 1985. In 1987 Microsoft's stock hit $90, catapulting its main owner, Bill Gates, who was just 31, onto a list of billionaires.

While Apple languished and IBM blundered, some startup computer manufacturers boomed. Michael Dell was still a student at University of Texas at Austin when in 1984 in his dormitory room he founded PCs Limited, later renamed Dell Computer. He decided to specialize in custom

PC-compatible computers. This relieved the customer of the tedious and risky business of assembling components to customize the machine. Dell also wanted to deal directly with the customer, initially by mail order only. It was a return to the business model of the early hobbyists. Dell's revenues rose exponentially. Dell's success relied on an automated supply-chain system that removed the need for inventories: its PCs were "made to order." Dell's success mirrored Compaq's success in the early 1980s. Both owed their low prices more to a distribution strategy than to a technological breakthrough.

Gateway 2000 was another company that was created by a young hobbyist, built to order, and sold directly to customers. It was formed in a South Dakota barn by Ted Waitt. In 1987, it introduced its first PC. In 1991, it was ranked the fastest growing company in the US.

All of them would soon have to battle on another front. In April 1985, Japanese manufacturer Toshiba launched its T1100, one of the earliest IBM-compatible laptops; it was the project of Atsutoshi Nishida. That machine set the standard in terms of features: internal rechargeable batteries, an LCD (Liquid Crystal Display) screen and a floppy-disk drive. HP had already debuted its first laptop in 1984, the HP-110, which was also IBM-compatible, running MS-DOS on the Intel 8086. Still, Toshiba took the idea to a new level.

Therefore there were several business models for the personal computer industry:

- Lock customers with a proprietary operating system (IBM and Apple);
- Copy the de-facto standard and get to market fast (Compaq); compete with Unix workstations (AT&T);
- Copy the de-facto standard and make to order "just-in-time" (Dell);
- Produce not just desktop PCs but also portable "laptops" (Toshiba), and;
- Focus on a cross-platform software platform (Microsoft).

Networks

As personal computers became more powerful and easier to use, the client-server architecture became a serious alternative to the monolithic mainframe. In client-server systems, the software application was split into a client portion, which ran on a personal computer, and a server portion, which ran on a more powerful computer. Many clients such as MS-DOS PCs or Macintosh machines were connected to servers. A Unix minicomputer was much easier to connect to than an IBM mainframe. The server hosted the database. By distributing software away from centralized mainframes and onto networked personal computers, companies created more flexible environments and saved money. Mainframes were rapidly abandoned. Software companies built fortunes by porting legacy system applications created for mainframes to minicomputers. Thousands of mainframe programmers of the Cobol generation lost their jobs to software engineers of the C-language and Basic generation. Basic became the language of choice on personal computers.

Computer networks began to proliferate, both within a corporation and among corporations, due to the Internet. A router is a computer-based device for routing and forwarding data to the computers of a network. Judy Estrin, a pupil of Vint Cerf at Stanford and a former Zilog engineer, had already started a company to sell routers, Bridge Communications in 1981 in Mountain View.

Stanford took the lead again. In 1981 Stanford had a team working on a project to connect all its mainframes, minis, LISP machines, and Altos. William Yeager designed the software on a PDP-11 and his ubiquitous student Andy Bechtolsheim designed the hardware. Leonard Bosack was a support engineer who worked on the network router that allowed the computer network under his management at the Computer Science lab to share data with another network at the Graduate School of Business. In 1984, Bosack and his wife Sandy Lerner, manager of the other lab, started Cisco in Atherton to commercialize the Advanced Gateway Server. It was a revised version of the Stanford router. Their product was developed in their garage and first sold in 1986 through word of mouth. They had correctly guessed that connecting networks to networks would become more important as more corporations needed to connect geographically distributed offices, each having its own network.

Other networking companies also launched. In 1983 Bruce Smith, a former executive at a satellite communications company, founded Network Equipment Technologies (NET) in Redwood City to provide high-end multiplexers to large companies. In 1985 two Xerox PARC engineers, Ronald Schmidt and Andrew Ludwick, started SynOptics in Santa Clara to develop Ethernet products. In 1985 Washington-based bar owner Jim Kimsey founded Quantum Computer Services that introduced a new business model. He provided dedicated online services for personal computers. One could use a Commodore personal computer to connect to a bigger computer where other applications could be found, such as videogames. In 1988, Quantum would add service for Apple and PC-compatible computers, and rename itself America Online (AOL).

In 1986, there were already 30 million personal computers in the US. Yet very few of them were "online" and capable of connecting to a service run on a remote computer because modems were slow and expensive. In 1987 US Robotics of Chicago unveiled a 9600-baud modem, but it cost $1,000.

Storage

Meanwhile, the saga of storage devices that had started with Alan Shugart's floppy disc continued to spawn new ideas and companies. In

1984, SUN had unveiled the Network File System (NFS), designed by Bill Joy and managed by Bob Lyon. It had a software component that allowed computers to access data storage over a Unix network. When DEC, HP, IBM, and eventually AT&T adopted NFS, it became an industry standard for distributing data storage over a computer network.

Middleware for local area networks such as NFS enabled new architectures for storing data. Auspex, founded in 1987 in Santa Clara by Adaptec's boss Larry Boucher, introduced the first data storage appliances for a computer network. Among the young engineers hired by Boucher were MIPS' file-system expert David Hitz and Chinese-born Berkeley and Stanford engineering alumnus James Lau.

Changing of the Guard

In the fast-moving Bay Area, a new generation was taking over and the old one was rapidly being buried. In 1987, National Semiconductor acquired Fairchild from Schlumberger, which had acquired it in 1979 with the whole of Fairchild Camera and Instrument. In the same year ComputerLand, valued two years prior at $1.4 billion, was purchased for a modest sum by a private equity firm. Zilog had long succumbed to Exxon and the managers of its historical Z80 era had already quit.

SUN was causing another revolution. Between 1986 and 1987, its revenues almost tripled. By the end of 1988, it would pass DEC in market shares of workstations (SUN 38.3%, DEC 23.1%, Apollo 16.7%, Hewlett-Packard 10.6%). SUN ended up eroding DEC's supremacy in the academic and then in the engineering market, which had traditionally been the bedrock of DEC's success.

SUN and DEC's business ideologies were quite different. DEC still belonged to the era of vertically integrated manufacturers that produced in-house virtually all the hardware and software components of the computer. SUN, by contrast, pioneered a manufacturing industry that relied on third parties to provide all the components. The DEC generation believed that a company needed to personally make the key components of its products. The SUN generation believed that such key components ought to be delegated to specialty shops in Silicon Valley and, eventually, around the world. In-house development was unlikely to match the same "best of breed" quality across the board guaranteed by a portfolio of specialized companies. SUN's departments were only in charge of designing, coordinating, assembling, and selling.

The complexity of creating a product had shifted from a network of internal laboratories to a network of external suppliers. What had changed was the pace of technological innovation. The small startup SUN had been able to introduce more products in its first five years in its market segment than a multi-billion dollar corporation like DEC. The DEC generation relied on proprietary components to keep the competition at bay. The SUN generation relied on the frenzied pace of product releases, knowing that each product was easy for the competition to clone but difficult to clone in time before a new product would make it obsolete. In the end, the SUN model greatly increased its revenues per employee. It also reduced its exposure to the risk of capital-intensive operations.

The SUN model would create a huge secondary economy in Silicon Valley of hyperspecialized companies that would never become household names despite achieving considerable revenues. Apple also adopted the SUN model, whereas HP managed to fare better than DEC even with the old model of vertical in-house integration. In 1987 SUN seemed to renege on its own "open-architecture" ideology when it switched from off-the-shelf hardware and software to its own RISC microprocessor, SPARC, and its own operating system, Solaris. However, it was still outsourcing the production of its components.

Cyberculture

In the 1980s, the media and the intelligentsia were fascinated by the possibilities of the "cyberspace," the invisible medium of data. Due to networks, data now traveled through space and lived a life of its own. William Gibson invented a whole new genre of science fiction with his novel "Neuromancer" in 1984, and he popularized the term "cyberspace." In 1983 Bruce Bethke had written the story "Cyberpunk," which introduced another term in the genre: the punk that roams cyberspace. The media had been creating a mythology of hackers, of software engineers who could manipulate programs and data. The media had also been speculating on the possibilities of Artificial Intelligence. All these threads resonated with a society that was haunted by the fear of a nuclear holocaust and an alienated urban life.

In January 1986 a "computer virus" nicknamed "Brain" started spreading among IBM PCs. Every time a user copied something from an infected floppy disc, the user also involuntarily copied the virus on the PC, which then replicated itself on any other floppy disc used by that machine. Computers had become vulnerable to contagious diseases just like living beings. The virus had been created in faraway Pakistan by the owners of Lahore's computer shop Brain. An earlier virus called "Elk Cloner" had done relatively little damage because it was confined to the Apple II world, but the widespread adoption of the IBM PC standard had created a whole new world of opportunities for digital contagion.

Synthetic Biology

Synthetic biology, which offered the prospect of creating genes, proteins, and even living creatures, started to arise. Synthetic biology is to biology what mechanical engineering is to physics: its goal is to build biological systems that do not exist in nature. In May 1985, Robert Sinsheimer organized a meeting of biologists in Santa Cruz to discuss the feasibility of sequencing the entire human genome. In a few months Leroy Hood's team at the California Institute of Technology in Pasadena refined an automated method to sequence DNA. It was the first automated DNA sequencer, which made it possible to sequence the entire human genome. Lloyd Smith was the main developer of the machine due to his background in both engineering and chemistry. Within one year that sequencer was launched on the market by Sam Eletr's Applied Biosystems in Foster City, which also provided an automated protein synthesizer, protein sequencer, and DNA synthesizer (these were easier technologies to develop). Leroy Hood's team included a young Mike Hunkapiller, who was also one of the first employees of Applied Biosystems.

A brand new discipline was born when in 1984 Steven Benner at the University of Florida created a gene encoding an enzyme, the first artificially designed gene of any kind. In 1988 Benner organized the conference "Redesigning the Molecules of Life', the first major conference on synthetic biology. Meanwhile a third company joined Alza and Genentech among the successes of the Bay Area's pharmaceutical industry. Michael Riordan of venture-capital firm Menlo Ventures founded Oligogen, later renamed Gilead Sciences, in August 1987 in Foster City. It would, after a number of acquisitions, experience exponential growth in the 1990s.

The Anthropology of High-Tech Individualism

Only a fraction of the high-tech workforce was born and raised in the Bay Area. The others were, by definition, "strangers." Some of them had come to study, and therefore could count on a network of friends from college. Many of them had come for work while in their 20s or 30s. Their social life was not easy in a region where individualism was pushed to the extreme. People lived alone most of the day, commuting by car (one person per car) because public transportation was inefficient, working in a cubicle, and living in apartments. The housemate was often a social choice, not an economic one: it was a chance to occasionally talk to somebody. Companies encouraged employees to mingle by throwing company parties. Some companies, notably SUN, even organized their workplace to mirror a college campus. Human connections tended to be very weak. Friendships tended to be rather superficial. Most people's "friends" were just random acquaintances who would not hesitate to "flake out" on an appointment.

The poverty of social life was, however, offset by the broad range of summer and winter activities that quickly became a feature of the regional psyche. The Bay Area was close to the skiing area of Lake Tahoe, the beaches of the Pacific coast, the forests and waterfalls of Yosemite, the deserts of Death Valley, and the mountains of the Sierra Nevada. Furthermore, this part of California enjoyed six months of virtually no rain, a strong motivation to spend weekends outdoors. During the week, people who lived in the ubiquitous apartment complexes could enjoy the annexed amenities, from the swimming pool to the gym.

The ethnic Babel, the appeal of the outdoors, and the apartment life caused a decline of quintessential American entertainment such as bowling, billiard, baseball, fishing, and hunting. Social events were monopolized by work-related issues. High culture was virtually non-existent, completely subcontracted to San Francisco and Berkeley. Restaurants, not politics, made news.

Silicon Valley engineers were also the users of the technology invented there. The region posted a higher percentage of users of computer technology than any other region of the world. An emblem of this recursive lifestyle was Fry's, the first electronic superstore that opened in 1985 in Sunnyvale, selling everything from cables to computers. The technology manufactured there had a direct influence on shaping the lifestyle of this heterogeneous workforce. In fact, it was a unifying factor. High-tech, not the church or the government, provided an identity to the community.

The volatility of the job market in Silicon Valley was even higher than in other parts of the US. The lifespan of a company was totally unpredictable. A sense of insecurity was inherent in the lives of these highly paid professionals. At the same time, it was a lot easier to land a high-tech job in Silicon Valley than anywhere else on the globe just because of the sheer number of high-tech companies. A sense of arrogance was therefore also inherent in the lives of this population. Sometimes the psychological relationship was upside down: the company had to be grateful that an engineer worked for it, whereas in the rest of the world it was usually the worker who was grateful to the company.

Insecurity and arrogance coexisted in the same mind, with wild swings from one to the other depending on the company's performance. A typical career consisted in a worker being parasitical on a company's success until that success began to taper off, and then he would jump onto another company's bandwagon. It was a career path of quantum jumps. It also implicitly required a process of lifelong training in order to avoid obsolescence. It wasn't just instability: it was accelerated and self-propelled instability.

Culture and Society

The main cultural event of those years in San Francisco was probably the WELL. Started in 1985 by Stewart Brand of the Whole Earth fame, the "Whole Earth Lectronic Link" (WELL) provided a virtual community of computer users, structured in bulletin boards for online discussions. Brand had just invented social networking. Its impact on the "alternative" lifestyle was significant. It was the first time that a computer-based system had such an impact on a computer-illiterate public. In 1986, Judy Malloy published the computer-mediated hyper-novel "Uncle Roger" on the

WELL. In 1983 Christina Augello founded the Exit Theatre, which became a reference point for the local performance scene.

The Whole Earth Catalog had provided the first link between the art crowd of San Francisco and the high-tech crowd of Silicon Valley. During the 1980s, the links multiplied: in 1981, Trudy Myrrh Reagan organized in San Francisco the first YLEM meeting of artists working with new technologies; in 1984, Roger Malina, an astronomer at UC Berkeley, established Leonardo in San Francisco to foster the integration of art and science, while Marcia Chamberlain at San Jose State University organized the first CADRE conference.

Science was never quite predictable in the Bay Area. In 1984, the "Search For Extraterrestrial Intelligence" (SETI) Institute, a non-profit organization supported by NASA and later by private philanthropists, opened its doors in Silicon Valley. It implemented what NASA Ames' "Project Cyclops" had recommended in 1971 under the leadership of Bernard Oliver.

In January 1985 Kevin Kelly launched the magazine "Whole Earth Review," the successor to Stewart Brand's "Whole Earth Catalog," except that it was now an opinion journal. It introduced virtual reality, the Internet, and artificial intelligence to the masses of Silicon Valley hackers. Its articles embodied the idealistic and futuristic aspects of software development in the Bay Area.

Driven by college radio stations and alternative magazines, music for young people underwent a major transformation. Despite the limitations of the instruments, the musical avantgarde was experimenting with techniques once reserved to the research centers. Rock music, ranging from avant-metal band Faith No More to avant-folk ensemble American Music Club, displayed a preference for destabilizing genres.

In 1986 Larry Harvey started the first "Burning Man" event on Baker Beach in San Francisco. By simply burning a sculpture, he started one of the most influential grass-roots festivals of the age. In a sense, it represented a fusion of the psychedelic and of the hobbyist cultures of the Bay Area. In a few years Burning Man moved to the desert and attracted thousands of independent artists willing to burn their art after displaying it. Somehow, that phenomenon mirrored the whole Silicon Valley experience (and, not coincidentally, would become extremely popular among Silicon Valley "nerds" who otherwise had no interest in art). "Burning Man," born out of a counterculture that reacted against what Silicon Valley represented, was an appropriate metaphor for what Silicon Valley represented.

A map of Silicon Valley in 2013, which originally just included the Santa Clara Valley from Gilroy to Palo Alto. Today it is a metaphysical space stretching from San Jose to San Francisco and Berkeley.

The Coastal Range of mountains fences much of Silicon Valley, and the western side can be quite green. Hiking and outdoor sports are popular.

Stanford's Quadrangle, the historic center of campus with its California ranch-style architecture, is known to students as "The Farm."

Stanford's "Engineering Corner," where the old radio and engineering labs were. Terman, Litton, Hewlett, Packard, and many others did their research here.

Lawrence Berkeley Labs overlooking UC Berkeley. This was the original Berkeley Radiation lab where the cyclotron was built and researchers perfected the electromagnetic enrichment of uranium.

Lee DeForest invented the audion to amplify electrical signals. Fleeing his Chicago creditors, in 1910 DeForest moved to San Francisco and got into radio broadcasting. A Stanford alumnus named Cyril Elwell used DeForest's technology to start Federal Telegraph Corporation (FTC), the first successful Silicon Valley startup.

Fred Terman (left) was a Stanford engineering professor, dean, and later provost from 1925 to 1965; he perfected the university-industry partnership model and encouraged students and professors to take leaves to build startup companies. His star students included Dave Packard, Bill Hewlitt, and Charlie Litton (right), a mechanical genius who breakfasted in the late afternoon, went to the office in evening, and worked till morning so he could have a productive day during the night's quiet hours.

The house and garage on 367 Addison Ave. where Bill Hewlett and Dave Packard started HP in 1938. Hewlett lived in the garage among the workspace, while Packard and his wife Lucille, who paid the rent with her stable job, lived in the house.

Inside the garage where Hewlett and Packard built their company; they first built and sold audio oscillators to Californian movie makers, including the Walt Disney Co. Photo courtesy of HP.

Bill Hewlett (left) and Dave Packard became best friends and business partners. They were both good engineers and managers, though Hewlett preferred to be the inside man while Packard was the outside man. They started the company with a meager pool of savings and grew it to be a multi-billion dollar company, selling electronic testing devices, calculators, and then later computers and printers. Photo courtesy of HP.

Georges Doriot was a Harvard Business School professor who started the first professional venture capital company, ARD. He mentored a generation of HBS students, like Charles Waite and Tom Perkins, who went on to start venture capital partnerships in Silicon Valley. Photo courtesy of the Harvard Baker Library.

William Shockley was a brilliant co-inventor of the transistor at Bell Labs. He moved back home to Palo Alto, seeking a warm climate to launch Shockley Transistor in 1955. Shockley was brilliant at recruiting technical talent and horrible at motivating and retaining them.

Shockley's old laboratory building where he launched his startup and alienated his employees with his tirades. A group called the "Traitorous Eight" left to start Fairchild Semiconductor. Leaving large companies to join startups is a Valley tradition.

The "Traitorous Eight" who founded Fairchild Semiconductor. From left: Gordon Moore, Sheldon Roberts, Eugene Kleiner, Robert Noyce, Victor Grinich, Julius Blank, Jean Hoerni, and Jay Last. They built a powerful company and then disbanded after the East Coast executives alienated them with slow decisions and scant sharing of the profits.

The old offices of Fairchild Semiconductor; many semiconductor entrepreneurs worked here in the late 1950s before leaving to start their own companies.

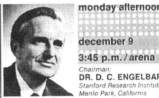

monday afternoon

december 9

3:45 p.m. / arena

Chairman:
DR. D. C. ENGELBART
Stanford Research Institute
Menlo Park, California

a research center for augmenting human intellect

This session is entirely devoted to a presentation by Dr. Engelbart on a computer-based, interactive, multiconsole display system which is being developed at Stanford Research Institute under the sponsorship of ARPA, NASA and RADC. The system is being used as an experimental laboratory for investigating principles by which interactive computer aids can augment intellectual capability. The techniques which are being described will, themselves, be used to augment the presentation.

The session will use an on-line, closed circuit television hook-up to the SRI computing system in Menlo Park. Following the presentation remote terminals to the system, in operation, may be viewed during the remainder of the conference in a special room set aside for that purpose.

Douglas Engelbart and his team developed computer-interface elements such as bit-mapped screens, the mouse, hypertext, collaborative tools, and precursors to the graphical user interface in the mid-1960s, long before the personal computer industry existed. On the right is the original announcement of the 1968 "Mother of all Demos," courtesy of Christina Engelbart and the Bootstrap Institute.

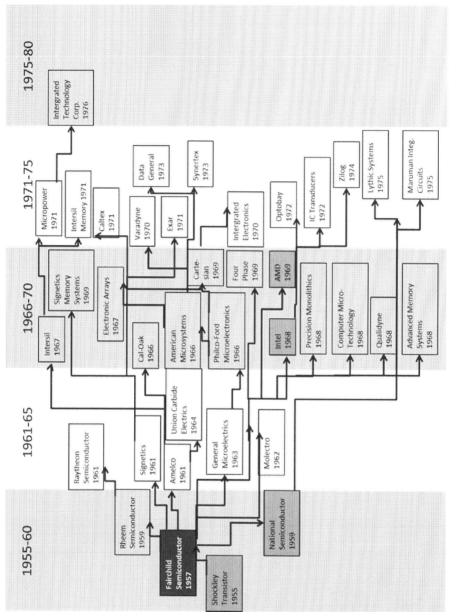

From Shockley's company came Fairchild Semiconductor and then a whole range of companies, as this Silicon Valley genealogy chart shows. Note that Shockley co-invented the transistor in 1947 at Bell Labs with John Bardeen and Walter Brattain. Image constructed from a SEMI diagram made with the help of Don Hoefler.

The first employee and two co-founders of Intel Corp: Andy Grove, Bob Noyce, Gordon Moore (left to right). They rebuilt their entire business from scratch after abandoning the DRAM market to focus on microprocessors. Photo courtesy of Intel Corp.

Intel's first office building-a one-story, modest dump that characterizes most Silicon Valley buildings quite well.

The Four Phase Founders in 1970, with Lee Boysel, a former Fairchild Semiconducter Engineer. They designed the AL1, a commercial microprocessor (an 8-bit CPU).

The preferred chip
Intel employs NutraSweet branding strategy

The Intel 4004 Chip in 1971. Intel Corp. launched its "Intel Inside" ad campaign in 1981, rebating money to Intel customers, who agreed to include the "Intel Inside" logo in print and TV ads. Intel redefined a market and built a global, consumer brand.

An Intel 8088 microprocessor from 1974; it started the microprocessor wars.

AMD's "White House" Headquarters-where the main competition to Intel was planned.

The HP-35 was Hewlett-Packard's first pocket calculator and the world's first scientific pocket calculator, with trigonometric and exponential functions. Introduced at $395, the HP-35 was available from 1972 to 1975. It was created after HP co-founder Bill Hewlett challenged his co-workers to create a "shirt-pocket sized HP-9100."

IBM's Almaden Labs, which started in San Jose but then moved to the hills above Silicon Valley, close to Stanford University. Here an army of PhD researchers developed photoresistors and the quantum mirage effect.

Atari's Pong videogame system in 1972 was the first successful arcade game. Atari co-founders Ted Dabney (left) and Nolan Bushnell, next to an original Pong console. Photo courtesy of the Computer History Museum.

Larry Sonsini of Wilson Sonsini Goodrich Rosati. The most powerful lawyer in Silicon Valley invented the model of cheaply serving startups with the hope of later servicing large tech companies.

Wilson Sonsini's law offices; sometimes called the "Death Star." Attorneys here worked in fiefdoms and targeted hi-tech startup clients.

Don Valentine was one of the most successful VCs in Silicon Valley. He developed an "aircraft carrier" method of investing, where a "carrier" company would sail with a fleet of other companies supporting it. Apple was a carrier and 13 other companies were the smaller ships to serve it (e.g. Tandon Corp. made disk drives for Apple's computers).

The IMSAI 8080 came out in1975 and copied the MITS Altair 8800 to become the first clone computer, kicking off a copy and re-engineering mentality that pervades Silicon Valley.

Xerox PARC's old Computer Science Laboratory (CSL). This is the building where the modern PC, laser printer, and Ethernet network were invented.

The PARC Computer Science Laboratory (CSL), circa1970 ca. One PARC institution was "Dealer," a weekly meeting in a lounge with sofas and bean bag chairs at lunch time. One person would be the "dealer" and set a topic for discussion. Topics were unconstrained, like how to take apart and re-assemble a bike, how programming algorithms are similar to kitchen recipes, or a presentation on the sociolinguistics of the Nepalese language and culture. Discussion and blunt talk were common, with people calling each other out with ejaculations like "bullshit" and "nonsense." Photo courtesy of the Palo Alto Research Center, Incorporated.

Bob Metcalfe of 3Com, a former Xerox PARC researcher, who invented the Ethernet to connect computers to each other. He left PARC for an IT job at Citibank and then started his own Ethernet networking company. Like many successful tech entrepreneurs, he later became an angel investor and then a VC at Polaris Venture Partners.

The Xerox Alto Computer in1973, the first true personal computer, copied by both Apple and IBM. The Xerox 9700 Electronic Printing System was introduced in 1977 as a 300dpi duplex Xerographic (Laser) printer. It could do 2 pages per second and for many years was the premier high volume page printer.

Steve Jobs' childhood home and garage, where the first Apple kits where assembled by Jobs, Wozniak, and some friends to be sold to Paul Terrell's Byte Shop in 1976.

Apple first started out in this dumpy building in Cupertino in the late 1970s. Before Steve Jobs died in 2011, he was building a $5bn mega-office which looked like a spaceship and would be the sleekest corporate headquarters in Silicon Valley.

Steve Jobs, Mike Markkula, and Steve Wozniak (left to right), the co-founders of Apple, showing off an early product at the Comdex computer show in Las Vegas during the 1980s. Most vendors put products on a plastic table; Jobs would exhibit his wares on purple velvet, as if he were presenting jewels.

Evans Hall on the UC Berkeley Campus, where researchers developed the BSD Unix and invented "vi".

3000 Sand Hill Road, Menlo Park, is near the Stanford University campus. Many of the most successful VCs had their offices in these buildings, where billions of dollars of venture money were managed.

Genentech's campus-the company ran its own bus and van service to get employees from San Francisco here quickly.

Genentech's founders Herb Boyer (left) and Bob Swanson were a biochemist and venture capitalist, respectively. They manufactured synthetic human insulin in 1978 and basically started the biotechnology industry. Photo courtesy of Genentech.

Images of Silicon Valley

Tom Perkins of KPCB (left) and Bill Draper III of Sutter Hill Ventures were two of the most successful venture capitalists. Perkins felt a VC was in the business of selling money to entrepreneurs and so needed to add value to differentiate oneself. He attributed his success to proactively incubating startups that he brainstormed with entrepreneurs, and not waiting for business plans to come in through the mail.

The First IBM PC was introduced in 1981 to compete with the Apple II. It was a major success, selling a million units in less than three years and generating large markets for other companies like Microsoft and Compaq (an IBM PC clone manufacturer).

Electronic Arts' offices in Redwood City showed that this game maker had a design sense. Sleek buildings like this were rare in Silicon Valley.

SUN's co-founders Vinod Khosla, Bill Joy, Andreas Bechtolsheim, and Scott McNealy (lef t to right), in 1982. They built a workstation using standard off-the-shelf hardware components and Unix, replicating the business model of the IBM PC. Photo courtesy of SUN Microsystems.

The co-founders of Software Development Laboratories (SDL) in 1978 were Ed Oates, Bruce Scott, Bob Miner, and Larry Ellison (left to right). SDL morphed into the database powerhouse Oracle, whose products are used by more than 95% of Fortune 500 companies. Photo courtesy of Oracle.

The Old Omex/Precision Instruments Building where Oracle Began as Software Development Laboratories. When the engineers in the startup had space allocated to them and needed to get their terminals strung to the computer room next door, they didn't have anywhere to string the wiring. Ellison walked in, picked up a hammer, and slammed a hole in the middle of the wall. He said, "There you go," and then walked away.

Oracle's campus in 2010, after three decades of success, is perhaps the sleekest office space in Silicon Valley. Ellison is known for his love of the Japanese aesthetic.

Bill Atkinson of General Magic helped develop the graphical user interface (GUI) and the Hypercard system in the 1980s. Meanwhile, Stewart Brand was producing the Whole Earth Catalog, which inspired a generation of techies with its back-to-nature advice and techno-utopian articles.

Two well-funded failures in the history of Silicon Valley were Go and Webvan.com. Go tried to launch pen computing in the early 1990s and failed. Webvan tried to sell groceries through the internet. The startup burned through $375 million in 3 years and was valued at $1.2 billion at the top of the bubble; it went bust within 12 months and fired 2,000 employees.

Jeff Hawkins (left), Founder of Palm Computing, who re-conceived the pen computer as the Palm Pilot, a personal digital assistant; he made millions in the late 1990s and the PDA later morphed into the smartphone. Marc Andreeson and Jim Clark (center and right) launched Netscape Communications in 1994 and made Mosaic Netscape available for download. Within a year, about 90% of Web users were browsing with Netscape's Navigator. Netscape went public in August 1995 even before earning money. By the end of its first trading day, the company was worth $2.7 billion and Clark had stock worth hundreds of millions.

Netscape's offices in 1995 were the epicenter of the Dot Com bubble, which ended in 2000, wiping out hundreds of billions in market value.

Yahoo!'s founders Jerry Yang and David Filo on Stanford's campus in the early 1990s. They launched a website dedicated to cataloging all the existing websites in some predefined categories and their company grew to dominate the early web.

An early Yahoo screenshot in 1994 showed that the founders valued simplicity. They made the web easy to navigate.

Yahoo!'s campus in 2010, when the company was facing decline and in the sights of angry activist shareholders, after the board turned down an offer from Microsoft to buy or license Yahoo!'s search business.

John Doerr, perhaps the most famous modern VC, was a top salesman at Intel who joined KPCB in 1980, funding companies such as Compaq, Netscape, Symantec, SUN Microsystems, drugstore.com, Amazon.com, Intuit, and Google, as well as failures such as Friendster and Go.

The 1,900-square-foot home at 232 Santa Margarita in Menlo Park, in whose garage Google started in 1998. This garage was only a few miles away from the garages where Yahoo! and Hewlett-Packard were founded.

Google co-founders Sergey Brin (center) and Larry Page (right), in a rare moment when they were not wearing jeans. They wisely brought on Eric Schmidt (left), a seasoned tech executive, in 2001 as Google's CEO, so the three could run the firm as a triumvirate. Schmidt convinced the founders that the best way to monetize their search engine was through sponsored ads.

An early Google screenshot from 1998 showed that the company was trying to reduce web clutter and give its users a minimalist interface.

Google's campus in 2010, formerly the Silicon Graphics' offices, where employees were given lavish perks like free massages, multiple free restaurants run by chefs, and unlimited snack food and van services to their neighborhoods. Google let many of its software engineers design their own desks or work stations with Tinker Toy-like pieces. Some had standing desks or even attached treadmills so they could walk while working. Employees expressed themselves by drawing or writing on walls.

YouTube's old offices in downtown Palo Alto, near the Stanford campus. Google acquired the loss-making YouTube in November 2006 for $1.65 billion, 21 months after it was started by some Stanford grad students.

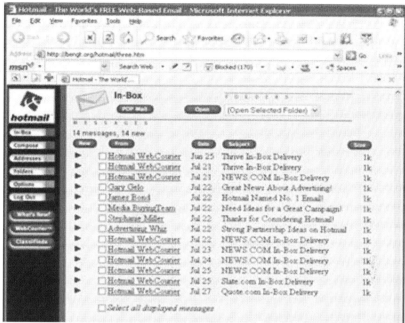

A screenshot of Hotmail, the first provider of web-based email. The company was created by two former Apple hardware engineers, Sabeer Bhatia and Jack Smith. Hotmail users checked their e-mail on the Web, regardless of where they were. Its model was so easy to understand that Hotmail signed up more than 8.5 million subscribers by December 1997, in just 18 months. It helped that Hotmail was free.

Craig Newmark created Craiglist in 1995 as a mailing list for 240 friends in San Francisco, covering of technology events, Internet jobs, apartments, lectures, restaurant reviews, and local events. After hitting a million page views a month, he launched a private company to provide a bare-bones website, which then destroyed the print classified ads business. Photo courtesy of Stephanie Canciello, Unali Artists.

Craigslist was run out of a Victorian house in San Francisco's Inner Sunset District from its start until 2010, when it moved to downtown San Francisco.

eBay's campus in a non-descript part of San Jose. Early employees had to assemble their own chairs and desks after being hired, due to the frugal culture created by the founders.

eBay founder Pierre Omidyar confers with CEO Meg Whitman. Omidyar built the web's first successful auction site and sold a broken laser pointer, which he was about to throw away, to a collector bought it for $14.83. A multi-billion dollar market was born.

Jimmy Wales formally established Wikipedia in 2003 as a non-profit foundation based in San Francisco. Wikipedia became a free, multilingual encyclopedia edited collaboratively by the Internet community. Within a few years, it would contain more information than the Encyclopedia Britannica and was another example of how utopian ideals percolated into the Internet world.

A Wikipedia screenshot in 2010, with its minimalist styling. Most of Wikipedia's operating budget was raised through voluntary donations.

The luckiest building in Silicon Valley was 165 University Ave, in Palo Alto, which had early startup tenants of Google, Paypal, Logitech, and other others. Downtown Palo Alto was the most pleasant and walkable part of Silicon Valley; the rest of the Valley was a drab set of office parks connected by old streets and highways.

Peter Thiel and Reid Hoffman were a co-founder and an early employee at Paypal, a payment firm sold to eBay in 2002; it spawned many other startups. Both men later became venture capitalists and public intellectuals, with Thiel funding Facebook and Hoffman launching LinkedIN.

Apple's Steve Jobs became the most successful creator ever of consumer tech products. He introduced the game-changing iPhone (top right), iPad (left), and MacBook Air (bottom right) within 5 years of each other, selling billions of dollars of hardware. Jobs perfected a form of product creation and marketing by following his intuition and ignoring customer feedback.

Apple's Infinity Loop and headquarters in 2010, where all the company's secret projects were developed, Willy-Wonka style. New projects were given code names and kept in secret sub-facilities behind multiple security rings.

Asian-born entrepreneurs slowly changed the ethnic makeup of Silicon Valley. Indian-born Vinod Khosla (right) co-founded SUN Microsystems and then became a successful VC. Taiwan-born Jen-Hsun Huang (left) and two SUN engineers left in 1993 to start Santa Clara-based Nvidia, a fabless semiconductor company, to design graphic chipsets for personal computers.

Twitter's offices in the SOMA district of San Francisco in 2010. This was one of the hottest parts of Silicon Valley after 2008, with the highest rents in the region. Other startups like Klout, Storify, and Huddle wanted to be close to Twitter to develop relationships that could convert to partnerships or an acquisition.

Twitter's co-founders, Evan Williams (left) and Jack Dorsey, were two of the most successful serial entrepreneurs in Silicon Valley. Dorsey was a proponent of wabi-sabi, a Japanese concept that beauty can be found in imperfection and impermanence, like a tweet.

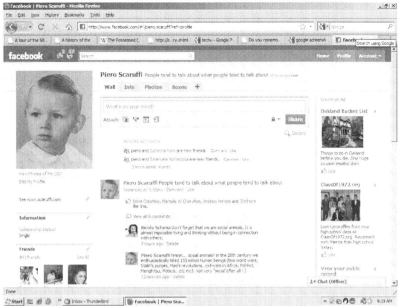

A Facebook screenshot in 2010. One reason Facebook succeeded where Friendster and MySpace failed was that Facebook standardized the layout of everyone's profile page, making the site much easier to use.

The Facebook Co-Founder and CEO Mark Zuckerberg, who wanted to change the world by making an invisible social graph transparent. His first business card read: 'I'm CEO, Bitch."

Facebook's original offices, where Zuckerberg would get to work in the afternoon and work till the early morning, often in pajama bottoms and a t-shirt. When the software code-writing got intense, he wouldn't let people leave for food, pounding the table and yelling: "No! We're in lockdown! No one leaves the table until we're done with this thing." Everyone was hungry.

Marissa Meyer (left) and Sheryl Sandberg were former Google executives who became the CEO of Yahoo! and the COO of Facebook. They brought a smooth professional management style to companies founded by boy-geeks and were two of the most admired executives in Silicon Valley in 2013. Meyer had a baby during her first few months on the job at Yahoo!.

Elon Musk, the entrepreneur that many considered to be the next Steve Jobs or Henry Ford. He built two revolutionary companies, SpaceX (private rockets to space) and Tesla (electric cars), while chairing the board of SolarCity (solar panels). Hollywood writers used him as the inspiration for the Tony Stark character in the "Iron Man" series.

The Tesla roadster in 2010. It was the only car to ever get a 99/100 rating in the important Consumer Reports Survey that evaluated cars.

A birds' eye view of Silicon Valley in 2010. Year-round sunny weather in a moderate temperature range was one reason many entrepreneurs were drawn to Silicon Valley. Other reasons were: the massive tech corporations (the engines) who could acquire startups; the best technical and scientific university system network in the world (Stanford, UC Berkeley, UCSF, San Jose State); the network of startup lawyers, incubators, and VCs; the frontier spirit of starting and failing; the openness to immigrants and other marginalized groups (nerds, geeks, gays, hackers, hippies, etc.); and the deep desire from engineers and scientists to build new companies to change the world.

22. Startups: Fab-less Firms, Networking, Mobility, and Nanotech (1987-90)

Outsourcing the Fab

By the late 1980s, software had trouble keeping up with the progress in hardware. Hardware indirectly enabled a lot of functions that software was not exploiting yet. So while Intel introduced the 80486 in 1989, containing 1.2 million transistors and performing 20 million instructions per second, IBM was right to ignore the new microprocessor. Meanwhile its competitors Compaq, Olivetti, and Zenith rushed to introduce 486-based computers.

However, the real news for Silicon Valley's semiconductor industry was not technological but logistical. In 1985 the government of Taiwan hired Chinese-born Texas Instruments' vice-president Morris Chang to run the Industrial Technology Research Institute (ITRI). Chang promoted the outsourcing of semiconductor manufacturing by US companies to Taiwanese companies. In 1987 he personally founded the Taiwan Semiconductor Manufacturing Corporation (TSMC). Taiwanese companies were able to slash costs, mainly because of cheap labor.

This led to the establishment in Silicon Valley of "fab-less" semiconductor companies, which were hardware companies that did not own a fabrication lab but instead used TSMC for the actual manufacturing process. The model was pioneered by Chips and Technologies and Xilinx, and particularly by their executives Gordon Campbell and Bernard Vonderschmitt. Cirrus Logic, founded in 1981 by Indian-born MIT alumnus Suhas Patil, and Adaptec, founded in 1981 by Laurence Boucher, were other early fab-less chip "manufacturers" in the Valley.

The fabless phenomenon became a form of inter-firm cooperation in disguise. Whenever a Silicon Valley manufacturer outsourced a project to a Taiwanese fab, it directly improved the Taiwanese plant both by injecting capital and by the project's new requirements. This indirectly constituted a favor to its competitor who would outsource next to the same plant. As long as this meant that the shared Taiwanese plant was going to be always better at serving one's needs, it was accepted that it would also be better at serving the competition's needs. It was like living in a polyandrous relationship in which it was accepted to share the same wife as long as that wife became better and better at being a helpmeet for all the husbands.

The Software Industry

The late 1980s witnessed a flurry of new computer models to replace the old text-only systems with graphical environments; they added more power and memory. The main beneficiaries were the software companies, whose power kept increasing.

However, no West Coast firm could compete with the giants of the East Coast. IBM remained by far the largest software company in the world. Only 13% of IBM's 1989 revenues came from software, but that corresponded to $8 billion. IBM's total revenues of $62 billion constituted about a third of the world's total revenues for hardware and software. The first software company to reach one billion dollar in sales was Computer Associates in 1989, based in New York and still mainly focused on applications for mainframe computers. Massachusetts-based Lotus, which had sold over four million copies of 1-2-3 by 1988, now trailed behind Oracle, with sales of $692 million in 1990. In January 1990, Microsoft released Office for Windows, which integrated Word, Powerpoint, and Excel. The days of Lotus's domination in the application business were numbered.

Data Management in the Bay Area

At the turn of the decade the largest software company in the Bay Area was Oracle. Its relational database management system had become the de-facto international standard after IBM had involuntarily legitimized SQL in the mid 1980s. The difference between IBM and Oracle is that Oracle had targeted minicomputers and notably Unix. In 1982, before IBM introduced the DB2, Oracle had 24 employees, a customer base of 75 companies, and revenues of $2.5 million. In 1987 revenues had reached the $100 million mark. In 1989 they skyrocketed to $584 million, and then they almost doubled in one year, just short of a billion dollars for the fiscal year ending in May 1990. This was one case in which a much bigger competitor had helped, not killed, the independent by legitimizing its better technology. Seattle-based Microsoft was slightly ahead of Oracle with revenues of $804 millions in 1989.

The other database manufacturers of the Bay Area were also booming. In 1988 Sybase became the darling of the stock market by introducing a client/server relational database, SQL Server, and signing a deal with Microsoft to port SQL Server to Windows. The joint project would lead to Microsoft's own namesake product. In 1989 Phil White took over at Informix and turned it around in a dramatic way to make it one of the Bay Area's most valuable companies.

Two other database companies thrived. First, Michael Pliner of networking company Sytek started Verity in April 1988. It was a spin-off from Advanced Decision Systems and largely staffed with MIT alumni such as Clifford Reid, to capitalize on ADS's text retrieval system for topic-based queries. Topic, initially designed for the Strategic Air Command of the Air Force by David Glazer and Phil Nelson, was one of the first commercial "search engines." Second, Legato, founded in September 1988 in Mountain View by Bob Lyon and Russell Sandberg, the SUN engineers who had helped Bill Joy create NFS, introduced a device to improve the performance of SUN's NFS. Yet it would soon become a leader in the more strategic field of cross-platform automatic data backup and recovery.

The increasing importance of sharing data across applications on a variety of software platforms in real time spawned a new industry of "middleware." In 1987, Boston-based Vivek Ranadive founded Teknekron Software Systems, which in 1997 would evolve into TIBCO and relocate to Palo Alto to market an "Information Bus" capable of shuttling mission-critical data between software programs. It rapidly digitized Wall Street's transactions.

At the hardware level, SanDisk was founded in 1988 by two EEPROM experts, Israeli-born Eli Harari and Indian-born Sanjay Mehrotra. It soon became a significant competitor of Asian leaders Toshiba and Samsung in the strategic field of flash memory cards.

Software for Manufacturing

The market for enterprise resource planning (ERP) software had been expanding rapidly. Corporations could run their entire business, from procurement to sales, via one monolithic system. SAP dominated that market. In the US, the leader was JD Edwards. Both their platforms ran on mainframes. That industry came to the Bay Area in 1987, when David Duffield founded PeopleSoft in the East Bay. PeopleSoft started with the idea of taking the human-resource management system developed for the mainframe by Duffield's previous company, Integral Systems. He had founded it in 1972 in New Jersey but relocated in 1976 to Walnut Creek, near Berkeley, to port a HR system to the client-server architecture. The product rapidly overtook the mainframe-based competition, generating revenues of $1.9 million in 1989 and $6.1 million in 1990. PeopleSoft went on to overtake JD Edwards and eventually absorb it.

Importantly for Silicon Valley, a new sector of software for manufacturing was being invented in Detroit. In 1982 General Motors began to plan a new car, the Saturn. GM had hired Wharton Professor Morris Cohen to improve its factories. Cohen's proposals went into the new Saturn factory, and basically amounted to linking all GM dealers with the factory's mainframe via satellite. Cohen had modeled GM's business as a series of "supply chains," each one representing a stream of "resources," such as raw materials and third-party components, towards a finished product that is delivered to the end customer. By doing that, the Saturn factory had built the first supply chain management (SCM) system, integrating suppliers, factories, and customers. A company named

Intellection (later renamed i2) was founded in Dallas in 1988 by two former Texas Instruments employees, Indian-born Sanjiv Sidhu and Myanmar-born Ken Sharma, to create an independent SCM software package called Rhythm. Needless to say, the border between ERP and SCM was blurred at best.

Locally in the Bay Area, there were many companies serving the needs of the semiconductor industry. For example, Rasna Corporation, founded in November 1987 in San Jose by engineers of IBM's Almaden Research Center, sold computer-aided engineering tools for the semiconductor industry. Their compnay was eventually purchased by Parametric Technology of Boston, which had just purchased CAD pioneers Evans & Sutherland.

Silicon Valley also missed the train on one of the most important innovations in manufacturing: 3D printing. The technology was originally introduced for "rapid prototyping" in 1986 by Charles Hull at 3D Systems in Valencia, located in the Los Angeles metropolitan area. This was the first 3D printer that a factory could actually install and use to create objects based on a file created with Computer-Aided Design/ Computer-Aided Manufacturing (CAD/CAM) software.

Unix and Internet

While Microsoft's operating systems were spreading from computer to computer, Unix continued to stumble. Unix had been stuck in a time warp of sorts after AT&T and SUN had taken separate roads with incompatible implementations. Just as AT&T and SUN commenced a truce in 1988, the war resumed on another front. IBM, DEC, Hewlett-Packard, and others formed the Open Software Foundation (OSF) to enact an open Unix standard, clearly a preemptive strike against the blossoming AT&T/SUN alliance.

Elsewhere in the US during the late 1980s, the trend towards networking continued at all levels. In 1988 Bellcore, the descendant of the glorious Bell Labs that AT&T had to abandon when the government broke it up in 1984, invented "Digital Subscriber Line" (DSL). It was a communications technology that provided broadband on a regular phone line. Price permitting, this allowed every household in the world to use their existing phone line to establish a high-speed connection with a computer. This enabled the transmission of bulky files, such as the ones produced by scanning a document or by a digital camera.

The Internet was still exclusive. In order to access it, a user needed an account (a login name and password) at a university or research laboratory or government agency. With few exceptions, the user interface was Unix, so the Internet user needed to be fluent in Unix commands. The old UUCP protocol was still the main way to provide access to Usenet and e-mail. UUCP was the invisible "language" spoken by the nodes of the Internet as they transferred and forwarded data.

The public internet started with the early internet service providers (ISPs). Rick Adams, a system administrator at the Center for Seismic Studies in Virginia, pioneered the idea of providing those UUCP-based services commercially to companies in 1987 when he founded Uunet, the first independent ISP. Initially it simply provided access to Usenet and e-mail, but in 1990 it also launched its AlterNet that made the Internet even easier to access. Uunet's customers were mainly companies that needed to do research on the Internet. At the same time in 1989 Barry Shein in Boston started the ambitiously named "The World," another pioneering ISP. Every small business willing to purchase a modem could get on the Internet. There was precious little for ordinary households on the Internet other than e-mail, but every household could do the same. In 1989 CompuServe, Ohio's pioneer of "dial-up" time-sharing services, connected its proprietary e-mail service to the Internet. This allowed its customers to exchange e-mail with Internet users. Cheap computer models with built-in models began to appear.

With public networks came the first dangers. In 1988, "Morris," the first Internet "worm," unleashed by graduate student Robert Morris at Cornell University, infected most of the Internet, an omen of the dangers of networking.

As computer networks mushroomed, it became economically unfeasible to provide every terminal user with expensive computers such as Unix workstations. In 1984 MIT had created the specifications for a "thin client," i.e. a very simple machine to connect to a network. Simply called "X," it created an industry of "X terminals." They also came to be associated with graphics because the X protocol mandated a graphical user interface (GUI) on the terminal and enabled the transmission and remote display of high-resolution images. These X terminals were therefore capable of displaying graphics generated on a server, and basically constituted a cheaper alternative to Unix workstations such as SUN. Network Computing Devices was founded in 1987 in Mountain View by Doug Klein and others, including a young Martin Eberhard, who had worked at San Jose's ASCII terminal maker Wyse Technology. It was soon run by Judy Estrin, a pupil of Vint Cerf at Stanford and the founder of Bridge Communications, to sell X terminals.

Meanwhile, collaborative software platforms called "groupware" became popular in the 1990s. Ray Ozzie and other former students of the University of Illinois's CERL, who had grown up with the online community PLATO Notes, ported Notes to the personal computer with funding from Lotus. The result in 1990 was Lotus Notes, a system for interconnected personal-computer users to share a project.

Laptops and Videogames

Two off-shoots of the personal computer were becoming increasingly significant in terms of revenues, and both were dominated by Japanese companies.

First, laptops were becoming important, especially to travelling business users. After Toshiba had revolutionized the field, there had also been rapid progress in creating smaller mobile computers with the power of a personal computer. In 1988 Compaq introduced its first laptop PC with VGA graphics, the Compaq SLT/286. In 1989 NEC released the UltraLite, an even lighter laptop, but still based on the older 8086 processor. Finally, in September 1989, Apple released the first Macintosh portable.

Laptops appealed to individuals who needed to work in different locations on the same data. Instead of having to connect to a mainframe whenever they needed to enter or access a record, the "mobile" workers were enabled by the laptop to carry that record with them. Initially the laptop was a success mainly with sales forces but it soon spread through the hierarchies and even became a status symbol for the executive management itself. In 1990 the number of mobile personal computers sold in the US skyrocketed to more than one million (versus eight million desktops).

Second, the leadership for videogame consoles had decisively shifted to Japan. In 1988 Sega introduced the Mega Drive/Genesis and in 1990 Nintendo introduced the Super Nintendo Entertainment System, both destined to sell tens of millions of units. No video console introduced in the US in those years would even remotely compete with the Japanese numbers.

However, a new concept was being born in the Bay Area that would have wide-ranging consequences. SimCity was a simulation game, first released in 1989 and created by game designer Will Wright for Jeff Braun's Maxis in Emeryville, near Oakland. It was different in that there was no winning and no losing, no enemies, and no weapons. A player simply created a city from scratch.

Biotech

The futuristic industries of the Bay Area, biotech and nanotech, were still growing slowly. In 1990 Swiss pharmaceutical giant La Roche acquired a majority stake in Genentech, which had become the largest biotech company in the world with revenues of about $400 million. The takeover legitimized the whole industry.

The government entered the picture of the bioscience in a grand way. In October 1988, the National Institutes of Health, in collaboration with the Department of Energy, established the Office for Human Genome Research. It was later renamed the National Human Genome Research

Institute (NHGRI). James Watson, one of the co-discoverers of the structure of DNA, was its first director. The US and other nations (eventually Britain, China, Japan, Germany, France, Canada and New Zealand) launched the International Human Genome Project with the mission to determine the sequence of the human DNA and to map the 25,000 genes of the human genome.

Nanotech

The term "nanotechnology" had been popularized by Eric Drexler's book "Engines of Creation - The Coming Era of Nanotechnology" (1986). "Nano" referred to technology that operates at the atomic and molecular scale, 100 nanometers or smaller. Materials are built from atoms. The configuration of the atoms can produce materials with completely different properties, like coal versus diamond, or sand versus silicon. Molecular manufacturing would open a new era for the fabrication of materials. This vision was originally propounded by theoretical physicist Richard Feynman in 1959.

Progress in nanotechnology was enabled by the invention of the Scanning Tunneling Microscope (STM) in 1981 that allowed scientists to work on individual atoms, and by the invention of the Atomic Force Microscope in 1986. In 1989 Don Eigler at IBM's San Jose Almaden labs carried out a spectacular manipulation of atoms that resulted in the atoms forming the three letters "IBM."

The problem with nanotechnology was that its tools were extremely expensive. The electron synchrotron nicknamed "Advanced Light Source" in construction at the Lawrence Berkeley Lab was designed to generate laser-like beams 10,000 times brighter than the brightest light ever produced on Earth. It was the ideal tool for exploring the structure of materials, for observing the nucleus of biological cells and for building subatomic microstructures; but even that wasn't "nano" enough.

The Culture of Risk

While all of this was going on, the Bay Area contributed relatively little to groundbreaking technological innovation. It was mostly incremental evolution.

The real innovation was on another dimension. Silicon Valley did not depend anymore on the military and its financial independence had created a new business model that questioned the old world order in many ways. Funding from the military had helped create a very stable hardware industry that, a few decades later, had spawned a new, highly unstable industry of small software companies. Behind it there was a new attitude towards risk that somehow may have been part of the regional psyche since the days of the Far West. Yet it was also due to the nature of the old semiconductor business.

Building chips had always been a tricky business. As chips got smaller and faster, that business began to border on magic. By the late 1980s, companies such as Intel had to build a completely new plant in order to create a new generation of semiconductors, and each new plant easily cost in the neighborhood of $1 billion. The smaller the chips were, the higher their demand for capital. At the same time these products had a very short lifespan, in most cases less than two years. During their lifetime these products were also subject to price wars that reduced their return on investment.

The rule of thumb in the 1980s was that 25% of the new electronics firms failed within a few years. Nonetheless, semiconductor components making memory chips, programmable logic, micro-processors, and custom-made circuits constituted the heart of the most successful appliances ever, from calculators to videogames. It was worth the risk.

Investors learned that it was a statistical game: invest in several startups, and only a few would survive, but those would make a lot of money for a short period of time. Any company that stayed in the business learned to live with high risk, aware that they could be gold mines today and broke in two years.

That culture of risk remained after its very creators had succumbed to it. The culture reincarnated in the software industry of the late 1980s. The creation of wealth continued and now depended on the venture capital available locally rather than on the defense industry. Many of the new investors were former startup founders themselves. They recycled their money in the same environment in which they had made it. They had been raised in that culture of risk.

And it was more than a culture. It was a whole infrastructure designed to promote, assist, and reward risk-takers in new technologies. That infrastructure consisted not only of laboratories, plants, and offices, but also of corporate lawyers, marketing agencies, and venture capitalists. Coupled with the continuous flow of international students from the local universities, this world represented an entire ecosystem at the service of a risk-taking culture.

Law firms, for example, specialized not only in incorporating startups and documenting the early funding process, but also in protecting intellectual property. No other region in the world boasted attorneys that were more efficient and skilled in protecting a company's intellectual property. This hidden economy of corporate lawyers pre-dated the boom of the 1980s. It certainly helped that California law always displayed a bias towards the small company. This was probably the legacy of having had to fight the East-Coast conglomerates in the old days when the West Coast did not have any large conglomerate. The task of defending California businesses was left to the state, and the state enacted laws to that extent. The best-known example was probably the law forbidding non-compete contracts that stopped employees of a firm from migrating to a competing firm. Other states allowed such contracts because the local conglomerates lobbied for them in the old days to protect their dominant status.

In the 1980s, Silicon Valley represented a significant demographic change for the US. There was a shift in political and economic power from the old industrial and financial capitals of the Northeast and Midwest towards a new pole of industry and finance based on the West Coast.

This had even wider geopolitical implications: the biggest competitor of California was Japan, not Western Europe. The old "Atlantic" economy, whose industrial and financial centers stretched from the East Coast and Midwest of the US to Western Europe, was being replaced by a new "Pacific" economy, whose industrial and financial centers stretched from the Far East to California and Texas. It wasn't just the technology that had moved to the Pacific, it was also the capital. The venture capitalists based in Menlo Park and San Francisco accounted for a rapidly growing share of the world's venture capital. In fact, the semiconductor industry, which was slowing down, would have dragged the Bay Area down with it if it weren't for the large amounts of capital available to a completely new industry, the software industry.

There was really no compelling reason for a software company to open business in the Silicon Valley. After all, Microsoft was based in Seattle, and Apple's computers supported many fewer third-party developers than Microsoft. IBM, still the largest hardware, software and consulting company in the world, was based far away. The reason that a new industry boomed in Silicon Valley was, ultimately, that there was a lot of talent and money around. The universities and companies of the region had attracted bright, highly educated brains from all over the US and the world. The combination of capital and brains replaced a declining industry with a booming one.

As a consequence, the symbiosis between venture capital and educational centers (Stanford, Berkeley, UCSF, and also San Jose State University, which churned out software engineers by the thousands) had become an addiction.

The downside, of course, was the temptation to generate a profit as quickly as possible. The great investor of the 1950s and 1960s, the US military, planned for the long-term. It had no interest in return on investment. The new investors of the 1980s had a short-term view of business. Investors began to promote corporate strategies that were focused not on innovation but on return on investment. This fear became national when Japan's MITI funded ambitious long-term projects that no Silicon Valley startup could possibly match because no investor would invest in long-term prospects.

However, the short-term approach helped translate well with the market for products. The Silicon Valley startup was usually "visionary" but grounded in the reality of technological feasibility and of market readiness. Furthermore, the Darwinian system of small startups as a whole was more likely to find a solution to a problem than, say, a large bureaucratic company. Progress was incremental but rapid.

The venture capital firms had created a ghost industry that evolved in parallel to the technological one. This ghost industry was focused on making money typically through one of two ways: the IPO where the startup goes public for a value much higher than the capitalist's investment, or an acquisition where a large company, often based outside the Bay Area, buys the startup for a price much higher than the capitalist's investment.

Venture capital firms did not incubate healthy, long-lasting businesses as much as they incubated their own prospects for profit. This ghost economy was purely concerned with IPOs and acquisitions, independently of the intrinsic (social, scientific, human) value of a startup's technology. It was as much a gamble to make money as stock gambling at Wall Street, except that the multiplicator could potentially be much bigger.

Considering the voracious nature of the whole process of IPOs and acquisitions, it is remarkable that Silicon Valley as a whole did generate real, groundbreaking products that triggered social changes all over the world.

The precarious lives of startups also created a culture of employment promiscuity. Engineers became accustomed to the idea that they may have to change jobs many times in their career. Each new job was a bet on the chances of a company. This culture created a further order of flexibility in that people were also more willing to change jobs on their own. A new startup could easily find the right brains to develop a new technology, whereas elsewhere in the world people were less prepared to switch jobs.

It helped that so many Silicon Valley residents were immigrants from other states or from other nations. They were not afraid to move to a new environment and start a new life. The goal in Europe and on the East Coast was the career: ascend the ladders of the company's hierarchy. This was hard to conceive in Silicon Valley, where a company's business life expectancy was much lower than its employee's biological life expectancy. The fact that people living in Europe and on the East Coast were, instead, more reluctant to change jobs was, in fact, an important factor in determining the evolution of their economies. Silicon Valley's dream was a linear progression from engineer in a startup to founder of a startup to investor in a startup. This dream encouraged people to take chances working for a startup, to take chances creating startups, and to take chances investing in startups. It was a self-fulfilling prophecy and a self-sustaining metabolic cycle.

Now that venture capitalists employed or were themselves technology specialists, their role had changed in a subtle way. A venture capitalist had always had a vested interest in helping the company he had funded. But the technology-savvy venture capitalist, totally immersed in the community of innovators and with strong ties to the academia, could do more. She had to become a knowledge broker, helping shape companies and their businesses through her network of contacts. Venture-capital firms had become more and more active in guiding if not running the business of their portfolio companies, going from whom to hire for the executive team to which companies to choose as partners.

Part of this passion for startups was also the legacy of the anti-establishment and therefore anti-corporate sentiment of the 1960s. Software, in particular, appealed to the long-haired alternative type of kid, being novel, invisible, and creative. It was at about this time that Silicon Valley witnessed the rise of a cult of personality that went beyond mere admiration. Jobs, Ellison, Noyce, and McNealy became more than founders or leaders; they became myths and prophets. The Fairchild founders had not been folk legends at all. The HP founders had been respected, but not over-hyped. They had been role models for a selected number of people who knew their responsible and dignified role in running the company.

On the other hand, the leaders of Apple, Oracle, Intel, and SUN acquired a semi-divine status in Silicon Valley. These mythical figures fought epic battles, typically against Bill Gates, Silicon Valley's bête noire. The local media chronicled their fantastic odysseys. Their charisma replaced the charisma of the engineers who had truly invented their technologies (the likes of Kirby, Faggin, Wozniak, and Bechtolsheim).

This phenomenon had a net effect on the ambitious youth of Silicon Valley. The trend had been shifting away from inventing a product to starting a company, with the emphasis on the business plan rather than on the technological breakthrough.

Culture and Society

None of this could have happened if the Bay Area had not continued attracting brainpower from all over the world. The old model of lifetime employment in a large, safe company still prevailed on the East Coast, in Western Europe, and in Japan. The West Coast, instead, spearheaded the preference for the small, dynamic company. Even if a startup didn't offer benefits, required one to work on weekends, and was likely to go bankrupt, it offered a big upside through equity. Silicon Valley's agile, dynamic and brutal Darwinian system won over all the other technology centers in the US and Europe. Silicon Valley came to embody the old myth of the "the land of opportunity" and therefore became an even bigger attractor for young educated people. Between 1970 and 1990 the population of San Jose alone almost doubled, from 445,779 to 782,248 people. In 1989 San Jose passed San Francisco in population. The San Francisco Bay Area was now officially a misnomer.

While it was attracting engineers, the Bay Area continued to attract artists and musicians who thrived on diversity. The collective of chamber, electronic, ethnic music that revolved around Lights In A Fat City and Trance Mission, or the iconoclastic collective of Thinking Fellers Union Local 282 were emblematic of what the Usenet had labeled "alt-rock." Visual artists formed the multidisciplinary gallery Luggage Store (properly the 509 Cultural Center) in 1987. This followed the Lab, which was also founded by interdisciplinary artists, which in turn followed the Capp Street Project, founded by Ann Hatch to promote avantgarde installations.

The strand of anti-technological spirituality was still proceeding in parallel with the monumental achievements of the high-tech industry: the two behaved like entangled Siamese twins. The human-potential movement that had mutated into the new-age movement was still quite popular in the Bay Area. In August 1987, psychedelic painter Jose Arguelles organized the Harmonic Convergence in Sedona, Arizona to celebrate what he believed to be a planetary alignment correlated with the Mayan calendar. Believers rushed to power centers, or vortexes, were the phenomenon would be maximized. One vortex was Mount Shasta, located 400 kilometers north of San Francisco. The Californian nuttiness always mutated into a different form.

Yet the Bay Area assumed a physiognomy that wouldn't change for a while. San Jose overtook San Francisco to become the biggest city of the Bay Area, but remained a major financial center and virtually its only cultural center. In terms of music, art, and culture, Berkeley was its eastern appendix, with UC Berkeley still producing a lively counterculture. During the 1980s, UC Berkeley was a unique center for alternative music, boasting three of the largest record stores in the world within the space of three blocks. It also had non-stop, improvised collective drumming in the lower Sproul Plaza. Next to it, Oakland was still a poor crime-ridden city. The East Bay between Oakland and San Jose was home to large immigrant communities from the Indian subcontinent and from Latin America.

Silicon Valley from San Jose to Mountain View was a breathtaking industrial area with few equals in the world. Virtually any non-residential street was lined with multi-story office buildings, a veritable "who's who" of the high-tech industry. North of Mountain View was the Peninsula, which included Stanford University. The human landscape around Stanford was quite different from the one emanating from Berkeley. It was less culturally extravagant and more business-oriented. The Peninsula contained some of the wealthiest communities in the world: Atherton, Woodside, Portola Valley, Menlo Park, Los Altos Hills, and Palo Alto itself (originally an industrial and student area, but which turned into an expensive town through tech wealth). An impressive amount of private capital was held in this area. The I-101 corridor was still industrial, especially between Redwood City and the San Francisco airport. It included Oracle and Genentech, but towards the hills the Peninsula was the habitat of new and old multimillionaires.

23. Surfers: The World-Wide Web, Netscape, Yahoo, Multimedia, and Bioinformatics (1990-95)

The World-Wide Web

The 1990s opened with one of the most influential inventions of all times: the Web. The British engineer Tim Berners-Lee of CERN, Geneva's high-energy physics laboratory funded by multiple European governments and the largest Internet node in Europe, realized that applying the hypertext paradigm to the Internet could create a worldwide network beyond the imagination of the original inventors of hypertext. He set out to define a HyperText Markup Language (HTML) to write hypertext documents linking each other. Berners-Lee implemented the server on a NeXT computer, and wrote the first client, a "browser" that he named "World-Wide Web." The server transferred ("served") webpages to the client according to a simple protocol, HyperText Transfer Protocol (HTTP). The browser was inspired by DynaText, developed in 1990 by Electronic Book Technologies.

HTML was nothing more than a language to "publish" a document. There had been many before. The HTML code tells the browser how to display the content of the page. Since its Version 6 in 1975, the first one to be released outside Bell Labs, the Unix operating system had included a widely used text-formatting system, "nroff." Since 1986, the scientific community had used LaTex, developed by Leslie Lamport at the SRI International, to produce technical papers. A world standard for these "mark up" languages had been defined in October 1986, the Standard Generalized Markup Language (SGML). HTML was, in fact, a more primitive relative of these languages. The real innovation was the "link" that, when the user clicked on it with the mouse, instructed the browser to jump from the current page to another page, hosted on the same or another computer (via the HTTP). This simple idea dramatically changed the user experience on the Internet. A major quantum leap in the high-tech industry had come from a government-funded laboratory.

The Web was disclosed to the broader Internet world in August 1991. In December 1991, physicist Paul Kunz set up the first World-Wide Web server in the US at the Stanford Linear Accelerator Center (SLAC). In April 1992 there was already another browser, Enwise, written for Unix by four Finnish students at the Helsinki University of Technology. The first major browser in the US was ViolaWWW, completed by Taiwanese-born student Pei-Yuan Wei at UC Berkeley in December 1992. It was a project inspired by the look and feel of Apple's Hypercard. These two were notable for being graphical browsers.

At just about the same time in December 1991, the US government got involved. It passed the High-Performance Computing and Communication Act, originally proposed by Senator Al Gore. Gore envisioned a "National Information Infrastructure" that would create a vast network of public and private information systems to deliver potentially all the information of the nation to potentially all the citizens of the nation. This law funded a number of research projects around the US, and in particular it funded the project for a graphical browser at the National Center for Supercomputing Applications of the University of Illinois. The employees in charge of it were Marc Andreessen and Eric Bina. Their goal was to create a user-friendly browser with a graphical user interface. They completed their Mosaic web browser in 1993.

Mosaic's graphical user interface made all the difference. It also made it easier to display documents containing both texts and images. Originally developed for UNIX, it was soon ported to Windows, turning any PC into a client for the World-wide Web. Andreessen found a job in Silicon Valley. There he met Silicon Graphics' founder Jim Clark who encouraged him to commercialize Mosaic through a startup. In April 1994, the duo launched Mosaic Communications Corporation, later renamed Netscape Communications, in Mountain View. In October 1994 Mosaic Netscape was available for download and within a year about 90% of World-wide Web users were browsing with Netscape's Navigator. Netscape went public in August 1995 even before earning money. By the end of its first trading day, the company was worth $2.7 billion and Clark had stock worth hundreds of millions.

In 1994 Berners-Lee introduced the Uniform Resource Locator (URL) to express the hierarchy of domain names of the Internet into World-wide Web names (e.g., www.stanford.edu). The most popular domain was ".com," which became known as "dot com." It was originally meant to identify commercial activities, as opposed to ".edu" (for educational institutions), ".gov" (for government agencies) and ".org" (for non-profit organizations). The craze that followed Netscape's IPO became known as the "dot-com craze."

Netscape did more than simply start a new gold rush. It made the Web easy to navigate for anybody, as long as they knew how to type on a keyboard and they could find a computer connected to the Internet. It leveled the playing field so that the illiterate computer user could browse the Web the same way that a pro did. Due to Netscape's browser, the shapeless and non-intuitive cluster of digital information that had accrued on the Internet became intelligible and meaningful to everybody. This in turn prompted more and more people to add content to the Web. It now became clear that one boom had enabled the other one: the personal computer boom of the 1980s had placed a computer in millions of households, and that now constituted the vast public of the Web. A key factor was that the Netscape browser was free for individuals and non-profit organizations. Netscape also protected the Internet from monopolies that would have loved to hijack it. Its browser used open standards and indirectly forced much larger corporations to adopt those same standards, thus avoiding the kind of wars that still plagued the world of operating systems.

Searching the Web

Meanwhile the World-wide Web had created another kind of application. Already in 1990, before anyone had heard of the Web, some students in Montreal had created a "search engine" named "Archie" to find sites on the Internet, which in those days were accessed via File Transfer Protocol (FTP). Many universities and companies experimented with search engines before Yahoo and Google dominated the field.

Before the Web took hold, the most popular way to catalog and transmit documents over the Internet was Gopher, created by Mark McCahill at the University of Minnesota and also debuted in 1991. Immediately, two applications were born to search Gopher catalogs: Veronica (in Nevada) and Jughead (in Utah). EINet's Galaxy, launched in January 1994 in Texas, was the first catalog of websites. WebCrawler, created by Brian Pinkerton at the University of Washington and launched in April 1994, was the first search engine for the web, a website that indexed and then searched the texts it found on the web. At about the same time Michael Mauldin at Carnegie Mellon University started the project Lycos to catalog pages of the web, which went live in July.

In 1993 the Web had clearly won over Gopher. A catalog of websites was casually circulating at Stanford University. In January 1995, the authors of that catalog, Stanford's students Jerry Yang and David Filo, launched Yahoo! (Yet Another Hierarchical Officious Oracle!), which was simply a website dedicated to cataloging all the existing websites in some predefined categories.

The Internet grew geometrically. In October 1994, the Internet already consisted of 3,864,000 hosts. It had increased in size by 61% in one year. The need for search tools was becoming obvious. Tools like Yahoo! greatly increased the usefulness of the Web: instead of knowing only the few websites run by friends, one could now find out about websites run by complete strangers.

The Internet was affecting culture and the public and writer Jean Armour Polly who coined the phrase "Surfing the Internet." Surfing soon became an activity for a growing population of Internet users. Some did it for entertainment and some did it for work or study. The Internet had existed for a long time. It took the Web to turn it into a major attraction. And, due to the Web, applications that had been around for more than a decade became widely popular (notably e-mail).

Email had created a powerful alternative to "snail" mail. A new technology would soon provide a powerful alternative to the telephone. The origins of instant messaging for personal computers go back at least to the CompuServe CB Simulator of 1980 and Q-Link, the original America OnLine chat system (acquired from PlayNET). However, instant messaging reached the masses and became a viable alternative to a phone call due to Tribal Voice (founded by John McAfee), ICQ, introduced by the Israeli company Mirabilis in 1996, and AOL Instant Messenger, launched by AOL in 1997. In theory, Netscape allowed anyone to see any website.

In practice, however, most people used services like America OnLine to access the Internet. AOL provided a simple way to connect a home computer to the Internet: the customer would receive a floppy disc in the mail with all the software needed to perform the magic. The price to pay was freedom. The customers of AOL would typically only see what AOL wanted them to see, i.e. an AOL-sanctioned subset of the World-wide Web. Most people were content to visit the AOL pages and rarely ventured outside the AOL world.

The Net Economy

For decades the Internet had been used only for research and entertainment. Commercial activity was discouraged from the Internet, which was viewed as a scientific tool and not as a shopping mall. It was still funded by a military agency and not for the use of consumers. Somehow the advent of the Web led to the relaxation of that ethos and the most shameless commercial activities began to surface (initially just individuals who took advantage of the network to buy/sell items). The impact on society was massive.

Technically speaking, commerce on the Internet violated usage regulations. However, most corporations maintained an Internet node and did so for business purposes. However, it was still a violation to blatantly market and sell products or services on the Internet (with the exception of the Usenet, because UUCP was administered separately). The Internet's backbone, the NSFnet, was run by the National Science Foundation (NSF). In 1992, the US government allowed commercial networks to link to the NSFnet, despite protests from the academia. The result was that in a few years the commercial networks made the NSFnet look expensive and obsolete. In 1995 the government finally decided to relieve the NSF of the responsibility for the backbone, therefore de facto legalizing commerce over the entire Internet.

The World-wide Web did not create e-business. Electronic commerce had existed before the Internet (notably, Electronic Data Interchange), and e-commerce had existed the Internet before the WWW. For example, in 1991 William Porter, who already owned a stock-brokerage firm in Palo Alto, founded E*trade to offer online electronic trading via AOL and

CompuServe. But the WWW basically provided a friendlier and free user interface, which encouraged many more businesses to go online. In 1994 the first online bank opened, First Virtual.

The venture capital world of Silicon Valley was ready for it. A number of founders of successful companies of the Bay Area had retired and had become venture capitalists themselves, so called "angels." Hans Severiens knew many of them and proposed that they joined forces. So in 1994 the "Band of Angels" was born. In the true spirit of Silicon Valley it wasn't just a scheme to pool money together. The primary goal was to pool knowledge together, not money. They met every month. They led the way.

Collaboration among venture capitalists had always been a trademark of Silicon Valley, and probably one of the reasons for its success. Frequently sharing a history in the Valley's high-tech industry, venture capitalists and angels formed a highly interconnected network of firms. Successful entrepreneurs became successful because of that network, and were expected to join the network after they had become successful. Since venture-capital firms frequently invested with other firms in the same startup, they depended on each other's well being. Since they invested in multiple companies at the same time, their main interest was not in a particular startup but in the broader picture. In a sense, the venture-capital world of Silicon Valley did not invest in a company but in Silicon Valley as a whole.

Finally, venture capital firms in Silicon Valley had a high degree of technological competence, either directly through their partners or indirectly through their consultants. Venture capitalists nurtured startups, shaping their management structure and providing advice at every stage of development. They relied on informal networks of high-tech specialists and knowledge workers. Venture capital had not grown much since the heydays of the microprocessor. It was about $3 billion in 1983. It was about $4 billion in 1994. Then it skyrocketed to $7.64 billion in 1995.

Netscape's dazzling IPO in August 1995 was a dividing line in the history of Silicon Valley, just like the 1956 founding of Shockley Transistor and the 1971 creation of the Intel microprocessor. Internet companies multiplied and many of them received shocking amounts of funding. It had never been so easy for a startup to go public. The dot-com craze had reinvented yet again the landscape of the Bay Area. This time the repercussions on Wall Street were direct and immediate. The new Silicon Valley propelled the technology-heavy stock index Nasdaq to the stars, creating wealth all over the world.

A software industry that was not glamorous but was becoming increasingly strategic had to do with Internet security. In particular, Midwestern entrepreneur Kevin O'Connor invested in Internet Security Systems, founded in 1994 by Georgia Tech student Christopher Klaus. The company would be purchased by IBM in 2006 for $1.3 billion.

Multimedia, Networking and Mobility

Progress in desktop publishing continued at an ever more rapid pace. Apple's most impressive product of those years was perhaps QuickTime, introduced in December 1991. It allowed developers to incorporate video and sound in Macintosh documents. A year later, Macromedia was born in San Francisco from the merger of Authorware, a seller of graphical programming environment, and MacroMind, whose Director software was a multimedia-authoring toolset. Director turned its users into "directors" of a film. It was a novel metaphor for building applications, mainly useful for creating the software of stand-alone kiosks. In 1993 Adobe Systems introduced the Portable Document Format (PDF) to create and view professional-quality documents, and the free Acrobat reader for it.

The boom of graphics applications led to a demand for better graphic processors. Santa Clara-based Nvidia was a fabless semiconductor company founded in 1993 by Jen-Hsun Huang and two SUN engineers to design graphic chipsets for personal computers.

Communications were also driving rapid progress. Cisco had entered the Ethernet switch business by acquiring Crescendo Communications in 1993 and Kalpana in 1994. By 1997 Ethernet switching was producing more than $500 million in annual revenues for Cisco. C-Cube, started in August 1988 in Milpitas by Weitek's Edmund Sun and Alexandre Balkanski, had already begun making chips for video compression technology (MPEG codecs).

Early cloud services were developd too. In 1990 Marc Porat at Apple started a project code-named Paradigm that aimed to build an innovative hand-held mobile device. In May 1990 Porat and two Apple software engineers, Bill Atkinson and Andy Hertzfeld, decided to start a company to develop the idea, General Magic. Their vision was now more ambitious. They wanted to put the power of a real computer into the hands of a casual mobile user. At the time this was technologically impossible, so they thought of creating a "cloud" of services running on interconnected devices: by roaming the cloud, even a simple, weak device could muster the computing power of a real computer. They came up with the Telescript programming language to write applications for hand-held device (a "personal intelligent communicator") that would physically and opportunistically spread onto remote computers but eventually deliver back a result to the user of the hand-held device. Telecom and infotech giants such as Sony, Motorola, Matsushita, Philips and AT&T invested in the idea. Commercially, it was a spectacular flop, but a new paradigm had indeed been introduced: "cloud computing."

EO was launched in 1991 by French-born C-Cube's executive Alain Rossmann to manufacture a personal digital assistant. It was also a cellular telephone using GO's PenPoint operating system that recognized handwritten commands (EO was the hardware arm of GO).

Meanwhile Apple invested in developing a pen-based tablet computer with software for handwritten recognition, eventually released in 1993 as the Newton platform. Newton was another flop, but launched the vogue for small, mobile personal digital assistants (PDAs) in Silicon Valley, a decade after the Psion. Incidentally, it was running the ARM processor from Britain. Newton failed but indirectly it helped ARM survive by targeting small devices. In 1991 HP too had entered that market with the Jaguar. Apple therefore was a late comer, but its MessagePad was the first device based on Newton and it came with a stylus and handwriting recognition. More importantly, it looked "cool."

Digital pictures and printing started to overtake the chemical photo variety. In 1990, Los Angeles-based Dycam, probably the first company founded to link electronic photography and computers, introduced the world's first digital camera, Model 1. It was capable of storing pictures as digital files on an internal one-megabyte RAM chip and of downloading them to a PC. The Kodak DCS100 arrived soon after. Meanwhile in 1990 Kodak had launched the Photo CD, a box to convert negatives or slides to image files on a CD, but it used a proprietary format instead of Jpeg. The first camera that could download images into a personal computer via the serial port was the Apple QuickTake 100, that could store up to 32 images at a resolution of 320x240 pixels on a flash memory. However, it was the Kodak DC40, introduced in 1995, that made the concept popular worldwide. In 1994, Epson introduced the Stylus Color, the world's first color inkjet printer that allowed households to print their own digital photos. Early digital cameras used an analog process to convert the image into a set of pixels. The process was originally invented at Bell Labs in 1969 by Willard Boyle and George Smith for computer data storage. Image sensors made of CMOS technology, the same technology used to make computer processors and computer memories, were invented in 1993 by Eric Fossum at NASA's Jet Propulsion Laboratory in southern California. Yet these Active Pixels Sensors (APS) would not become popular until the 2000s.

In a rare instance of cross-industry collaboration, IBM, Intel, Microsoft, Compaq, DEC, and others joined together to define a Universal Serial Bus (USB) for personal computers, eventually introduced in 1996. It would make it a lot easier to connect peripherals to computers, and it would enable gadgets such as digital cameras to be treated like computer peripherals. By 2009 more than three billion devices would have a USB port.

In 1982, a European consortium of national telecommunications agencies, notably France Telecom and Deutsche Bundespost, had joined to create a common standard for mobile phone communications, the Groupe Special Mobile (GSM). They had envisioned that every mobile phone would be equipped with an integrated circuit, called a Subscriber Identity Module (SIM) card, to contain information about the user, so that the information would be independent of the mobile phone and therefore portable across phones. The first SIM card was made in 1991 in Germany by Giesecke & Devrient for the Finnish wireless network operator Radiolinja, the one that launch the first GSM service (now renamed Global System for Mobile Communications), heralding the second generation (2G) of mobile telephony, which was digital instead of analogic. Meanwhile, Qualcomm in San Diego was developing a different technology, CDMA, launched in 1992, but adopted only in North America, and eventually sold to Japan's Kyocera.

Cell-phone technology came to the Bay Area in 1992, when Martin Cooper of Motorola established ArrayComm in San Jose to improve the capacity and coverage of cellular systems. While not particularly successful, ArrayComm would train and spread alumni in the region.

Smartphones to access the internet were in the making. Redwood City-based Unwired Planet (later renamed Phone.com and Openwave) pioneered a mobile Internet browser technology called a microbrowser. It developed Handheld Device Markup Language (HDML), basically an HTML for handheld devices. While most companies in the mobile-phone business were busy adopting the "push" paradigm of SMS, Openwave adopted its own "pull" paradigm. One year later Openwave and three giants of mobile communications (Ericsson, Motorola and Nokia) would turn HDML into WML (Wireless Markup Language), the international standard for cell phones to access the Internet.

Speech-recognition technology would turn out to be crucial for the user interfaces of mobile devices, and one of the main research centers was the old SRI International. Michael Cohen led a team that developed the technology used in the Air Travel Information System (ATIS), a project originally funded by the DARPA. The technology combined two in-house backgrounds, one in voice recognition and one in natural language processing. In 1994, Cohen quit and founded Nuance in Menlo Park; it would become one of the leaders in the sector. Nuance would be licensed by Siri for the Apple iPhone and Cohen would be hired by Google in 2004.

IBM versus Microsoft

Microsoft continued to dominate the operating-system market. In May 1990, Windows 3.0 finally had the success that had eluded previous versions of Windows. The difference was that Windows now boasted a vast portfolio of well-tested applications, starting with Microsoft's own Word, Excel, and Powerpoint. Windows 3.0 gained widespread third-party support. When 3.1 was released in April 1992, three million copies were sold in just two months. When Windows 95 was released in August 1995, the frenzy was even bigger. In 1991, Microsoft had revenues of $1,843,432,000 and 8,226 employees. Bill Gates was becoming one of the richest men in the country. More importantly, millions of computer users were abandoning the text commands of MS-DOS for the overlapping windows, the pull-down menus and the mouse clicks of Windows.

The holy alliance between IBM and Microsoft that had turned Microsoft into a software powerhouse came abruptly to an end in 1990. Microsoft realized that Windows 3.0 was a much more successful product than OS/2 could ever become. It was available on a lot more platforms, it was sold pre-loaded by a lot of computer manufacturers, and it boasted a fast-growing catalog of third-party applications. On the other hand, OS/2 was sponsored only by IBM and it was much more expensive. Microsoft decided to part ways and continue its focus on Windows. IBM had lost its grip on the computer industry: for 1992, it reported a loss of $4.96 billion, the highest in US history up to that point. In January 1993, as one stock kept rising while the other one kept plunging, Microsoft's market value ($26.78 billion) passed IBM's ($26.76 billion), though IBM still employed many more people and still had revenues of $64 billion. The market just didn't believe that IBM's business model had a future.

Digitalk and ParcPlace had introduced commercial versions of the object environment Smalltalk and had created a small but devoted following for it. In 1991 IBM launched its own Smalltalk-based project that in 1995 yielded the object-oriented environment VisualAge. Apple, in turn, had started Pink, a project to design an object-oriented operating system written in the object-oriented version of C, the C++ programming language. In 1992 IBM and Apple banded together and formed Taligent in Cupertino with the goal to complete Pink and port it to both platforms. The whole plan was widely viewed as an anti-Microsoft move, now that Microsoft was a common enemy. Again the project failed, but it yielded at least one intriguing idea: the "People, Places and Things" metaphor that provided procedures for these three categories to interact at a high level of conceptualization.

The onslaught of Windows could not be stopped. Microsoft became the largest software company in the world with annual sales in 1994 of over $4 billion. It even began to draw the attention of the US government, which feared a monopoly in software. The US government forced Microsoft to be less "evil" towards the competition, but it was only the beginning of a series of lawsuits and investigations into Microsoft practices both in the US and in Europe.

The rise of Microsoft and the decline of the traditional giants of IT came at a price: the shrinking research lab. When the IT and telecom worlds were ruled by the likes of IBM and AT&T, the research laboratories were huge and their ambitions were huge. Those labs invented the transistor, the Internet, the programming language, the operating system, the hard disk, the relational database, and Unix. Microsoft's research laboratories invented nothing. AT&T's descendants, the regional Bell companies and the new telecom companies, invented nothing. IBM and AT&T did not need to acquire other companies: their products came from their research labs. Microsoft and later Google bought their most famous products from startups. Their cash did not buy them great research teams: it bought them great intellectual-property lawyers who filed patents for countless trivial features of their products, a tactic meant to discourage competitors from venturing into the same areas of development. The Microsoft era was the era of the business plan: companies relied on a business plan, not on technological innovation, in order to achieve domination. No wonder that they did not produce anything comparable with the transistor or the many inventions of IBM.

In Silicon Valley, in particular, the rate at which companies were created and destroyed was one practical explanation for why the old-fashioned research lab became less and less viable. It was basically inherent to the Silicon Valley model of frenzied growth that no single company could afford to have a long-term plan, and especially one that was not focused on any one product. Life expectancy was very low. And the only way to prolong your life was to live day by day. It was the law of the wilderness transferred from the lawless towns of the Far West to the high-tech industry. That was, ultimately, the lesson learned from the experience of Xerox PARC.

Free Unix

While the great Unix wars were still going during 1991, a Finnish student named Linus Torvalds developed a new Unix kernel, called Linux. He equipped it with GNU tools when GNU did not offer a kernel yet. In this way Torvalds had accomplished what Stallman had advocated: a free and open-source version of Unix. However, initially the only support came from independents, certainly not from the big corporations who were fighting the Unix wars. In 1994, Marc Ewing, a graduate from Carnegie Mellon, completed his Red Hat Linux and started Red Hat in North Carolina. In January 1993 Novell itself bought all the rights to the Unix source code from AT&T for $150 million.

Storage

One company tried to compete with storage specialists such as the East-Coast giant EMC and the Japanese colossus Hitachi. Network Appliance was an Auspex spin-off founded in 1992 in Sunnyvale by David Hitz and James Lau. They conceived of data storage devices as a new type of appliance that could be shared by all the computers of a local area network. Data storage over Ethernet was a simple concept but also a gold mine that allowed NetApp to double revenues every year throughout the 1990s. Theirs was a Copernican revolution: instead of using expensive custom hardware to run a general-purpose operating system as fast as possible, they used standard hardware running proprietary software that did only one thing: store and retrieve data.

Enterprise Resource Planning (ERP)

ERP and supply chain management (SCM) were ripe for growth in the Bay Area. PeopleSoft added a financial module in 1992, pushing revenues up to $575 million in 1994. Next it added a manufacturing module in 1995, after acquiring the supply chain management system developed by Red Pepper Software, pushing revenues to $816 million in 1997. It was one of the most sensational success stories of the client-server era. Red Pepper had been founded in 1993 in San Mateo by Monte Zweben, a former scientist at NASA's Ames Research Center, where he had developed an artificial intelligence-based scheduling system for NASA's Kennedy Space Center.

In 1993 former Oracle sales executive Thomas Siebel started Siebel to market a software application for sales force automation, the first step towards customer relationship management (CRM). Meanwhile, in 1992, SAP had launched R/3, moving its ERP system from the mainframe to a three-tiered client-server architecture and to a relational database. It was an immediate success. In 1994 SAP's revenues increased 66% and then 47% the following year to $1.9 billion, three times what they had been in 1991.

Competing Economic Models

In 1991, the US computer industry posted its first "trade deficit:" more computer technology was imported than exported in dollar value. The dynamics of the various regions were wildly different. In the US, the computer industry was constantly changing, with large companies disappearing overnight and new giants emerging almost as quickly. In Europe, on the other hand, the computer market was dominated by old bloated companies: Nixdorf in Germany, Bull in France, ICL in Britain, and Olivetti in Italy.

The Europeans had generally been more eager to jump on the bandwagon of "open systems," despite the fact that their revenues largely depended on proprietary custom design, notably in operating systems. Their business model typically emphasized the one-stop shopping experience for their customers, and those customers were typically very large businesses (notably banks).

Europeans preferred to sell "solutions" rather than individual pieces of hardware and software, a solution being a tailored combination of hardware and software. For many years these components had been made in house. It was basically a scaled-down and nationalistic version of the IBM business model. They could successfully compete against IBM because of two factors: political protection from national governments, and national non-English languages in an age in which only a tiny minority of Europeans understood English. They all employed hardware and software from the US, but they made a point of changing the name and the interface to turn it into a proprietary product. Their products could be very creative. Olivetti, in particular, had developed a Unix-like real-time operating system, Multi-functional Operating System (MOS), designed by Alessandro Osnaghi and initially implemented at their Cupertino labs. They mostly endorsed Unix as an alternative to IBM and joined the Open Systems Foundation.

However, the large computer manufacturers of Europe had started declining rapidly. In 1982, Bull was nationalized by the French government. In 1990, German conglomerate giant Siemens acquired Nixdorf, the Japanese conglomerate Fujitsu acquired 80% of ICL, and Olivetti struggled to survive (it would capitulate in the mid-1990s). The transition to open systems turned out to be a form of mass suicide.

Europe did not fare much better in the realm of software: only SAP began a worldwide power, dominating the ERP sector even in the US. Japan managed to become a powerhouse of hardware but failed to make a dent in software.

However, it was unclear where the US computer industry derived its advantage. After all, the World-wide Web was "invented" at CERN by a pan-European team, and Finland was the first country to implement a GSM network. If one had to name a region that was forward-looking, it wouldn't be Silicon Valley but Switzerland, the world's most energy-efficient economy, that had pioneered both "greentech" (renewable energy, "green" buildings, waste management, sustainable transportation) and biotech since the late 1980s. Nonetheless, only a specialist in Swiss affairs could name a Swiss company, and even that specialist would probably not be able to name a single Swiss invention of the era.

The overall economic model clearly played a role. The German economic model favored gradual innovation and long-term planning (the kind of thinking that was useful, say, in metallurgy). In contrast, the US model favored disruptive innovation in real time. Silicon Valley was the ultimate implementation of the US philosophy.

At the same time, the Silicon Valley model was not just unbridled capitalism as often depicted elsewhere. For example, in 1993 leaders from government, business, academia, and the community established the Joint Venture Silicon Valley Network. They sponsored the Economic Development Roundtable (later renamed the Silicon Valley Economic Development Alliance) and other initiatives to make the region as business-friendly as possible, while another spin-off, Smart Valley, helped schools, local government and community centers get on the Internet.

Intel benefited from the booming market for personal computers, and in 1992 became the world's largest semiconductor company, ahead of NEC and Toshiba. Its revenues had doubled in five years, reaching $8 billion. It was taking its revenge against the Japanese that almost bankrupted it a few years earlier.

Biotech
Because of the success of Genentech, the biotech industry was expanding in the Bay Area, albeit at a modest pace. In 1990 Michael West from the University of Texas' Southwestern Medical Center in Dallas started Geron with funding from oil-industry tycoon Miller Quarles. He wanted a "cure" aging (in other words, discover immortality). In 1992, the company relocated to Menlo Park, where West had found more venture capital. In 1998, Geron's scientists, led by Calvin Harley, would isolate human embryonic stem cells but never get any closer to marketing immortality. In 1992, Calgene, a spin-off of UC Davis, near Sacramento, created the "Flavr Savr" tomato, the first Genetically Manufactured Food (GMF) to be sold in stores.

The science of biotech itself, however, was progressing rapidly. First, the Human Genome Project was finally underway. In 1992, the saga of Craig Venter began. Venter was raised in the San Francisco peninsula and had joined the National Institutes of Health in Maryland, which at the time still run by James Watson as a traditional biomedical center. In 1992 Venter, frustrated that the center wouldn't move faster towards automation of genetic processing, quit his job and the Human Genome Project to set up The Institute for Genomic Research (TIGR) a few kilometers away, in Rockville. It was funded by venture capitalist Wallace Steinberg of New Jersey with $70 million over seven years and staffed with many of Venter's old coworkers at the NIH. Meanwhile, Steinberg hired William Haseltine, who had pioneered research on AIDS at Harvard University since the 1970s in collaboration with Robert Gallo of the National Cancer Institute, who a few years later would discover the cause of AIDS, HIV. Steinberg put Haseltine in charge of a new company named Human Genome Sciences (HGS), the business plan being that Venter's TIGR would create a database of genetic information and Haseltine's HGS would sell it to pharmaceutical companies.

This was a bold plan because until then no biomedical company had ever made a profit by simply selling information. It corresponded to a vision of future medicine as "bioinformatics." In 1993, HGS sold its genetic database to SmithKline Beecham for $125 million. In 1995 Robert Fleischmann of TIGR used research by Nobel laureate Hamilton Smith of Johns Hopkins University in nearby Baltimore to sequence or "map" the genome of a free-living organism, the bacterium Haemophilus Influenzae, responsible for ear infections. This success triggered a series of genome sequencing projects around the US.

Other researchers were working hard at products too. Stephen Fodor was doing research at the Affymax Research Institute, a pharmaceutical company founded in 1988 by Alza's Zaffaroni in Palo Alto, on fabricating DNA chips using the same manufacturing techniques used to make semiconductors. Meanwhile, Peter Schultz was a pioneer in combinatorial chemistry at the Lawrence Berkeley Lab. They both wanted to overcome the slow pace at which genetic testing was carried out and find a method for simultaneously testing thousands of molecules. With help from Zaffaroni, the duo started Affymetrix in Santa Clara in 1992 to produce "gene-chips," the biological equivalent of electronic chips, by printing a huge number of DNA molecules on a silicon wafer. The first DNA chip came out in 1994. Along the same lines in 1992 South African-born geneticist Sydney Brenner joined Applied Biosystems' founder Sam Eletr to start Lynx Therapeutics in Hayward. The company developed a massively parallel method for simultaneous interrogation of multiple DNA samples in a single test.

After the Human Genome Project had enumerated all human genes, the next step would be to understand what those genes mean. Molecular Applications Group, founded in 1993 in Palo Alto by Stanford's biologists Michael Levitt and Christopher Lee, applied the techniques of data-mining software to genetic information in order to help biotech companies figure out the function of a protein from its DNA.

The business potential of human-genome science was obvious from the beginning to pharmaceutical companies: knowing how the genome works would allow medicine to understand which ones cause which diseases, and possibly how to cure them.

The first "genomic" startup to have an IPO was the invention of a New York venture-capital firm. In 1991 a group had acquired a St Louis-based biotech startup, Invitron, founded by scientist Randall Scott. Then they had transformed it into Incyte Pharmaceuticals, a Palo Alto startup. In 1994 Incyte launched a service for personal genomics, LifeSeq. It was accessible by yearly subscription for several million dollars and basically contained two databases: a catalog of genes of the genome, and a catalog of where each was expressed and what its probable function was. LifeSeq had actually been constructed for Incyte by consulting biotech firm Pangea Systems. Pangea later introduced a search engine for genetic databases, and eventually put it online as DoubleTwist.

Another major sequence repository for bioinformatics was GenBank (Genetic Sequence Data Bank), created in 1982 as a successor to Los Alamos' Sequence Database. It was maintained for a while by IntelliGenetics until 1989 when it was assigned to the newly created National Center for Biology Information. Finally, UniGene was a database of transcript sequences, also maintained by the National Center for Biotechnology Information.

Some progress was made in "solving" aging. In 1993, Cynthia Kenyon, a pupil of Brenner at Cambridge University now at UCSF, discovered that a single-gene mutation could double the lifespan of the roundworm Caenorhabditis Elegans. This finding stimulated research in the molecular biology of aging.

The media focused on biotechnology for pharmaceutical applications ("red biotech") and for genetically-modified food ("green biotech"). But there was also a third application: biotechnology to produce biochemicals, biomaterials, and biofuels from renewable resources ("white biotech").

This latter technology was based on fermentation and biocatalysis. It typically required "bioreactors" fueled with tailored micro-organisms (e.g. yeast, fungi and bacteria) to convert crops or other organic materials into sugars and then into useful chemicals. The "products" of white biotech ranged from sophisticated ingredients for red and green biotech to bulk chemicals such as biofuels. The promise was to replace the synthetic, petroleum-based materials that had become popular in the 20th century with biodegradable materials. These would also require less energy to manufacture and create less waste when disposed.

Greentech

Another nascent industry had to do with energy: fuel cells. Their promise was to open an era of environmentally clean power plants. In 1991 United Technologies Corporation, a large East-Coast defense contractor, became the first company to market a fuel-cell system, mainly used by NASA in the Space Shuttle. Meanwhile, research on lithium batteries at the Lawrence Berkeley Lab spawned the startup PolyPlus Battery, which opened offices in Berkeley in 1991.

The Anthropology of the Digital Frontier

Ironically, all the technological changes had not changed the nature of society in Silicon Valley all that much. It still embedded the "frontier" model: most individuals were single and male. Most immigrants were male, whether coming illegally from Mexico to clean swimming pools or legally from India to write software. The main difference from the old days of the frontier was that they, at some point, would bring their wives with them. The national immigrants, coming from other states of the US, were mostly male at the lab level and almost exclusively male in the engineering and executive jobs. Graduates from San Jose State University in the late 1990s were still only 18% female. Women, however, did not just stay home: more and more women studied business, law, and marketing, all professions that could potentially lead to highly paid jobs. The "saloon," too, had changed dramatically: the new saloon was itinerant, located at the home or in a bar where a party was being thrown, and the party was often meant as a business opportunity (an event to find a new job, not an event to find a wife).

Spare time was still limited, with many people working weekends and even holidays. The standard package granted only two weeks of vacation, and immigrants used them mostly to visit family back home. The real vacation often came in the form of a "sabbatical" of six or twelve months. It was difficult to take a few days off during a product's lifecycle. It was easier to just take six months and be replaced by someone else during that period. At the same time there was increased pressure to know the world, because business was increasingly international. And the world was increasingly the countries touched by the Pacific Ocean, not the Atlantic Ocean.

After many venture capitalists moved to Menlo Park in the 1980s and Palo Alto in the 1990s, San Francisco lost its role as the financial center of the Bay Area. It resumed its old role as the entertainment hub for the frontier. Silicon Valley engineers and entrepreneurs moved to San Francisco for, essentially, the nightlife. Compared with the sterilized and structured lifestyle of Silicon Valley, where people's main forms of entertainment were the gym and the movie theater (or, at home, the videogame and the video) and everything closed at 10PM, San Francisco promised a "wild" lifestyle.

However, Palo Alto itself was rapidly becoming an ideal concentration of restaurants, cafes and stores, most of them lining up on University Avenue, the continuation of Stanford University's Palm Drive. It had lost its "student town" charm and become one of the most expensive places to live. The nearby Stanford Shopping Center was becoming the most celebrated shopping experience in the whole Bay Area.

Mountain View, which historically had no fewer influential startups, proceeded to create something similar to University Avenue in its "intellectual" heart, Castro Street. It was originally lined with bookstores, via a seven-block renovation project that ended in 1990.

Culture and Society

The marriage of the World-wide Web and of the utopian WELL culture recast old debates about personal freedom into the new distributed and government-operated digital medium. Notably, the Electronic Frontier Foundation was formed in San Francisco in July 1990 by three people: Lotus founder Mitch Kapor; John Perry Barlow, a former lyricist for the Grateful Dead now turned libertarian activist; and by Usenet and GNU veteran John Gilmore, to defend civil liberties on the Internet.

In 1993 Kevin Kelly, the publisher of the "Whole Earth Review", co-founded the magazine "Wired", where he continued to deal with the interaction of technology, culture and society. It had been preceded by a far more radical publication, "Mondo 2000," started in 1989 by Ken Goffman in Berkeley. It was a glossy magazine devoted to underground cyberculture that dealt with both the technology of the Internet age and the "smart drugs" of the rave age.

The 1990s were the age of the raves, all-night dance parties often held illegally in abandoned warehouses. The longest economic expansion in the history of the US helped fuel the decade-long party. The music scene expanded dramatically yielding not pop stars but all sorts of alternative concepts: prog-rock trio Primus, folk-rock combo Red House Painters, acid-rock project Subarachnoid Space, stoner-rockers Sleep, the surreal electroacoustic act of the Thessalonians and electronic/digital composer Pamela Z.

The visual arts were also expanding dramatically, fueled by a growing art market. A new generation of art galleries emerged in the early 1990s, such as the Catharine Clark Gallery and the Yerba Buena Center for the Arts. San Francisco continued to specialize in creating niche, subculture movements, as opposed to high-brow art and music. The 1990s witnessed a boom in mural and graffiti art, notably Ricardo "Rigo 23" Gouveia, Margaret Kilgallen, Barry McGee ("Twist") and Ruby "Reminisce" Neri. Students from the San Francisco Art Institute originated the "Mission School," an art movement centered in the Mission district that was inspired more by street art than by museum art. They often built their artworks with found objects. Chris Johanson emerged from this crowd. In 1990 even the San Francisco main dump began a program of artists in residence. Harrell Fletcher and Jon Rubin, both students at the College of Arts and Crafts, opened a "gallery" in Oakland where they created art installations about the neighborhood using neighborhood residents. In 1995 Amy Franceschini founded the artist collective Futurefarmers to promote participatory art projects.

San Francisco was also becoming the hub of one of the most vibrant design schools in the world, due to designers such as the four Michaels: Michael Vanderbyl, Michael Manwaring, Michael Cronin and Michael Mabry. While the first graphic designer to embrace the Macintosh was April Greiman in Los Angeles, San Francisco was the base of Rudy Vanderlans, who started Emigre (the first major magazine that used the Mac), and of John Hersey, another pioneer of computer-based graphic design.

However, the Bay Area that had witnessed the hippies and the punks was falling into the hands of high-tech nerds. As its universities graduated thousands of software and hardware engineers every year, thousands more immigrated into the area. The age witnessed another wave of immigration of youth from all over the world, just like 30 years earlier. But, unlike in 1966, this time the drivers were not "peace and love" but vanity and greed.

The metropolitan area of the Bay Area expanded dramatically in all directions, but especially southward and eastward. Its population was cosmopolitan and young. Agriculture had definitely been wiped out. The demographic change made the Bay Area even more tolerant and open-minded. In 1993, the political science professor Condoleezza Rice became Stanford University's youngest, first female, and first non-white provost.

24. Funder Builders: The Heyday of Venture Capital (1978-2000)

Venture Capital after the New ERISA Rules, 1978-1990

The big money came into venture capital a second time after government action. In 1978, venture capital experienced its first major fundraising year, as the industry raised approximately $750 million. Two government-related factors were important. First, in 1978 Congress cut capital gains taxes from 49.5% to 28% per the 1978 Revenue Act, encouraging investing. Second and more importantly, in 1979 the US Labor Department relaxed certain of the ERISA restrictions, under the "prudent man rule," thus allowing corporate pension funds to invest in riskier asset classes like venture capital. Pension funding rose from $100-200 million annually in the 1970s to an amount greater than $4 billion by the end of the 1980s.

The public successes of the venture capital industry in the 1970s and early 1980s (e.g., Digital Equipment Corporation, Apple Inc., Genentech) fueled the creation of many new venture capital investment firms. From around 225 firms in 1979, there were over 650 firms by the end of the 1980s. Each firm searched for the next Apple Computer. While the number of firms multiplied, the capital managed by these firms increased by only 11% from $28 billion to $31 billion over the course of the decade.

Still, the 1980s were difficult times. The growth of the industry lead to poor deals with bad pricing: VCs funded bad projects led by inexperienced entrepreneurs. Venture capitalists overinvested and started under-monitoring companies. Returns started declining and venture firms began posting losses for the first time. In addition to the increased competition among firms, several other factors hurt returns. The market for initial public offerings cooled off in the mid-1980s before collapsing after the 1987 stock market crash. Also foreign companies, particularly from Japan and Korea, flooded early stage companies with capital.

Investor herding was very clear in the Winchester disk drive industry. During the late 1970s and early 1980s, venture capitalists invested $400 million in 43 disk drive companies. Many went public, and companies raised $800 million through IPOs in 1983. By mid-1983, the twelve publically traded disk drive companies had a market value of $5.4 billion, a 4x sales-to-earnings ratio, and a 50x price-to-earnings ratio. But by the end of the year, profits fell by 98% and the market cap of those 12 fell to $1.4 billion.

The industry changed in response to the changing conditions. US corporations that had sponsored in-house venture investment arms, including General Electric and Paine Webber, either sold off or closed these arms. Additionally, venture capital arms within Chemical Bank and Continental Illinois National Bank, among others, began shifting their focus. They went from funding early stage companies toward investments in more mature, "growth" companies. Industry founders J.H. Whitney & Company and Warburg Pincus began to transition toward leveraged buyouts and growth capital, following KKR and Foerstmann Little.

Two young investors stood out in the 1980s and 1990s. Both became partners at KPCB: John Doerr and Vinod Khosla.

Doerr grew up in Missouri, studied electrical engineering at Rice, and earned his Harvard MBA in 1976. He was an engineer and project manager at Intel and then got bored. He talked his way onto the sales team and became one of the top salesmen. Once, to close a microprocessor deal, he even threw a lawnmower into a deal. After Intel, Doerr joined KPCB in 1980, funding companies such as Compaq, Netscape, Symantec, SUN Microsystems, drugstore.com, Amazon.com, Intuit, and Google, as well as failures such as Friendster and Go.

After joining KPCB, Doerr would hang out in Stanford's Margaret Jacks Hall and talk with engineers and scientists about their work. He attended the meetings of the Computer Forum, entrepreneurship clubs, and conferences of various kinds to meet inventors like Jim Clark, Forrest Baskett, and Andy Bechtolsheim. Doerr engaged former Stanford faculty and alums, who then referred their students to him. Doerr went on to back key people who would become famous entrepreneurial names, such as: Larry Page, Sergey Brin, Eric Schmidt (Google); Jeff Bezos (Amazon); Scott Cook, Bill Campbell (Intuit); Andy Bechtolsheim, Scott McNealy, Bill Joy, & Vinod Khosla (Sun).

Doerr was known for his frenetic, almost superhuman energy. He was a rail-thin man in slacks and a rumpled blue blazer, with a lump of hair falling across his forehead. As SUN CEO Scott McNealy once said about Doerr: "John Doerr is the Eveready Bunny on steroids and hardwired to the Hoover Dam power plant. He burns brighter than mere mortals yet is one of the most human people I know. Everyone should have a friend like John." Doerr drove a minivan and flew in a private jet. Sometimes people saw him rushing to a conference, simultaneously holding a conversation with others around him and talking on a cell-phone and tapping an e-mail on another. Doerr would state that his most important criterion in looking at a company was the quality of the team: "I always turn to the biographies of the team first. For me, it's team, team, team." Doerr believed it wasn't just the individual people that mattered, but their sum as a team, their mix of experience, personalities, and chemistry. Great teams had ideally worked together before and were in short supply.[34]

Doerr also followed Tom Perkin's philosophy in taking an active role in venture investing, in being a "company builder" and not just a banker. He conceptualized his role as assembling new teams of entrepreneurs and scientists, or funding good "speedup" teams like Intuit, Amazon.com, and Shiva. He saw his role as a recruiter who entrepreneurs paid in stock for the right to help them build a team. All parties worked like crazy to make the stock valuable. One example was Jim Clark starting Netscape, who had more than enough money to build the team himself. However, Clark needed the help in team-building, and so put together a team with Doerr within 20 days after a financing round: five vice-presidents and a CEO. Within two years they had a hundred million dollars of revenue in a quarter and were the 18th largest software company and the most rapidly growing ever.[35]

One of Doerr's coups was recruiting an entrepreneur to leave his company and join Doerr's own team as a partner at KPCB.

Vinod Khosla grew up in New Delhi, India and received degrees from IIT Delhi, Carnegie Mellon, and the Stanford GSB. He founded his first startup, Daisy Systems, after finishing his MBA, and in 1982 he founded SUN Microsystems along with his Stanford classmates Scott McNealy and Andy Bechtolsheim, along with UC Berkeley computer science graduate student Bill Joy. Khosla served as the first Chairman and CEO of SUN Microsystems from 1982 to 1984, when he left the company to become a venture capitalist, eventually joining KPCB in 1986 due to Doerr's invitation.

While at KPCB, Khosla and other partners at the firm took over on Intel's monopoly with Nexgen/AMD (the only microprocessor to have significant success against Intel, sold to AMD for 28% of AMD). Then Khosla helped incubate the idea and business plan for Juniper Networks to successfully take on Cisco's dominance of the router market. Finally, Khosla was also involved in the formulation of the very early advertising based search strategy for Excite, and from there also helped to transform the moribund telecommunications business and its archaic SONET implementations with Cerent (sold to Cisco for $7 billion). In 2004, Khosla left KPCB to form Khosla Ventures. He was driven by the need for flexibility and a desire to be more experimental, to fund sometimes imprudent "science experiments," and to take on both "for profit" and for "social impact" ventures. Khosla was not always a success: he played a key role with several of the tech industry's most spectacular failures, including Asera, Dynabook, and others.

[34] Malone, Michael S. "John Doerr's Startup Manual." Fast Company, February 28, 1997. http://www.fastcompany.com/magazine/07/082doerr.html.
[35] Brockman, John. "The Coach: John Doerr." Edge Digerati. http://www.edge.org/digerati/doerr/index.html.

The Venture Capital Funding Process

Venture capitalists are selective in their investments, conducting wide but not necessarily deep due diligence. A venture capital firm may receive thousands of solicitations a year, conduct a few hundred meetings, and invest in 2 to 6 companies a year. One estimate from the Kauffman Foundation is that less than 1% of ~600,000 new employer businesses created in the US every year take venture funding. Only 16% of companies had venture funding of those in the Inc. 500 list of fastest growing young companies from 1997-2007.

Venture capitalists have tried to articulate what they search for, and this seems to vary. One top venture investor, Bill Gurley of Benchmark Capital, listed the following as key points he wanted to learn initially about a company in meetings:

- Quality of the idea – this is from both an economic standpoint and a defensibility standpoint.
- Quality of the founder(s) – smart, motivated, goal oriented (or as Doriot said: "You will get nowhere if you do not inspire people.")
- Mode of operation – frugal vs. excessive.

Gurley's claim was that all the multi-billion dollar companies started in Silicon Valley after 1960 had venture funds backing them, with few exceptions like Salesforce.com and Siebel. Another venture capitalist, Ray Rothrock of Venrock, examined profit and loss forecasts, unit analysis, and projected balance sheets, but most importantly, wanted a strong team and large new market. Generally venture firms sought target returns in the 40% to 80% range, depending on the stage of financing. Finally, John Doerr of KPCB searched for four factors in new ventures: missionary, not mercenary, leaders who were top-notch and passionate; large, rapidly-growing and under-served markets; reasonable levels of financing; and team execution with a sense of urgency, as time was the most important resource for the technorati.

There were typically six stages of financing offered by venture firms, and this roughly corresponded to the stages of a company's development (dollar amounts below are approximate):

- Seed Money: Low level financing of $50,000 to $1 million, this was used to prove a new idea, and could be provided by angels or smaller venture firms;
- Start-up: Early stage firms that needed funding of $500,000 to $2 million for expenses associated with marketing and product development;
- First Round: Funding for early manufacturing and sales, usually $1 million to $10 million;
- Second Round: Working capital in the $2 million to $20 million for early stage companies that were selling products/services but were not yet turning a profit;

- Third Round: Also called mezzanine financing, this was expansion money for a newly profitable company, and could range from $5 million to $50 million.
- Fourth Round: Also called bridge financing, this financed the "going public" process, and could range from $5 million to $100 million or more.

Because there were no public exchanges listing their securities, private companies met venture capital firms and other private equity investors in several ways, including: warm referrals from the investors' trusted sources and other business contacts; investor conferences and symposia; and summits where companies pitched directly to investor groups in face-to-face meetings.

So what was the value-add of a venture capitalist in a world of creative destruction? As Don Valentine stated, most venture capitalists have to fund companies started by newbies, twenty-somethings with no prior management experience. Hence the venture capitalist helped the young CEO/founder learn how to manage, rent a building, pick a health insurance plan, find sales prospects, and generally access an infrastructure of other services. People like Valentine helped the founders get introduced to "a great lawyer, a great banker, a great search firm, a great accounting firm" and so on. They made these basic things easy for people who had never done it before and didn't particularly care about these crucial but boring details.[36]

In the case of DEC and Doriot, Olsen reached out to Doriot for advice on numerous issues, including hiring senior people, marketing products, and dealing with bankers. For example, one piece of advice Doriot gave regarding marketing, according to Harlan Anderson, was to not lay a circuit board on a bare desk, but to put it on a sheet of purple velvet, like a jeweler.

So what made for a successful venture investor? Dick Kramlich of NEA once said in an interview: "If you look at what makes a good venture capitalist, my view is this: On a spectrum of intuition and analysis, you ought to be two-thirds intuition, one-third analysis." Kramlich believed intuition is honed over time by making mistakes, and that one of the biggest mistakes was waiting too long for all the information to come in. One interesting point that Bill Draper added was time focus. Most venture capitalists tend to spend money on their bad companies, the duds, to save principal. However a better strategy was to focus on the winners. Basically, Kramlich suggested investors ought to kill or neglect the sick early on and focus on the strong.

---

[36] Valentine, Donald T. "Interview with Don Valentine," Silicon Genesis: An Oral History of Semiconductor Technology. April 21, 2004, Menlo Park, California.
http://silicongenesis.stanford.edu/transcripts/valentine.htm.

The Internet Boom and Bust

By the end of the 1980s, venture capital returns were relatively low, especially in comparison with their leveraged buyout brethren which had a debt-fueled decade of success. Venture firms had competed for hot startups, had taken poor companies into IPOs, and had generally destroyed capital.

After a shakeout of venture capital managers, the more successful firms retrenched. They focused on improving operations at their portfolio companies rather than continuously making new investments. Results would begin to turn very attractive, successful and would ultimately generate the venture capital boom of the 1990s. Professor Andrew Metrick once referred to the 1980-1995 period as the "pre-boom period" in anticipation of the boom that would begin in 1995 and last through the bursting of the Internet bubble in 2000.

The late 1990s were a boom time for venture capital, as firms on Sand Hill Road in Menlo Park and Silicon Valley benefited from a huge surge of interest in the nascent Internet and other computer technologies. IPOs of stock for technology and other growth companies soared and venture firms posted large returns.

The prototypical "dot-com" company's business model relied on a network effect business model, like railroads or telephone companies which own a network and have a de facto monopoly. The internet company would operate at a sustained net loss to build market share (mind share, click-throughs, impressions, etc.). These companies offered their services or end product for free, expecting they could build enough brand awareness and users to charge for services or ads later. During the loss period, the companies relied on venture capital and especially initial public offerings of stock to pay their expenses while having no source of income at all. The amount of cash they consumed for a unit of time (week, quarter, year) was their "burn rate," and their "runway" was the period of time they had till they consumed all their cash and went bust. The novelty of the technologies these companies touted, combined with the difficulty of valuing the companies, sent many stocks to dizzying heights. Entrepreneurs became very rich, as did venture capitalists. On paper.

Yet many companies failed due to excess. Some great examples of investor excess during the boom were:

- Webvan.com, which tried to sell groceries through the internet; it burned through $375 million in 3 years, was valued at $1.2 billion at the top of the bubble before going bust within 12 months and firing 2,000 employees.
- Kozmo.com, a competitor to Webvan trying delivery services, which raised $280 million from investors and went bust 2 years later, also firing 2,000 people.

- Pets.com, a pet supply store, which lost $147 million in 9 months in 2000 and then fired its 300 employees who were mostly hired the year before.
- eToys.com, which racked up $247 million of debt before going bust in 2001.
- Drkoop.com, started by a Reagan-era Surgeon General, which raised $89 million in its 1999 IPO only to go bust in 2001.
- Boo.com, which spent $188 million in just six months in an attempt to create a global online fashion store; it went bankrupt in May 2000 and sold its assets for $2 million.
- Startups.com, which was the "ultimate dot-com startup"; it went out of business in 2002. No one knew what the company would sell.
- GeoCities, which was purchased by Yahoo! for $3.6 billion in January 1999. Yahoo! closed GeoCities on October 26, 2009.
- GovWorks.com, the doomed dot-com featured in the documentary film Startup.com, which went from dozens of employees to bust.
- Hotmail, founded by Sabeer Bhatia, which was sold to Microsoft for $400 million; at that time Hotmail had 9 million members.
- InfoSpace, which had stock in March 2000 at a price of $1,305 per share, but by April 2001 its price had crashed down to $22 a share.
- The Learning Company, which was bought by Mattel in 1999 for $3.5 billion; sold for $27.3 million in 2000.
- Broadcast.com, which was sold by its owner Mark Cuban to Yahoo for $5.7 billion in 1999; it was later shut down.

Historically, the dot-com boom can be seen as similar to a number of other technology-inspired booms of the past including railroads in the 1840s, automobiles and radio in the 1920s, transistor electronics in the 1950s, and biotech in the 1980s.

The Nasdaq crash and technology slump that started in March 2000 shook virtually the entire venture capital industry as valuations for startup technology companies collapsed. Over the next two years, many venture firms had been forced to write-off large proportions of their investments and many funds were significantly "under water" (the values of the fund's investments were below the amount of capital invested). Venture capital investors sought to reduce the size of commitments they had made to venture capital funds and in numerous instances, investors sought to unload existing commitments for cents on the dollar in the secondary market.

The post-boom years represented just a small fraction of the peak levels of venture investment reached in 2000. Yet funding was still greater than the levels of investment from 1980 through 1995. As a percentage of GDP, venture investment was 0.058% percent in 1994, peaked at 1.087% (nearly 19x the 1994 level) in 2000 and ranged from 0.164% to 0.182 % in 2003 and 2004. The revival of an Internet-driven environment, due to deals such as eBay's purchase of Skype, the News Corporation's purchase of MySpace.com, and the very successful Google.com and Salesforce.com IPOs, helped revive the venture capital environment.

Two types of venture investors epitomized the 1990s. The first was the institutional type, exemplified by Benchmark Capital. Benchmark was founded in 1995 by a few venture capitalists, including Bob Kagle from TVI, Andy Rachleff and Bruce Dunlevie from Merill Pickard, and the entrepreneur Kevin Harvey. Benchmark's initial $5 million investment in eBay was worth over $4 billion in mid-1999, at the boom's peak. The five Benchmark partners focused on early-stage companies and had other hits such as Ariba, PlanetRx, and Scient. They had an equal partnership structure, and asked limited partners for a premium (30%) carry payout. One interesting philosophical point of theirs was that venture capital is a service business more than an investment business, that the entrepreneurs are at the center of the universe and the venture capitalists serve them.

The second type of venture investor was the lone investor with operating experience, exemplified by Kavitark Ram Shriram. He was a founding board member and one of the first angels in Google. Shriram grew up in Chennai, India, went to Michigan for his MBA, and then worked in Bell Northern Research Labs. He came to the Valley in the early 1980s because of the much better weather than freezing Minnesota. He then left the corporate world for a series of startups. He joined Netscape in 1994 before they shipped products or posted revenue. He drove the many partnerships and channels that Netscape employed to get distribution for its browser and server products. Netscape was a place where he learned about the momentum that came from two key things: a young team of driven tech people working till 2-3AM in the morning; and the size of a market opportunity where "we could taste blood. That gives you an adrenalin rush like no other."Shriram left as Netscape fell apart and founded Junglee in 1997, which Amazon.com bought in 1998. He served as an officer of Amazon.com working for Jeff Bezos.

Shriram invested in Google after David Cheriton, a Stanford computer science professor, gave the founders a $100,000 check written on the porch of his home (other early investors were Andy Bechtolsheim and Ron Conway). Shriram at one point owned a few million shares, and invested in InMobi, StumbleUpon, Zazzle, & Mevio. Ram Shriram started Sherpalo in 2000 to fund early stage ventures.

Shriram's basic philosophy as an investor was that you needed to be prepared and in the right space; then you needed to get lucky. As he expounded in a radio interview, an entrepreneur needs to both work hard and get lucky. But getting lucky meant preparing and strategically being in the right place. Shriram said "I can't say I got lucky at Netscape, I got lucky at Amazon, I got lucky at Google; it doesn't happen that way. You typically will need to be discriminating enough to find the right opportunity."

Shriram's best single investment of the late 1990s, a serendipitous angel check to Google, was a highly uncertain bet. He couldn't tell how big the opportunity was, he didn't know the revenue model, and he couldn't even see the execution challenges. But focusing on execution was what mattered and "luck plays a small role. If you put all your eggs in the luck basket, then you should just go play the lottery."[37]

The toughest thing, however, was learning to live with mistakes, especially painful and costly ego and people mistakes. A venture capitalist both needed a healthy ego and needed to keep it in check and listen so he could learn. People issues mattered most as a "lot of mistakes that go on in the life of the company have to do with people judgments. The hardest thing is people judgments." Finding people for the right stage of the company, both in hiring and firing, was the hardest. Often having the founder step aside for a professional CEO could be a difficult challenge.[38]

Other examples of famous lone investors included David Cheriton of Stanford (the world's only billionaire professor still teaching full-time), Peter Thiel (of eBay, Facebook, and LinkedIn fame), Ron Conway, Esther Dyson, Chris Dixon, and so on.

---

[37] Bhatt, Kamla. "Listen to Google's first investor." LiveMint, December 4, 2008. http://www.livemint.com/Articles/PrintArticle.aspx?artid=507C367E-C1E7-11DD-AB22-000B5DABF613.
[38] Ibid.

25. Dot Com Failures: Startups that Went Bust in the Tech Boom (1991-2000)

The Tech Boom and Startup Failures

All bubbles are the same; yet specific bubble assets may vary from government bonds to railroad shares, or from technology stocks to mortgage securities and houses. Also, charlatans and fraudsters mix with genuine innovators who fumbled upon a product or business model that satisfied consumers' needs.

Charles Kindleberger documented a pattern behind bubbles in his 1978 book titled "Manias, Panics, and Crashes." First a displacement of some sort comes, like a new technology or practice, such as the transcontinental railroad or the Internet/Web technology. This radically improves the outlook for a segment of the economy. People take advantage of the opportunity, fueling a boom that fuels itself on easy access to cash. For railroads, promoters sold stock and bonds to far-away European investors. For the Internet, early venture capitalists cashed out large sums of money only to raise a hundred times more from far-away East Coast investors to speculate with.

The positive feedback loop continues till there is pure speculation – assets are bought only to be sold at a higher price to other buyers in heat, with prices completely removed from any indicators of fundamental value like revenues, earnings, or dividends. Often promoters invent dubious metrics. For railroads, track miles laid was often used, without any reference to the value of moving freight over those miles (a railroad to nowhere moving nothing will take investors nowhere). For the Internet, dubious measures like page impressions and click-throughs were used to justify outrageous future revenue potential and so valuations.

Finally, speculation runs its course and a quick downturn ensues. Swindles make the news. This leads to revulsion and a complete drying up of funds, a negative feedback loop that is sharp and discontinuous, inducing a selling panic. For railroads, stock price crashes led to revelations of management embezzlement or poor stewardship. For the Internet, after stock option vesting periods ended, insiders cashed out and left companies burning cash on a quick trail to bankruptcy.

After the technology bubble burst, many traded Internet companies lost 75%+ of their 52-week market capitalization high price; most trimmed expenses or laid off workers. It was rare to see an industry evaporate as quickly and completely as Web stocks did. In 2000, CNNfn.com asked the research firm Birinyi Associates to calculate the market value of the 280 stocks in the Bloomberg US Internet Index at their respective 52-week highs and their 2000 market value. The combined market values of the 280 stocks had fallen to $1.19 trillion from $2.95 trillion at their peak. The loss was $1.76 trillion.

However, not all failed companies are obviously flawed. Most had a plausible premise or genuine innovation that never quite met their customers' pain points and willingness to pay, or they were too early to the market. This chapter presents six examples of investor excess and entrepreneurial fumbling during the 1990s Tech Bubble:

- Webvan.com, which tried to sell groceries through the Internet; it burned through $375 million in 3 years, was valued at $1.2 billion at the top of the bubble before going bust within 12 months and laying off 2,000 employees.
- eToys.com, which racked up $247 million of debt before going bust in 2001.
- Pets.com, which in 1999 went from IPO to liquidation in 268 days and burned over $80 million in wasteful advertising.
- The Learning Company, bought by Mattel in 1999 for $3.5 billion and later sold for $27.3 million in 2000.
- GeoCities, purchased by Yahoo! for $3.6 billion in January 1999. Yahoo! closed GeoCities on October 26, 2009.
- Broadcast.com, whose owner Mark Cuban sold to it Yahoo for $5.7 billion in 1999, after which, Yahoo shut the site down.

Webvan and Scaling Losses Fast

Webvan.com was based on a simple idea. Busy people don't like waiting in lines to buy groceries; they would rather buy them online and have them delivered home as Amazon.com does. It was a simple hypothesis that proved to be unfounded – busy people wouldn't pay enough to make such a business profitable, and the service wasn't that convenient. Webvan tried to sell groceries through the Internet and then deliver them with its system of warehouses and vans. It burned through $375 million in 3 years, and was valued at $1.2 billion at the top of the bubble before going bust within 12 months and laying off 2,000 employees.

Webvan first started in the San Francisco market with an Oakland distribution center. However, that location was always deeply unprofitable. Yet the company chose to raise money and scale to other markets. Its "smart money" backers included Benchmark Capital, Softbank, Sequoia Capital and, through its HomeGrocer acquisition, former Netscape Communications CEO Jim Barksdale of The Barksdale Group. The right startup course would be to stay small and perfect a profitable model, or shut down a failed experiment after losing small amounts of capital. Instead, the backers decided to go big and lose money on a large scale, building infrastructure for an unproven business model. "Get big fast" is a suicidal and sociopathic motto if a company is losing gobs of money as a small venture.

Yet in a mere 18 months, Webvan raised $375 million in an IPO, expanded from the San Francisco Bay Area to eight US cities, and built a gigantic infrastructure from the ground up. Webvan signed a $1 billion contract with Bechtel Corp. to build a string of high-tech warehouses worth about $30 million each. Webvan came to be worth $1.2 billion (or about $30 per share at its peak), and it touted a 26-city expansion plan. It acquired competitor HomeGrocer in June 2000.

Webvan's problem was that the grocery business had razor-thin margins and Webvan was never able to attract enough customers to justify its spending spree. The company had an overly complex website, and the service was not as convenient as it billed itself. Customers had to order everything a day or more in advance and set a time window when they would be home so Webvan could deliver this stuff. However, their core customers were very busy people who didn't know exactly where they would be a day or two from now, so it was a hassle. Logistics was a problem, as delivering perishables was much harder than compact hard goods like books and CDs. Adoption was slow, as a 2000 Jupiter survey found that only 2% of Web users had bought groceries online in the last year. The model was, however, loved by working parents and busy stay-at-home parents. Eventually Webvan went bankrupt in July 2001, putting 2,000 people out of work, giving stockholders worthless paper, and leaving San Francisco's new ballpark with a Webvan cup holder at every seat.

The CEO George Shaheen, formerly head of Andersen Consulting, had left before the bankruptcy. Under the terms of his "retirement package," Shaheen got 50% of his base salary and target bonus for the rest of his life, or about $375,000 annually. The payments would continue to be sent to Shaheen's wife should he die first. Unfortunately, the company died before either of them did.

eToys.com and Poor Planning

eToys.com had a similar model to Webvan.com. It was founded in 1997 as a hassle-free alternative to crowded toy stores. eToys was a concept from Idealab, the Pasadena, California, incubator that helped launch a group of publicly traded Internet firms including: GoTo.com, CitySearch, NetZero, and Tickets.com. Other backers included Highland Capital Partners and Sequoia Capital Partners. eToys launched its initial public offering in May 1999, raising $166 million at a price of $20 per share. In October 1999, the stock hit a high of $84.25, briefly giving the company an $8 billion valuation, more than its largest bricks-and-mortar competitor, Toys "R" Us.

eToys sales soared from $700,000 in 1997 to $150 million in 1999. Yet costs climbed even faster, pushing the break-even point to $900 million annually. During the holiday season of 1999, eToys drew more customers than the Web sites of Toys "R" Us and Amazon.com, according to traffic figures from Jupiter Media Metrix. However, eToys spent $220 million in advertising to generate $215 million in sales.

In December 2000, it became clear that holiday sales projections would not be met. Sales would be about half of what was expected and eToys reported an $86 million operating loss. In early January 2001, the company closed two warehouses and laid off 70% of its workers. The stock was eventually halted at 9 cents per share and the company declared bankruptcy, with $247 million of debt. eToys closed in March 2001. KB Toys bought its intellectual assets, including the web domain name, for $3.4 million (KB later went bankrupt too).

Though popular with consumers, eToys failed for many reasons. First, it had an exorbitant cost structure and was squeezed by the entry of Amazon.com, Toys "R" Us, and other big players into the online toy business. Much like Pets.com, eToys spent millions on advertising, marketing, and technology which didn't pan out. Second, the company rushed to expand and market itself at every opportunity. In 1999, it decided to enter the new market of baby-oriented products, in addition to children-based products and toys already in its online catalog, by acquiring BabyCenter, Inc., a web-based community offering baby products and information content for parents. This was a major integration project of distribution and customer service operations, requiring funds when eToys was still operating at a loss. In February 1999, eToys expanded into the European market with the opening of etoys.co.uk and purchase of a subsidiary in the Netherlands, as well as added service to Canada. This immensely increased the inventory, logistics, and facility costs. Third, eToys also carried a high variety of items, yet at any given time only had a few big name toy products, which drive sales. Many of their toys, however, were small and not worth the shipping costs required, thus not yielding any margins but instead generating great inventory expenses and logistics nightmares.

Pets.com and Outrageous Ad Spends

Pets.com sold pet supplies on the Internet. It began operations in February 1999 and closed in November 2000, one of the shortest lives for any publically traded company (from IPO to liquidation in 268 days). It was started by Greg McLemore and eventually run by star marketing executive Julie Wainwright, with funding from the venture capital firm Hummer Winbald. The company's strategy was to get publicity fast, and so it started with a five city advertising campaign and then expanded the campaign to ten cities by Christmas 1999. The company mascot, a sock puppet, was well-received and featured in a Macy's Thanksgiving Day parade and a Super Bowl commercial.

However, the business was a mess. During its first fiscal year (February to September 1999) Pets.com earned revenues of $619,000, yet spent $11.8 million on advertising. Most products were sold at a deep loss under cost, and shipping costs for heavy bags of pet food were high. Pets.com was never able to give pet owners a compelling reason to buy supplies online. After they ordered dog food, a customer had to wait a few days to actually get it. But the dog often needed to eat right away!

Amazon.com helped Pets.com raise $82.5 million in an IPO in February 2000 before collapsing nine months later. At its peak, the company had 320 employees, of which 250 were employed in warehouses across the US. The Pets.com management stayed on to provide an orderly wind down of operations and liquidation of assets. During this period, CEO Julie Wainwright received $235,000 in severance on top of a $225,000 "retention payment" while overseeing the closure. Unfortunately, her husband asked for a divorce the same week the company filed for bankruptcy.

The Learning Company and Lipstick on a Pig

In 1998, Mattel's CEO Jill Barad was under pressure to go digital and increase revenues from electronic toys, as most of Mattel's sales came from hard goods (plastic toys like Barbie dolls) and not interactive goods (anything electronic or web/Internet related). So she bought The Learning Company (TLC) in December 1998 for a $3.6 billion dollar stock swap. TLC had some popular computer game "edu-tainment" titles like Reader Rabbit and Carmen Sandiego, plus TLC's 1998 revenues were a respectable $850 million. This created good "optics," as it moved Mattel's electronic/interactive sales above $1 billion. Yet the deal went bad right away, with TLC losing money from day one, nearly $300 million in 1999 and about $1 million a day in 2000. Clearly the due diligence on the deal was non-existent, as sales fell far below estimates and accounts receivables jumped soon, suggesting accounting manipulations.

Kevin O'Leary and Michael Perik, founders of a Canadian software company called Softkey International Inc., had created TLC over the previous decade by acquisitions of smaller companies. Softkey had published a CD-ROM version of the Sports Illustrated swimsuit calendar, and its owners famously stated that creating software titles was no different from blending new flavors of cat food. Their strategy was to cut prices and increase distribution and revenues. They did not generate any profit. Their last and biggest deal, it seems, was selling out near the market top. They put lipstick on their pig and sold it for billions.

Barely two years after the purchase, Mattel sold TLC for $27.3 million in September 2000 to Gores Technology Group, a private equity firm. Barad was ousted that year with a $50 million dollar "golden parachute" compensation package.

GeoCities and Users without Monetization

Creating a website and finding a place that would host it was still a bit too complicated for the masses, but it got a lot easier and even free in 1995 when David Bohnett and John Rezner launched GeoCities in Los Angeles (the original name was BHI, Beverly Hills Internet). GeoCities basically created a web within the Web. It became a free place for users to put content such as text, pictures, and music, and so have personal web pages; it exploded in popularity. The site may have been the first mainstream example of an open, participatory, and personal Internet. A year later, it had thousands of users and over 6 million monthly page views. The GeoCities web was first structured in six virtual neighborhoods. Users (known as "homesteaders") could choose a neighborhood and an address within that neighborhood. GeoCities automatically created a webpage for each homesteader and provided an easy way for the homesteader to customize it. In 1996 GeoCities had 29 "neighborhoods," which were groupings of content created by its users. Examples included: "Augusta" for golf, "SiliconValley" for computers, "Pentagon" for military, and "Rainforest" for conservation. The company went public in August 1998, listing on the NASDAQ exchange with the code GCTY. The IPO share price was $17, rising rapidly after launch to a peak of over $100. By 1999 GeoCities was the third-most visited website on the World Wide Web, behind AOL and Yahoo.

In January 1999, Yahoo! acquired Geocities for $3.6 billion, even though Geocities had a quarterly loss of $8 million. Yahoo laid off most of Geocities 300 employees. Users became angry as Yahoo! claimed it owned all rights and content, and then reversed itself. Also innovation stopped, as Rezner noted: "The Yahoo sale was sort of bittersweet -- obviously, financially, it was great... Nothing ever happened. GeoCities stagnated from Day One." Rezner was experimenting with search algorithms similar to Google and user profile pages similar to Facebook; yet nothing came of it.

In 2001, Yahoo introduced a for-fee premium hosting package. Each package included storage, domain names, a set-up fee, and so on. Basic service could collectively cost members about $122 per year; premium service offered double the storage space, data transfer, etc. for $158. Thrifty members could continue to use GeoCities for free, but their sites would be plagued by annoying ads. ComScore stated that Geocities had 18.9 million unique visitors from the US in March 2006. In March 2008 Geocities had 15.1 million unique US visitors. In March 2009 Geocities had 11.5 million unique visitors, a 24% decline from March 2008. Yahoo closed GeoCities on October 26, 2009, despite the fact that it was one of the top 200 most trafficked sites, according to metrics tracker Alexa.

GeoCities was the first proof that you could have something really popular and still not make any money on the Internet. Having traction, eyeballs, and users wasn't enough – a company needed a successful monetization model. This lesson was learned well by Google and Facebook. Google perfected a targeted ad model which was perfect for search, while Facebook seemed to be perfecting a model of digital goods, ads, and micropayments.

Broadcast.com and the Sale of Nothing for Billions

Broadcast.com was founded as the web radio company AudioNet by Chris Jaeb in September 1995, and later taken over by Mark Cuban and Todd Wagner. Cuban was an entrepreneur who started his first company, MicroSolutions, right out of college. Despite minimal computer experience, he became immersed in technical details and market research. He used strategies that would become staples of his business style: brand building, using a top-flight sales team, and pursuing exclusive partnerships doggedly. Cuban sold MicroSolutions to CompuServe for $6 million in 1990, when it had annual revenues of $30 million, and he retired. Retirement didn't last long. Cuban and college-buddy Wagner took over AudioNet so they and their buddies could hear Indiana Hoosiers basketball games on the web. Within four years, Broadcast.com went public in mid-1998. The stock price soared to $62.75 a share in its first day of trading. The company had piped content from about 100 TV stations, 500 radio stations, and thousands of artists to millions of PC users worldwide. Meanwhile, operating losses went from $3 million in 1996 to $16 million in 1998. Yet in 1999, Cuban gracefully sold Broadcast.com to Yahoo! for $5.7 billion. Just like its purchase of GeoCities, Yahoo! had done another horrendous deal (to be fair, with outrageously overpriced stock of its own).

Over the next few years Yahoo split the services previously offered by Broadcast.com into separate services, such as Yahoo Radio, Yahoo Launchcast for music, and Yahoo Platinum for video entertainment. Yahoo Radio and Platinum were eventually shut down, as pirated content, copyright issues, and dis-satisfied third-party content providers made the services too much of a liability (problems that Google's YouTube faced a decade later). As Broadcast.com politely put it in its 1999 annual report: "We may be subjected to claims for negligence, copyright, patent, trademark, defamation, indecency and other legal theories based on the nature and content of the materials that we broadcast." Yahoo also couldn't keep Cuban, just as it didn't keep other entrepreneurs whose companies it acquired, like Viaweb's Trevor Blackwell and Paul Graham or Geocities' David Bohnett.

Cuban received $1.7 billion of stock, and sold most of it. He then spent a record $280 million to buy the Dallas Mavericks in January 2000. Said Cuban with a smirk after doing the deal of the decade: "I've been a hustler all my life… One of my favorite sayings is, 'No balls, no babies.' I learned that from a Las Vegas blackjack dealer."

26. iBoomers: Google, Hotmail, Java, the Dotcoms, High-speed Internet, and Greentech (1995-98)

Searching the Internet

Netscape's billion-dollar IPO started the "dot-com bubble" of the late 1990s. Visionaries all over the world envisioned the Internet as a vehicle that would revolutionize business. The Internet would reduce the importance of the "brick and mortar" physical store and create new ways for companies to market and sell their products online. Consumers could shop online from a vast worldwide catalog.

Sensing a lethal threat, in August 1996 Microsoft, which so far had contributed nothing to the Internet, introduced its own browser, Internet Explorer. It was bundled for free with the Windows operating system. Many observers interpreted this as a strategy to destroy Netscape, whose browser was not available for free, while it was still small. Microsoft's move not only fatally wounded Netscape, which AOL eventually bought for $4.2 billion, but also preempted any other company from developing a browser for the Windows operating system. Internet Explorer had been quickly packaged by recycling code from the commercial version of Mosaic marketed by Spyglass (the business arm of the University of Illinois). Microsoft also acquired in January 1996 the tool developed by Boston's Vermeer Technologies for building websites, FrontPage. Eventually, the US government would force Microsoft to unbundle Internet Explorer from the Windows operating system, but it would be too late to save Netscape.

Search engines were still at the forefront of the Internet revolution. The Bay Area quickly generated startups in that field. In February 1995, Steve Kirsch launched the search engine Infoseek, based in Sunnyvale. It pioneered "cost-per-impression" and "cost-per-click" advertising. Yet the company's main claim to fame was that it hired Li Yanhong, the engineer who in 1999 moved to China and co-founded the Chinese search engine Baidu.

Six Stanford students started the project Architext in February 1993. It changed its name to Excite when it launched in December 1995. Excite was notable for being started by a team without a product. The six kids founded the company before deciding what to do with it. The initial investors, Geoff Yang and Vinod Khosla, were instrumental in turning Graham Spencer's tool for searching text archives into a search engine for the Web, an idea that had not occurred to the founders. Due to a deal with Netscape, Excite went on to become the number-two search engine and the fourth most visited website in the world. They became the poster children of venture capitalists' often repeated but rarely applied motto that it is wiser to fund a great team than a great idea.

DEC had opened a research center in Palo Alto. The center created an internal search engine called AltaVista, made available to the Web in October 1995. AltaVista had a more sophisticated technology than previous search engines, notably Louis Monier's crawler (the software that roams the Web looking for documents); it allowed users to input natural-language queries. In 1997 it even introduced automatic language translation via Babel Fish, based on the old Systran system. DEC was the only one of the computing giants to enter the search business: Microsoft ignored the field, as did IBM and AT&T.

David Patterson and others at UC Berkeley had obtained DARPA funding for a project called Network of Workstations (NOW) that envisioned a supercomputer built out of networked personal computers and workstations (a forefather of cluster computing). That architecture was used by Eric Brewer and his graduate student Paul Gauthier to create the fastest search engine yet, Inktomi. HotBot, launched in May 1996, was based on Inktomi's technology and quickly overtook AltaVista as the number-one search engine.

None of the early players figured out how to make money with searches. Their main asset was traffic from the millions of Internet users who accessed the webpage of the search engine, but none of these startups figured out how to turn traffic into profits. They morphed into general-purpose portals, the Web equivalent of a shopping mall.

Yahoo!, meanwhile, was happy to use other people's search technology: first Open Text (a spin-off of the University of Waterloo in Canada), then AltaVista, and then Inktomi. Yahoo! went public in April 1996. In the first hour of trading, its value reached $1 billion. Not bad for a company that so far had revenues of $1.4 million and had lost $643,000.

An alternative approach to indexing the Web was pursued by the Open Directory Project (originally Gnuhoo), a public index of websites launched in June 1998 by SUN employees Rich Skrenta and Bob Truel. It was a collaborative effort by thousands of volunteer editors, initially modeled after the old Usenet. ODP was acquired by Netscape in October 1998. It surpassed Yahoo!'s directory sometime in 2000.

Google was founded in 1998 by two Stanford students, Larry Page and Russian-born Sergey Brin. They launched a new search engine running on Linux; it was an offshoot of a research project begun in 1996. The amount of information available on the Web was already causing information overload, and the issue was how to find the information that was really relevant. Google ranked webpages according to how "popular" they were on the Web (i.e. how many webpages linked to them). Google went against the trend of providing ever more sophisticated graphical user interfaces: the Google user interface was minimal text. In 1999, Google had eight employees. Their first "angel" investor was Andy Bechtolsheim of SUN. Then, in June 1999, they obtained $25 million from Sequoia Capital and Kleiner-Perkins.

Outside the Bay Area, the most significant player was perhaps InfoSpace, founded in March 1996 by former Microsoft employee Naveen Jain, who built an online "yellow pages" service, also offering "chat rooms" where users could exchange live text messages.

These companies did not invent search technology. Search technology had existed for a while. Verity was the main vendor of tools for searching text archives. However, companies like Verity, that had pioneered the field and were getting rich by selling text search to the corporate world, were too busy maintaining their legacy applications to think about making a Web version of their tools. There was still a huge divide between software companies working in the old off-line world and the software companies working in the new on-line world. The former did not quite understand the Web yet and, in fact, would never catch up. The wheel had to be reinvented by young inexperienced kids because the older, experienced, skilled, and competent experts were stuck in a time warp.

Getting Online

The explosion of interest in the Internet meant an explosion of internet service providers (ISPs). The government helped the commercial boom of the Internet in yet another way. In 1994, the National Science Foundation commissioned four private companies to build four public Internet access points to replace the government-run Internet backbone: WorldCom in Washington, Pacific Bell in San Francisco, Sprint in New Jersey, and Ameritech in Chicago. Then other telecom giants entered the market with their own Internet services, which they often subcontracted to smaller companies. By 1995 there were more than 100 commercial ISPs in the US. The user had to pay a monthly fee and was sometimes also charged by the hour. Some ISPs simply gave users remote access to a Unix "shell" running on the ISP's server. Services based on SLIP (Serial Line Internet Protocol), the first protocol (1988) devised for relaying Internet Protocol packets over "dial-up" lines, and later PPP (Point-to-Point Protocol) implied that the user was given a modem and had to dial a phone number (sometimes a long-distance number) to reach the ISP.

In 1995 the leading ISPs were: Uunet (annual revenues of almost $100 million), which targeted companies willing to pay $1,000 a month for Internet service; Netcom ($50 million revenues), which skyrocketed from zero to 400,000 subscribers in its first year due to a simpler pricing scheme, a flat fee for 400 hours, targeting the consumer market; and PSINet. Also in 1995 telecom giant AT&T unveiled its ISP service, called WorldNet, which copied Netcom's flat-rate model. Soon Pacific Bell, a regional telephone company, began offering Internet access to most of the four metropolitan areas of California (Bay Area, Los Angeles, Sacramento, San Diego).

The number of ISPs in the nation passed 3,000 at the beginning of 1997, and about 1,000 more were born in the next six months. By the year 2000, Uunet, the first and still the largest ISP, running 500,000 kilometers of fiber and cable, owned about 30% of the Internet's infrastructure. Dial-up pioneer CompuServe was a distant second. Metricom, founded in Los Gatos in 1985, pioneered the business of a wireless ISP in 1994 when it launched Ricochet Networks and offered service to Cupertino households. By 1996 it was covering the whole Bay Area. At the other end of the dial-up connection, companies like Ascend Communications of Alameda (near Oakland) made fortunes by selling equipment to manage dial-up lines; it was acquired in 1999 by Lucent for $20 billion.

The one piece of equipment that almost everybody needed was the modem. US Robotics was an example of a company that never bent to the standards. While its modems used proprietary protocols, it managed to become the leader in its sector. In 1997 3Com purchased US Robotics for $6.6 billion.

Browser-based Computing

Unless one worked for a university or research laboratory, an individual's e-mail was run by her or his ISP. When a user subscribed to the service, the ISP gave the user one or more e-mail addresses. The user had to install software on the home computer that periodically downloaded email messages. Starting with Soren Vejrum's WWWMail, several attempts had been made at providing an email service that could be accessed from a browser.

Hotmail was the first big winner. In July 1996, two former Apple hardware engineers, Sabeer Bhatia and Jack Smith, funded by venture capitalist Tim Draper of Draper Fisher Jurvetson, launched Hotmail. It liberated the Internet user from the slavery of the ISP. Hotmail was a website. Hotmail users checked their e-mail on the Web, regardless of where they were. E-mail had just become location-independent. Even better: e-mail "traveled" with the user, because it could be accessed anywhere there was a web browser. Its model was so easy to understand that Hotmail signed up more than 8.5 million subscribers by December 1997, in just 18 months. It helped that Hotmail was free. Microsoft bought Hotmail in December 1997 for about $400 million.

Another secondary business created by the emergence of the browser had to do with a browser's "plug-ins." A plug-in was a piece of software written by someone else that was incorporated into the browser to add a functionality that was not present in the original browser. One could add and remove plug-ins at will, thus customizing the browser. Macromedia released two of the most popular and innovative plug-ins for Netscape's browser Navigator: Shockwave in 1995, an evolution of Director to display videos; and Flash Player in 1996, an evolution of the animation tool FutureSplash acquired from FutureWave. Most plug-ins were free.

In 1995 SUN launched Java, originally developed by James Gosling. It was both an elegant object-oriented programming language and a virtual machine. The advantage of a virtual machine is that any application written for it runs on any physical machine on which the virtual machine has been ported. Java basically recycled the concepts made popular among older software engineers by Smalltalk. Language-wise, the nearest relative to Java was NeXT's Objective-C. Java, however, specifically targeted the new world of the Internet, for no other reason than portability of applications. SUN gave away Java for free and Netscape soon introduced a feature to process webpages that contained "applets" written in Java.

The promise of Java as the Esperanto of the Internet was such that venture-capital firm Kleiner-Perkins hastily created a $100 million fund to invest in Java startups. Supported by a growing number of companies, notably IBM and Oracle, Java indeed became the language of choice for Internet applications. The more the Internet grew, the more Java grew. Eventually it started threatening the decade-old supremacy of the C language.

A web server is a software tool that transfers ("serves") pages of the World Wide Web to clients via the Hypertext Transfer Protocol (HTTP). It is the foundation of a Web-based application. The browser wars between Netscape and Microsoft also extended to the web server in 1995 when Microsoft introduced a free add-on to its NT operating system, Internet Information Server. It competed against Netscape's web server that cost $5,000. WebLogic, formed in 1995 in San Francisco, launched an application server for the Java 2 Enterprise Edition (J2EE). It was acquired in 1998 by San Jose-based BEA, founded by Chinese-born former SUN manager Alfred Chuang. Another pioneering Java application server was delivered by Steve Jobs' NeXT in 1995: WebObjects. It was also an object-oriented rapid application development environment.

Building Bricks

Many of the tools required by Internet-based applications were available for free. In 1995 in Oregon a veteran of the Smalltalk environment, Ward Cunningham, who had his own software consulting business, created WikiWikiWeb, the first "wiki." It was an online manual of reusable software programming methods maintained in a collaborative manner on the Internet. Soon there would be "wikis" for everything. A wiki is an online knowledge-base that is created, edited, and maintained by a community of users. Any member of the community is allowed to change the content of any webpage of the knowledge-base from within an ordinary browser. The knowledge-base has no single author. It continuously evolves as more knowledge is provided by the users.

Meanwhile, a community of Unix developers launched the Apache server in 1996 as open-source software. The project extended and refined the web server implemented by Robert McCool at the government-funded National Center for Supercomputing Applications of the University of Illinois at Urbana-Champaign. Apache made it possible for anybody to start a website on their own home or office computer, thus increasing the amount of content and the number of applications that reached the Web.

In 1997 the World Wide Web Consortium (W3C), founded in October 1994 at MIT by Tim Berners-Lee as the international standards organization for the Web, introduced the XML standard for exchanging documents on the Web. In 1998 a struggling Netscape that was being strangled by the free Microsoft browser and the free Apache server decided to license the code of its browser for free as open source so that anybody could use it to build a better browser. Thus began the project "Mozilla." It was a desperate survival strategy.

Hotmail's Exponential Growth

Hotmail grew its user base faster than any media company in history and so in an instructive case study. The founders were both hardware engineers, not software engineers. This was a case in which the idea came from a user viewpoint, not from a technology viewpoint. They needed a way to bypass the company's firewall and figured out how to do it. Many software engineers could have done the same because they knew the Web technology well enough but simply did not come up with the idea because they personally didn't need it. Being hardware engineers helped Hotmail's founder deliver a sturdy no-nonsense "product." Software engineers are artists who proceed by trial and error, and are not terribly concerned if their product has bugs (one can always fix the bugs later). Hardware engineers cannot afford bugs: every time a mistake is made, the cost is huge. Therefore Hotmail's founders naturally delivered something that was ready to be used by millions of people. About 100,000 people signed up for Hotmail in the first three months. Most new software needs a lot of tweaking before it gets it right: theirs didn't need any tweaking. Hotmail was a case in which the cultures of hardware and software converged and leveraged each other.

Hotmail, like Yahoo, was also another story that showed the unprecedented power of the Internet to spread news by word of mouth. Email, the very nature of Hotmail's business, was also the most powerful grass-roots tool ever to spread information. Hotmail's founders did two things to further improve its efficiency. First, they added a tagline to every email that invited the recipient to join Hotmail. Second, they gave each and every user an email address that contained "hotmail.com" so that each recipient would know (even without reading the tagline) that Hotmail existed. Both were useful for "branding"; but neither would have worked if

Hotmail had not been useful and usable. Users spread the gospel that there was a simpler, better, and cheaper way to do email.

Hotmail's concept (Web-based email, or "webmail") was a very easy concept to copy. It was copied by many companies that were much larger. Hotmail, however, proved how difficult it was to catch up. Precisely because the Internet medium was so unique in rapidly multiplying users, it created a de-facto standard even before the industry could do so. Once it became a de-facto standard, a startup such as Hotmail enjoyed a huge advantage even over much larger companies such as Microsoft. The advantage was such that the larger company would have to invest millions in R&D and marketing for several years to match the startup. Indirectly this also ended up discouraging large companies from trying to catch up with successful startups: much cheaper to just buy them for outrageous prices. Rocketmail became Hotmail's main competitor after being a partner (they built Hotmail's directory of registered users). Eventually, Yahoo bought Rocketmail in 1997, to compete against Microsoft.

Finally, Hotmail bet on advertising as a viable source of revenues. Hotmail failed to prove that concept: it was never profitable. Yet it represented one more step towards proving it. Hotmail's founders realized that email was even more powerful than Yahoo to generate "click-throughs" (actual visits to the advertised website). Indirectly, Internet start-ups realized that advertising had become a key component of capitalist society. One could almost claim that more creativity was going into marketing a product than in designing it. That industry had been consistently looking for innovative advertising vehicles: the newspaper, the nickelodeon, the radio and the television. The Internet boom took place at precisely the time when advertising was booming too. Cable television revenues had an 82% growth rate in 1994-95. The Web was also capable of delivering interactive advertising. And its advertising led straight to the store (through a mouse click, i.e. a "click-through").

Ads were perceived by the masses as a negative feature. Many startups failed because they were perceived to be too "commercial" once their web-based services started displaying too many ads. It was a tricky balance. On the one hand, startups needed the revenues from ads that were proportional to the number of people visiting their websites. But on the other hand, ads were making their websites less attractive and therefore reducing the number of visitors. Websites without any ads were more likely to earn the trust of the Internet public than websites with ads. However, the Internet public was not willing to turn that "trust" into financial support: websites that tried to charge a fee for each visit were even less likely to survive than websites that displayed ads. The Internet public was an odd beast: it wanted information without advertising, but it was not willing to pay for that information in any other manner. The good news for Internet startups is that the costs of operation were very low (Hotmail had 15 engineers when it was bought by Microsoft for $400 million).

Internet startups that followed the "free service" model indirectly adopted the view that their real product was the user base. A car manufacturer makes a car and makes money by selling the car. Many websites offered a web-based service that was only an excuse to create a large user base, and then they made money by selling advertising to corporations interested in selling whatever products or services to that user base, or by upselling a different kind of service to that user base.

The Net Economy: 1995

Dotcom companies soon appeared in every sector of society; electronic commerce spread quickly. Some examples are detailed below.

Amazon.com: In 1995 Jeff Bezos, a former Wall Street hedge fund executive who had relocated to Seattle, launched Amazon.com as the "world's largest bookstore," except that it was not a bookstore but a website. Amazon was the quintessential declaration of war to the "brick and mortar" store.

Craigslist.com: It was launched in 1995 by Craig Newmark from his San Francisco residence, provided a regional advertising platform (initially only for the Bay Area) that quickly made newspaper classified obsolete since it was free and reached more people. It became a cult phenomenon, spreading by word of mouth. Newmark refused investments and offers to sell.

Xing Technology: Based in southern California, it developed the first live audio and video delivery system over the Internet, StreamWorks, i.e. a system to play an audio or video file while it is downloaded from the Internet. Xing was acquired by RealNetworks in 1999, a firm formed in Seattle by ex-Microsoft executive Rob Glaser in 1995, who had introduced the RealAudio "streaming" audio software. These two companies enabled live broadcasts on the Internet.

Viaweb (Yahoo Stores): In 1995 New York-based computer scientists Paul Graham and Robert Morris started Viaweb. It was a website to create online stores which made it easier for many people to get into e-commerce. It was also one of the first Web-based applications: it ran on a server and was controlled by the user by clicking on the links of a webpage displayed on a browser. Viaweb was similar to what had been done with X-terminals to run X-Windows (the browser being the equivalent of the X terminal).

eBay: In 1995 French-born Armenian-Iranian and former General Magic's engineer Pierre Omidyar founded AuctionWeb (renamed eBay in 1997), a website to auction items. The idea was that strangers would buy from strangers whom they never met and with no direct contact. By the end of 1998 eBay's auctions totaled $740 million.

Other companies ventured into Internet telephone, security, and website development tools. In 1995 the Israeli company VocalTec released the first commercial Internet phone software, i.e. a system capable of dispatching telephone calls over the Internet. In 1995 Kevin O'Connor, with the money he made at Internet Security Systems, started Internet Advertising Network (IAN), which later acquired and retained the name of the DoubleClick system of New York's Internet ad agency Poppe Tyson. Indian-born Samir Arora, who had managed Hypercard at Apple, founded NetObjects in 1995 in Redwood City to develop tools for people to build their own websites.

In 1995 only 15% of Internet users in the US were women. Yet two New York media executives saw that the number was growing and that women were not served adequately by the new male-dominated medium. Candice Carpenter and Nancy Evans founded the female-oriented portal iVillage in June 1995. Furthermore, corporate lawyer Stacy Stern co-founded FindLaw, a portal for law-related information, the first time that case law was made easily accessible to the US public.

Some also started thinking about the possibility of combining Internet and the television. In July 1995, former Apple and General Magic employee Steve Perlman founded Artemis Research, later renamed WebTV. He wanted to build a set-top box based on custom hardware and software which would allow a television set attached to a telephone line to plug into an Internet service using a dial-up modem and to browse the Web via a thin client. The goal was to turn the World-wide Web into a home appliance. The WebTV set-top box was introduced in September 1996 by Sony and Philips; it was not very successful but it pioneered the idea of accessing the Web via a consumer electronics device instead of a workstation or personal computer. In April 1997, Microsoft acquired WebTV. The dotcom boom also boosted the stock of e-learning, a field pioneered by Stanford in the 1960s. However, very few of the startups of the era survived, notably Saba, founded in 1997 in Redwood Shores by Oracle's executive Bobby Yazdani.

At this point the "users" of a dotcom service were typically technology-savvy professionals, especially those raised on Unix. At the time not everybody was connected to the Internet, not everybody had access to high-speed lines, and not everybody understood what the World-Wide Web was. In 1996 there were 14 million households in the US with Internet access, almost all of them on dial-up lines. Even in 1998, when the number of users in the US had skyrocketed to 75 million, the vast majority still used dial-up services. Ordinary people were still reluctant to use email, let alone sophisticated ecommerce websites. Many households were just beginning to get familiarized with computers.

The Net Economy: 1996-97

A few big Web innovations were push technology and subscription models. In February 1996 Pointcast, founded by Christopher Hassett, started a fad for "push" technology with its software that gathered information from the Web and then displayed it on a personal computer, which amounted to basically the opposite of surfing. With push, a software agent sends information to the user instead of the user searching the Web. Marimba, a spin-off of SUN's Java group founded in 1996 in Mountain View by Arthur van Hoff and Jonathan Payne and headed by Kim Polese, offered subscription-based software distribution so that one could automatically get updates to its applications.

The movie industry was helped by an early Web subscription-model business named Netflix. In August 1997 Reed Hastings, who had been selling tools for programmers with his first startup Pure Software, founded Netflix in Scotts Valley, between San Jose and Santa Cruz. He wanted to rent videos, initially on DVD, via the Internet. DVD rentals were a direct strike against movie theaters, one of the pillars of social life in the 20th century. Netflix upped the ante by removing even the DVD store and allowing movie buffs to simply order movies online. The movie still required a physical device, the DVD, but was delivered at home.

The world was being mapped and made available. In 1997, Jim Gray of Microsoft, working with Aerial Images of North Carolina, created the web-based mapping service TerraServer that also offered satellite images from the United States Geological Survey (USGS) and Russia's space agency Sovinformsputnik. In 1996 Chicago-based GeoSystems Global launched the web-based mapping service MapQuest that also provided address matching. In 1996, Jim Clark of Silicon Graphics fame founded Healtheon to create software for the health-care system to "map" treatment data.

The Net Economy: 1998-99

As technology became more reliable, applications became more sophisticated too, spreading to broadcasting, books, and groceries. In 1998 UC Berkeley Professor Abhay Parekh founded FastForward Networks to provide radio and television broadcasting over the Web. NuvoMedia was founded that same year in Palo Alto to sell the Rocket eBook. It was a paperback-sized handheld device to read digital books downloaded from online bookstores ("ebooks"). Another e-book reader was introduced at the same time by rival SoftBook Press, founded by Amiga's videogame guru James Sachs and by publishing industry executive Tom Pomeroy in 1996 in Menlo Park. The two startups were eventually purchased by Rupert Murdoch's media conglomerate.

At the moment that companies started doing business on the Web, it became important to have reliable services to display webpages in real time. Akamai, founded in 1998 by MIT student Daniel Lewin, replicated content to servers located around the world in order to minimize the time it took to deliver it to the end users.

The New Nature of Innovation

The semiconductor boom had largely been the making of one legendary company. Fairchild Semiconductor gave birth to more than 50 semiconductor startups. The vast majority of Silicon Valley engineers working in semiconductors during the 1960s had worked at Fairchild at one time or another. The history of the semiconductor industry in Silicon Valley is the Fairchild genealogical tree. The semiconductor boom largely consisted in the refinement of one technology. It was a very vertical kind of technological development.

The age of Apple, Cisco, SUN, and Oracle was different. This boom was more diversified. The inventions of Apple, Cisco, SUN, and Oracle had little in common. Furthermore, neither of them gave rise to a significant genealogical tree. Compared with Fairchild Semiconductor, relatively few startups were created by former Apple, Cisco, SUN, or Oracle engineers, and fewer survived or stayed independent (Salesforce.com is one of the rare few). No major company of the size of Intel emerged from any of these. What each of them created was a chain of suppliers. There was a vertical economy that relied on them but the boom was becoming more horizontal.

The dotcom age was completely horizontal. The dotcom boom was wildly diversified. It wasn't just the refinement of a technology, but the application of a technology to many different applications in wildly different fields. The dozens of dotcoms were exploring a vast landscape. Some dotcoms refined previous ideas like search or social networking, but most of them did not refine a previous application at all: they were the first to implement that application on the Web. If someone else had preceded them, there was no relationship between the two sets of engineers; there were no Fairchild-Intel relationships. The Internet resettled Silicon Valley in a new landscape, and the dotcom boom was mostly about exploring this new landscape and finding gold mines in it.

One reason that dotcoms did not bother to refine previous dotcoms' inventions, like semiconductor startups had done in the 1970s, was that there were so many opportunities. Why compete with an existing dotcom? Another reason that dotcoms did not bother to refine previous dotcoms' inventions was outsourcing: the job of refinement was best left to India.

Network Neutrality

The dotcom boom owed a lot to a fundamental principle of the Internet, never encoded in a law but tacitly accepted by the whole community. The network had to be company-neutral and application-agnostic. The network was simply a highway that anybody could use. There was no VIP lane. No matter how large and powerful a corporation was, it had to use for its ecommerce activities the very same network that the poorest student was using to set up her personal website. The Internet had been conceived to be as general as possible and with no particular application in mind. The dotcom boom was a boom of applications, not of platforms. The innovation went into the applications. The platform was roughly still the same as in the 1980s if not the 1970s.

The application boom was driven by the neutrality of the Internet. First of all, that neutrality protected the small Internet startup from the "brick and mortar" corporation. Everybody could get a fair chance in the marketplace, a fact that was not true in the "brick and mortar" economy where large businesses could use a plethora of tactics to hurt smaller newcomers.

Secondly, the network allowed the producer, the creator of a Web-based service, to offer its "product" directly to the consumer, the user. There was no need for an intermediary anymore. In the traditional economy users shopped for the products that an intermediary had decided to deliver to the store. It was not the user who decided which products would show up at the store: it was a chain of intermediaries starting from the product planning division all the way down to the store owner. The Internet removed the whole chain. People were creating applications on the Web, and users were deciding which ones became successful.

In the "brick and mortar" economy a corporation decided which product to sell and then proceeded to publicize it. In the "net" economy, instead, it was the user who decided which "product" to use. The marketing for that product, its website, was the "buzz" created within the community of users. There was no advertisement publicizing a website, no salesman selling it door to door, and no store displaying it on its window.

Getting Online Part II

Internet dial-up services were multiplying, but dial-up access was slow. Two technologies appeared at the end of the 1990s to remedy the problem. The US government made another important decision for the future of the Internet in 1996. The "Telecommunications Act" allowed cable television providers to offer Internet services. Milo Medin, a former NASA scientist, and tycoon William Randolph Hearst III started At Home Network (@Home), technically a joint venture between TCI (the largest cable operator in the US) and the venture capital firm Kleiner Perkins. Their mission was to deliver Internet broadband to a million homes by the first quarter of 1997. The high-speed cable ISP was born. In 1997 US West launched the first commercial Digital Subscriber Line (DSL) service in Phoenix. Cable Internet used the cables laid down for cable television. DSL used the ordinary telephone lines. Neither was widely available at the time.

The obvious beneficiaries of the age of networking were the companies that specialized in networking hardware. By the mid-1990s the three Silicon Valley giants Cisco, 3Com, and Bay Networks (formed by the merger of SynOptics and Billerica) had achieved $1 billion in revenues. Indian-born Pradeep Sindhu, a former semiconductor scientist at Xerox PARC, founded Juniper Networks in 1996 in Sunnyvale to manufacture high-end routers in direct competition with Cisco. When it went public in 1999, its IPO was one of the most successful in history, turning it overnight into a $4.9 billion company.

The astronomical growth of Internet communications also created demand for high-speed fiber-optic cables to connect not only research centers, but also millions of ordinary homes.

Fiber optics cables are made of thin glass wires. Optical switches convert the digital signals into light pulses. The light pulses are transmitted over these optical cables instead of the copper wires of the traditional telephone lines. The boom for optical cables began in 1996, when the US government enacted the Telecommunications Act that deregulated the telecom market. This created ferocious competition among local and global telecom companies at the same time that the pundits predicted an exponential rise in broadband need due to the advent of the Web.

It is not a coincidence that the capacity of optical cables almost doubled every six months starting in 1992 until in 2001 they achieved a bit rate of 10 terabits per second. Lucent, a 1995 spin-off of AT&T and Canadian giant Nortel, which had deployed the world's first commercial fiber-optic link in 1980, dominated the market. In 1999 Nortel and Lucent together owned more than 50% of the $12.3 billion market, a market that had just grown by 56% from 1998.

There was big money even in acquisitions. In 1999 Cisco acquired Cerent of Petaluma for $7.4 billion and became the third power. Meanwhile Nortel bought Xros of Sunnyvale in 2000 for $3.25 billion. In 1988, the Southern Pacific Railroad began installing fiber-optic cable along its lines and in 1995 it spawned Qwest, headquartered in Denver, Colorado. By 1999 it had revenues of $3.92 billion. Aerie Networks of Denver raised $100 million of venture capital in its first two years. Sycamore Networks, located in Massachusetts, was worth $29.1 billion in September 2000.

Silicon Valley became one of the hotbeds of optical technology. A spin-off of Optivision founded in 1997 in San Jose by Indian-born Rohit Sharma, ONI Systems was one of the first to go public. Then came the deluge: Kestrel Solutions of Mountain View; Lightera Networks of Cupertino; Calient of San Jose; Mayan Networks of Mountain View; Amber Networks of Fremont; Zaffire of San Jose; Luminous Networks of Cupertino; Luxn of Sunnyvale and others.

The world was suddenly awash in fiber-optic cables. This overcapacity, not mandated by governments but simply the result of business miscalculations, dramatically lowered the cost of broadcasting information, thereby increasing the motivation to broadcast information. The fiber-optic rush created on the Internet the equivalent of the freeway system created by the US government in the 1950s. It did so rapidly and at no cost to the taxpayer. The cost was political. The vast fiber-optic infrastructure did more than connect the nation electronically: it connected the nation to India too, thus accelerating the process of outsourcing IT jobs to India.

Cyberculture and Cybersociety

The Internet was also beginning to be used for cultural purposes. The online magazine Salon was founded in 1995 in San Francisco by David Talbot, a former editor for the San Francisco Examiner. In April 1999 Salon would purchase the glorious WELL. The term "blog" came to be associated with websites run by an individual who published content on a more or less regular basis, the Web equivalent of a television talk show or of a newspaper column. In 1998 Bob Somerby, an op-ed writer for the Baltimore Sun, started "The Daily Howler," the first major political blog. In September 1997, Rob Malda launched Slashdot, a website catering to an audience of the open-source hobbyists ("news for nerds") that provided an index of stories published by other websites or magazines, the first news aggregator.

Anthropologists were excited about the convergence of the virtual communities enabled by cyberspace and the technology of virtual reality that had matured since the pioneering years. In 1994, Ron Britvich in southern California created WebWorld, later renamed AlphaWorld and then again renamed Active Worlds. In it people could communicate, travel, and build. Bruce Damer was a former member of the Elixir team in LA. Inspired by the hippie communes of the 1960s, they had purchased a ranch in the Santa Cruz Mountains south of Silicon Valley, established the Contact Consortium in 1994. In 1996 the ranch yielded three-dimensional virtual-reality environments such as a virtual town (Sherwood Forest) and a virtual university (The U).

The Anthropology of Transience

Silicon Valley's real, non-virtual society was characterized by transience at all levels. People were coming and going. Companies were being started and closed. This society of transience created a landscape with no monuments. Not even rich people cared for building monuments. In a place that had no great buildings, a company's sign might become a landmark. Buildings were to be destroyed so nobody felt the need to start a building meant to last forever like all civilizations had done before.

This "flatness" of the world created a strange contradiction: there was no visible sign of Silicon Valley's grandeur. The greatness of Silicon Valley was defined by products designed in corporate rooms and built in laboratories that were hidden from the public. People could read about what made Silicon Valley great but there was no exterior manifestation to prove it. The office buildings of Intel, Hewlett-Packard, Oracle, and Apple were almost incognito. Dubai was erecting one skyscraper after another and Shanghai would soon begin to do the same. The Roman and the British empires had left countless public buildings to celebrate their triumphs. Silicon Valley, by contrast, didn't even have a landmark of the kind that any midsize city in the US could boast of, like Seattle's Space Needle or St Louis' Arch. A tour of Silicon Valley's historical buildings was a tour of garages and offices. Silicon Valley was "inside," not "outside."

It was not that these rich individuals and companies were reluctant to spend their money. They did spend. In the 1990s Silicon Valley contributed more than one billion dollars to charitable causes. However, the typical contribution was in the form of philanthropy. A company or an individual was more likely to spend a fortune in a "project" (whether helping the poor in Africa or helping a local organization) than in a building. It was all part of the mindset of transience: a project does not depend on a physical location.

Civic life was, in fact, often shaped by philanthropy rather than planned by government. Silicon Valley's very beginning had been shaped by an act of philanthropy and not by an act planned by the government: Stanford University.

Bubble Deals

The business model that became ubiquitous among dotcom startups was about becoming popular and cool, not necessarily making money. The dotcom startup was after market share, not profits. In other words, the competition was about getting as many users as possible, typically by providing a service for free, hoping that eventually the large number of users would also bring in revenues. Therefore the typical dotcoms were operating at a net loss. Very few actually had a plan on how to make money. Most of them envisioned a day when they could charge a fee for their services, but the trend was obviously in the opposite direction, with more and more companies waiving fees for their online services. Netscape, for example, made Navigator available for free in January 1998. A different avenue to profitability was taken by the dotcoms that began to sell advertising space on their websites, notably Geocities in May 1997.

In the second half of the 1990s there were more than 100 venture capital firms at work in the Bay Area. The five most prominent were Accel, Kleiner Perkins Caufield & Byers, Crosspoint Ventures, Sequoia Capital, and Hambrecht & Quist. In 1998, Taiwanese computer manufacturer Acer opened Acer Technology Ventures to invest in Silicon Valley startups.

The new wave of software companies had further changed the demographics of Silicon Valley with a significant injection of brains from Asia. By 1998, Chinese and Indian engineers ran about 25% of Silicon Valley's high-tech businesses, accounting for $16.8 billion in sales and

58,000 jobs. But the bubble was getting frothy. In November 1998 Netscape surrendered and was purchased by AOL. It was a bad omen for the dotcoms.

27. Other Boomers: The Y2K Bug, Wi-Fi, Personal Digital Assistants, and DNA Mapping (1995-98)

The Y2K Bug

At the same time that the dotcoms were booming, another factor contributed to a dramatic increase in software revenues: the Y2K phenomenon. "Y2K" was an abbreviation for "Year 2000." The vast majority of business software for large computers had been written in the 1960s and 1970s and then was ported to new generations of computers. Because of the limitations of storage at the time and because very few people expected those applications to last that long, most business programs could run only until 1999. The applications had no way to represent a date beyond 1999 (the commonly used two-digit abbreviation of the year, for example "55" instead of "1955," would turn the year 2000 into the year 1900).

Panic spread when the corporate world realized what that meant. As the world entered a new century, unpredictable glitches could bring down the world economy and cause all sorts of disasters. Virtually all the business software in the world had to be rewritten, or at least analyzed to make sure there was no "Y2K bug." At one point, the Gartner Group estimated the cost of fixing the Y2K bug at $600 billion.

This was a boon for software companies that serviced legacy applications. So much code needed to be rewritten that, globally, one of the main beneficiaries of the Y2K panic was India. Since 1991, it had begun liberalizing its protectionist economy, and it boasted a large and cheap English-speaking IT workforce. US companies had to outsource millions of lines of code to Indian companies. India's National Association of Software and Service Companies (Nasscom) estimated that India's software exports in 1998-99 reached $2.65 billion, growing at a yearly rate of over 50%. Y2K-related projects accounted for $560 million or about 20% of the total.

The Y2K economy fueled the software industry at the same time that the Internet was moving it, thus generating an economic bubble on top of another bubble. The mayhem was so loud that very few people realized that the year 2000 was the last year of the 20th century, not the first year of the 21st century. That honor belonged to the year 2001: for the age of the computer anything with a zero at the end ought to be a beginning, not an end. The second millennium of the Christian calendar lasted only 999 years (the first millennium had been from year 1 to 1000, i.e. 1000 years).

A 1999 article by international consultant Peter de Jager in the reputable magazine Scientific American concluded: "I believe that severe disruptions will occur and that they will last perhaps about a month." Highly educated people stockpiled food and water, and some decided to spend the last day of the year in bunkers. The apocalypse would come, but it would come a few weeks later, in March 2000, and it would have little to do with the way computers represent dates.

Software Tools

Meanwhile, the proliferation of software startups in Silicon Valley was not limited to the Internet and the Y2K bug. In 1998, Stanford's scientist Mendel Rosenblum was working on SimOS, a project to create a software simulator of hardware platforms. Such software would be able to run the operating systems written for those hardware platforms. Rosenblum and others founded VMware to pursue that mission. In May 1999, they introduced VMware Workstation, which was not a workstation but a SimOS-like software environment (a "virtual machine"). It allowed a Unix machine to run the Windows operating system and all of its applications. Eventually they would broaden the idea to allow one physical computer to run multiple operating systems simultaneously. Server virtualization had already been popular in the mainframe era, but Rosenblum was the first one to implement it on smaller computers.

Red Hat had become the darling of the Linux world. In 1998 it merged with Sunnyvale-based Cygnus Solutions, founded in 1989 by John Gilmore and Michael Tiemann to provide tools for Linux. When Red Hat finally went public in August 1999, it achieved one of the biggest first-day gains in the history of Wall Street. Meanwhile, Marc Fleury started the Georgia-based JBoss project for a Java-based application server; JBoss would be acquired by Red Hat in 2006.

The Internet and Y2K booms on top of the pre-existing software boom increased the need for software development environments. One of the paradigms that took hold was Rapid Application Development (RAD), originally championed by James Martin at IBM in 1991 but fitting very well the frantic world of Silicon Valley. Instead of developing an application top-down, RAD calls for the immediate creation of a working prototype followed by a series of incremental improvements, similar to what nature does. Delphi, released by Borland in 1995, was an early example of a development environment for RAD. Java also called for a new type of development environment. Visual Cafe, released by Symantec in 1997, was another example. There continued to be a proliferation of software tools to overcome the dearth of software engineers and the pressure to deliver ever faster.

In those years, supply chain management was brought to the Bay Area. Agile Software, founded in 1995 in San Jose by Bryan Stolle, sold a suite to help firms manage bills of materials (BOMs). Ariba was started in 1996 in Sunnyvale; it automated the procurement process. Both pioneered business-to-business (B2B) commerce over the Internet. Supply chain management was as hot as ERP. Sales of i2's Rhythm went from $26 million in 1995 to $65 million in 1996, and in 1999 i2 would boast a 13% share of the $3.9 billion supply-chain software market. ERP was already well established in the Bay Area due to PeopleSoft and Oracle, although the German companies continued to dominate. In 1997 the total revenues for the ERP software market was $7.2 billion, with SAP, Baan, Oracle, J.D. Edwards, and PeopleSoft accounting for 62% of it.

The Computer Market at the Turn of the Century

For the time being the evolution of computers was largely independent of the dotcoms. Thirty-four million households owned a computer in 1996 in the US, justifying IBM's purchase of Lotus Development, one of the many moves that realigned IBM towards the world of personal computers. In 1997, IBM's revenues were $68 billion, but now a big chunk of them came from technical support to its aging mainframes, a business that employed 160,000 people. IBM introduced a new generation of mainframes based on Intel microprocessors, the Netfinity series.

Compaq was the rising star. In 1994, it had overtaken IBM in personal-computer sales. In 1997, the year it shipped 10 million personal computers and laptops, Compaq's revenues skyrocketed to $24.6 billion. Compared with Dell and Gateway, Compaq was most successful with corporate customers. In the second half of the 1990s, it moved aggressively to capture that market from IBM. In 1997 Compaq acquired Tandem Computers and their line of fault-tolerant servers, a move that gave Compaq more credibility in mission-critical business applications. Compaq then acquired Digital Equipment Company (DEC), which had been struggling to adjust to the new world of personal computers. DEC was certainly in trouble: despite reducing its workforce to 50,000 people from a peak of 130,000, DEC still employed about 65% more people than Compaq to generate about 50% lower revenues. However, DEC's products included both high-end servers priced at $1 million and up and low-end servers priced under $100,000, plus workstations. More importantly, 45% of its revenues came now from services: DEC's technical and customer support was a worldwide army of 25,000 people. That was exactly what Compaq needed to take on its rival IBM.

Dell broke in with an edge in PCs and Toshiba built one in laptops. In 1996 Dell began selling its computers via its website. The website used NeXT's just released WebObjects technology. It allowed consumers and businesses to order directly, and even to customize the configuration of their PC. By spring 1999 Dell had erased the US sales gap with Compaq (Compaq 16.8%, Dell 16.4%), although Compaq continued to sell more units abroad. The market for laptop computers was dominated by Toshiba, which in 1997 enjoyed a market share of 20.4%. Toshiba also introduced the first DVD player in 1996.

Compared with the fortunes of IBM, Compaq, Dell, and Toshiba, the two Silicon Valley giants, Hewlett-Packard and Apple, had a mixed record. Since 1995 HP had become one of the most successful personal-computer manufacturers. It owned more than 50% of the market for printers in that market. And it looked very aggressive: in 1994 it had partnered with Intel to develop a 64-bit processor (code-named "Merced") that promised to be a dramatic departure from Intel's x86 architecture. However, when it was eventually released in 2001 with the official name of Titanium, it was a flop because in the meantime Intel had released a faster x86-based processor, the Pentium. Apple had allied with IBM and Motorola in 1994 to use their PowerPC microprocessor for a new line of high-end Macintoshes. In 1996 it purchased NeXT and the Unix-based NextStep operating system with WebObjects technology, a Java-based application server for rapid object-oriented software development of Web-based applications. Steve Jobs was back at Apple. In 1997 Apple followed Dell in using WebObjects to create a website (the "Apple Store") to sell customized machines directly to the end customer. However, Apple was bleeding. It couldn't compete with the DOS/Windows-based computers and in 1999 it laid off 2,700 of 11,000 employees.

A Wireless Future

The new semiconductor companies often targeted emerging niche markets. In 1994 wireless pioneer Proxim had introduced a product to let ordinary computers exchange data via the ether, which truly inaugurated the era of office wireless networks. In May 1998 John Hennessy and Teresa Meng of Stanford University opened in Santa Clara a startup named Atheros that specialized in chipsets aimed at wireless local area networks, later known as "Wi-Fi networks" from the industry standard adopted in 1999. As wireless LANs moved to the home, this would turn out to be a lucrative market. Marvell was started in 1995 in Santa Clara by Indonesian-born Sehat Sutardjia, his Chinese-born wife Weili Dai and his brother Pantas. It was a fabless maker of semiconductors used in data storage and mostly serving Asian companies. Marvell too would rapidly jump onto the wireless bandwagon.

Gadgets

This was also the age of the gadgets propelled by digital technology but decoupled from the computer industry. In the arena of videogames, in 1995 Sony introduced the Playstation, one of the most popular platforms of all times. In 1998, sales of videogame consoles in the US alone amounted to $6.2 billion, which dwarfed the sales of videogame software on personal computers ($1.8 billion). The situation had reversed itself one more time, and now the videogame console was rapidly gaining, due to a combination of lower prices and much improved performance.

Progress in graphics video, animation, and audio continued at a rapid pace. In 1995 the Moving Picture Experts Group (MPEG) of the International Organization for Standardization (ISO) published the "mp3" standard (more properly, MPEG-1 Layer 3) for digital audio and video compression, largely based on the 1989 thesis of German student Karlheinz Brandenburg. Mp3 had been designed to compress video and audio into the bit-rate of a CD. While Mp3 proved inadequate for videos, it became a very popular format for digital music. In March 1998, Korean-based Saehan Information Systems released the MPMan F10, the first portable Mp3 player, capable of storing nine songs.

Digital media companies proliferated around San Francisco's South of Market (SoMA) district, an area previously known mostly for night-clubs and abandoned warehouses that was now nicknamed "Multimedia Gulch." More than 35,000 people worked in the multimedia sector in San Francisco in 1999. Many of them were self-employed or worked for small companies and there were almost 1,000 multimedia businesses. The Multimedia Gulch briefly transplanted Silicon Valley's model to the "city."

Ironically, the company that had pioneered 3D graphics in the Bay Area was the exception to the general euphoria. Silicon Graphics' spectacular growth peaked in 1995; its market capitalization reached $7 billion in 1995 and revenues were $2.2 billion. However, the company began a rapid decline as it seemed to live in a different world where the Internet did not exist. It mostly specialized in visual effects for Hollywood.

A successful movie, John Lasseter's "Toy Story," premiered in November 1995 and made history for being the first feature-length computer-animated film. Lasseter, a former Walt Disney animator, worked at Lucasfilm under Ed Catmull to make a groundbreaking computer-animated short, "The Adventures of Andre and Wally B" (1984), for which they used a Cray supercomputer. When Jobs purchased Lucasfilms in 1986 and turned it into Pixar, Lasseter was given the power and freedom to invest in that technology, but it took almost a decade to come out with a full-length film. Personal computers, instead, had to live with humbler features. For example, in 1997 RealNetworks introduced RealVideo to play videos on a computer, but it still used a proprietary format.

Gadgets started to infringe on TV. TiVo was introduced in the Bay Area in 1998 by former Silicon Graphics engineers Jim Barton and Mike Ramsay and funded by Geoff Yang and Stewart Alsop. It was a digital video recorder capable of digitizing and compressing analog video signal from a television set and of storing it onto a computer's hard-disk. At that point, the television viewer was able to do with television programs what a computer user could do with data. It was a relatively simple idea but it changed forever the definition of "live event" and ended the age in which all viewers were synchronized on the same program.

A hyped event of 1996 in Silicon Valley was the release of a hand-held pen-based computer called Palm Pilot. It was a computer with no keyboard, whose user interface was simply a screen on which the user could write in natural language. The founder of Palm, Jeff Hawkins, had studied automated hand-written text recognition at UC Berkeley. It was the first pen-based user interface to gain wide acceptance. In 1998 the Palm Pilot had almost 80% of the market for palm-sized computers; the next year it would enjoy four consecutive quarters of triple-digit revenue growth. Palm had already been purchased by US Robotics in 1995, which then merged with 3Com in June 1997.

The most sensational high-tech product introduced abroad in 1996 was probably Nokia's 9000 Communicator, which invented the category of "smart phones." Palm had tried to create a "personal digital assistant" (PDA) starting with a computer. Finnish conglomerate Nokia, the world leader in mobile phones, started with a mobile phone, adding computer capabilities based on an Intel 386 processor running Berkeley Softworks' GEOS operating environment on top of DOS. In 1997, Psion, the British company that had invented the personal digital assistant, adopted the ARM processor in its Series 5 in conjunction with a brand new operating system that was later renamed Symbian, a joint venture with Ericsson, Nokia, Panasonic, and Motorola.

One of the most daring gadgets introduced in the mid-1990s was a by-product of the feud between Microsoft and Oracle. In 1996 Oracle introduced a disk-less desktop computer, the network computer. Larry Ellison preached a world in which data did not have to reside in the house or the office of the user, but could reside on the Internet. Ellison envisioned a future in which the computing power was on the Internet and the user's machine was simply a tool to access that computing power. Indirectly, this was also a world in which desktop computers had no need for Microsoft's operating systems. The net computer was the counterpart to General Magic's hand-held device, and yet another premonition of "cloud computing." Alas, it also became another embarrassing Silicon Valley flop.

Biotech

In biotech the state-of-the-art moved fast. The Human Genome Project had been slow to get started, like all big projects, but at last in April 1996 human DNA sequencing began in earnest at several universities funded by the National Institute of Health. Most of these research centers were using the sequencing machines of Applied Biosystems, acquired by East-coast pharmaceutical giant Perkin-Elmer. Also in 1996, Sydney Brenner founded the Molecular Sciences Institute in Berkeley while Monsanto, a multinational food corporation, acquired Calgene.

For the media, 1996 was the year of cloning. A team assembled by Ian Wilmut at the Roslin Institute in Britain cloned "Dolly" the sheep, the first time that a mammal had been cloned in a lab from adult cells. The experiment was centered on the ideas of Keith Campbell, who in 1995 had already succeeded in cloning a pair of lambs, albeit from embryonic cells. In May 1999, Geron of Menlo Park bought the rights on Roslin's nuclear-transfer technology for $25 million.

PE Biosystems, the new name of Applied Biosystems after being acquired by Perkin-Elmer, had become a wealthy company with revenues of $871 million by 1998. It sold sequencing machines to the centers of the Human Genome Project. The company's new President, Michael Hunkapiller, a former assistant of Leroy Hood at CalTech, boldly attacked his academic customers by deciding to launch a private project to decode the human genome before the Human Genome Project. Basically, he was convinced that the result depended on his machines, not on the army of biologists of the research centers, and that private industry would be more efficient than government bureaucracies. He hired a man who shared his passion for automated genetic processing, Craig Venter of Maryland's Institute for Genomic Research, where the first sequencing ("mapping") of a living being's genome had been carried out in 1995. Venter had fallen out with Haseltine after their mutual investor Steinberg had died in 1997, since Venter was more interested in the science and Haseltine in creating a multibillion-dollar pharmaceutical conglomerate.

In May 1998, Michael Hunkapiller and Venter set up a new company, Celera Genomics, which soon relocated to the Alameda, near Oakland. Technically, both Biosystems of Foster City and Celera Genomics of Alameda were owned by Applera, a spin-off of Perkin-Elmer's Life Sciences Division which in 2000 also became the official new name of Perkin-Elmer. However, in 2006, Applera renamed itself Applied Biosystems and spun off Celera Genomics. It was a confusing business story that still left two tightly related companies, one engaged in building machines and the other one in using those machines to sequence DNA. The main investor in both was Cuban-born businessman Tony White, the head of their parent company who had brokered the deal between Venter and Hunkapiller. Celera Genomics hired a staff of distinguished scholars, including Nobel laureate Hamilton Smith, and bought 300 of Applied Biosystems' most advanced machines to create the world's largest automated factory for mapping DNA.

Other companies were also important. The Israeli-born computer scientist Victor Markowitz, who had developed a data management system for genome databases at the Lawrence Berkeley Labs, founded the bioinformatics company Gene Logic in Berkeley in 1997 to market a database management system for gene expression data to biotech companies.

In 1997 the Department of Energy established the Joint Genome Institute (JGI) in an industrial park in Walnut Creek, northeast of Berkeley, to coordinate the three main biological laboratories involved in genomics: Lawrence Berkeley Labs, Lawrence Livermore Labs, and Los Alamos, located in New Mexico. In 2010, JGI would hire Victor Markowitz of Gene Logic as chief information officer.

The local universities were central to biotech's development. In the 1990s Stanford held 124 biotech patents, SRI International had 50, and the University of California as a whole had 321 (mainly at Berkeley and San Francisco). Some private companies had many patents too: Genentech 335, Incyte 322, Alza 238, Syntex 168, Chiron 167. Genentech's former employees had opened more than thirty Bay Area-based startups. South San Francisco, where the Genentech campus was located, had become a major R&D center for biomedicine. For example, Exelixis and Cytokinesis had been started in 1997 a few blocks from Genentech. Investment in biotech companies peaked at $1 billion in the year 2000, up from $668 million in 1999. Between 1995 and 2000, $3 billion in venture capital had created 71 startups. At the beginning of 2000 the Bay Area's 90 publicly-traded biotech companies reached a market capitalization of $82 billion. Meanwhile, in 1998 James Thomson at University of Wisconsin and John Gearhart at Johns Hopkins University reported that they had grown human embryonic stem cells.

As biotech boomed, nanotechnology finally began to take off in the second half of the 1990s. One important startup was NeoPhotonics, founded in 1997 by Timothy Jenks and specializing in photonic integrated circuits. A merge of biotech and nanotech (Micro-Electro-Mechanical Systems or MEMS) took place in 1996 with the founding of Cepheid in Sunnyvale. The company's goal was to build machines that perform rapid molecular testing, typically to detect infectious disease and cancer, i.e. to provide DNA test results when and where they are needed.

Culture and Society

San Francisco's counterculture reacted again in its own idiosyncratic manner to the capitalistic culture of Silicon Valley. Since Silicon Valley had adopted the religion of ever faster and cheaper products, in 1996, Stewart Brand of Whole Earth fame and Danny Hillis, who had designed the supercomputer Connection Machine at MIT, established the "Long Now Foundation" to promote slower and better thinking, long-term thinking.

Meanwhile, pop and dance musicians such as Dan Nakamura, Matmos, Kit Clayton, Kid 606, Blectum From Blechdom and Irr. App. (Ext.) were pushing the envelope of digital music, showing what could be done with a simple laptop, while the psychedelic tradition survived in Devendra Banhart.

During the 1990s the population of the Bay Area grew by 13%. The San Francisco- Oakland- San Jose metropolitan region had seven million people in 2000, making it the fifth largest metropolitan area in the US.

The Anthropology of the Untouchables

In the 1990s the median income in Santa Clara County was almost twice the median income in the US, but within the Valley the income gap kept increasing. There were at least three classes with widely different income levels.

The common laborers, such as the security guards who worked night shifts, the cleaning people, and the clerks of the gas stations, had a low income. It was difficult for them to afford the cost of living of the Bay Area. Many of them resided in the East or South Bay, where rent was cheaper, and many of them lived in old-fashioned familiar groupings. They were not very visible: you had to take one of the freeways into the Bay Area very early in the morning to see them commute to work from distant places.

Then there was the huge mass of engineers, who could afford a nice car and a nice apartment. However, the cost of living was such that many of them shared a house or an apartment with someone else. Those who bought a house most likely bought a town home in a subdivision. Each subdivision provided long lines of identical homes with minimal separation from each other. These were the most visible inhabitants of the valley, stuck in traffic during rush hours.

The upper class consisted of the rich: either hereditary rich or beneficiaries of the computer boom. Their company was acquired, their company's stock had skyrocketed, or they were just highly paid executives. This third class was much larger than in any other part of the world. Entire areas of Atherton, Woodside, Portola Valley, and Los Gatos were carpeted with multimillion-dollar homes.

And yet the lower class was dreaming of sending its children to school so that they would become engineers, and the engineering class was dreaming of becoming millionaires, so both castes happily accepted their subordinate roles.

Finally, there was the old generation who bought a home in the 1960s and lived a much more relaxed life in single-family detached houses, most of them with a swimming pool and a large backyard. They paid very little for their house before the computer boom. During the 1990s, as they began to retire, many of them sold their homes to the younger generation of the computer boom. This generation of ordinary middle-class families quietly faded away, enjoying the profits from their investment in real estate but rapidly obsolete in the digital age.

28. Googlers: A Case Study on Google from Search Startup to Big Brother (1995-2013)

Google the Startup

In the fall of 1995, Larry Page and Sergey Brin met at Stanford University. Page was a 22-year old University of Michigan grad and Brin was a 21-year old Stanford student assigned to show him around. Upon meeting and conversing, they disagreed about almost everything they discussed, but Brin convinced Page to come to Stanford. As PhD students the next year, they began collaborating on a search engine called BackRub, which operated on Stanford's servers for more than a year. It eventually took up too much bandwidth and the university complained. In 1997, they renamed BackRub "Google" (a play on the word "googol," a mathematical term for the number represented by the numeral 1 followed by 100 zeros). Brin and Page intended that the term reflect their mission to organize a seemingly infinite amount of information on the web.

The website started to grow in popularity, suggesting it could be commercialized. In August 1998, Brin and Page convinced SUN Microsystems co-founder Andy Bechtolsheim to write a check for $100,000 to an entity that didn't exist yet: a company called Google Inc. They quickly set up a workspace in Susan Wojcicki's garage at 232 Santa Margarita, Menlo Park and filed for incorporation in California on September 4, 1998, so they could cash the check. They hired Craig Silverstein, a fellow Stanford computer science grad student, as their first employee and worked on optimizing the site. By December, PC Magazine praised Google for having "an uncanny knack for returning extremely relevant results." The magazine gave Google its top spot for search engines for its Top 100 Web Sites for 1998.

By February 1999 Google outgrew the garage office and moved to new space at 165 University Avenue in Palo Alto, Silicon Valley's "luckiest" building, with just 8 employees. Some accounts suggest that Page and Brin wanted to return to their studies and offered to sell the company then for $1 million to Excite and Yahoo; both companies turned down the offer. Instead, in June the founders accepted a $25 million venture investment from Sequoia Capital and Kleiner Perkins, when John Doerr and Michael Moritz joined the board. This investment and its follow-on ones would prove to be the highest returning investment made in the world in the decade of the 1990s, worth between $40 to $75 billion in 2007 at Google's market capitalization peak (only eBay came close from a total dollar perspective). The company used the money to move to its first Mountain View location, a city south of Palo Alto that would become its home base. To emphasize its fun culture, Google hired Charlie Ayers, the former Grateful Dead cook, in November 1999 as its first chef in a cook-off (his stock options would be worth millions by 2005). Offering nice perks to win the Valley's talent war was a key part of Google's early cultural DNA; the food perk was offered before the company was even profitable. By May 2000, Google had sites in 10 languages, including: French, German, Italian, Swedish, Finnish, Spanish, Portuguese, Dutch, Norwegian, and Danish. The company also won two important Webby Awards: Technical Achievement (voted by judges) and People's Voice (voted by users). A great service was born, but it was not a business. It hadn't been monetized, as user searches had not been translated to profits. Yet the company was different and becoming successful.

Google's success came from following a few key principles, later codified into its corporate philosophy. The first principle was to focus on the user; all else would follow. A focus on providing the best user experience possible, and not badgering the user with ads or irrelevant information, was a key edge when most companies did the opposite. The homepage interface was clear and simple. The second principle was "fast is better than slow," and required the company to respect users' time. So the pages loaded instantly. Google's founders could honestly say: "We may be the only people in the world who can say our goal is to have people leave our homepage as quickly as possible." All ads were clearly marked as such and tastefully kept aside, and also relevant and not distracting. Third, Google basically did one thing "really, really well" by initially focusing on search and not many other lines of business.

Google the Business

Google's big break came in June 2000. Yahoo decided to get out of the search technology business and so contracted to make Google its default search provider. It was a big mistake in hindsight. Google had then built the first billion-URL index to become the world's largest search engine. In October Google finally launched its first product, Google AdWords, with 350 customers. The self-service ad program offered online activation with a credit card, keyword targeting, and performance feedback. More importantly, in March 2001 the founders brought on Eric Schmidt as chairman of the board of directors; they named him CEO in August, so the three could run the firm as a triumvirate. In the summer the firm launched Image Search, offering access to 250 million images, and opened its first international office in Tokyo, the first of many offices around the world. The index size had grown to 3 billion web documents. Google's technology was clearly superior in many ways to the technology of the other web-search contenders. In January 2001 Google hired Wayne

Rosing, a Silicon Valley veteran who had overseen the Lisa at Apple and Java at SUN. In February Google completed its first acquisition, an archive of the old Usenet, dating back to 1995, to create an extra application (Google Groups). It was the same tactic used in the past by Microsoft to create its portfolio of applications. Venture capitalists John Doerr of Kleiner-Perkins and Michael Moritz of Sequoia Capital became more involved in steering the business of the company. In 2002 Google got the support of AOL, the new owner of Netscape and a rival of Microsoft.

The biggest internal argument was how to directly monetize search queries, and whether contextual ads directed at a search would be helpful or a distraction. They tested a service in 2000 allowing advertisers to put up "sponsored links" at low-risk, as Google would only charge if a user clicked on a link. Wanting to keep the integrity of the service, the ad had to be relevant to the search terms; otherwise there would be no ad and initially 85% of searches had no ads.

The Faustian deal for Google's rapid success was AdWords, a pay-per-click advertising system, by far its main source of revenues. Google had started selling "sponsored links" in 2000, a practice already followed by their rivals. This was a manual process involving a salesperson and it mainly targeted large corporations. AdWords, introduced in 2002, was mostly automated and, because it slashed the price of posting an ad on the Web, it targeted medium and small businesses that had been reluctant to advertise on the Web. In the end, Google decided to roll its ad interface out, and in February 2002 the company released a major overhaul for AdWords, including new cost-per-click pricing. This was one of the most cost-effective ways of reaching desirable customers in the history of advertising, as people with search terms had "revealed intent/preferences;" users basically showed they wanted to learn about, and maybe buy, something specific. It allowed advertisers to make a guess on how to hook the user. It was also a money-making machine, one of the most profitable companies ever. Google's revenues went from $400 million in 2002 to $1.4 billion in 2003, $6.1 billion in 2005, and $16.5 billion in 2007. Net income grew from $100 million in 2002 to $4.2 billion in 2007. More than 95% of its revenue still came from the text ads.

The days of a commercial-free Web were not only over: Google de-facto turned the Web into an advertising tool that incidentally also contained information. The business model was the ultimate in cynicism. Millions of website editors spread all over the world added content to the Web on a daily basis, and Google used that colossal amount of free content as a vehicle to sell advertising services to businesses. Web surfers used Google to search for information, but Google "used" them to create the audience that justified the amount it charged for advertising. Both the producers of content and the consumers of content were getting no money out of this splendid business model. Intermediaries had always made money in business, but this case was different. Google was an intermediary of sorts in the flow of content from producer to consumer and was making money even though there was no money transaction between producer and consumer. The money was coming from an external entity that wanted to sell its products to the consumer. Every time someone added a webpage to the Web it made Google more powerful. Unlike traditional intermediaries, which made money by charging a fee per each transaction, Google never charged the user anything for searching. Yahoo and Excite had already understood the power of this business plan but Google was the one that implemented it to perfection.

Google's real innovation was in the field of advertising. In June 2003 Google introduced AdSense, designed by Paul Buchheit. It was a vast technological improvement over AdWords: content-targeted advertising. AdSense was capable of "understanding" the topic of a webpage and therefore automatically assign to it the relevant ads among all the ads provided by paid advertisers. By systematically monitoring the behavior of its search engine's users, Google had invented an automated system with three aims: first, for advertisers to create more effective ads; second, for Google itself to display more relevant ads; and third, for users to view the most relevant ads. The traditional ad in a newspaper had mostly been a one-sided decision, based on what an advertiser wanted to print and how much it was willing to pay, mediated by one of the newspaper's salespeople. In Google's world the ad became a computer-mediated deal among three entities: the advertiser, Google's AdSense, and the user. Basically, AdSense created an infinite feedback loop that allowed advertisers to continuously improve their adverts, and at the same time promoted a race among advertisers to develop the "fittest" ad in a sort of Darwinian process. If previous progress in search-based advertising had lowered the barrier from large corporations to small businesses, AdSense enabled any content provider, from established news media to the smallest website on a rock star run by a teenage fan, to monetize its content. Of course, this also led to an alienating process in which very serious texts were being used to publicize trivial products (famously AdSense associated ads about plastic bags with the news of a murderer who had stuffed its victim's body parts in a plastic bag). The new landscape for advertisers was the whole behavior of the user, that Google monitored as much as possible through the user's searches. Thus, for example, someone dying of cancer and desperately searching the Web for medicines and devices would automatically be turned by AdSense into a golden business opportunity for any company advertising those medicines and those medical devices.

Yahoo! had lost part of its sheen, but still generated yearly revenues of $1.6 billion in 2003 (up from $953 million in 2002), with an astronomical yearly growth and market value. In 2003 it acquired Overture/GoTo, nurtured by Los Angeles-based incubator Idealab, and introduced the "pay per click" business model for advertisers instead of the traditional "per view" model. GoTo had also introduced the idea of letting advertisers bid to show up higher in the results of a search (the "pay-for-placement" model).. In 2006 revenues would reach $6.4 billion. Note that the dotcom companies were mainly selling ads. The initial dotcom business plan of simply becoming popular had eventually worked out: all you needed was a large audience, and then the advertisers would flock to your website. What was missing in the 1990s was the advertisers.

Except for the few headline stories, the new Silicon Valley startup was very different from the exuberant ones of the 1990s. The term "ramen profitable" was coined by venture capitalist Paul Graham to refer to a startup that makes enough money to pay the bills while the founders aim for a big score.

Google's goal was to make money without doing evil. This was a balance between being a business generating revenue from search and ads, while making sure the core service wasn't compromised and that ads were relevant to searches. The early "Don't Be Evil" motto was coined by Paul Bucheit, the engineer behind Gmail, after a July 2001 meeting of early employees to state the company's core values. It began with clichés like: "Treat Everyone with Respect," for example, or "Be on Time for Meetings." The engineers in the room, who were very anti-corporate, were rolling their eyes because they hated specific rules and wanted a single, generalized statement. That's when Paul Buchheit blurted out what would become perhaps the most unique corporate motto ever. Buchheit said: "All of these things can be covered by just saying, 'Don't Be Evil." The message stuck and was embraced by the founders, for example, when considering whether to enter and exit the China market. Or as Page said: "When you are making decisions, it causes you to think. I think that's good."

Much was being said of Google's ethics that allowed employees vast freedom to be creative. However, almost all of Google's business was driven by acquisition of other people's ideas. Gmail, developed internally by former Intel employee Paul Buchheit and launched by invitation only in April 2004, was not much more than Google's version of Hotmail. What made it popular was the hype caused by the "invitation-only" theatrics, plus the large amount of storage space offered. Google Checkout, introduced in June 2006, was a poor man's version of PayPal. Google Streetview, introduced in 2007, was quote similar to Vederi's ScoutTool (StreetBrowser), launched in 2000. So Vederi sued. Google's Android operating system for smartphones, acquired in 2005 from the namesake startup and introduced in 2007, was widely believed (not only by Steve Jobs) to be a diligent but uninspired imitation of the iPhone's operating system. The "semantic" improvement to the Google search engine of 2009 was due to the Orion search engine, developed in Australia by Israeli-born Ori Allon an acquired in 2006.

Google replicated Microsoft's model. Its own research labs were incredibly inept at inventing anything original, despite the huge amount of cash poured into them. That cash mostly bought them patents on countless trivial features of their products, a tactic meant to prevent innovation by the competition. What drove Google's astronomical growth was the business strategy, not the inventions.

Google kept releasing other products after ads. It released a set of APIs, enabling developers to query more than 2 billion Web documents and program in their favorite environment (Java, Perl, or Visual Studio). This was followed with the successful launch of Google News in September 2003, with 4000 news sources, and the launch in January 2004 of Orkut (Google's social networking service, with modest success in places like Brazil, but a failure in the US). At that point the search index hit a new milestone: 6 billion items, including 4.28 billion web pages and 880 million images. In 2002 Google acquired Blogger and in 2004 they acquired Keyhole (a CIA-funded startup), the source for their application Google Earth. More than a search engine, Google was expanding in all directions, becoming a global knowledge provider.

Three interesting elements of the Google corporate culture were: data-driven experimentation, scalability, and redundancy. First, everything was tested with hypotheses, data collection, analysis, and then more experiments. The exact placement of text and ads on a search results screen was measured, along with font size, color, and other minute variables. Google even did eye-tracking research on user groups to see where a user's attention was focused on a page.

For scalability, the idea was to apply machine intelligence to a search problem, and then apply it on a very large scale. The goal was to use software algorithms and automation and minimize human involvement in the end product, as it applied to billions of transactions. Scalability also became evident when Google decided to build its server hardware and infrastructure early on by itself, instead of using outside mainframes or servers. Page and Brin first assembled their own machines with generic, standard parts, and this "in house" hardware mentality continued as Google grew bigger. One advantage Google had was that many dot.com server farms were going bust around 2001, so Google could buy their data centers at "fire sale" prices. Multiple server farms in disparate locations, like Dalles, Oregon or Lenoir, North Carolina, were opened for redundancy. By 2012 Google probably operated the largest cluster of computer server farms in the world, far larger than any single government. By late 2006, analysts estimated Google had about 500,000 to one million servers. Each server farm cost about $600 million to open. By 2012, the number had presumably crossed 2 million servers over dozens of locations globally; the exact number was a closely-guarded corporate secret.

Google the Multinational Monopolist

Google grew and prospered, dwarfing even the excesses of the dotcom bubble. In 2003 Google had 10,000 servers working nonstop to index the Web (14 times more servers than employees). In March 2004 Google moved to a large facility called the "Googleplex" at 1600 Amphitheatre Parkway in Mountain View. This gave the 800+ employees a campus environment and prepared the company for an initial public offering (IPO). This took place on August 18, 2004, when 19,605,052 shares of Class A common stock were issued and started trading at $85 per share. The IPO showed the founders' determination and creativity in a few ways. First, it was a dual-share IPO, so the founders retained voting control over the company and could think long-term. Second, it was a Dutch auction IPO, something that went against the Wall Street norm, but which the founders thought was more efficient. Finally, the IPO raised $2,718,281,828 (reflecting the mathematical constant "e," which is 2.718281828).

By October 2004, the company launched Google Desktop Search to help people search for files and documents stored on their hard drive using Google technology. It was the first of many encroachments on Microsoft's monopoly on operating systems and desktop office software. The company also launched Gmail in April 2004, a revolutionary service challenging Yahoo's mail service and Microsoft's Hotmail for many reasons. First, Gmail offered many times more the amount of storage, a multiple in the hundreds. Second, its search functionality and speed of operation were much better than the competitors, due to an Ajax interface, which later became the de facto standard for webmail. Third, it was entirely free! The launch itself was an excellent viral marketing campaign, where new users had to be invited in; open access Gmail wasn't available till April 2007. One final benefit of Gmail was that a profitable ad technology, AdSense, was developed by the Gmail team and later used with other products like Blogger.

After Gmail, Google launched four products, three of which were revolutionary. The minor product was the beta version of Google Scholar, a free service for searching scholarly literature such as peer-reviewed papers, theses, books, preprints, abstracts, and technical reports. While buggy, it worked much better than previous types of scholarly search tools.

More importantly, in December 2004 the company began the Google Print Program (later named Google Books). It aimed to scan and digitize the libraries of Harvard, Stanford, the University of Michigan, Oxford, and the New York Public Library, the largest research libraries in North America and the UK. Only the University of Michigan, under the brave leadership of President Mary Sue Coleman, gave unfettered access to its books in and out of copyright. The project began when Page and Marissa Mayer, a Google exec, ran an experiment by turning the pages of a 300-page book, one by one, by the cadence of a metronome. They found that 40 minutes was needed, and with this data they estimated the cost of scanning 30 million books at $50 per book to be about $1.5 billion. Google Books was the first attempt to create a universal library since the Library of Alexandria was destroyed in the third century CE; Project Gutenberg and the Million Book Project were precursors that moved too slowly. It was a monumental endeavor of global human history, and the initiative started at a Silicon Valley company. The project was promptly bogged down by short-sighted American lawyers and publishers. The company had a goal to finish digitizing every book in WorldCat, the union catalogue of 25,000 libraries worldwide, by 2015.

Of equal importance was the launch of Google Maps in February 2005. The API was made open that June, allowing developers to embed Google Maps on many kinds of mapping services and sites, and therefore destroying Yahoo Maps in a contest for dominance. Google Maps would grow to allow anyone to map any route they wanted in the developed world, and eventually to even see street views. Both Books and Maps were audacious programs that exemplified Google's principles that "There's always more information out there" to digitize and make accessible and that "the need for information crosses all borders." Books and Maps would eventually try to reach many languages in many countries. MapQuest, the pioneering Web-based mapping service acquired by AOL in 2000, lost to Google Maps because the latter allowed third-party developers to add information to the map and use the map in their own software. The time-consuming process of scaling a web application was more easily done by "exploiting" the Internet community of software developers.

Finally, Google Translate was disclosed in May 2005. Google had prepared an algorithm by using multilingual documents from the UN, with 200 billion word pairs and phrasings. The statistical machine algorithm was self-teaching and gave accurate and often fluid translations of difficult languages like Chinese and Arabic. The company placed the algorithm in a contest run by the NIST standards agency of the US government, and it scored 1st among 11 entrants. Google's data centers spare memory were used for massive parallel processing, as hard drives couldn't handle the load of statistical machine translation and the trillions of permutations involved. By the spring of 2007, Google offered first rate translations of 23 languages, not only from non-English to English, but also translation between any pairing of languages.

Google was well-positioned for the decade by focusing on mobile search, analytics, and on attracting talent through perks. In June 2005 the company launched Google Mobile Web Search, specially formulated for viewing search results on mobile phones; mobile Gmail was launched later in the year. Mobile would prove to be very important for the company's long term strategy, as the Web moved to cloud services, multiple devices, and enhanced mobility. Google got this trend earlier than most when it formulated this principle: "You don't need to be at your desk to need an answer . . . people want access to information wherever they are, whenever they need it." The company also released Google Analytics (formerly Urchin) to help websites measure site visits and the impact of marketing campaigns. Meanwhile the company offered perks like lectures (Authors@Google), free gourmet food, massages, gaming, and so on.

Meanwhile, both Yahoo and Microsoft were being left behind. Google went from 47% of the search market in April 2002 to 58% in January 2008. Yahoo went from 21% to 22%. A Microsoft employee, Robert Scoble, blogged in 2004 about how Google's search results were better than MSN Search. Meanwhile, when a star Microsoft developer, Mark Lucovsky, told CEO Steve Ballmer, that he was leaving for Google, Ballmer threw a chair across his office and said he was going to "bury" Google's Eric Schmidt. According to the SF Chronicle, Ballmer blurted: "I'm going to fucking kill Google."

Google did make mistakes. A few failures over the growth years tempered the company. Google News was launched in 2003 and updated in 2005, but by 2007 it only drew 30% of the traffic of Yahoo News, which had human editors. It seemed that larger datasets did not make the algorithm better at identifying important or relevant news articles. Google Finance to search financial information was launched in March 2006 but was a bust compared to Yahoo Finance and Bloomberg. A free citywide WiFi service launched in August 2006 didn't go anywhere. More controversially, Google spent $1.65 billion in October 2006 to acquire YouTube, an online video company, after its own Google Video service fizzled. YouTube by some estimates still lost $300-500 million a year in 2009. By 2012 it was still unclear whether YouTube and its offshoot, GoogleTV, would be a failure or a large success. One thing was evident; Google was a dominant player in web video, with a strong network effect position.

Failures were made less painful by playfulness of employees, like the April Fool's Day joke of 2006 (an annual tradition). Google launched a new (fake) product, Google Romance: "Dating is a search problem." In honor of the company's popularity and penetration, the Oxford English Dictionary (OED) added "Google" as a verb.

Google also mounted a more serious attack on Microsoft, first by acquiring Writely, a web-based word processing application that would become the core of Google Docs, to challenge Microsoft Word and Office. It also started Google Calendar to challenge Outlook, and acquired Picasa Web Albums, to allow users to upload and share photos online. When Docs were attached to a premium version of Gmail, a new product, Google

Apps was created, and sold for $50 a year per user to university accounts and eventually companies. By the first quarter of 2007, this was a $37 million business. Google Apps was a formidable first attempt at a Software as a Service (SaaS) or "cloud" product, where applications are run from Internet servers (the "cloud") and not from a user's desktop.

By July 2008, Google's indexing system for processing links showed the firm had 1 trillion unique URLs, with the number of individual web pages growing by several billion pages per day. Page and Brin were adamant that their algorithm would not be tampered with by human hands, but they did allow human evaluators to judge the relative quality of results from different algorithmic tweaks. This was used to improve the final algorithm. Google Streetview, launched in May 2007, also allowed Maps users to actually see and walk through streets. The service was created by sending hundreds of trucks with cameras through all the major cities of the US, and eventually the world. For the first time, anyone in China or India could "walk" through NYC, LA, Paris, London, or any other global city. More ominously, the firm continued its attack on Microsoft by launching a new browser, Chrome, in September 2008, following the launch of Google Docs and Spreadsheets in October 2006; presentations were added the next year.

Google was quirky. In October 2008, right before the US Presidential election, it released a draft proposal to wean the US off of coal and oil for electricity use and to reduce oil use by cars 40% by 2030. That same month, employees in Mountain View built a zip line to travel across the small Permanente Creek separating a few of the company's buildings (one can imagine the lawyers at any other company killing such an idea). This illustrated the company's principle that "you can be serious without a suit." It was a minor detail, but like most startups in Silicon Valley, employees could actually wear anything they wanted in a Google office, within the bounds of hygiene. The company celebrated freedom.

The biggest challenge Google faced after 2008 was losing talent. Key employees left to start companies externally, and many felt the intimate atmosphere of the company had faded. Common reasons included a lack of smaller community at Google, or a lack of incentives that a startup could provide; an entrepreneur could work to the bone but potentially be rewarded by millions. In March 2009, Google launched its own venture capital arm to at least track and invest in talent across Silicon Valley. Time will tell if this strategy works.

By late 2010, Google showed a 23% year-over-year profit growth and had promising developments in search-linked advertising, its Android mobile phone platform, and advertising development for YouTube and Google TV. Also, Google launched other amazing projects in 2010 like the Google Car, driven by a machine algorithm over 140,000 miles of road with minimal human control. This would be an early entry into the operating system of a car in a potential future world where all cars drive themselves, and computer systems in cars tend to human needs. Google also decided to invest up to $5 billion with others in offshore wind energy in a project called the Atlantic Wind Connection. One potential use would be to power its East Coast server farms with green energy, both "doing good" and securing a reliable power source in case coal or natural gas power plants became too expensive or had a breakdown (a risk mitigation and energy redundancy motive).

One remarkable fact about Google, a company built on search relevance, was that Page, Brin, and Schmidt had an estimate for how long their company will be relevant. Given Google's mission to organize all the world's information, they estimate it would take 200-300 years to get all the world's information, including all scientific facts, information on human emotions, memories in people's brains, and non-factual information, collected and organized. With about 14 years having passed by 2012, the company was only about 3-4% there. Yet the founders and their team were thinking big and thinking about the long-term; something rare for any human endeavor.

Google vs Apple vs Facebook vs Amazon vs...

During the 2000s, Google largely represented the battle between the Web-based world against the desktop-based world of Microsoft. Google won this ideological battle, as even Microsoft was beginning to move towards cloud-based applications. Yet Google made little money out of it. Mostly it was the big virtualization platforms that were benefiting from this epochal switch in computing platforms. Google and Facebook were growing due to business plans that relied almost exclusively on selling advertising. They both offered a free service: in Google's case, many free services. Their services were based on content (text, images, videos, posts) provided for free by millions of "volunteers" (the internet public). Both companies made money by selling advertising space to companies eager to publicize their products to the viewers of all that content. Neither Google nor Facebook was creating any content. They existed as parasites off of other people's content. Neither had found a way to make money other than through advertising techniques. From a strategic point of view, though, there was a difference between the two.

Google's search engine had been invincible for a few years, but by the end of the decade it was increasingly weaker than other kinds of businesses. It was becoming apparent to Google's own management that the switching cost for a user to adopt one of the newer and perhaps better search engines was virtually zero. The network effect of a search engine is low by definition: a network effect is how much the value of the product depends on the number of users using it. On the contrary, Facebook enjoyed both high switching costs that kept users from leaving and so its network effect was very high. It was no surprise then that in 2011, Google announced Google+, its second attempt at establishing a viable social-networking platform after the embarrassing Buzz and Wave failures. By then, Facebook had passed 750 million users.

At the same time, Google invested in the smartphone market. In July 2008, Apple had launched the App Store for iOS applications (an iOS device was an iPhone, iPod Touch or iPad). By July 2011, the App Store had 425,000 apps uploaded by thousands of third party developers, downloaded 15 billion times on 200 million iOS devices. By then Google's equivalent, the Android Market, had 250,000 applications, downloaded 6 billion times on 135 million Android devices; more importantly, the Android store was growing faster. Google was activating new Android devices at the rate of 550,000 per day. By the end of 2011 Android smartphones owned 46.3% of the market and Apple iPhones owned 30%, leaving RIM (14.9%) and Microsoft (4.6%) way behind: there was now one area in which Silicon Valley alone beat the rest of the world.

Google's management, probably aware that Google's successes tended to be the ones acquired from others as opposed to the ones developed internally, launched Google Ventures, the venture-capital arm of the company. Basically, it was beginning to make sense for Google to invest its huge cash reserves into other companies rather than into Google's own R&D. Google was trying yet another revolutionary business model: to become an incubator of startups (infotech, biotech and cleantech). As an incubator, it offered a much more powerful infrastructure than a venture capitalist could, starting with office space at its Googleplex and computing power in its gargantuan server farm. Google even offered a huge bonus ($10,000 in 2011) to any employee who suggested a startup resulting in an actual investment. Three major development platforms were competing for world domination: the Facebook Platform (launched in 2007), the iPhone App Store (2008) and the Android platform (2007).

The company that was rapidly losing its sheen was Yahoo!. Its advertising business remained strong but Yahoo! had done the opposite of Google: it invested in creating content, even hiring journalists and bloggers. Yahoo! had basically moved towards becoming a media company at a time when Google and Facebook had been moving towards the more cynical model of purely exploiting the content created by their users. In a sense, Yahoo! still believed in quality at a time when Google and Facebook were proving that quality did not matter anymore and that advertising revenues depended almost exclusively on quantity. To make matters worse, Yahoo! had not contrived a way to have its users disclose personal information the way Google and Facebook had, which meant that Google and Facebook could offer targeted advertising to their advertising customers, encroaching on as much privacy as tolerated by the law.

Yahoo! alumni were more creative than the company itself. In 2009, two Yahoo! executives, Brian Acton and Jan Koum, founded WhatsApp in Santa Clara to provide instant messaging over the Internet Protocol for smartphones (Android, BlackBerry, iPhone, etc). While Facebook and Google were not paying attention, WhatsApp did to SMS what Skype had done to the old telephone service: it turned it into a computer application. By the end of 2009, Whatsapp already had one million users; but that was just the beginning of its meteoric rise. One year later they were ten million, and by the end of 2012 Whatsapp had passed the 200 million users mark.

Another front in the multiple wars that Google was fighting was the intellectual-property front. In November 2010, a consortium including Microsoft, Apple, Oracle, and EMC paid $450 million for 882 networking-software patents owned by Novell, or about $510,000 per patent. They were not interested in Novell's technology, but simply in protecting themselves from potential lawsuits. In June 2011, a consortium that included Microsoft, Apple, Ericsson, Sony, EMC, and Research In Motion purchased the 6,000 patents for wireless communication owned by bankrupt telecom company Nortel. They paid $4.5 billion, or $750,000 for each patent. Microsoft now co-owned the Nortel patents for voice services and the Novell patents for Linux, while Apple co-owned the Nortel patents for manufacturing and semiconductors and Oracle owned the patents for Java (acquired from SUN). Google's Android service was left naked and subject to lawsuits. In August 2011, Google paid $12.5 billion for Motorola's smartphone business in order to acquire its 24,500 patents, which was about $510,00 per Motorola patent. The purpose became clear a few days later: Apple had levied multiple lawsuits against Android-based smartphone manufacturers like HTC and Samsung, accusing them of "copying" the iPhone, and now HTC was in a position to sue Apple using some of the patents purchased by Google.

During the second decade of the century Silicon Valley was devastated by such patent wars. Google, Apple, Oracle and others filed patents by the thousands, bought even more, and then filed lawsuits against each other. A patent was becoming a weapon of mass destruction: the richest corporations could file patents about the most trivial of ideas and use it to prevent competitors from implementing entire families of products. The main losers were the small companies and the startups; they did not have an army of attorneys to file patents and did not have an army of attorneys to fight the big corporations in court. We will never know how many inventors were on the brink of creating revolutionary products and either gave up, were forced to give up, or were acquired by bigger companies. The process of filing a patent was considered ridiculous by the very corporations that indulged in it, but there was no chance of changing it; those same corporations hired an army of lobbyists in Washington to counter any attempt to rectify a clearly flawed process. A patent is a license to sue. It rarely represents a true innovation. In most cases it represents the exact opposite: an impediment to innovation, and even a blunt threat to anyone who dares innovate. Companies that have limited cash were forced to spend much of it fighting lawsuits instead of spending it to fund research and development. More and more money was being spent to fund lawyers than to fund research, and Google was a large player in the game.

29. Monopolists: A Case Study on eBay, Google, Facebook, and Companies with Network Effects (1998-2013)

Explaining Network Effects

The most overhyped concept in Silicon Valley, especially when an Internet startup pitches venture capitalists in a Monday morning meeting, is that of a "network effect." A company's product shows a positive network effect when more usage of the product by any user increases the product's value for other users, and sometimes all users. As five companies have shown, finding and building a company around a network effect can create much social value and lead to a monopolistic position, like a 19th century railroad. The difference is that an Internet startup can create billions of dollars of wealth from little initial capital: a few servers run by some engineers. eBay, Craigslist, Google, Facebook, and Yelp have shown that proper execution can generate a network effect to make something socially useful and monetize the value being created.

The classic example illustrating a network effect is the cell phone network: the more people that have cell phones, the more useful a cell phone becomes to each person on the network. Some Internet businesses naturally lead themselves to network effects, like operating systems and browsers. The concept was first formally studied in the context of long-distance telephony in the 1970s (as part of the AT&T antitrust case), and researchers have uncovered empirical evidence of network effects in products as diverse as spreadsheets, databases, networking equipment, and DVD players.

Two specific types of network effects are interesting. First, indirect network effects occur when the use of a product spawns the production of other valuable, complementary goods. The two classic examples of this are: a computing platform like Apple's computers and its peripherals (the disk drives, keyboards, and other devices to connect to them); a cloud platform like the Facebook or Salesforce.com platform, and the apps built for them (Zynga's games or Jigsaw's contact data application). In an indirect network effect, one network acts like a host, and its success positively affects that of another entity, a parasite. Second, two-sided network effects occur when the increase in use by one set of users increases the value of a complementary product to a very distinct set of other users. Hardware software platforms (like the Windows-Intel combination) or matching services (like OKCupid's dating service or eBay's auction service, connecting buyers and sellers) show indirect network effects. Neither product is dependent on the other, but the success of one strongly affects the other.

eBay and Marketplace Networks

On Labor Day weekend in 1995, computer programmer Pierre Omidyar wrote the code for what he called an "experiment." What would happen if everyone in the world had equal access to a single global marketplace? Omidyar tested his new auction website, AuctionWeb, by posting a broken laser pointer, which he was about to throw away. To his surprise, a collector bought it for $14.83.

The sale of a broken laser pointer was the beginning of a radical transformation in commerce. At the beginning Omidyar ran it for free because his expenses were so low. When traffic became high and his web services company started charging him for the bandwidth, he decided to charge sellers a small fee: 5% for items sold below $25, and 2.5% for items above that. He didn't know if it would work, as no payment system existed. He found out it did work over the next few weeks as he got envelopes filled with nickels and dimes scotch-taped to index cards, not to mention crumpled dollar bills. One key innovation was a feedback forum where buyers could rate the honesty and efficiency of sellers, as the entire site was based on trust and reputation.

Other auction sites had existed, but their models were structurally flawed. Some had users bidding by email. Others had no search function or categories, so buyers had to spend much time searching. One serious competitor was OnSale, launched by the entrepreneur Jerry Kaplan, in May 1995. While OnSale had a lead in 1996, with four times the dollar transaction of AuctionWeb, its structural flaw was that it took possession of goods it sold as a middleman, usually remainder items or computers. While OnSale could control the customer experience better, it required a higher expense structure and complicated logistics.

As the site took off, Omidyar hired his first employee, Chris Agarpao, to help him handle the website's operations. In 1996, Omidyar hired his second employee, Jeff Skoll, as President of the company. Around the same time, Omidyar quit his day job at General Magic. Soon revenue topped $10,000 in a single month. By year-end, Gross Merchandise Volume (GMV), the amount sold on the site, was $7.2 million, with 41,000 users. To some extent, AuctionWeb was built on Beanie Babies, a popular group of collectible, mass-produced, plush bean-bag toys made by Ty Warner (Legs the Frog, Flash the Dolphin, Patti the Platypus, etc.).

There were a few key reasons why AuctionWeb succeeded at this point. First, auction theory suggests that auctions aren't an efficient way to sell most goods. But auctions are great for goods whose prices are theoretically indeterminate, like collectibles or antiques, where value is in the eye of the beholder. Second, AuctionWeb connected distant buyers and sellers much better than other options: flea markets, collector shows, and antique shops. Early collectors groups like Barbie or Star Trek fans flocked there. Third, AuctionWeb was extremely thrifty, unlike most dot.com startups. Salaries were low, office supplies were rationed, and the first thing a new employee had to do was assemble his or her cheap chair and desk. Meanwhile, gross margins were above 80%. Finally, AuctionWeb had a true first mover advantage. Registered sellers developed reputations, which made them sticky on the site. Buyers had no other place to go with as large a selection of sellers and goods. Eventually the lock-in became so strong that no other site could compete.

In 1997 AuctionWeb was officially retired for "eBay," and eBay hosted more than 200,000 individual auctions per month, compared with 250,000 auctions in all of 1996. That same year the Beanie Babies craze represented 6.6% of eBay.com's volume, or roughly $500,000. eBay ended the year with GMV of $95 million and 341,000 users. The company also took a venture capital investment from Benchmark Capital, though it didn't need the money. It did need the credibility to attract more talented engineers and seasoned management as it scaled. The next year, the company recruited Meg Whitman, a former Bain consultant and Disney strategy executive, as President and CEO. Later, eBay went public on NASDAQ on September 24, 1998, when its shares went up 163.2% to close at $47.375, up $29.375 from its target price of $18 a share. Gross profit margins were 88%, compared to 22% at Amazon.com. Omidyar, Skoll, and Whitman became billionaires, measured by paper wealth, the next year. The money meant little: Omidyar still drove his beat-up Volkswagen Cabriolet and Skoll kept his old Mazda while he kept living in a rental group house.

From 1998 to 2005, the firm's GMV of $700 million and 2.1 million users grew to $44.3 billion and 181 million users. The company expanded to a number of international locations and in 2000 made public the first of several Application Programming Interfaces (APIs), allowing developers to build custom interfaces and functionality. In 2000 the company acquired Half.com, a marketplace for used books, movies, music and games (one of its main competitors). It also introduced a "Buy It Now" feature, allowing buyers to shop at a fixed price. By 2001, eBay was even used to sell a Gulfstream jet for $4.9 million — the highest-priced item sold to date on eBay. One side effect of eBay was that prices for collectibles fell as amateurs listed them more alongside professionals. One study by Auctionbytes.com showed that prices fell 25%. For example, 1,314 auctions of Swarovski crystal pieces in one year had an average selling price of $51.61; a year later, 8,023 auctions had an average price of $38.03. eBay was making the market more liquid and efficient for "garage and attic" collectibles.

eBay had three important strategic acquisitions. First was Paypal in 2002, the web's leading payment system. Next in 2004 eBay Inc. acquired

Marktplaats.nl, the Netherlands' leading online classifieds site. This was to lead to the launch in 2005 of Kijiji, a local classifieds site available in nearly a dozen countries. Finally in 2005 eBay acquired Skype, the leading voice-over-the Internet telephone company (besides Vonage).

Some failed acquisitions were Rent.com in 2005 (the leading Internet listing site for rental housing in the US) and Shopping.com that same year. The company's employees topped 10,000. By 2007, eBay acquired StubHub, the world's largest online ticket marketplace, and expanded Kijiji to 200 US cities. Also Paypal accounted for 8% of all e-commerce worldwide. A year later, John Donahoe was named President and CEO of eBay Inc., succeeding Meg Whitman. PayPal opened its platform, PayPal X, becoming the first major global payments company open to third-party development. In 2009, eBay acknowledged that Skype was not critical to it and so sold the company to a group of investors, but retained a 30% stake; Microsoft ended up with control of Skype. At year-end 2009, eBays GMV was $57.2 billion, with over 90 million users. At the same time Paypal had a net total payment value of $71.6 billion with over 81 million users. In 2010 eBay relaunched its Kijiji classifieds site as eBayClassifieds.com, with some user and technology enhancements, but Craigslist was still far ahead.

After Whitman left, CEO John Donahoe was recasting Ebay into a retail and financial services outfit anchored around its core online marketplace and PayPal payments divisions. First, he expanded into retail logistics and services with the 2011 acquisition of GSI Commerce. Second, he followed Paypal's growth as a financial services company specializing in payments, controling the digital wallet and mobile payments from smartphones. eBay estimated that marketplace revenue would grow to $11.5 billion by 2015 while PayPal would generate $10.5 billion.

Craigslist and Classified Ad Networks

In 1995, an engineer named Craig Newmark began e-mailing out a list of technology events and opportunities to friends and acquaintances. It had Internet jobs, apartments, lectures, restaurant reviews, and local events. The list grew from about ten people to 240, the maximum e-mail ceiling on CCs, so Newmark moved to a listserv. Newmark had to give it a name. As he was a former network engineer for IBM and Schwab, he wanted to call it "SF-events." This was perfect for the nerd lacking interpersonal skills, someone with a tough time connecting and who was much more comfortable in e-mail than in person-to-person contact. But a friend responded: "To hell with that, don't make it fancy, just keep it Craigslist" (what everyone was calling it).

Craigslist soon passed a million page views a month. Newmark was using PERL-based code that converted e-mails to Web pages so that he could instantly publish friends' postings. An early decision was to turn down ads from Microsoft Sidewalks. Ads violated Newmark's philosophy, which was an absence of judgment, openness to human variety and needs, a desire to be amused, and near-complete indifference to the profit motive or traditional business values. The site grew to be a place for classified postings (for apartments, goods, jobs) and community listings (events, groups, thoughts).

Newmark's worldview was based on a simple belief: "People are good and trustworthy and generally just concerned with getting through the day... The purpose of the Internet is to connect people to make our lives better. We are just trying to give people a break." If most people are good and have simple needs, all one had to do to serve them well was build a minimal infrastructure allowing them to get together and work things out for themselves. All additional features were superfluous and hurtful. The site had a clean and unpretentious look, without graphics, like an early Internet application; its minimalist design was elegant.

Newmark left his day job in 1999 and incorporated the site, giving away 25% to a staffer, Phillip Knowlton. Newmark believed that Craigslist was a community trust that belonged to everyone. If he were to own the whole thing, he could develop a big ego and get "middle-aged crazy." He also decided against running Craigslist as a nonprofit, which would have required him to learn and follow too many rules (ironically, non-profits could be more complicated to run than for-profits, due to government rules). Newmark reasoned no one could stop him from giving away his money if he made too much of it.

In late 1999 the Tech Bubble started to burst. In 2000, after the implosion, Newmark hired Jim Buckmaster, a shy, black-haired coder who had been working at a dead start-up called Creditland. At that point the site was limited to San Francisco. Buckmaster took the initiative to launch it in Boston in June 2000 and two months later in New York, Chicago, L.A., Seattle, and Washington, D.C. All were launched with no marketing or publicity, as a public service and not as a business. Buckmaster shortly pushed it out to 34 countries. When Buckmaster joined, every posting had to be manually reviewed and approved by a staffer; not an efficient or scalable model for a technology business. Buckmaster also implemented a self-posting system, in which a user sends himself an e-mail and approves the listing; then it was published. This was soon coupled with a flagging system so offensive posts could automatically be removed through group consensus. Buckmaster also expanded the categories to include child care, political and legal discussion forums, the Missed Connections list, and a category called "Men Seeking Sex." Later, Newmark changed the title of this controversial group to "Casual Encounters," inspired by the TV show "Sex and the City." After only eleven months on the job, Newmark made Buckmaster his President and CEO, as he didn't want to administer the site and growing business.

Craigslist grew headily and started to decimate its key competitors, which were local newspaper classifieds. Many newspapers weren't even aware of Craigslist's existence from 1999-2004 while it destroyed one of their core revenue sources. Sometimes a site for a new city grew very slowly for a long time. But eventually the listings would hit a certain volume, a network effect tipping point, after which the site took off. As classifieds made up nearly 50% of big-city newspapers' revenues, Craigslist weakened the industry at its foundations, with one estimate being that revenue from newspaper classified ads was off nearly 50% from 1999 to 2009 (a drop of almost $10 billion). Consider the social wealth and productivity gain: it was much easier for people to post and search classified ads, but the cost to society went from about $10 billion to $100 million (Craigslist's estimated 2009 revenues). Hence Craigslist provided a much better service for 1/100th the cost. That is the promise of any great Internet-based, network-effect business.

In 2004, Knowlton sold his 28% stake to eBay million for $16 million (a very bad business decision, as the stake would easily be worth ten times that amount in 5 years). About another $16 million went to Craigslist for additional special rights, including the ability to veto certain corporate actions. The two companies initially claimed they had a good relationship. But then eBay tried to expand its own classified service, Kijiji, while Google launched Google Base. In 2008, eBay would even sue Craigslist as a minority shareholder, a battle that would continue into 2010. The sharks were circling but could get nowhere in the end.

Craigslist was one of the strangest network-effect monopolies in internet history. Customers were happy to be locked in by fees set at zero for nearly all the services. The for-profit company was happy operating as a public service and generally did not cooperate with other businesses or upgrade the technology or user interface. In August 2004, Craigslist began charging $75 to post listings in San Francisco and $25 to post openings in New York and LA. Even by 2012, the only postings that cost money to place on the site were job ads in some cities ($25 to $75), apartment listings by brokers in New York ($10), and advertisements in some adult categories, partly to keep records for police investigators. By 2005, Fortune estimated the company made more than $20 million a year. In 2009, Craigslist's largest category was New York apartments, where it posted more than half a million listings a month. There was still no banner advertising.

From 2006 to 2009, the open social forum created controversy. In July 2005, the SF Chronicle criticized Craigslist for allowing irresponsible dog breeders to sell pit bulls in the Bay Area. In August 2007 Atlanta's mayor wrote to the company to looking into ads that may have involved child prostitution. In February 2008, a Michigan woman was charged with using Craigslist to hire a contract killer to murder a romantic rival in Oroville, California. In April 2009, Boston police arrested a 23-year old Boston

University medical student, Philip Markoff, for robbing and murdering a woman who advertised her massage services on Craigslist in Boston.

Yet the site grew and solidified its network monopoly. By 2009, it got more than 3 billion page views per month (10 million actual users a month), ranking it seventh on the Net, not so far behind Google and eBay; but over 90% of its audience was estimated to be in the US by Alexa, a web analytics firm. No other classified site came close, let alone few other websites on the Internet. Craigslist got more traffic than either eBay or Amazon.com, which had 16,000 employees and more than 20,000, respectively. By 2010, Craigslist had about 30 employees, with a revenue-per-employee ratio of over $3 million, more than most investment banks in the US.

Craigslist could be one of the most effective businesses in the world, by any conventional measure: revenues per employee, return on equity, profit margins, etc.. Craigslist earned large amounts of cash, more than $100 million in 2009, by one estimate. It clearly used society's resources much more effectively than most web companies, and housed its offices in a small Victorian home in the gritty Sunset district of San Francisco (the servers were distributed at other locations for redundancy). Yet the owners' ethic was to be thrifty.

Newmark was a rich man who shunned the trappings of wealth. In refusing to take the company public or to sell any display advertising, Newmark stepped away from many millions. His ownership share was between 30% to 49%. But as an owner of a private company, he would answer to no one other than users. When anybody reminded Newmark of his net worth, he replied that there was nothing he would care to do with that much money: he already had a parking space for his car, a hummingbird feeder, a small home with a view, and a shower with strong water pressure. What else was necessary for life? Contrast this with the Boeing 747 jet the Google founders bought, while they simulated a green lifestyle driving Priuses and Teslas.

One big criticism of Craigslist was that it wouldn't cooperate with anyone, including government officials or other startups. If a developer built a third-party application designed to make Craigslist work better, Buckmaster and his crew often erected technical roadblocks to shut the site down. Numerous local governments have excoriated and even sued Craigslist for taking a fairly robust, libertarian stance in its policies.

All the day-to-day management of Craigslist was run by Buckmaster in 2012. The long-running Silicon Valley war between logical engineers and emotional marketers has been settled at Craigslist. The company had no marketers, but only programmers, customer service reps (Craig being an important one), and accounting staff. Craigslist had no sales, human resources, or business development group or staff. Even better, there were no meetings. The staff communicated by email and IM. This was a nice environment for techie employees, as Buckmaster said: "Not that we're a

Shangri-La or anything, but no technical people have ever left the company of their own accord."

Newmark had a presence as a guiding founder and an evangelist. He also worked customer service hard. In 2008, Newmark got about 195,000 email messages. He estimated that roughly 60% were spam. He read all the rest and replied to many. Newmark cared about the details, about executing all the little things users would like the site to do. Newmark replied: "I'm not interested in politics, I'm interested in governance. . . Customer service is public service."

Google's Search and Contextual Ad Dominance through Network Effects

Google's core search technology made it a natural monopoly, both for information search on the Internet and contextual ads. Many of its other applications, like Gmail, Maps, Books, and so on, reinforced that status. A natural monopoly existed when there was great scope for economies of scale to be exploited over a very large range of output (here search indexing and queries). Power lines were a good example of a natural monopoly; only one set was needed for any community, and duplication is wasteful and inefficient.

Search was a classic network effect service. The more people that used a search engine and clicked on results, the better a search engine could be at optimizing results and so have more relevant results, attracting more users. As a result of a positive network effect, with current search algorithms only one firm should dominate. Some argued that Gmail and other applications were also used to reinforce the strength in search and contextual ads, as Google mined users' email boxes for useful information and targeted them based on it.

Two types of consumers co-existed in the online ad market and they were joined at the hip. The individual surfer used a search engine, e-mail services, and other applications to find content and get targeted results (ads could come up with the search results, or on the content page through an ad network). The online ad buyer was also a consumer, interested in targeting her ad to the surfer, and she cared about clickthrough, cost-per click, revenues per click, and other measures of how effective an ad was. If the individual surfer stopped using Google, the ad buyer would find Google's targeted search and ad networks less valuable.

For Google users, the charge for the service was nothing; it was free. But what search companies were fighting over was the quality of the search results and the output of queries; they competed to provide the best service to users. Search quality was measured by criteria such as: not being overinclusive or underinclusive in the results; time to execute the search; ranking priority (more relevant sites should have a higher priority); description of results (brief, on-point results are better). If a company's output, the total number of queries and the queries per searcher, was high, then the search engines could extract more money from ad buyers.

Clearly, quality and range of services drove output; the more powerful, relevant, fast, or comprehensive a search engine was, and the better the ancillary services like e-mail, aggregated news, etc., the more likely it was to attract new searchers. Over time, most users switched to Google's services because they offered the most (e.g. the most e-mail storage), the best search engine from a technical viewpoint, and what many thought were the best other ancillary services like Maps and messaging.

Ad buyers cared about prices only as they related to their metrics of value received such as cost per impression (CPM), cost per click (CPC), and cost per acquisition (CPA). For example, ad buyers wanted their profits from a conversion to exceed their cost-per-click, or want to get a large audience, so care about impressions. The five search companies competed weakly; only Yahoo and Google really competed. Ad buyers generally split their spending dollars between all five networks, and the mix tended to closely track search engine share (so as of July 2010, ComScore measured 66% to Google, 17% to Yahoo, and 11% to MSN). While online ad buyers also cared about the quality of service given by online media reps, and service was generally poor, in the end they cared the most about the number of users on a network.

Google dominated the search world because it had a better product. As of July 2010, it had over 65% of the retail search query market (measured by ComScore – by hits, it had a larger sample and measures it at about 70%). If you counted the wholesale search that Google did for Ask.com, AOL, MySpace, eBay, and others, the market ratio was 71% to 74%. For other countries, like most of Western Europe, Google's search shares were generally above 90%; the only major countries it didn't dominate were China, Japan, South Korea, and Russia. But this was just the technology share. Even the current US antitrust chief at the Justice Department in 2010 admitted Google was the dominant online advertiser and had "lawfully" obtained its monopoly.

Google dominated the business of search even more than just the technology; at the core the business consisted of contextual advertising. The Q1 2009 search advertising revenues showed Google had $5,510 million, Yahoo $399 million, and Microsoft $151 million; the total was about $6,060 million. The Q1 2010 search advertising revenues showed Google had $6,770 million, Yahoo $343 million, and Microsoft $119 million total to about $7,232 million. Hence Google's market share of Q1 2009 and Q1 2010 was about 91% and 94% respectively.

On the technology side, it was impossible for most companies to enter search. Because most search algorithms optimized based on past users' searches, network effects prevent new engines from being as powerful as the dominant few. By collecting terabytes of data on past searches, e-mail records, and web crawls, the dominant core engines had erected an enormous barrier to entry. Alternatively, economies of scale could be a reason. Google, Microsoft, and Yahoo spent billions of dollars on massive server farms from which they could gather data from web crawls and consumer behavior. Their purpose was to optimize search algorithms.

These high sunk costs made it unlikely that other companies would enter the market; hit-and-run entry just wasn't possible. It would take years to build server farms, program a successful algorithm, and then build the critical mass of users so that your algorithm would succeed. While it was possible that a silver-bullet optimization algorithm could use a completely different method than web crawls and past queries, that seemed unlikely for the near future.

Facebook and the Inevitability of One Social Network

In February 2004, Mark Zuckerberg and co-founders Dustin Moskovitz, Chris Hughes, and Eduardo Saverin launched TheFacebook.com from their Harvard dorm room. Zuckerberg had previously turned down offers of about $1 million for a music recommendations company called Synapse so he could go to college at Harvard. There, he developed addictive apps like CourseMatch, to let students pick courses based on what their friends were in, and FaceMash, a comparison site where users could compare the faces of Harvard undergrads for hotness (the administration shut it down quickly). Because of notoriety from this, Zuckerberg was approached by three upperclassmen: Divya Narendra and twins from Greenwich, Connecticut, Cameron and Tyler Winklevoss. They wanted his help for a site that they had been working on, called Harvard Connection. Zuckerberg helped them but he soon abandoned their project in order to build his own site, theFacebook.com.

The site was an immediate hit, and, at the end of his sophomore year, Zuckerberg dropped out of Harvard to run it. Narendra and the twins felt cheated. In 2008, Facebook reached a $65 million settlement with them after they sued claiming Zuckerberg stole their idea. Or as Cameron Winklevoss said of Zuckerberg: "He stole the moment, he stole the idea, and he stole the execution." By 2010, the settlement had failed and the parties were back in court. After launching at Harvard and spreading like a frat party invitation to freshmen on a Friday night, Facebook quickly expanded to Stanford, Columbia, and Yale.

Seeing something potentially big, the Facebook founders moved their base of operations to Palo Alto, California in March 2004, sleeping on friends' couches. Zuckerberg insisted they weren't simply creating another online tool for college kids to check each other out. Rather he saw Facebook as a "social utility." He explained that one day everyone would be able to use it to locate people on the web; it would be a truly global digital phone book. Zuckerberg was also hoping peer pressure would eventually lead to a network effect. By September, Facebook had nearly 1 million active users, growing to more than 800 college networks by year end. The company also raised $12.7 million in venture capital from Accel Partners, possibly the best venture capital investment of that year, and maybe the decade. Zuckerberg's business card read: "I'm CEO, Bitch."

Through 2005, the service expanded to high school networks and went to international schools, reaching 5.5 million active users by October 2005. Seeing the company's scary, viral growth, the founders raised another $27.5 million from Greylock Partners, Meritech Capital Partners, and other firms. In August 2006, nearly two and half years after its founding, Facebook finally opened to the world and expanded registration so anyone could join. The company introduced a News Feed and Mini-Feed service with additional privacy controls, and a share feature later in the year.

One achievement was that Facebook destroyed earlier competitors like MySpace and Friendster. A major reason was that money was never Zuckerberg's top priority; rather, he wanted the creative control to create a great product that would shape millions of people's lives. So in 2005, when MTV Networks considered buying Facebook for seventy-five million dollars, he turned them down. The next year both Yahoo! and Microsoft offered much more. Zuckerberg turned them all down again. Terry Semel, the former CEO of Yahoo!, tried to buy Facebook for a billion dollars in 2006 and reflected: "I'd never met anyone—forget his age, twenty-two then or twenty-six now—I'd never met anyone who would walk away from a billion dollars. But he said, 'It's not about the price. This is my baby, and I want to keep running it, I want to keep growing it.'" Semel couldn't believe it.

Social networking had first started in April 1995 when Cornell University students Stephan Paternot and Todd Krizelman launched theGlobe.com, an online community that expanded the old concept of the Usenet. In November 1998, theGlobe.com went public. On its first trading day the price of its stock closed at 606% the initial share price, setting an all-time record for IPOs; still, the company failed after the dot com crash, leaving MySpace, Friendster, and Facebook to capitalize on the concept. In 1997, Stanford University's engineering students Al Lieb and Selina Tobaccowala founded Evite, a free website to manage invitations. A milestone for web-based social networking software was SixDegrees.com, launched in 1997 by New York's corporate lawyer Andrew Weinreich and named after the hypothesis that all human beings are linked by at most six connections. A user could link to friends and family and reach people beyond the first level of connection. At the peak it had one million registered users. Still, none of these had a Zuck.

Zuckerberg dreamt of a platform, the Holy Grail. By March 2007, Facebook reached 20 million active users and soon launched a Facebook Platform with 65 developer partners and over 85 applications. The platform strategy would be key, as attracting developers creates another network effect by making a platform more useful, attracting more users, and so more developers looking for an audience or customer group. Zynga (social games), Pencake (online quizzes), and JibJab (online stickers and greeting cards) built their entire models around Facebook users. In July 2007, Facebook and Microsoft expanded an existing advertising deal (the primary source of Facebook's revenues at that point) to cover international markets; Microsoft also took a $240 million equity stake in Facebook. More importantly, Facebook launched Facebook Platform for Mobile. Facebook reached over 50 million active users by July. In October 2007, Facebook launched Facebook Ads as an early step to monetizing its audience. By April 2008, Facebook reached over 100 million active users (note that its user growth doubled in less than a year).

Facebook's stunningly fast growth was due to network effects. As it grew larger, its utility increased (like a classic cell phone network). Other social networks became less useful (would you want to be on the network with all your friends, or the one with just a quarter?). Eventually, it seemed inevitable that only one social network would win, and it would be Facebook. Even countries where other social networks dominated, like Germany's StudiVZ, would eventually lose out; Facebook stole the lead in 2010.

Zuckerberg described the network effect power of Facebook as the "social graph," the network of connections and relationships between people on the service. Zuckerberg said: "As Facebook adds more and more people with more and more connections it continues growing and becomes more useful at a faster rate. We are going to use it spread information through the social graph." The end effect of the social network was that groups of people and social applications could achieve exponential growth. So developers could create social apps off the Facebook base to create more value, without having to reconstruct the social graph all by themselves. For example, Facebook had information on all the birthdays of a person's friends around the world. Every time a friend's birthday approached, Facebook notified a user. One app, called BarTab, allowed a Facebook user in San Francisco to buy his friend in Boston a beer over Facebook, by giving the friend a credit, which he could redeem in an actual bar. So Facebook acted as an information storage tool and a mnemonic device. A developer could create a tool to leverage the social graph and this particular data point to do a commercial action, like buy a beer. Facebook and BarTab profited by taking a cut of every drink sold.

In August 2008, Facebook launched Facebook Connect, a revolutionary technology to let users log on to company websites using their Facebook logins. This would make a Facebook account a form of personal ID on the Web (privacy settings included), and appeal to advertisers for many reasons. First, when a user logged on to a third-party site using Facebook Connect, that activity could be reported on her friends' news feeds (a de facto endorsement). Second, the tool made it easy for users to invite their friends to check out the advertiser's site. As an example, Starbucks used Facebook to ask people to donate five hours of time to volunteer work. Third, if a user signed in using a Facebook account, a new screen, a hybrid of Facebook and an advertiser's page, popped up with information on how to find local deals, with a tab on the page asking the user to "help spread the word." If the user clicked on it her entire address book of Facebook friends would come up. This allowed her to recommend the advertiser page with a few clicks.

Monetization of users was key for Facebook; it happened, but more slowly than expected. The potential was vast, as Facebook could eavesdrop on every phone or e-mail conversation of its users. That was similar to what all the wall posts, status updates, 25 Random Things, quizzes, and picture tagging on Facebook in 2010 amounted to. They offered a semipublic way of exposing things people were interested in doing, buying, and trying. However, traditional online ads on Facebook and other social-networking sites failed. Banner ads on Facebook sold for as little as 15 cents per 1,000 clicks (compared with, say, $8 per 1,000 clicks for an ad on a targeted news portal such as Yahoo Auto). Marketers believed that Facebook users ignored most traditional ads. By February 2009, Facebook reached over 200 million active users. Later in April, Digital Sky Technologies made a $200 million investment for preferred stock at a $10 billion valuation.

Talented managers and hackers were also germane to the Facebook strategy. In the early years, Facebook ran through a series of senior executives and was unstable; even Zuckerberg's close friends wouldn't stay. Zuckerberg would get to work in the afternoon and work till the early morning, often in pajama bottoms and a t-shirt. When the software code-writing got intense, he wouldn't let people leave for food, pounding the table and yelling: "No! We're in lockdown! No one leaves the table until we're done with this thing." Everyone was hungry.

Things calmed down in March 2008 when Zuckerberg hired Sheryl Sandberg, a Google executive who was the chief of staff for Lawrence Summers when he was Secretary of the Treasury. She had helped build Google's money-minting AdWords program. Sandberg joined Facebook as the company's COO and she recruited executives from eBay, Genentech, and Mozilla. The company also got YouTube's former chief financial officer, Gideon Yu, as CFO. A flood of former Google employees soon arrived, too. In July 2009, Facebook acquired FriendFeed for about $50 million; it was a promising social network startup headed by some talented ex-Googlers, notably Paul Buchheit and Bret Taylor (who became Facebook's CTO). Importantly, the board was packed with old media luminaries (Washington Post publisher Don Graham and venture capitalist Jim Breyer) along with Silicon Valley technology mensches (PayPal co-founder and major Valley angel Peter Thiel and Netscape founder Marc Andreessen). Facebook was thus winning the talent war against Google.

In 2012, the company was still dominated by Zuckerberg, who many called "Mark" or "Zuck." His desk was near the middle of the office, near his personal glass-walled conference room and within arm's length of senior employees like Sandberg. Before arriving each morning, Zuckerberg worked out with a personal trainer. He came to work in blue jeans, a t-shirt, and a fleece. He was intimately involved in almost every new product and feature, often obsessing about them. He left his daily schedule open from 2PM to 6PM so he could meet with coders working on new projects. Debate was an important part of meetings and Zuckerberg was a good listener. He was often one of the last people to leave the office, working nights and weekends with the other coders.

As the growth continued, Facebook kept innovating. In August 2009, Facebook reached over 300 million active users and crossed the 500 million mark by August 2010; revenues were estimated in the $550 million to $700 million range. In spring 2010, Facebook introduced the Open Graph. Users reading articles on Nytimes.com could see which articles their Facebook friends read, shared, and liked. Zuckerberg hoped users would eventually read articles, visit restaurants, and watch movies based on what their Facebook friends recommended. This would reduce the need for online critics or even Google or Netflix algorithms.

More broadly, Zuckerberg imagined Facebook as becoming a layer underneath almost every electronic device. A user could turn on her TV and see that five of her Facebook friends were watching "Mad Men," and that her parents taped a PBS documentary "The Shakers" for her. She could buy a Coach handbag with a single click, using her Facebook credentials, and a select group of her friends would be notified and encouraged to look at similar bags. All her friends could visit all the places she had visited recently and vice versa.

The ultimate promise of Facebook was that for many people it replaced rolodexes, cellphones, e-mail, messaging, and the annual Christmas card. Zuckerberg and his team had repeatedly shunned profit and increasingly larger buyout offers. Instead they focused on designing a service that delivered more utility to its users. When asked, "Why don't you sell the company?" he responded, "I don't really need the money. And anyway, I don't think I'm ever going to have an idea this good again." Eventually, as the thinker Piero Scaruffi pointed out, every person in the world would have access to the Internet and a Facebook account. Theoretically, one could then "friend" the entire world and then send a message to the entire world at a click of a button. This was something no government or human being could do in human history, and it raised the question: What would you say to the entire world?

The dark side of Facebook, like any new technology, was also apparent. In July 2010, a security researcher released a file containing the names, profile addresses, and unique identification numbers of more than 100 million Facebook users. The information was collected via a public directory Facebook made available that lists users who shared at least some of their profile information with everyone on the Internet. Although the information in the file was freely available online through search engines and Facebook's own directory, the organized list of names and identification numbers in it could make it easier for others to compile users' e-mail addresses, locations, or other data they have made available. This was a powerful weapon for abusive governments or just malign marketers.

Facebook went public with an initial public offering (IPO) on May 18, 2012. It was one of the biggest in technology, with Facebook sporting a peak market capitalization of over $104 billion. However, the stock fell by nearly 50% in 3 months, showing that it was overhyped and that good businesses can trade at horribly inflated valuations.

Yelp and Critical Review Networks

Yelp was conceived in the summer of 2004 after its two founders, Russ Simmons and Jeremy Stoppelman, hung out at an incubator started by Max Levchin, a Paypal co-founder. They were looking for a consumer Internet idea and decided they could duplicate the Yellow Pages online. When Stoppelman got sick and needed a local doctor, he turned to friends for recommendations and help. The first version of the site came out in October 2004; its aim was to help friends ask other friends for recommendations. The idea was "online word of mouth" but the actual mechanism of the site was painful, noisy, and spammy. People hated it as they weren't promised a response from their friends, and friends were often annoyed by questions to which they lacked answers. The founders saw that users like to write their own reviews, and re-centered the site around that in February 2005. The site took off from then, and the $1 million in seed financing was enough for it to get traction in San Francisco first, then the Bay Area and other metro regions (the founders consciously mimicked Craigslist).

By November 2008, Yelp had 4 million reviews written and 15 million visitors a month, outgrowing competitors like Citysearch, ZagatOnline, or Chowhound. Again, the network effect was at play. The larger a site became, the more useful and powerful it would be, until its competitors were forced into being irrelevant. Niche sites like Angie's List (a local rating website for service providers like doctors and plumbers) could try to carve a narrow spot, but were unlikely to succeed. More than 80% of Yelpers were under age 40, so they were early adopters. Yelp also created a community of elite Yelpers who wrote great reviews and got recognition, top placement, and invitations to free marketing events (with lots of food and drink).

Yelp's business model was based around soliciting restaurant "sponsorships." For a modest fee, a restaurant could keep one favorable review, marked "sponsor," at the top of the list. The company still kept unfavorable reviews on the site, unless they were clearly fakes. For example, the Fifth Floor restaurant in San Francisco, which had one Michelin star, paid Yelp $300 a month for such a sponsorship. Meanwhile, Fifth Floor's top two Yelp reviews, including the sponsored one, were highly positive. But three others of those in the top 10 were negative. Some local papers reported that Yelp sales representatives had promised to move or remove negative reviews for advertisers. Users themselves have discovered that reviews have disappeared. This tarnished both the service and the business.

In February 2009, Google had discussions to buy Yelp for more than $500 million, not bad for a company started with $31 million in venture funding. Yelp had more than 300 employees, of which more than 200 did sales, and 2009 revenues of about $30 million. After the deal didn't go through, Google started competing aggressively by starting a robust aggregator of local reviews, Google Places, buying the reviewer Zagat, and using Yelp's own reviews for unlicensed content. By January 2013, Yelp had about 100 million monthly visits to the site.

30. Survivors: Paypal, Wikipedia, and Genomics (1999-2002)

The Bubble Bursts

The party was wild. The dotcom boom was driving all sorts of indicators through the roof.

Between 1998 and 1999 venture-capital investment in Silicon Valley firms increased more than 90% from $3.2 billion to $6.1 billion. In 1999 there were 457 IPOs in the US. The vast majority of the companies that went public were high-tech startups and about 100 were directly related to the Internet. An impressive number were based in Silicon Valley. The US had 250 billionaires and thousands of new millionaires had been created in just one year. Microsoft was worth $450 billion, the most valued company in the world, even if it was still many times smaller than General Motors. Bill Gates was the world's richest man with a fortune of $85 billion. In 2000 the number of public companies in Silicon Valley reached 417; venture-capital investment in the US peaked at $99.72 billion or 1% of GDP, mostly going to software (17.4%), telecommunications (15.4%), networking (10.0%) and media (9.1%).

One of the worst deals ever in the history of Silicon Valley took place in January 1999, when @Home acquired a struggling Excite for $6.7 billion. It was at the time the largest Internet-related merger yet. Later that year Excite refused to buy for less than one million dollars the technology of a new search engine developed by two Stanford students, Google.

A symbolic event took place in January 2000 when America Online (AOL), the pioneer of dial-up Internet access, acquired Time Warner, the world's largest media company. A humble startup of the "net economy" had just bought a much larger company of the old "brick and mortar" economy. At one point or another in the early months of 2000s, Microsoft, Cisco, and Intel all passed the $400 billion mark by market valuation, and the only company of the old economy that could compete with them was General Electric.

Then came the financial crash of March 2000. The dotcom bubble burst even faster than it had expanded. Within 30 months (between March 2000 and October 2002) the technology-heavy Nasdaq lost 78% of its value, erasing $4.2 trillion of wealth. The losses in Silicon Valley were astronomical. In 2001 there were only 76 IPOs.

There were multiple causes for the inflated values of dotcom stocks and then their crash. One was certainly the gullible and inexperienced "day traders" who enthusiastically purchased worthless stocks. Another one was the incompetent or dishonest Wall Street analysts who created ad-hoc reports to justify the aberrations of those worthless stocks. A final boost may have come from the US central bank, the Fed, which pumped more money into the system in late 1999 so that people had cash and wouldn't need to stockpile more for a Y2K Armageddon.

If this were not enough, the large IT companies based on the East Coast were probably hurt more by the end of the Y2K panic than by the dotcom crash. The first of January of 2000 came and went without any apocalypse. The Y2K paranoia was rapidly forgotten, as if it had never existed. The last day of December of 1999 would remain the best day ever to fly, because planes were empty: people were so afraid that airplanes would crash all over the world. Unfortunately, the Y2K paranoia had created an easily predictable "boom and bust" situation. Billions of dollars had been spent in acquiring new hardware and software before 1999, but all of this, by definition, came to an end one minute after midnight. It was one of the few cases in which a "bust" was widely advertised before it happened.

There was no question that the dotcom bubble had gone out of control, but the drop in IT investment after the Y2K scare exacerbated the problem. The direct impact of the stock-market crash was on jobs. Half of all dotcoms shut down. The other half had to restructure to live in a new age where growth was proportional to and not independent of profits. They needed to make money; with falling real revenues, the only solution was to cut costs.

Silicon Valley learned how to trim costs in the early 2000s. On top of the layoffs due to cost cutting, there were three additional problems. First of all, the number of software engineers coming out of universities had massively increased to keep up with demand; now there were no jobs for these young graduates. Second, Silicon Valley companies had begun outsourcing jobs to India: 62% of India's exports of software in 2000 went to the US. Third, the US government had just bent to the demands of the IT industry to increase the number of visas for foreign IT workers, causing a flood of immigrants: 32% of Silicon Valley's high-skilled workers were foreign-born in 2000, and mostly from Asia. These combined factors caused the first massive decline in employment in the Bay Area since the end of the Gold Rush era.

The 2001 recession was significant because California and the Bay Area had been largely immune from recessions since the Great Depression. Recessions in California tended to be milder, while recoveries were faster and stronger. In 2001 the opposite happened: California fared a lot worse than the rest of the nation.

Out of the Ruins

The Nasdaq crash did not mean that the Internet was already dying. On the contrary, in 2000 it was estimated that 460 million people in the world were connected to the Internet and that 10 billion e-mail messages a day were exchanged over the Internet. In 2001 alone, 42 million users traded

$9.3 billion worth of goods on eBay. For the first time, even a small business in a remote town could reach a market of millions of people. To mention just one emblematic statistic, Merrill Lynch reported that trades by institutional clients over its e-commerce platforms amounted to $1.9 trillion in 2000. According to the US Census Bureau, the grand total of e-commerce was just short of one trillion dollars in 2000. 94% of e-commerce was Business-to-Business (B2B), basically the Internet-based version of the decade-old Electronic Data Interchange. Retail e-sales of Business-to-Consumer (B2C) goods were only $29 billion in 2000, but in the following years they would increase rapidly, with a double-digit year-over-year growth rate.

Some of the most innovative ideas for the Web emerged out of the Bay Area right in the middle of the crisis. In February 1999, Marc Benioff founded Saleforce.com to move business applications to the Internet, pioneering "cloud" computing, where users don't need to own a computer in order to run a software application. eHow.com was founded in March 1999 to provide a practical encyclopedia to solve problems in all sorts of fields via articles written by experts in those fields. Friendster was launched in March 1999 in Morgan Hill, south of San Jose, by Jonathan Abrams; it allowed people to create "social networks." Blogger.com, founded in August 1999 by Evan Williams and Meg Hourihan, enabled ordinary Internet users to create their own "blogs," or personal journals.

Even music search was affected. Tim Westergren, an alumnus of Stanford's Center for Computer Research in Music and Acoustics (CCRMA), had devised a search engine for music called Savage Beast and had launched the Music Genome Project to archive songs based on their musical genes: the search engine simply looked for songs whose genome was similar to a given song. That project website evolved into Pandora, an Internet-based streaming radio simulator that "broadcast" music based on the listener's preference. Given a song, Pandora produced a customized radio program of similar songs.

When in 2000 Yahoo opted for Google's search engine, Inktomi read the ink on the wall, that Google was going to wipe out the competition, and decided to invest in a new field: streaming media. Inktomi paid $1.3 billion for FastForward Networks, which specialized in large-scale delivery of radio and television broadcasting over the Web in the wake of Seattle's RealNetworks. Listen.com launched Rhapsody, a service that provided streaming on-demand access to a library of digital music; RealNetworks acquired Listen.com in 2003.

Virtual Money

The late boom bought dreams of virtual money. German-born Peter Thiel, founder of the conservative student magazine Stanford Review and a successful stock trader, funded Confinity in December 1998 in Palo Alto with two editors of the Stanford Review, Luke Nosek and Ken Howery.

The company was the brainchild of cryptography expert Max Levchin. He was a Ukrainian Jew from Chicago who brought with him a group of University of Illinois alumni, including Russel Simmons and Jeremy Stoppelman. Their goal was to develop a system for Palm Pilot users to send ("beam") money to other Palm Pilot users, i.e. to make payments without using cash, cheques, or credit cards.

The first entities to be impressed by Confinity were European: Nokia and Deutsche Bank used Confinity software to "beam" from a Palm Pilot their $3 million investment in the company to Thiel. Meanwhile, X.com had been founded also in Palo Alto by South African-born Elon Musk in March 1999 after he had sold his first company, Zip2, which had software powering websites for news companies. X.com offered online banking services including a way to email money. In 2000, Confinity and X.com merged to form PayPal. Confinity's original concept evolved into a web-based service to send money over the Internet to an e-mail address, therefore bypassing banks and even borders. Thiel's utopian vision of a universal currency was embedded in much anti-government rhetoric that reflected the traditional anti-establishment mood of the Bay Area from a right-wing perspective.

However, ironically, PayPal quickly had to devote most of its efforts to fight fraud. For example, to make sure that the user was a human being and not a program, Dave Gausebeck and Levchin resurrected a technique invented by AltaVista in 1997. Their display blurred and distorted characters and asked the users to enter them on the keyboard. Basically it was a reverse Turing test (a machine that tries to figure out if it is talking to a human), which became popularly known as CAPTCHA (Completely Automated Public Turing test to tell Computers and Humans Apart).

PayPal's success was immediate. It beat all its competitors that had preceded it in trying to help consumers sell and buy over the Internet. Paypal was another case, like Netscape before it, of the public choosing a standard before either government or corporations could do so. In October 2001, PayPal already boasted 12 million registered users. Its IPO in early 2002 netted $1.2 billion dollars. The establishment, however, struck back: both banks and local governments tried in every legal way to derail PayPal. Eventually, PayPal found that the only way to survive was to sell itself to eBay in July 2002, for $1.5 billion.

PayPal was an impressive nest of talents, and extremely young ones among its 200 employees. Levchin was 26 at the IPO, Musk was 31, and Thiel was the oldest at 35. Half of those 200 would quit by 2006 and found or staff new startups. In December 2002, Reid Hoffman of PayPal launched LinkedIn in Mountain View, the main business-oriented social networking site. In 2002 PayPal's co-founder Elon Musk founded Space Explorations Technology or SpaceX to develop space transportation; in December 2010, his Falcon 9 would become the first private spaceship to orbit Earth. Roelof Botha became a partner at Sequoia Capital, and Thiel started his own venture-capital fund, Clarium Capital. In the following years, former PayPal employees would start Yelp (Jeremy Stoppelman and Russel Simmons in 2004), YouTube (Chad Hurley, Steven Chen and Jawed Karim in 2005), Slide (Max Levchin in 2005), and Halcyon Molecular (Luke Nosek in 2009). It was not just a mafia, as the "Paypal Mafia" was widely known in Silicon Valley, but a self-sustaining and cooperative group, because it included venture capitalists, entrepreneurs, managers, and engineers.

Winners and Losers

Many of the established Silicon Valley companies did well through the recession. For example, Oracle in 2000 abandoned the client-server architecture in favor of the browser-based architecture and in the first quarter of 2001 posted growing revenues of $2.3 billion. Siebel at that time owned almost 50% of the customer relationship management (CRM) market in 1999 and minted money.

Advanced Micro Devices (AMD) beat Intel to a historical milestone. In February 2000, its Athlon microprocessor broke the 1000 megahertz (1 gigahertz) barrier. Intel's Pentium III (running at the same speed) came out a few months later. However, 2001 was a bad year for the sector. Revenues for the semiconductor industry plunged more than 30% in 2001, with Intel alone declining 21% from $33.7 billion in 2000 to $26.5 billion.

British chip manufacturer ARM had been selling embeddable RISC chips since 1991, and in 1998 its technology was mature enough that it was licensed by Qualcomm for its cell-phone technology. By 2001, ARM dominated the market for embedded RISC chips, particularly for cell-phone applications. Only Intel, IBM, AMD and Taiwan-based fabless VIA owned a license for Intel's x86 technology, while ARM had made it very easy for anyone to license its technology. Besides the merits of its chip, its business model was friendlier to manufacturers interested in developing their own custom processors. It was no surprise that dozens of other companies had done so.

The first uber-successful smartphone focused on e-mail and telephony. In 1999, the Canadian company Research In Motion, a spin-off of the University of Waterloo, introduced the Blackberry smart-phone. It was a hand-held device with a real keyboard that allowed users to check e-mail, make phone calls, send text messages, and browse the Web. The telephone had just been turned into a wireless email terminal, and email had become a mobile service. Silicon Valley took notice and in October 2002 Danger, founded by former WebTV's employee Andy Rubin, released the mobile phone Hiptop, later renamed T-Mobile Sidekick. Palm was in troubled waters: by the end of 2001, its revenues had collapsed 44%.

The large computer firms were changing. In July 1999, Hewlett-Packard appointed Carly Fiorina as CEO: she became the first female CEO of a company listed in the Dow Jones Industrial Average, another tribute to the Bay Area's propensity to encourage diversity. In May 2002, Hewlett-Packard acquired Compaq, becoming the largest manufacturer of servers, the second largest computer company in the world after IBM, and the only serious contender for Dell in the personal-computer market. It looked like after the breathtaking ups and downs of the personal-computer market, the company that was still standing was from the older generation. Because Compaq had purchased DEC, HP now contained a division that contained a division that was the old rival DEC. Symbolically, this represented the end of the war between Silicon Valley and Boston. At the peak of that war nobody would have imagined that some day DEC would end up being just a small division within a Silicon Valley company. And DEC had been the very originator of the "Route 128" boom in the Boston area.

The other surviving giant of the old generation, IBM, had pretty much left the personal-computer market, but it dominated software services. In 2000 software and services accounted for 50% of IBM's business. The history of computer manufacturing looked like a vast graveyard of distinguished names, from Univac to DEC to Compaq.

Corporate Tech

Web-based commerce was there to stay and some of the obscure winners of those years were companies that could see beyond the temporary debacle. In particular, e-commerce, being entirely software-driven, lent itself to better analytics. During the following decade a huge number of startups would try to capitalize on this fact, continuing a trend towards retail sales optimization that had been going on in Corporate America ever since. DemandTec, founded in 1999 in San Mateo by Stanford professor Hau Lee and economist Mike Neal, became one of the leaders in analytical software tools for retailers, or Consumer Demand Management (CDM) software. Such products performed a behind-the-scene scientific study of shoppers' behavior on the Web to help e-retailers with their pricing and marketing strategies. This was also one of the early applications of cloud computing coupled with large-scale data management.

Consumer Multimedia

A sector that showed promise was the whole consumer multimedia business. Photography had gone digital due to ever-cheaper digital cameras. Music had gone digital, especially when free software allowed music fans to "rip" CDs into mp3 files. And digital formats for videos were beginning to spread. Consumers needed two things: applications to display and play these digital files, and storage to save them. In 1999, IBM released a 37.5-gigabyte hard-disk drive, at the time the world's largest. Seagate Technology, which had been purchased for $3 billion by Veritas

Software, specialized in storage management software; it smashed IBM's record with the Barracuda 180-gigabyte hard drive. 3PAR was founded in 1999 in Fremont by former SUN executive Jeffrey Price and Indian-born former SUN chief architect Ashok Singhal to deliver shared storage devices. It utilized allocation strategies of "just-enough" and "just-in-time" for increased efficiency. In 1995, the Israeli company M-Systems, founded in 1989 by Dov Moran, had introduced the first flash-memory drive, and in 1999 it introduced the first USB flash drive, marketed as "a hard disk on a keychain." That was the birth of flash-based solid-state drives, an alternative with no movable parts to the electromechanical hard-disk drives that had movable parts, including a spinning disk; it was going to revolutionize the industry.

Meanwhile, in 2000 Microsoft demonstrated the Windows Media Player to play both music and videos. In January 2001, Apple responded with its iTunes software. In October 2001 Apple chose a completely different route: it launched a consumer device, the iPod, to play music files. It was basically a "walkman" for mp3s with a five-gigabyte internal hard-disk.

The history of P2P, one of the big innovations of the era, was mostly based outside the Bay Area. Shawn Fanning, a student at Boston Northeastern University, came up with the idea of a Web-based service to distribute mp3 files, i.e. music, over the Internet. His Napster went online in June 1999. It allowed consumers all over the world to share music files, thus circumventing the entire music industry. The music industry reacted with a lawsuit that eventually shut down Napster in July 2001. It was too late to stop the avalanche, though. Napster inspired a new generation of similar Web-based services, except that the new generation improved Napster's model by using Peer-to-Peer (P2P) architectures.

A P2P service basically facilitates the transfer of files between two computers, but does not physically store the file in between the two computers. Kazaa, for example, was developed in Estonia by Ahti Heinla, Priit Kasesalu and Jaan Tallinn, and introduced in March 2001 by the Dutch company Consumer Empowerment. In July 2001 San Francisco resident Bram Cohen unveiled the P2P file sharing protocol BitTorrent, soon to become the most popular service of this kind. It was faster than previous P2P services because it downloaded a file from many different sources at the same time (if multiple copies were available on multiple servers). These whiz kids became heroes of the counterculture for defying the music industry.

Gaming was also undergoing a dramatic transformation. In 1996 the San Francisco Chronicle's website had introduced "Dreadnot," a game built around a fictional mystery that took place around real locations in San Francisco. It featured real people and used phone numbers, voice mailboxes, email addresses, and other websites; it was an interactive multiplatform narrative. It was the first "alternate reality game" and it was free. A few years later, in nearby Redwood City, a team of game designers at Electronic Arts began working on "Majestic," that eventually debuted in July 2001, the first "alternate reality game" for sale. In keeping with the theme of the genre, it was credited to two fictional game designers, Brian Cale and Mike Griffin. These games involved the real life of the players, and therefore Electronic Arts marketed it with the motto "It plays you." The game that launched the genre on a planetary scale was Microsoft's "The Beast" that debuted a few weeks before "Majestic."

Wireless and Encryption

Radio Frequency Identification (RFID), a wireless technology that used radio waves to track items, had been invented in the 1970s but was largely forgotten. In 1998, MIT professors David Brock and Sanjay Sarma developed Internet-based UHF RFID that made it feasible for top retailers such as Wal-mart to deploy RFID technology extensively, typically for inventory purposes within supply chain management. Wal-mart eventually mandated RFID to all its suppliers by 2005. Among the early manufacturers of RFID products was Alien Technology, founded by Stephen Smith, a professor of electrical engineering at UC Berkeley.

RFID found another application in contact-less credit cards (or "blink technology"). These were credit cards with an embedded RFID microchip that didn't need to be swiped but simply waved. The idea was pioneered by the Octopus card in Hong Kong in 1997 to pay for public transportation and by oil company Mobil's Speedpass keychain in 1997 for gasoline pumps.

The market leaders were in Europe and in Japan. The European market was dominated by Mifare, developed in 1994 in Austria by Mikron (Mifare meaning "MIkron FAre collection system") and acquired by Dutch conglomerate Philips in 1998, while Sony's FeliCa, introduced in 1996, ruled in Japan. Both were proprietary technologies because they had been introduced before the international standard was decided.

Encryption for digital communications had been born in the Bay Area but owed its improvement to Israeli scientists. Adi Shamir, who had invented the crucial RSA algorithm for PKI, proposed a simpler form of encryption in 1984: Identity-Based Encryption (IBE), in which the public key is some unique information about the identity of the sender (typically, the person's email address). The first practical implementation of IBE was the work of Stanford Computer Science professor Dan Boneh in 2001. Two of his students, Rishi Kacker and Matt Pauker, started Voltage in 2002 in Palo Alto to develop security software for corporate customers.

Wikipedia

The website that would have the biggest impact on society, Wikipedia, started in the Midwest. In 1996, Chicago-based options trader Jimmy

Wales had co-founded Bomis, a website of pornographic content for a male audience. At the same time, he was preaching the vision of a free encyclopedia and, using Bomis as his funding source, he had Larry Sanger as the editor-in-chief of this Nupedia, which debuted in March 2000. The concept was aligned with Richard Stallman's Free Software Foundation, except that it was not about software but about world knowledge.

Next came the wiki. In January 2001 Sanger decided to add a "wiki" feature to let contributors enter their texts. Wikis had become popular in corporate intranets as ways to share knowledge, basically replacing the old concept of "groupware." This method proved a lot more efficient than the traditional process of peer review, and therefore "Wikipedia" (as Sanger named it) was already surpassing Nupedia in popularity. Wales realized that Wikipedia was the way to go, abolished Nupedia, and opened Wikipedia to everybody. Formally established in 2003 as a non-profit foundation based in San Francisco, Wikipedia became a free, multilingual encyclopedia edited collaboratively by the Internet community. Within a few years, it would contain more information than the Encyclopedia Britannica ever dreamed of collecting. It was another example of how utopian ideals percolated into the Internet world.

Larry Sanger left to join the Digital Universe Foundation based in Scotts Valley. It was founded in 2002 by Utah-based entrepreneur Joe Firmage, a former Novell executive, and by German-born astrophysicist Bernard Haisch. Its mission was to create a more reliable web-based encyclopedia, Digital Universe (originally called OneCosmos).

The "copyleft movement" was a new intellectual trend shaped on the Web. It rejected the ways of big media corporations that retained all rights and thus stifled creativity. Larry Lessig, a law professor at Stanford Law School, founded the Creative Commons in 2001 in San Francisco to promote sharing and diffusing creative works through less binding licenses than the traditional "all rights reserved" copyright. Lessig went on to found the Center for Internet and Society (CIS) at Stanford "to improve Internet privacy practices."

Uploading

The key difference between this generation of the Web's users and the previous generation was not so much in the number of people who were browsing but in the number of people who were uploading content to it.

Digital content had been around for decades. The vast majority of archives in the developed world had already been converted to databases. Large amounts of text had been scanned and digitized. New text was almost all in digital form. No other appliance since the ice box had disappeared so rapidly from households like the typewriter did in the 1990s. The telex had been replaced by e-mail. Newspapers and magazines had converted to digital composition. And now an increasing number of individuals were producing digital texts at an exponential pace, whether students writing their essays for school or adults writing letters to friends. Digital cameras and digital recorders were flooding personal computers with digital images and sounds. Napster-like services were popularizing the idea that a song is a file.

All this digital material was available, but it had been largely kept private on someone's home or work computer. The browser and the search engine, by definition, had encouraged people to "download" information from the Web, not to "upload" information to it. Wikipedia, blogs, P2P tools, social networking sites and soon YouTube and Flickr heralded an era in which the rate of uploading was going to almost match the rate of downloading. In fact, uploading was becoming a form of entertainment in itself. The 1990s had been the age of democratizing the Internet. The 2000s witnessed the democratization of the "uploading:" more and more individuals began to upload their digital content to the Web in what became one of the most sensational processes of collective knowledge creation in the history of humankind.

In this scenario, the business model of America OnLine (AOL) was terribly outdated. Warner, originally a film production company, had merged in 1990 with publisher Time. Then Time Warner had entered the cable television business by acquiring Ted Turner's TBS in 1996. The media conglomerate now owned films, TV shows and articles. Then in 2000 AOL purchased Time Warner and AOL Time Warner was born, the first media conglomerate of the Internet age that was making everything from cinema to email. The idea was to couple content and online distribution. It failed because AOL was rapidly losing its grip on the World-wide web as the era of dial-up access was being replaced by the era of Digital Service Lines (DSL) and cable broadband. There was no need anymore for AOL's dial-up service, which came with the limitation of being able to see only the part of the World-wide Web that AOL owned.

Biotech

Unfortunately, the dotcom crash also affected the biotech industry. Funding for biotech startups collapsed after reaching a peak of $33 billion in 2000. It didn't help that Bill Haseltine's Human Genome Sciences, one of the most hyped startups on the East Coast, turned out to be an embarrassing bluff. It raised a huge amount of money before the dotcom crash, but it did not introduce any pharmaceutical product. Luckily, philanthropy offset the retreat of the venture capitalists. In 2000, Victoria Hale, a former Genentech scientist, started the first non-profit pharmaceutical company, the Institute for OneWorld Health, in San Francisco. In 2000, the Bill and Melinda Gates Foundation became the world's largest foundation, and specifically addressed biotechnology.

Biofuels too began to attract capital. In 2002 Codexis was founded as a spin-off from drug developer Maxygen. Amyris Biotechnologies, founded in 2003 by some Berkeley scientists, raised over $120 million in venture capital in a few years due to the Institute for OneWorld Health.

In 2000 the US government-funded Human Genome Project and the privately funded Celera made peace and jointly announced that they had succeeded in decoding the entire human genome. Enumerating the genes of human DNA enabled a new discipline: genomics, the study of genes. In particular, biologists were interested in finding out which genes cause which diseases, and how to create a predictive medicine or just how to develop smarter diagnoses. In other words, Celera and the HGP had produced billions of bits of information, but the next task was to interpret that information and apply it to understanding human diseases. This implied that someone had to scavenge that mass of information looking for useful bits. Silicon Genetics was founded in 2000 in Redwood City by Australian-born mathematician Andrew Conway of Stanford's Biochemistry Department to focus on "expression software," software tools to investigate gene expression.

DoubleTwist, Human Genome Sciences and Invitron were examples of companies that revised their business plan accordingly. They were biomedical companies trying to sell not pharmaceutical drugs but information and analysis. That was the bioinformatic side of the biotech business. Then there was the genomic side of the business, which analyzed a specific person's genome against that mass of annotated information.

An important step towards personal genomics was the establishment in October 2002 of the International HapMap Consortium. It was a collaboration among research centers (Canada, China, Japan, Nigeria, Britain, and four in the US, including UCSF) to create a "haplotype map" of the human genome. This map was about SNPs (Single-Nucleotide Polymorphisms). SNP means that a nucleotide of the DNA can have different values in different individuals of the same species. The 10 million or so SNPs that exist in human populations explain why some people are more likely to develop a certain disease than others. In 2002, Jeffrey Trent of the National Human Genome Research Institute, established the non-profit Translational Genomics Research Institute in Arizona.

The sequencing of the human genome made the database of Palo Alto-based pioneer Incyte partially irrelevant, but Incyte continued to acquire biotech startups and in 2000 launched an online version of Lifeseq that offered information about a gene's functions at a more affordable price. DoubleTwist, instead, succumbed to the double whammy of the dotcom crash and the sequencing of the human genome.

The media seized on the announcement in October 2001 by Advanced Cell Technology (ACT) that it had cloned the world's first human embryo, angering President George W. Bush, who opposed human cloning on religious grounds. ACT was a spin-off of the University of Massachusetts founded by James Robl whose lab there had been the first to clone calves from somatic cells. The team included Jose Cibelli, a pupil of Robl who had experimented with nuclear transfer to rejuvenate cells, Robert Lanza, who was working on clones of endangered species. Their goal was actually to generate embryonic stem cells that were needed for controversial medical research.

Meanwhile, an important milestone was achieved by synthetic biology. In July 2002, Eckard Wimmer's team at University of New York at Stony Brook created the first synthetic virus by cloning the polio virus from its chemical code that they had simply downloaded from the Web. The pharmaceutical industry kept growing in the area around South San Francisco, fueled in no small part by Stanford's School of Medicine. For example, in 2002 Israeli-born professor Daria Mochly-Rosen started KAI Pharmaceuticals.

Neurotech

There was also renewed interest in artificial intelligence, a field that had markedly declined since the heydays of the 1980s. However, the action came mostly from futurists and intellectuals rather than from practitioners, and the funding came from philanthropists rather than the academia or the government. The Singularity Institute for Artificial Intelligence (SIAI), devoted to super-human intelligence, was founded in 2000 in San Francisco by Eliezer Yudkowsky, while in 2002 Jeff Hawkins of Palm Computing founded the Redwood Neuroscience Institute in Menlo Park.

With great potential, the Stanford Artificial Intelligence Laboratory was quietly experimenting with robots and in 2005 would win the "Grand Challenge," a race of driver-less cars funded by the DARPA in the Nevada desert, with its Stanley, a modified Volkswagen Touareg.

Greentech

Times of economic crisis had always been good for imagining completely new business sectors. An emerging theme in Silicon Valley was energy, especially after the 2001 terrorist attacks that highlighted how vulnerable the US was to the whims of oil-producing countries. In 2001, KR Sridhar, an alumnus of India's prestigious National Institute of Technology who had worked on NASA's Mars mission, founded Ion America (renamed Bloom Energy in 2006) in Sunnyvale to develop fuel-cell technology to generate environmentally-friendly electricity. Within a few years, it had raised $400 million in venture capital money. Its fuel cells were based on beach sand. Each unit cost between $700,000 and $800,000. Google and eBay were among the early adopters of these fuel-cell power generators. Fuel cells opened up the possibility of liberating individuals from the slavery of power plants and transmission grids.

NanoSolar was the first solar energy company based in Silicon Valley, and it collaborated with Stanford University and Lawrence Berkeley

National Laboratories. They developed an ink capable of converting sunlight into electricity; it became the foundation for its family of flexible, low-cost and light-weight solar cells.

Nanotech

Nanotechnology, on the other hand, seemed to benefit from the dotcom crash, as venture capitalists looked elsewhere to invest their money. The US government enacted a National Nanotechnology Initiative in 2001, which helped fuel the sector. New startups in Silicon Valley included Nanosys, founded in 2001 to produce "architected" materials, and Innovalight, founded in 2002 and specializing in solar cell technology. Venture capitalists saw opportunities in the convergence of biotech, infotech, and nanotech. However, the nano hype mainly resulted in books and organizations with pompous titles, such as "Kinematic Self-Replicating Machines" (2004) by Robert Freitas and Ralph Merkle.

In the old tradition of government intervention to boost high-tech investments, the Central Intelligence Agency (CIA) set up an odd not-for-profit venture-capital firm in Menlo Park, called In-Q-Tel, in 1999. It would invest in leading-edge technologies such as nanotech and biotech. One of their investments in Silicon Valley was in Keyhole, which developed a geospatial data visualization tool (software to display three-dimensional images of satellite images).

Bionics

The Bay Area's passion for creating a society as inclusive as possible had always made it a friendly place for disabled people, particularly around the Berkeley campus. In 2000, DARPA decided to fund a project at UC Berkeley's Robotics and Human Engineering Laboratory. It built technology capable of mobilizing paralyzed people. These "exoskeletons," named BLEEXes (Berkeley Lower Extremity Exoskeletons), were lightweight battery-powered artificial legs that helped a disabled person not only to walk but also to carry a heavy load. The first BLEEX was introduced in 2003. In 2005, the director of that laboratory, Homayoon Kazerooni, founded a company, Berkeley ExoWorks (later renamed Berkeley Bionics), to commercialize the devices. In 2010 Berkeley Bionics would introduce eSuit, a computer-controlled suit to make paralyzed people walk. Transformative technologies were quietly emanating from the Valley.

The Anthropology of E-socializing

Email became pervasive in the 1990s. Email and the Web came rapidly to be used not only for business but also for personal matters, fun, and family. High-tech tools were not social in themselves but the people who produced them and used them daily discovered their "social" value. They soon came to be used as social tools too to replace the lacking social life of Silicon Valley; to create networks of soccer players, hikers, music listeners, etc. This "discovery" that high-tech tools were valuable for building social networks would have widespread implications. It also meant that individuals came to be progressively more and more often plugged into the network.

Email developed a new mindset of interaction with the community: it allowed people to delay a response, to filter incoming messages, to assign priorities. Of course, this had already been made possible by answering machines; but email was written and was stored on the computer. Email also allowed a message to have multiple recipients, which led to the creation of mailing lists. In other words, email increased control over personal communications.

Electronic socializing also helped remove some of the ethnic barriers that still existed. In 1997, more than 80% of newborn babies had parents of the same ethnic group. For a region with such a large percentage of foreign-born people, it was surprising that the ethnic background still mattered so much. The advent of e-socializing removed some of the formalities that one expected from friends.

High-tech also fostered mobility of information at the expense of mobility of bodies. Telecommuting became more common, if not widespread. Telecommuters lived and worked in the same place: the home office. And they worked when inspired. They had no work hours, as long as they delivered their task by the deadline. Teleconferencing and telecommuting further reduced personal interactions. Co-workers became invisible although present 24 hours a day. On one hand, high-tech tools made one reachable anywhere any time. On the other hand, it also estranged one from the community.

Silicon Valley's engineers were the first users of their technologies. But the opposite was also true: Silicon Valley's engineers could also be the last users of technologies developed in other regions. For example, the rate of adoption of cellular phones was a lot slower than in Europe.

One reason why the virtual community was so successful was that the physical community was so unsuccessful. Silicon Valley was a sprawling expanse of low-rise buildings but it did not have an identity as a community (other than the identity of not having an identity). San Jose, in particular, had become one of the richest cities in the nation. It was, however, not a city, but just an aggregate of nondescript neighborhoods that had grown independently over the years. In true Silicon Valley fashion, the city decided to create a downtown area overnight that would introduce a flavor of European lifestyle. It spent almost one billion dollars to create a large shopping, dining, and entertainment complex strategically located at the border with Santa Clara and Cupertino. In 2002, Santana Row opened for business. It was totally artificial.

The Myth

The Cold War had ended in 1991 with a complete conversion of the communist world to capitalism. Throughout the 1990s, due to the dotcom boom and to the favorable global political environment, there was much discussion about how to export Silicon Valley's model to other regions of the world, notably Singapore, India, and China. Nobody found quite the right formula, although they all took inspiration from many aspects of Silicon Valley.

In the US itself there were different opinions on how to foster innovation. For example, Microsoft's former research head, Nathan Myhrvold, founded Intellectual Ventures in 2000; it was a secretive enterprise with a business model to purchase as many patents as possible in just about every imaginable field. But the emphasis was more on filing patents than on incubating viable companies. Owning a huge portfolio of patents is mainly a legal business, involving armies of intellectual-property attorneys, and it can be lucrative because any other company trying to develop a product in the same sector will have to buy the related patents. Of course, this "patent trolling" business hampers rather than fosters innovation because many smaller companies will never even think of venturing into a field for which a billion-dollar venture fund owns a patent. Regardless of the philanthropic merits of encouraging inventors from all over the world, Silicon Valley looked down on this kind of approach: it was artificial and it did not create a real integrated networked economy.

Microsoft's co-founder Paul Allen had pioneered this approach in 1992 when he had established the Palo Alto-based Interval Research Corporation. It was a technology incubator that made no products but filed a lot of patents that were used 18 years later to sue just about every major company in the Web business.

31. Lost Funders: Venture Capital Struggling in the Aughties (2001-12)

Acquisitions over IPOs and Angels over Venture Capital

The venture capital industry struggled in the Aughties. Large venture firms funded many companies from 2003 to 2007, but exits were few and returns for the decade from 2001 to 2011 were dismal. The biggest shift after the bust of the Internet bubble was that the vast majority of venture capital-backed exits were through M&A sales to "strategic" corporate investors, and not IPOs (roughly 80% M&A to 20% IPO).

One reason for the smaller number of IPOs was the decline of the small investment bank, which thrived in the US in the 1970s and 1980s. Many died off through the 1990s, including Robertson Stephens in 2001, which was shut down in an act of spite by its parent company, FleetBoston, even though Robertson bankers offered to buy the company for millions of dollars. Most of the banks were in San Francisco or New York City, and included names such as: C.E. Unterberg Towbin; Marron, Eden & Sloss; Carter Berlind; Potoma & Weill; Fahnestock; Wessels, Arnold; Adams Harkness & Hill; Robertson Stephens; Montgomery Securities (the old firm with that name); Laird & Company; D.H. Blair; Raymond James; Black & Company; Robinson Humphrey; Loeb Rhoades & Company; G.H. Walker; and Hambrecht & Quist. These firms were willing to raise $3 million to $50 million to take smaller startups public, such as Intel. They made a viable aftermarket for the shares. Yet during the Tech Bubble, most of the smaller investment banks either consolidated or went bust.

A second reason was Sarbanes-Oxley, the post-Enron US regulation that imposed tough reporting requirements and accounting controls on public firms. Smaller public firms just couldn't handle this, as it added to the legal and accounting costs for both the firm and the investment bank. Some believed that the minimum economic level for an IPO in 2010 was a $50 million offering at a $250 million market value.

With IPOs becoming difficult, startups had to be acquired by strategic corporate buyers. Between 2000 and 2009, the biggest corporate acquirers were Cisco (48), IBM (35), Microsoft (30), EMC (25), Oracle (23), Broadcom (18), Symantec (18), HP (18), Google (17), and SUN (17); they took center stage. Clearly, the Silicon Valley engines were driving the startup process and were higher on the food chain, consuming energetic young companies as they matured.

By decade-end, a few venture capital firms, like New Enterprise Associates Inc., could close large funds ($2.5 billion for NEA XIII, which collected 17% of all US venture capital funds in 2009). Many were predicting the demise of the venture capital industry; even the NEA partners wished the industry would shrink, at least to narrow their competition. Observers pointed out that it had been 14 years, as of early 2012, since the venture capital industry returned more capital than it consumed, and there were few mega-exits in the aughties. Google was still the largest exit until the Facebook IPO.

Yet most venture capitalists, like Alan Patricof or Paul Kedrosky, believed the future was in small funds and $20 million to $100 million exits by sale to corporate acquirers. Small partnerships like First Round Capital and Baseline Ventures started building a model with $100,000 to $2 million seed-stage investments, with the hope of exits in the $20 million to $100 million range. Their model was to invest for a 5% to 12% stake, and not the typical 25% to 40% bite a venture investor took. Yet even smaller institutions, like Paul Graham's Y-Combinator targeted the ideal first-time entrepreneur (techie males, ages 18-26) for fields where scaling was easy (Web 2.0 or "web services"). Y-Combinator offered $10,000 to $20,000, took a small 2% to 6% stake, and then gave support and a "Startup School" program to get their young men (and few women) into the world of entrepreneurship.

Another interesting model was Plug and Play, started by the Amidi family. Their incubator provided startups physical space, computing power, seminars, and so on; it received equity and often charges for the use of facilities, but at an amount under the market rate. Google, Paypal, Logitech, and Danger were once tenants in their famous building on 165 University Avenue (with a rug shop on the bottom floor, for retail).

According to SVB Financial Group's Startup Outlook 2010 Survey, 80% of startups had less than 50 employees. The majority of them were in software/Internet (42%), life sciences (32%), and hardware (13%). In the depths of the 2008-2009 recession, the biggest concerns of companies were access to capital, the business climate, government regulation, IP protections, and access to talent. Anecdotally, venture investors still liked e-commerce, Internet, and cloud services companies because of capital efficiency. Yet a new generation of companies under the "cleantech/greentech" rubric started attracting capital, and firms like KPCB and Khosla Ventures started leaving software/Web 2.0 for these greener fields. Geographically, in 2009 the Bay Area factored 45% of all investment dollars. By comparison, New England had only 10%, Southern California had 9%, the New York metro area had 5%; then there was the rest of the country.

Time would tell which model was better: small or large, capital efficient-investing or capital-intensive investing. Perhaps there would be winners in both spaces. Yet the venture capital industry would have to prove itself, as it hit a trough for financial returns.

Financial Returns from Venture Capital Investing

Financial returns in the aughties were dismal, falling to 2.59% for the decade ending September 30, 2011. This number turned positive only in 2011 and 2012 due to IPOs like LinkedIN, Facebook, and Zynga. The data for the decade ending Sept. 30, 2011 from Cambridge Associates, an industry data firm and consultant, showed poor end-to-end pooled mean net returns to limited partners (this is what the industry uses to approximate average annual compounded returns for all investors):

Period ending 9/30/2011	End-to-end Pooled Mean Net to LPs (%)
One Year	20.93
Three Year	4.93
Five Year	6.72
Ten Year	2.59
Fifteen Year	27.26
Twenty Year	19.38

Note: The data uses 1,327 US venture capital funds from 1981 to 2011.

The data, when analyzed by year or decade, told an interesting story. Lean years of 1980s: After an anecdotally great decade of the 1970s, much of the 1980s' returns (the first to be rigorously tracked) were weak. From 1981 to 1986, returns ranged from 8.5% to 14.5%. This wasn't horrible, but it compared poorly with public equity indices, which had amazing years with lower risk and complete liquidity.

Fat years of 1990s: The industry took off afterwards, and funds with vintage (starting) years of 1987 to 1998 did spectacularly well, with returns from 12.4% to 99.3% (note that a handful of funds drastically changed the averages, pulling them up by a factor of 2x). Or as Joshua Lerner, a Professor at Harvard Business School, found out by analyzing returns, net of fees, for 1,252 U.S. venture funds going back to 1976, the median return for top-quartile firms was 28%. That included the huge profits of the Tech Boom, which no one expected would recur. The median return for all venture funds was just under 5%, or worse than what Treasury bonds would have given investors over that period. Lerner's lesson: "If you're not with the good guys, it's not worth playing." The industry went from investing $7.3 billion in 1995 to $100.4 billion in 2000, per NVCA industry statistics.

Lean years of 2000s: The aughties were a nightmare for investors. Returns ranged from a high of 4.3% to lows of around -4%. Amounts invested ranged from $20 billion to the $30 billion in the aughties, but fell to $17.8 billion in 2009. More vintages had negative returns than positive returns. In private, the most sophisticated limited partners had conversations about cutting the venture investments to small amounts, or perhaps about leaving the industry all together.

Venture Capitalists Giving Back to Society (or Cashing in Claim Checks)

Generally, venture capitalists have made few, large philanthropic gifts; as a group, they don't seem to be as generous as entrepreneurs. Both venture capitalists and entrepreneurs have generated enormous amount of societal wealth, and their bank accounts act as "claim checks" on society's resources. Early great entrepreneurs, like Hewlett and Packard at HP and Noyce and Moore at Intel, exemplified a down-to-earth philosophy best stated by Warren Buffett, who didn't have a guilt problem with money.

Buffett saw his money as representing an "enormous number of claim checks on society," which were little pieces of paper he could turn into consumption. Buffett stated that if he wanted to, he could "hire 10,000 people to do nothing but paint my picture every day for the rest of my life." While GDP would go up, the utility of the product would be zero and he would be taking away resources that could go to medical research, nursing, startup creation, teacher support, or other productive activities. Luckily, Buffett had few worldly material wants (homes, yachts, cars, etc.) and so virtually all his claim checks would go to charity when he died. These entrepreneurs gave most of their wealth back to society. The Hewlett, Packard, and Moore Foundations were multi-billion dollar charities doing good works across the US in the fields of education, health care, and so on.

Many venture capitalists, however, were stingy. This stinginess appeared early, as Georges Doriot left most of his wealth, nearly $52 million consisting mostly of Digital stock in 1987, to a private trust; Doriot and his wife, however, did generously support the French Library in Boston. In comparison, Digital Founder Ken Olsen gave millions to Gordon College and other charities, mostly in line with his Christian conservative beliefs.

Yet a handful of venture capitalists made large donations to public institutions as a sign of maturity and their responsibility of giving back to society. Mike Moritz, a partner at Sequoia Venture Capital, gave $50 million to his alma mater, Christ Church College at Oxford University, in 2008 (Moritz made early investments in both Yahoo and Google). Another Sequoia partner, Mark Stevens, gave $22 million in 2004 to the School of Engineering at his alma mater, USC. Bill Draper formed the Draper

Richards Foundation with $20 million to give grants and support to social entrepreneurs, such as Chris Balme and the Spark Program, which helped educate and motivate under-privileged youth through internships.

Sadly, many venture capitalists continued to have a gilded age mentality of Porsches and mansions. One example was Tom Perkins, with his multiple homes, a $10 million condo in the Millennium Tower in San Francisco, a Bugatti car collection, and a 289-foot (88 meters) luxury, sailing yacht called the Maltese Falcon, which cost between $150-250 million to build. Perkins sold it to a hedge fund manager in 2009 as he got older and it became more difficult to run the boat and pay its high costs.

32. Aughties Failures: A Case Study on Startups that Died of Indigestion (2001-10)

Aughties Failures

The aughties were a tough decade for startups in Silicon Valley. Few companies had multi-billion dollar IPOs and the preferred exit was a sale to a large corporation. It was a better decade for the large, established companies, the engines of the Valley, but even some of them stumbled. Novalux Corp. was a startup failure that lingered from the technology bubble and showed what startups were poor at doing (manufacturing complicated technologies). Friendster and MySpace were early social networking sites that managed to bungle a billion-dollar opportunity and lose to Facebook. The biggest and most controversial failure was Yahoo!'s descent from "King of the Internet" in 2000 to a dud company by 2012.

Novalux's Microchip Laser

Novalux Corp. was funded in 1998, at the height of the Internet bubble but dragged on for 10 years, consuming about $193 million in venture funding before it went bust. Aram Mooradian was a laser scientist at MIT who invented a supercharged microchip laser, which he thought could apply to HD TVs, fiber-optic data transmissions, and even blood sampling in doctors' offices. Mooradian raised $2.5 million from Vanguard Ventures and Crescendo Ventures and set up an office in San Mateo, California to raise even more money ($109 million) from CSFB, Crescendo, and Telesoft Partners. The company remained in planning mode with no product. It then hired 160 employees and built a fabrication facility, only to find that its potential customers, optical networking integrator companies like Lucent and Nortel, were cutting back their budgets in the telecom implosion of 2001. The company fired 40% of its workforce and filed for bankruptcy in March 2003.

Yet Novalux lived on. A new group of backers, including Morgan Stanley, Doll Capital Management, and Dynafund, took control and put in another $33 million to build chips for HD TVs and computer monitors. A 2005 financial report projected sales of $86 million by 2008. However glitches kept the product from being built well. Mooradian also suffered a heart attack in 2006 that destroyed his kidneys (requiring him to go on dialysis treatments for life). As customers bailed again in 2007, the venture investors gave up and sold the company to the Australian startup Arasor for $7 million. Mooradian in hindsight thought the company's mistake was trying to manufacture, as opposed to developing and testing chips and then licensing the technology to much larger companies. A nimble startup has no manufacturing edge over firms like Intel or Toshiba.

Friendster and MySpace: Early Social Networking Failures

Friendster and MySpace show that getting to a space early, and even becoming big, don't guarantee success. Technology startups in areas with a low barrier to entry, like social networking, need to create some sort of lock-in effect, generally through a genuine network effect, and they need to execute well. The story of the failure of Friendster and MySpace is bracing. Both companies came close to dominating the market but ultimately lost to Facebook.

In 2002, Jonathan Abrams, a former Netscape software engineer, started Friendster in Morgan Hill, California, so that he could meet girls more easily. It was a way to surf through his friends' address books for good-looking girls. Incidentally, Facebook had a similar beginning when its founder Mark Zuckerburg wanted the same ability to surf the Harvard undergraduate class yearbook; this shows that the carnal desires of male nerds can result in technologies that profoundly change society. The Friendster site took off and Google offered Abrams $30 million in 2003 for the company (an amount in Google stock that would later be worth over $1 billion). With many venture capitalists raising his hopes, he foolishly refused and instead raised about $15.4 million by 2003. Kleiner Perkins' John Doerr and Benchmark Capital's Bob Kagle (venture capitalist royalty) were early backers and board members, while star angels like Peter Thiel and Ram Shriram took stakes too.

The problems started there. Abrams has reportedly stated that he had a sound business plan which foundered when the investors replaced him in April 2004, a few months after funding the company; they messed everything up. The average board member was older than 50 and didn't understand the nuances of the technology. However, Doerr stated that investors "understood the opportunity [but]… the company didn't seize that opportunity." Doerr claims that Abrams was too young to handle growing a company, hire people, build territories, and so on.

The product suffered as the web site became slow; it took over 40 seconds to load a single page, the core service. Meanwhile the board focused on Internet phone service and other ancillary services like multiple languages and advertising. A series of CEOs came and left, lasting only a few months each. One key decision was to keep the service "closed"; that is, users had to post their real pictures, have real profiles, and could only connect to friends of friends.

MySpace, in contrast, was started in early 2004 by two Los Angeles music fans. It had a simple "open" system, where anyone could connect with anyone else. MySpace focused on giving users a free space to post their text, music, and video, and to simply connect. The company started to attract many more users than Friendster, and the owners sold it to News Corp. for $580 million in July 2005.

Friendster ran out of cash in late 2005. It never developed a realistic monetization strategy, to turn its free users into paid customers or generate healthy revenue streams from ads. Investors had a tough choice but decided to double-down. From 2006 to 2008, Friendster raised another $33 million and started to focus on the operational issues and core product. But the company had already lost the lead; it decided to try and focus on older users and Asian users. Friendster was acquired by MOL Global, a Malaysian company, for $26.4 million in 2009, and Facebook bought some of Friendster's social networking patents for $40 million in 2010.

MySpace quickly degenerated after the acquisition, both operationally and in terms of strategic direction. The company allowed users to pollute their web pages with photos, graphics, and video, giving the whole experience a cluttered and childish "teen-angst" look. MySpace also had sexual predator problems, not to mention problems with spammers, viruses, and pornography. The company let disorganized advertising in, further debasing the user experience. Arguably the biggest mistake MySpace made was de-emphasizing Web 2.0 as a strategy and applications made by third-party developers.

From 2008 to 2010, Facebook roared past MySpace and Friendster, acquiring 50 million to 200 million users in record time; it had more than 500 million active users by mid-2010 and over a billion by early 2013. Facebook had a semi-closed network. Users could choose how open or closed they wanted their pages to be. Facebook kept the design simple and standardized, giving users some ability to customize but not to clutter; it kept the user experience simple and clean; and it developed other sources of revenues besides ads, like applications such as games and utility tools, encouraging third-party developers. Facebook also excelled at the very difficult task of building communities, starting with user's school connections, and then spreading to every type of group imaginable. Friendster never got the execution right for it, and MySpace's users were more like solitary islands than members of a large group.

Yahoo!'s Drift from Search

Arguably the biggest failure of the 2000s was Yahoo! Corp., despite its stellar success in the 1990s. Yahoo started as a student hobby of David Filo and Jerry Yang. Both were doctoral candidates in Electrical Engineering at Stanford University and they created their guide to the Internet in a campus trailer in February 1994. Shortly after starting, they were spending more time on their lists of favorite links, not to mention categories and sub-categories, than on their doctoral dissertations. The site started out as "Jerry and David's Guide to the World Wide Web" but became Yahoo! (reportedly an acronym for "Yet Another Hierarchical

Officious Oracle!"). Word spread quickly from Stanford Internet users across the country, and Yahoo! had its first million-hit day in the fall of 1994, translating to almost a 100,000 unique visitors. Yahoo! was essentially a search company, helping Internet surfers find information and websites.

Yang and Filo believed they had a startup opportunity on their hand. In March 1995, the pair incorporated the business and met with dozens of Silicon Valley venture capitalists. They received nearly $2 million from Sequoia Capital in April 1995, and hired a management team of Tim Koogle (a Motorola executive) as CEO and Jeffrey Mallett (founder of Novell's WordPerfect consumer division) as COO. Yahoo! raised a second round of funding in fall 1995 from Reuters Ltd. and Softbank. Quickly after, Yahoo! launched a successful IPO in April 1996, raising $33.8 million. The company had a total of 49 employees.

Yahoo!'s most important strategic decision from 1996 to 1998 was to be a portal, and not a directory provider or search company. It tried to compete with MSN, Lycos, Excite, AOL, and other web portals offering a range of services like free e-mail, games, news, horoscopes, and messaging. The company acquired Four11's Rocketmail in March 1997 and Classicgames.com later in 1997, not to mention the disastrous GeoCities acquisition in 1998. Yahoo!'s biggest mistake, clear in hindsight, was to not pursue Internet search aggressively early on. Instead of buying the rights to Google's search algorithms for less than $2 million in 1998, they licensed the technology in June 2000, letting Google develop an edge. At the height of the dotcom bubble, Yahoo! had a market capitalization value of over $140 billion, despite having 1999 profits of just $61 million. It was a peak to which the company would never return.

Yahoo! did survive the Internet bust, but its stock fell from a high of $119 to a low of $8, a 93% loss. After the bust, Yahoo! partnered with a few broadband telecom companies and decided it needed to be more robust at search. In April 2001, the founders brought in Terry Semel (a Warner Brothers veteran) as CEO to improve its relationship marketing, content development, and media strategy. He thoughtfully and methodically expanded the company beyond search and banner ads to make money from charging for services like mail, stores, games, and online dating. Semel's strategy was to focus on monetizable content, while trying to stay abreast of technology by buying promising startups. Yahoo! even tried generating content for a while, with a web-based TV show and original content like "Kevin Sites in the Hot Zone."

On the technology side, Yahoo! acquired Inktomi in December 2002, Overture in July 2003 (its best acquisition by far, in terms of solid technology driving revenues and profits), and AltaVista soon after, while dropping Google search results in February 2004 for its own technology. A key purchase was Flikr in March 2005, which remained one of the web's top photo sharing sites. At the same time, a large blunder was failing to acquire Facebook for more than $1 billion in 2006. This was a major failure in the execution of Semel's strategy, though the actual strategy was sound.

By 2007, Yahoo! had fallen behind. Its ad platform and search engine were not as effective as Google's, and more importantly, Yahoo! failed the talent war. The most talented engineers went to Google, as it offered them the most freedom and the best perks (free corporate cafeterias with celebrity chefs, free corporate shuttles around the Bay Area, massages, visiting lecturers, etc.). So Google developed strong tech-heavy products like Gmail, Google Maps, and Picasa, all of which beat their Yahoo! counterpart.

Besides falling behind in search, Yahoo! lost out on three major Internet trends: social networking, which Facebook came to dominate; user-generated content, which companies like Yelp! and Demand Media took over; and finally, cloud computing, where Salesforce.com and Amazon built a strong presence. One success, however, was Yahoo! Finance, which remained the best free website for financial information from 2000 to 2012. Semel left in June 2007, and was followed by three CEOs in three years (Susan Decker, Jerry Yang, and Carol Bartz).

In February 2008, Microsoft Corp. made an unsolicited bid of $45 billion to acquire Yahoo!, mostly for its search technology (this would be 75 times Yahoo!'s 2009 profits of nearly $600 million). Google stepped in offered to again offer its search technology to Yahoo! in a revenue sharing deal, which by one analyst's estimate would increase Yahoo!'s cash flow 25% annually (a short run boost but a potential long run strategic blunder). Yahoo!'s Yang rejected both offers as being too low, only to see Yahoo!'s market capitalization value fall even lower over the next few years. Eventually, in 2009 Yahoo! struck a deal where Microsoft's new Bing search engine would power Yahoo!'s search and they would share revenues. This again took Yahoo! out of the technology "megawatt war," requiring thousands of services and a deep operational back end, into front-end competition of content and services. Again, Yahoo! seemed to be falling further behind in social networking, cloud computing, and mobile computing, the most promising directions in which the Web was growing. Carol Bartz, Yahoo!'s CEO in 2010, recognized that Yahoo! needed to be on all platforms. Yet she didn't make it clear whether Yahoo! was a search and technology company, a content company, or something else. She did define Facebook and Google as Yahoo!'s main competitors. While her primary goal was user growth in new markets like Asia (with monetization to come later), Yahoo! still lacked the focus of its two main competitors. So in 2010 Yahoo! did not a reached a terminal point, but it seemed like its relative decline would continue.

In 2012, an activist board member replaced Bartz with Marissa Meyer, a top Google executive. Meyer's turnaround strategy would be watched carefully, but the odds were heavily against her.

33. Downsizers: Facebook, YouTube, Web 2.0, and Tesla Motors (2003-06)

Distributed and Small

The early 2000s were an age of downsizing. Silicon Valley companies had to learn the art of cost cutting. Startups had to learn the art of actually developing a product and selling it. Once again, the beneficiary was India. Creating a lab in India, where software engineers earned a fraction of Silicon Valley engineers, was a relatively painless way to dramatically cut costs. By 2005 more than 50% of all jobs outsourced by Silicon Valley companies went to India.

There were other lessons to be learned too. In July 2003 AOL spun off Mozilla. It was originally founded by Netscape to foster third-party development on the browser under a free open-source license. It quickly built a reputation as a new browser. The first chair of the Mozilla Foundation was Lotus' founder Mitch Kapor. The lesson learned by Netscape through Mozilla was that the open-source model works, but it is a Darwinian process, and, just like in nature, it works very slowly. The Mozilla community hated Microsoft's Internet Explorer and therefore loved the Netscape browser. Unfortunately, this meant that dozens of people added features to Mozilla to the point that it became famously fat and slow.

Mozilla needed a re-birth. This came in 2002 when a new batch of developers, mainly Stanford students, produced a "lighter" version of the Mozilla browser. It was eventually named Firefox. Firefox was indeed a state-of-the-art browser that could match IE, whose team Microsoft had just disbanded anyway in 2001. Yet precious time had been lost. In 2003 Microsoft's Internet Explorer (IE) owned 95% of the browser market.

Computing devices had been getting smaller since the first Eniac was unveiled. That trend had never really stopped. It just proceeded by discontinuous jumps: the minicomputer was a significant downsizing from the mainframe, and so was the personal computer from the minicomputer. The laptop, however, was just a variation on the personal computer, the only major difference being the screen. In 2005, sales of notebook computers accounted for 53% of the computer market; the traditional desktop computer was on the way out. IBM pulled out of the market for desktop computers. There was a clear trend towards a portable computing device, but the laptop per se did not truly represent a quantum leap forward, just a way to stretch the personal-computer technology to serve that trend.

At the same time, sales of smart phones were booming too, but there was a lesson there. In 2004, Motorola introduced the mobile phone Razr, an elegant-looking device that by July 2006 had been bought by over 50 million people, propelling Motorola to second position after Nokia. Yet sales started dropping dramatically in 2006. Motorola learned the hard way an important rule of the cell phone market: phones went in and out of fashion very quickly. There was room for more players, and Silicon Valley had largely been on the sidelines until then. No Silicon Valley company was part of the consortium formed in 2004 to develop and promote Near Field Communication (NFC), basically the smartphone equivalent of the old RFID. This was a method to allow smartphones to exchange data by simply pointing at each other at close range. The founders were Nokia, Philips, and Sony. It would take seven years for Silicon Valley to catch up, when Google would introduce the technology in its NFS-enabled smartphones.

The positive note for the dotcoms was that the Web was spreading like a virus all over the world. By 2006 Google had indexed more than eight billion pages, coming from the 100 million websites registered on the Web. In March 2006, the English version of Wikipedia passed one million articles. The Internet was being accessed by 1.25 billion people in the world. The dotcom bubble had not been completely senseless: one just had to figure out how to capitalize on that massive audience.

By 2005 Yahoo!, Google, America OnLine (AOL) and MSN (Microsoft's Network) were the four big Internet "portals," with a combined audience of over one billion people. Never in history had such a large audience existed. Never in history had Silicon Valley companies controlled such a large audience; most of that billion used Google and Yahoo!. There were only two threats to the Internet: spam (undesired marketing emails) and viruses (malicious software that spread via email or downloads and harmed computers).

Intel capitalized on the popularity of the Web with a new generation of microprocessors. Wi-Fi became a household name after Intel introduced the Centrino for laptops in March 2003. From that point on a laptop would be associated with wireless Internet as much as with mobility.

Mobile television, already available in South Korea since 2005, spread worldwide in a few years, finding millions of customers in Asia, Africa, and Latin America. Ironically, the West lagged behind, and in 2012 mobile TV was still a rarity in the US. But even in this case Silicon Valley was actually at the vanguard: the leading mobile TV chip maker, Telegent Systems, a fabless company founded in 2004 by LSI Logic's inventor Samuel Sheng, was based in Sunnyvale.

Social Networking

Initially, instead, the idea behind the dotcoms had been to transfer commerce to the Web; hence e-commerce. This was a more than viable business, but, in hindsight, it lacked imagination. It soon proved to be viable mostly for the already established "brick and mortar" corporations.

It took a while for the dotcoms to imagine what one could "sell" to one billion people spread all over the world: social networking. For the first time in history it was possible for one billion strangers to assemble, organize themselves, discuss issues, and act together.

Social networking was another practical implementation of Metcalfe's law that the value of a network of users increases exponentially with each new user. Three important companies were Facebook, Ning, and Twitter.

Facebook and Ning overlapped a little. In February 2004 Harvard student Mark Zuckerberg launched the social-networking service Facebook. It soon spread from college to college. Weeks later Zuckerberg and friends relocated to Silicon Valley and obtained funding from Peter Thiel of PayPal. Somehow this one took off the way that previous ones had not. Facebook started growing at a ridiculously fast pace, having signed up 100 million users by August 2008 on its way to becoming the second website by traffic after Google by the end of the decade. In 2005 Gina Bianchini and Netscape's founder Marc Andreessen launched Ning, a meta social-networking software. It allowed people to create and customize their own social networks. Inktomi's founders Brian Totty and Paul Gauthier formed Ludic Labs in San Mateo in 2006, a venture devoted to social media software for consumers and businesses that launched offerfoundry.com, talkfilter.com and diddit.com.

Last but not least, in 2006 Evan Williams and Jack Dorsey created the social-networking service Twitter, where people could post short live updates of what was going on in their life. A "tweet" was limited to 140 characters. That limit reflected the way people wanted to communicate in the age of smart phones: very brief messages. Twitter soon became popular for current events the way CNN had become popular during the first Gulf War.

The Unix and in particular Linux world had been the first example of a social networking platform. It was used to refine the platform itself. Facebook and the likes simply adopted the concept and transferred to it the sphere of private life.

Facebook's sociological impact was massive. For example, Facebook offered a "Like" button for people to applaud a friend's statement or picture, but did not offer a "Dislike" button. Facebook was creating a society in which it was not only rude but physically impossible to be negative. The profile picture of the Facebook user was supposed to be a smiling face. The whole Facebook society was just one big collective smile. The Web's libertarian society was turning into a global exercise in faking happiness. After all, the French historian Alexis de Tocqueville had warned in 1840 in his study "Democracy in America" that absolute freedom would make people lonely and desperate. In a sense, social networking universes like Facebook were testing the possibility of introducing a meta-level of behavioral control to limit the absolute freedom enabled by the Web.

Google, eBay, Facebook and Twitter shared one feature that made them such incredible success stories was: simplicity. Initially, they all had a humble, text-only "look and feel" in the age of graphic design, banners, chat rooms, and so on. All that Twitter had needed to change the world was 140 characters.

Your Life Online

In November 2005, a group of former Paypal employees, all still in their twenties, got together to launch a new website, YouTube. The Stanford student founders were based in San Mateo and funded by Roelof Botha of Sequoia Capital, another PayPal alumnus. The concept sounded innocent enough. It was just a way for ordinary people with an ordinary digital videocamera to upload their videos to the Web. It turned out to be the perfect Internet video application. By July 2006, more than 65,000 new videos were being uploaded every day, and more than 100 million videos were viewed by users worldwide every day. Eleven months after its founding, Google bought YouTube for $1.65 billion.

YouTube did more than simply help people distribute their videos worldwide: it ushered in the age of "streaming" media. "Streaming" means to watch a video or to listen to a recording in real time directly from its Web location as opposed to downloading it from the Web on one's computer. YouTube's videos were "streamed" to the browser of the viewer. YouTube did not invent streaming, but it demonstrated its power over cable television, movie theaters, and any previous form of broadcasting videos to the masses.

Another idea that matured in the 2000s was Internet-based telephony. Skype was founded in Europe in 2003 by Niklas Zennstroem and Janus Friis to market a system invented by Kazaa's founders. Internet users were now able to make free phone calls to any other Internet user, as long as both parties had a microphone and a loudspeaker in their computer. The lesson learned in this case was that telephony over the Internet was a major innovation for ordinary consumers, not companies, but ordinary consumers could not afford suitable computers until the 2000s. Skype was not charging anything for the service, so, again, the business model was just to become very popular all over the world.

E-commerce

The net economy was, however, recovering from the dotcom burst. For example, Amazon lost a staggering $2.8 billion between 1995 and

2001. Its first profit was posted at the end of 2001, and it was a mere $5 million. But in 2005 it posted revenues of $8.5 billion and a hefty profit, placing it inside the exclusive club of the "Fortune 500." In 2006 its revenues would top $10.7 billion. In 2007, its sales would increase a stunning 34.5% over the previous year. eBay's revenues for 2006 reached $6 billion. Netflix's revenues were up 48% from the previous year, just short of one billion dollars, and it had almost six million subscribers.

It took a while before the business world understood the benefits of selling online: it makes it easier to track customers' behavior and fine-tune your marketing to attract more customers or to attract more advertisers. The amount of data generated world-wide had been increasing exponentially for years, and those data were mostly ending up on the Internet. Enerprise software was ridiculously inadequate to dealing with that avalanche of data. A new kind of application, launched by serial entrepreneurs Rob Das and Erik Swan in 2002 in San Francisco, filled that niche: analyze customer behavior in real time and churn out business metrics data.

Digital Entertainment

A lesson was arising from the massive amount of music downloaded both legally and illegally from the Internet. In 2003, the file-sharing system Rapidshare was founded in Germany, the file-sharing system TorrentSpy went live in the US, and a BitTorrent-based website named "The Pirate Bay" opened in Sweden. In 2005 Megaupload was founded in Hong Kong. In 2006 Mediafire was founded in the US. These websites allowed people to upload the music that they had ripped from CDs, and allowed the entire Internet population to download them for free. The "fraud" was so extensive that in 2006 the music industry in the US (represented by the RIAA) filed a lawsuit against Russian-based Internet download service AllOfMP3.com for $1.65 trillion. Needless to say, it proved impossible to stop half a billion people from using free services that were so easy to use. Music downloading became a pervasive phenomenon.

Apple's iTunes store, opened in April 2003, was the legal way to go for those who were afraid of the law, and by the end of 2006, half of Apple's revenues was from sales of the iPod, one of the most successful devices in history. Digital videos came next, although the sheer size of the video files discouraged many from storing them on their home computers.

The lesson to be learned was twofold. One lesson was for the media companies: it was virtually impossible to enforce copyrights on digital files. The other lesson was for the consumers: it was wishful thinking that one could digitize a huge library of songs and films because that would require just too much storage. A different system was needed, namely streaming.

The phenomenon of digital music downloading was another premonition of an important change in computing. From the viewpoint of the "downloader," the whole Web was becoming just one huge repository of music. Its geographical location was irrelevant. It was in the "cloud" created by multiple distributed servers around the world.

The situation was quite different in the field of books. In the late 1990s, companies such as SoftBook Press and NuvoMedia had pioneered the concept of the e-book reader. Microsoft and Amazon had introduced software to read ebooks on personal computers. Amazon simply purchased the technology in 2005 from the French company Mobipocket that had introduced it in 2000. That was at the time when there were virtually no ebooks to read. This changed in 2002 when two major publishers, Random House and HarperCollins, started selling digital versions of their titles. Amazon became and remained the main selling point for ebooks, but "ebookstores" began to appear elsewhere too, notably BooksOnBoard in Austin, Texas that opened in 2006. In October 2004, Amazon had hired two former Apple and Palm executives, Gregg Zehr (hardware) and Thomas Ryan (software), who in turn hired mostly Apple and Palm engineers, and had started a company in Cupertino called Lab126 to develop a proprietary $400 hand-held e-book reader, the Kindle. It was eventually introduced in November 2007. The Kindle was not just a software application but a custom device for reading books. That device, conceptually a descendant of the Palm Pilot, was the device that tilted the balance towards the ebook.

The company that democratized video was instead based in San Francisco: Pure Digital Technologies, originally founded by Jonathan Kaplan to make disposable digital cameras. In May 2006, it launched the Flip video camera, sold in popular department stores at an affordable price. Designed for direct conversion to digital media and particularly for Internet video sharing, it helped countless unskilled users of the Internet become amateur filmmakers. In just 18 months, PDT sold 1.5 million of its one-button camcorders and became the leader of that market. PDT showed that the smartphone was going to threaten the existence of entire lines of products, well beyond voice communication.

The Bay Area had a mixed record in the field of photography, with only the Flip gaining ephemeral momentum for a few years. Lytro was founded by Stanford's computational mathematician Ren Ng in 2006 and based in Mountain View. It aimed at designing more than a cheaper better camera: it went for the light-field cameras, a camera capable of capturing much more information and therefore of creating a much richer digital representation of the scene. The most obvious benefit was to be able to refocus the image after having taken the picture. The technology had been originally invented at the MIT Media Lab. Yet it a Stanford University team that perfected it made it fit for the consumer market.

The Aging Internet

The dramatic success in the 2000s of the new business models of Netflix (videos), YouTube (videos), Apple (music), Facebook (news), Google (news) and Twitter (news) was beginning to bring out a fundamental problem of the Internet. All these services depended on the ability to distribute content over the Internet Protocol (IP). In other words, the Internet was increasingly being used as a media distribution network to access data. Unfortunately, it had been designed to be a (host-to-host) communications network. The Internet was becoming simultaneously the world's greatest distribution network and one of the world's worst distribution networks.

Nobody was proposing to dump the Internet yet, but it was obvious that the system needed to be tweaked. In particular, the router had to be reinvented. In 2006, Xerox PARC came up with Content Centric Networking (CCN), a project under the direction of Van Jacobson of Cisco and the Lawrence Livermore Laboratory. CCN was an idea already pioneered by Ted Nelson in 1979 and developed by Dan Cheriton at Stanford in 1999 Scott Shenker at UC Berkeley in 2006. It aimed at redesigning the Internet around data access.

Serving the Old Economy

Some sectors, like business software and Oracle, had little to learn from the dotcom revolution. In the 2000s, Oracle represented an old-fashioned business model, the one that targeted "brick and mortar" companies. However, the Web had not slowed down the growth of software demand by the traditional companies that manufactured real products: it had increased it. They all needed to offer online shops backed by the fastest and most reliable database servers.

The escalating transaction volumes for e-business were good news for Oracle. Oracle was the undisputed leader in providing database management solutions, but these companies also demanded ERP systems and CRM systems. Oracle proceeded to acquire two Bay Area companies that had been successful in those fields: PeopleSoft (2004) and Siebel (2005). Now Oracle could literally connect the plant of a company to its corner offices and even to its traveling salesmen. In 2005 the total revenues of ERP software were $25.5 billion, with SAP making $10.5 billion and Oracle $5.1 billion. Oracle's founder and CEO, Larry Ellison, was estimated to be worth $18.7 billion in 2004, one of the richest people in the world.

Robots and Avatars

Recovering from the dotcom crash, Silicon Valley was more awash with futuristic ideas than ever before. In 1999, Philip Rosedale had founded Linden Lab to develop virtual-reality hardware. In 2003 Linden

Lab launched "Second Life," a virtual world accessible via the Internet in which a user could adopt a new identity and live a second life. In 2005, Andrew Ng at Stanford launched the STAIR (Stanford Artificial Intelligence Robot) project to build robots for home and office automation by integrating decade-old research in several different fields. In 2006, early Google architect Scott Hassan founded Willow Garage to manufacture robots for domestic use.

The emphasis on virtual worlds had a positive effect on the US video-game industry. After losing the leadership to Japan in the mid-1980s, the US recovered it in the 2000s because Japanese videogames were not as "immersive" as the ones made by their US competitors. For example, the simulation game "The Sims," created by SimCity's creator Will Wright for Maxis in February 2000, had become the best-selling PC game of all times within two years of its release. With the exception of Nintendo, which successfully introduced the Wii home console in 2006, Japanese game manufacturers were losing market shares for the first time ever. The Wii popularized hand-held motion-sensitive controllers, which led to a new generation of videogame consoles controlled by gestures and spoken commands.

However, the next big thing in videogames was online virtual worlds in which users created "second-life" avatars and interacted with each other, like Habbo Hotel and Gaia Online; the former was launched in February 2003 by Derek Liu in San Jose. Both became extremely popular, involving millions of users spread all over the world. In February 2006, Alyssa Picariello even established a website to chronicle life in Gaia Online: the Gaiapedia.

Mobile Payments

The "electronic wallet" was another application of the smartphone. Nokia pioneered the combination of smartphone and RFID with the Nokia 5140 in 2004. That was the first GSM phone integrated with RFID reading capability. The Japanese used mainly Sony's FeliCa chip for their electronic wallets; by the end of 2009 Sony had shipped more than 400 million FeliCa chips. In 2004, Sony and Philips Semiconductors developed Near Field Communication (NFC) and Nokia joined them in founding the NFC Forum. Like RFID, NFC was a wireless technology for short-range communications between electronic devices. The main advantage was that it was cheaper and easier to implement, and therefore should foster mobile payments using a smartphone. NFC chips allowed for two-way communication instead of only one way. In 2007, Nokia unveiled the first fully integrated NFC phone, the Nokia 6131 NFC, while Sony and NXP were still holding on to their proprietary standards FeliCa and Mifare. This is when Bay Area inventors entered the fray. Blaze Mobile, founded by telecom veteran Michelle Fisher in 2005 in Berkeley, invented the NFC payment sticker in 2006. Bling Nation, founded in 2007 in Palo Alto by

Argentinian serial entrepreneur Wenceslao Casares and Venezuelan economist Meyer Malka, developed a sticker for smartphones with an embedded NFC chip to charge purchases to a Paypal account.

In 2009, Jack Dorsey, a co-founder of Twitter, started Square and designed a "reader" that allowed anybody with a mobile phone to make a payment and anybody with a mobile phone and a Square-provided "cash register" to accept it with no cash, credit cards, RFID, or receipt. These startups, quite simply, understood that mobile users carry a computer with them, not just a phone. In fact, they even carry a GPS that knows their location. Since its founding, Square has signed up more than a million merchants and will process more than $5 billion in transactions in 2013.

The original pain point behind Square came from a personal story. One of Dorsey's former bosses was Jim McKelvey, a glass blower, who remarked during a phone conversation that he had lost a recent sale of a $2,500 blown-glass bathroom faucet because his customer could pay only with a credit card because he was calling from Panama. As McKelvey told this tale to Dorsey, both of them had iPhones pressed to their ears. Dorsey knew smartphones had more processing power than entire banks did in the 1960s and he surmised they should easily be able to process credit card payments.

Dorsey was an autodidact following Steve Job's path, with interests ranging from CB radio to blue jeans to maps and journal keeping. He was a big fan of the Japanese design concept of wabi-sabi, which found beauty in imperfection and impermanence. Keith Rabois, an early PayPal executive and the COO at Square said of Dorsey: "There are three things you need to do as a CEO-founder. Think strategically, drive design, and drive technology. Jack is the only person in the Valley I've met who's all three." Dorsey also split his time between Twitter and Square, like Jobs did between Pixar and Apple at one point.

Engineering the Future

The Web was only a decade old but high-profile critics were already complaining that it was inadequate. Berners-Lee in person had written an article in 2001 explaining the need for a "Semantic Web" in which a webpage would be able to declare the meaning of its content. In 2004 the first "Web 2.0" conference was held in San Francisco to promote the idea that the Web had to become an open platform for application development, with such development increasingly decentralized and delegated to the users themselves. The term had originally been coined in 1999 by San Francisco-based writer Darcy DiNucci. In the beginning of the Web one could only be either a producer or a consumer of webpages. The user of a browser was a passive viewer of webpages. Web 2.0 aimed for "active" viewers of webpages. A Web 2.0 webpage is a collaborative effort in which the viewers of the page can modify it and can interact with each other. Wikipedia was an example of a Web 2.0 application. Google's search indirectly was too, since it relied on a "page ranking" algorithm that was based on what was linked by millions of webpages all over the world.

The first widely publicized example of Web 2.0 was Flickr, a photo-sharing service that allowed users to "tag" photos, both their own and other people's. It was founded in February 2004 by game industry veterans Caterina Fake in San Francisco and Stewart Butterfield in Vancouver. Unlike Ofoto and Snapfish, whose websites were just ways to encourage people to print photos, Flickr understood that in the age of ubiquitous camera phones and social networking the real value was in sharing photos across the community. Soon people started taking pictures precisely for the purpose of posting them on Flickr, pictures that they would not otherwise have taken.

Yahoo! was the first major dotcom to invest in Web 2.0. It acquired Flickr in March 2005 and introduced in June its own My Web service, which allowed webpage viewers to tag and share bookmarks. Then in December it bought the most popular website for social bookmarking and tagging, Del.icio.us (originally started by Wall Street financial analyst Joshua Schachter in 2003). Basically, Yahoo! wanted to present itself as a "social search" that was fine-tuned by humans as they browsed the web, as opposed to Google's impersonal algorithmic search.

The technical underpinning of Web 2.0 consisted of free tools such as Ajax (Asynchronous JavaScript and XML), a concept invented in 2003 by Greg Aldridge in Indiana. Ajax was a platform for website developers to create interactive web-based applications (essentially HTML, XML and JavaScript).

In a nutshell, the goal was simple: to allow the viewer to make changes to a webpage on a browser without reloading the whole page. This, obviously, had been done before: JavaScript, among other tools, had been available in Netscape's browser since 1996, and web-based applications were already pervasive during the first dotcom boom but most of them went out of business quickly. Amazon allowed users to post reviews of books since the very beginning. However, Web 2.0 had a more ambitious vision: that the Web could be viewed as a platform for creating applications, a platform that would eventually replace the individual computer.

Blogging started to democratize too. Matt Mullenweg in San Francisco introduced in 2003 a new popular platform for people to create their own website or blog: Wordpress. The reason it spread like wildfire is that it was maintained as "open source" by a growing community of volunteers. In June 2003 Mark Fletcher, already the founder of ONElist (acquired by Yahoo! in 2000), launched Bloglines, the first Web-based news aggregator.

Digg, founded in November 2004 by serial entrepreneur Jay Adelson in San Francisco, pioneered the idea of letting visitors vote stories up or down (i.e., "digging" or "burying"), thus bridging the world of news aggregators and social networking.

TechCrunch was founded in June 2005 by Michael Arrington out of his home in Atherton to publish high-tech news and gossip about Internet startups. An even more powerful kind of criticism was leveled at the Web: it did not contain enough "semantic" information about its own data. According to Danny Hillis of the Connection Machine fame, it contained information, not knowledge, and what was needed now was a knowledge web. In July 2005 he established Metaweb, a company that proceeded to develop what in March 2007 became Freebase, an open, free and collaborative knowledge base. For all practical purposes it worked just like Wikipedia, except that its output was a set of structured data, or, better, "meta-data." Google later acquired Metaweb.

Biotech

Biotechnology was becoming main-stream and synthetic biology was the new frontier, though its goal was not clear. Yet the businessmen behind it envisioned the possibility of building new living species (initially just bacteria) that would perform useful industrial or domestic functions. It would exist just as electronics had led to devices that performed useful industrial and domestic functions - the word "military" was carefully omitted. Scientists in synthetic biology were actually not very interested in cloning existing species: why not use existing species then? They were interested in modifying existing organisms to create organisms that do not exist in nature. Genetic engineering is about replacing one gene, whereas synthetic biology is about replacing entire genomes to generate "reprogrammed organisms" whose functions are different from the original ones (because the DNA instructions have changed).

Synthetic biology exploited the power of microbes to catalyze a sequence of biological reactions that transform a chemical compound into another compound. The first synthetic biology conference was held at MIT in 2003. A year later, Codon Devices was the first company to commercialize synthetic biology; it was founded by MIT Professor Drew Endy. In 2006 Jay Keasling inaugurated the world's first synthetic biology department at the Lawrence Berkeley Laboratory. UCSF also became a major center of biological research. In 2003 Christopher Voigt founded a lab to program cells like robots to perform complex tasks, and in 2005 UCSF opened an Institute for Human Genetics.

One example of synthetic biology that captured the attention of the media in April 2005 was the announcement that Keasling had successfully converted yeast into a chemical factory by mixing bacteria, yeast, and wormwood genes. This "factory" was capable of turning simple sugar into artemisinic acid, the preliminary step to making an extremely expensive anti-malarial drug, artemisin. Artemisinin was commonly extracted from a plant. The goal of synthetic biology was now to create "designer microbes" by selecting genes based on which protein they encode and the path they follow. Some day, synthetic biology could even replace industrial chemistry, which relies on a sequence of chemical reactions to manufacture materials.

Craig Venter's saga continued. After disagreements with Celera's main investor Tony White, in January 2002 Venter left Celera taking Hamilton Smith with him. In 2003, they synthesized the genome of a virus with just eleven genes; unlike the artificial polio virus at Stony Brook, it truly behaved like a virus. With a keen sixth sense for money and publicity, in September 2004 Venter started his own non-profit institute in both Maryland and California (San Diego) to conduct research in synthetic biology and biofuels. In particular, he worked on building the genome of a bacterium from scratch and on inserting the genome of one bacterium into another. Bacteria are the simplest living organisms, made of just one cell.

Bioinformatics continued to thrive. Two former Silicon Genetics executives, Saeid Akhtari and Ilya Kupershmidt, started NextBio in Cupertino in 2004 to create a platform to perform data mining on public and private genomic data.

Nanotech

Nanotechnology was still a mystery. While returns were low and nano startups routinely switched to more traditional manufacturing processes, during both 2006 and 2007 venture-capital firms invested more than $700 million in nanotechnology startups.

A promising avenue was to wed "nano" and "green," a mission particularly nurtured in Berkeley. NanoSolar engineers formed the core of Solexant, founded in 2006 in San Jose by Indian-born chemist Damoder Reddy and by Paul Alivisatos, Professor of Chemistry and Materials Science at UC Berkeley. Alivisatos was also the director of the Lawrence Berkeley Laboratory to manufacture printable thin-film "quantum dot" photovoltaic cells using a technology developed at the Lawrence Berkeley Laboratory. This was held to be the next generation of solar technology: flexible, low-cost, and high-yield.

Other solar research was promising too. Michael Crommie, a scientist at the Materials Sciences Division at the Lawrence Berkeley Laboratory and a professor of physics at UC Berkeley, was working on solar cells the size of a single molecule. Canadian nanotechnology specialists Ted Sargent of the University of Toronto developed a "quantum film" capable of a light-capturing efficiency of 90%, as opposed to 25% for the CMOS image sensors employed in digital cameras. In October 2006 he founded InVisage in Menlo Park to make quantum film for camera phones.

Greentech

Skyrocketing oil prices and concerns about climate change opened a whole new range of opportunities for an environmentally friendly energy generation, nicknamed "greentech" or "cleantech." Of the traditional kinds of renewable energy (wind power, solar power, biomass, hydropower, biofuels) solar and biofuel emerged as the most promising. At the same time, the US started investing in fuel-cell companies in 2005 with the goal of fostering commercial fuel-cell vehicles by 2020. By 2008 it had spent $1 billion. California embarked on a project to set up a chain of stations to refuel hydrogen-driven vehicles, despite the fact that the state had only 179 fuel-cell vehicles in service in 2007.

Silicon Valley entrepreneurs and investors delved into projects to produce clean, reliable, and affordable energy. A startup that focused on renewable fuels was LS9, founded in 2005 in South San Francisco to create alkanes (a constituent of gasoline) from sugar by Harvard Professor George Church and Chris Somerville, the director of UC Berkeley's Energy Biosciences Institute; it was financed by Vinod Khosla and Boston-based Flagship Ventures.

Cars were another interesting sector. After selling their e-book company NuvoMedia, in 2003 Martin Eberhard and Marc Tarpenning founded Tesla Motors in Palo Alto to build electrical cars. In 2006 they introduced the Tesla Roadster, the first production automobile to use lithium-ion battery cells. In 2004 SUN's co-founder Vinod Khosla, who had joined venture capital firm Kleiner Perkins Caufield & Byers, founded Khosla Ventures to invest in green-technology companies. One year later another SUN co-founder, Bill Joy, replaced him at Kleiner Perkins Caufield & Byers to invest in green technology. Sebastian Thrun at Stanford built the robotic car that in 2005 won a DARPA "race" in a California desert. Thrun was then hired by Google to work on autonomous vehicles that, in following years, would be seen driving over California highways with only one person in the car: the passenger. Driver-less cars, once implemented, could become a technology that saves tens of thousands of lives and hundreds of billions of wasted costs from human error and freeway congestion.

Another legendary "serial entrepreneur" of Silicon Valley, Marc Porat of Go fame, turned to building materials for the "green" economy focused on reducing energy consumption and carbon emission. Some startups included: Serious Materials (2002) in Sunnyvale for eco-friendly materials; CalStar Cement (2007), a spin-off of the University of Missouri based in the East Bay (Newark) that manufactured eco-friendly bricks; and Zeta Communities (2007) in San Francisco for pre-assembled homes that operate at net-zero energy.

Meanwhile, UC Berkeley and the Lawrence Berkeley Laboratory launched a joint "Helios Project" for artificial photosynthesis, i.e. to convert sunlight into fuel.

Culture and Society

The arts mirrored progress in the high-tech industry. The 2000s were the decade of interactive digital art, pioneered by the likes of Camille Utterback. In 2005 the Letterman Digital Arts Center opened in San Francisco to house Lucasfilm's lab. The first Zer01 Festival for "art and technology in the digital age" was held in San Jose in 2006, sponsored by San Jose State University's CADRE. Stephanie Syjuco's counterfeit sculptures, Lee Walton's web happenings, and Amy Balkin's ecological projects referenced the issues of the era. In 2000, Fecalface.com was launched to support the alternative art scene (later also a physical gallery, the Fecal Face Dot Gallery). The Adobe Books Backroom Gallery, another epicenter of new art, opened in 2001. The Mission School's mission of mural paintings and found-object sculpture was being continued by Andrew Schoultz and Sirron Norris. Dave Warnke focused on stickers and hand-painted posters, Sandro "Misk" Tchikovani specialized in three-dimensional letters, and Damon Soule explored mixed media on found wood.

Hacker parties had always been popular in Silicon Valley but during the 2000s they reached new height, both in terms of size and enthusiasm. In May 2005 a group of high-tech geeks convened at the Hillsborough house of David Weekly, a Stanford graduate who was working on his startup (later incorporated as PBwiki). That was the first "SuperHappyDevHouse", a concept that soon became popular in Silicon Valley: a casual meeting in a casual environment of creative engineers to work in the same building on their pet projects. Unlike the many networking events, the goal was not necessarily to publicize one's idea or to meet other people: it was to go home having written some actual software or at least come up with ideas for some software. Unlike hacker competitions, it was not about showing one's dexterity at coding. And, unlike the raves of San Francisco, it was not a wild party of drinking and drugs; quite the opposite in fact. It was a way to create a more stimulating environment than the cubicles of an office, and, in fact, more similar to the dormitory of a university campus. The idea would spread internationally within a few years. The ambition was to emulate the success of the Homebrew Computer Club of the 1970s, although the similarity was mostly superficial.

The Anthropology of Pan-Ethnic Materialism

The cultural diversity of the Bay Area continued to ablate religious certainties. A person's loyalty to her religious group was undermined by the proximity of so many other religious groups (in the workplace, at shared homes, in sport activities). This led to an increasingly higher degree of flexibility in choosing one's faith. The new-age movement, with its syncretic non-dogmatic view of spirituality, had left its own influence on the region, even though its message was now being interpreted in a more materialistic manner. For many people, religion was to be shaped by how one wanted to behave. For example, greed and promiscuity were definitely "in" for the vast majority of independently religious people. Religious axioms that constrained one's lifestyle were not particularly popular. Religious practices that were perceived as beneficial to one's mind and body were. Thus Zen retreats and yoga classes were popular even among people who did not believe in Buddhism.

The Santa Clara Valley had traditionally been a Catholic region. It had become a unique experiment within the Catholic world: a Catholic region with sizeable minorities of other religious groups that were not poor segregated immigrants, as was the case in Italy or France, but who lived on equal footing with the original Catholic families. Both the percentage and the level of integration were unique among Catholic regions.

The time and attention usually devoted to religious functions were translated to the high-tech world. The public rituals of religion were replaced by public rituals of lectures and high-tech symposia. The mass in a church was replaced by a business or technology forum. The technology being produced downplayed the cultural differences. People tended to recognize themselves more strongly as workers of a company than as members of a religious or ethnic group.

Those who had predicted the demise of Silicon Valley had completely missed the point. In 2005, Silicon Valley accounted for 14% of the world's venture capital but less than 0.03% of the world's population. San Jose's population of 912,332 had just passed San Francisco and San Jose had become the tenth largest city in the US. The Bay Area as a whole was the largest high-tech center in the world with 386,000 high-tech jobs in 2006.

34. Sharks: The iPhone, Cloud Computing, Location-based Services, Social Games, and Personal Genomics (2007-2013)

The Decline of the Computer

The late 2000s were the age of streaming media, smart phones, and cloud computing; all trends pointed towards the demise of the "computer" as it had been known for 50 years.

Music and file sharing were at the bleeding edge. In 2008 digital music downloads grew by 25%, to $3.7 billion (including 1.4 billion songs). This accounted for 20% of all music sales, but the music industry estimated that over 40 billion songs were illegally file-shared, which meant that 95% of the market for digital music downloads was underground. In 2009, file-sharing services ranked among the Internet's most popular websites: Rapidshare was 26th and Mediafire was 63rd. In 2009 BitTorrent accounted for at least 20% of all Internet traffic. The numbers were so large that it was hard to believe all these people were criminally motivated. It was instead an important signal that people like to download files instead of buying physical objects. Movies, on the other hand, were encoded in very large files: it was more effective to "stream" them than to download them. Here, too, the public was sending the message that the physical object was becoming redundant.

As images, music, and videos proliferated at increasingly higher resolutions, the demand for storage became prohibitive. At the same time that the demand for remote downloads increased, network bandwidth was increasing rapidly. It then became sensible to think of keeping the files on the Internet instead of downloading them on the home computer. In the past, the main reason to download them before viewing them had just been that the network was "slow." Once the network became fast enough, using a home computer to store multimedia files became redundant, and consumers started playing them directly from the Internet. For example, Netflix had become the main movie rental-by-mail service and launched its streaming feature in January 2007. In just two years its catalog grew to more than 12,000 titles (movies and television episodes). In March 2010 YouTube broadcast the Indian Premier League of cricket live worldwide, the first major sport competition to be broadcast live on the Internet.

Smart phones that allowed browsing the Web and exchanging e-mail had become very popular, notably the BlackBerry and the Razr, but the brutally competitive field was not for the faint of heart. In June 2007 Apple, which after the iPod had become the master of fashionable devices, introduced the iPhone. It immediately captured the imagination of the younger generation. In 2008, Apple also introduced the "App Store," where independent software developers could sell their applications for the iPhone (by March 2013 there were an estimated 800K apps and about 50 billion downloads).

In 2007, Google began freely distributing Android. It was a Linux-based open-source operating system for mobile phones that had originally been developed by a Palo Alto stealth startup named Android and founded by Andy Rubin and others. Google also created the Android Marketplace to compete with the App Store (by March 2013 it had 675,000 applications for Android-based devices). Motorola was the first company to deliver an Android-based smart phone, the Droid, and reaped the benefits: it shipped 2.3 million units in the first quarter of 2010, thus resurrecting itself after the collapse of the Razr. In 2010 Taiwanese cell-phone manufacturer HTC entered the Android market with its Incredible phone and so did Samsung with its Galaxy S. Every Android manufacturer had little control on its future, though, because the success of its device depended on Google's whims and on the whims of the carrier (Verizon, AT&T and Spring being the main ones).

At the beginning of 2010, Research In Motion was estimated to have 42% of the market, followed by Apple with 25%, Microsoft with 15% and Android-based devices with 9%. Android sales in the first three months of 2010 accounted for 28% of all smart phone sales, ahead of iPhone's 21% but still behind BlackBerry's 36%.

The loser was Palm, which released its Pre at the same time as Apple released the iPhone. It didn't have the heft to compete with Google and Apple, and in April 2010 was sold to HP. In March 2008 John Doerr of Kleiner Perkins launched a $100 million venture-capital fund, the iFund, for iPhone applications, crediting the iPhone as an invention more important than the personal computer because it knew who the user was and where s/he was.

Apple's iOS was a hit because of its multi-touch technology, but that was hardly an Apple invention. Touch-screen technology had come from Europe, and it had been in Britain (at Xerox's EuroPARC) that sixteen years earlier Pierre Wellner had designed his multi-touch "Digital Desk" with multi-finger and pinching motions. Then a pair at the University of Delaware founded Fingerworks to commercialize a technology to help people with finger injuries use a computer. Fingerworks had gone on to sell a full line of multi-touch products, notably the iGesture Pad in 2003. Apple had acquired Fingerworks' multi-touch technology in 2005. The iOS, unveiled in January 2007 was a Unix-like operating system that incorporated that technology: one-finger swipe to scroll horizontally, a finger tap to select an object, a reverse two-finger pinch (an "unpinch") to enlarge an image, and so on. Incidentally, in 2001 Paul Dietz and Darren Leigh at Mitsubishi Electric Research Labs (MERL) in Boston had even developed a multi-touch interface that could even recognize which person is touching where, called "DiamondTouch."

It was easy to predict that soon more users would access the Internet from mobile devices than from desktop computers. In 2009, almost 90% of households in the US owned a cell phone. Yet the average time of voice minutes per call (1.81 minutes) was lower than in 2008, despite the fact that millions of households were disconnecting their land phone lines. At the beginning, voice conversation was the only application for cell phones. Then came text messaging, Web browsing, navigation, and so forth.

Text messaging, in particular, proved to resonate with the psychology of the digital age. It was less time-consuming and disruptive than a voice call, even if it took longer to type a message than to say it. Voice communication was rapidly becoming an afterthought, while a myriad of applications were becoming the real reason to purchase a "phone." The purpose of a cell phone was more data than voice. Handset design was less and less "cheek-friendly," more and more palm-friendly, because people were not supposed to "hear" but to "see" with their cell phone. In 2012, the cell phones from Nokia were to the Apple and Android smart phones what typewriters were in the age of the personal computer.

Phones were penetrating other key devices. In 2008 Chrysler pioneered the router system that installed the Internet even in cars by connecting a cellular device to a wireless local-area network. At the end of 2009, there were already 970,000 cars equipped with Internet access.

In May 2010, a symbolic event took place when Apple's market capitalization ($227 billion) passed Microsoft's ($226 billion). In August 2011 Apple passed ExxonMobil to become the most valuable company in the world based on market capitalization, though this would not last.

Towards Computing as a Utility

At the same time the traditional computer was attacked by the paradigm of "cloud computing." This was Internet-based computing in which the computers are hidden from the users and computing power is delivered on demand, when needed, just like electricity is delivered to homes when and in the amount needed. Public cloud storage had been legitimized in 2006 when Amazon had introduced its Simple Storage Service, or S3, service that anyone could use. Box was founded near Seattle in 2005 by Aaron Levie and Dylan Smith but soon relocated to Silicon Valley (Los Altos), decided to use its own servers and to target the corporate world. Dropbox, founded in 2007 by MIT students, created a friendlier service based on S3. Cloud computing was typically built on "virtual" infrastructures provided by "hypervisors," or virtual-machine monitors, that allowed multiple operating systems to run concurrently on a single computer, enabling any application to run anywhere at any time.

The pioneer and leader of virtualization had been Vmware. Its 2008 revenues increased 42% to $1.9 billion, and new hypervisors were offered by Oracle (VM, introduced in 2007 and based on open-source Xen technology), Microsoft (Hyper-V, introduced in 2008), and Red Hat (Enterprise Virtualization, introduced in 2009). The virtual-machine monitor Xen was developed in 2003 at the University of Cambridge by Ian Pratt's team and acquired by Florida-based Citrix Systems in October 2007. In August 2010 Hewlett-Packard offered $1.6 billion to acquire 3PAR, specialized in data storage for cloud computing shared by multiple companies ("utility storage").

There were only four companies selling the kind of storage required by cloud computing: IBM, Hitachi, 3PAR, and EMC. EMC was based in Boston, but in 2003 had acquired three Silicon Valley success stories: Documentum, Legato, and VMware. EMC represented yet another business in which Silicon Valley had largely failed to lead. Founded in 1979 by Richard Egan and Roger Marino to make memory boards for minicomputers, in 1990 EMC had introduced a data storage platform for mainframe computers, Symmetrix. It was the right time: the explosion of data that came with the Internet created a demand that only data storage systems like Symmetrix could satisfy.

The next step after virtualizing the operating system and the databases was to virtualize the network, which was precisely the mission of Palo Alto-based Nicira Networks, a 2007 spin-off of a joint Stanford-Berkeley project.

Virtualization allowed a "farm" of computing power to create a virtual machine for a customer, no matter where the customer was located. A computing environment (made of disparate software and hardware components) could be dynamically configured to represent several different machines, each assigned to a different customer. This "multi-tenant system" was conceptually similar to a power plant: it supplied computing power over the Internet to multiple customers the way a power plant supplied electricity over the electric grid to multiple customers.

For decades, software and hardware manufacturers had relied on business plans that envisioned selling the very same system to multiple customers who were using it to perform identical tasks. Ubiquitous and cheap broadband was fostering an era in which a "computing utility" could provide that service (hardware and software) to all those customers over the Internet, with no need for those customers to purchase any of the components; they just paid a monthly fee.

Knowledge production was becoming centralized the way energy production had become centralized with the invention of the electrical grid (spreading the power created by a power plant) and the way food production had become centralized 5000 years earlier after the invention of the irrigation network. Each "network" had created a new kind of economy, society and, ultimately, civilization.

Social networking too was destined to become a "utility" of sorts for businesses. The idea of collaboration software over the Web had been pioneered by startups such as Jive Software, founded in 2001 by two students from the University of Iowa, Matt Tucker and Bill Lynch, and originally based in New York. In the age of Facebook it was renamed "enterprise social network service" and embraced by startups such as Yammer, originally developed in 2007. This platform hinted at the first major revolution in ERP since SAP's glorious R3.

Google vs. Microsoft vs. Facebook

The 1990s had been the decade of Microsoft. Microsoft owned the operating system, and it owned the most popular applications. Microsoft's success relied on the concept of the personal computer: one user, one application, one computer. Web-based computing represented the first serious challenge to Microsoft's business model. Due to increased bandwidth and more sophisticated Internet software, it had become possible to create applications that ran on websites and that users could access via their Web browser. It was basically a client-server architecture, except that the "server" was potentially the entire Internet, and the client was potentially the entire human population.

Cloud computing was on-demand Web-based computing. The concept was pioneered by startups such as Salesforce.com. In February 2007, Google targeted Microsoft's core business when it disclosed a humbler version of cloud computing, Google Docs. That suite could be accessed by any computer via a Web browser, and included a word-processor and a spreadsheet program (both acquired from independent companies, respectively Upstartle and 2Web Technologies). One could already imagine the end of the era of the operating system, as the Web replaced the need for one. A computer only needed a browser to access the Web, where all other resources and applications were located.

Microsoft was still dominant and powerful. In 2008 Microsoft Windows owned almost 90% of the operating system market for personal computers, while Google owned almost 70% of the Internet search market. The future, though, seemed to be on Google's side. In May 2013, Microsoft's IE commanded 50% of the browser market, followed by Firefox with 18% and Google's own Chrome (first released in September 2008) with 17%. That was a steep decline from the days when IE was ubiquitous.

On the other hand, Google's revenues depended almost entirely on third-party advertising. The "war" between Google and Microsoft was well publicized, but the war between Google and Yahoo! was probably more serious for Google's immediate future. In 2007 Google paid $3.1 billion for DoubleClick, the New York-based company that dominated "display advertising." This was the method favored by Yahoo! when Google was piling up millions with its keyword ads. As the quality of browsers and computers improved, Yahoo!'s glamorous ads became more and more popular, and they were served by DoubleClick. By acquiring it, Google struck at the heart of Yahoo!'s business. And now Google had all the pieces to create an "advertising operating system." In 2009 Yahoo! owned 17% of the market for display ads, followed by Microsoft at 11% and AOL at 7%.

Google's strategy became even more aggressive in 2010 when it started acquiring aggressively. Notably, it purchased BumpTop, the three-dimensional GUI developed since 2006 by University of Toronto's student Anand Agarwala, and Plink, a visual search engine developed by two Oxford University's students, Mark Cummins and James Philbin. Chrome OS was first released in November 2009. It was a variant of the Linux-based operating system Ubuntu that was developed in Britain by Mark Shuttleworth's Canonical. At the same time, the products that Google engineers truly invented and that the company widely hyped, such as the social networking platform Buzz and the groupware Wave, were embarrassing failures.

Google's technology was consistently inferior to what the Silicon Valley landscape was producing. For example, Superfish, started in 2006 in Palo Alto by Israeli-born semiconductor-industry veteran Adi Pinhas and A.I. guru Michael Chertok, launched in 2010 a visual search tool that, unlike Google Goggles, was able to recognize pictures regardless of perspective, lighting, distance and so forth.

The effect of Google's domination of the search-engine market was the same as the effect of Microsoft's domination of the personal-computer operating-system market: to stifle innovation. Google had built its reputation on returning webpages based on their "relevance." Now it was mostly returning commercial websites that had little relevance to the search string, and the ubiquitous Wikipedia (for which one was better off just searching within Wikipedia itself). A very relevant article written by a scholar was very unlikely to show up in the first page of results. The "irrelevance" of Google's searches was mainly driving an entire economy based on advertising products and services. And, of course, the fact that the Web was being littered with the ubiquitous "Google Adwords" hardly represented a welcome change. Most of the text and images that flooded a user's screen constituted commercial ads (in ever more creative and invasive fashions). Due to the proliferation of Google AdWords, the Web was becoming not only unsearchable but also unreadable.

Alas, Google had a virtual monopoly on web search: any search engine that was truly committed to "relevance" had scarce chances of success against Google, just like any operating system for personal computers against Microsoft.

The line-up of winners in the cloud world was small. In 2009 Microsoft was still the largest software company in the world with revenues of $50 billion, while Google's revenues were "only" $22.8 billion. Google had already passed IBM's software revenues ($22 billion), Oracle ($17.5 billion) and SAP ($15.3 billion, and the most troubled of all of these). By comparison, the wildly popular Facebook only made an estimated $550 million in 2009. At one point in March 2010 Microsoft was the second largest company in the US, with a market capitalization of $256 billion, following oil producer Exxon ($315 billion) and followed by a fast-growing Apple ($205 billion) that had passed the retail giant Walmart ($205 billion). Google's market capitalization was $184 billion.

Those numbers sent two messages, both adverse to Microsoft. The personal computer was being attacked simultaneously on two fronts, by the smart phone and by web-based computing. In April 2010, Apple further weakened the personal computer when it introduced the tablet computer iPad, which sold one million units in less than one month.

Another battlefront was television. In 2010, Google released an open platform for television sets that was the home-video equivalent of its mobile-phone platform Android. It was another attempt to marry content and hardware, something that only Apple had successfully achieved so far but with a proprietary platform. Not being a maker of hardware, Google chose again to offer an open platform. The first hardware partner to sign up was Japanese conglomerate Sony. Sony had a history of championing networked television. An early adopter of WebTV, Sony had introduced already in 2000 a product called AirBoard, a tablet computer that let users watch television, surf the Internet, view photos and wirelessly control several gadgets. Sony wasn't interested as much in TV-based web surfing (the feature provided by the alliance with Google) as in video and music streaming, i.e. selling its content (not just a piece of hardware) to the consumers. Sony owned a vast library of films and music. Google did not make any hardware and did not own any content. Google had become a giant by simply facilitating the connection between the hardware and the content, but now it was debatable who owned the future: the company that laid the cable connecting a device to some content or the companies making the device and providing the content?

The wild card in this scenario was Facebook. It began the year 2009 with 150 million users and grew by about one million users a day, the fastest product ever to reach that many users in just five years. In May 2007, Facebook had announced an open platform for third parties to develop applications. This amounted to a Copernican revolution: applications were no longer written for an operating system but for a social network. This event spawned a new industry of widget makers for the Facebook platform, notably RockYou (originally RockMySpace), founded in Redwood City in 2006 by Lance Tokuda and Jia Shen. However, Facebook was also being widely criticized for its ever-changing privacy policies after having contributed to distribute all over the world sensitive personal information of millions of people. It had basically become the premier stalking tool in the world.

The price paid by users of social networking platforms was a massive dissemination of private information. By the late 2000s there was so much information available on the Web about individuals that it was natural to put together a person's lifestyle just by browsing her name. A new kind of application, social network aggregators, was soon born to help that process. In 2006, a group of Stanford students based in Mountain View, including Harrison Tang, came up with such an idea and developed Spokeo. In October 2007, former Google employees including Paul Buchheit (the creator of Gmail and AdSense) and Bret Taylor (the creator of Google Maps) launched FriendFeed, capable of integrating in real time information posted on social media. In July 2009 it was acquired by Facebook.

Facebook indirectly also set a new standard for creating a startup. In the fall of 2007, B. J. Fogg, an experimental psychologist who was running the Persuasive Technology Lab at Stanford, instructed his students to create Facebook applications with the only goal of having as many people as possible use them in as short a period of time as possible. The students were forced to create no-frills applications whose main asset was that they were easy to use and spread around. That class alone created a number of millionaires because many of those applications became hits on the Facebook ecosystem. These Stanford CS student authors went on to join successful companies. They had just hit on a new formula to create a successful product: just make it easy to use and spread virally. You can always refine it later.

In April 2012, Facebook paid $1billion for tiny San Francisco-based startup Instagram, a mobile photo-sharing service for the iPhone that had been introduced in October 2010 by Kevin Systrom (formerly at Google) and Brazilian-born Mike Krieger. Another social networking platform for photo sharing and messaging, specifically designed for the iPhone and later mobile devices in general was Path, launched in San Francisco by Shawn Fanning of Napster fame and by former Facebook executive Dave Morin. What initially distinguished Path from Facebook was that it limited your number of friends to fifty.

Location was becoming important again. Craigslist had been the last major Web-based service to address the geographic community, while almost every other major service addressed the virtual community of the whole Web. The trend was reversed by the end of the decade. In 2010 Facebook belatedly added Places, a location-based service. It was similar to Foursquare, founded in 2007 in New York by Dennis Crowley and Naveen Selvadurai, and Gowalla, launched in 2009 from Austin, Texas by Josh Williams and Scott Raymond. These services basically let friends equipped with mobile devices know each other's location. Meanwhile, Google rolled out Realtime Search that performed location-based filtering of status updates, for example to find out what is going on in a town. In 2011 Google tried to acquire discount-coupon site Groupon, launched in November 2008 in Chicago by Andrew Mason. Groupon brokered deals between consumers and local stores. Maybe it was not "Google versus

Microsoft" after all, but "Google versus Facebook." Incidentally, in 2010 eBay acquired shopping engine Milo, which kept track of which goods were available in neighborhood stores.

Because of Google and Facebook, the way people used the Internet had changed dramatically since the day that Marc Andreessen had created the Netscape browser. Nonetheless, the browser had not changed much since those days. Microsoft's Internet Explorer, Mozilla's Firefox, Google's Chrome, and Apple's Safari had simply copied the concept, the look and the buttons of the original, barely introducing collateral features.

A startup that tried to "upgrade" the browser to the age of Facebook was Mountain View-based RockMelt, founded in November 2008 by Eric Vishria and Tim Howes, both former employees of networking company Opsware before it was acquired by Hewlett-Packard. It also marked Marc Andreessen's returns to his roots, since he was the main financial backer of RockMelt. RockMelt represented the typical paradigm shift that periodically shook Silicon Valley. In this case the victim was Facebook. Instead of having the Facebook user look at the Internet through the filter of his Facebook page and his friends' Facebook pages, RockMelt allowed the user to view the Facebook world and many other popular services (e.g., real-time news) as an extension of the browser.

The other thing that had not changed much since the invention of the Web was the search engine. While Google dominated the field, its search engine was largely agnostic about the contemporary boom of social networks. The emergence of "social search" technology was well represented by Blekko, founded in Redwood Shores in June 2007 by Rich Skrenta. He was the high-school hacker who had created the first personal-computer virus in 1982; the SUN guru who had created the Open Directory Project; and the entrepreneur who had created Topix. It was basically a hybrid approach that mixed the traditional machine-powered search engine with the human-powered wiki. Nor was Facebook a dogma in its space. In March 2010, former Google employee Ben Silbermann launched the image bookmarking system Pinterest out of Palo Alto. Within two years it was second only to Facebook and Twitter among social networking platform. The key difference was that it organized networks of people around shared interests, not social connections.

Facebook was also coming under attack because of its loose security policies. Furthermore, Facebook's content was exclusive to the Facebook website, and there was a deliberate attempt by Facebook to isolate the Facebook user from the rest of the Internet world. While dissatisfaction was pervasive, the people who dared to take on Facebook were almost always technology enthusiasts based outside the Bay Area. In 2004 Chicago-based developer Michael Chisari, started Appleseed, the first open source social networking engine. In 2007 Belgium-based developer Laurent Eschenauer announced OneSocialWeb. This one was based on XMPP, the technology behind Instant Messaging. David Tosh and Ben

Werdmuller, two researchers at the University of Edinburgh in Britain, founded Elgg in 2004. The most hyped by the media of this generation of open-source social networks was Diaspora, developed by four New York University students.

The Bay Area Giants

The other giants of Silicon Valley were left scrambling for an exit strategy during these times of upheaval. In 2008, Hewlett-Packard purchased Texas-based giant Electronic Data Systems (EDS) in a shift towards services, and in 2009 Xerox followed suit by purchasing Affiliated Computer Services. HP also purchased Palm, now a struggling smart-phone maker. The value of Palm was twofold: an operating system designed for cloud computing; and an application development environment based on a drag-and-drop metaphor. By 2006, HP had finally passed Dell in worldwide personal-computer shipments (16.5% market share versus Dell's 16.3%), while Gateway had disappeared, having been bought in 2007 by Acer of Taiwan. For the first time, a Silicon Valley company ruled the personal-computer market. Oracle, instead, still aiming mainly at the corporate world, acquired middleware experts BEA in 2008 and decided to enter the hardware market by purchasing a struggling SUN in 2009.

However, the glory of becoming the biggest personal-computer maker in the world did not mean much at a time when Apple's tablet was crippling personal-computer sales, and in August 2011 HP announced that it was going to spin off (i.e. exit) its personal computer business. This came at the same time when HP dumped the recently acquired Palm and at the same time that HP acquired British database application company Autonomy. Autonomy and EDS represented the future of HP, not personal digital assistants and personal computers.

In 2010 a new player emerged in the battle for the mobile operating system, and, while it was not based in the Bay Area, it relied on technology developed by a Bay Area startup. Long ridiculed for its lack of design style and and for its long list of flops (the Bob desktop metaphor, the Spot wristwatch, the Tablet PC, the Ultimate TV, the Zune music player, the Kin smartphone), Microsoft finally got it right with the mobile operating system Windows Phone: it was derived from the Danger technology that they had acquired from the same man who sold Android to Google, i.e. Andy Rubin.

Cloud computing started to take hold even in corporate settings. In 2009, Cisco partnered with Massachusetts-based EMC, the largest provider of networked storage in the world, to found Acadia and convert the old data-centers of the corporate world to cloud computing. In the same year Cisco introduced its first line of servers, the Unified Computing System. It competed directly with HP and IBM while upping the ante by integrating VMware's virtualization software (that now allowed to move applications from one server to another at the click of a mouse). At the beginning of 2010 Cisco posted its best quarter ever, with sales of $10.4 billion. Intel was largely immune to the turmoil: in 2010 it posted record sales again. In March 2009 AMD spun off its manufacturing unit to create GlobalFoundries. Within a year it became the world's second largest silicon-chip foundry company after Taiwan's TSMC.

However, the next battleground for chips would be in the mobile space. British chip manufacturer ARM still dominated cellular-phone applications which required all-day battery life. Third-generation cellular phones were being integrated with video, music, and gaming and this triggered a boom in chips for mobile devices. Ironically, both Intel and AMD had exited that market in June 2006. Intel had sold its ARM-based technology to Marvell, and AMD had sold its MIPS-based technology to Raza Microelectronics. In 2010 Intel reentered the market with both an in-house project and the acquisition of German-based Infineon. ARM chips were already powering devices such as Sony television sets, the Amazon e-reader Kindle, and hotel keycard locks, and analysts foresaw a future in which thousands of small devices would need ARM chips to interact among themselves and to retrieve information from the Internet. In 2009, ARM was a $0.5 billion corporation versus Intel's $35 billion, but the trend was towards ARM's small low-power chips. Intel took action in November 2010: for the first time it manufactured someone else's chips (San Jose-based fab-less Achronix, a competitor of XIlinx and Altera in the high-end accelerating chip market). Intel also entered the market traditionally dominated by Taiwanese and Chinese factories. It was unlikely this was due to a desire to enter the brutal market of contract manufacturing and more likely a desire to learn new markets.

The boom of smartphones also benefited makers of Wi-Fi chips, such as Atheros and Marvell: 56 million Wi-Fi-enabled cellular phones shipped in 2008 (a 52% increase over the previous year). More than 54 million smartphones were sold in the first quarter of 2010, an increase of 56% over the previous year.

It was not unusual for Silicon Valley to be late on innovation, but this was embarrassing for a region named after silicon. All the big providers of chips for smartphones (San Diego-based Qualcomm, Texas Instruments, Korea-based Samsung, Irvine-based Broadcom) except for Marvel were based outside the Bay Area. Even Apple's iPhone used a chip manufactured by Samsung. It was the same for all the providers of wireless telecommunications networks: Verizon was based in Philadelphia, AT&T was based in New Jersey, Sprint was based in Kansas (although its origins were in the Bay Area), T-Mobile was the subsidiary of Deutsche Telekom, and Clearwire was founded in 2003 in Seattle.

Social Games

Virtual worlds were booming. The audience for pioneering virtual worlds such as Gaia Online and Habbo had passed five million monthly active users. The next front was the social network. Launched in May 2008 and only accessible as an application on Facebook, the virtual world YoVille passed five million monthly active users in March 2009. By allowing people to create "second-life" avatars and interact with each other, YoVille de facto created a new concept: a virtual social network within the real social network. The success of YoVille spawned a generation of browser-based "social games" running on Facebook. YoVille itself was acquired in July 2008 by Zynga, founded in July 2007 in San Francisco by serial entrepreneur Mark Pincus. In June 2009 Zynga released FarmVille, a shameless clone of the Facebook-based social game Farm Town that was introduced by Florida-based Slashkey a few months earlier. In 2010 FarmVille had become the most popular Facebook game, boasting more than 50 million users. Zynga also introduced Mafia Wars (2009), a shameless copy of another pioneering social game, David Maestri's Mob Wars, that had debuted on Facebook in January 2008 (Maestri was still an employee at Freewebs). Six months after the release of Playfish's Restaurant City from Britain, Zynga released Cafe World.

Competitors soon started retaliating by copying Zynga's games too. While Zynga kept churning out clones of popular games, the founder of Freewebs, Shervin Pishevar, opened Social Gaming Network (SGN) in January 2008 in Palo Alto to develop original social games for the Facebook platform. Whatever the strategy, the Bay Area was becoming again the epicenter for videogame evolution. By 2010, Apple was promoting the iPhone itself as a gaming platform, further eroding Nintendo's console-based empire.

Videogames were still selling strongly. Activision was setting one record after the other, selling 4.7 million copies of "Call of Duty - Modern Warfare 2" on its first day in 2009 and 5.6 million copies of "Call of Duty - Black Ops" on its first day in 2010 (grossing more than $650 million worldwide during the first five days of sales). In December 2010, Activision's Cataclysm sold 3.3 million copies in the first 24 hours. Note that the "Call of Duty" games were developed by Infinity Ward in southern California (Encino) using the id Tech 3 engine developed by in Texas by PC game pioneer John Romero and others at Id Software. The technological breakthroughs were coming from somewhere else.

Videogames had become a huge industry, a phenomenal economic success. However, the state of the videogame craft was not all that advanced if one considered that videogames still relied on the original idea: create something that stimulates interest via the two primal impulses (kill and make money, given that sex was off limits) and make it as addictive as possible so people will come back for the sequel. Zynga's "FarmVille" was an addictive game exploiting the pulse to get rich, and hits like "Call of Duty" were addictive by exploiting the pulse to kill. This was not exactly high art. In 2008, San Francisco-based game designer Jonathan Blow released "Braid", a videogame for Microsoft's Xbox. The concept was completely different. Blow focused on his own aesthetic values, on sophisticated scripting and subtle psychology. Blow conceived the videogame as an art (not "art" as in "craft" but "art" as in "Michelangelo" and "Van Gogh"). He then invested the profits into producing an even more "artistic" game, "The Witness", introduced in March 2012.

The very notion of how to play a videogame was changing. OnLive was launched in March 2009 in Palo Alto by Apple alumnus and WebTV founder Steve Perlman, after seven years of work in stealth mode. OnLive, which went live in June 2010, was out to disrupt the videogame console by providing videogames on demand to any computer. The videogames were hosted on the "cloud" of the Internet instead of requiring the user to purchase them on physical cassettes. This was advertised as "5G wireless." Earlier, 2G in 1992 marked the transition from analog to digital voice; 3G in 2001 enabled Internet browsing; 4G provided basic video streaming; and 5G was meant to provide high-definition video streaming.

In 2010 the first blockbuster of iPhone videogaming took off. Angry Birds, developed by Finnish game developer Rovio Mobile, founded in 2003 by three students from Helsinki University of Technology (Niklas Hed, Jarno Vakevainen and Kim Dikert). Introduced in December 2009, it sold over 12 million copies in just one year.

The world of gaming was shaken in 2012 when Ouya, founded in San Francisco by Julie Uhrman, announced an Android-powered open-source gaming console. Unlike other platforms, that charged game developers, Ouya promised no licensing fees, no retail fees and no publishing fees. While less powerful than the best-selling consoles of the time (like Microsoft's Xbox 360 and Sony's PlayStation 3), Ouya was promising a whole new world of games, not confined to the big developers. In July 2013, Ouya raised more than $2.5 million in just 8 hours on Kickstarter.

As 3D motion-control and motion-sensing products started to become affordable and therefore popular (e.g., Microsoft's Kinect, a motion sensing input device introduced in 2010 for the Xbox videogame console, based on technology originally developed by PrimeSense in Israel), the idea was copied in the Bay Area by a new generation of startups, notably San Francisco-based Leap Motion, founded in 2010 by David Holz and Michael Buckwald, whose product allowed users to interact with their computer by gesturing at it.

The Empire

Looking at the numbers, Silicon Valley had never been healthier than it was in 2008, before the big worldwide financial crisis struck. It had 261 public companies and countless startups. eBay was selling $60 billion worth of goods in 2007, a figure higher than the GDP of 120 countries of the world. In 2007 venture capitalists invested $7.6 billion in Silicon Valley and an additional $2.5 billion in the rest of the Bay Area. The Bay Area boasted the world's highest concentration of venture capitalists. Silicon Valley's share of venture-capital investment in the US reached 37.5% at the end of 2009 (compared, for example, with New York's 9.2%). Silicon Valley had 2.4 million people (less than 1% of the US's population) generating more than 2% of the US's GDP, with a GDP per person of $83,000.

The rest of the Bay Area was equally stunning: by 2009 the Lawrence Berkeley Labs alone boasted 11 Nobel Prize winners, more than India or China, and UC Berkeley boasted 20. So the tiny town of Berkeley alone had 31, more than any country in the world except the US, Britain, Germany, and France. Add Stanford's 16 and UCSF's 3 for a grand total of 50 in a region of about 19,000 square kilometers, smaller than Belize or Slovenia. In 2006 the Bay Area received three Nobel prizes out of nine: one each to Stanford, Berkeley, and UCSF. In the last 20 years the winners included: Richard Taylor of Stanford University (1990), Martin Perl of Stanford University (1995), Douglas Osheroff of Stanford University (1996), Steven Chu of Stanford University (1997), Robert Laughlin of Stanford University (1998), and George Smoot of the Lawrence Berkeley Labs (2006) for Physics; William Sharpe of Stanford University (1990), Gary Becker of Stanford University (1992), John Harsanyi of UC Berkeley (1994), Myron Scholes of Stanford University (1997), Daniel McFadden of UC Berkeley (2000), Joseph Stiglitz of Stanford University (2001), George Akerlof of UC Berkeley (2001), and Oliver Williamson of UC Berkeley (2009) for Economics; Sydney Brenner (2002), the founder of the Molecular Sciences Institute in Berkeley, Andrew Fire of Stanford University (2006), and Elizabeth Blackburn of UCSF (2009) for Medicine; Roger Kornberg of Stanford University (2006) for Chemistry; Saul Perlmutter of Lawrence Berkeley Lab (2011) for physics; and Brian Kobilka of Stanford (2012) in Chemistry.

The Bay Area was more than a region: it was an economic empire. The number of jobs that had been outsourced to countries like India probably exceeded the number of jobs created in Silicon Valley itself. And the relationship with the rest of the world was as deep as it could be. A study by Duke University found that 52% of Silicon Valley's high-tech companies launched between 1995 and 2005 had been founded by at least one immigrant. This phenomenon was probably a first in history. At the same time investors flocked from all over the world. For example, in 2008 Taiwanese conglomerate Quanta invested into two Silicon Valley's "fab-less" startups: Tilera (founded in October 2004 by Anant Agarwal) and Canesta (founded in April 1999 by Cyrus Bamji, Abbas Rafii, and Nazim Kareemi).

Neurotech

In neurotech, the new approach was based on computational power. In practice, the cumbersome, slow, and expensive computers of the 1960s had forced computer scientists to focus on models, whereas now the small, fast and cheap processors of the 2010s were encouraging computer scientists to use brute force. The availability of colossal amounts of information on the Web made this change of strategy even more appealing. For example, Stanford's professor Andrew Ng led a team at Google that wired 16 thousand processors to create a neural net capable of learning from Youtube videos. The new approach contained little that was conceptually new, just a lot more computing power. The "deep belief networks" at the core of the "deep learning" of these systems was an evolution of the old "neural network" of the 1980s and it had mostly been done by Geoffrey Hinton at the University of Toronto.

The sensation in robotics was coming from Boston. In 2012, Rethink Robotics, founded in 2008 by one of the most celebrated robot scientists in the world, Rodney Brooks, introduced Baxter, a low-cost programmable industrial robot that promised to make robots affordable for small companies. Progress in Artificial Intelligence was also coming from an idea originally advanced by Carver Mead at the California Institute of Technology (Caltech) in 1990. He wanted to build processors that look like the brain. In 2008, Dharmendra Modha at IBM's Almaden Labs launched a project to build such a "neuromorphic" processor, i.e. made of chips that operate like neurons.

More prosaic applications were needed in the age of smart phones, cloud computing and social networking. SRI International's Artificial Intelligence Center, that had already spawned Nuance in the 1990s, spawned Siri in the new century. Adam Cheyer was the leader of a software project (code-named CALO/PAL) to develop a personal assistant capable of learning and self-improving. Founded in 2007 by Cheyer with Dag Kittlaus (a telecom executive from Norway) and Tom Gruber (an alumnus of Stanford's Artificial Intelligence Lab), Siri launched a virtual personal assistant for mobile devices that was acquired by Apple in 2010.

New Zealand-born Oxford-educated physicist Sean Gourley and Bob Goodson (Yelp's first employee and a YouNoodle co-founder) started Quid in San Francisco in September 2010. Quid developed a global intelligence platform for tackling large unstructured data sets (initially about high-tech innovation, i.e. about Silicon Valley startups).

The groundbreaking technologies feeding the social-networking frenzy kept coming from other regions, though. For example, face-recognition came to the masses via Face.com, launched in May 2010 by an Israeli company founded by Moti Shniberg, who had previously founded the pattern-recognition firm ImageID in 1998, and by Gil Hirsch. They turned their technology into a smartphone application (KLiK) and a Facebook application (Photo Finder), both real-time facial recognition programs capable of automatically identifying friends in photos (Face.com was acquired by Facebook in 2012).

Virtual Reality

The Bay Area had pioneered virtual reality but then pretty much lost interest in it. It was now sitting on the side while major developments were bringing the technology to the general audience: mass market immersive-reality devices such as Sony's head-mounted display HMZ-T1, introduced in november 2011; mass-market tracking devices such as the Microsoft Kinect, launched in november 2010 and originally conceived to allow gamers to interact with the Xbox 360 game console via gestures; and mass-market lenticular printing (that creates the illusion of three dimensions or the effect of a changing image as it is viewed from different angles) by companies such as Futuredisplay, founded in 2003 in South Korea.

Biotech

Biotech, just like infotech, was moving towards the individual, which in its case meant personal genomics for predictive medicine. Navigenics was founded in Foster City in November 2007 by cancer specialist David Agus and Dietrich Stephan of the Translational Genomics Research Institute to provide genetic testing for predisposition to a variety of diseases. It was still an expensive service but the rapid cost reduction in DNA chips and the knowledge derived from the Human Genome Project helped bring it closer and closer to the masses. New biotech startups included iZumi Bio, founded to develop products based on stem-cell research (2007) and iPierian, founded to develop products based on cellular reprogramming (2007). In 2009, Swiss pharmaceutical giant LaRoche purchased Genentech for $46.8 billion.

The cost of a personal genetic test-kit was $3 billion in 2003, and there was only one (the Human Genome Project). In 2009 the cost had decreased to $48,000. It was made by San Diego-based startup Illumina, formed in 1998 by venture-capital firm CW Group to commercialize a system developed at Tufts University. In 2009, Complete Genomics was founded in March 2006 in Mountain View. It announced a genome-sequencing service for under $5,000.

The genesis of this company spoke loud about the mature state of the industry. One of the founders was serial entrepreneur Clifford Reid, co-founder of Sunnyvale-based information-retrieval startup Verity in 1988 and of San Mateo-based digital video communications company Eloquent in 1996. The other founder was Serbian-born biologist Radoje Drmanac, who had participated in the Human Genome Project since 1991 and had later co-founded Sunnyvale-based biotech startup Hyseq. By the end of 2009 only about 100 human genomes had ever been sequenced. Complete

Genomics planned to sequence 5,000 human genomes in 2010, 50,000 genomes in 2011 and 1 million genomes by 2014.

Human-genome sequencing firms were proliferating, each using a different technique and each focusing on different data. 23andme, founded in April 2006 in Mountain View by former Affymetrix executive Linda Avey and by Sergey Brin's wife Anne Wojcicki, analyzed parts of the human genome to derive useful medical information. Its kits were priced under $500 by 2010. Halcyon Molecular, founded by Michael and William Andregg in Arizona in 2003 and relocated to Mountain View in 2008, hired PayPal's Luke Nosek in September 2009 and set a goal to sequence individual genomes in a few minutes and for less than $100. In 2007 the Bay Area boasted about 700 biomedical companies.

However, the promises of the Human Genome Project were still largely unrealized. In particular, the thesis that genes cause diseases had sent biologists hunting for the common variants in the genome of individuals who are affected by the same health problems. Ten years later, the "common variant" strategy was being attacked by an increasing number of scientists, throwing into disarray the whole industry of personal genomics.

Meanwhile, life was being made in the lab. Venter's new venture heralded the birth of synthetic biology as a business. In May 2010 Hamilton Smith's team at the Craig Venter Institute in Maryland achieved another milestone in synthetic biology by building a bacterium's DNA from scratch in the lab. He then transplanted it into the cell of a host bacterium of a different species, where the artificial DNA took control of the host cell and started replicating. The resulting living being behaved like the species made of synthetic DNA. It was the first time that a living cell was being regulated entirely by artificially manufactured DNA. They had just managed to reprogram a living being. That living being's parent was a computer. This event opened the doors to an industry that would design custom bacteria on a computer and then build them in the lab.

Eventually, one could envision a day when individuals would be able to program a living organism on a handheld device connected to the lab and order the living organism on the fly. This vision was becoming possible in reality because all the economic factors were converging. It was becoming increasingly easier to sequence ("map") the DNA of an organism, a fact that resulted in ever larger databases of genomes of existing organisms. It was becoming increasingly cheaper to synthesize ("build") DNA molecules. Both processes were a lot faster than they used to be, due to their rapid computerization. The only tool that was missing for a broader availability of life synthesis was a tool to edit the DNA sequences. The other tool that a wary humankind would have liked to see was the equivalent of the "undo" feature of computers. The media frenzy around this event resembled the media frenzy of the 1950s when computers were labeled as "electronic brains" that would eventually take over the world. Now it was bacteria which were bound to take over the world. Venter's next target was algae. Bacteria are single-cell organisms. So are algae. Algae can be used to make biofuels, because they can make carbon dioxide into fuels by photosynthesis.

Drew Endy at Stanford University was working on creating a catalog of "biobricks" that synthetic biologists could use to create living organisms. His model clearly mirrored the way the personal-computer industry got started, with hobbyists ordering kits from catalogs advertised in magazines and then assembling the computer in their garage. In 2012, a Stanford bioengineering team led by Markus Covert produced the first complete computer model of a free-living organism, the bacterium Mycoplasma genitalium.

Greentech

On the greentech front, in 2008 solar technology accounted for almost 40% of worldwide private investments in greentech, followed by biofuels at 11%. In the US, venture capitalists invested a grand total of $4 billion into "green-tech" startups in 2008, which was almost 40% of all investments in high-tech in the US. The solar-energy company Solyndra was started in May 2005 in Fremont (East Bay) by Chris Gronet, formerly an executive at Applied Materials that manufactured equipment for the semiconductor industry. By 2009 Solyndra had $820 million in venture funding and more than a billion dollars in product orders. In March 2009, the Department of Energy helped Solyndra build a 500-megawatt factory for cylindrical solar cells at the cost of $733 million; but then Solyndra went bankrupt in September 2011 leaving behind mostly doubts about the whole industry. In 2007 Google's founders established Google.org, the non-profit arm of Google, to fund greentech startups. In 2008 they invested in eSolar, a Pasadena-based manufacturer of solar thermal plants, and in AltaRock Energy, a Sausalito-based firm tapping geothermal energy.

Solar startups multiplied after President Obama's blessing. Twin Creeks Technologies, founded in 2008 in San Jose by veterans of the semiconductor industry such as Indian-born Siva Sivaram and Venkatesan Murali; and Cogenra Solar (originally called SkyWatch Energy), a spin-off of semiconductor manufacturer Applied Materials led by Gilad Almogy, started in 2009 in Mountain View and was funded by Vinod Khosla.

Innovation, as often in the past, was not really coming from Silicon Valley, though. The big news in greentech came from Boston-based 1366 Technologies (founded by MIT professor Ely Sachs in 2007), that developed a more accurate way to cast the silicon wafers for solar cells so that solar cells can be produced at lower costs. This company was leapfrogging Silicon Valley startups using a typical Silicon Valley model: partnership with the DARPA to bring the technology to maturity and then application to a commodity product. A different kind of "greentech" was represented by the companies that aimed at serving the "green" market. Simbol Materials was founded in 2008 in Pleasanton by Luka Erceg and Scott Conley; it hired geochemists from the Lawrence Livermore National Laboratory and bought technology from that lab to produce lithium from geothermal brines, the best source of renewable energy.

More interesting were the many attempts at fundamentally changing the way people behave. For example, in 2008 Simon Saba founded his own company in San Jose to design and manufacture a mass-market sport electric car. He envisioned the Saba as a Tesla for ordinary families.

The potential for linking infotech and greentech did not go unnoticed. German giant SAP had pioneered the field with software to perform carbon accounting, energy auditing, safety management and resource planning, soon followed by archrival Oracle. Anticipating legislation about climate change (that would penalize the emission of greenhouse gases) a few Bay Area startups entered the space of software for energy and emission management to help companies control their "carbon footprint." Hara was founded in 2008 by former SAP executive Amit Chatterjee and run by Oracle alumni. In January 2009, Tom Siebel, the founder of Siebel Systems who had become a passionate advocate of net-zero energy homes, launched C3 with a board that comprised former secretary of state Condoleezza Rice and Shankar Sastry, the dean of engineering at UC Berkeley. UC Berkeley had nurtured the science of energy conservation. One of its scientists, Charlie Huizenga, had founded already in 2005 Adura Technologies, whose software aimed at monitoring and optimizing the lighting of a building.

Cold Fusion

In 1985, the US, the Soviet Union, Japan, and the European Union had launched a joint project to build the International Thermonuclear Experimental Reactor (ITER). The hope was that it would lead to a power plant fueled by fusion. ITER had been designed according to the Soviet tomahawk reactor invented by Soviet physicists Igor Tamm and Andrei Sakharov.

The holy grail of nuclear fusion, however, was "cold fusion," i.e. fusion that does not require the high temperatures generated by such an expensive reactor. In March 1989 Stanley Pons, a chemist at the University of Utah, and Martin Fleischmann from the University of Southampton in Britain had announced that they had achieved "cold fusion," i.e. nuclear fusion at room temperature (about 20 degrees Celsius). Within a few months the scientific community had come to consider it a bluff, which discredited the entire field. Meanwhile, ignored by the media, in 1989 New Zealand electrochemist Michael McKubre had just begun to study cold fusion at SRI International. For about two decades the field had virtually been silenced by mainstream science. By the end of the 2000s interest had returned, as cold fusion would solve the problem of energy forever. Construction of ITER, mostly funded by the European Union, finally began in 2008 in southern France after India, mainland China, and South Korea had joined the original quartet. At the same time mainstream science began to accept the results on "cold fusion" that Michael McKubre's lab had achieved.

Meanwhile, hot fusion remained the scientifically proven way to go. The Livermore Labs were entrusted in 1997 with the National Ignition Facility (NIF). The project required high-power lasers to trigger nuclear fusion in the hydrogen fuel. The term "ignition" refers to the point when more energy is generated than is consumed by the plant. The Lawrence Livermore National Laboratory basically planned to simulate the nuclear fusion of a star (more than 100 million degrees Celsius, hotter than the center of the sun) with the world's most powerful laser.

Lasers

One of the great scientific endeavors of the 2000s was a joint project among CalTech, MIT, and Stanford to detect gravitational waves: the Laser Interferometer Gravitational-Wave Observatory (LIGO). The most expensive project ever funded by the National Science Foundation (NSF), LIGO became operational in August 2002 in two observatories located 3,000 kilometers apart (Louisiana and Washington state). The experiment required the most precise measurement ever. Capitalizing on laser amplification studied by Robert Byer's team at Stanford, Ueda Kenichi in Japan developed transparent ceramic laser for high-energy applications that, in turn, led to Northrop Grumman's announcement in 2009 that it had created a 100-kilowatt laser, an impressive achievement for a discipline that in 1984 could only produce two-milliwatt lasers. This combination of high precision and high energy was unprecedented in history. Livermore Labs' researchers realized that the technology could also serve the purpose of the National Ignition Facility (NIF).

Lasers were also employed at the Lawrence Berkeley Labs to create a new generation of "miniature" particle accelerators. In 2006 Wim Leemans's team accelerated electrons to a billion electronvolts (1GeV) in a distance of centimeters rather than hundreds of meters. The next project was the Berkeley Lab Laser Accelerator (BELLA), in which a laser would produce one-quadrillion watts (one billion million watts) for a millisecond, enough to accelerate electrons to an energy level of 10 GeV in a distance of just one meter.

Meanwhile, SLAC inaugurated the Linac Coherent Light Source (LCLS) that in April 2009 produced the world's brightest X-ray laser (X-rays being much higher-frequency radiations than microwaves). It was now technically possible to pinpoint a biological cell, and, generally speaking, explore matter at the molecular scale.

Culture and Society

The future was more mysterious than ever, even though these technologies diverged in so many directions. The debate about the future permeated many Bay Area circles, mostly centered on oracles of the future ("futurists"). Taking inspiration from the private International Space University (ISU), founded by MIT professors in 1987, in 2009 OCR inventor Ray Kurzweil and ISU's founder Peter Diamandis started the Singularity University, located at Moffett Field. It basically bestowed academic credentials upon futurists. Sometimes the futurists' rhetoric was oddly reminiscent of the post-hippie new-age spirituality of the 1970s, except that now it was focused on achieving immortality. Scientists at the Singularity University speculated that in the future immortality could be achieved by downloading one's consciousness onto a computer.

The Seasteading Institute, founded in 2008 in Sunnyvale by Patri Friedman, envisioned cities floating in the middle of the ocean as utopian libertarian communities to experiment with alternative social systems.

The arts reacted seemingly by discarding the whole notion of a future, by embracing in fact a playful tone even when they confronted tragic themes. Al Farrow used guns and bullets to sculpt his "Cathedral" (2007). In 2010 Scott Sona Snibbe, one of the many Bay Area practitioners of immersive interactive art, turned one of his interactive software artworks, Gravilux, into an application for the iPhone and iPad. It was downloadable for free from the iTunes store: within weeks it became a worldwide success. At the intersection of art and science, in 2001 neuroscientist Semir Zeki had founded the Institute of Neuroesthetics in Berkeley, and in 2008 Piero Scaruffi started the Leonardo Art Science Evenings (LASERs) in San Francisco.

Berkeley's passion for "including" disabled people culminated in 2010 with the inauguration of the Ed Roberts campus, a place not only devoted to people with disabilities but designed by architect William Leddy to make sure that anyone (anyone) could use it, even blind people without arms or legs.

An important ideological change was taking place inside the Bay Area's universities about using new digital media to export knowledge to the rest of the world. For example, Khan Academy was launched by Salman Khan to make a free K-12 education available through short instructional videos on YouTube. Copying that idea in 2011, Stanford professors Peter Norvig and Sebastian Thrun created free courseware on the Web that could be accessed by students worldwide. In 2011 Sebastian Thrun quit Stanford to start the online university Udacity that would educate tens of thousands of students worldwide for free. Also in 2011 two Stanford researchers, Andrew Ng and Daphne Koller, whose free Web-based courseware had already been used by more than 100,000 students, launched their own startup, Coursera, aiming at providing interactive courses from Stanford, UC Berkeley, the University of

Michigan, the University of Pennsylvania and Princeton University in all sorts of disciplines.

Meanwhile, the ever-shifting demographics of the Bay Area were experiencing another major make-up. This time, they were Muslims. Most of them came from the Indian subcontinent and chose Fremont as their new hometown. In October 2006, an Afghan woman wearing the Muslim head scarf was killed in a brazen daylight shooting. That tragic incident put Muslims on the social map of the Bay Area. The Zaytuna Institute, the first Muslim liberal arts institution in the US, had been founded by Shaykh Hamza in 1996 in Berkeley. The first Bay Area Muslim Film Festival had been held in March 2004 in Berkeley. The Muslim population of the Bay Area was estimated at 250,000 in 2008.

The success of Paypal, Facebook and the likes had transformed Palo Alto from a student town to a startup town. Mountain View, the first beneficiary of the dotcom since the days of Netscape and Yahoo and now the heartland of Google, was on its way to become another exclusive community. Silicon Valley had expanded north (to Oracle's Redwood City and to Genentech's South San Francisco) but not quite north to the intellectual hubs of Berkeley and San Francisco that, despite nurturing several startups, never quite experienced the same ebullient business creativity, as if to prove that a startup needs irresponsible thinking more than it needs worldly erudition.

The Anthropology of the Age of Self-awareness

The 2000s were the decade when Silicon Valley was obsessed with itself. The Tech Museum of Innovation opened in 1998 in San Jose, and the Computer History Museum opened in 2003 in Mountain View. Silicon Valley had always been a bit surprised of being a world-famous phenomenon. The Stanford Silicon Valley Archives reopened in 1999 at the Green Library and began amassing donations of documents from companies and individuals. As many of its original founders were reaching the age of the memoir, Silicon Valley was becoming a self-celebratory phenomenon. In another act of self-celebration, in 2006 Julie Newdoll of YLEM gave a commission to sculptor Jim Pallas, who specialized in plywood hitch-hikers. She wanted sculptures of six founding fathers of Silicon Valley (DeForest, Hewlett, Packard, Shockley, Terman, and Noyce) to be dispatched around the US equipped with tracking devices.

This society saturated with high-tech was still humane. A few events were emblematic of the anti-technological reaction that was more pervasive than ever, despite appearances. First was the growing popularity of the outdoors. A store like REI, founded in 1938 in Seattle by a group of mountaineers, became a conglomerate due to its success in the Bay Area, where it maintained eight locations. It specialized in sporting goods, notably for hiking, climbing, and biking. The Bay Area had always been obsessed with fitness (and the gym had become ubiquitous) but this went beyond fitness. Silicon Valley engineers used their spare time to train for the epic hikes of Yosemite and the High Sierra, as well as for marathons, bike races, and triathlons, no matter how unprepared they were.

The "Burning Man" festival had moved to an isolated corner of the Black Rock desert in Nevada where it had completely lost its "counterculture" status. It was now one of the most advertised and expensive events of the year. But it was a futuristic, urban experiment. During the Labor Day weekend in September, tens of thousands of people, mostly from the Bay Area, set up a tent city, lived in it, and were stimulated to be creative and spontaneous. Then they simply "undid" it all, leaving no traces behind. Burning Man had become famous for its fantastical and participatory art installations that were meant to be burned at the end of the festival and for its picturesque costumes and body art of the crowd. But it was becoming more interesting as a self-organized community. Burning Man had originally been studied as a semi-religious ritual of purification and communion by the high-tech generation, but now it was also studied as a city powered by solar energy and motorized by biodiesel. It was decorated with the arts instead of billboards, and cleaned by the citizens themselves. By comparison, the European equivalent was the "Love Parade," which was really just a big party of music, alcohol, and drugs.

And then there was the end of the world. The cycles of the Maya calendar end with the year 2012. This and other coincidences led to the formation of theories about some kind of impending apocalypse that became a favorite topic of discussion among engineers who had never cared about Maya history (and, alas, probably didn't really know who the Maya were). Growing awareness of the role of technology in shaping society was mirrored by growing moral anxiety. In October 2011, a new class of corporation was created in California, the "benefit corporations", which are corporations whose charters specifically mandate the pursuit of ethical and environmental goals instead of giving priority to maximizing the financial return to shareholders.

While these phenomena could be viewed as reactions to the materialism of high-tech business, they were also emblematic of a shift towards more superficial hobbies. Knowledge-driven hobbies had been replaced by skills-driven hobbies: salsa dancing, mountain biking, snowboarding, marathon running, etc. This shift translated into a rapid collapse of the independent bookstores, several of which were vestiges of the counterculture of the 1960s. It wasn't just the online bookstore that killed them: it was also a rapidly declining audience for high-brow culture. In 2001 Printers Inc. in Palo Alto closed. Kepler's in Menlo Park almost closed in 2005 but was saved by a grass-roots campaign. In 2006, both Cody's in Berkeley and A Clean and Well Lighted Place in Cupertino had to shut down. Maybe it was also a sign that the digital generation demanded a different vehicle than the traditional paper book.

In reality, there were increasingly big differences between the various poles of the Bay Area. Long work hours and maddeningly slow traffic were progressively isolating Silicon Valley from the rest of the Bay. Silicon Valley was a region of low-rise residential buildings and town-home parks organized in geometric neighborhood that were largely self-sufficient. Therefore the need to visit other parts of the Bay was minimal. The distances between Silicon Valley and the artistic world of San Francisco, the political world of Berkeley, and the scientific world of Stanford, had increased dramatically. No wonder that Silicon Valley was infamous for no cultural variety: everybody read the same book, watched the same movie, and sang the same song. Its inhabitants were too isolated from culture. Silicon Valley was giving a new meaning to the word "provincial."

For a long time the engineering world had been fundamentally male. The 21st century began with an increasing number of women joining the ranks of engineers. There was also significant progress in promoting women to executive jobs. Young female executives included Sheryl Sandberg (1969), chief operating officer of Facebook, and Marissa Mayer (1975), a vice-president at Google who then became the CEO of Yahoo!. However, there still was no female Steve Jobs or Mark Zuckerberg.

This society was still very transient. In 1992, unemployment in Silicon Valley had reached 7.4%. In 2000 it had declined to 1.7%. One year later it had increased to 5.9%. By 2007 it was down again. It was not the same people who left and came. Those who left probably never came back. It was terribly difficult to resettle in the Bay Area after one left it, both in terms of real estate (home prices tended to skyrocket during a recovery due to a chronic shortage of housing) and in terms of employment. It was easy for a recent immigrant or fresh graduate to take a risky job, but difficult for someone who already had a career somewhere else. Silicon Valley was the one region of the world whose identity was not defined by the people who lived in it, because they changed all the time.

However, perhaps the most unique aspect of culture and society in the San Francisco Bay Area was that there was absolutely no building reflecting the booming economic, technological, and political power. Rarely had human civilization been so invisible. There was no breathtaking skyscraper, no imposing monument, no avantgarde city landmark. Silicon Valley and the rest of the Bay did not invest a single penny in advertising its own success. In March 2012, the New York Times estimated that all fine arts museums of San Francisco combined ranked 13th in the nation for investments in new acquisitions, even behind the Princeton Art Museum, with a total that was less than 10% of what the Metropolitan Museum of New York alone spent.

The Gift Economy

At the end of the Great Recession of 2008, economists were beginning to understand one important factor among the causes of the chronic unemployment in the US: free community content. In 2006 YouTube only had 60 employees, but they were managing 100 million videos. YouTube's employees were not making the videos: millions of people around the world were donating them to YouTube. If a Hollywood studio had decided to create 100 million videos, it would have had to hire hundreds of thousands of people to act them, direct them, produce them, edit them, and upload them. In 2004, Craigslist only had ten employees moderating more than a million advertisements posted every month. A newspaper handling the same amount of advertisements would have to hire hundreds of editors. In 2005 Flickr only had nine employees, but they were managing a repository of millions of pictures. Those pictures were taken around the world, edited, uploaded, documented and even organized by millions of users. A magazine that decided to create a similar repository of pictures would have to hire thousands of photographers, tour guides and editors. In 2005 Skype only had 200 employees, but they were providing telephone service to more than 50 million registered users. Any telecom in the world that provided a comparable service employed tens of thousands of technicians, operators, accountants, etc. One of the fundamental discoveries of the "net economy" had been that users of the Web around the world are happy to contribute content for free to websites willing to accept it.

This phenomenon obviously displaced workers who used to be paid to create that very content. This phenomenon was not creating joblessness but merely unemployment: it was creating unpaid jobs. Millions of people worked (some of them for many hours a day) to create and upload content to other people's businesses (such as Wikipedia, Facebook, Twitter, Flickr and YouTube). They were working, but they were not employed. They worked for free, out of their own will. Not even slaves did that. Indirectly, the Web had created a broad new class of knowledge workers: volunteer amateur editors. Their net effect was to displace the existing knowledge workers, such as photographers, journalists, actors, directors, researchers, writers, librarians, musicians, as well as all the engineers and clerical staff who provided services for them.

When thousands of knowledge workers lose their job, i.e. when their purchasing power collapses, inevitably this has a repercussion on the entire economy and creates further ripples of unemployment. Every time someone adds a line to Wikipedia, a professional knowledge worker becomes less indispensable and more disposable. Every time someone adds a picture to Flickr, a video to YouTube, news on Twitter, a notice on Facebook, or an ad on Craigslist, the job of a professional becomes more vulnerable. In the past each wave of technological innovation had come with a wave of new jobs that replaced the old ones.

Society had to train millions of users of word processors to take the place of million of typists. Companies had to churn out computers instead of typewriters, a process that involved hiring more people. In fact, each wave of technological progress typically created new opportunities for knowledge workers, and this class therefore expanded rapidly, creating more employment and higher incomes. The expansion was still happening: there ware now millions of people making videos instead of just a few thousands, and there ware now millions of people taking pictures and millions posting news. The difference was that this time they didn't ask to be paid: they were doing it for free.

Therefore businesses could operate with a minimal staff: the old knowledge workers were replaced by free labor. Therefore the number of knowledge workers was still increasing, but the number of those who were paid for their work was shrinking dramatically.

It was an illusion that YouTube was run by only a handful of employees. YouTube "employed" millions of "employees." It just so happened that 99% of them were happy to work, providing content, for free. Therefore there was no need anymore to actually hire people to create content. Protectionists were complaining that developing countries were "dumping" cheap products on the US market that caused US companies to go out of business. Protectionists were screaming at "unfair trade." But the real enemy of employment was free labor. Nothing kills jobs faster and more permanently than free labor. That is a form of competition that was coming from inside the US society, an accidental by-product of technological progress.

This accidental by-product was actually the dream of socialist utopians. The net economy had created production tools that were available for free to everybody. That was precisely Marx's definition of socialism: the collective ownership of the means of production. This accidental by-product was also the dream of the hippie utopians of the San Francisco Bay Area. In the 1970s Stewart Brand of the WELL had imagined precisely such a virtual community of people engaged in the free production and exchange of knowledge goods: a community of people investing their time and sharing their content for free. The utopian society of Marx and Brand had materialized as a "gift economy" (a term coined in 1985 by Lewis Hyde and applied to the net economy in 1998 by Richard Barbrook) in which a few businesses provided the means of production to a mass of millions of volunteer amateur editors.

The free labor of these many worker ants allowed a very small number of queens to get extremely rich while causing millions of middle-class families to lose their income.

The irony is that they were often the same people. The very person who uploads a picture, a text or a video for free is the person who will (directly or indirectly) need to look for another (often less remunerative) job as a (direct or indirect) consequence of that act of free labor.

The Internet had indeed democratized society. Everybody could now start their own business. At the same time the Internet had increased the value of knowledge, another step in the progress of human civilization from survival-based goods to knowledge-based goods. The problem was that the Internet had also democratized knowledge production: everybody could now provide content, and they were willing to do it for free.

The net economy was, in fact, rapidly evolving towards an economy of one-man operations. There were now Web-based tools available to build, run, and monetize a business that only required limited technical skills and no more than a few days of work. One person alone could create an assembly line entirely on the Web to produce a mass-market product/service (in the same category as YouTube, Flickr and Craigslist). That assembly line did not employ any worker other than the founders who assembled it. Once the one-person business was up and running, its success mainly depended on how many people were willing to contribute content for free, i.e. how much free labor you could harvest on the Internet. One could foresee a future when a startup would require even fewer founders. If successful in attracting millions of amateur content providers, it would employ even fewer people, and only those very few would benefit financially from its success.

In the age of smartphones and email, there was another victim: physical proximity was no longer a necessity for a startup. There was no need to be based, say, in Palo Alto, where the cost of living was so high. The time had come for geographically distributed startups. For example, StackOverflow was founded in 2008 by Jeff Atwood in Berkeley and Joel Spolsky in New York, and employed people in different states.

These startups of the "gift economy" were annoyed by the pressures of investors. Therefore it came as no surprise that in April 2010 Jared Cosulich and Adam Abrons founded Irrational Design with the explicit goal of not seeking venture capital. The "business plan" of the startup was to be creative, with no specific product in mind. Venture capitalists were perceived as hijacking the minds of the founders to focus on a lucrative product. Irrational Design was emblematic of a generation that aimed for precisely the opposite: let the minds of the founders invent at will, with no regard for market response or potential acquisitions. For example, in July 2002 eBay paid $1.5 billion for PayPal, a tiny unprofitable online payment service; in October 2006 Google paid $1.65 billion for YouTube, a video uploading site that had no revenue; in April 2012, Facebook paid $1 billion for Instagram, a photo-sharing service for mobile devices that had no revenue and only a handful of employees.

The traditional economy had tended to concentrate wealth in the hands of a few large companies that had run giant empires of hundreds of thousands of employees around the world. The gift economy was rapidly concentrating wealth in the hands of a few individuals who ran giant empires of tens of millions of unpaid amateurs.

The Assembly Line Model of Startup Funding

The first boom of Silicon Valley's venture capital world took place in the mid-1980s when large semiconductor companies needed money to build "fabs" (short for "fabrication plants"). A fab is an extremely expensive project that requires hundreds of millions of dollars. The age of one-man startups, though, did not require such massive investments. The returns as a percentage could be even higher with a much smaller investment. Unlike fabs, that need an accurate plan of implementation, Web-based startups could adjust their functions in real time based on user's feedback. So all one needed to start a company was just a good idea and a rudimentary website.

At the end of the 2000s it was getting so easy and cheap to start a company that the business of funding companies was beginning to resemble an assembly line. When car manufacturing became cheap enough, Ford built an assembly line and launched the first mass-market car. Something similar was happening in Silicon Valley in 2010 in the business of manufacturing startups. Sometimes angels would invest without even having met the founders in person.

This logic was being pushed to the extreme limit by a new generation of angel investors who were sometimes barely in their 30s. The Google, Facebook, and PayPal success stories, plus all the startups that they acquired, had created plenty of very young millionaires and even some billionaires. Google acquired more than 40 companies in 2010 alone. The young founders could comfortably retire, but it was "cool" to become angel investors and help other young founders get started and get rich. These new angels were "kids" compared with the veterans of 3000 Sand Hill Road. Yet many of these kids felt that they could more accurately guess the future of the world and jumped into the game passionately. Needless to say, these kids tended to fund startups that were started by kids even younger than them.

The mindset of both investors and founders was very different from the mindset of investors and founders of the 1980s. The credentials of a founder were often based on popularity, not on a professional business plan. In fact, these new investors "hated" the Wall Street type of founder. They loved, on the other hand, the "cool" kid. The successful founder was someone who could create "buzz" on the Internet about his or her idea, even if he or she had no clue how to monetize that idea. It was, in a sense, the psychology of the high school transplanted into the world of finance. The intellectual idealism of the early Internet was being replaced by the subculture of high-school gangs, albeit one that abhorred drugs and violence.

The new angels, in turn, were not professionals educated by Stanford or Harvard in the subtleties of economics; they were former "cool" kids. They invested based on their instinct, trying to guess who would become the next cool kid. To some extent the venture capital business had always been a statistical game: you invest in ten startups hoping that just one makes it big. But it had always been backed by some (economic) science. It was now becoming pure gambling. The psychology required from an angel investor was more and more similar to the psychology of the gambler who spent the day in front of a slot machine in Las Vegas casinos. The inception of this new kind of venture capitalism was commonly taken to be 2005, when Paul Graham started Y Combinator in Mountain View and incubated eight seed-stage startups.

Another significant change in the way startups are funded took place when the "crowd-funding" website Kickstarter launched in 2008 in San Francisco. The concept had been pioneered by the New York-based music company ArtistShare: raise money among ordinary people to fund a (music) event. Kickstarter transferred the concept into the world of the Bay Area startups with amazing success. By May 2013, Kickstarter had funded more than 99,000 projects that had raised more than $630 million dollars. Kickstarter got further help from the government when the JOBS Act was enacted in April 2012. It made it legal for smaller investors to fund a company and with fewer restrictions.

Last but not least, the early adopters too were of a different kind than for previous generations of products. The early adopter of an Intel product or of an Oracle product was a multinational corporation. The early adopter of an Apple gadget was a professional with a good salary, and typically a technology-savvy one. Now the early adopter of a website like a social networking platform was, instead, just a kid himself. The early adopter was not paying anything to use the "product" (the social networking platform). Therefore the profile of the early adopters was, for the first time ever, disconnected from their financial status and instead related to how much spare time they had and were willing to spend on the Internet. The early adopters were typically very young. These "kids" created the "buzz." They established the credentials of a new platform. The adult audience followed the trend set by a very young audience.

The Big-Brother Web

Google, Facebook, and other cloud companies justified their new features on the basis of providing "better services," but in reality they were providing better services mainly to marketers. The multinational marketers (such as WPP Group) were now in control of the Web. They drove the new features of the most popular websites. For that reason Google and Facebook were improving the "services" of tracking what people do on the Internet. In theory, this vast database of individual behavioral patterns was meant to provide a personalized experience on the Internet. In practice, its motivation was economic. Marketers were willing to pay more for advertising on platforms that tracked individual behavior. For the marketers it meant the difference between a shot in the dark and targeted advertisement. Targeted ads were obviously much more valuable. Google's and Facebook's founders kept swearing that there was no "Big Brother" in the future of their worlds, but a sort of Big Brother was precisely the ultimate outcome of their business plan.

One major event created even more anxiety. In August 2010, Google signed a deal with Verizon that basically terminated the "net neutrality" principle. The Internet had been born as a noncommercial platform. Therefore it had been easy to enforce a principle that every piece of data, no matter how powerful its "owner," should move at the same speed through the vast network of nodes that physically implement the Internet. That principle was never codified in a law, but it had been respected even during the dotcom boom, allowing, for example, Amazon to grow at the expense of the traditional bookstore chains and Netflix to hurt the business of the traditional movie theater chains. The Google-Verizon deal represented a major departure because it specifically stated that the age of wireless access to the Internet was different in nature. Since the future of the Internet was obviously to be wireless, this was not a hypothetical scenario: it was a promise.

Changing Nature of Innovation

Significant changes were occurring in the very focus of innovation. Technological innovation was no longer what it used to be, especially for the software industry. Silicon Valley had become the testbed for extremely complex system engineering (rather than the testbed for new ideas). The real value was to be found not in the products themselves (their features and their looks) but in the complexity that surrounded and enabled their success. Oracle (the distributed ERP system), Apple (especially iTunes), Cisco (the network to connect customers with more than 40,000 specialized channel partners), Google (billions of simultaneous searches and videos), HP and VMware (the cloud), and Facebook (billions of simultaneous posts) were ultimately engaged in solving very complex problems of scale. The customer paid for a product (or sometimes didn't even pay for it), but in reality the customer was buying an infrastructure. For example, Google's great innovation in its early years was the search engine, but the rest of Google's history was largely a history of acquiring or copying other people's ideas: the real contribution by Google consisted in turning rudimentary platforms (such as Android and Maps) into formidable robust distributed platforms.

The big Silicon Valley companies (notably Google and Oracle) were now growing through acquisition. They specialized in turning around not businesses but platforms. They had become extremely efficient reengineering factories.

The hardware industry was prospering but knowing that physical limits were going to be reached soon. In particular, it was getting more and more difficult to achieve faster speeds without generating unmanageable heat. Increasing the clock speed of a chip also increases its consumption which also increases the heat it generates. The stopgap solution had been to squeeze multiple processors on the same chip, but that was becoming impractical too. There was a general feeling that the age of the CMOS transistor was about to come to an end. For some the solution was to move away from transistors. Stan Williams at Hewlett-Packard was working on "memristors" based on titanium dioxide. Transistors are "volatile", i.e. they must be continually powered in order to preserve information, whereas "memristors" would be a nonvolatile technology, that only needs to be powered when "reading" or "writing" information (changing its state or checking its state). At Stanford University the Robust Systems Group led by Subhasish Mitras was researching nanocircuits: the smaller the circuit, the smaller its demand for power and the heat it generates. Mitras was experimenting with carbon nanotubes.

The change here reflected the new dynamics of the computer industry. In the past change had been driven by the demands of bureaucratic, military or space applications, i.e. by government demand, and to some extent by the needs of corporate America. Now change was driven by the insatiable appetite of consumer electronics.

Another concept that had not changed in decades was the one underlying magnetic data storage. In 2011 Andreas Heinrich's team at IBM's Almaden Research Center reduced from about one million to 12 the number of atoms required to store a bit of data. In practice, this meant the feasibility of magnetic memories 100 times denser than the most popular hard disks and memory chips.

Quantum computing was, instead, still largely ignored in Silicon Valley. The idea of using the odd features of Quantum Physics to create supercomputers dated from 1982, when one of the greatest physicists, Richard Feynman, speculated that a computer could store information by exploiting precisely the principles of quantum superposition (that a particle can be in two states at the same time) using "qubits" (quantum bits) instead of binary bits. In 1994 Peter Shor at Bell Labs proved an important theorem: that a quantum computer would outperform a classic computer in a category of difficult mathematical problems. In 1997 British physicist Colin Williams and Xerox PARC's Scott Clearwater published "Explorations in Quantum Computing", a book that actually described how a quantum computer could be built. Vancouver's D-Wave, founded in 1999 by quantum physicists Geordie Rose and (Russian-born) Alexandre Zagoskin of the University of British Columbia, aimed at doing precisely that. In February 2007 D-Wave finally demonstrated its Orion prototype at the Computer History Museum in Mountain View. In 2009, Yale professor Steven Girvin unveiled a macroscopic quantum processor (quantum processors were supposed to be very microscopic). In May 2011, D-Wave announced the sale of its first commercial quantum computer, purchased by Lockheed for the Quantum Computing Center that it established with the University of Southern California in Los Angeles, although purists debated whether it qualified as a real "quantum" computer.

The Electronic Empire and its Resource Needs

The world economy was hit hard in September 2008 by a financial crisis that started in the US, due to reckless banking speculation. The crisis was mostly a Wall Street problem, but it dragged down the entire economy. However, high-tech companies in the Bay Area did relatively well, most of them reemerging after two years unscathed. The dotcom crash had been useful to teach them how to trim costs quickly in the face of an economic downturn.

Silicon Valley had traditionally been indifferent to national and especially internationally events. Even the various wars that the US fought (World War I, World War II, Korea, Vietnam, the first and second Iraqi wars, Afghanistan) were perceived as distant echoes and, quite frankly, as business opportunities. This happened despite the strong anti-war sentiment of San Francisco and Berkeley, yet another contradiction in the ideological dynamics of the Bay Area. This was true because of the relative isolation of California, but also because for a long time Silicon Valley's core business did not need anybody else. Silicon is the second most abundant chemical element of the Earth's crust after oxygen.

The entire industry of semiconductors had a large advantage over other industries: its primary element was cheap and widely available. There was no need for wars in the Gulf War and no wild spikes in prices like for gold. Software had an even smaller resource footprint: a software engineer just needed two fingers to type on a keyboard. Until the 1990s, Silicon Valley saw the rest of the world either as a market or as an outsourcing facility.

The age of the cell phone, of the videogame, of the digital camera, and of the digital music player, instead, relied on another material, tantalum, which was far less abundant. Tantalum was obtained from coltan (columbite-tantalite) and one country held the largest reserves of coltan: the Democratic Republic of Congo. That nation also held another record: the bloodiest civil war since 1998. Reports started circulating that the civil war was funded by the smuggling of coltan towards the Western companies that needed it for their consumer electronics products. At the same time stories also appeared of the terrible work conditions in the Chinese factories of Shenzhen, where hundreds of thousands of low-paid workers assembled electronic devices for US manufacturers (notably Apple).

Meanwhile, lithium batteries, widely used in mobile electronic devices, obviously relied on lithium being available and cheap. Yet about 50% of the world's reserves of lithium were based in Bolivia, which had just elected a socialist president with an anti-US agenda. China had become the biggest producer of "rare earths" (vital to cell phones, laptops and greentech) and pressure was mounting to reopen the Californian mines that used to dominate the world markets. The 50 million tons of electronic waste generated worldwide each year were mostly sent for disposal to developing countries where valuable metals were converted into scrap metal for resale at the cost of human lives and environmental disasters.

At the same time California was going through very turbulent financial times for the first time in its history. It had one of the highest unemployment rates in the country, slow growth, and a chronic budget deficit. Silicon Valley had risen from the 1940s to the 1990s in a state that was booming. Now it was embedded in a state that was failing. Putting it all together, Silicon Valley was no longer insulated from global politics as it had been for decades.

It was not a coincidence that in 2010 two of its most popular executives, Meg Whitman and Carly Fiorina, entered the national political scene. Even more relevant was the role of Silicon Valley technology which influenced world events. In 2009, Iranian youth took to the streets using Twitter to coordinate and assemble protests against their rigged national elections. In 2010, students armed with cell phones and social networking software overthrew the Tunisian dictator. Later in 2011, a webpage created by Google executive Wael Ghonim indirectly started the mass demonstrations against the regime in Egypt. In response to the events, the Egyptian government took down the Internet within its borders. A few days later Google launched a special service to allow the protesters in Egypt to send Twitter messages by dialing a phone number and leaving a voice mail: the purpose was not to help Twitter (a competitor) make money, but to help the protesters win the revolution. Silicon Valley was becoming a political player largely independent of any government.

Silicon Valleys in Time

If a historian specializing in technological evolution had examined the world a century ago, she would have never bet her money on a primitive, underpopulated, and underdeveloped region like the San Francisco Bay Area. She might have picked a place in the US (most likely Boston, New York or Philadelphia), but more likely a place in Western Europe, probably somewhere between Oxford and Cambridge. With 20/20 hindsight everybody has a theory about why it all happened in "Silicon Valley." Yet most of those theories are easily disproven if one studies other regions of the world: the same conditions existed somewhere else and to an even greater degree.

One needs to spend more time analyzing the previous cases of economic, technological, and cultural booms. Three obvious candidates are Athens in the 5th century BC, Firenze (Florence) of the Renaissance, and the eletrical Berlin of a century ago.

There was little that made Athens truly special. Other cities might have succeeded better than Athens, particularly the ones on the coast of what is today Turkey that were the cradle of Greek civilization. However, Athens was probably the nicest place to live: the attitude of its citizens was different, somewhat eccentric for those times. Eventually it was that attitude that led to the invention of democracy and capitalism.

It may have been easier to predict Firenze's ascent given that the city had been getting richer since at least the 12th century. However, who would have bet on a city state within peninsular Italy, which was mostly famous for endemic warfare? And if you had to pick an Italian city-state why not Venice that was creating a little empire, not surrounded by dozens of city-states like Florence was in Tuscany, and that constituted a crucial link between the superpower of Constantinople and Western Europe? Again, what stands out is the attitude of the Florentines: if you liked adventure and innovation, it was nicer to live in Florence than in greedy, narrow-minded Venice. Eventually Florence did produce more liberal regimes and enlightened dictators instead of Venice's faceless dogi.

The "electrical Berlin" of the early 20th century came out of a black hole: Germany did not even exist 30 years earlier. Germany was the last place in Europe that was still politically divided in tiny medieval-style states the late 19th century. When Germany got unified, the spirit of unification certainly fueled nationalistic pride but, again, there was hardly anything special about German science and technology up to that point. There was indeed something special about German philosophy and German poetry, but one can argue it actually went against progress. What was unique about Berlin at that time was the enthusiasm of its population: the attitude, again, was indeed unique. In all three places it was the attitude (the spirit) of the population that was markedly different from the norm. In all three places that attitude rewarded the independent in ways that were not the norm, and it instituted a stronger degree of meritocracy than elsewhere.

The same might be true also for the San Francisco Bay Area. The great universities, the mass immigration and the venture capital (knowledge, labor and money) came later. What was already there was the spirit of the American frontier, the self-reliance of the eccentric independent explorer that later would become the hobbyist and the hacker.

Silicon Valleys in Space

There have been many attempts to recreate Silicon Valley in other countries. It is worth examining the ones in Western Europe that at the time led the world in universities, immigrants, and capital.

France created Sophia Antipolis, a technology park in Southern France. First of all, it was created by the French government with a socialist-style centralized plan. The region has become a magnet for foreign IT companies that want a foothold into Europe, but hardly the creator of domestic startups that the Bay Area is in the US. There are a few factors that make a huge difference: there is social pressure to join big corporations, not to start small companies; if you do open your own company, failure is terminal; very few foreign talents have been (permanently) attracted to the area; on the contrary many of the French talents trained there have emigrated to the US where they did start the kind of company that they would not start in France. Note that, by all accounts, the quality of life in southern France matches if not surpasses the quality of life in California.

The Munich metropolitan area in southern Germany has become another high-tech hub. In this case, the German government did not quite plan a Silicon Valley per se: it was the defense industry that brought advanced manufacturing to the area in ways not too different from how the defense industry bootstrapped Silicon Valley's high-tech industry. The advanced manufacturing that led to the success of companies like BMW transformed an essentially rural community in Bavaria into a high-tech hub. Here there are also excellent educational institutions: the Fraunhofer Institute and the Max Planck institute, that provide world-class public education. The quality of life is quite high by European standards and the weather is much better than in most of Germany. The socialist underpinning here is represented by the fact that the main "venture capitalist" has been Bayern Kapital, an arm of the state government. The region has indeed spawned a varied fauna of infotech, biotech, and cleantech startups just like in Silicon Valley. The region has also avoided the brain-drain that consumes most of Western Europe: relatively few German entrepreneurs and engineers have moved to the US. However, this region too has failed to attract significant numbers of foreign talents.

Four factors made Germany completely different from the Bay Area. First of all, Germany's fundamental problem was the high cost of its labor, about ten times the cost of labor in China in 2010. Therefore the whole nation was engaged in a collective distributed project to devise ever more efficient ways to manufacture goods. Therefore both universities and corporations focused their research on innovating in the manufacturing process, rather than innovating through the products made by those processes. The German system was biased towards perfecting existing technology rather than creating new technology. RWTH Aachen spent billions of euros to create a technology park that specializes in just manufacturing techniques. Stanford's technology park was never meant for just one specific application of technology. Secondly, the relationship between industry and academia was always different in Germany than in the US. German corporations funded academic research that was very specific to their needs, whereas universities in the US received money that was generically for research. This meant that the transfer of know-how from academia to industry was much smoother and faster in Germany than in the US, but at the same time the students were raised to become workers and then managers in the existing corporations rather than start new creative businesses. Thirdly, Germany's big success story could also be a curse. Germany achieved an impressive degree of distribution of high education, spreading world-class research institutes all over its territory. The Max Planck Institute had 80 locations in 2010, the Fraunhofer Society had 60. Yet this also meant that most of the bright scientists, engineers and entrepreneurs didn't need to move to another city, as they could find a top-notch technological centers right where they lived. Silicon Valley was mainly built by immigrants from other US states and from abroad. It was one place where everybody converged to do high-tech because most of the rest of the country did not have the conditions that are favorable to the high-tech industry. Germany provided them almost to dozens of regions, therefore none of them can become the equivalent of Silicon Valley. Finally, and this is true for all of continental Europe, German industry had to deal with a strong anti-technological and anti-capitalist sentiment that was created over the decades by an alliance of socialists, environmentalists, hippies, philosophers, psychologists, and so forth.

So far the main success stories of Europe have come from these regions: SAP (Heidelberg), ARM (Cambridge) and Nokia (Oulu). The European region that came closest to resembling Silicon Valley (although at a much smaller scale) was Oulu in northern Finland, where more than a thousand startups were born in the 2000s, most of them in wireless technology, but also in biotech, cleantech and nanotech.

Israel was, actually, the country with the highest venture capital per person in the entire world ($170 compared with $75 in the US in 2010). Its startups focused on the military, communications, agricultural and water technology that were essential for the country's survival. Many of these startups were acquired by Silicon Valley companies. None of these startups managed to grow to the point of becoming an international player.

Asia's High-Tech Industry

In the second half of the 20the century, Japan was the only country that competed with the US in terms of mass-scale innovation that changed the daily lives of billions of people. Japanese inventors created the transistor radio (1954), the quartz wristwatch (1967), the pocket calculator (1970), the color photocopier (1973), the portable music player (1979), the compact disc (1982), the camcorder (1982), the digital synthesizer (1983), the third-generation videogame console (1983), the digital camera (1988), the plasma TV set (1992), the DVD player (1996), the hybrid car (1997), mobile access to the Internet (1999), the Blu-ray disc (2003), and the laser television set (2008). However, Japanese innovation mostly came from conglomerates that were very old: Mitsubishi (1870), Seiko (1881), Yamaha (1887), Nintendo (1889), Fujitsu (1934), Canon (1937), Toyota (1937), Sony (1946), NTT (1952), etc.

With the exception of the media hub in Tokyo that was mostly devoted to pop culture, there was no major industrial cluster in Japan that could compare with Silicon Valley. Tokyo's "high-tech" regions were the traditional industrial hubs that grow around big companies, like Aichi, the location of Toyota's main plant and of many Toyota suppliers, Hiroshima, Sendai, Yonezawa. Later a sort of Silicon Valley emerged in Fukuoka, in the far south of Japan (Kyushu island) due to a cluster of universities (Kyushu University, Kyushu Institute of Technology, Kitakyushu University, the Institute of Systems & Information Technologies) and mostly for the semiconductor industry.

South Korea followed a similar path to high-tech innovation. Like Japan it relied mainly on well-established companies like Samsung. Korea's environment was hostile to foreign companies and there was little interaction between universities and industry, with professors more similar to government bureaucrats than to incubators of ideas or coaches of entrepreneurs.

However, South Korea also had two regions that looked a bit like Silicon Valley. In 1973, South Korea established the Korea Advanced Institute of Science and Technology at Daedeok, south of Seoul. This area began to attract R&D labs and eventually to spin off startups. It therefore came to be known as "Daedeok Valley" and officially as Daedeok Science Town. The software industry, instead, assembled around Teheran Road in Seoul (between Gangnam Station and Samseong Station), nicknamed "Teheran Valley", a three-km stretch that probably got the majority of South Korean venture-capital investment during the dotcom boom.

In terms of process, however, Taiwan was the real winner. In 1973 Taiwan established the Industrial Technological Research Institute (ITRI) to develop technologies that could be turned into goods for foreign markets, an institute that would spawn dozens of semiconductor firms, starting with UMC in 1980 and TSMC in 1987, and then the Hsinchu Science-based Industrial Park, established in 1980 about 88 kms from Taipei, near four universities. In 20 years, more than 100 companies were formed by graduates of those universities. Taiwan was also the place where venture capital took off in Asia and was also the first place that implemented the feedback loop between university and corporate R&D typical of Boston and Silicon Valley. TSMC launched the independent silicon-chip foundry, that turned Taiwan into Silicon Valley's main destination for outsourcing chip manufacturing, and which in turn helped create a vibrant chip-design industry with companies such as MediaTek and NovaTek.

Japan, Korea, and Taiwan have not attracted highly educated immigrants from elsewhere like Silicon Valley did. The only Asian country to do so was Singapore. It is not a coincidence that Singapore was also the country that invested the most in attracting foreign businesses and their know-how. Singapore too developed an advanced venture-capital industry and fostered interaction between its universities and the private industry. Still, none of these countries created a vibrant software industry like Silicon Valley.

China was a late-comer and capitalized on its neighbors' many experiments, avoiding Japan's model because it simply did not have the kind of old established manufacturing and financial giants that Japan had. The idea of a "Chinese Silicon Valley" came to nuclear scientist Chen Chunxian of the Academy of Sciences after a 1979 trip to California. Back home in 1980, he tried unsuccessfully to start a privately-funded Advanced Technology Service Association just outside Beijing. However, the Academy took up his idea and began to play the role of incubator for high-tech startups, one of which would become Lenovo, most of them based along the ten-km Zhongguancun Street. The idea appealed to both staff and students of the two leading universities of Beijing, Peking University and Tsinghua University, who needed to make more money than the tiny government salaries and subsidies. Finally, in 1988, the government gave its blessing and the whole region came to be called Zhongguancun Science Park. In little over than a decade, massive government incentives created thousands of new companies, the vast majority in software and telecommunications.

In 2008 the US entered the Great Recession while Asia was still booming. Nonetheless, in 2010, Asians overcome Hispanics as the largest group of immigrants to the US. That is Asia's single biggest failure. People were leaving the continent by the hundreds of thousands even at a time when Asia looked like a land of opportunities and the US was widely considered on the way out as a world power. One had to wonder what it would take to reverse the tide if the biggest economic crisis in 70 years didn't do it.

The Importance of Process and of Evolution

The most important event in the modern history of Asian industry, however, may predate all of this. In 1953, Taiichi Ohno invented "lean manufacturing" (or "just-in-time" manufacturing) at Japan's Toyota. That was one of the factors that turned Toyota into a giant success story and eventually into the largest car manufacturer in the world. More importantly, it created the mindset that the process is often more important than the product. When ITRI's president Morris Chang launched Taiwan's Semiconductor Manufacturing Company (TSMC), the first independent silicon-chip foundry in the world, to serve the "fabless" companies of the US, he simply applied that mindset to the computer industry and realized that one could decouple the design and the manufacturing. That does not mean that only the design is creative: the design would not lead to a mass-market product without a highly efficient manufacturing process that lowers the cost and improves quality.

From the point of view of the Asian suppliers, what was really revolutionary (and not just evolutionary) was the process, not the product. The fabless process and the offshore customer-service process were the real breakthroughs, not the new laptop model or the new operating system.

Without significant progress in Asia in the industrial process many great success stories of Silicon Valley products may have not happened at all. The world viewed from Silicon Valley was a world centered on the place where a product was designed and marketed. The world viewed from Japan, Taiwan, and Korea was a world centered on the industrial centers that could manufacture products based on whatever design, faster, cheaper and better. The world viewed from India was a world centered on the army of software engineers that could deliver software based on whatever needs, faster, cheaper and better. From the Asian viewpoint, it was the increasing evolutionary efficiency of the "builders" that allowed Silicon Valley to create "revolutionary" products and new markets. For example, despite being a relatively small economy and boasting virtually no invention that ordinary people can name, Taiwan rapidly became the fourth country in the world for patents filed (after the US, Japan, and Germany); and Japan rapidly became the country with the highest percentage of GDP spent in R&D.

That "evolution" stemmed from a mindset driven by incremental progress, the equivalent of new releases of an operating system, each one enabling a whole new range of features and prices for the next product to capture the headlines. From the viewpoint of Asia, ideas for "revolutionary" products are actually easy. What is difficult is "making" those products, not imagining them.

Furthermore, it is debatable which region and system has yielded more "revolutionary" products. The argument that small companies and Silicon Valley rule is an opinion, not a fact. The perception is that, in Japan, innovation was driven only by big companies. That perception is true. What is not true is the perception that the source of innovation was significantly different in the US. It is easy to forget that Silicon Valley has invented very little. Most of the things that changed the high-tech world, from the transistor to the disk drive, were invented by big companies like AT&T and IBM. Many of the really revolurionary ones, like the computer, the Internet, the World Wide Web, were invented by government labs. Blaming Japan for relying too much on big companies and big government means not knowing what Silicon Valley actually does, which is not to invent much technology. In fact, the rigid bureaucratic big-company system of Japan has invented a lot more than Silicon Valley. And it has arguably created more wealth for ordinary people, turning a poor country into one of the richest countries in the world.

The Western Contribution to the Success of Asia's High-tech Industry

Part of the success of Asia was obviously made in Silicon Valley: the fiber-optics boom of the 1990s helped collapse the cost of a leased telecom line between California and Bangalore, and then the Voice Over IP technology of the early 2000s made it irrelevant. Without this simple improvement in the cost of communications India's software industry would not have picked up the way it did. The dotcom boom introduced dozens of online services that eliminated the distance factor and therefore helped remote firms compete with local firms. Even the passion for industry standards that has always been a peculiarity of the US ended up favoring those abroad who wanted to create critical mass for their services of outsourcing.

The US government has indirectly been proactive in creating opportunities for Asian firms. When Bell Labs invented the transistor, it was under government pressure that its owner AT&T decided to license transistor technology at a low price to anybody who wanted it, including the company that later became Sony. It was under government pressure that IBM decided to "unbundle" the software applications from its mainframe computers, thereby spawning a software boom worldwide. It was the government that created and funded the Arpanet, which went on to become the internet and the backbone of the global outsourcing movement.

The biggest gift of the West to Asia was perhaps the revolution in management that had started in earnest in the 1920s but got a phenomenal boost in the 1990s with the collapse of the communist world and the boom of free trade. The US boasted the most advanced class of business administrators in the world in terms of maximizing profits (at least short term), and their discipline almost inevitably took them to outsource both manufacturing and services. One of the tools that they used was also a Western invention: ERP software to manage complex sophisticated distributed supply chains.

And, of course, it was the US and its allies that had taught Asia to speak English: India, Hong Kong, and Singapore had been British colonies, while Taiwan, South Korea, and Japan had been militarily occupied by the US at one point or another. The language turned out to be an important factor in leapfrogging ahead of the Europeans.

Another, less obvious, reason why it was so easy for Asian companies to do business with Silicon Valley is that Silicon Valley and the high-tech industry in general was less innovative than it appeared to be to consumers: both software and hardware products tended to follow a predictable evolutionary path that it was easy for such sophisticated suppliers of services to anticipate the required building blocks.

In brief, those successful regions of Asia that had traditionally valued higher education, especially in engineering and science, enjoyed enlightened state planning. They placed an emphasis on electronics while Europe was still focused on cars and appliances. They boasted workforces with strong work habits, guaranteeing quality and reliability, and were largely non-ideological. They didn't view capitalism as evil, like large segments of the European public, and did not harbor religious or ethnic hostilities towards Westerners.

The Missing Ingredients in Asia

However, nothing like Silicon Valley has emerged in East Asia. One simple reason for this is that it is not only startup founders who have to be visionary in order to achieve technological breakthroughs: venture capitalists have to be visionary too. In Singapore, for example, they are government bureaucrats. Asia has a tradition of keeping the money in the hands of trusted and prudent bureaucrats. The US has a tradition of letting the reckless, successful, self-made man be the one who funds the next big thing.

However, that cannot be the whole story. For example, Japan never created a vibrant software industry. But it would be unfair to blame it only on the economic and political system: very few startups in Silicon Valley were founded by Japanese immigrants, despite the fact that the number of Japanese engineers working in Silicon Valley has always been significant. Compare that with the incredible percentage of Indian and Chinese immigrants who started companies. And this is despite the fact that Japanese students are routinely ranked higher than Indian and Chinese students in standardized tests internationally.

It might look surprising that a country like Singapore, that appears to be a lot more "modern" than the San Francisco Bay Area, contributed less to technological innovation than Silicon Valley. Singapore is a model of urban design and management. Silicon Valley is decades behind Singapore, meaning that it would probably take a century for Silicon Valley to catch up with Singapore's infrastructure projects, not to mention to match Singapore's architectural wonders. It's not only the subway and the quality of roads that are superior in Singapore: the Singaporean citizens are way more "high-tech" than their peers in Silicon Valley. Singaporeans had cell phones when they were still a rarity in Silicon Valley. Silicon Valley still has to match the Internet speed that Singaporeans have been enjoying for years.

People in Silicon Valley got the first taste of mobile payments a decade after it became commonplace in Singapore. However, hard as it may have tried, Singapore produced no Apple, Oracle, Google, or Facebook. The reason might be the very concept of what high-tech is. In Silicon Valley people need just a cubicle to work and a car to get there, given the horrible public transportation. They are perfectly happy living in a culturally poor place of ugly buildings and restaurant chains. In Singapore people expect a town that is comfortable; a nice place to live in. High-tech is a means to an end just like concrete and plastic. It is part of the urban fabric. It is one of the elements that contribute to making Singapore a model of urban design and management. In Silicon Valley, people are willing and even excited to be worked to death like slaves for the privilege of being part of the high-tech world that designs the tools of tomorrow, and for a tiny chance of becoming the next billionaire. In Singapore, there is nothing particularly prestigious about working in high tech. Prestige comes from using tech to do something that is relevant to society. Silicon Valley assumes that one can change the world just by releasing a new device or a new website that will spread virally. Singapore assumes that one can change the world by adopting whichever the best available tools are at the moment, and it is largely irrelevant who invented them; just like it's irrelevant who makes the blue jeans or the shoes that became popular after independence.

35. Conclusions about Silicon Valley and its Future

The Morphing Computer

The computer that drives a smartphone in 2013 is nearly a million times cheaper, a hundred thousand times smaller, and thousands of times more powerful than a mainframe of the 1970s. In less than four decades, the computing power that one can buy with the same amount of money has increased a billion times. The amount of data that one can store for $100 has also multiplied astronomically. A person can buy one terabyte for $100 in 2012 versus 28 megabytes for $115,500 in 1961 (the IBM 1301 Model 1); note that one tera is one million megas. The number of documents that one can print and mail has also increased by several orders of magnitude. The speed at which a document is transmitted has decreased from days to milliseconds, down nine orders of magnitude. The amount of free information available to the user of a computer has escalated from the documents of an office in the 1960s to the 30 billion webpages of the Web in 2013.

Originally, computing meant speed. A computer was a machine capable of performing computations in a fraction of a second that would have required many humans working for many days. Fifty years later, this simple concept has led to a completely different understanding of what computing meant. Computing power now means two things: access to an overwhelming amount of knowledge, and pervasive worldwide communication. The former has created a knowledge-based society, in which problems are solved by tapping into a vast and dynamic archive of knowledge; in a sense, the same utopia as artificial intelligence. The latter has created virtual communities. It is not obvious anymore how these two effects related to computing speed, the original purpose of computers.

The computer has transformed human society into a digital society, in which humans are creators, archivists, relayers, and browsers of digital data which encode world facts into Boolean algebra. It is a vastly more efficient way of encoding the world than the previous paper-based society. At the same time progress in telecommunication technology, and in particular the convergence of telecom and IT, has turned the innocent phone into an all-encompassing personal assistant that is only marginally used for voice communication.

The Valley Does Development, Little Research

Silicon Valley is widely viewed as the symbol of this revolution.

However, computers were not invented in Silicon Valley and Silicon Valley never had the largest hardware company or the largest software company in the world. Silicon Valley did not invent the transistor, integrated circuit, personal computer, Internet, World-Wide Web, the browser, the search engine, and social networking. Silicon Valley also did not invent the phone, cell phone, and smartphone. But, at one point in time or another, Silicon Valley was instrumental in making them go "viral," in perfecting a product the world wanted.

Silicon Valley's startups excelled at exploiting under-exploited inventions that came out of large East Coast and European R&D centers and somehow migrated to the Bay Area. AT&T, an East Coast company, invented semiconductor electronics and Shockley ported it to Mountain View. IBM, an East Coast company, invented data storage at its San Jose laboratories. Xerox, an East Coast company, perfected human-machine interfaces at its Palo Alto Research Center. The government invented the Internet and chose the SRI as one of the nodes. CERN, a European center, invented the World-wide Web and the first US server was assigned to the SLAC, and so forth.

In fact, Silicon Valley's largest research centers were never truly "research" centers but rather "R&D" (research and development) centers. They were more oriented towards the "D" than the "R." Nothing was comparable to AT&T's Bell Labs or to IBM's Watson labs, each of which produced Nobel Prize winners, unlike, say, HP Labs or Xerox PARC. One could argue that the "R" of Silicon Valley was done at Stanford University and UC Berkeley, but even those two research centers produced no monumental invention in the realm of high technology, nothing comparable to the transistor or to the World-Wide Web. They were much better at incubating businesses than at inventing the technology for those businesses.

Don't look at Silicon Valley to guess what the next big thing in high-tech will be: it is being invented somewhere else. Silicon Valley will pick it up if it promises to revolutionize the lives of ordinary people or workers.

There are many places in the world where much more sophisticated technology is created, from nuclear power plants to airplanes. But personal computers, web services, and smartphones have changed our lives in a more invasive and pervasive manner. Somehow those are the technologies in which Silicon Valley excels. It is not about the complexity and sophistication of the technology, but about the impact it will have on human society. In a sense, Silicon Valley "loves" socially destabilizing technologies. Silicon Valley has a unique, almost evil, knack for understanding the socially destabilizing potential of an invention and then making lots of money out of it. That's, ultimately, what people mean when they talk of Silicon Valley as a factory of innovation.

There was nothing intrinsic in the Silicon Valley model that made it work for computers in particular. Whatever it was, that model worked for high-tech in general. Silicon Valley represented a platform for perennial innovation that could be applied to other fields as well (such as biotech and greentech). It coincidentally started with "infotech," the first massively destructive industry since the electrical revolution.

The Silicon Valley model until 2000 could be summarized in three mottos: "question authority," "think different," and "change the world." Silicon Valley did not exist in a vacuum. It paralleled important sociopolitical upheavals that started in the San Francisco Bay Area and then spread all over the world, such as the free-speech movement and the hippie movement. Alternative lifestyles and utopian countercultures had always been in the genes of the Bay Area, starting with the early pioneers of the Far West. The propensity towards independence and individualism predates Silicon Valley's startups. That propensity led to the "do it yourself" philosophy of the hobbyists who started Silicon Valley. The hobbyists came first. Then came the great engineering schools, the massive government investment, the transfer of technology from academia to industry, and, at last, massive private investment. All of this would not have happened without that anti-establishment spirit which propelled the Bay Area to the front pages of newspapers worldwide during the 1960s. Many of today's protagonists of Silicon Valley are, consciously or not, part of or children of the generation that wanted to change the world. They did.

The history of the high-tech industry in the Bay Area, from Philo Farnsworth to Peter Thiel, is largely the history of a youth culture, just like the "other" history of the Bay Area, from the Gold Rush to the hippies, is a history of a youth culture. The protagonists were often extremely young, and almost invariably contributed the most significant ideas in their youth, just like rock musicians or mathematicians. One cannot separate the evolution of that youth culture and the evolution of the high-tech industry: they are each other's alter ego. In fact, the two biggest technological waves and financial bubbles were started by young people for a market of young people (personal computers and Internet, i.e. hobbyists and dotcoms). They represented the ultimate feedback loop of youth culture.

The eccentric independent is truly the protagonist of this story. Silicon Valley could not have happened in places that were not friendly towards the eccentric independent. For example, Europe was a place where employees had to wear a suit and tie in order to succeed. Therefore Europe created an upper class of people who were better at dressing up, and not necessarily the ones who were more knowledgeable, competent, and creative. In the Bay Area even billionaires wore blue jeans and t-shirts before and after becoming billionaires. Silicon Valley could not have happened on the East Coast either, for the same reason that the hippies and the free-speech movement were not born on the East Coast: the Bay Area was permeated by a unique strand of extravagant and idiosyncratic anti-establishment sentiment and by a firm belief in changing the world. The one place that came close to replicating Silicon Valley was Route 128 near

Boston, which was also the second most anti-establishment place in the nation.

However, the East Coast was similar to Europe and dissimilar from Silicon Valley in another respect: vertical instead of horizontal mobility. Europe and the East Coast encouraged employees to think of a career within a company, whereas Silicon Valley encouraged employees to think of switching jobs all the time. In Europe there was little motivation to hire someone from another company, since one could not recycle that person's skills legally, and it was even illegal to start a new business based on what one learned at a company. Hence Europe created big companies where people's main motivation was to get promote to higher and higher positions; and, typically, away from engineering. This praxis had the double effect of "detraining" engineers as they were shuffled around in search of better-sounding titles, and typically landed non-technical positions while limiting the flow of knowledge to the internal departments of a company. However, in Silicon Valley, engineers continuously refined their technical skills as they moved from company to company while at the same time facilitating a flow of knowledge from company to company.

Perhaps this was the ultimate reason why in Europe an engineering job was considered inferior to a marketing job or even to sales jobs, while in Silicon Valley the status symbol of being an engineer was only second to the status symbol of being an entrepreneur; and so was the salary. In Europe, marketing and sales people made more money and had better prospects than engineers. Europe converted tens of thousands of bright engineering talents into mediocre bureaucrats or sales people in suits and ties while Silicon Valley converted them into advisers to the board or founders of companies, in blue jeans and T-shirts.

It certainly didn't help Europe that it relied so much on the three "Bs" (big government, big labor, and big corporations) while Silicon Valley despised all three. However, the history of Silicon Valley and of computing in general shows that big government can be the greatest engine of innovation when it is driven by national interest, typically in times of war. Big corporations do work when they can afford to think long-term; for many years most innovation in computers came from AT&T and IBM, and in Silicon Valley they came from Xerox. Big labor was always absent from Silicon Valley, but in a sense it was volunteered by the companies themselves, like the HP model.

The role of big government, big corporations, and big labor in the success of Japan and Britain is instructive. The Japanese computer industry had to start from scratch in the 1950s. The failing British computer industry had pioneered computers in the 1940s and had all the know-how necessary to match developments in the US. In both cases the government engaged in sponsoring long-term plans and in brokering strategic alliances among manufacturers, and in both cases initial research came from a government-funded laboratory. However, the outcomes were completely opposite: Japan created a vibrant computer industry within the existing conglomerates, whereas Britain's computer industry self-destroyed within two decades.

Last and most importantly, the Bay Area managed to attract brains from all over the world. The competitive advantage derived from immigration was immense. Brains flocked to the Bay Area because the Bay Area was "cool." It projected the image of a dreamland for the highly educated youth of the East Coast, Europe and Asia. Because the Bay Area was underpopulated, those immigrants came to represent not an isolated minority but almost a majority, a fact that encouraged them to behave like first-class citizens and not just as hired mercenaries. The weather and money certainly mattered, but what attracted all those immigrants to the Bay Area was, ultimately, the anti-establishment spirit applied to a career. It made work feel like it wasn't work but a way to express one's self.

And, as usual, luck has its role: had William Shockley grown up in Tennessee instead of Palo Alto, maybe he would have never dreamed of starting his company in Mountain View, and therefore neither Fairchild nor Intel nor any of the dozens of companies founded by his alumni and the alumni of his alumni would be based in the Bay Area, or in California at all. All the reasons usually advanced to explain why Silicon Valley happened where it happened neglect the fact that the mother of all "silicon" startups was based there simply because Shockley wanted to go back where he grew up.

Some myths about Silicon Valley have been exaggerated and some truths have been downplayed. Mentorship, to start with, was not as important as claimed by the mentors. It was customary that the founder of a successful company received funding to start another company. This did work in terms of profitability, because the star-appeal brought both investors and customers, but it rarely resulted in technological breakthroughs. Recycling a successful entrepreneur was just an advanced form of marketing. In practice, the vast majority of quantum leaps forward in technology were provided by young newcomers who knew very little about the preexisting business.

One factor in the evolution that is often underestimated is how important the shortcomings of the established industry leaders have been to foster innovation. Apple completely missed the advent of the Internet, Google completely missed the advent of social networking, and Facebook will soon completely miss the "next big thing." Each of these blunders helped create a new giant and an entire new industry. If Apple had introduced a search engine in 2000, perhaps Google would never have existed, and if Google had introduced a social-networking platform in 2004, perhaps Facebook would never have existed. Each of them had the power to easily occupy the new niche, except that they failed to notice it. In most cases the founders and CEOs of Silicon Valley companies are visionaries in the narrow field in which they started, but not very skilled at noticing seismic shifts in the overall landscape.

The Bay Area was uniquely equipped with the mindset to subvert rules and embrace novelty. However, history would have been wildly different without the government's intervention. The Bay Area constitutes a prime example of technologies that moved from military to civilian use. The initial impulse to radio engineering and electronics came from the two world wars, and was largely funded by the military.

The first wave of venture capital for the high-tech industry was created by a government program. It was the US and UK governments that funded the development of the computer, and NASA was the main customer of the first integrated circuits. The Internet was invented by the government and then turned into a business by the government. Generally speaking, the federal government invested in high-risk long-term projects while venture capitalists tended to follow short-term trends. The US government was the largest venture capitalist of Silicon Valley, and the government of the US was also the most influential strategist of Silicon Valley; whereas, one could argue, venture capitalists mainly created speculative bubbles. However, even the "bubble ideology" has a positive function in Silicon Valley: it accelerates business formation and competition. It is difficult to tell which of those factors were essential to Silicon Valley becoming what it became.

There's another element to the success of Silicon Valley that is hard to quantify: the role of chance in creativity. Because of its lifestyle and values, Silicon Valley has always maximized the degree of chance. Work is often viewed as play, not duty. Fun and ideals prevail over money and status. Hence chance, hence creativity. From this point of view the importance of the arts is often underestimated: the Bay Area was famous as a refuge for "crazy" artists way before it became known as an incubator of startups. Like every other phenomenon in the world, Silicon Valley does not exist in a vacuum.

A tough question is why Silicon Valley worked for some sectors and not for others. It failed in laser applications, although it had a head start, and it never made a dent into factory automation, despite a head start in robotics. Perhaps the individual is not enough: it takes a community of inventors. The defense industry created that community for the radio engineering and the semiconductor industry. The venture capitalists are creating it for biotech and greentech. Factory automation, however, despite the potential of causing one of the most dramatic changes in human society, was largely left to heavy industry that was not based in the Bay Area. The Defense Department created that community elsewhere. The Japanese government created it in Japan. Nobody ever created it in Silicon Valley. The whole premise of numeric control (coupling processors with sensors) remains largely alien to Silicon Valley.

Conclusions about Silicon Valley and its Future

There have been attempts at creating "Silicon Valleys" around the world: Malaysia's Multimedia Super Corridor, Dubai's Internet City, Bangalore's eCity, China's Zhongguancun Science Park, etc. The closest thing to Silicon Valley outside the US has probably been Singapore, whose GDP of $182 billion in 2008 is less than half of the Bay Area's GDP of $427 billion. However, venture capitalists invested $1,370 per capita in the Bay Area in 2006 versus $180 per capita in Singapore and $107 per capita in New York state. Another close second could be Israel, a country rich with venture capitalists and high-tech companies; but Israel has been entangled in the perpetual political turmoil of the Middle East.

The only country that can compete with the US in terms of mass-scale innovation that has changed the daily lives of billions of people is Japan. However, Japanese innovation has mostly come from conglomerates that are a century old: Sony, Seiko, Yamaha, Nintendo, Fujitsu, Canon, Toyota, Mitsubishi, etc. It is hard to find a Japanese company that emerged due to a new technology and became a major player. The whole phenomenon of venture capitalists and high-tech startups has been trivial in Japan.

Many have written about the role of East Asian governments in the astronomical growth of their economies. Few have written about how much those economies owe to Silicon Valley. Both the venture capitalists and the startups of Silicon Valley contributed to creating the very economic boom of East Asia that then they set out to exploit. Silicon Valley literally engineered the high-tech boom in Taiwan and mainland China as much as those governments did. Those economies have become not what they wanted to become but precisely what Silicon Valley needed: highly efficient futuristic science parks with all the tools to cheaply and quickly mass produce the sophisticated components needed by Silicon Valley companies. The same is true for India: the large software parks such as the one in Bangalore have largely been shaped by the demand of software coming from Silicon Valley, not by a government-run program for the future of software technology. Whenever such programs exist, they often embody precisely the goal to serve the demand coming from the US. The "Golden Projects" of mainland China of the 1990s, that created the high-tech infrastructure of that country, would have been pointless without a major customer. That customer was Silicon Valley.

Asians point out that in 2009 their continent employs 1.5 million workers in the computer industry while the US employs only 166,000. That is true. But they forget to add that most of those 1.5 million jobs were created by Silicon Valley. Foxconn (Hon Hai Precision Industry) was founded in Taiwan in 1974 by Tai-Ming "Terry" Gou to manufacture plastic. In 1988, it opened a pioneering factory in China's then experimental city Shenzhen, became the world's largest manufacturer of electronics by 2009, with revenues of $62 billion. It dwarfed Apple and Intel, employing 800,000 people. However, its main customers were Apple, Intel, Cisco and Hewlett-Packard, besides Sony, Microsoft and

495
Conclusions about Silicon Valley and its Future

Motorola. In 2005 Taiwanese companies produced 80% of all personal digital assistants, 70% of all notebooks, and 60% of all flat-panel monitors.

This, of course, also translated into an interesting and somewhat unnerving social experiment: Silicon Valley was generating and investing ever larger sums of money, but creating an ever lower number of jobs. The investment and the profit were based here, but the jobs were based "there" in Asia. In fact, the Bay Area's unemployment rate in 2012 was close to 10%, one of the highest in the entire world. One could see a future when the low-level workers of the high-tech industry would start moving out of Silicon Valley towards Asia. The same was true of the other industries, from energy to biotech.

As China is rapidly emerging as an economic world power, its government has spent more than any other country in creating technology parks. It's unclear whether China as it is now exists will create its equivalent to Silicon Valley. One reason is that millions of websites are banned in China. Here are some of the consequences. First, there is an enormous amount of know-how that doesn't percolate through Chinese society. Second, it is impossible to raise a generation of creative kids when they can only "consume" what the government selects and mandates; it is a recipe for raising very dumb citizens. Third, no educated foreigner dreams of emigrating to China for the rest of his life such as millions of foreigners decide to move to California. Three key factors in the success of Silicon Valley are automatically removed when a government decides to ban websites at will: know-how, creativity, and immigration.

This is just one of the many changes that have dramatically altered what Silicon Valley used to be, and that makes nostalgic people pessimistic about the future. There are other examples. The creative eccentric of the 20th century has been replaced by a generation of disciplined but unimaginative "nerds" who would be helpless without a navigation system and a cell phone (or just without air conditioning). Government intervention in high-tech has been scaled down (as a percentage of the industry), with the result that there is less investment in long-term projects, and the public mood against "big government" leaves few hopes that the trend can be reversed any time soon.

One major trend is that immigration laws, economic downturns, and a chronically weak dollar have greatly reduced the number of graduate-level immigrants from other developed countries. The ones who come to study in the US and would like to stay have a hard time obtaining a work visa. The time-consuming and humiliating procedure to obtain a green card discourages even those who do obtain a work visa. It is impressive how many of the innovators of the Bay Area were not natives of the Bay Area. Immigration has been a true engine of innovation. At the same time, the tightly knit community of Silicon Valley has been ruined by the massive immigration of opportunists who don't have that spirit, and by the outsourcing of jobs to India that has disenfranchised the engineer from her/his company.

The two recessions of the 2000s created a culture of extreme pragmatism in the industry. The proverbial family-style management pioneered by HP has turned into a 60-hour workweek with virtually no vacation days and indiscriminate layoffs whenever needed. Both companies and employees have become opportunists instead of idealists.

The growing power of lawyers introduced another degree of distortion in the system: the chances of being laid off by a company are becoming inversely proportional to how much one is willing to pay for an attorney. An attorney is more likely to obtain something from a company on behalf of an employee than the employee through her or his work. This is beginning to replicate the problems that Europe has with unionized labor, except that it is much more expensive to defend one's job in the Bay Area through a lawyer than to defend one's job in Europe through the unions.

The academic environment offers mixed news. On one hand, Silicon Valley's stellar technical schools still act as an incubator of startups. On the other hand, each college and university has greatly expanded the activities for students to the point that it has become a walled city. Students do not find the time to stick their neck outside the campus. This does not encourage interaction with other cultural environments. One can argue that such a closed system is designed to create hyper-specialists and stifle creativity.

Meanwhile, the infrastructure of Silicon Valley and of the US in general risks falling behind the ones in the most advanced European countries of Asia and Europe. Gone are the days when it was Asians and Europeans who would marvel at the transportation, the technology, and the gadgets of Silicon Valley. It is now the other way around. Silicon Valley does not have anything that even remotely resembles the futuristic clean and fast public transportation of Far Eastern metropolises (the magnetic levitation trains, the multi-layered monorails, the bullet trains). Its households have to live with one of the slowest and most expensive "high-speed" Internet services in the world. Cellular phone coverage is poor everywhere and non-existent just a few kilometers outside urban areas. US tourists abroad marvel at what the Japanese and the Germans can do with their phones. South Korea plans to connect every single home in the country at one gigabit per second by the end of 2012, which is about 85 times the average speed provided to Silicon Valley homes in 2011 by the number one Internet provider, whose marketing campaing labels it as "blazing speed."

There are other fields in which the Bay Area suffers from national diseases. Obtuse immigration laws are keeping away the best brains of the world and sending away the ones that manage to graduate in the US. And this happens at a time when countries from Canada to Chile have programs in place to attract foreign brains. At the same time, a growing wealth gap has created an educational system that disproportionally favors the children of the rich: if a student graduates from Stanford, it's likely she is from a rich family, not necessarily a world-class student.

Unlike the other high-tech regions of the world, the boring, nondescript, urban landscape of Silicon Valley was the epitome of no creativity, no originality, no personality, and no style. It is difficult to find another region and time in history that witnessed an extraordinary industrial boom without producing a single building worthy of becoming a historical monument. Finally, the high-tech industry of the Bay Area has produced no Nobel Prize, unlike, say, the Bell Labs, another high-tech power-house.

There is another dimension in which Silicon Valley has changed significantly. Until the 2000s, Silicon Valley had never witnessed a case in which the leaders of a technological or business revolution where all based in Silicon Valley itself. Intel was dominant in microprocessors, but its competitors (Motorola, the Japanese) were located outside California. HP was a major personal-computer maker but its competitors were located outside California (IBM, Compaq, Dell, the Japanese and Taiwanese). Apple and Netscape were briefly dominant in their sectors but they were quickly defeated by the Microsoft world. Oracle faced competition from IBM in databases and from SAP in ERP.

The 2000s, instead, have witnessed an increasing concentration of power in Silicon Valley, as the companies vying for supremacy have become Google, Apple, and Oracle. Google is becoming the monopolist of web search. Apple is becoming the reference point for hand-held communication devices. Oracle is becoming the behemoth of business software. Each of them is trying to impose not only its products but also its view of the world as the world moves towards cloud computing. Google is Internet-centric. Apple is device-centric. Oracle is server-centric. Each indirectly assumes that their business models are not compatible: two have to die. It is the first time in the history of Silicon Valley that not two but three local firms are engaged in such a deadly struggle. This constitutes a moral rupture in the traditional "camaraderie" of Silicon Valley.

The 2010s were also the first time ever that Silicon Valley was not about "being small" but being big: Intel (the number-one semiconductor company), Oracle (number one in ERP), Apple (most valuable company in the world), Google (by far number one in web search), Facebook and LinkedIN (number one and two in social networking), Cisco (number one in routers), and HP (number one in personal computers). These were large multinational corporations, the kind that did not exist in Silicon Valley in the old days. Silicon Valley was originally about "being small." As Silicon Valley becomes a place for big corporations, the attitude towards risk-taking might change too.

However, the exuberant creativity boom of the previous decades has left a durable legacy: a culture of risk-taking coupled with a culture of

Conclusions about Silicon Valley and its Future

early adoption of new inventions. And it is more than a culture: it is a whole infrastructure designed to promote, assist, and reward risk-takers in new technologies. That infrastructure consists not only of laboratories and plants, but also of corporate lawyers, marketing agencies, head hunters, and, of course, investors. After all, the culture of "inventing" was never all that strong in the Bay Area, whereas the culture of turning an invention into a successful product has always been its specialty; and it may even be stronger than ever.

It has become easier than ever to start a company. The entry point is getting lower and lower. It is inevitable that sooner or later Silicon Valley will produce the Mozart of the Web, a child prodigy who will create a successful tech business at age 8 or 10.

Silicon Valley is the engine of a world in which people are plugging into the Web because of a smartphone, searching for information because of Google, socializing on the Web because of Facebook, shopping on the Web because of eBay, and paying on the Web because of PayPal. Soon that world will also offer biotech tools for "human life extension" and greentech devices for ubiquitous low-cost energy.

Silicon Valley is not booming anymore: it has become the very process of booming. Silicon Valley was an alternate universe. It is now gobbling up the rest of the universe.

36. A Timeline of Silicon Valley

Lines in parentheses are events that did not occur in the Bay Area but affected the development of computers.

(1885: William Burroughs develops an adding machine)

1887: The Lick Observatory is erected near San Jose, the world's first permanently occupied mountain-top observatory

(1890: Hermann Hollerith's tabulator is chosen for the national census)

1891: Leland and Jane Stanford found Stanford University near Palo Alto

(1906: Lee DeForest invents the vacuum tube)

1906: The San Francisco earthquake and fire

1909: Stanford University's President David Starr Jordan invests $500 in Lee DeForest's audion tube, the first major venture-capital investment in the region

1909: Charles Herrold in San Jose starts the first radio station in the US with regularly scheduled programming

1909: Cyril Elwell founds the Federal Telegraph Corporation (FTC) in Palo Alto to create the world's first global radio communication system

(1911: Hollerith's Tabulating Machine Company is acquired by a new company that will change name to International Business Machines or IBM in 1924)

1915: The Panama-Pacific International Exposition is held in San Francisco, for which Bernard Maybeck builds the Palace of Fine Arts in San Francisco

1916: General Motors opens a large Chevrolet automobile factory in Oakland

1917: Edwin Pridham and Peter Jensen found the electronics company Magnavox in Napa

1921: Ansel Adams publishes his first photographs of Yosemite

1925: Frederick Terman joins Stanford University to teach electronics and electrical engineering and encourages his students to start businesses in California

(1925: Burroughs introduces a portable adding machine)

(1925: AT&T and Western Electric form the Bell Labs in New York)

1927: Philo Farnsworth invents all-electronic television broadcasting while in San Francisco

(1927: Fritz Pfleumer in Germany invents magnetic tape)

1929: The physicist Robert Oppenheimer joins UC Berkeley

1931: Ernest Lawrence designs the first successful cyclotron and founds the Lawrence Berkeley Laboratories

1933: The Navy opens a base at NAS Sunnyvale (later renamed Moffett Field)

1934: The first lesbian nightclub opens in San Francisco, "Mona's"

(1935: Germany's AEG introduces the first tape recorder)

1936: San Francisco builds the longest bridge in the world, the "Bay Bridge"

1936: Joe Finocchio opens the gay bar "Finocchio's" in San Francisco

(1936: John Lawrence, brother of Lawrence Berkeley Labs' founder, starts the Donner Laboratory to conduct research in nuclear medicine

(1937: Alan Turing describes a machine capable of performing logical reasoning, the "Turing Machine")

1937: Stanford University's Professor William Hansen teams with brothers Sigurd and Russell Varian to develop the klystron tube, used in the early radars

1937: The Golden Gate Bridge is completed in San Francisco

(1938: John Atanasoff at Iowa State College conceives the electronic digital computer)

1939: Fred Terman's students, William Hewlett and David Packard, start a company to produce their audio-oscillator

1939: Walt Disney becomes the first customer of Hewlett-Packard, purchasing their oscillator for the animation film "Fantasia"

1939: Ernest Lawrence is awarded the Nobel Prize in Physics

1939: The US government establishes the Ames Aeronautical Laboratory (later renamed Ames Research Center) at Moffett Field

1941: Stanford University's Professor Fred Terman is put in charge of the top-secret Harvard Radio Research Laboratory

1941: Glenn Seaborg and Edwin McMillan at UC Berkeley produce a new element, plutonium

1942: The US government launches the "Manhattan Project" to build a nuclear bomb under the direction of Robert Oppenheimer

1942: The health-care organization Kaiser Permanente is founded in Oakland

(1943: Tommy Flowers and others build the Colossus, the world's first programmable digital electronic computer)

(1943: Warren McCulloch and Walter Pitts describe an artificial neuron)

1944: Frank Malina founds the Jet Propulsion Laboratory (JPL)

1944: Alexander Poniatoff founds Ampex

(1944: Howard Aiken of IBM unveils the first computer programmed by punched paper tape, the Harvard Mark I)

(1945: Vannevar Bush proposes the "Memex" desk-based machine)

(1940: John Von Neumann designs a computer that holds its own instructions)

(1945: IBM establishes the Watson Scientific Computing Laboratory (later Watson Research Center) at Columbia University in New York)

1946: The Stanford Research Institute is founded

1946: Blacks constitute about 12% of Oakland's population

(1946: The first venture capital firms are founded in the U.S., American Research and Development Corporation (ARDC) by former Harvard Business School's dean Georges Doriot, J.H. Whitney & Company by John Hay Whitney, Rockefeller Brothers by Laurance Rockefeller (later renamed Venrock)

1946: John Northrop and Wendell Stanley of UC Berkeley are awarded the Nobel Prize in Chemistry

1946: Fred Terman returns to Stanford University as the dean of the engineering school and founds the Electronics Research Lab (ERL), mostly founded by the US military

(1946: The first non-military computer, ENIAC, or "Electronic Numerical Integrator and Computer," is unveiled, built by John Mauchly and Presper Eckert at the University of Pennsylvania

(1947: AT&T Bell Telephone Laboratory's engineers John Bardeen, William Shockley and Walter Brattain demonstrate the principle of amplifying an electrical current using a solid semiconducting material, i.e. the "transistor")

(1947: Norbert Wiener founds Cybernetics)

(1947: John Von Neumann describes self-reproducing automata)

1947: Ampex introduces a magnetic tape recorder

1948: The Varian brothers found Varian Associates

(1948: Claude Shannon founds Information Theory and coins the term "bit")

(1949: William Giauque of UC Berkeley is awarded the Nobel Prize in Chemistry)

1950: Turing proposes a test to determine whether a machine is intelligent or not

(1950: Remington purchases Eckert-Mauchly Computer)

1951: The Stanford Industrial Park is conceived

1951: Glenn Seaborg and Edwin McMillan of UC Berkeley are awarded the Nobel Prize

(1951: The first commercial computer is built, the Univac)

(1951: A team led by Jay Forrester at MIT builds the "Whirlwind" computer, the first real-time system and the first computer to use a video display for output)

1952: IBM opens its first West Coast laboratory in San Jose (later Almaden Research Center)

1952: Felix Bloch of Stanford University is awarded the Nobel Prize in Physics, the first for Stanford

1952: The Atomic Energy Commission establishes a Livermore Laboratory as a branch of the UC Berkeley's Radiation Laboratory

1953: Varian is the first tenant of the Stanford Industrial Park

1953: The CIA finances a project named "MkUltra" to study the effects of psychoactive drugs

1953: Electronics manufacturer Sylvania opens its Electronic Defense Lab (EDL) in Mountain View

1953: Lawrence Ferlinghetti founds a bookstore in San Francisco, "City Lights," that becomes the headquarters of alternative writers

(1954: Remington Rand introduces UNIVAC 1103, the first computer with magnetic-core RAM)

(1954: IBM introduces its first computer model, the 704)

1954: David Bohannon opens the Hillsdale Shopping Center, a suburban shopping mall

1955: The Stanford Research Institute demonstrates the ERMA computer

1956: IBM's San Jose labs invent the hard-disk drive

Mar 1956: UC Berkeley Professor Harry Huskey designs Bendix's first digital computer, the G-15

(1954: George Devol designs the first industrial robot, Unimate)

1955: The first conference on Artificial Intelligence is held at Dartmouth College, organized by John McCarthy

1955: The "Daughters of Bilitis" is founded in San Francisco, the first exclusively Lesbian organization in the US

1955: Stanford University hires Carl Djerassi

1955: Allen Ginsberg's recitation of his poem "Howl" transplants the "Beat" aesthetic to San Francisco

1955: Private investors or "angels" (including John Bryan, Bill Edwards and Reid Dennis) establish "The Group" to invest together in promising companies

(1955: Alexander Schure founds the New York Institute of Technology)

(1955: Remington Rand merges with Sperry to form Sperry Rand)

1955: Stanford University merges the Applied Electronics Laboratory and the Electronics Research Laboratory into the Systems Engineering Laboratory under the direction of Fred Terman and focusing on electronic warfare

1956: William Shockley founds the Shockley Transistor Corporation in Mountain View to produce semiconductor-based transistors to replace vacuum tubes, and hires Robert Noyce, Gordon Moore and others

1956: Charles Ginsburg of Ampex Corporation builds the first practical videotape recorder

1956: Aircraft-company Lockheed opens an electronics research laboratory in the Stanford Industrial Park and a manufacturing facility in Sunnyvale

(1956: Werner Buchholz of IBM coins the term "byte")

(Apr 1957: John Backus of IBM introduces the FORTRAN programming language, the first practical machine-independent language)

Oct 1957: Several engineers (including Robert Noyce and Gordon Moore) quit the Shockley Transistor laboratories and form Fairchild Semiconductor in Mountain View, using funding from Fairchild Camera and Instrument

(1957: ARDC invests $70,000 in Digital Equipment Corporation (DEC)

(1957: Max Mathews begins composing computer music at Bell Laboratories)

1957: Dean Watkins of Stanford's ERL founds Watkins-Johnson, one of the first venture-capital funded companies in the Santa Clara Valley

(1957: Allen Newell and Herbert Simon develop the "General Problem Solver")

(1957: Frank Rosenblatt conceives the "Perceptron," a neural computer that can learn by trial and error)

(1957: Morton Heilig invents the "Sensorama Machine," a pioneering virtual-reality environment)

(1957: Former SAGE engineer Ken Olsen founds the Digital Equipment Corporation)

1957: Rockefeller Brothers invests in Fairchild Semiconductor, the first venture-funded startup of the Bay Area

(1958: Jack Kilby at Texas Instruments invents the integrated circuit, a micro-sized silicon device containing a large number of electronic switches)

(1958: Charles Townes of Columbia theorizes about an optical laser and his student Gordon Gould builds one and names it "LASER" or "Light Amplification by the Stimulated Emission of Radiation")

1958: Draper, Gaither and Anderson is founded, the first professional venture-capital firm in California

1958: NASA opens a research center near Mountain View

1959: The first commercial Xerox plain-paper photocopier goes on sale

1959: Eveready (later renamed Energizer) introduces the alkaline battery

1959: Jean Hoerni at Fairchild Semiconductor invents the planar process that enables great precision in silicon components, and Robert Noyce at Fairchild Semiconductor designs a planar integrated circuit

1959: Dancer and mime Ron Davis founds the San Francisco Mime Troupe

1959: Arthur Kornberg of Stanford University is awarded the Nobel Prize in Medicine

1959: Emilio Segre and Owen Chamberlain of the Lawrence Berkeley Labs are awarded the Nobel Prize for the discovery of the antiproton

1959: Frank Chambers founds the venture-capital company Continental Capital

1959: GTE buys Sylvania

1959: Several Stanford students volunteer to take part in the CIA project "MkUltra" to study the effects of psychoactive drugs

(1960: William Fetter of Boeing coins the expression "computer graphics")

(1960: Digital Equipment introduces the first minicomputer, the PDP-1 (Program Data Processor), that comes with a keyboard and a monitor

(1960: Theodore Maiman of the Hughes Research Laboratory demonstrates the first working laser)

1960: Donald Glaser of the Lawrence Berkeley Labs is awarded the Nobel Prize

1960: Wayne Thiebaud at UC Davis pioneers "pop art"

1960: John McCarthy speculates that "computation may someday be organized as a public utility"

(1961: Joe Orlicky of JI Case pioneers Material Requirements Planning or MRP)

1961: Laurence Spitters founds Memorex

(1961: Max Palevsky forms Scientific Data Systems)

(1961: Charles Bachman at General Electric develops the first database management system, IDS)

(1961: Philco unveils the first head-mounted display)

(1961: Fernando Corbato at MIT creates the first working time-sharing system, CTSS or "Compatible Time Sharing System," that allowed to remotely access a computer, an IBM 7090/94)

(1961: IBM owns more than 81% of the computer market)

(1961: General Motors unveils "Unimate," the first industrial robot)

1961: Robert Hofstadter of Stanford University is awarded the Nobel Prize in Physics

1961: Melvin Calvin of the Lawrence Berkeley Labs is awarded the Nobel Prize

1961: Tommy Davis founds one of Santa Clara Valley's first venture-capital firms with Arthur Rock, Davis & Rock

1962: The San Francisco Tape Music Center for avantgarde music is established by composers Morton Subotnick and Ramon Sender

(1962: Paul Baran proposes a distributed network as the form of communication least vulnerable to a nuclear strike)

(1962: Steve Russell and others at MIT implement the computer game "Spacewar" on a PDP-1)

1962: Stanford University founds the Stanford Linear Accelerator Center (SLAC)

1962: Bill Draper and Franklin Johnson form the venture-capital firm Draper and Johnson Investment Company

1962: Michael Murphy founds the "Esalen Institute" at Big Sur to promote spiritual healing

(1962: The first commercial modem is manufactured by AT&T)

1963: Douglas Engelbart at the Stanford Research Institute builds the first prototype of the "mouse"

1963: John McCarthy moves to Stanford

1963: Syntex, a pioneer of biotechnology, moves from Mexico City to the Stanford Industrial Park

(1963: The "American Standard Code for Information Interchange" or "ASCII" is introduced

(1963: Ivan Sutherland of MIT demonstrates "Sketchpad," a computer graphics program, and the first program ever with a graphical user interface)

(1964: IBM introduces the first "mainframe" computer, the 360, and the first "operating system," the OS/360)

1964: Syntex introduces the birth-control pill

1964: Tymshare starts one of the most popular time-sharing service and creates a circuit-switched network

(1964: Robert Moog begins selling his synthesizer)

1964: Mario Savio founds the "Free Speech Movement" and leads student riots at the Berkeley campus

1964: Bill Draper and Paul Wythes form Sutter Hill Ventures

1964: MkUltra's alumnus Ken Kesey organizes the "Merry Pranksters" who travel around the country in a "Magic Bus," live in a commune in La Honda and experiment with "acid tests" (LSD)

(1964: John Kemeny and Thomas Kurtz (at Dartmouth College) invent the BASIC programming language)

(1964: American Airlines' SABRE reservation system, developed by IBM, is the first online transaction processing

1964: Former Sylvania employee Bill Perry founds computer-based electronic-intelligence company ESL

1965: Gordon Moore predicts that the processing power of computers will double every 18 months ("Moore's law")

Sep 1965: Ben Jacopetti inaugurates the Open Theater as a vehicle devoted to multimedia performances for the Berkeley Experimental Arts Foundation

1965: Owsley "Bear" Stanley synthesizes crystalline LSD

1965: Ed Feigenbaum implements the first "expert system," Dendral

1965: Lotfi Zadeh invents Fuzzy Logic

1965: George Hunter of the Charlatans introduces the "light show" in rock concerts

1965: Former Ampex employee Ray Dolby founds the Dolby Labs while in Britain (relocating it to San Francisco in 1976)

1965: Ron Davis of the San Francisco Mime Troupe publishes the essay "Guerrilla Theatre"

1965: The Family Dog Production organizes the first hippie festival in San Francisco

1965: Terry Riley composes "In C," music based on repetition of simple patterns ("minimalism")

1965: Edward Feigenbaum leads development of the expert system "Dendral" at Stanford University

(1965: The Digital Equipment Corporation unveils the first successful mini-computer, the PDP-8, which uses integrated circuits)

(1965: European computer manufacturer Olivetti introduces the first affordable programmable electronic desktop computer, the P101)

1966: Stewart Brand organizes the "Trips Festival" putting together Ken Kesey's "Acid Test," Jacopetti's Open Theater, Sender's Tape Music Center and rock bands

1966: John McCarthy opens the Stanford Artificial Intelligence Laboratory (SAIL)

1966: The first "Summer of Love" of the hippies is held in San Francisco, and a three-day "Acid Test" is held in San Francisco with the Grateful Dead performing

1966: Hewlett-Packard enters the business of general-purpose computers with the HP-2115

1966: Willie Brown organizes the Artists Liberation Front of San Francisco-based artists at the Mime Troupe's Howard Street loft

1966: The first issue of the San Francisco Oracle, an underground cooperative publication, is published

1966: Emmett Grogan and members of the Mime Troupe found the "Diggers," a group of improvising actors and activists whose stage was the streets and parks of the Haight-Ashbury and whose utopia was the creation of a Free City

1966: Huey Newton, Bobby Seale, Angela Davis and other African-American activists found the socialist-inspired and black-nationalist "Black Panther Party" at Oakland

1966: There are 2,623 computers in the US (1,967 work for the Defense Department)

1966: Donald Buchla develops a voltage-controlled synthesizer for composer Morton Subotnick, the Buchla Modular Electronic Music System

1966: The Asian Art Museum of San Francisco is inaugurated

(1967: Jack Kilby (at Texas Instruments) develops the first hand-held calculator)

1967: A "Human Be-In" is held at the Golden Gate Park in San Francisco

1967: Monterey hosts a rock festival

1968: Stewart Brand publishes the first "Whole Earth Catalog"

1968: David Evans and Ivan Sutherland form Evans & Sutherland

1968: Philip Noyce, Gordon Moore and Andy Grove found Intel ("Integrated Electronics") to build memory chips

(1968: The hypertext system FRESS created by Andries van Dam at Brown University for the IBM 360 introduces the "undo" feature)

(1968: ARDC's investment in Digital Equipment Corporation (DEC) is valued at $355 million

(1968: Computer Science Corp becomes the first software company to be listed at the New York stock market)

(1968: Dutch mathematician Edsger Dijkstra writes "GO TO Statement Considered Harmful")

(1968: Barclays Bank installs networked "automated teller machines" or ATMs)

1968: John Portman designs the Embarcadero Center in San Francisco

1968: William Hambrecht and George Quist found the investment company Hambrecht & Quist in San Francisco

1968: Frank Malina founds Leonardo ISAST in Paris, an organization devoted to art/science fusion

1968: John Bryan and Bill Edwards found the investment company Bryan & Edwards

1968: Doug Engelbart of the Stanford Research Institute demonstrates the NLS ("oN-Line System"), the first system to employ the mouse

1968: Luis Alvarez of the Lawrence Berkeley Labs is awarded the Nobel Prize

1969: Gary Starkweather of Xerox invents the laser printer

1969: Xerox buys Scientific Data Systems (SDS)

1969: Advanced Micro Devices is founded by Jerry Sanders and other engineers from Fairchild Semiconductor

1969: The Stanford Research Institute (SRI) demonstrates Shakey the Robot

1969: Frank Oppenheimer founds the San Francisco Exploratorium as a museum of science, art and human perception

1969: Construction begins at 3000 Sand Hill Road, in Menlo Park, soon to become the headquarters of the venture-capital community

(1969: Ted Codd of IBM invents the relational database)

1969: Bell Labs unveils the Unix operating system developed by Kenneth Thompson and Dennis Ritchie

1969: The computer network Arpanet is inaugurated with four nodes, three of which are in California (UCLA, Stanford Research Institute and UC Santa Barbara)

1969: Leo Laurence in San Francisco calls for the "Homosexual Revolution"

1969: Four Stanford students found ROLM to design computers for the military

1970: Intel introduces the first commercially successful 1K DRAM chip

1970: 1970 Lee Boysel at Four Phase Systems designs the AL1, a commercial microprocessors (an 8-bit CPU)

1970: The first "San Francisco Gay Pride Parade" is held in San Francisco

1970: Gays and lesbians start moving to the "Castro" district of San Francisco in large numbers

(1970: The first practical optical fiber is developed by glass maker Corning Glass Works)

(1970: Edgar Codd at IBM introduces the concept of a relational database)

1970: Five of the seven largest US semiconductor manufacturers are located in Santa Clara Valley

1970: Xerox opens the Palo Alto Research Center or PARC

1970: Alan Kay joins Xerox PARC to work on object-oriented programming

1970: Charles Walton invents Radio Frequency Identification (RFID)

1970: Stanford's Ed Feigenbaum launches the Heuristic Programming Project for research in Artificial Intelligence

1971: Cetus, the first biotech company, is founded in Berkeley

1971: Pierluigi Nervi builds St Mary's Cathedral in San Francisco

1971: Berkeley's nuclear physicist Donald Glaser founds Cetus Corporation, the first biotech company of the Bay Area

1971: Film director George Lucas founds the film production company Lucasfilm

1971: David Noble at IBM invents the floppy disk

1971: Nolan Bushnell and Ted Dabney create the first arcade video game, "Computer Space"

1971: Ted Hoff and Federico Faggin at Intel build the first universal microprocessor, a programmable set of integrated circuits, i.e. a computer on a chip

1971: Intel unveils the first commercially available microprocessor, the 4004

1972: At least 60 semiconductor companies have been founded in Silicon Valley between 1961 and 1972, mostly by former Fairchild engineers and managers

1972: European manufacturer Olivetti establishes an Advanced Technology Centre (ATC) in Cupertino

1972: Intel introduces the 8008 microprocessor, whose eight-bit word allowed to represent 256 characters, including all ten digits, both uppercase and lowercase letters and punctuation marks

1972: Magnavox introduces the first videogame console, the "Odyssey"

1972: Nolan Bushnell invents the first videogame, "Pong," an evolution of Magnavox's Odyssey, and founds Atari

1972: Venture-capitalist company Kleiner-Perkins, founded by Austrian-born Eugene Kleiner of Fairchild Semiconductor and former Hewlett-Packard executive Tom Perkins, opens offices in Menlo Park on Sand Hill Road, followed by Don Valentine of Fairchild Semiconductor who founds Capital Management Services, later renamed Sequoia Capital

1972: Electronics writer Don Hoeffler coins the term "Silicon Valley"

(1972: A novel by David Gerrold coins the term "computer virus")

(1972: The Global Positioning System (GPS) is invented by the US military, using a constellation of 24 satellites for navigation and positioning purposes)

(1972: Ray Tomlinson at Bolt, Beranek and Newman invents e-mail for sending messages between computer users, and invents a system to identify the user name and the computer name separated by a "@")

(1972: IBM engineers in Mannheim, Germany, found Systemanalyse und Programmentwicklung or SAP)

1972: Bruce Buchanan leads development of the expert system "Mycin" at Stanford University

1972: European computer manufacturer Olivetti opens a research center in Cupertino (the "Advanced Technology Centre")

1973: Lynn Hershman creates the first site-specific installation, "The Dante Hotel"

1973: Efrem Lipkin, Mark Szpakowski, and Lee Felsenstein start the "Community Memory," the first public computerized bulletin board system

1973: Stanley Cohen of Stanford University and Herbert Boyer of UCSF create the first recombinant DNA organism, virtually inventing "biotechnology"

(1973: Automatic Electronic Systems of Canada introduces the "AES-90," a "word processor" that combines a CRT-screen, a floppy-disk and a microprocessor)

(1973: Vietnamese-born engineer Andre Truong Trong Thi uses the 8008 to build the computer Micral)

(1973: Japan's Sharp develops the LCD or "Liquid Crystal Display" technology)

1973: Intel introduces a CPU named 8088

1973: William Pereira builds the Transamerica Pyramid in San Francisco

(1973: Martin Cooper at Motorola invents the first portable, wireless or "cellular" telephone)

1973: Vinton Cerf of Stanford University coins the term "Internet"

1973: Xerox PARC's Bob Metcalfe coins the term "Ethernet" for a local area network

1973: The Arpanet has 2,000 users

1973: Gary Kildall in Monterey invents the first operating system for a microprocessor, the CP/M

1974: Ed Roberts invents the first personal computer, the Altair 8800

1974: Donald Chamberlin at IBM's San Jose laboratories invents SQL

1974: Xerox's PARC unveils the "Alto," the first workstation with a "mouse"

1974: Spectra-Physics builds the first bar-code scanner ever used in a store

1974: Paul Flory of Stanford University is awarded the Nobel Prize in Chemistry

1974: Reid Dennis and Burton McMurtry found the investment company Institutional Venture Associates

1974: Philips acquires Magnavox

1974: Tommy Davis launches the Mayfield Fund

1974: Vint Cerf of Stanford and others publish the Transmission Control Protocol (TCP)

1974: The Ant Farm art collective creates the installation "Cadillac Farm"

(1974: The Polish geneticist Waclaw Szybalski coins the term "synthetic biology")

1975: Xerox PARC debuts the first GUI or "Graphical User Interface"

1975: Advanced Micro Devices introduces a reverse-engineered clone of the Intel 8080 microprocessor

1967: John Chowning at Stanford University invents frequency modulation synthesis that allows an electronic instrument to simulate the sound of orchestral instruments

1975: John Chowning and Leland Smith at Stanford found a computer music lab, later renamed Center for Computer Research in Music and Acoustics (CCRMA)

(1975: Ed Catmull and Alvy Ray Smith establish the Computer Graphics Laboratory at the New York Institute of Technology)

(1975: Ed Roberts in New Mexico introduces the Altair 8800 based on an Intel microprocessor and sold as a mail-order kit)

(1975: Bill Gates and Paul Allen develop a version of BASIC for the Altair personal computer and found Microsoft)

1975: Steve Wozniak and others found the "Homebrew Computer Club"

(1975: John Holland describes genetic algorithms)

1976: Steve Wozniak and Steve Jobs form Apple Computer and build the first microcomputer in Jobs' garage in Cupertino.

1976: Stanford University researchers (Martin Hellman, Ralph Merkle and Whitfield Diffie) describe the concept of public-key cryptography

1976: Bill Joy writes the "vi" text editor for Unix

1976: William Ackerman founds Windham Hill to promote his "new age" music

1976: Burton Richter of Stanford University is awarded the Nobel Prize in Physics

1976: Biochemist Herbert Boyer and venture capitalist Robert Swanson found Genentech, the first major biotech company

(1976: Ed Catmull and Fred Parke's computer animation in a scene of the film "Futureworld" is the first to use 3D computer graphics)

1976: Institutional Venture Associates splits into two partnerships, McMurtry's Technology Venture Associates and Dennis' Institutional Venture Partners

1976: ROLM introduces a digital switch, the CBX (a computer-based PBX)

(1976: MOS Technology introduces the 6502 processor)

1977: Steve Jobs and Steve Wozniak develop the Apple II using the 6502 processor

1977: Bill Joy at UC Berkeley ships the first BSD version of Unix

1974: IBM's San Jose laboratories unveils the relational database system System R

1977: 27,000 people are employed in the Semiconductor industry of Silicon Valley

1977: San Francisco's city supervisor Harvey Milk becomes the first openly gay man to be elected to office in the US

1977: George Coates founds his multimedia theater group, Performance Works

1977: UC Berkeley develops the "Berkeley Software Distribution" (BSD), better known as "Berkeley Unix," a variant of the Unix operating system

Aug 1977: Larry Ellison founds the Software Development Laboratories, later renamed Oracle Corporation

1977: Atari introduces a videogame console, the 2600, based on the 6502 processor

1977: Dave Smith builds the "Prophet 5," the world's first microprocessor-based musical instrument, the first polyphonic and programmable synthesizer

(1977: Dennis Hayes of National Data Corporation invents the PC modem, a device that converts between analog and digital signals)

(1978: Toshihiro Nishikado creates the first blockbuster videogame, "Space Invaders")

1978: The rainbow flag debuts at the San Francisco Gay and Lesbian Freedom Day Parade

(1978: Mark Pauline founds the Survival Research Laboratories

1978: Apple launches a project to design a personal computer with a graphical user interface

1978: Atari announces the Atari 800, designed by Jay Miner

1979: Dan Bricklin develops VisiCalc, the first spreadsheet program for personal computers

1979: Larry Michels founds the first Unix consulting company, Santa Cruz Operation (SCO)

1979: Michael Stonebraker at UC Berkeley unveils a relational database system, Ingres

1979: University of California at Berkeley launches the "Search for Extraterrestrial Radio Emissions from Nearby Developed Intelligent Populations" project or "Serendip"

1979: Lucasfilm hires Ed Catmull from the New York Institute of Technology to lead the Graphics Group of its Computer Division

1979: Kevin MacKenzie invents symbols such as :-), or "emoticons," to mimic the cues of face-to-face communication

1979: John Shoch of Xerox's PARC coins the term "worm" to describe a program that travels through a network of computers

1980: The Arpanet has 430,000 users, who exchange almost 100 million e-mail messages a year

1980: John Searle publishes the article on the "Chinese Room" that attacks Artificial Intelligence

1980: Sonya Rapoport creates the interactive audio/visual installation "Objects on my Dresser"

1980: The largest semiconductor manufacturers in the world are: Texas Instruments, National, Motorola, Philips (Europe), Intel, NEC (Japan), Fairchild, Hitachi (Japan) and Toshiba (Japan).

1980: Seagate Technology introduces the first hard-disk drive for personal computers

1980: Doug and Gary Carlston found the videogame company Broderbund

1980: Paul Berg of Stanford University is awarded the Nobel Prize in Chemistry

1980: Polish writer Czeslaw Milosz of UC Berkeley is awarded the Nobel Prize in Literature

1980: Integrated circuits incorporate 100,000 discrete components

1980: The Usenet is born, an Arpanet-based discussion system divided in "newsgroups"

1980: Apple goes public for a record $1.3 billion

1980: UC Davis researchers found biotech company Calgene

1980: John Doerr joins Kleiner, Perkins, Caufield, and Byers

1980: Ed Feigenbaum and others found IntelliGenetics (later Intellicorp), an early Artificial Intelligence and biotech startup

(1980: Sony introduces the double-sided, double-density 3.5" floppy disk that holds 875 kilobyte)

1980: Onyx launches the first microcomputer running the Unix operating system

1981: The Xerox 8010 Star Information System is the first commercial computer that uses a mouse

1980: David Patterson and Carlo Sequin launch a RISC (Reduced Instruction Set Computer) project at UC Berkeley

1981: John Hennessy starts a RISC project at Stanford University

1981: Ed Feigenbaum and others found Teknowledge, the first major startup to develop "expert systems"

1981: Arthur Schawlow of Stanford University is awarded the Nobel Prize in Physics

1981: Roger Malina relocates Leonardo ISAST from Paris to San Francisco

1981: Jim Clark of Stanford University and Abbey Silverstone of Xerox found Silicon Graphics in Sunnyvale to manufacture graphic workstations

(1981: The IBM PC is launched, running an operating system developed by Bill Gates' Microsoft)

1981: Andreas Bechtolsheim at Stanford University builds a workstation running Unix and networking software

1982: John Warnock and Charles Geschke of Xerox PARC develop PostScript and found Adobe to commercialize it

(1982: John Hopfield describes a new generation of neural networks)

(1982: Thomas Zimmerman of IBM Almaden builds the first commercially-available dataglove

1982: Stanford students Andy Bechtolsheim, Vinod Khosla and Scott McNealy (a former Onyx employee) and former Berkeley student Bill Joy found SUN Microsystems, named after the "Stanford University Network," to manufacture workstations

1982: Apple's employee Trip Hawkins founds Electronic Arts to create home computer games

1982: John Walker founds Autodesk to sell computer-aided design software

1982: Gary Hendrix founds Symantec

(1982: Nastec introduces the term "Computer-Aided Software Engineering (CASE)" for its suite of software development tools)

1983: The Lotus Development Corporation, founded by Mitchell Kapor, introduces the spreadsheet program "Lotus 1-2-3" for MS-DOS developed by Jonathan Sachs

1983: Gavilan, founded by Manuel Fernandez, former CEO of Zilog, introduces the first portable computer marketed as a "laptop"

1983: Crash of the videogame console market

1983: Compaq introduces the Portable PC, compatible with the IBM PC

1983: The Transmission Control Protocol and Internet Protocol or "TCP/IP" running on Unix BSD 4.2 debuts on the Arpanet, and the Arpanet is officially renamed Internet

1983: Paul Mockapetris invents the Domain Name System for the Internet to classify Internet addresses through extensions such as .com

1983: Apple introduces the "Lisa," the first personal computer with a graphical user interface

1983: Henry Taube of Stanford University is awarded the Nobel Prize in Chemistry

1983: The Musical Instrument Digital Interface is introduced, based on an idea by Dave Smith

(1983: William Inmon builds the first data warehousing system)

1983: Gerard Debreu of UC Berkeley is awarded the Nobel Prize in Economics

(1983: Nintendo releases the Family Computer, renamed Nintendo Entertainment System in the U.S.)

1984: Cisco is founded by Leonard Bosack and Sandra Lerner

(1984: Michael Dell, a student at University of Texas at Austin, founds PCs Limited, later renamed Dell, to sell custom PC-compatible computers by mail-order only)

1984: The Search for Extraterrestrial Intelligence (SETI) Institute is founded by Thomas Pierson and Jill Tarter

1984: Robert Gaskins and Dennis Austin develop "Presentation," an application to create slide presentations (later renamed "PowerPoint")

1984: The "Search For Extraterrestrial Intelligence" or SETI Institute is founded

1984: Michael McGreevy creates the first virtual-reality environment at NASA Ames

(1984: Nicholas Negroponte and Jerome Wiesner found MIT Media Lab)

(1984: General Motors builds a factory that uses Supply Chain Management software)

(1984: Wavefront introduces the first commercial 3D-graphics software)

1984: Hewlett-Packard introduces the first ink-jet printer

1984: Apple introduces the Macintosh, which revolutionizes desktop publishing

(1984: William Gibson's novel "Neuromancer" popularizes the "cyberpunks")

(1984: The CDROM is introduced by Sony and Philips)

(1984: Psion introduces the first personal digital assistant)

(1984: The CADRE laboratory ("Computers in Art, Design, Research, and Education") is established at San Jose State University

(1984: Fujio Masuoka at Toshiba invents flash memory, a cheaper kind of EEPROM)

1985: Stewart Brand creates the "Whole Earth Lectronic Link" (or "WELL"), a virtual community of computer users structured in bulletin boards for online discussions

1985: Digital Research introduces GEM (Graphical Environment Manager), a graphical-user interface for the CP/M operating system designed by former Xerox PARC employee Lee Jay Lorenzen

(1985: Microsoft releases Windows 1.0 for MS-DOS)

(1985: Commodore launches the Amiga 1000, a 16-bit home computer with advanced graphical and audio (multimedia) designed by former Atari employee Jay Miner and running a multitasking operating system and GUI designed by Carl Sassenrath)

1985: Richard Stallman founds the non-profit organization "Free Software Foundation" (FSF)

1985: Hewlett-Packard introduces the LaserJet, a printer for the home market

1985: Jobs and Wozniak leave Apple

(Jul 1985: Aldus introduces PageMaker for the Macintosh, the first system for desktop publishing)

1985: A crisis in the semiconductor industry is brought about by the dumping of cheaper Japanese products

(1985: Richard Stallman releases a free operating system, "GNU")

1985: Warren Robinett, Scott Fisher and Michael McGreevy of NASA Ames build the "Virtual Environment Workstation" for virtual-reality research, incorporating the first dataglove and the first low-cost head-mounted display

(1985: Microsoft ships the "Windows" operating system)

(1985: Jim Kimsey founds Quantum Computer Services (later renamed America Online) to provide dedicated online services for personal computers)

1985: The Arpanet is renamed Internet

1985: Jaron Lanier founds VPL Research, the first company to sell Virtual Reality products

1985: Robert Sinsheimer organizes a meeting in Santa Cruz of biologists to discuss the feasibility of sequencing the entire human genome

1986: Apple's co-founder Steve Jobs buys Lucasfilms' Pixar, that becomes an independent film studio run by Ed Catmull

1986: A book by Eric Drexler popularizes the term "nanotechnology"

(1986: Phil Katz invents the zip compression format for his program Pkzip)

(1986: A virus spread among IBM PCs, nicknamed "Brain")

1986: Larry Harvey starts the first "Burning Man" on Baker Beach in San Francisco

1986: Judy Malloy publishes the computer-mediated hyper-novel "Uncle Roger" on the WELL

1986: Renzo Piano builds the California Academy of Science in San Francisco

1986: Yuan Lee of the Lawrence Berkeley Labs is awarded the Nobel Prize

1987: Chris Langton coins the term "Artificial Life"

1987: Jerry Kaplan and others found GO Corporation to manufacture portable computers with a pen-based user interface

1987: David Duffield and Ken Morris found PeopleSoft to manufacture Enterprise Resource Planning (ERP) applications

(1987: The JPEG (Joint Photographic Experts Group) format is introduced)

(1987: Linus Technologies introduces the first pen-based computer, WriteTop)

1987: Bill Atkinson at Apple creates the hypermedia system HyperCard

1987: The largest semiconductor manufacturers in the world are Japan's NEC, Japan's Toshiba and Japan's Hitachi

(1987: Uunet becomes the first commercial Internet Service Provider, ISP)

1988: "Morris," the first digital worm, infects most of the Internet

1988: Steven Benner organizes the conference "Redesigning the Molecules of Life', the first major conference on synthetic biology

(1988: 1988: Digital Subscriber Line (DSL) that provides broadband on a phone line is invented by Bellcore)

1989: UC Berkeley introduces the "BSD license," one of the first open-source licenses

1989: Adobe releases Photoshop

(1989: Barry Shein founds the first Internet Service Provider, "The World," in Boston)

1990: Richard Taylor of Stanford University is awarded the Nobel Prize in Physics and William Sharpe of Stanford University is awarded the Nobel Prize in Economics

1990: Between 1970 and 1990 the population of San Jose has almost doubled, from 445,779 to 782,248

(1990: Dycam introduces the first digital camera, Model 1)

(1990: Microsoft announced that it will stop working on OS/2)

(1990: The "Human Genome Project" is launched to decipher human DNA)

(1990: Michael West founds the biotech company Geron that pioneers commercial applications of regenerative medicine

(1990: Tim Berners-Lee of CERN invents the HyperText Markup Language "HTML" and demonstrates the World-Wide Web)

(1990: The first Internet search engine, "Archie," is developed in Montreal)

1990: LaRoche acquires a majority stake in Genentech

(1991: The World-Wide Web debuts on the Internet)

(1991: United Technologies Corporation becomes the first company to market a fuel-cell system)

(1991: Microsoft has revenues of $1,843,432,000 and 8,226 employees)

(1991: Finnish student Linus Torvalds introduces the Linux operating system, a variant of Unix)

(1991: Paul Lindner and Mark McCahill of the University of Minnesota release "Gopher," a software program to access the World-Wide Web)

1991: Pei-Yuan Wei introduces a "browser" for the world-wide web, Viola

1991: Apple introduces QuickTime

1992: Macromedia is founded in San Francisco

1992: Intel becomes the world's largest semiconductor manufacturer, passing all its Japanese rivals

(1992: The first text message is sent from a phone)

1992: The "Information Tapestry" project at Xerox PARC pioneers collaborative filtering

(1992: The Electronic Visualization Lab at the University of Illinois Chicago creates a "CAVE" ("Cave Automatic Virtual Environment"), a surround-screen and surround-sound virtual-reality environment (graphics projected from behind the walls that surround the user)

(1992: SAP launches R/3, moving its ERP system from mainframe to a three-tiered client-server architecture and to a relational database)

1992: Gary Becker of Stanford University is awarded the Nobel Prize in Economics

1992: Calgene creates the "Flavr Savr" tomato, the first genetically-engineered food to be sold in stores

(1992: Jean Armour Polly coins the phrase "Surfing the Internet")

(1992: Thomas Ray develops "Tierra," a computer simulation of ecology)

1993: Stanford University's Professor Jim Clark hires Mark Andreessen

1993: Condoleezza Rice becomes Stanford's youngest, first female and first non-white provost

1993: Thomas Siebel founds Siebel for customer relationship management (CRM) applications

1993: Steve Putz at Xerox's PARC creates the web mapping service Map Viewer

1993: The first "Other Minds Festival" for avantgarde music is held in San Francisco

1993: Broderbund introduces the videogame "Myst"

1993: Adobe Systems introduces Acrobat and the file format PDF (or Portable Document Format)

1993: Marc Andreessen develops the first browser for the World Wide Web (Mosaic)

1994: John Harsanyi of UC Berkeley is awarded the Nobel Prize in Economics

(1994: Mark Pesce introduces the "Virtual Reality Modeling Language" or VRML)

1994: The "Band of Angels" is founded by "angels" to fund Silicon Valley startups

(1994: University of North Carolina's college radio station WXYC becomes the first radio station in the world to broadcast its signal over the Internet)

1994: The search engine Architext (later Excite) debuts

1994: There are 315 public companies in Silicon Valley

1995: Stanford student Jerry Yang founds Yahoo!

1995: Salon is founded by David Talbot

1995: Netscape, the company founded by Marc Andreessen, goes public even before earning money and starts the "dot.com" craze and the boom of the Nasdaq

(1995: Microsoft introduces Internet Explorer and starts the browser wars)

1995: John Lasseter's "Toy Story" is the first feature-length computer-animated film

(1995: The MP3 standard is introduced)

1995: Mario Botta builds the Modern Museum of Art in San Francisco

1995: Martin Perl of Stanford University is awarded the Nobel Prize in Physics

(1995: The Sony Playstation is introduced)

1995: Ward Cunningham creates WikiWikiWeb, the first "wiki," a manual on the internet maintained in a collaborative manner

1995: SUN launches the programming language Java

1995: Piero Scaruffi debuts his website www.scaruffi.com

1995: Craig Newmark starts craigslist.com on the Internet, a regional advertising community

(1995: Amazon.com is launched on the Web as the "world's largest bookstore," except that it is not a bookstore, it is a website)

1995: The At Home Network (@Home) is founded by William Randolph Hearst III

1996: Sabeer Bhatia launches Hotmail, a website to check email from anywhere in the world

(1996: Dell begin selling its computers via its website)

1996: Steve Jobs rejoins Apple

1996: Jeff Hawkins invents the Palm Pilot, a personal digital assistant

Timeline

1996: Stewart Brand and Danny Hillis establish the "Long Now Foundation"

1996: Douglas Osheroff of Stanford University is awarded the Nobel Prize in Physics

1996: Macromedia introduces Flash

(1996: The first DVD player is introduced by Toshiba)

(1996: GeoSystems Global launches the web mapping service MapQuest that also provides address matching) Donnelley began making maps with computers in the mid-1980s to generate maps for customers. Much of that code was adapted for use on the Internet to create the MapQuest web service

(1996: The Apache HTTP Server is introduced, an open-source web server)

(1996: 1996: Monsanto acquires Calgene)

(1996: Nokia introduces the first smartphone)

1996: Sydney Brenner founds the Molecular Sciences Institute in Berkeley

1996: Brent Townshend invents the 56K modem

(1997: Andrew Weinreich creates SixDegrees.com, the first social networking website)

(1997: US West launches the first commercial DSL service in Phoenix)

1997: Reed Hastings founds Netflix to rent videos via the Internet

1997: The XML standard for exchanging documents on the World-Wide Web is introduced

(1997: Myron Scholes of Stanford University is awarded the Nobel Prize in Economics

1997: Steven Chu of Stanford University is awarded the Nobel Prize in Physics

1997: Evite is founded by Stanford engineering students Al Lieb and Selina Tobaccowala

(1997: The total revenues for ERP software market is $7.2 billion, with SAP, Baan, Oracle, J.D. Edwards, and PeopleSoft accounting for 62% of it)

1998: Stanford's scientist Mendel Rosenblum and others found Vmware

1998: NuvoMedia introduces the Rocket eBook, a handheld device to read ebooks

1998: Netscape makes its browser Navigator available for free in January 1998.

1998: Chinese and Indian engineers run about 25% of Silicon Valley's high-tech businesses, accounting for $16.8 billion in sales and 58,000 jobs

1998: SoftBook Press releases the first e-book reader

1998: Saul Perlmutter's team at the Lawrence Berkeley Lab discovers that the expansion of the universe is accelerating

1998: Celera, presided by Craig Venter of "The Institute for Genomic Research" (TIGR), is established to map the human genome (and later relocated to the Bay Area)

1998: Netscape launches the open-source project "Mozilla" of Internet applications

1998: Robert Laughlin of Stanford University is awarded the Nobel Prize in Physics

1998: America Online acquires Netscape

1998: Pierre Omidyar founds eBay, a website to auction items

1998: Two Stanford students, Larry Page and Russian-born Sergey Brin, launch the search engine Google

1998: Yahoo!, Amazon, Ebay and scores of Internet-related startups create overnight millionaires

1998: Peter Thiel and Max Levchin found Confinity

(1998: Jorn Barger in Ohio coins the term "weblog" for webpages that simply contain links to other webpages)

(1998: Jim Gray creates the web mapping service TerraServer that also offers satellite images)

(1998: Bob Somerby starts "The Daily Howler," the first major political blog)

(1998: Taiwanese computer manufacturer Acer opens Acer Technology Ventures to invest in Silicon Valley startups

1999: Camille Utterback's "Text Rain" pioneers interactive digital art

1999: Between 1998 to 1999 venture capital investments in Silicon Valley firms increases more than 90% from $3.2 billion to $6.1 billion

1999: Google has 8 employees

(1999: Total revenues for supply-chain software are $3.9 billion, with i2 owning 13% of the market)

1999: Siebel owns almost 50% of the CRM market

1999: Friendster is launched by Jonathan Abrams

1999: Blogger.com allows people to create their own "blogs," or personal journals

1999: Marc Benioff founds Saleforce.com to move business applications to the Internet, pioneering cloud computing

1999: Philip Rosedale founds Linden Lab to develop virtual-reality hardware

1999: The world prepares for the new millennium amidst fears of computers glitches due to the change of date (Y2K)

(1999: The recording industry sues Shawn Fanning's Napster, a website that allows people to exchange music)

1999: 100 new Internet companies are listed in the US stock market

1999: The US has 250 billionaires, and thousands of new millionaires are created in just one year

(1999: Microsoft is worth 450 billion dollars, the most valued company in the world, even if it is many times smaller than General Motors, and Bill Gates is the world's richest man at $85 billion)

1999: At Home acquires Excite, the largest Internet-related merger yet

2000: The NASDAQ stock market crashes, wiping out trillions of dollars of wealth

2000: Victoria Hale, a former Genentech scientist, starts the first non-profit pharmaceutical company, the Institute for OneWorld Health

2000: Venture-capital investment in the US peaks at $99.72 billion or 1% of GDP, mostly to software (17.4%), telecommunications (15.4%), networking (10.0%) and media (9.1%)

2000: 32% of Silicon Valley's high-skilled workers are foreign-born, mostly from Asia

(2000: Software and services account for 50% of IBM's business)

2000: Daniel McFadden of UC Berkeley is awarded the Nobel Prize in Economics

2000: There are 417 public companies in Silicon Valley

2000: 10 billion e-mail messages a day are exchanged over the Internet

2000: Confinity and X.com merge to form Paypal, a system to pay online

2000: The government-funded Human Genome Project and the privately-funded Celera jointly announce that they have decoded the entire human genome

(2000: Dell has the largest share of worldwide personal computer sales)

2001: Apple launches the iPod

2001: Listen.com launches Rhapsody, a service that provides streaming on-demand access to a library of digital music

2001: KR Sridhar founds Bloom Energy to develop fuel-cell technology

2001: Nanosys is founded to develop nanotechnology

2001: Semir Zeki founds the Institute of Neuroesthetics

2001: Joseph Stiglitz of Stanford University is awarded the Nobel Prize in Economics

2001: George Akerlof of UC Berkeley is awarded the Nobel Prize in Economics

2001: Jimmy Wales founds Wikipedia, a multilingual encyclopedia that is collaboratively edited by the Internet community

2001: Hewlett-Packard acquires Compaq

2002: Ebay acquires Paypal and Paypal cofounder Elon Musk founds SpaceX to develop space transportation

2002: Bram Cohen unveils the peer-to-peer file sharing protocol BitTorrent

2002: Sydney Brenner is awarded the Nobel Prize in Medicine

2002: Codexis is founded to develop biofuels

(2003: Skype is founded in Europe by Niklas Zennstroem and Janus Friis to offer voice over IP, a system invented by Estonian engineers)

2003: Matt Mullenweg launches a platform for people to create their own website or blog, Wordpress

2003: Linden Lab launches "Second Life," a virtual world accessible via the Internet

2003: Amyris Biotechnologies is founded to produce renewable fuels

2003: Christopher Voigt founds a lab at UCSF to program cells like robots to perform complex tasks

2003: Martin Eberhard and Marc Tarpenning found Tesla to build electrical cars

(2003: The first synthetic biology conference is held at MIT)

2004: Mark Zuckerberg founds the social networking service Facebook at Harvard University (soon relocated to Palo Alto)

2004: Mozilla releases the browser Firefox, created by Dave Hyatt and Blake Ross

(2004: Drew Endy of MIT founds Codon Devices to commercialize synthetic biology)

2004: Oracle buys PeopleSoft

2004: Google launches a project to digitize all the books ever printed

2004: UC Berkeley establishes a Center for New Media

2004: Vinod Khosla of venture capital firm Kleiner Perkins Caufield & Byers founds Khosla Ventures to invest in green-technology companies

2005: Adobe acquires Macromedia

2005: San Jose's population of 912,332 has passed San Francisco, and San Jose is now the tenth largest city in the US

2005: Andrew Ng at Stanford launches the STAIR project (Stanford Artificial Intelligence Robot)

2005: Oracle acquires Siebel

2005: Gina Bianchini founds Ning

2005: Google launches the web mapping system Google Earth that also offers three-dimensional images of terrain

2005: More than 50% of all jobs outsourced by Silicon Valley companies go to India

2005: UCSF opens the "Institute for Human Genetics"

2005: The Letterman Digital Arts Center opens in San Francisco

(2005: Sales of notebook computers account for 53% of the computer market)

2005: Sales of notebook computers account for 53% of the computer market

2005: Yahoo!, Google, America OnLine (AOL) and MSN (Microsoft's Network) are the four big Internet portals with a combined audience of over one billion people worldwide

2005: Silicon Valley accounts for 14% of the world's venture capital

2005: 52.4% of Silicon Valley's high-tech companies launched between 1995 and 2005 have been founded by at least one immigrant

(2005: Total revenues of ERP software are $25.5 billion, with SAP making $10.5 billion and Oracle $5.1 billion)

2005: Ebay acquires Skype

2005: Solar-energy company Solyndra is founded

2005: SUN's founder Bill Joy joins venture-capital firm Kleiner Perkins Caufield & Byers to invest in green technology

2005: Former Paypal employees Chad Hurley, Steve Chen and Jawed Karim launch YouTube

2006: Jack Dorsey creates the social networking service Twitter

2006: The Bay Area is the largest high-tech center in the US with 386,000 high-tech jobs

2006: YouTube is bought by Google for $1.65 billion

2006: Jay Keasling inaugurates the world's first Synthetic Biology department at the Lawrence Berkeley National Laboratory

2006: Lyndon and Peter Rive found SolarCity

2006: The first Zer01 Festival is held in San Jose

2006: Roger Kornberg of Stanford University is awarded the Nobel Prize in Chemistry, Andrew Fire of Stanford University is awarded the Nobel Prize in Medicine, and George Smoot of the Lawrence Berkeley Labs is awarded the Nobel Prize in Physics

2006: Tesla Motors introduces the Tesla Roadster, the first production automobile to use lithium-ion battery cells

2006: The World-Wide Web has 100 million websites

2006: Google acquires YouTube

2006: Walt Disney acquires Pixar

2006: Scott Hassan founds Willow Garage to manufacturer robots for domestic use

2007: 48% of Apple's revenues come from sales of the iPod

2007: Apple launches the iPhone

2007: Forrester Research estimates that online retail sales in the US reached $175 billion

2007: The biotech company iZumi Bio is founded to develop products based on stem-cell research

2007: The biotech company iPierian is founded to develop products based on cellular reprogramming

2007: The world's largest vendors of personal computers are HP, Dell, Taiwan's Acer, China's Lenovo and Japan's Toshiba

2008: The Silicon Valley has 2.4 million (less than 1% of the U.S.'s population) generating more than 2% of the U.S.'s GDP, with a GDP per person of $83,000

2008: Microsoft Windows owns almost 90% of the operating system market for personal computers, while Google owns almost 70% of the Internet search market

2008: For a few months San Francisco issues marriage license to same-sex couples

2008: Venture capitalists invest $4 billion into green-tech startups in 2008, which is almost 40% of all US investments in high-tech

2008: Taiwanese conglomerate Quanta invests into Silicon Valley startups Tilera and Canesta

2008: Hewlett-Packard purchases Electronic Data Systems in a shift towards services

2008: There are 261 public companies in Silicon Valley

2009: Oracle buys SUN

2009: Google's market value is more than $140 billion

2009: BitTorrent accounts for at least 20% of all Internet traffic

2009: Facebook has 150 million users in January and grows by about one million users a day, the fastest product ever to reach that many users in five years

2009: President Barack Obama appoints Steve Chu, director of the Lawrence Berkeley Laboratory, to be Secretary of Energy

2009: Tesla Motors obtains a $465-million loan from the US government to build the Model S, a battery-powered sports sedan

2009: Elizabeth Blackburn of UCSF shares the Nobel prize in Medicine and Oliver Williamson of UC Berkeley shares the Nobel prize in Economics

2009: Thomas Siebel founds energy startup C3 LLC

2009: Xerox purchases Affiliated Computer Services in a shift towards services

2009: Microsoft is the largest software company in the world with revenues of $50 billion, followed by IBM with $22 billion, Oracle with $17.5 billion, SAP with $11.6 billion, Nintendo with $7.2 billion, HP with $6.2 billion, Symantec with $5.6 billion, Activision Blizzard with $4.6 billion, Electronic Arts with $4.2 billion, Computer Associates with $3.9 billion, and Adobe with $3.3 billion.

2010: Google is worth $180 billion

2010: YouTube broadcasts the Indian Premier League of cricket live worldwide

2010: Apple is worth $205 billion, third in the US after Exxon and Microsoft

2010: HP purchases Palm, a struggling smartphone maker

2010: The Lawrence Livermore National Laboratory plans to simulate the nuclear fusion of a star (more than 100 million degrees Celsius, hotter than the center of the sun) with the world's most powerful laser, called the National Ignition Facility

2010: Microsoft's IE has 59.9% of the browser market, followed by Firefox with 24.5% and Google Chrome with 6.7%

2010: Apple introduces the tablet computer iPad that sells one million units in less than one month

2010: SAP buys Sybase

2010: The smarphone market grows 55% in 2010, with 269 million units sold worldwide

2011: The largest notebook vendors in the world are Acer, ASUS, Dell, HP and Samsung, but Apple is the single largest notebook vendor in the world, with a 20% market share, if one also considers notepads

2011: Apple's AppStore has 425,000 apps, downloaded 15 billion times, on 200 million iOS devices, while Google's Android Market has 250,000 applications, downloaded 6 billion times, on 135 million Android devices

2011: Apple surpasses ExxonMobil to become the most valuable company in the world based on market capitalization

2011: Google acquires Motorola's smartphone business

2011: Sony introduces the head-mounted display HMZ-T1

2011: Android own 46.3% of the smartphonemarket, Apple iPhones 30%, RIM 15% and Microsoft 4.6%

2011: The world buys almost 60 million tablet computers, of which 66.6% are Apple iPads, 28.8% are Androids and 1.3% are Research in Motion (QNX/BlackBerry)

2011: James Ellenbogen's team at MITRE unveils the world's first nanoelectronic processor

2012: Facebook has 7 billion visits a month, Twitter 182 million, Pinterest 104 million, LinkedIn 86 million, Tagged 72 million and Google+: 61 million, and Facebook users average 405 minutes per month, Pinterest and Tumblr users 89 minutes, Twitter 21 minutes, Google+ 3 minutes

2012: Pinterest becomes the third largest social network in the USA after Facebook and Google+

2012: Facebook acquires Instagram

2012: Facebook acquires Face.com

2012: Facebook goes public, the biggest high-tech IPO in history

2012: Android-based smartphones made by Samsung, HTC and others account for 75% of the market, whereas Apple's share is 14.9%

2012: Google has 85% of worldwide search engine use, followed by Yahoo with less than 8%, Bing with less than 5%, Baidu with less than 2%

2012: Microsoft's Internet Explorer is the most used browser with more than 55% of users, followed by Firefox with 20%, Chrome with 17%

2012: South Korea's Samsung sells twice as many smartphones as Apple and five times more than Nokia

2012: SpaceX launches the first commercial flight to the International Space Station

37. Bibliography

We present below what is likely the most complete bibliography on Silicon Valley. Most of the sources for this book came from articles, interviews, books, and personal contacts. Much of the literature we consulted on Silicon Valley is still in journal and newspaper articles, along with a range of relevant books. We generally found that the Stanford and UC Berkeley university library systems were superb and had all the resources we needed.

Wikipedia turned out to be the worst possible "source." Most of its articles are simply press releases from corporate PR departments, with all the omissions and distortions that they deem appropriate for their business strategies. On the other hand, vintage magazines and newspapers were an invaluable source of information and analysis. If websites like Wikipedia are going to replace the magazines and newspapers of the past, the loss to scholarship will be large. The most persistent marketing department or fan will decide what information will be available to future generations.

Many good books exist, but with a limited perspective because they rely heavily on interviews with the "protagonists." Our experience is that interviews with the protagonists are only a semi-reliable way to assess what truly happened. The protagonists generally hold a biased view of the events, and sometimes just don't properly remember basics such as dates, places, names, etc. We searched for narratives from "antagonists" and other third-party sources, along with primary documents for proof (invoices, contracts, etc.).

BOOKS & MONOGRAPHS

General History

Caddes, Carolyn. Portraits of Success: Impressions of Silicon Valley Pioneers. Palo Alto: Tioga Publishing Company, 1986.

Cerruzzi, Paul E. A History of Modern Computing. Cambridge, Mass.: MIT Press, 2000.

Chan, Sucheng, Spencer Olin & Thomas Paterson. Major Problems in California History. New York: Wadsworth Publishing, 1996.

Chandler, Alred D. Inventing the Electronic Century: The Epic Story of the Consumer Electronics and Computer Science Industries. New York: Free Press, 2001.

Cowan, Ruth Schwartz. A Social History of American Technology. New York: Oxford University Press, 1996.

Cringely, Robert X. Accidental Empires: How the Boys of Silicon Valley Make Their Millions, Battle Foreign Competition, and Still Can't Get a Date. New York: Harper, 1992.

Cumings, Bruce. Dominion from Sea to Sea: Pacific Ascendancy and American Power. New Haven, CT: Yale UP, 2009.

Dallman, Peter. Plant Life in the World's Mediterranean Climates: California, Chile, South Africa, Australia, and the Mediterranean Basin. Berkeley, CA: Univ. of California Press, 1998.

Davidow, Michael & Michael Malone. The Virtual Corporation: structuring and revitalizing the corporation for the 21st century. New York: HarperCollins, 1992.

Englisch-Lueck, Jan. Cultures@SiliconValley. Stanford: Stanford UP, 2002.

Florida, Richard. The rise of the creative class: And how it's transforming work, leisure and everyday life. New York: Basic Books, 2002.

Freiberger, Paul & Michael Swaine. Fire in the Valley: The Making of the Personal Computer, Collector's Edition. New York: McGraw Hill, 1999.

Gilder, George. Microcosm: A Prescient Look Inside the Expanding Universe of Economic, Social and Technological Possibilities within the world of the Silicon Chip. New York: Touchstone Books, 1989.

Hanson, Dirk. The New Alchemists: Silicon Valley and the Microelectronics Revolution. Boston: Little, Brown & Co., 1982.

Johnson, Paul. A History of the American People. New York: HarperCollins, 1998.

Kaplan, David A. The Silicon Boys and their Valley of Dreams. New York: Perennial, 2000.

Kenney, Martin. Understanding Silicon Valley: the Anatomy of an Entrepreneurial Region. Stanford: Stanford UP, 2000.

Lecuyer, Christophe. Making Silicon Valley: innovation and the growth of high tech, 1930-1970. Cambridge, MA: MIT Press, 2006.

Lee, Chong-Moon, William F. Miller, et al. The Silicon Valley edge: a habitat for innovation and entrepreneurship. Stanford: Stanford University Press, 2000.

Levy, Steven. Hackers: Heroes of the Computer Revolution. Garden City, NY: Doubleday, 1984.

Macaulay, David. The New Way Things Work. Boston: Houghton-Mifflin, 1998.

Malone, Michael. Betting It All: The Entrepreneurs of Technology. New York: Wiley, 2002.

Malone, Michael. The Valley of Heart's Delight: A Silicon Valley Notebook 1963-2001. New York: Wiley, 2002.

Markoff, John. What the Dormouse Said: How the Sixties Counterculture Shaped the Personal Computer Industry. New York: Penguin, 2005.

McClellan, James E. and Dorn, Harold. Science and Technology in World History: An Introduction. Baltimore: Johns Hopkins University Press, 1999.

McKendrick, David G., Richard F. Doner, & Stephan Haggard. From Silicon Valley to Singapore: Location and Competitive Advantage in the Hard Disk Drive Industry. Stanford, CA: Stanford University Press, 2000.

McLaughlin, John, Leigh Weimers & Ward Winslow. Silicon Valley - 110 Year Renaissance. Palo Alto, CA: Santa Clara Historical Association, 2008.

Morgan, Jane Electronics in the West: The First Fifty Years. Palo Alto, CA: National Press Books, 1967.

Pellow, David & Lisa Park. The Silicon Valley of Dreams: Environmental Injustice, Immigrant Workers, and the High-Tech Global Economy. New York: NYU Press, 2002.

Bibliography

Pellow, David Naguib & Lisa Sun-Hee Park. The Silicon Valley of Dreams: Environmental Injustice, Immigrant Workers, and the high-Tech Global Economy. New York: New York University Press, 2002.

Preer, Robert W. The Emergence of Technopolis: Knowledge-intensive technologies and regional development. New York: Praeger, 1992.

Rogers, Everett M. & Judith K. Larsen. Silicon Valley Fever. New York: Basic Books, 1984.

Roszak, Theodore. From Satori to Silicon Valley. San Francisco: Don't Call it Frisco Press, 1986.

Saxenian, AnnaLee. Local and Global Networks of Immigrant Professionals in Silicon Valley. San Francisco: Public Policy Institute of California, 2002.

Saxenian, AnnaLee. Regional Advantage: Culture and Competition in Silicon Valley and Route 128. Cambridge, MA: Harvard University Press, 1994.

Schmieder, Rich. Rich's Guide to Santa Clara County's Silicon Valley. Palo Alto: Rich Enterprises, 1982.

Starr, Kevin. California: A History. New York: Modern Library, 2007.

Starr, Kevin. Coast of Dreams. New York: Vintage, 2006.

Turner, Fred. From Counterculture to Cyberculture: Stewart Brand, the Whole Earth Network, and the Rise of Digital Utopianism. Chicago: U. of Chicago Press, 2008.

Vance, Ashlee. Geek Silicon Valley: The Inside Guide to Palo Alto, Stanford, Menlo Park, Mountain View, Santa Clara, Sunnyvale, San Jose, San Francisco. Guilford, CT: Globe Pequot Press, 2007.

Wong, Bernard P. The Chinese in Silicon Valley: Globalization, Social Networks, and Ethnic Identity. Lanham, MD: Rowman & Littlefield, 2005.

Corporations, Startups, and Entrepreneurs

Amelio, Gil & William L. Simon. On the Firing Line: My 500 Days at Apple. New York: HarperBusiness, 1998.

Angel, Karen. Inside Yahoo!: reinvention and the road ahead. New York: John Wiley and Sons, 2002.

Asen, Ben. Me by Me: The Pets.com Sock Puppet Book. New York: Simon & Schuster, 2000.

Ashbrook, Tom. The Leap: A Memoir of Love and Madness in the Internet Gold Rush. Boston: Houghton Mifflin, 2000.

Auletta, Ken. Googled: The End of the World as We Know It. New York: Virgin Books, 2010.

Bashe, Charles & Johnson, L.R. IBM's Early Computers. Boston: MIT Press, 1989.

Battelle, John. The search: how Google and its rivals rewrote the rules of business and transformed our culture. London: Nicholas Brealey, 2006.

Benioff, Marc. Behind the Cloud. New York: McGraw Hill, 2009.

Bernstein, Jeremy. Three Degrees above Zero: Bell Labs in the Information Age. New York: Charles Scribner's Sons, 1984.

Binder, Gordon. Science Lessons: What the Business of Biotech Taught Me About Management. Boston: Harvard Business School Press, 2008.

Brandt, Richard. Inside Larry and Sergey's Brain. New York: Portfolio, 2009.

Brock, Gerald W. The US Computer Industry: A Study of Market Power. New York: Ballinger, 1975.

Brown, Clair and Greg Linden. Chips and Change: How Crisis Reshapes the Semiconductor Industry. Cambridge, Boston: MIT Press, 2009.

Bunnell, David & Adam Brate. Making the Cisco Connection: The Story Behind the Real Internet Superpower. New York, NY: Wiley, 2000.

Bunnell, David and Adam Brate. Making the Cisco Connection: The Story Behind the Real Internet Superpower. New York: Wiley, 2000.

Bylinsky, Gene. The Innovation Millionaires: how they succeed. New York : Charles Scribner's Sons, 1976.

Carlton, Jim. Apple: The Inside Story of Intrigue, Egomania, and Business Blunders. New York: Random House, 1997.

Carroll, Paul. Big Blues: The Unmaking of IBM. New York: Crown Publishers, 1993.

Chutkow, Paul. Visa: The Power of an Idea. Chicago: Harcourt, 2001.

Clark, Jim & Owen Edwards. Netscape Time: The Making of the Billion-Dollar Start-up That Took on Microsoft. New York: St. Martin's Press, 1999.

Cohen, Adam. The Perfect Store: Inside eBay. New York: Back Bay, 2003.

Cohen, Scott. Zap! - The Rise and Fall of Atari. New York: McGraw-Hill, 1984.

DeLamarter, R.T. Big Blue, IBM's Use and Abuse of Power. New York: Dodd, Mead & Co., 1986.

Deutschman, Alan. The Second Coming of Steve Jobs. New York: Broadway Books, 2000.

Bibliography

Drazin, Charles, Erik Portanger, & Ernst Malmsten. Boo Hoo: $135 Million, 18 Months... a Dot.Com Story from Concept to Catastrophe. New York: Random House, 2001.

Farman, Irvin. Tandy's Money Machine: How Charles Tandy Built Radio Shack into the World's Largest Electronics Chain. New York: Mobium Press, 1992.

Ferguson, Charles H. High Stakes, No Prisoners: A Winner's Tale of Greed and Glory in the Internet Wars. New York: Three Rivers Press, 2000.

Fisher, Franklin M. & J. McKie. IBM and the US Data Processing Industry: An Economic History. New York: Praeger, 1983.

Frank Rose (1990), West of Eden: The End of Innocence at Apple Computer, Penguin Books

Fried, Jason and David Heinemeier Hansson. Rework. New York: Random House, Inc., 2010.

Gilder, George. Telecosm: How Infinite Bandwidth Will Revolutionize Our World. New York: Simon and Schuster, 2000.

Gilder, George. The Silicon Eye. New York: WW Norton & Co., 2006.

Gilder, George. The Spirit of Enterprise. New York: Simon and Schuster, 1984.

Hall, Mark & John Barry. Sunburst: The Ascent of Sun Microsystems. New York: Contemporary Books, 1990.

Hertzfeld, Andy. Revolution in the Valley. Sebastopol, CA: O'Reilly Books, 2005.

Hiltzik, Michael. Dealers of Lightning: Xerox PARC and the Dawn of the Computer Age. New York: Harper Paperbacks, 2000.

Hock, Dee. Birth of the Chaordic Age. San Francisco: Berrett-Koehler Publishers, 1999.

Hsieh, Tony. Delivering Happiness: A Path to Profits, Passion, and Purpose. New York: Business Plus, 2010.

Hughes, Sally. Genentech: The Beginnings of Biotech. Chicago: Univ. of Chicago Press, 2011.

Isaacson, Walter. Steve Jobs. New York: Simon & Schuster, 2011.

Jackson, Eric M. The PayPal Wars: Battles with eBay, the Media, the Mafia, and the Rest of Planet Earth. Los Angeles, CA: World Ahead Pub., 2004.

Jackson, Tim. Inside Intel: Andy Grove and the rise of the world's most powerful chip company. New York: Dutton, 1997.

Kaplan, Jerry. Startup: A Silicon Valley Adventure. New York: Penguin Books, 1996.

Kaplan, Philip J. F'd Companies: Spectacular Dot-Com Flameouts. New York: Simon and Schuster, 2002.

Killen, Michael. IBM: The Making of the Common View. New York: Harcourt Brace Jovanovich, 1988.

Komisar, Randy. The Monk and the Riddle: The Education of a Silicon Valley Entrepreneur. Cambridge, MA: Harvard Business School Press, 2000.

Kounalakis, Markos. Defying Gravity: The Making of Newton. Hilsboro, OR: Beyond Words Pub., 1993.

Kunkel, Paul. AppleDesign: The Work of the Apple Industrial Design Group. New York: Graphics Inc., 1997.

Lay, Beirne. Someone Has To Make It Happen: The Inside Story of Tex Thornton, The Man Who Built Litton Industries. Englewood Cliffs, N.J.: Prentice Hall, 1969.

Linzmayer, Owen. Apple Confidential 2.0. San Francisco: No Starch Press, 2004.

Littman, Jonathan. Once Upon a Time in ComputerLand: The Amazing, Billion-Dollar Tale of Bill Millard. Los Angeles: Price Stern Sloan, 1987.

Livingston, Jessica. Founders at Work. Berkeley, CA: Apress, 2007.

Malone, Michael S. Bill & Dave: How Hewlett and Packard Built the World's Greatest Company. New York: Penguin Portfolio, 2007.

Malone, Michael S. Infinite loop: how the world's most insanely great computer company went insane. New York: Doubleday, 1999.

Manes, Stephen & Paul Andrews. Gates: How Microsoft's Mogul Reinvented an Industry--and Made Himself the Richest Man in America. New York: Touchstone, 2002.

Maureen D. McKelvey. Evolutionary Innovations: The Business of Biotechnology. New York: Oxford University Press, 1996.

Maxwell, Fredric Alan. Bad Boy Ballmer: The Man Who Rules Microsoft. New York: Harper, 2003.

McKendrick, David G., Richard F. Doner, Stephan Haggard. From Silicon Valley to Singapore: Location and Competitive Advantage in the Hard Disk Drive Industry. Stanford: Stanford UP, 2000.

Moritz, Michael. Return to the Little Kingdom: How Apple and Steve Jobs Changed the World. New York: Overlook, 2009.

Osborne, Adam & John Dvorak. Hypergrowth: The Rise and Fall of Osborne Computer Corporation. Berkeley, CA: Idthekkethan Pub. Co., 1984.

Packard, David. The HP Way. New York, HarperBusiness, 1995.

Bibliography

Paulson, Ed. Inside Cisco: The Real Story of Sustained M&A Growth. New York: Wiley, 2001.

Pisano, Gary. Science Business: The Promise, the Reality, and the Future of Biotech. Boston: HBS Press, 2006.

Pugh, Emerson W. Building IBM: Shaping an Industry and Its Technology. Boston: MIT Press, 1995

Real, Mimi, Glynnis Thompson Kaye & Robert Warren. A Revolution in Progress: A History of Intel to Date. Santa Clara, CA: Intel Corporation, 1984.

Reid, T.R. The Chip: How Two Americans Invented the Microchip and Launched a Revolution. New York: Random House, 2001.

Rifkin, Glenn & George Harrar. The Ultimate Entrepreneur: The Story of Ken Olsen and DEC. Boston: Prima Publishing, 1990.

Rodgers, T.J. No-Excuses Management: Proven Systems for Starting Fast, Growing Quickly, and Surviving Hard Times. New York: Doubleday Business, 1993.

Schein, Edgar. DEC Is Dead, Long Live DEC: The Lasting Legacy of Digital Equipment Corporation. San Francisco: Berrett-Koehler, 2003.

Sculley, John & John A. Byrne. Odyssey: Pepsi to Apple. New York: HarperCollins, 1989.

Sheff, David. Game Over: How Nintendo Zapped an American Industry, Captured your Dollar, and Enslaved your Children. New York: Random House, 1993.

Sidhu, Inder. Doing Both: How Cisco Captures Today's Profit and Drives Tomorrow's Growth. London: FT Press, 2010.

Slater, Robert. The Eye of the Storm: How John Chambers Steered Cisco Through the Internet Collapse. New York, NY: HarperBusiness, 2003.

Southwick, Karen. High Noon: The Inside Story of Scott McNealy and the Rise of Sun Microsystems. New York: Wiley, 1999.

Sporck, Charles. Spinoff: A Personal History of the Industry that Changed the World. Saranac Lake, NY: Saranac Lake Pub., 2001.

Steiglitz, Ken. Snipers, Shills & Sharks: eBay and Human Behavior. Princeton, NJ: Princeton University Press, 2007.

Steven Levy (1994), Insanely Great: The Life and Times of Macintosh, the Computer That Changed Everything

Stross, Randall. Planet Google: One Company's Audacious Plan To Organize Everything We Know. New York: Free Press, 2008.

Symonds, Matthew & Larry Ellison. Softwar: An Intimate Portrait of Larry Ellison and Oracle. New York: Simon and Schuster, 2004.

Tedlow, Richard. Andy Grove: The Life and Times of an American. New York: Portfolio, 2006.

Vettel, Eric J. Biotech: The Countercultural Origins of an Industry. Philadelphia: University of Pennsylvania Press, 2006.

Vise, David & Mark Malseed. The Google Story. New York: Delacorte Press, 2005.

Wallace, James and Jim Erickson. Hard Drive. Bill Gates and the Making of the Microsoft Empire. New York: Wiley, 1992.

Waters, John K. John Chambers and the Cisco Way: Navigating Through Volatility. New York: Wiley, 2002.

Watson, Thomas J., Jr. and Peter Petrie. Father, Son & Co.: My Life at IBM and Beyond. New York: Bantam Books, 1990.

Wilson, Mike. The Difference Between God And Larry Ellison*: Inside Oracle Corporation. New York: William Morrow, 1997.

Wolff, Michael. Burn Rate: How I Survived the Gold Rush Years on the Internet. New York: Simon & Schuster, 1998.

Wozniak, Steve & Gina Smith. iWoz: From Computer Geek to Cult Icon: How I Invented the Personal Computer, Co-Founded Apple, and Had Fun Doing It. New York: W. W. Norton & Company, 2006.

Young, Jeffrey S. & William L. Simon. iCon Steve Jobs: The Greatest Second Act in the History of Business. New York: John Wiley & Sons, 2005.

Yu, Albert. Creating the Digital Future: The Secrets of Consistent Innovation at Intel, New York: Free Press, 1998.

Yuen, Albert. Bill & Dave's Memos. A Collection of Bill Hewlett and David Packard's Writings. Palo Alto: 2DaysofSummer Books, 2006.

Bibliography

Venture Capital and Service Professionals

Ante, Spencer E. Creative Capital: Georges Doriot and the Birth of Venture Capital. Boston: Harvard Business Press, 2008.

Bagley, Constance E. & Craig Dauchy. The Entrepreneur's Guide to Business Law. New York: Thomson/Southwestern/West, 2003.

Doerflinger, Thomas M. & Jack L. Rivlin. Risk and Reward: Venture Capital and the Making of America's Great Industries. New York: Random House, 1987.

Doriot, Georges F. Manufacturing class notes: Harvard Business School, 1927-1966. Board of Trustees, The French Library in Boston, 1993.

Draper, William H. The Startup Game: Inside the Partnership between Venture Capitalists and Entrepreneurs. New York: Palgrave, 2011.

Filipp, Mark R. Covenants Not to Compete, 2nd ed. New York: John Wiley & Sons, 2001.

Finkel, Robert & David Greising. The Masters of Private Equity and Venture Capital. New York: McGraw Hill, 2009.

Galanter, Marc & Thomas Palay. Tournament of Lawyers: The Transformation of the Big Law Firms. Chicago: University of Chicago Press, 1991.

Gompers, Paul, & Josh Lerner. The Venture Capital Cycle, 2nd ed. Cambridge, MA: MIT Press, 2004.

Gupta, Udayan. Done Deals. Venture Capitalists Tell their Stories. Boston: HBS Press, 2000.

Kaplan, David A. Mine's Bigger, Tom Perkins and the Making of the Greatest Sailing Machine Ever Built. New York: Harper Collins, 2007.

Kindleberger, Charles P. Manias, Panics, and Crashes: A History of Financial Crises. New York: Wiley, 1978.

Longstreth, Bevis. Modern Investment Management and the Prudent Man Rule. Oxford: Oxford University Press, 1986.

Lowe, Janet. Warren Buffett Speaks: Wit and Wisdom from the World's Greatest Investor. New York: Wiley, 1997.

Mahar, Maggie. Bull! A History of the Boom, 1982-1999. HarperCollins, 2003.

Metrick, Andrew. Venture Capital and the Finance of Innovation. New York: John Wiley & Sons, 2007.

McCahery, Joseph A. & Luc Renneboog. Venture Capital Contracting and the Valuation of High-technology Firms. New York: Oxford UP, 2004.

Perkins, Tom. Valley Boy: The Education of Tom Perkins. New York: Gotham Reprint, 2008.

Rivlin, Gary. The Godfather of Silicon Valley: Ron Conway and the Fall of the Dot-Coms. New York: At Random, 2001.

Stross, Randall E. eBoys. New York: Ballentine,2000.

Weisel, Thomas & Richard Brandt. Capital instincts: life as an entrepreneur, financier, and athlete. Hoboken, NJ: Wiley, 2003.

Wilmerding, Alex. Term Sheets & Valuations - A Line by Line Look at the Intricacies of Venture Capital Term Sheets & Valuations. New York: Aspatore Books, 2006.

Wilson, John. The New Ventures, Inside the High Stakes World of Venture Capital. New York: Addison-Wesley Publishing, 1985.

Science, Technology, and Universities

Abbate, Janet. Inventing the Internet. Cambridge, MA: MIT Press, 1999.

Balk, Alfred. The Rise of Radio, from Marconi through the Golden Age. New York: McFarland and Co., 2005.

Bardini, Thierry. Bootstrapping: Douglas Engelbart, Coevolution, and the Origins of Personal Computing. Stanford CA: Stanford University Press, 2000.

Barley, Stephen R. & Gideon Kunda. Gurus, hired guns and warm bodies: itinerant experts in a knowledge economy. Princeton: Princeton University Press, 2004.

Bassett, Ross Knox. To the Digital Age: Research Labs, Start-up Companies, and the Rise of MOS Technology. Baltimore: John Hopkins UP, 2002.

Berners-Lee Tim & Mark Fischetti. Weaving the Web: The Original Design and Ultimate Destiny of the World Wide Web by Its Inventor. San Francisco: Harper, 1999.

Berube, David. Nano-Hype: The Truth Behind the Nanotechnology Buzz. Amherst, NY: Promotheus Books, 2005.

Birchler, Urs W. and Monika Butler. Information Economics. London: Routledge, 2007.

Bresnahan, Timothy & Alfonso Gambardella (ed.). Building High Tech Clusters, Silicon Valley and Beyond. Cambridge: Cambridge University Press, 2004.

Campbell-Kelly, Martin & William Aspray. Computer: A History of The Information Machine, Second Edition. New York: Westview Press, 2004.

Campbell-Kelly, Martin. From airline reservations to Sonic the Hedgehog: a history of the software industry. Cambridge, MA: MIT Press, 2003.

Carr, Nicholas. The Big Switch: Rewiring the World. New York: Norton, 2009.

Castells, Manuel. The Rise of the Network Society. Malden, MA: Blackwell, 1996.

Ceruzzi, Paul E. A History of Modern Computing (2nd Edition). Cambridge: MIT Press, 2003.

Chandler, Alfred D., Jr. Inventing the Electronic Century: The Epic Story of the Consumer Electronics and Computer Science Industries. New York: Free Press, 2001.

Cool, Jennifer. Communities of Innovation: Cyborganic and the Birth of Networked Social Media. Los Angeles: USC Libraries, 2008.

Ferguson-Reid, Edna. Why 2k? - A Chronological Study of the (Y2K) Millennium Bug: Why, When and How Did Y2K Become a Critical Issue for Businesses. New York: Universal Publishers, 1999.

Finn, Bernard, Robert Bud & Helmuth Trischler. Exposing Electronics. Amsterdam, Netherlands: Harwood Academic, 2000.

Flamm, Kenneth. Creating the Computer: Government, Industry, and High Technology. Washington, DC: Brookings, 1988.

Gillmor, Stewart. Fred Terman at Stanford: building a discipline, a university, and Silicon Valley. Stanford: Stanford UP, 2004.

Goldberg, Adele. A History of Personal Workstations. New York: ACM Press, 1988.

Kaiser, David. Becoming MIT: Moments of Decision. Cambridge, MA: MIT UP, 2010.

Koren, Leonard, Wabi-Sabi: for Artists, Designers, Poets & Philosophers. Berkeley: Stone Bridge Press, 1994.

Krugman, Paul. Geography and Trade. Cambridge, Mass.: MIT Press, 1991.

Lammers, Susan M. Programmers at Work. Redmond, WA: Microsoft Press, 1986.

Leslie, Stuart W. The Cold War and American Science: The Military-Industrial-Academic Complex at MIT and Stanford. New York: Columbia UP, 1993.

Lojek, Bo. History of semiconductor engineering. New York: Springer, 2006.

Lowen, Rebecca S. Creating the Cold War University: The Transformation of Stanford. Berkeley: University of California Press, 1997.

Moody, Glyn. Rebel Code: Linux and the Open Source Revolution. London: Alan Lane, 2001.

Nohria, Nitin & Robert G. Eccles (editors). Networks and Organizations: Structure, Form, and Action. Boston: HBS Press, 1992.

O'Mara, Margaret Pugh. Cities of Knowledge: Cold War Science and the Search for the Next Silicon Valley. Princeton: Princeton UP, 2004.

Rheingold, Howard. Tools for Thought: The History and Future of Mind-Expanding Technology. Cambridge, MA: MIT Press, 2000.

Riordan, Michael & Lillian Hoddeson. Crystal Fire: The Birth of the Information Age. New York: Norton, 1997.

Rowen, Henry, et al. "Making IT: The Rise of Asia in High Tech." Stanford: Stanford UP, 2006.

Shapiro, Carl & Hal Varian. Information Rules: A Strategic Guide to the Network Economy. Cambridge, MA: HBS Press, 1999.

Shy, Oz. The Economics of Network Industries. Cambridge, UK: Cambridge UP, 2001.

Stigler, George. Production and Distribution Theories. New York: Macmillan Company, 1941.

Stratton, Julius A. et al. Mind and Hand: The Birth of MIT. Cambridge, MA: MIT UP, 2005.

Swedin, Eric G. & David L. Ferro. Computers: The Life Story of a Technology. Baltimore: Johns Hopkins University Press, 2007.

Yost, Jeffrey. The Computer Industry. Santa Barbara, CA: Greenwood Press, 2005.

Young, Jeff. Forbes Greatest Technology Stories. New York: Wiley, 1998.

Zachary, G. Pascal. Endless Frontier: Vannevar Bush, Engineer of the American Century. New York: The Free Press, 1997.

Zhang, Junfu & Nikesh Patel. The Dynamics of California's Biotechnology Industry. San Francisco: Public Policy Institute of California, 2005.

Zook, Matthew A. The Geography of the Internet Industry: Venture Capital, Dot-Coms, and Local Knowledge. Malden, MA: Blackwell Pub., 2002.

INTERVIEWS, SPEECHES, & ORAL HISTORIES

Bowes, William K. Jr. "Early Bay Area Venture Capitalists: Shaping the Economic and Business Landscape," conducted by Sally Smith Hughes in 2008, Regional Oral History Office. The Bancroft Library, University of California, Berkeley, 2009.

Crowther, William. OH 184. Oral history interview by Judy E. O'Neill, 12 March 1990, Cambridge, Massachusetts. Charles Babbage Institute, University of Minnesota, Minneapolis. http://www.cbi.umn.edu/oh/pdf.phtml?id=97

Draper, William H. III. "Early Bay Area Venture Capitalists: Shaping the Economic and Business Landscape," oral history conducted by Sally Smith Hughes in 2009, Regional Oral History Office, The Bancroft Library, University of California, Berkeley, 2008.

Draper, William H. III. "Venture Capital Greats - Draper, William H. III" an oral history conducted and edited by Mauree Jane Perry, National Venture Capital Association, Venture Capital Oral History Project, October, 2005.

Gurley, Bill. "Startup 128: An Interview with Bill Gurley of Benchmark," interviewed by Joseph Ansanelli, June 28, 2009. http://www.ansanelli.com/blog/?p=1118

Hambrecht, William R. "Early Bay Area Venture Capitalists: Shaping the Economic and Business Landscape ," conducted by Sally Smith Hughes in 2010, Regional Oral History Office, The Bancroft Library, University of California, Berkeley, 2011.

Jobs, Steve. "Stanford Commencement Speech 2005." Available online: http://www.stanford.edu/class/ee204/Apple2008.html.

Johnson, Franklin P. "Bay Area Venture Capitalists: Shaping the Economic and Business Landscape" conducted by Sally Smith Hughes in 2008. Regional Oral History Office, The Bancroft Library, University of California, Berkeley, 2009.

Kramlich, C. Richard. "Venture Capital Greats: A Conversation with C. Richard Kramlich," interviewed by Mauree Jane Perry on August 31, 2006, in San Francisco, California. National Venture Capital Association, Arlington, Virginia.

McMurtry, Burton J. "Early Bay Area Venture Capitalists: Shaping the Economic and Business Landscape," an oral history conducted by Sally Smith Hughes in 2009, Regional Oral History Office, The Bancroft Library, University of California, Berkeley, 2009.

Minck, John. Inside HP: A Narrative History of Hewlett-Packard from 1939-1990. http://www.hpmemory.org/an/pdf/Hpnar30.pdf

Myers, Gibson S. "Early Bay Area Venture Capitalists: Shaping the Economic and Business Landscape," an oral history conducted by Sally Smith Hughes in 2008, Regional Oral History Office, The Bancroft Library, University of California, Berkeley, 2009.

Norberg, Arthur L., Charles Suskind, & Roger Hahn. "Frederick Emons Terman, Interviews," 1975. Joint project of Bancroft Oral History Project and Stanford Oral History Project, published 1984.

Packard, David. "How Bill Hewlett and I Wound Up in a Palo Alto Garage." The Scientist, 1986.

Patricof, Alan. "Another View: V.C. Investing Not Dead, Just Different" NY Times Dealbook, February 9, 2009, http://dealbook.blogs.nytimes.com/2009/02/09/another-view-vc-investing-not-dead-just-different/

Perkins, Thomas J. "Early Bay Area Venture Capitalists: Shaping the Economic and Business Landscape," an oral history conducted by Sally Smith Hughes in 2009, Regional Oral History Office, The Bancroft Library, University of California, Berkeley, 2010.

Robertson, Sanford R. "Early Bay Area Venture Capitalists: Shaping the Economic and Business Landscape," an oral history conducted by Sally Smith Hughes in 2010, Regional Oral History Office, The Bancroft Library, University of California, Berkeley, 2011.

Rock, Arthur. "Early Bay Area Venture Capitalists: Shaping the Economic and Business Landscape," conducted by Sally Smith Hughes in 2008 and 2009. Regional Oral History Office, The Bancroft Library, University of California, Berkeley, 2009.

Rothrock, Ray. "Startup 130: 10 Questions for Ray Rothrock of Venrock," interviewed by Joseph Ansanelli, August 18, 2009. http://www.ansanelli.com/blog/?p=1205

Sonsini, Lawrence . "Early Bay Area Venture Capitalists: Shaping the Economic and Business Landscape," an oral history conducted by Sally Smith Hughes in 2010, Regional Oral History Office, The Bancroft Library, University of California, Berkeley, 2011.

Strassmann, Paul A. OH 172. Oral history interview by Arthur L. Norberg, 26 May 1989. Charles Babbage Institute, University of Minnesota, Minneapolis. http://www.cbi.umn.edu/oh/pdf.phtml?id=338.

Terman, Frederick. Interviews conducted by A. L. Norberg, Charles Susskind, and Rodger Hahn, History of Science and Technology Project, Bancroft Library, University of California, Berkeley. 1978.

Terman, Frederick. Frederick Emmons Terman Papers (SC0160). Department of Special Collections and University Archives, Stanford University Libraries, Stanford, Calif.

Terman, Sibyl W. "Personality of the month: F. E. Terman," The Link (Stanford Electronics Laboratories), December 1955.

Valentine, Donald T. "Interview with Don Valentine," Silicon Genesis: An Oral History of Semiconductor Technology. April 21, 2004, Menlo Park, California. http://silicongenesis.stanford.edu/transcripts/valentine.htm.

Valentine, Donald T. "Newsmaker: Legendary venture capitalist looks ahead," interviewed by Alorie Gilbert. CNET News, Nov. 17, 2004. http://news.cnet.com/Legendary-venture-capitalist-looks-ahead/2008-1082_3-5466478.html

Valentine, Donald T. "Early Bay Area Venture Capitalists: Shaping the Economic and Business Landscape," an oral history conducted by Sally Smith Hughes in 2009. Regional Oral History Office, The Bancroft Library, University of California, Berkeley, 2010.

Winograd, Terry. OH 237. Oral history interview by Arthur L. Norberg, 11 December 1991, Cambridge, Massachusetts. Charles Babbage Institute, University of Minnesota, Minneapolis. http://www.cbi.umn.edu/oh/pdf.phtml?id=16

Wythes, Paul. "Paul Wythes Interview," Conducted and edited by Mauree Jane Perry. National Venture Capital Association Venture Capital Oral History Project, 2006. http://digitalassets.lib.berkeley.edu/roho/ucb/text/wythes_paul_donated.pdf

NEWSPAPERS, MAGAZINES, & JOURNAL ARTICLES

General History

American Electronics Association. "Cyberstates 2002: A State-by-State Overview of the High-Technology Industry." Washington DC, 2002.

American Electronics Association. "Cyberstates 2001." Washington DC, 2001.

Angel, David P. "The Labor Market for Engineers in the US Semiconductor Industry." Economic Geography 65, April 1989, pp. 99-112.

Armour, John & Douglas Cumming. "The Legislative Road to Silicon Valley." Oxford Economic Papers, Vol. 58, 2006, pp. 596-635. http://ssrn.com/abstract=473593 or doi:10.2139/ssrn.473593

Blank, Steve. Hidden in Plain Sight: The Secret History of Silicon Valley (Rev4). Dec. 2009. http://www.slideshare.net/fullscreen/sblank/secret-history-of-silicon-valley-rev-4-dec-09/1http://steveblank.com/secret-history/.& http://steveblank.com/secret-history/.

Ewing Marion Kauffman Foundation. "Business Dynamic Statistics: Tracking Annual Changes in Employment for Growing and Shrinking Businesses." Accessed October 12, 2009.

Gershon, Dianne. "The economic impact of Silicon Valley's immigrant entrepreneurs." Nature 405, 598, June 1, 2000. http://www.nature.com/nature/journal/v405/n6786/full/405598a0.html.

Gilson, Ronald J. 1999. "The Legal Infrastructure of High Technology Industrial Districts: Silicon Valley, Route 128, and Covenants Not to Compete." New York University Law Review 74(3), pp. 575-629.

Hyde, Alan Stuart. "How Silicon Valley Has Eliminated Trade Secrets (and Why This is Efficient)" SSRN, January 1997. http://ssrn.com/abstract=5185

Hyde, Alan Stuart. "Working in Silicon Valley: Economic and Legal Analysis of a High-Velocity Labor Market." University of Illinois at Urbana-Champaign's Academy for Entrepreneurial Leadership Historical Research Reference in Entrepreneurship, 2003. http://ssrn.com/abstract=1511553

Hyde, Alan. 1998. "Silicon Valley's High-Velocity Labor Market." Journal of Applied Corporate Finance 11(2), pp. 28-37.

Lemos, Rob & Erdin Beshimov. "East Meets West - 5 Observations on Silicon Valley from an MIT Sloan Perspective." Silicon Valley Watcher, Jan. 12, 2010. http://www.siliconvalleywatcher.com/mt/archives/2010/01/east_meets_west.php.

Mendonca, Lenny, Diana Farrell, et al. "Sustaining the Bay Area's Competitiveness in a Globalizing World." Bay Area Council, March 2008. http://www.bayeconfor.org/media/files/pdf/BayAreaProfile2008.pdf

Norberg, A.L. "The origins of the electronics industry on the pacific coast." Proceedings of the IEEE, Volume 64, Issue 9, Sept. 1976, pp. 1314 – 1322.

Public Policy Institute of California. "Silicon Valley's Skilled Immigrants: Generating Jobs and Wealth in California." Research Brief, Issue #21, June 1999.

Public Policy Institute of California. "Silicon Valley Immigrants Forging Local and Transnational Networks." Research Brief, Issue #56, April 2002.

Saxenian, AnnaLee. "Silicon Valley's New Immigrant Entrepreneurs." University of California, Santa Cruz, Working Paper 15, May 2000.

Bibliography

Stangler, Dane & Robert E. Litan. "Where Will The Jobs Come From?" Kauffman Foundation Research Series: Firm Formation and Economic Growth, November 2009. http://www.kauffman.org/uploadedFiles/where_will_the_jobs_come_from.pdf

US Census Bureau. "Business Dynamic Statistics." Accessed October 12, 2009.

Wadhwa, Vivek, AnnaLee Saxenian, Ben Rissing, & Gary Gereffi. "Skilled Immigration and Economic Growth." Applied Research in Economic Development 5, no. 1, May 2008, pp. 6-14.

Wadhwa, Vivek, AnnaLee Saxenian, Richard Freeman, and Salkever Alex. "Losing the World's Best and Brightest. Research Report." Ewing Marrion Kauffman Foundation, 2009.

Weil, Thierry, "Silicon Valley Stories." CERNA Working Paper 2009-1, January 2009. http://hal.archives-ouvertes.fr/docs/00/48/82/00/PDF/Silicon_valley_stories_CWPS_2009-1.pdf

Corporations, Startups, and Entrepreneurs

"A Tangled Webvan." Supermarket Strategic Alert Special Report, 2001.

"Cisco was top acquirer of past decade." San Jose Business Journal, January 6, 2010. http://sanjose.bizjournals.com/sanjose/stories/2010/01/04/daily44.html?s=du&ed=2010-01-06

"Oracle Anniversary Timeline," Profit Magazine, May 2007, p. 26-30

"Return of the Prophet." Economist, June 28, 1997, p. 66.

Ahl, David H. "Osborne Computer Corporation." Creative Computing," Vol. 10, No. 3, March 1984, p. 24.

Ballmer, Steve. "Microsoft Withdraws Proposal to Acquire Yahoo (Letter)." May 3, 2008. http://www.microsoft.com/presspass/press/2008/may08/05-03letter.mspx.

Ballmer, Steve. "Microsoft Proposes Acquisition of Yahoo! for $31 per Share." Feb. 1, 2008. http://www.microsoft.com/presspass/press/2008/feb08/02-01CorpNewsPR.mspx

Bannon, Lisa. "Boss Talk: Santa's Middleman Takes Stock—In Critical Season for eToys, CEO Lenk Affirms Faith In Eventual Profitability." WSJ, December 8, 2000, B1.

Bannon, Lisa. "E-Commerce(A Special Report): The Lessons We've Learned—Toys: Rough Play—Consumers like buying toys online; But that hasn't made it a great business yet." WSJ, October 23, 2000, R21.

Barnes, Cecily. "eToys files for Chapter 11." CNET News, March 7, 2001.

Boehret, Atherine. "Testing Souped-Up Search Functions." WSJ, March 26, 2008, D4. http://online.wsj.com/public/article/SB120648944687663981-72vQKsD0lg1izTzOInM4LLptwYQ_20090326.html?mod=rss_personal_technology

Ira Boudway. "Rocket Man: Should Elon Musk Doubters Think Again?" Bloomberg Businessweek, May 22, 2012, http://www.businessweek.com/articles/2012-05-22/rocket-man-should-elon-musk-doubters-think-again#r=lr-fs

Brand, Stewart. "Spacewar." Rolling Stone, December 7, 1972.

Brandt, Richard, and Evan I. Schwartz, "The Selling Frenzy That Nearly Undid Oracle," Business Week, December 3, 1990.

Brandt, Richard, Otis Port, and Robert D. Hof. "Intel: The Next Revolution." BusinessWeek, September 26, 1988, p. 74.

Broadcast.com 1998 SEC Form 10-K 405 filing, 3-30-1999, http://www.sec.gov/Archives/edgar/data/1061236/0000950134-99-002266.txt.

Bylinsky, Gene. "Intel's Biggest Shrinking Job Yet." Fortune, May 3, 1982, p. 250.

Calore, Michael. "Gmail Hits Webmail G-Spot." Wired, April 1, 2004.

Campbell, Shawn. "Yahoo SM vs. Google AdWords." SearchEngineGuide, June 7, 2005. http://www.searchengineguide.com/shawn-campbell/yahoo-sm-vs-google-adwords.php.

Cave, Andrew. "Mattel sale ends $3.6bn fiasco." Telegraph UK, Sept. 30, 2000. http://www.telegraph.co.uk/finance/4467013/Mattel-sale-ends-3.6bn-fiasco.html

Claburn, Thomas. "Bots Helped To Boost Microsoft Live Search Gains." InformationWeek, July 12, 2007.http://www.informationweek.com/news/internet/search/showArticle.jhtml;jsessionid=PYE AKXVTKKRY4QSNDLRSKH0CJUNN2JVN?articleID=201001092&_requestid=167631.

Clark, Tim. "Inside Intel's Marketing Machine." Business Marketing, October 1992, pp. 14-19.

Cleland, Scott. "Why Google's Search Ad Monopoly is Understated." Precursor Blog, May 4, 2010. http://precursorblog.com/content/why-googles-search-ad-monopoly-understated

Clifford, Stephanie. "A Web Shift in the Way Advertisers Seek Clicks." NY Times, April 21, 2008. http://www.nytimes.com/2008/04/21/business/media/21online.html?_r=1&ex=1366516800&en=aee220abd02bd289&ei=5088&partner=rssnyt&emc=rss&oref=slogin.

ComScore Press Release. "ComScore Releases February 2008 US Search Engine Rankings." March 19, 2008. http://www.comscore.com/press/release.asp?press=2119.

ComScore Press Release. "ComScore Releases July 2010 US Search Engine Rankings."August 17, 2010,

Bibliography

http://www.comscore.com/Press_Events/Press_Releases/2010/8/comScore_Releases_July_2010_U.S._Search_Engine_Rankings.

Cook, William J.. "Shifting into the Fast Lane," US News & World Report, January 23, 1995, p. 52.

Corcoran, Elizabeth. "Reinventing Intel." Forbes, May 3, 1999, pp. 154-59.

Couretas, John & Aaron Robinson. "GM, Ford to Do More Purchasing on Web," Crain's Detroit Business, November 8, 1999, p. 7.

Darnton, Robert. "Google & the Future of Books." NYRB, February 12, 2009. http://www.nybooks.com/articles/archives/2009/feb/12/google-the-future-of-books/

Delaney, Kevin & Matthew Karnitschnig. "Google Offers to Help Yahoo Fight Off Microsoft." WSJ, February 4, 2008.

Diaz, Sam. "Yahoo's search strategy: We're not fighting "the megawatt war." ZDNet, August 25, 2009. http://www.zdnet.com/blog/btl/yahoos-search-strategy-were-not-fighting-the-megawatt-war/23161

Diaz, Sam. "Yahoo's search strategy: We're not fighting "the megawatt war." ZDNet, August 25, 2009. http://www.zdnet.com/blog/btl/yahoos-search-strategy-were-not-fighting-the-megawatt-war/23161

Dignan, Larry. "Mattel/The Learning Co. in $3.8B merger." ZDNet.com, December 14, 1998. http://www.zdnet.com/news/mattelthe-learning-co-in-38b-merger/101179

Dolan, Kerry A. "Purple People." Forbes, Sept. 1, 2003. http://www.forbes.com/forbes/2003/0901/072_print.html

Farber, Dan. "Facebook's Zuckerberg uncorks the social graph." ZDNet, May 24, 2007. http://www.zdnet.com/blog/btl/facebooks-zuckerberg-uncorks-the-social-graph/5156

Farmer, Melanie Austria & Greg Sandoval. "Webvan delivers its last word: Bankruptcy."CNET News, July 9, 2001.

Fisher, Lawrence. "Mattel Decides to Put on Sale Software Unit Bought in May." NY Times, April 4, 2000.

Foley, Stephen. "The Big Question: Is Google gaining a monopoly on the world's information?" The Independent, February 19, 2010.

Foremski, Tom. "Thought Leader: Valley Veteran Bill Coleman On Failure And The Guild Of Entrepreneurs . . ." Silicon Valley Watcher, March 5, 2009. http://www.siliconvalleywatcher.com/mt/archives/2009/03/thought_leader_7.php.

Francisco, Bambi. "A Yahoo year for Terry Semel." CBS MarketWatch.com, Sept. 18, 2003.

Garland, Susan B. & Andy Reinhardt. "Making Antitrust Fit High Tech." BusinessWeek, March 22, 1999, p. 34.

Glasner, Joanna. "EToys: Going Down Slowly." Wired, Feb. 16, 2001. http://www.wired.com/techbiz/media/news/2001/02/42030#ixzz0wEtTgJ58

Glasner, Joanna. "Why Webvan Drove Off a Cliff." Wired, July 10, 2001. http://www.wired.com/techbiz/media/news/2001/07/45098#ixzz0wEGpej1O

Goldman, Abigail. "California; Mattel Settles Shareholders Lawsuit For $122 Million The El Segundo-Based Toy Maker Closes The Books On Itsill-Fated $3.5-Billion Purchase Of Learning Co." Los Angeles Times, December 6, 2002.

Gottlieb, Carrie. "Intel's Plan for Staying on Top." Fortune, March 27, 1989, p. 98.

Greene, Jay. "Microsoft's New Bet on Search." Businessweek, September 27, 2007. http://www.businessweek.com/technology/content/sep2007/tc20070926_626712.htm?campaign_id=rss_daily.

Guide to the Charles Vincent Litton papers, 1912-1972. UC Berkeley: Bancroft Library, BANC MSS 75/7 c, 1912-1972.

Haislip, Alex. "Zappos CEO Wanted To Stay Independent, Sequoia Wanted Liquidity—Sources," PE Hub, July 22, 2009. http://www.pehub.com/45388/zappos-ceo-wanted-to-stay-independent-sequoia-wanted-liquidity-sources/

Hansell, Saul. "Yahoo Says It Is Backing Away From TV-Style Web Shows." NY Times, March 2, 2006. http://www.nytimes.com/2006/03/02/technology/02yahoo.html

Hatlestad, Luc. "The Greatest Show on Earth," Red Herring, August 1997.

Helft, Miguel. "Jobs Says Apple's Approach Is Better Than Google's." NY Times Bits Blogs, October 18, 2010. http://bits.blogs.nytimes.com/2010/10/18/steve-jobs-our-approach-is-better-than-googles/

Helft, Miguel. "Will Apple's Culture Hurt the iPhone?" NY Times, October 17, 2010.

Hempel, Jessi. "How Facebook is taking over our lives." Fortune, March 11, 2009. http://money.cnn.com/2009/02/16/technology/hempel_facebook.fortune/index.htm

Hoefler, Don. Semiconduct Family Tree." Electronic News. July 8, 1968. http://archive.computerhistory.org/resources/still-image/PENDING/X3665.2007/Fairchild/FSC_ENews_Hoefler_July68.pdf

Bibliography

Hof, Robert D., Larry Armstrong, & Gary McWilliams. "Intel Unbound." BusinessWeek, October 9, 1995, p. 148.

Hoffman, Thomas. "Intranet Helps Market Shift; Web Data Mart Expands Bank Investment Service." Computerworld Magazine, May 25, 1998.

Hormby, Tom. "The Amiga Story: Conceived at Atari, Born at Commodore." Low End Mac, Nov. 1, 2006. http://lowendmac.com/orchard/06/amiga-origin-commodore.html

Hormby, Tom. "The Story Behind Apple's Newton." Low End Mac, Feb. 7, 2006. http://lowendmac.com/orchard/06/john-sculley-newton-origin.html

Hsieh, Tony. "Why I Sold Zappos." Inc., June 1, 2010. http://www.inc.com/magazine/20100601/why-i-sold-zappos_Printer_Friendly.html

Junnarkar, Sandeep. "Yahoo completes Broadcast.com acquisition." CNET News, July 20, 1999. http://news.cnet.com/Yahoo-completes-Broadcast.com-acquisition/2100-1023_3-228762.html

Kincaid, Jason. "Founders At Work: Uncovering The Truth Behind A Hotmail Founder's Claims." TechCrunch, Feb 23, 2009.

Kirkpatrick, David. "Intel Goes for Broke." Fortune, May 16, 1994, pp. 62--68.

Kirkpatrick, David. "Intel's Amazing Profit Machine." Fortune, February 17, 1997.

Kirkpatrick, David. "Mr. Grove Goes to China." Fortune, August 17, 1998, pp. 154-61.

Kirkpatrick, Marshall. "MySpace: We don't need Web 2.0." TechCrunch, Sept. 12, 2006, techcrunch.com/2006/09/12/myspace-we-dont-need-web-20

Klepper, Steven. "Silicon Valley: A Chip off the Old Detroit Bloc." Draft paper presented at the Entrepreneurship and Innovation Conference, Copenhagen, CBS, Denmark, June 17 - 20, 2008. http://www2.druid.dk/conferences/viewpaper.php?id=4145&cf=29

Krigel, Beth. "Yahoo completes GeoCities acquisition." CNET News, May 28, 1999. http://news.cnet.com/2100-1023-226485.html

La Monica, Paul. "Semel out as Yahoo! CEO." CNNMoney.com, June 18 2007. http://money.cnn.com/2007/06/18/news/companies/yahoo_semel/

Lessin, Jessica, et al. "Apple vs. Google vs. Facebook vs. Amazon." WSJ, Dec. 25, 2012, http://online.wsj.com/article/SB10001424127887324677204578188073738910956.html?mod=WSJ_hpsMIDDLENexttoWhatsNewsSecond#printMode

Levy, Steven. "The Many Sides of Jack Dorsey." Wired, June 22, 2012, http://www.wired.com/business/2012/06/ff_dorsey/all/

Lohr, Steve. "In Sun, Oracle Sees a Software Gem." NY Times, April 20, 2009. http://www.nytimes.com/2009/04/21/technology/companies/21sun.html

Maloney, Janice. "Larry Ellison Is Captain Ahab and Bill Gates Is Moby Dick." Fortune, October 28, 1996.

Mandese, Joe. "Google Study Finds Packaged Goods Spots Perform At 'Parity' Online Vs. TV." ONLINE MEDIA DAILY, Apr 1, 2008. http://publications.mediapost.com/index.cfm?fuseaction=Articles.showArticleHomePage&art_aid=79646.

Markoff, John. "An 'Unknown' Co-Founder Leaves After 20 Years of Glory and Turmoil." NY Times, September 1, 1997. http://www.nytimes.com/1997/09/01/business/an-unknown-co-founder-leaves-after-20-years-of-glory-and-turmoil.html?pagewanted=print

Markoff, John. "Google Cars Drive Themselves, in Traffic." NY Times, Oct. 9, 2010. http://www.nytimes.com/2010/10/10/science/10google.html?adxnnl=1&pagewanted=print&adxnnlx=1288670663-EK5zwUMrO2ZskiQxnzqk+g.

Markoff, John. "Silicon Duo to Take on Microsoft." International Herald Tribune, December 14, 1998.

McCarthy, Caroline. "Facebook: One Social Graph to Rule Them All?" CBS/AP/CNet News, Apr. 21, 2010. http://www.cbsnews.com/stories/2010/04/21/tech/main6418458.shtml.

McGirt, Ellen. "How Cisco's CEO John Chambers Is Turning the Tech Giant Socialist." Fast Company, September 16, 2008. http://www.fastcompany.com/magazine/131/revolution-in-san-jose.html

McNeil, Donald G. "Eat and Tell." NY Times, November 5, 2008. http://www.nytimes.com/2008/11/05/dining/05yelp.html?pagewanted=print

Mehta, Stephanie. "Behold the server farm! Glorious temple of the information age!" Fortune, August 1, 2006. http://money.cnn.com/magazines/fortune/fortune_archive/2006/08/07/8382587/index.htm

Milian, Mark. "GeoCities' time has expired, Yahoo closing the site today." LA Times Blog. October 26, 2009. http://latimesblogs.latimes.com/technology/2009/10/geocities-closing.html

Miller, Claire Cain. "Google Said to Be Near a Yelp Deal." NY Times, December 18, 2009.

Miller, Claire Cain. "The Review Site Yelp Draws Some Outcries of Its Own." NY Times, March 3, 2009. http://www.nytimes.com/2009/03/03/technology/start-ups/03yelp.html?pagewanted=print

533
Bibliography

Miller, Claire Cain. "The Review Site Yelp Draws Some Outcries of Its Own." NY Times, March 3, 2009. http://www.nytimes.com/2009/03/03/technology/start-ups/03yelp.html?pagewanted=print

Miller, Rich. "The Fully Operational iDataCenter." Data Center Knowledge, Oct. 24, 2010. http://www.datacenterknowledge.com/archives/2010/10/24/video-the-fully-operational-idatacenter/

Morrison, Scott. "Yahoo Chief Defends Her Site, Strategy." WSJ, June 25, 2010.

Mossberg, Walter S. "Apple iPad Review: Laptop Killer? Pretty Close." WSJ All Things Digital, March 31, 2010. http://ptech.allthingsd.com/20100331/apple-ipad-review/.

Olsen, Stefanie & Margaret Kane. "Yahoo to buy Overture for $1.63 billion." CNET News, July 14, 2003. http://news.cnet.com/2100-1030_3-1025394.html

Paczkowski, John. "Departing Sun Co-Founder to Employees: 'Kick Butt and Have Fun!'" All Things D, Digital Daily, January 26, 2010. http://digitaldaily.allthingsd.com/20100126/sun-co-founder-to-employees-kick-butt-and-have-fun/

Palmer, Jay. "Zero Hour." Barron's October 4, 1999, pp. 33--34, 36.

Perkins, Anthony. "Oracle CEO Larry Ellison on Building the Multimedia Library." Red Herring, May 1994.

Pita, Julia. "The Arrogance Was Unnecessary." Forbes, September 2, 1991.

PricewaterhouseCoopers. "Internet Advertising Revenues Again Reach New Highs, Estimated to Pass $21 Billion in 2007 and Hit Nearly $6 Billion in Q4 2007." February 25, 2008. http://www.iab.net/about_the_iab/recent_press_releases/press_release_archive/press_release/195115.

Reinhardt, Andy, Ira Sager, and Peter Burrows. "Intel: Can Andy Grove Keep Profits Up in an Era of Cheap PCs?" BusinessWeek, December 22, 1997.

Reinhardt, Andy. "Who Says Intel's Chips Are Down?" BusinessWeek, December 7, 1998, p. 103.

Reinhardt, Andy. "The New Intel: Craig Barrett Is Leading the Chip Giant into Riskier Terrain." BusinessWeek, March 13, 2000, p. 110.

Ristelhueber, Robert. "Intel: The Company People Love to Hate." Electronic Business Buyer, September 1993, pp. 58-67.

Rivlin, Gary. "Wallflower at the Web Party." NY Times, Oct. 15, 2006.

Roberts, H. Edward & William Yates. "Altair 8800 minicomputer." Popular Electronics, January 1975.

Rosenblatt, Richard. "Former MySpace Chairman Richard Rosenblatt's Advice To The New Executive Team." TechCrunch, May 4, 2009. http://techcrunch.com/2009/05/04/former-myspace-chairman-richard-rosenblatts-advice-to-the-new-executive-team/

Rowley, James. "Antitrust Pick Varney Saw Google as Next Microsoft (Update2)." Bloomberg, February 17, 2009.

Rusli, Evelyn. "Yelp's CEO On Google: We Were Suprised...I Don't Think It's A Permanent Situation." TechCrunch, July 31, 2010.

Schiffman, Betsy. "A Community That Stays Together, Pays Together." Forbes, August 28, 2001. http://www.forbes.com/2001/08/28/0828yahoo.html

Schlender, Brent. "Javaman: The Adventures of Scott McNealy." Fortune, October 13, 1997.

Schlender, Brenton R. "Software Tiger: Oracle Spurs Its Fast Growth with Aggressive Style." Wall Street Journal, May 31, 1989.

Schonfeld, Erick. "Kijiji" Isn't Kutting It. How about eBay Classifieds?" TechCrunch, Feb 28, 2009. http://techcrunch.com/2009/02/28/kijiji-isnt-kutting-it-how-about-ebay-classifieds/

SF Chronicle, July 18, 2010. http://articles.sfgate.com/2010-07-18/news/21988334_1_free-e-editions-print-paper

Shankland, Stephen. "Oracle buys Sun, becomes hardware company." CNet News, January 27, 2010. http://news.cnet.com/8301-30685_3-20000019-264.html

Sharpe, Ed. "Hewlett-Packard The Start -2." Southwest Museum of Engineering, Communications and Computation. http://www.smecc.org/hewlett-packard_the_start__-2.htm

Sharpe, Ed. "Hewlett-Packard, The Early Years." Southwest Museum of Engineering, Communications and Computation. http://www.smecc.org/hewlett-packard,_the_early_years.htm

Sharpe, Ed. "The Life of Fred Terman." Southwest Museum of Engineering, Communications and Computation, Vol. 3, Iss. 1. http://www.smecc.org/frederick_terman_-_by_ed_sharpe.htm

Steel, Emily. "Sizing Up a Post-Yahoo Ad Landscape." WSJ, April 11, 2008, B7. http://online.wsj.com/article/SB120787375527206619.html?mod=technology_main_whats_news

Stoppelman, Jeremy. "For Yelp, Locals Aren't Yokels." Newsweek, Oct. 21, 2009. http://www.newsweek.com/2009/10/21/for-yelp-locals-aren-t-yokels.html

Swartz, Jon. "EXECUTIVE SUITE: Losing's not an option for Cuban." USA Today, April 26, 2004. http://www.usatoday.com/money/2004-04-25-cuban_x.htm

Bibliography

Tam, Pui-Wing, et al. "Startups Adjust to Web's Down Cycle." WSJ, Dec. 23, 2012, http://online.wsj.com/article/SB10001424127887324296604578177541652032424.html?mod=go oglenews_wsj&_nocache=1357622123002&user=welcome&mg=id-wsj#printMode.

Temple, James. "Craigslist suit may challenge Whitman campaign." TechCrunch, Sep 12, 2006.

The Precursor Blog, May 4, 2010. http://precursorblog.com/content/why-googles-search-ad-monopoly-understated

Thomas, Owen. "Exclusive: 18 new ways Mark Zuckerberg rules social networking." VentureBeat, August 4, 2010.

Thompson, Bob. "Search Me? Google Wants to Digitize Every Book. Publishers Say Read the Fine Print First." Washington Post, August 13, 2006, http://www.washingtonpost.com/wp-dyn/content/article/2006/08/12/AR2006081200886_pf.html.

Torget, John W. "Learning from Mattel," Tuck School of Business at Dartmouth, Case no. 1-0072, 2002.

Ulanoff, Lance. "Is Google a Monopoly?" PCMag, May 9, 2007.

Ashlee Vance . "Elon Musk, the 21st Century Industrialist." Bloomberg Businessweek, September 13, 2012, http://www.businessweek.com/articles/2012-09-13/elon-musk-the-21st-century-industrialist

Vargas, Jose Antonio. "The Face of Facebook." New Yorker. September 20, 2010. http://www.newyorker.com/reporting/2010/09/20/100920fa_fact_vargas?printable=true#ixzz0zR vbAHqK

Varian, Hal. "Our Secret Sauce." The Official Google Blog, Feb. 28, 2008. http://googleblog.blogspot.com/2008/02/our-secret-sauce.html.

Weiss, Philip. "A Guy Named Craig." New York Magazine, Jan 8, 2006.

Wells, Alicia. "TNS Media Intelligence Reports US Advertising Expenditures Grew 0.2 Percent in 2007." TNS Media Intelligence, March 25, 2008. http://www.tns-mi.com/news/03252008.htm.

Whoriskey, Peter. "CBS Scores on the Web With March Madness." Wash. Post, April 17, 2008, D01. http://www.washingtonpost.com/wp-dyn/content/article/2008/04/16/AR2008041603481.html?referrer=emailarticle.

Wilson, John W. "Intel Wakes Up to a Whole New Marketplace in Chips." BusinessWeek, September 2, 1985, pp. 73.

Wolf, Gary. "Why Craigslist Is Such a Mess." Wired, August 24, 2009.

Wolverton, Troy. "Pets.com latest high-profile dot-com disaster." CNET News, Nov. 7, 2000. http://news.cnet.com/2100-1017-248230.html

Worthen, Ben & Brent Kendall. "Justice Department Sues Oracle for Fraud." WSJ, July 30, 2010. http://online.wsj.com/article/SB10001424052748703578104575397573983263294.html

Venture Capital and Service Professionals

"American Keiretsu." Red Herring, January 31, 1998. http://www.redherring.com/Home/8219

"Making a Difference for 30 Years--1962-1992." Jefferies & Company, Inc., http://www.jefo.com, 1998.

"Mercenaries vs. Missionaries: John Doerr Sees Two Kinds of Internet Entrepreneurs." Knowledge@Wharton, April 13, 2000.

"NEA closes 13th fund with $2.5B." San Jose Business Journal, January 6, 2010. http://sanjose.bizjournals.com/sanjose/stories/2010/01/04/daily53.html?f=et79&jst=e_cn_lk&ian a=&s=du&ed=2010-01-06

"Top 100 Venture Capital Firms, Early Stage." Entrepreneur Magazine, 2008. http://www.entrepreneur.com/vc100/stage/early.html

Abate, Tom. "Moritz gives $50 million to Oxford." SF Chronicle, June 17, 2008. http://articles.sfgate.com/2008-06-17/business/17165214_1_sequoia-venture-capital-chief-executive-eric-schmidt-bay-area-venture

Allbritton, Chris. "Silicon Valley's Man with a Mission Faces Off Against Microsoft ...." Los Angeles Times, May 10, 1998, p. 2.

Ante, Spencer E. "Michael Moritz: Lessons from a Long-Ball Hitter." Bloomberg Businessweek, February 25, 2009.

Appleyard, Bryan. "Nassim Nicholas Taleb: the prophet of boom and doom." Sunday Times, June 1, 2008. http://business.timesonline.co.uk/tol/business/economics/article4022091.ece

Baum, Geoff. "Accountant, Lawyer, Banker, Flack." Forbes, August 25, 1997, pp. 99-100.

Bhatt, Kamla. "Interview with Ram Shriram: Part 1." LiveMint, November 30, 2008.

Bhatt, Kamla. "Listen to Google's first investor." LiveMint, December 4, 2008. http://www.livemint.com/Articles/PrintArticle.aspx?artid=507C367E-C1E7-11DD-AB22-000B5DABF613

Brandt, Richard L., "Interview: Gary Reback." Upside, February 1998, pp. 92-94.

535
Bibliography

Brockman, John. "The Coach: John Doerr." Edge Digerati. http://www.edge.org/digerati/doerr/index.html

Calvey, Mark. "Culture shock -- J.P. Morgan jolts Hambrecht & Quist."

Cambridge Associates LLC. "US Venture Capital Index And Benchmark Statistics, Non-Marketable Alternative Assets." December 31, 2009.

Castilla, Emilio. "Networks of venture capital firms in Silicon Valley." Intl. Journal of Tech. Mgmt, 25, Part ½, 2003, pp. 113-135.

Christie, Les. "The ABCs of a unique IPO - The hottest tech IPO in years will be run as a 'Dutch Auction.'" CNN Money, April 29, 2004.

Connon, Heather. "Gags-to-riches tale of the Welsh wizard who bet on YouTube." The Observer, October 15, 2006.

Cox, Rob. "A History Lesson With Merrill Deal." Breakingviews/NY Times, January 23, 2009.

Davies, Erin. "Silicon Valley Law." Fortune, August 3, 1998, pp. 219-20, 222.

Deger, Renee. "Alive and Kicking." The Recorder, June 06, 2002. http://www.law.com/jsp/ca/PubArticleCA.jsp?id=900005369500&slreturn=1&hbxlogin=1.

Fabrikant, Geraldine. "Lionel Pincus, Who Helped Bring Investors to Private Equity, Dies at 78." NY Times, October 11, 2009, A24.

Fineberg, Seth A. "Congress Approves Revised Rollover Law." Venture Capital Journal, August 1, 1998, p. 1.

Friedman, Thomas L. "Start-Ups, Not Bailouts." NY Times, April 3, 2010, WK9.

Fryer, Bronwyn. "The Firm." Gentry, July 1998, pp. 71-75.

Gompers, Paul. "The Rise and Fall of Venture Capital." Business and Economic History, Vol. 23, no. 2, Winter 1994.

Green, M. B. "Venture Capital Investment in the United States 1995-2002." The Industrial Geographer 2(1), 2004, pp. 2-29.

Gross, Daniel. "The Dot-Firm's Dot-Bomb: How a leading West Coast law firm killed itself." Slate, Jan. 31, 2003. http://www.slate.com/id/2077953.

Helft, Miguel. "Rental Building's Good Karma Nurtures Success." NY Times, September 14, 2007.

Horne, William W. "A Maverick Matures." American Lawyer, September 1996.

Kahn, Joseph & Patrick McGeehan. "Chase Agrees to Acquire Hambrecht & Quist." NY Times, September 29, 1999.

Kedrosky, Paul. "Right-sizing the US Venture Capital Industry." Ewing Marion Kauffman Foundation, June 10, 2009. http://www.kauffman.org/uploadedFiles/USVentCap061009r1.pdf

Ken Wilcox. "Startup Outlook 2010." SVB Financial Group. April 19, 2010. http://www.svb.com/10096/Special_Report__Startup_Outlook_2010/

Khan, Amina. "Venturing Gone Awry." Forbes, Jan. 29, 2009. http://www.forbes.com/2009/01/29/novalux-venture-midas-technology_0129_flop.html

Kirsner, Scott. "Venture capital's grandfather." The Boston Globe, April 6, 2008.

Kleinbard, David. "The $1.7 trillion dot.com lesson." CNN Money, November 9, 2000. http://money.cnn.com/2000/11/09/technology/overview/

Kurtzman, Joel. "PROSPECTS; Venture Capital." New York Times, March 27, 1988.

Lashinsky, Adam. "Kleiner bets the farm." Fortune, July 24, 2008.

Lueck, Thomas J. " High Tech's Glamour Fades for Some Venture Capitalists." New York Times, February 6, 1987.

Malone, Michael S. "John Doerr's Startup Manual." Fast Company, February 28, 1997. http://www.fastcompany.com/magazine/07/082doerr.html

Marshall, Matt & Michael Bazeley. "Q&A with Kleiner Perkins Caufield & Byers." San Jose Mercury News, Nov. 13, 2004.

Miller, Claire Cain. "A New Kind of Venture Capitalist Makes Small Bets on Young Firms." NY Times, September 21, 2008.

Miller, Claire Cain. "Blair to Join Venture Firm as Adviser on Technology." NY Times, May 24, 2010. http://www.nytimes.com/2010/05/25/technology/25blair.html?dbk.

Murphy, Tom. "Merger Hits 'Wall Street West' Powerbase Shifting To Charlotte, N.C." CBS MarketWatch, April 4, 1998.

Neidorf, Shawn. "Silicon Valley Lawyers Embrace VC-Like Role." Venture Capital Journal, October 1, 1999, pp. 35-37.

O'Brien, Tia. "Top VC Doerr apologizes for helping fuel dot-com frenzy." San Jose Mercury News, July 15, 2001.

Parloff, Roger. "Scandals rock Silicon Valley's top legal ace." Fortune, November 17, 2006. http://money.cnn.com/magazines/fortune/fortune_archive/2006/11/27/8394382/index.htm.

Pollack, Andrew. "Venture Capital Loses Its Vigor." New York Times, October 8, 1989.

Bibliography

Pratt, Tom. "Jefferies' Equity Effort Expands into New Issues." Investment Dealers Digest, April 19, 1993, p. 14.

PricewaterhouseCoopers/National Venture Capital Association. "MoneyTree™ Report, Data: Thomson Reuters." Reuters, Jan. 22, 2010.

Reiner, Martha L. "Innovation and the Creation of Venture Capital Organizations." Business and Economic History, Second Series, Volume Twenty, 1991, http://www.h-net.org/~business/bhcweb/publications/BEHprint/v020/p0200-p0209.pdf

Reiner, Martha L. "The Transformation of Venture Capital: A History of Venture Capital Organization in the United States." Ph.D. Dissertation, University of California, Berkeley, 1989.

Rivlin, Gary. "A Counselor Pulled From the Shadows." NY Times, July 30, 2006. http://query.nytimes.com/gst/fullpage.html?res=9402E7D7123FF933A05754C0A9609C8B63&sec=&spon=&pagewanted=print.

Schwimmer, Anne. "Something to Cheer About." Investment Dealers Digest, September 27, 1993, pp. 16-21.

Sweeney, Jack. "Busy Plaintiffs Keep Silicon Valley on Edge." Computer Reseller News, November 28, 1994, p. 1.

Toal, Brian A. "New Jefferies Energy Group Gets Off to Fast 1993 Deal Pace." Oil & Gas Investor, October 1993, pp. 16-22.

Vrana, Deborah. "Jefferies' New Age: When Frank Baxter Took Over in the '80s." Los Angeles Times, March 22, 1998, p. D-1.

Wild, Joff. "The Battle for Clients in the Golden State." Managing Intellectual Property (London), May 1996, p. 14.

Wilson Sonsini Goodrich and Rosati, "The Entrepreneurs Report: Private Company Financing Trends," Summer 2009. http://www.wsgr.com/publications/PDFSearch/entreport/Summer2009/private-company-financing-trends.htm.

Zuckerman, Sam. "Big S.F. Bank Sold to Chase In New York: Hambrecht & Quist caters to Silicon Valley." SF Chronicle, September 29, 1999.

Science, Technology, and Universities

Adams, Stephen B. "Regionalism in Stanford's Contribution to the Rise of Silicon Valley." Enterprise and Society 4(3), 2003.

Adams, Stephen B. "Stanford and Silicon Valley, Lessons on becoming a high-tech Region." California Management Review, 48(1), 2005, pp. 29-51.

Arthur, W. B. "Increasing returns and the new world of business." Harvard Business Review, 1996, pp. 100-109.

Arthur, W. B. "Positive feedbacks in the economy." Scientific American 262, 1990, pp. 92-99.

Besen, S. M. & J. Farrel. "Choosing how to compete: Strategies and tactics in standardization." Journal of Economic Perspectives 8, 1994, pp. 117-31.

Blank, Steve. "Hidden in Plain Sight: The Secret History of Silicon Valley." Computer History Museum, Presentation on Nov. 20, 2008. http://www.slideshare.net/startuplessonslearned/steve-blanks-secret-history-of-silicon-valley-talk-at-computer-history-museum-112008-presentation, and http://www.youtube.com/watch?v=hFSPHfZQpIQ.

Blum, Walter, "The Grand Vizier of the age of electronics: Terman of Stanford," San Francisco Examiner, 24 March 1963.

Bush, Vannevar. "As We May Think." The Atlantic, July 1945. http://www.theatlantic.com/magazine/archive/1969/12/as-we-may-think/3881/

Campbell-Kelly, Martin. "The History of the History of Software." IEEE Annals of the History of Computing 29 #4, Oct.-Dec. 2007, pp. 40-51.

Chou, D. and O. Shy. "Network effects without network externalities. International Journal of Industrial Organization." 8, 1990, pp. 259-270.

Church, J and N. Gandal. "Complementary network externalities and technological adoption." International Journal of Industrial Organization 11, 1993, pp. 239-260.

Comins, Michael. "Ad Networks vs. Ad Servers, IMediaConnection, May 26, 2004. http://www.imediaconnection.com/content/3523.asp

David, P. A. "Clio and the economics of QWERTY." American Economic Review 75, 1985, pp. 332-37.

Economides, Nicholas. "The Economics of Networks." International Journal of Industrial Organization, October 1996.

Elder, Rob. "The man who discovered electronic gold at Stanford," San Jose Mercury-News, 2 October 1977.

Bibliography

Ellis H. S. and W. Fellner. "External economies and diseconomies." American Economic Review 33, 1943, pp. 493-511.

Farrell J. and G. Saloner. "Standardization, compatibility, and innovation." Rand Journal 16, 1985, pp. 70-83.

Farrell, Joseph & Paul Klemperer. "Coordination and Lock-In: Competition with Switching Costs and Network Effects." Handbook of Industrial Organization, Volume 3, Edited by M. Armstrong and R. Porter.

Gandal, Neil. "Network goods (empirical studies)." The New Palgrave Dictionary of Economics, Second Edition. Eds. Steven N. Durlauf and Lawrence E. Blume. Palgrave Macmillan, 2008. The New Palgrave Dictionary of Economics Online. Palgrave Macmillan. 23 August 2010.

Glover, Frederic O. "Dr. Terman's paper trail," Sandstone and Tile, Winter, 1979.

Katz, Michael and Carl Shapiro. " Network externalities, competition, and compatibility." American Economic Review 75, 1985, pp. 424-440.

Katz, Michael and Carl Shapiro. " Systems competition and network effects." Journal of Economic Perspectives 8, 1994, pp. 93-115.

Katz, Michael and Carl Shapiro. " Technology adoption in the presence of network externalities." Journal of Political Economy 94, 1986, pp. 822-841.

Kay, Alan C. "The Early History of Smalltalk." ACM Sigplan Notices, 28 No. 3, 1993, p. 69.

Kenney, Martin. "California Universities and Internet-based Entrepreneurship." Berkeley Roundtable on the International Economy, UC Berkeley, July 21, 2003. http://www.stanford.edu/dept/HPST/TimLenoir/Startup/VolumeDrafts/14_Kenney_CalUniversiti esAndEntrepreneurship.pdf

Klemperer, Paul. "Network goods (theory)." The New Palgrave Dictionary of Economics, Second Edition. Eds. Steven N. Durlauf and Lawrence E. Blume. Palgrave Macmillan, 2008.

Klemperer, Paul. "Network goods (theory)." The New Palgrave Dictionary of Economics. Second Edition. Eds. Steven N. Durlauf and Lawrence E. Blume. Palgrave Macmillan, 2008. The New Palgrave Dictionary of Economics Online. Palgrave Macmillan. 23 August 2010.

Knight, Frank. "Some fallacies in the interpretation of social cost." Quarterly Journal of Economics 38, 1924, pp. 582-606.

Lecuyer, Christophe. "Hewlett-Packard and Stanford University." Feb. 4, 2003. http://www.stanford.edu/dept/HPST/TimLenoir/Startup/VolumeDrafts/08_Lecuyer_Stanford-and-HP.pdf.

Leibenstein, H. "Bandwagon, snob, and Veblen effects in the theory of consumer's demand." Quarterly Journal of Economics 64, 1950, pp. 183-207.

Lenoir, Timothy, Nathan Rosenberg et al. "Inventing the Entrepreneurial University: Stanford and the Co-Evolution of Silicon Valley." Stanford SIEPR, Aug. 2003, http://www.stanford.edu/dept/HPS/TimLenoir/Startup/VolumeDrafts/Lenoir_IntroductionDraft.pdf.

Lenoir, Timothy. "Terman and Early Venture Capital." Stanford Univ. unpublished manuscript, 2003.

Lenoir, Timothy. "The Terman Model: Steeple Building and a Recipe for Distinction." Stanford Univ. unpublished manuscript, 2003.

Leonard-Barton, Dorothy. "Core capabilities and core rigidities: a paradox in managing new products," Strategic Management Journal, 13:111, 1992.

Liebowitz, S. J. and Stephen Margolis. "Are network externalities a new source of market failure?" Research In Law And Economics 17, 1995, pp. 1-22.

Liebowitz, S. J. and Stephen Margolis. "Market processes and the selection of standards." Harvard Journal of Law and Technology 9, 1996, pp. 283-318.

Liebowitz, S. J. and Stephen Margolis. "Path dependence, lock-in and history." Journal of Law, Economics and Organization 11, 1995, pp. 205-226.

Liebowitz, S. J. and Stephen Margolis. "The fable of the keys." Journal of Law and Economics 33, 1990, pp. 1-26.

Liebowitz, S.J. and Stephen E. Margolis. "Network Externalities (Effects)." http://wwwpub.utdallas.edu/~liebowit/palgrave/network.html

Medeiros, Frank A. "The Sterling years at Stanford: a study in the dynamics of institutional change," Ph.D. dissertation, Stanford University, 1979.

Moody, James & Martina Morris. "Social networks, economic relevance of." The New Palgrave Dictionary of Economics. Second Edition. Eds. Steven N. Durlauf and Lawrence E. Blume. Palgrave Macmillan, 2008. The New Palgrave Dictionary of Economics Online. Palgrave Macmillan. 23 August 2010.

Noyce, R.N., and M.E. Hoff. "A History of Microprocessor Development at Intel." IEEE Micro 1 #1 Feb. 1981, pp. 8-21.

Bibliography

Paine, Adelaide. "Dr. Frederick Emmons Terman: Vice President, Provost, Stanford University," The Microwave Journal, March 1961.

Rosenberg, Nathan, Brent Goldfarb, & Jeannette Colyvas. "Stanford Inventive Activity: Report to Dean Kruger (Confidential)." Stanford Univ. unpublished manuscript, Fall 2002. http://www.stanford.edu/dept/HPST/TimLenoir/Startup/VolumeDrafts/03_Rosenberg-Colyvas-Goldfarb_MeasuringInventiveness.pdf

Rowen, Henry S. & Rebecca Sheehan. "The GSB and Silicon Valley." Stanford Univ., Sept. 2002. http://www.stanford.edu/dept/HPST/TimLenoir/Startup/VolumeDrafts/10_Rowen-Sheehan_GSB.pdf

Salzman, Ed. "One man sparks Peninsula electronics boom," Oakland Tribune, May 1961.

Sharpe, Ed. "The Life of Frederick Terman." SMEC Vintage Electrics Vol #3, Issue #1, 1991. http://www.smecc.org/frederick_terman_-_by_ed_sharpe.htm

Wall, Aaron. "History of Search Engines: From 1945 to Google 2007 (2007)." http://www.searchenginehistory.com/

Wall, Wall. "How Search Engines Work: Search Engine Relevancy." June 13, 2006. http://www.seobook.com/relevancy/.

Williams, James C. "Frederick E. Terman and the rise of Silicon Valley." International Journal of Technology Management, Volume 16, Number 8 / 1998, pp. 751 – 760.

WEBSITES

"eBay History." Ebayinc History. n.d. Web. 3 Feb. 2013. http://www.ebayinc.com/history

"A History of Innovation: The Events and People that Shaped Intel." Intel Corporate Archives. n.d. Web. 3 Feb. 2013. http://www.intel.com/about/companyinfo/museum/archives/index.htm

"A VC: Musings of a VC in NYC." Fred Anderson Blog. 3 Feb. 2013. Web. 3 Feb. 2013. http://www.avc.com/

"Chris Dixon's Blog." Chris Dixon Blog. n.d. Web. 3 Feb. 2013. http://cdixon.org/

"CNet News." CNet News, n.d. Web. 3 Feb. 2013. http://news.cnet.com/

"EDGAR Company Search." US Securities and Exchange Commission. 11 Feb. 2010. Web. 3 Feb. 2013. http://www.sec.gov/edgar/searchedgar/companysearch.html

"Gartner IT Research." Gartner Corp. IT Research Portal, n.d. Web. 3 Feb. 2013. https://www.gartner.com/login/loginInitAction.do?method=initialize

"GigaOM." GigaOM News, n.d. Web. 3 Feb. 2013. http://gigaom.com/

"Google Milestones." Google Corporate Information. n.d. Web. 3 Feb. 2013. http://www.google.com/corporate/milestones.html

"History of Science and Tecnology Sources, UC Berkeley" n.d. Updates and expands Rider's and Lowood's "Guide to Sources in Northern California for History of Science and Technolog" published by the Office for History of Science and Technology in 1985. Web. 3 Feb. 2013. http://bancroft.berkeley.edu/collections/hstc/about.html

"How to Change the World: A Practical Blog for Impractical People." Guy Kawasaki Blog. 24 Aug. 2010. Web. 3 Feb. 2013. http://blog.guykawasaki.com/

"Latest Industry Statistics – Venture Capital." National Venture Capital Association. 1 Feb. 2013. Web. 3 Feb. 2013. http://www.nvca.org/index.php?option=com_content&view=article&id=78&Itemid=102

"New Emerging Technology News and Trends: GigaOM Tech News." GigaOm. 3 Feb. 2013. Web. 3 Feb. 2013. http://gigaom.com/

"Paul Graham Essays." Paul Graham Website. n.d. Web. 3 Feb. 2013. http://www.paulgraham.com/articles.html

"Research Library: Collection Highlights." History San Jose, Silicon Valley from a to z. n.d. Web. 3 Feb. 2013. http://www.historysanjose.org/research/library/collection_highlights.html

"Sandstone and Tile." Stanford Historical Society. n.d. Web. 3 Feb. 2013. http://histsoc.stanford.edu/STbackfiles.shtml

"Santa Clara Valley Historical Association: Recording Silicon Valley's History and the High-Technology Revolution." Santa Clara Valley Historical Association. n.d. Web. 3 Feb. 2013. http://www.siliconvalleyhistorical.org/home

"Secret History of Silicon Valley." Steve Blank. n.d. Web. 3 Feb. 2013. http://steveblank.com/secret-history/

"Silicon Genesis: An Oral History of Semiconductor Technology." Stanford University. 3 Dec. 2008. Web. 3 Feb. 2013. http://silicongenesis.stanford.edu/complete_listing.html

"Silicon Valley 150." San Jose Mercury News. n.d. Web. 3 Feb. 2013. http://www.siliconvalley.com/sv150

Bibliography

"Silicon Valley History Online." California State Librarian. n.d. Web. 3 Feb. 2013. http://www.siliconvalleyhistory.org/

"Secret History of Silicon Valley." Steve Blank's Blog. 23 Sept. 2010. Web. 3 Feb. 2013. http://steveblank.com/category/secret-history-of-silicon-valley/

"Stanford University Libraries Special Collections & University Archives, Finding Aids. n.d. Web. 3 Feb. 2013. http://www-sul.stanford.edu/depts/spc/findaids.html

"TechCrunch." TechCrunch. 3 Feb. 2013. Web. 3 Feb. 2013. http://techcrunch.com/

"The Official Google Blog: Insights from Googlers into our Products, Technology, and the Google Culture." Google Corp. 3 Feb. 2013. 3 Feb. 2013. http://googleblog.blogspot.com/

"The Stanford Silicon Valley Archives: Selected Holdings." Stanford University. n.d. Web. 3 Feb. 2013. http://svarchive.stanford.edu/holdings.html

"Timeline of Computer History." Computer History Museum. n.d. Web. 3 Feb. 2013. http://www.computerhistory.org/timeline/

"UC Berkeley Bancroft Library Finding Aids." UC Berkeley Library, n.d. Web. 3 Feb. 2013. http://bancroft.berkeley.edu/collections/findingaids.html

"UC Berkeley Regional History Office (Business History - Venture Capitalists – Science, Medicine, and Technology)." UC Berkeley Library, n.d. Web. 3 Feb. 2013. http://bancroft.berkeley.edu/ROHO/collections/subjectarea/index.html

"Venture Capitalists Oral History Project." Bancroft Library (UCB) Oral Histories. 4 Aug. 2010. Web. 3 Feb. 2013. http://bancroft.berkeley.edu/ROHO/projects/vc/transcripts.html

"VentureBeat: Interpreting Innovation." VentureBeat. n.d. Web. 3 Feb. 2013. http://venturebeat.com/

"Welcome to the Digibarn Computer Museum." Digibarn. n.d. Web. 3 Feb. 2013. http://www.digibarn.com/

"ZDNet: Technology, News, Analysis, Commentary." ZDNet News, n.d. Web. 3 Feb. 2013. http://www.zdnet.com/

Alphabetical Index

@Home, 362, 406
1366 Technologies, 463
23andme, 462
2Web Technologies, 450
3270, 179
3Com, 362
3PAR, 412, 449
4004, 170
8010 Star Information System, 190
AARON, 183
Abrams Jonathan, 408
Abrons Adam, 472
Acadia, 455
Accel, 365
ACE, 75
Acer, 365, 455
Achronix, 456
Ackerman William, 194
Acorn, 216, 232
ACT, 416
Activision, 211, 457
Adams Ansel, 34, 86
Adams Rick, 310
Adaptec, 186, 306
Adelson Edward, 436
Adelson Jay, 440
Adobe Books Backroom Gallery, 444
Adobe, 155, 212, 323
ADR, 212
ADS, 214, 307
AdSense, 379
Adura Technologies, 464
Advanced Memory Systems, 122
AdWords, 378
Aerial Images, 360
Aerie Networks, 363
AES, 171
Affiliated Computer Services, 455
Affymax Research Institute, 330
Affymetrix, 331, 462
Agarawala Anand, 451
Agarwal Anant, 459
Agile Software, 368
Agus David, 461
Ahti Heinla, 412
AIDS, 214
Aiken Howard, 59, 76
Ajax, 440
Akamai, 360
Akerlof George, 459
Akhtari Saeid, 442
Aldridge Greg, 440
Aldus, 236, 251
Alexander Sam, 76
Alivisatos Paul, 442
Allen Paul, 174, 420
Allison David, 93

Almaden Research Center, 178
Almogy Gilad, 463
Alsop Stewart, 371
Altair, 174
AltaRock Energy, 463
AltaVista, 352, 409
Altera, 213, 256
AlterNet, 310
Alto, 17, 19, 23-24, 45, 47-49, 52-53, 143-162, 179, 190, 213-15, 227, 233-34, 240, 258, 376, 399
Alvarez Luis, 39
Alza, 134, 181, 261, 374
Amazon, 434, 436, 440
Amazon.com, 358
Amber Networks, 363
AMD, 123, 177, 410, 456
Amdahl Gene, 76, 105
Amelco, 111
Amelio Gil, 241
American Anti-Imperialist League, 33
American Music Club, 263
Ameritech, 353
Ames Aeronautical Laboratory, 39
Amgen, 194
Amiga, 252
Ampex, 59, 82, 113, 187
AMT, 111
Amyris Biotechnologies, 415
and, 437
Anderson Fred, 92
Andreessen Marc, 289, 319, 433
Andregg Michael and William, 462
Android, 447
Angry Birds, 458
Ant Farm, 118, 183
AOL, 258, 366, 406, 431
Apollo, 191, 215, 259
Apple Lisa, 154, 155, 232-35, 240
Apple Macintosh, 152, 154, 155, 222, 227, 232-35, 240-43
Apple Newton, 27, 221, 222, 223, 224, 225, 243
Apple, 17, 19, 27, 96, 102, 103, 146, 154-62, 167, 176, 210, 213-48, 254, 323, 335, 370, 387-88, 390, 412, 446, 448, 452
Applera, 373
Appleseed, 454
Applied Biosystems, 194, 261, 372
Applied Materials, 463
APT, 90
Archie, 320
Architext, 351
ARD, 62, 67-74
Arguelles Jose, 317
Ariba, 368
ARM, 216, 410, 456

Alphabetical Index

Armour Polly Jean, 320
Arneson Robert, 116
Arora Samir, 359
ARPA, 106
Arpanet, 107, 189, 218
ArrayComm, 325
Arrington Michael, 441
Arrowhead Computers, 176
Artists Liberation Front, 117
Artzt Russell, 212
Ascend Communications, 354
Ashton-Tate, 211, 237
Asilomar Conference, 181
Asset Management, 133
AT&T, 32, 43, 60, 77-80, 104, 135, 189, 191, 217, 309, 326, 327, 353, 363
Atanasoff John, 43
Atari, 99, 102, 133, 213, 221-22, 228, 231-32
Atheros, 370, 456
Atkinson Bill, 254, 323
Atsutoshi Nishida, 257
Augello Christina, 263
Auspex, 259
Autodesk, 211
Avey Linda, 462
Baan, 369
Babel Fish, 352
Bachman Charles, 104
Backus John, 89
Baer Ralph, 133
Baidu, 351
Baillie Bruce, 116
Bakalar David, 79
Balkanski Alexandre, 323
Balkin Amy, 444
Ballmer Steve, 384
Bamji Cyrus, 459
Banhart Devendra, 374
Bar-Hillel Yehoshua, 88
Baran Paul, 106, 134
Bardeen John, 60, 145
Barton Jim, 216, 371
BASIC, 105
Bass Charlie, 188
Bauer Walter, 136
Bay Counties Wireless Telegraph Association, 32
Bay Networks, 362
BBN, 172, 194
BCC, 145
BEA Systems, 26, 205, 206
BEA, 355, 455
Beach Thompson, 31
Bechtolsheim Andy, 215, 258, 336-37, 342, 353, 376
Becker Gary, 459
Bell Earl, 115
Bell Gordon, 114
BELLA, 465
Benchmark Capital, 338, 342, 345, 392, 427
Bendix, 80, 123
Benioff Marc, 408

Benner Steven, 261
Bennett Tom, 177
Berg Paul, 181
Berg Peter, 142
Berkeley Bionics, 418
Berkeley Lab Lawrence, 312
Berkeley Labs Lawrence, 373
Berkeley National Laboratory Lawrence, 441
Berkeley, UC 18-19, 22, 24, 49, 95, 97, 120, 125, 146-49, 159, 206, 227, 266, 283, 337
Berners-Lee Tim, 318, 356
Berners-Lee, 439
Bessemer Securities, 133
Bethke Bruce, 260
Bezos Jeff, 336, 342, 358
Bhabha Homi, 85
Bhardwaj Vinod, 156
Bhatia Sabeer, 354
Bianchini Gina, 433
Bina Eric, 319
Biogen, 194
Bischoff Elmer, 86
Bishop Amasa, 85
BitTorrent, 412
Black Panther Party, 117
Blackberry, 410
BlackBerry, 446
Blackburn Elizabeth, 459
Blectum From Blechdom, 374
BLEEX, 418
Blekko, 454
Bloch Felix, 39, 84
Blogger, 381
Blogger.com, 408
Bloglines, 440
Bloom Energy, 417
Bohnett David, 349
Bolt, Beranek and Newman, 217
Bomis, 414
Borland, 211, 368
Bosack Leonard, 258
Botha Roelof, 409, 434
Boucher David, 251
Boucher Larry, 186
Boucher Laurence, 306
Boyer Herbert, 181, 193
Boyle Willard, 324
Boyse Lee, 170
Boysel Lee, 110, 122
Brainerd Paul, 236
Brand Stewart, 117, 228, 262, 374
Brandenburg Karlheinz, 371
Brattain Walter, 60
Bravo, 179
Brenner Sydney, 331, 372, 459
Brewer Eric, 352
Bricklin Dan, 184
Bridge Communications, 258
Brin Sergei, 27, 376, 381, 385, 386
Brin Sergey, 27, 336, 352, 376
Britvich Ron, 364
Broadcast.com, 341, 345, 350

Brobeck William, 39
Brobeck, 158, 163
Broderbund, 189
Broughton James, 41
Brower David, 141
Brown Alex, 97, 164, 165
Brown Willie, 117
Bryan & Edwards, 133
Bryan James, 253
Bryan John, 91, 133
BSD, 191
bubble, 165, 167, 221, 340, 344-45, 421, 426, 429
Buchheit Paul, 379, 380, 453
Buchholz Werner, 105
Buchla Don, 116
Buckmaster Jim, 394, 395, 396
Buffett Warren, 424
Bull, 328
BumpTop, 451
Burning Man, 263
Burroughs William, 30
Burroughs, 35, 105, 123
Burton McMurtry, 171
Bush Vannevar, 37, 43, 45, 50, 58, 60, 145, 227
Bushnell Nolan, 133, 213
Butterfield Stewart, 440
Byer Robert, 465
Byers Brook, 101
Byte Shop, 176
C-Cube, 323
C3, 464
CADRE laboratory, 252
Cafiero Luca, 156
CALDIC, 82
Calgene, 194, 330, 372
Calient, 363
CalStar Cement, 443
Campbell Bill, 225, 336
Campbell Gordon, 306
Campbell Keith, 373
Canesta, 459
Canion Rod, 209
Cannon Ed, 76
Canyon Cinema, 116
Capital Management Services, 171
Capp Street Project, 317
Carlston Doug, 189
Carmen Albert Pruden, 29
Carpenter Candice, 359
Casio, 171
Castro District, 118
Catharine Clark Gallery, 334
Catmull Ed, 178, 190, 252, 371
Catz Safra, 203, 206
CCRMA, 183, 408
CDC, 94
CEIR, 90
Celera Genomics, 373
Celera, 416
Cepheid, 374

Cerent, 363
Cerf Vinton, 173
CERN, 318
Cetus, 134, 194
Chad Hurley, 410
Chamberlain Marcia, 263
Chamberlin Donald, 178
Chambers Frank, 93
Chang Morris, 306
Chatterjee Amit, 464
Chen Steven, 410
Cheriton Dan, 437
Chertok Michael, 451
Chips and Technologies, 306
Chiron, 194, 374
Chisari Michael, 454
Chowning John, 183
Chu Steven, 459
Chuang Alfred, 355
Church George, 443
Cibelli Jose, 416
CICS, 135
Cirrus Logic, 306
Cisco, 17, 102, 206, 258, 323, 337, 362-63, 406, 421, 455
Citrix Systems, 449
Clarium Capital, 410
Clark Jim, 178, 215, 289, 319, 336, 360
Clark Wes, 107
Clayton Kit, 374
Clement Lewis, 32
CMOS, 110
Coates George, 195
COBOL, 89
Codd Edgar, 178
Codexis, 415
Codon Devices, 441
Cogenra Solar, 463
Cohen Bram, 412
Cohen Harold, 183
Cohen Morris, 308
Cohen Stanley, 181
Cohn Robert, 213
Coleman Bill, 26
Collins Jess, 87
Colossus, 59
Colter Mary, 35
Comeau Charles, 253
Commodore Amiga, 221, 222
Commodore, 171, 177, 209, 232, 252
Compaq, 209, 256, 306, 369, 411
Complete Genomics, 461
Compression Labs, 185
Compton Karl, 62
CompuServe, 135, 310, 354
Computer Associates, 307
Computer Sciences, 90
Computer Shack, 176
Computer Usage Company, 89
ComputerLand, 259
Confinity, 408
Conner Bruce, 87

Conner Finis, 186
Consumer Empowerment, 412
Contact Consortium, 364
Content Centric Networking, 437
Context Management Systems, 210
Continental Capital, 93
Conway Andrew, 416
Conway Ron, 342, 343
Cook Paul, 83
Cooley, 22, 158, 162
Cooper Martin, 174, 325
Corbato Fernando, 104, 135
Corfield Nick, 251
Corrigan Wilfred, 213
Cosulich Jared, 472
Cowell Henry, 35, 41
CP/M, 175, 209
Craigslist, 358, 390-96, 404
Cray Seymour, 76, 94
CRC, 80
Creative Commons, 414
Creeley Robert, 86
Crescendo Communications, 156, 323
Crick Francis, 94
Crommie Michael, 442
Crosspoint Venture, 133, 365
Crowley Dennis, 453
CSC, 137
Cuban Mark, 341, 345, 350
Cullinane John, 136
Cullinet, 212
Cummins Mark, 451
Cunningham Ward, 355
Cygnus Solutions, 368
Cypress Semiconductor, 213
Cypress, 256
Cytokinesis, 374
Dabney Ted, 133
Dahl Ole-Johan, 145
Dalmo Manufacturing Company, 59
Dalmo, 62
Damer Bruce, 364
Danger, 410
Data General, 114
Data Technology Corporation, 185
Davis & Rock, 93
Davis Angela, 117
Davis Ron, 116, 117
Davis Tommy, 92, 93, 96, 98
dBase, 211
de Castro Edson, 114
De Forest Roy, 116
Dead Kennedys, 195
DEC, 70-71, 90, 113, 148, 155, 215-16, 259,
339, 352, 369
DeFeo Mary-Joan "Jay", 87
DeForest Lee, 30, 45, 283
del.icio.us, 440
Dell Michael, 256
Dell Computer, 369, 411, 455
Dennard Robert, 122
Dennis Reid, 91, 171

Devol George, 88
Diamandis Peter, 466
Diaspora, 455
Diebenkorn Richard, 86
Dietrich Stephan, 461
Digg, 440
Diggers, 117
Digigraphics, 91
Digital Research, 175
Digital Universe Foundation, 414
Digitalk, 155
Dijkstra Edsger, 137
DiNucci Darcy, 439
Dion Norman, 186
Dixon Chris, 22, 163, 343
Dixon Maynard, 34
Djerassi Carl, 86, 109, 195
Documentum, 156, 449
Doerr John, 65, 100, 224, 292, 336-38, 376-
78, 427, 447
Dolby Labs, 113
Dolby Ray, 82
Doriot Georges, 62, 65-73, 90, 96, 100, 269,
338, 339, 424
Dorsey Jack, 301, 433
Dostert Leon, 88
DoubleClick, 359, 450
DoubleTwist, 416
Dougherty Brian, 252
Draper & Johnson, 93
Draper Bill, 18, 95-97, 113, 339, 424
Draper William, 92
Draper, Gaither and Anderson, 92
Dreadnot, 412
Drexler Eric, 312
Drmanac Radoje, 461
Drori Zeev, 111
Duffield David, 308
Duncan Robert, 62, 86
Dwight Herb, 115
Dycam, 324
Dynabook, 190
Dynamical Systems Research, 237
Dysan, 186
E-Tek Dynamics, 185
E*trade, 321
eBay, 17, 162, 342-43, 358, 376, 390-98,
402, 417, 435
Eberhard Martin, 310, 443
Eckert-Mauchly Computer Corporation, 76
Eckert Presper, 60
Eckert Wallace, 77
Eckert, 75, 76
EDM, 91
EDS, 107, 455
EDVAC, 75
Edwards Bill, 91, 133
Eigler Don, 312
Eimac, 37
EINet, 320
Eitel-McCullough, 62
Eitel Bill, 37

Elbourn Bob, 76
Electronic Arrays, 111
Electronic Arts, 212, 413
Electronic Frontier Foundation, 333
Eletr Sam, 194, 261, 331
Elgg, 455
Elixir, 155
Elk Cloner, 214
Ellenby John, 209
Ellis Jim, 189
Ellison Larry, 187, 196-207, 277-78
Ellison, 437
Eloquent, 461
Elwell Cy, 45
Elwell Cyril, 31
EMC, 449, 455
EMISARI, 173
Endy Drew, 441, 463
Engelbart Douglas, 82, 106, 109, 114, 120, 134, 145-47, 151, 227, 254, 271
English Bill, 146, 148, 227
ENIAC, 59
Ennis Earle, 32
Enwise, 318
EO, 323
Epson, 209, 324
Epstein Bob, 188
ERA, 76
ERISA, 65, 103, 335
Esalen Institute, 116
Esalen, 195
Eschenauer Laurent, 454
eSolar, 463
Estridge Donald, 208
Estrin Judy, 258, 310
Etak, 213
Ethernet, 173, 190
eToys, 341, 345, 346, 347
Evans & Sutherland, 178, 215, 252
Evans Arthur, 183
Evans David, 178
Evans Nancy, 359
Everson George, 39
Everson William, 62
Evite, 400
Ewing Marc, 327
Excite, 351, 406
Exelixis, 374
Exxon, 259, 452
Facebook, 17, 21-22, 27, 162, 320-3, 343, 349-50, 386, 390, 399, 400-03, 426-33, 452-54
Faggin Federico, 110, 124, 170, 177
Fairchild Semiconductor, 17, 65, 71, 92, 96, 100-01, 112, 121, 191, 232, 259, 270-72
Fairchild, Sherman, 71, 96, 121
Faith No More, 263
Fake Caterina, 440
Family Dog Production, 117
Fanning Shawn, 412
Farina Don, 93, 111
Farmer Randy, 254

Farnsworth Philo, 39
Farrow Al, 466
FastForward Networks, 360, 408
Fecalface.com, 444
Federal Telegraph Corporation, 31
Federal Telegraph, 17, 45, 46
Feigenbaum Ed, 109, 132, 191, 214
Felsenstein Lee, 172, 175, 209
Fenwick and West, 158, 162
Ferguson Phil, 111
Ferlinghetti Lawrence, 86
Fernandez Manuel, 209
Feynman Richard, 312
Filo David, 320
Filo, David, 428, 429
FindLaw, 359
Finocchio Joe, 41
Fiorina Carly, 410, 478
Fire Andrew, 459
Firmage Joe, 414
First Virtual, 322
Fisher Gerhard, 37
Fisher Research Laboratories, 37
Fisher Scott, 253
Flanders Ralph, 62
Flavr Savr, 330
Fleischmann Martin, 464
Fleischmann Robert, 330
Fletcher Harrell, 334
Fletcher Mark, 440
Fleury Marc, 368
Flickr, 440
Flip, 436
Flow-matic, 76
Flowers Tommy, 59
Fodor Stephen, 330
Fogg BJ, 453
Forrester Jay, 77
FORTRAN, 89
Fossum Eric, 324
Four Phase Systems, 122, 170
Foursquare, 453
Fox Terry, 182
Foxconn, 494
FrameTechnology, 251
Franceschini Amy, 334
Frankston Bob, 184
Free Software Foundation, 217, 414
Free Speech Movement, 116, 175
Freewebs, 457
Freitas Robert, 418
French Gordon, 175
FRESS, 134
Fried Howard, 182
Friedman Patri, 466
FriendFeed, 453
Friendster, 336, 400, 408, 426-28
Friis Janus, 434
Fry Thornton, 43
Fuller Leonard, 32, 38
Furness Thomas, 253
Fylstra Daniel, 184

Gaither Rowan, 92
Galactic Empire, 189
Gallo Robert, 330
Garrett Jesse James, 440
Gaskins Robert, 251
Gates Bill, 130, 152, 154, 174, 202, 208, 224, 227, 238, 242, 256, 406
Gateway, 369, 455
Gausebeck Dave, 409
Gauthier Paul, 352, 433
Gavilan, 210
Gay Pride Parade, 183
Gearhart John, 374
GenBank, 331
Gene Logic, 373
Genentech, 20, 99, 101, 162, 167, 193, 261, 311, 330, 335, 374, 402
General Electric, 81, 83
General Magic, 323
GeoCities, 341, 345, 349, 350, 429
George Harry, 251
GeoSystems Global, 360
GeoWorks, 252
Geron, 330, 373
Geschke Charles, 212
Geschke Chuck, 155
Ghonim Wael, 478
Giannini Amadeo, 33
Giauque William, 84
Gibson William, 260
Gifford Jack, 93, 213
Gilbert Walter, 194
Gilmore Jack, 77, 91
Gilmore John, 333, 368
Ginsberg Allen, 86
Ginsburg Charles, 82
Ginzton Ed, 61, 109, 219
Gismo, 88
Glaser Donald, 134
Glaser Rob, 358
Glazer David, 308
Gleason Madeline, 62
GlobalFoundries, 456
Gmail, 380, 382, 383, 384, 397, 430
GNU, 217, 327
GO Corporation, 254
Go PenPoint, 221
Goad Walter, 194
Goetz Martin, 136
Goldberg Adele, 145, 156
Google Apps, 385
Google Books, 382
Google, 17-22, 27, 159-68, 196, 247-49, 293-94, 336, 342-43, 349-50, 376-432, 447, 450-51, 463
Gopher, 320
Gorrell Leslie, 39
GoTo, 380
Gould Gordon, 115
Gouveia Ricardo "Rigo 23", 334
Gowalla, 453
GPS, 193

Graham Paul, 20, 350, 358, 380, 422, 474
Grateful Dead, 117
Gray Jim, 360
Gray Percy, 34
Greenwald Sidney, 76
GRiD Systems, 209
Grogan Emmett, 117
Gronet Chris, 463
Group f/64, 40
Group, 91
Groupon, 453
Grove Andy, 19, 96, 120-31, 273
GUI, 17, 143, 150-55, 222, 227, 240
Haefner Walter, 107, 212
Haisch Bernard, 414
Halcyon Molecular, 410, 462
Halcyon, 35
Hale Victoria, 415
Hambrecht & Quist, 133, 365
Hambrecht and Quist, 158
Hambrecht William, 133
Hamlin Edith, 40
Hamza Shaykh, 467
Hannah Marc, 215
Hanratty Patrick, 90
Hansen Armin, 34
Hansen Bill, 39, 61
Hansen William, 42
Hara, 464
Hardin Garrett, 141
Harley Calvin, 330
Harmonic Convergence, 317
Harrison Lou, 41
Harsanyi John, 459
Hart Peter, 191
Harvard Mark I, 59
Harvey Larry, 263
Haseltine Bill, 415
Haseltine William, 330
Hassan Scott, 438
Hassett Christopher, 359
Hastings Reed, 360
Hatch Ann, 317
Haueter Ruth, 76
Hauser Herman, 232
Hawkins Jeff, 289, 417
Hawkins Trip, 212
Hayes Dennis, 188
Hayes Microcomputers Products, 188
Healtheon, 360
Hedrick Wally, 87
Heilig Morton, 88
Heintz Ralph, 37, 39
Heiser Dick, 176
Hendrix Gary, 211
Hennessy John, 216, 370
Herbst Theatre, 195
Herrold Charles, 31
Hershman Lynn, 182
Hertzfeld Andy, 323

Hewlett-Packard, 17-18, 44-72, 81, 95-100, 112-14, 123, 132, 158, 162, 206, 222-32, 240, 251, 259, 267-8, 309, 370, 410, 421, 424, 455
Hewlett, William, 42, 267-8
HGS, 330
Hillis Danny, 374
Hitachi, 209
Hitz David, 259, 327
Hobart James, 115
Hoeffler Don, 171
Hoerni Jean, 92, 93, 111
Hoff Ted, 124, 170
Hoffman Mark, 188
Hoffman Reid, 409
Hofmann Hans, 40
Hollerith Hermann, 30
Homebrew Computer Club, 175, 209
Honey Stan, 213
Honeywell, 105, 123
Hood Leroy, 261, 373
HotBot, 352
Hotmail, 21, 97, 341, 354, 382
Hourihan Meg, 408
Howery Ken, 408
Howes Tim, 454
Howlett Eric, 253
Hsieh, Tony, 74
Huang Jen-Hsun, 300, 323
Huizenga Charlie, 464
Human Be-In, 118
Human Genome Project, 312, 330, 372, 416
Hunkapiller Michael, 373
Hunkapiller Mike, 261
Huskey Harry, 80
Huxley Aldous, 116
HyperCard, 254
Hyseq, 461
i2, 309
IBM, 17, 35, 59, 70-96, 104, 105, 107, 123-45, 152-56, 160, 178-79, 196, 197, 206, 208, 224-25, 235-41, 256, 307, 326, 369, 393, 411, 421
ICL, 328
Idealab, 380
IDS, 104
Illumina, 461
Immigrant, 24, 25
Imogen Cunningham, 40, 86
IMP, 107
IMS, 108, 178
IMSAI, 233
In-Q-Tel, 418
Incyte Pharmaceuticals, 331
Incyte, 374, 416
Indredible, 447
Informatics, 136
Informix, 188, 307
Infoseek, 351
InfoSpace, 353
Ingalls Dan, 145
Ingres, 178, 187
Inktomi, 352

Innovalight, 418
Institutional Venture Associates, 171
Institutional Venture Partners, 171
Integral Systems, 308
Integrated Device Technology, 185
Intel Corp., 17-20, 68, 96, 120-31, 153-54, 170, 185, 202, 222-26, 231, 240-45, 255, 273-74, 306, 329, 336-37, 390, 406, 410, 421, 424, 427, 432, 456
Intellectual Ventures, 420
Intellicorp, 191, 214
Interleaf, 251
International Business Machines, 35
Internet Security Systems, 322
Intersil, 111
Interval Research, 420
InVisage, 442
Invitron, 331
iPad, 452
iPhone, 224, 243-47, 447
iPierian, 461
iPod, 243-46, 412
IPTO, 106
Ireland David, 183
Irr. App. (Ext.), 374
Irrational Design, 472
Itek, 91
ITER, 464
iVillage, 359
iZumi Bio, 461
Jacobson Van, 437
Jacopetti Ben, 117
Jain Naveen, 353
Java, 355
JBoss, 368
Jefferson Airplane, 117
Jeffries Corp., 165, 169
Jenks Timothy, 374
Jensen Peter, 32
JGI, 374
Jobs Steve, 27, 65, 102, 152-56, 190, 205, 213, 222-48, 252, 370
Johanson Chris, 334
Johnson Franklin, 133
Joint Venture Silicon Valley Network, 329
Jones Fletcher, 90
Joy Bill, 191, 215, 443
JPEG, 252
Jughead, 320
Juniper Networks, 363
KAI Pharmaceuticals, 417
Kalpana, 156, 323
Kaplan Jerry, 224, 248, 254, 391
Kaplan Jonathan, 436
Kapor Mitch, 224, 333, 431
Kareemi Nazim, 459
Karim Jawed, 410
Kasesalu Priit, 412
Kay Alan, 144, 148-50, 156, 190, 254
Kazaa, 412
Kazerooni Homayoon, 418
KCLD, 98

Keasling Jay, 441
Kelly Kevin, 263, 333
Kemeny Gyorgy, 104
Kenichi Ueda, 465
Kent Adaline, 40
Kepes Gyorgy, 114
Kerouac Jack, 86
Kesey Ken, 87, 117
Kestrel Solutions, 363
Keyhole, 381, 418
Khan Academy, 466
Khan Ali Akbar, 118
Khan Salman, 466
Khosla Vinod, 18, 25-27, 215, 286, 300, 336-37, 443, 463
Kid 606, 374
Kilburn Tom, 75
Kilby Jack, 93, 114
Kildall Gary, 175
Kilgallen Margaret, 334
Kimsey Jim, 258
Kindle, 436
King Laura, 187
Kinkead Reiling, 416
Kirby Jack, 120
Kirsch Steve, 251, 351
Klaus Christopher, 322
Klein Doug, 310
Kleiner-Perkins, 171, 193, 215, 353, 447
Kleiner Eugene, 92, 171
Kleiner Perkins Caufield & Byers (KPCB), 65, 99, 100, 101, 336, 337, 338, 362, 365, 422, 443
Knoll Thomas, 155
Kodak, 252, 324
Komag, 185
Kornberg Roger, 459
Kos Paul, 183
Kottke Daniel, 190
Kovacs Gregory, 219
KR Sridhar, 417
Kramlich Dick, 73, 103, 339
Krizelman Todd, 400
Kubie Elmer, 89
Kupershmidt Ilya, 442
Kurtz Thomas, 105
Kurzweil Ray, 179, 466
Kwamie Floyd, 111
Lab, 317
Lab126, 436
Lam Research, 185
Lamantia Philip, 62
Lamond Pierre, 111
Lane Ray, 201, 203, 204
Lange Dorothea, 40, 86
Lanier Jaron, 254
Lanza Robert, 417
Lashlee Hal, 210
Lasseter John, 371
Lau James, 259, 327
Laughlin Robert, 459
Lawrence Ernest, 38

Lawrence Livermore Laboratory, 84
Learning Company, 341, 345, 348
Leary Timothy, 117
Leddy William, 466
Lee Christopher, 331
Leemans Wim, 465
Legato, 308, 449
Leghorn Richard, 91
Lerner Sandy, 258
Lesk Mike, 189
Lessig Larry, 414
Letterman Digital Arts Center, 444
Levchin Max, 409
Levin Joe, 76
Levitt Michael, 331
Levy Jim, 211
Lewin Daniel, 360
Licklider Joseph, 106
Lieb Al, 400
Lightera Networks, 363
Lights In A Fat City, 317
Lightwave, 219
LIGO, 465
Lin Fu-Kuen, 194
Linear Technology, 213, 256
LinkedIn, 343, 409
Linus Technologies, 254
Linus Torvalds, 327
Linux, 327, 368, 447
Linvill John, 219
Lion John, 118
Lipkin Efrem, 172
Lippincott Donald, 39
Lippman Andy, 253
Lisa, 213
Listen.com, 408
Litton Charles, 32, 37, 42, 46-7, 62, 83, 267
Lawrence, Roberts, 134, 217
Lockheed, 81, 112
Long Now Foundation, 374
Lord Chip, 118, 183
Lotus, 210, 307, 369
Lowe William, 208
LS9, 443
LSI Logic, 213, 256
Lucas George, 190
Lucasfilm, 252, 254, 371, 444
Lucent, 363
Ludic Labs, 433
Ludwick Andrew, 258
Luggage Store, 317
Luminous Networks, 363
Luxn, 363
Lynx Therapeutics, 331
Lyon Bob, 259, 308
Lytro, 436
Machine Intelligence Corporation, 211
Macintosh, 236
Macromedia, 323, 354
MADDIDA, 76
Madey John, 182
Maestri David, 457

Magic Theatre, 118, 195
Magnavox, 32, 133, 213
Magnetophon, 59
Magnuski Hank, 189
Maiman Ted, 115
Malda Rob, 364
Malina Roger, 263
Malloy Judy, 262
MapQuest, 360
Marconi Guglielmo, 30
Marden Ethel, 76
Marimba, 360
Marioni Tom, 183
Markkula Mike, 93, 231, 234
Markowitz Victor, 373, 374
Marsh Bob, 175
Martin James, 368
Martin Peter, 85
Marvell, 370, 456
Masuoka Fujio, 256
Mathews Arthur, 34
Matmos, 374
Mauchly John, 60
Mauchly, 75, 76
Mauldin Michael, 320
Maxim, 213, 256
Maxis, 311
Maxygen, 415
Mayan Networks, 363
Maybeck Bernard, 35
Mayfield Fund, 171
Mazzola Mario, 156
McCahill Mark, 320
McCarthy John, 88, 106, 109
McClure Michael, 86
McCollum John, 228
McConnell John, 141
McCool Robert, 356
McCullough Jack, 37
McCune Brian, 214
McFadden Daniel, 459
McGee Barry, 334
McGreevy Michael, 253
McKenna Regis, 111
McKubre Michael, 464
McMillan Edwin, 39, 58, 84
McMullen Jim, 111
McNealy Scott, 215
McNeilly Mike, 111
Mediafire, 435
Medin Milo, 362
Mediterranean weather, 23
Memex, 60
Memorex, 82, 113, 133
Menlo Ventures, 261
Merkle Ralph, 418
Merritt Chase William, 34
Merry Pranksters, 117
Metcalfe Bob, 150, 154, 172, 188, 280, 433
Metricom, 354
Meyer Frederick, 34
Michels Larry, 191

Micral, 172
Micro-Electro-Mechanical Systems, 219
Micron, 255
Microsoft Corp., 17, 21, 126, 128-30, 154-56,
165-66, 174, 191, 202-03, 208, 222-27, 239-
51, 256, 307, 325-7, 341, 351, 382-85, 394,
398-401, 406, 412, 421, 430, 447-51
Milk Harvey, 195
Millard William, 174, 176
Milo, 454
Miner Bob, 187, 196-201, 217, 221
Miner Jay, 232, 252
Minsky Marvin, 88, 106
MIPS, 216
MITS, 171, 174
MK-Ultra, 87
Mobipocket, 436
Mochly-Rosen Daria, 417
Mockapetris Paul, 217
Molectro, 111
Molecular Applications Group, 331
Monier Louis, 352
Monsanto, 372
Montalvo Villa, 41
Montgomery Securities, 158, 164-67, 421
Moore Gordon, 19-20, 92, 96, 112, 120-31,
143, 273, 424
Moritz Michael, 74, 378, 424
Morley Grace, 40
Morningstar Chip, 254
Morris Robert, 310, 358
Morris, 310
Morse Stephen, 185
Morton Jack, 79
Morton Paul, 82
MOS Technology, 177
Mosaic, 319, 351
Moseley Tim, 59
Mother of All Demos, 146, 151, 227
Motorola, 79, 92, 111, 174-77, 185, 255, 432,
447
Mozilla, 356, 431
MPEG, 371
MS-DOS, 208
Muir John, 33
Mullenweg Matt, 440
Mullin Jack, 59
Mullis Kary, 194
Mumford John, 133
Murali Venkatesan, 463
Murphy Michael, 116
Murray-Hopper Grace, 59, 76, 89
Musk Elon, 409
Myhrvold Nathan, 237, 420
MySpace, 342, 398-400, 426-28
Naimark Michael, 253
Nakamura Dan, 374
Nall James, 93, 111
NanoSolar, 417
Nanosys, 418
Napster, 412
National Semiconductor, 111, 177, 255, 259

Alphabetical Index

Nauman Bruce, 116
Navigenics, 461
NCR, 35, 105, 123, 209
NEC, 329
Negroponte Nicholas, 114
Nelson Phil, 308
Nelson Ted, 106, 134, 254, 437
NeoPhotonics, 374
Neri Manuel, 87
Neri Ruby "Reminisce", 334
NET, 258
Netflix, 360, 435
NetObjects, 359
Netscape Communications, 158-59, 167, 202, 289-90, 319, 336, 342, 345, 351, 355-56, 403, 427, 431
Network Appliance, 327
Network Computing Devices, 310
Network effect, 126-29, 340, 384, 390, 395-404, 427
Newdoll Julie, 467
Newell Allen, 88
Newmark Craig, 358, 393-97
Newton Huey, 117
Newton John, 156
NeXT, 239-44, 355, 369
NextBio, 442
Ng Andrew, 438
Ng Ren, 436
Nicira Networks, 449
Ning, 433
Nintendo, 256
Nishi Yoshio, 255
Nixdorf, 328
Noble David, 133
Nokia, 409
Noorda Ray, 211
Norman Bob, 93
Norris Sirron, 444
Nortel, 363
Northrop John, 84
Northrop, 465
Norvig Peter, 466
Nosek Luke, 408, 410, 462
Noskowiak Sonya, 40
Novalux Corp., 426
Novell, 211, 327
NOW, 352
Noyce Bob, 92-96, 120-31, 238, 273, 424
Nupedia, 414
NuvoMedia, 360
NVCA, 21, 22, 103, 423
Nvidia, 323
Nygaard Kristen, 145
O'Connor Kevin, 322, 359
Obata Chiura, 40
Octel Communications, 213
Octopus, 135
Odyssey, 133
Ohno Taichi, 107
Oliver Bernard, 263
Oliveros Pauline, 116

Olivetti, 114, 209, 306, 328
Olsen Ken, 90, 91, 184
Olson Peter, 213
Omidyar Pierre, 358, 391, 392
ONElist, 440
OneSocialWeb, 454
OneWorld Health, 415
ONI Systems, 363
OnLive, 458
Onyx, 191
Open Directory Project, 352
Open Software Foundation, 309
Open Theater, 117
Openwave, 325
Oppenheimer Robert, 38, 58, 84
Oracle, 17, 26, 162, 165, 187, 196-207, 217, 277-78, 307, 369, 372, 388, 410, 421, 429, 437, 449, 455
Orchard Hayes, 90
Orlicky Joe, 107
OS/2, 326
Osborne Adam, 209
Osborne Varian John, 35
Osborne, 209
Osheroff Douglas, 459
Osnaghi Alessandro, 329
Overture, 380
Ozzie Ray, 310
P101, 114
P2P, 412
Packard David, 17, 42-56, 100, 158, 206, 224, 229, 238-40, 424
Page Larry, 27, 49, 54, 159, 336, 352, 376, 380-86
Palevsky Max, 80, 105, 136
Palm Pilot, 409
Palm, 447, 455
Palmer Ralph, 76
Pandora, 408
Pangea Systems, 331
Panofsky Pief, 109
Pansophic Systems, 137
Pansophic, 212
PARC Xerox, 17, 143-57, 172, 190, 223, 227, 233, 279-80, 327, 437
ParcPlace, 156
Parekh Abhay, 360
Park David, 86
Parson John, 87
Partnerships, 73
Paternot Stephan, 400
Patil Suhas, 306
Patricof Alan, 422
Patterson David, 216, 352
Patterson Tim, 208
Pauline Mark, 195
Payne Jonathan, 360
PayPal, 409, 433
Paypal, 434
PC, 208
PDP, 114
PE Biosystems, 373

Peddle Chuck, 177
PeopleSoft Inc., 205, 206
PeopleSoft, 308, 328, 369, 437
Perceptron, 88
Perkin-Elmer, 372
Perkins Tom, 19, 100-101, 158, 164-65, 171, 425
Perl Martin, 459
Perlegos George, 185
Perlman Steve, 359, 458
Perot Ross, 107
Perrine Fred, 29
Perry Barlow John, 333
Perry Bill, 83, 112, 193
Petersen Kurt, 219
Peterson Sidney, 41
Pets.com, 341, 345, 347, 348
Pfleumer Fritz, 59
Phelan James, 41
Philbin James, 451
Philips, 209, 256, 359
Photoshop, 155
Piazzoni Gottardo, 34
Picture System, 178, 215, 252
Pilot ACE, 75
Pincus Mark, 457
Pincus Warburg, 103, 336
Pinhas Adi, 451
Pinkerton Brian, 320
Pirate Bay, 435
Piscopo Joseph, 137
Pishevar Shervin, 457
Pixar, 371
Pixley Frank, 34
Planet Drum, 142
PLATO, 173
Pliner Michael, 307
Plink, 451
Poduska William, 215
Pointcast, 359
Polese Kim, 360
PolyPlus Battery, 332
Pomeroy Tom, 360
Pong, 133
Poniatoff Alexander, 59
Pons Stanley, 464
Porat Marc, 323, 443
Porter William, 321
PostScript, 212
Potter David, 255
Poulsen Valdemar, 31
PowerPoint, 251
Pratt Haraden, 32
Pratt Ian, 449
Precision Instruments, 187
Price Jeffrey, 412
Pridham Edwin, 31, 32
Primus, 333
Prnet, 189
Processor Technology, 175
Project Cyclops, 263
Project Genie, 106

Project Stretch, 105
Proxim, 189, 370
Psion, 372
Pure Digital Technologies, 436
Pure Software, 360
Pyramid Technology, 216
Quanta, 459
Quantum Computer Services, 258
Quarles Miller, 330
Quist George, 133
Qwest, 363
Radical Faeries, 183
Raduchel Bill, 191
Rafii Abbas, 459
RAMAC, 83
Ramsay Mike, 371
Randolph Hearst III William, 362
Randolph Hearst William, 33
Rapidshare, 435
Rapoport Sonya, 195
Raskin Jef, 154, 227, 232
Rasna Corporation, 309
Rat Bastard Protective Association, 87
Ratliff Wayne, 210
Raychem, 83, 162
Raydac, 81
Raymond Scott, 453
Raytheon, 79, 92
Razr, 446
Reagan Trudy Myrrh, 263
RealNetworks, 358, 371, 408
Red Hat Linux, 327
Red Hat, 368, 449
Red House Painters, 333
Red Pepper, 328
Reddy Damoder, 442
Reenskaug Trygve, 190
Regitz Bill, 123
Reid Clifford, 307, 461
Reimers Niels, 109
relational database, 17, 196, 198
Remington Rand, 35, 76
Research In Motion, 410, 447
Residents, 194
Rexroth Ken, 86
Rexroth Kenneth, 62
Rezner John, 349
Rhodes Ida, 76
Rice Condoleezza, 334, 464
Riddle Mike, 211
Riley Terry, 116
Riordan Michael, 261
Ritchie Dennis, 135
Rizzoli Achilles, 40
Roberts Ed, 174
Robertson Sandy, 100, 165, 166, 167, 169
Robinson Herbert, 90
Robl James, 416
Rock Arthur, 18, 68, 71, 92-97, 102-05, 121, 237
Rockefeller Laurance, 62, 91
Rocketmail, 357

RockMelt, 454
RockYou, 452
Rodgers TJ, 160
ROLM, 188
Rosati Mario, 133
Rosedale Philip, 437
Rosekrans John, 195
Rosen Charlie, 132
Rosenblatt Frank, 88
Rosenblum Mendel, 368
Rosing Wayne, 378
Ross Douglas, 90
Rossmann Alain, 323
Rothko Mark, 86
Rubin Andy, 410, 447
Rubin Jon, 334
Rukeyser Muriel, 62
Runnymede Sculpture Farm, 195
Russell Steve, 104, 133
Ryan Harris, 30
Ryan Thomas, 436
Saba Simon, 464
SABRE, 104
Sachs Ely, 463
Sachs James, 360
Sachs Jonathan, 210
Saehan Information Systems, 371
SAGE, 77, 89, 104
Sakharov Andrei, 464
Saleforce.com, 408, 450
Salon, 364
San Francisco Mime Troupe, 116
Sand Hill Road, 19, 99, 197, 340
Sandberg Russell, 308
Sandberg Sheryl, 302
Sanders Jerry, 93, 123, 177
Sanger Fred, 194
Sanger Larry, 414
SAP, 178, 328, 369
Sargent Ted, 442
Sassenrath Carl, 252
Sastry Shankar, 464
Savio Mario, 116
Scaruffi Piero, 466
Scelbi, 172
Schachter Joshua, 440
Schawlow Arthur, 115
Scheller Richard, 193
Schlumberger, 191, 259
Schmidt Benno, 62, 66, 67
Schmidt Eric, 336, 377, 384
Schmidt Ronald, 258
Scholes Myron, 459
Schoultz Andrew, 444
Schultz Peter, 330
Sciences Gilead, 261
SCO, 191
Scott Bruce, 187, 217
Scott Randall, 331
Sculley John, 222-25, 235, 237
SDC, 89
SDS, 105, 136

Seaborg Glenn, 39, 58, 84
SEAC, 75
Seagate Technology, 186, 411
Seale Bobby, 117
Searle John, 191
Seasteading Institute, 466
Second Life, 438
Seeger Charles, 35
Segre Emilio, 39
Selfridge Oliver, 88
Selvadurai Naveen, 453
Sematech, 256
Sequin Carlo, 216
Sequoia Capital, 16, 26, 99, 101, 171, 345-46,
353, 365, 376, 409, 429, 434
Serious Materials, 443
SETI Institute, 263
Severiens Hans, 322
Shannon Claude, 60
Shao Howard, 156
Share, 89
Sharma Ken, 309
Sharma Rohit, 363
Sharp Phillip, 194
Sharp, 171, 209
Sharpe William, 459
Shein Barry, 310
Sheldon John, 89
Shen Jia, 452
Sheng Samuel, 432
Shepard David, 88
Shepard Sam, 195
Shima Masatoshi, 170
Shima, 177
Shockley William, 23, 53, 60, 91, 120, 269-
70
Shogren Joan, 116
Shriram, Ram, 342, 427
Shugart Alan, 133, 186
Shugart Technology, 186
Shuttleworth Mark, 451
Sidhu Sanjiv, 309
Siebel Thomas, 328
Siebel Tom, 464
Siebel, 410, 437
Siebel,, 410
Signetics, 93
Silicon Genetics, 416
Silicon Graphics, 191, 215, 371
Silverstone Abbey, 215
SimCity, 311
Simmons Russel, 409, 410
Simon Herbert, 88
Simonyi Charles, 151-54, 179, 251
Sinclair, 209
Sindhu Pradeep, 363
Singhal Ashok, 412
Singularity Institute, 417
Singularity University, 466
Sinsheimer Robert, 260
Sippl Roger, 187
Sivaram Siva, 463

SixDegrees.com, 400
Sketchpad, 104
Skrenta Rich, 214, 352, 454
Skype, 434
SLAC, 109, 175, 465
Slashdot, 364
Slashkey, 457
Slayton Joel, 252
Sleep, 333
Slide, 410
Smalltalk, 145, 155, 190, 326
Smart Valley, 329
Smith Bruce, 258
Smith Dave, 189
Smith George, 324
Smith Hamilton, 330, 373, 442, 462
Smith Jack, 354
Smith Julius, 239
Smith Lloyd, 261
Smoot George, 459
Snibbe Scott Sona, 466
Snyder Gary, 86
Social Gaming Network, 457
SoftBook Press, 360
Software Development Laboratories, 187
Software Plus, 210
Software Publishing, 251
Sol-20, 175
Solectron, 185
Solexant, 442
Solyndra, 463
Somerby Bob, 364
Somerville Chris, 443
Sonsini Larry, 133, 159-62, 277-78
Sony, 79, 186, 209, 256, 359, 370
Soule Damon, 444
Souza Larry, 194
Space Invaders, 189
Spacewar, 104, 149
SpaceX, 409
Spectra-Physics, 115
Spectra Diode Labs, 219
Sperry Corporation, 42
Sperry Rand, 105
Spicer Jack, 86
Spitters Laurence, 82, 113
Spokeo, 453
Sporck Charles, 93
Sporck Charlie, 111
Spreckels Rudolph, 32
Sprint, 353
Sproul Hall Sit-In, 117
SQL, 178
SRS, 219
SSEC, 60
Stackpole Ralph, 41
Stallman Richard, 217
Stanford Industrial Park, 81
Stanford Leland, 28
Stanford, 18, 19, 22, 44-55, 95-99, 125, 144-47, 153, 159, 227, 238-39, 265, 336-43, 376, 382, 399, 428

Stanley Owsley, 117
Stanley Wendell, 84
Starr Jordan David, 29
Stauffacher Frank, 41, 87
Steinberg Wallace, 330
Steinberg, 373
Stephens Robertson, 158, 166, 167, 421
Stern Stacy, 359
Stibitz George, 43
Stieglitz Alfred, 86
Stiglitz Joseph, 459
Stolle Bryan, 368
Stone Ellery, 32
Stonebraker Michael, 178, 187
Stoppelman Jeremy, 409, 410
Strands Mildred, 116
Subarachnoid Space, 333
Subotnick Morton, 116
Summer of Love, 117
Sun Edmund, 185, 323
SUN, 190-91, 215, 259, 286, 309, 355, 455
Superfish, 451
Survival Research Laboratories, 195
Sutardjia Pantas, 370
Sutardjia Sehat, 370
Sutherland Ivan, 104, 106, 178, 190, 253
Sutter Hill Ventures, 113
SWAC, 80
Swanson Robert, 193
Sybase, 188, 307
Sycamore Networks, 363
Syjuco Stephanie, 444
Sylvania, 79, 83
Symantec, 211, 368
Symbian, 372
SynOptics, 258, 362
Syntex, 374, 415
System R, 178, 187
System/360, 105
SYSTRAN, 114
Systran, 352
Szpakowski Mark, 172
Szybalski Waclaw, 181
T-Mobile, 410
Tabulating Machine Company, 35
Tai-Ming "Terry" Gou, 494
Talbert Dave, 110, 111
Talbot David, 364
Tallinn Jaan, 412, 434
Tamm Igor, 464
Tandem Computers, 186
Tandem, 369
Tandy, 209, 232
Tang Harrison, 453
Tape Music Center, 116
Tarpenning Marc, 443
Tate George, 210
Taylor Bob, 106, 143-48, 155
Taylor Bret, 453
Taylor Norman, 77, 91
Taylor Richard, 459
Tchikovani Sandro "Misk", 444

TCP, 173
TechCrunch, 441
Technology Venture Associates, 171
Teknowledge, 214
Telegent Systems, 432
Telesystems, 189
Teresa Meng, 370
Terman Frederick, 18, 32, 37, 44-58, 61, 95-99, 267
TerraServer, 360
Terrell Paul, 176
Tesla, 443
Texas Instruments, 79, 92, 111, 171, 177, 189, 232, 255
Thacker Charles, 145, 179
theGlobe.com, 400
Thessalonians, 334
Thiebaud Wayne, 116
Thiel Peter, 408, 433
Thinking Fellers Union Local 282, 317
Thompson Kenneth, 135
Thomson James, 374
Thornton Tex, 83
Thrun Sebastian, 443, 466
Tiemann Michael, 368
TIGR, 330
Tilera, 459
Time Warner, 406
Titus Jon, 172
TMS, 107
Tobaccowala Selina, 400
Tokuda Lance, 452
Toma Peter, 114
Tomlinson Ray, 172
Tong Richard, 214
TorrentSpy, 435
Tosh David, 454
Toshiba, 255-57, 329, 370
Toshihiro Nishikado, 189
Totty Brian, 433
Townes Charles, 115
TRADIC, 80
Tramiel Jack, 252
Trance Mission, 317
Transensory Devices, 219
Transitron Electronics, 79
Transitron, 92
Trent Jeffrey, 416
Treybig James, 186
Trubshaw Roy, 254
Truel Bob, 352
Truong Trong Thi Andre, 172
Truscott Tom, 189
TSMC, 456
Tuck James, 85
Turing Alan, 43
Twin Creeks Technologies, 463
Twitter, 301, 433
Tymshare, 107
U.S. Robotics, 258, 354
Uccel, 107, 212
UCLA, 147

UCSF, 18, 19, 101
Uemura Masayuki, 256
Ungermann Ralph, 177, 188
Unified Computing System, 455
UniGene, 331
Unimate, 88
United Technologies, 332
Univac, 76, 123
Unix, 135, 191, 192, 309, 327
Unwired Planet, 325
Upstartle, 450
URL, 319
US West, 362
USB, 324
Usenet, 189
Utterback Camille, 444
Uunet, 310, 354
Valentine Don, 16, 65, 93, 101-03, 111, 171, 231, 339
van Dam Andries, 134
Van Dyke Willard, 40
van Hoff Arthur, 360
Varian Associates, 109
Varian Russ, 39, 42
Varian Russell , 35
Varian Sigurd, 42
Varian, 62, 81, 82, 115
VAX, 216
Vederi, 380
Vejrum Soren, 354
Venrock, 62, 67, 68, 102, 338
Venter Craig, 330, 373
Venter, 442, 462
Venture capital, 64-72, 95, 103, 341
Veritas Software, 412
Verity, 307
Vermeer Technologies, 351
Veronica, 320
Viaweb, 358
Villierme Henry, 87
ViolaWWW, 318
Vishria Eric, 454
VisiCalc, 184
VisualAge, 326
VLSI Technology, 213, 256
VMware, 368, 449, 455
Vmware, 448
VocalTec, 358
Voigt Christopher, 441
Von Neumann John, 60, 88
von Neumann John, 75
Vonderschmitt Bernard, 306
Voulkos Peter, 116
VPL Research, 254
Wagner Frank, 136
Waitt Ted, 257
Wales Jimmy, 414
Walker John, 211
Walmart, 452
Walton Lee, 444
Wang An, 78
Wang Charles, 212

Wang, 186
Wanlass Frank, 110
Warnke Dave, 444
Warnock John, 178, 212
Warren Jim, 176
Watkins-Johnson, 92
Watkins Dean, 92
Watson Eugene, 115
Watson James, 94, 312, 330
Watson Thomas, 35
Watts Alan, 85
Wavefront, 251
Web 2.0, 439
WebCrawler, 320
WebLogic, 355
WebTV, 359
Webvan, 340, 345, 346
Wei Pei-Yuan, 318
Weili Dai, 370
Weinreich Andrew, 400
Weisel Thomas, 165-68
Weitek, 185
WELL, 262, 364
Werdmuller Ben, 455
West Michael, 330
Westergren Tim, 408
Western Electric, 79
Western Wireless Equipment Company, 32
Weston James, 40
Whalen Philip, 86
Wharton Tom, 359
Wheelon Bud, 113
Whirlwind, 77
White Minor, 86
White Tony, 373, 442
Whitman Meg, 478
Whitney & Company, 62
Whitney Jock, 62
Whole Earth Review, 263
Widlar Bob, 110, 111
Wiener Norbert, 60
Wikipedia, 413, 432, 451
WikiWikiWeb, 355
Wiley William, 116
Williams Evan, 301, 408
Williams Frederick, 75
Williams Josh, 453
Williamson Oliver, 459
Willow Garage, 438
Wilmut Ian, 373
Wilson John, 133
Wilson Sophie, 216
Wilson Sonsini (WSGR), 22, 158-66
Wimmer Eckard, 417
Windham Hill, 194
Windows, 237, 325
WML, 325
Wojcicki Anne, 462
Wordpress, 440
World, 310
WorldCom, 353
Wozniak Steve, 19, 102, 175-76, 228-33

Wright Will, 311
Wyly Sam and Charles, 107
Wyse, 310
Wythes Paul, 96-97, 113
X.com, 409
Xavier Martinez, 34
Xen, 449
Xenix, 191
Xerox, 17, 143-57, 213, 223-34, 240, 455
Xilinx, 213, 256, 306
Xing Technology, 358
XML, 356
Xros, 363
Y-Combinator, 422
Y2K, 367, 407
Yahoo!, 17, 19, 102, 196, 320, 341-52, 376-402, 408, 424, 426-32, 440, 450
Yang Geoff, 371
Yang Jerry, 320, 428-30
Yanhong Li, 351
Yeager William, 258
Yelp, 390, 404-10, 430
Yerba Buena Center for the Arts, 334
YLEM, 467
YouTube, 410, 434
YoVille, 457
Z Pamela, 334
Zadeh Lotfi, 113
Zaffaroni Al, 86, 109, 134, 330
Zaffire, 363
Zappos, 74
Zehr Gregg, 436
Zeki Semir, 466
Zenith, 306
Zennstroem Niklas, 434
Zer01 Festival, 444
Zeta Communities, 443
Zilog, 177, 185, 209, 232, 259
Zimmerman Thomas, 254
Zip2, 409
Zuckerberg Mark, 27, 399-403, 433
Zuse Konrad, 43
Zweben Monte, 328
Zworkyn Vladimir, 39
Zynga, 457

Made in the USA
Lexington, KY
15 July 2013